SCHOLARS OF CONTRACT LAW

This book, like its predecessor, provides a counter-balance to the traditional focus on judicial decisions by exploring the contribution of legal scholars to the development of private law. The work of a selection of leading scholars of contract law from across the common law world, ranging from Sir Jeffrey Gilbert (1674–1726) to Professor Brian Coote (1929–2019), is addressed by legal historians and current scholars in the field. The focus is on the nature of the work produced by the scholars in question, important influences on their work, and the impact which that work in turn had on thinking about contract law. The book also includes an introductory chapter and an afterword that explore connections between the scholars and recurrent themes.

The process of subjecting contract law scholarship to sustained analysis provides new insights into the development of contract law and reveals the central role played by scholars in that process. And by focusing attention on the work of influential contract scholars, the book serves to emphasise the importance of legal scholarship to the development of the common law more generally.

Also available from Hart Publishing:

Scholars of Tort Law
Edited by James Goudkamp and Donal Nolan

Scholars of Contract Law

Edited by
James Goudkamp
and
Donal Nolan

•HART•
OXFORD • LONDON • NEW YORK • NEW DELHI • SYDNEY

HART PUBLISHING

Bloomsbury Publishing Plc

Kemp House, Chawley Park, Cumnor Hill, Oxford, OX2 9PH, UK

1385 Broadway, New York, NY 10018, USA

29 Earlsfort Terrace, Dublin 2, Ireland

First published in Great Britain 2022

A catalogue record for this book is available from the British Library.

A catalogue record for this book is available from the Library of Congress.

Library of Congress Control Number: 2022943750

ISBN: HB: 978-1-50993-846-9
ePDF: 978-1-50993-848-3
ePub: 978-1-50993-847-6

Typeset by Compuscript Ltd, Shannon
Printed and bound in Great Britain by CPI Group (UK) Ltd, Croydon CR0 4YY

FSC www.fsc.org MIX Paper | Supporting responsible forestry FSC® C013604

To find out more about our authors and books visit www.hartpublishing.co.uk. Here you will find extracts, author information, details of forthcoming events and the option to sign up for our newsletters.

Preface

THIS VOLUME IS the second instalment in a series of edited collections concerned with scholars of private law. It follows *Scholars of Tort Law*, which was published in 2019. We found the work on *Scholars of Contract Law* rewarding and have again been privileged to collaborate with an outstanding cohort of contributors.

We had intended that drafts of the chapters that comprise this volume would be the subject of discussion and debate at a two-day workshop in Oxford but, alas, the Covid-19 pandemic precluded this from happening. Instead, the drafts were discussed in four online seminars that took place in April and May 2021. This model still permitted a lively dialogue that we hope the contributors found constructive. One advantage of proceeding virtually was that we were able to include more friends and colleagues in the proceedings than might otherwise have been possible. In addition to the contributors, we were very pleased to welcome to the workshops Hugh Beale, Anirudh Belle, John Cartwright, Mindy Chen-Wishart, Jordan English, Birke Häcker, Hector MacQueen, Ewan McKendrick, Edwin Peel, Francis Reynolds, Simon Whittaker and Mimi Zou. Their contributions greatly enriched the debates that took place.

In preparing the book for publication we incurred debts of gratitude to William Wong for his editorial assistance, to Elizabeth Wells for helping us to locate certain hard-to-find sources and to the University of Oxford Law Faculty's Research Support Fund for providing financial backing. We are also grateful to Victoria Broom for her excellent copyediting work and to Hart Publishing (particularly Sinead Moloney and Tom Adams) for their customary efficiency and continuing support of the project of which this volume forms a part.

James Goudkamp
Donal Nolan
6 July 2022

Contents

Contributors

Andrew Burrows is a Justice of the Supreme Court of the United Kingdom.

Hugh Collins is Cassel Professor of Commercial Law at the London School of Economics and Political Science.

James Gordley is the WR Irby Chair in Law at Tulane University Law School.

James Goudkamp is Professor of the Law of Obligations at the University of Oxford and a Fellow of Keble College, Oxford.

Gregory Klass is Frederick J Haas Professor of Law and Philosophy at Georgetown University Law Centre.

Michael Lobban is Professor of Legal History at the London School of Economics and Political Science.

Catharine MacMillan is Professor of Private Law at King's College London.

Joanna McCunn is a Senior Lecturer in Law at the University of Bristol.

Jonathan Morgan is Reader in English Law at the University of Cambridge and a Fellow of Corpus Christi College, Cambridge.

Donal Nolan is Professor of Private Law at the University of Oxford and a Fellow of Worcester College, Oxford.

Todd D Rakoff is Byrne Professor of Administrative Law at Harvard Law School.

Robert Stevens is Herbert Smith Freehills Professor of English Private Law at the University of Oxford and a Fellow of Lady Margaret Hall, Oxford.

Warren Swain is Professor of Law at the University of Auckland.

William Twining is Emeritus Quain Professor of Jurisprudence at University College London.

Stephen Waddams is University Professor at the University of Toronto.

Table of Cases

Table of Legislation

Australia

Canada

European Union

France

Germany

India

New Zealand

United Kingdom

United States

1

Scholars of Contract Law: Individuals and Themes

JAMES GOUDKAMP AND DONAL NOLAN

I. INTRODUCTION

THIS BOOK IS the second in a series of edited collections concerned with scholars of private law and follows the publication in 2019 of the inaugural volume on *Scholars of Tort Law* ('*STL*').[1] The reviews of *STL* provided some reassurance that the project on which we have embarked with this series is a worthwhile one.[2] We hope that readers of this second volume on *Scholars of Contract Law* will agree. In this introductory chapter we begin by reprising certain of the more important points about the project as a whole that we made in the introduction to *STL*,[3] before considering the implications of our methodology for this volume in particular. We go on to offer some observations on the individual scholars discussed in the book and to explore some key themes which run through the chapters that follow. This introductory chapter should be read in conjunction with William Twining's fascinating afterword (chapter 15), in which he combines personal recollections of, and observations on, some of the scholars who are considered in this volume with broader reflections on contract law scholarship past and present.

The *Scholars of Private Law* project was born of the belief that in the common law world insufficient attention has been paid to the role played by scholars in legal development, as compared with the role played by judges and the cases the judges decide. Hence the project explores and highlights the importance of scholarship in the development of private law, by focusing on the contribution

[1] J Goudkamp and D Nolan (eds), *Scholars of Tort Law* (Oxford, Hart Publishing, 2019).

[2] See N McBride [2020] *CLJ* 183; M Wilde (2020) 41 *Journal of Legal History* 221; B McDonald (2020) 42 *Sydney Law Review* 483; P Vines [2021] *University of New South Wales Law Journal Forum* 1; TT Arvind (2021) 37 *Professional Negligence* 114.

[3] J Goudkamp and D Nolan, 'Pioneers, Consolidators and Iconoclasts: The Story of Tort Scholarship' in *STL* (n 1).

which individual scholars have made to particular subject areas. In our view, the project both complements and is complemented by other work focused on the role of scholars in legal development in both common law and civilian systems.[4] Research of this kind not only serves to underline the part played by legal scholarship in legal development, but may also enable legal academics and their employing institutions to achieve a more historically informed understanding of the role of legal scholars themselves, and hence perhaps to challenge contemporary assumptions about the value of law schools and those who work in them. In the words of Susan Bartie:

> Better understandings of the efforts and endeavours of our predecessors – examining their ambitions and priorities – provides material which may be used to challenge dominant narratives and values, and encourages legal academics to develop an appreciation of a broader range of activities, perhaps with the ultimate goal of liberating law schools and universities from current ways of thinking about their role in society … A discipline that has little history or tradition and no real understanding of its identity or where it comes from is vulnerable to external policies that fail to thoughtfully respond to the needs of society. It is at greater risk of losing its sense of self.[5]

The *Scholars of Private Law* project is not overtly biographical in nature but should instead be understood primarily as an exercise in intellectual history.[6] Hence, while many of the contributors to the two volumes so far completed understandably include in their chapters a short biographical sketch of the scholar under scrutiny, this is not the main focus of enquiry, but is instead designed to set the scene for the discussion of the scholar's contribution to the discipline that follows. Our primary interest lies not in the details of the scholar's life, therefore, but in the scholar's influences and motivation, the nature of their scholarly contribution, and their influence on the law and on future scholarship. At the same time, we of course recognise that no sharp dividing line can be drawn between the life and the work, and it is certainly possible in some cases to identify life experiences that may help us to understand a particular scholar's motivation or focus.[7]

The choice of scholars whose contribution is explored and assessed is bound to be controversial, and so it is important that we emphasise that our approach to this difficult question was the same as in *STL*. We wish to draw attention

[4] See, eg, S Grundmann and K Riesenhuber (eds), *Private Law Development in Context: German Private Law Scholarship in the 20th Century* (Cambridge, Intersentia, 2018); S Bartie, *Free Hands and Minds: Pioneering Australian Legal Scholars* (Oxford, Hart Publishing, 2019).

[5] Bartie (n 4) 4–6.

[6] Though the categories of course overlap, and we certainly have no quibble with the characterisation of our project as belonging to 'a sub-genre of … legal biography': V Barnes et al, 'On Legal Biography' (2020) 41 *Journal of Legal History* 115, 120.

[7] For example, it seems likely that Fleming James's experiences as a lawyer working for a railroad company during the Great Depression influenced his tort scholarship, and it has been argued that the single-mindedness with which he pursued his 'loss-spreading' agenda was attributable to his being the son of a missionary: see G Calabresi, 'Professor Fleming James Jr (1904–1981)' in *STL* (n 1).

to three particular matters in that regard. First, the project is not a comparative one, and hence only common lawyers are included. In the case of contract, this meant that we excluded from the list of possible subjects two continental scholars whose impact on the common law of contract is of the highest order of significance, namely Robert Joseph Pothier and Friedrich Carl von Savigny. The influence of Pothier and Savigny on the common lawyers discussed in this volume will, however, be readily apparent from the chapters that follow, and is also addressed later in this chapter.[8] Second, we again excluded scholars who are still alive and research active, since we consider it important that the work of a scholar be considered in its entirety. And third, as with *STL* we consulted with our contributors to determine which scholar would be their subject, although the final list of scholars is in large measure down to their individual choices. Having said that, had it been necessary to do so, we would have intervened to ensure that certain scholars were considered, on the basis that their omission would have left too large a hole in what is in a sense the story of contract law scholarship in the common law world. That list would certainly have included the Englishmen Sir Frederick Pollock and Sir William Anson and the Americans Samuel Williston and Arthur Corbin. One final point that arose in connection with the contract project is that we decided to focus in this volume on scholars of general contract law, rather than scholars whose principal interest lay in the application of general contractual principles in more specific contexts, such as sales, insurance or carriage. Hence there are no chapters on the leading lights of commercial law scholarship, such as Judah Benjamin, Sir Mackenzie Chalmers and Karl Llewellyn, despite their undoubted contributions to the general law of contract.[9] (We hope that these scholars will feature in a later volume on scholars of commercial law.)

In any case, as with *STL* we consider that the list of scholars who are considered in this volume is defensible, although one criticism that could fairly be made of the list (no doubt among others) is that it is somewhat Anglo-centric. In our view, the most obvious omission is probably Oliver Wendell Holmes.[10] It was originally intended that there would be a chapter on Holmes, but unfortunately the contributor in question had to withdraw from the project for personal reasons. Some readers may also be surprised to see no discussion of Christopher Columbus Langdell, or of influential modern schools of American contract scholarship, such as the Wisconsin school, the Chicago school – and economic analysis more generally – and the new formalists, although to some extent these omissions are explicable by the ongoing research activity of the

[8] See pp 34–36 ('Civilian Influences').

[9] On Llewellyn and contract, see A Schwartz, 'Karl Llewellyn and the Origins of Contract Theory' in JS Kraus and SD Walt (eds), *The Jurisprudential Foundations of Corporate and Commercial Law* (Cambridge, Cambridge University Press, 2000).

[10] There is already a substantial body of work on Holmes's contract scholarship: see, eg, PJ Kelley, 'A Critical Analysis of Holmes's Theory of Contract' (2000) 75 *Notre Dame Law Review* 1681.

principal figures.[11] And while the book is somewhat skewed towards English scholars, there are yet others who could quite plausibly have been included, such as John Joseph Powell, the author of the first published work on the common law of contract,[12] and Joseph Chitty, whose name remains attached to the leading English practitioners' work, nearly two centuries after he published the first edition of his contract treatise in 1826.[13] It would be invidious to try to draw up a more comprehensive list of 'missing scholars', and indeed such a task would surely be an impossible one. We hope that it will be enough to emphasise that the volume is not intended as a 'pantheon' of leading common law contract scholars, but as a work of intellectual history, in which the contributors focus their attention on a scholar in whom they have a particular interest, and whose contribution to the law of contract they consider merits sustained analysis and evaluation.

It will be apparent to those familiar with *STL* that the temporal scope of this volume is considerably wider, since while the earliest of the tort scholars to be considered was Thomas McIntyre Cooley (whose principal work on tort law was published in 1879), the main works of the first three scholars considered here significantly predate Cooley's, in the case of Sir Jeffrey Gilbert by almost two centuries. That is no coincidence. We explained in the introduction to *STL* that the scope of that book rested on a distinction 'between the study of causes of action, cases and so on that are now treated as part of tort law, and "tort law" as a subject of study in its own right'.[14] Hence we excluded from the tort project writers (such as Sir William Blackstone) who worked at a time before tort came to be recognised as a distinct legal category in the second half of the nineteenth century. By contrast, it is arguable that contract was already an established legal category in England by the early eighteenth century. Admittedly, there is very little discussion of contracts in the early eighteenth-century work on English law by Thomas Wood,[15] or in Blackstone's mid-century *Commentaries*.[16] And as Stephen Waddams says, this indicates that 'Blackstone did not visualise contracts as a body of controlling principles from which legal obligations were derived', but that 'he thought of contracts as "part of" several different areas

[11] In the case of the Wisconsin school, the omission is ameliorated somewhat by the extensive discussion of the work of Stewart Macaulay in J Braucher et al (eds), *Revisiting the Contracts Scholarship of Stewart Macaulay: On the Empirical and the Lyrical* (Oxford, Hart Publishing, 2013) and in the chapters by Brian Bix, and Elizabeth Mertz and Lawrence Friedman in D Campbell (ed), *Stewart Macaulay: Selected Works* (Cham, Springer, 2020). As for Langdell, see DP O'Gorman, 'Langdell and the Foundation of Classical Contract Law' (2022) 70 *Cleveland State Law Review* 459.

[12] JJ Powell, *An Essay upon the Law of Contracts and Agreements* (London, J Johnson and T Whieldon, 1790).

[13] H Beale (ed), *Chitty on Contracts*, 34th edn (London, Sweet & Maxwell, 2021). The first edition was published in 1826: J Chitty, *A Practical Treatise on the Law of Contracts Not Under Seal* (London, S Sweet, 1826).

[14] Goudkamp and Nolan (n 3) 4.

[15] See W Swain, *The Law of Contract 1670–1870* (Cambridge, Cambridge University Press, 2015) 31.

[16] W Blackstone, *Commentaries on the Laws of England* (Oxford, Clarendon Press, 1765–69).

of the law – a means of effecting various legal consequences – and hence to be found in several different places' on his map of English law.[17] However, the unpublished work of Gilbert, along with *A Treatise of Equity*[18] (attributed to Henry Ballow, and containing extensive discussion of contracts), shows that 'early 18th-century English lawyers did have a clear concept of what constituted a contract',[19] and hence the devotion of a chapter to Gilbert in a volume on scholars of contract law seems to us to be justified.

II. THE SCHOLARS

In the introduction to *STL* we divided the scholars considered in that volume into three categories: pioneers, consolidators and iconoclasts. We do not employ the same typology here, as in our view it works much less well when it comes to the scholars considered in this collection. Nor do we simply consider each scholar in the order in which they appear in the book (*viz* by birth date). Instead, we have grouped them in the discussion that follows along roughly chronological lines, but with some variations, in a way that we hope will best enable us to highlight continuities and differences between them, as well as allowing us to focus on two particularly interesting pairings on either side of the Atlantic, namely Pollock and Anson in England, and Williston and Corbin in the United States. One advantage of this way of proceeding is that a strict chronological treatment by order of birth date would give rise to some difficulties, especially in the case of Anson and Pollock, since although Anson was born before Pollock, Pollock's principal work on contract predates Anson's, and for this and other reasons the latter was clearly more influenced by the former than vice versa. Similarly, for reasons that we hope will become apparent, it makes sense to consider Patrick Atiyah alongside Friedrich Kessler and Ian Macneil, and hence before his Oxford predecessors Geoffrey Cheshire and Cecil Fifoot and his Oxford contemporary Sir Guenter Treitel. The classification that we employ is therefore as follows: Gilbert, Colebrooke and Leake; Anson and Pollock; Williston and Corbin; Kessler, Macneil and Atiyah; and Cheshire and Fifoot, Treitel and Coote.

A. Gilbert, Colebrooke and Leake

The principal works of the three early English contract scholars considered in this book were written between the early 1700s and the mid-nineteenth century.

[17] S Waddams, 'Nineteenth-Century Treatises on English Contract Law' in A Fernandez and MD Dubber (eds), *Law Books in Action: Essays on the Anglo-American Legal Treatise* (Oxford, Hart Publishing, 2012) 127.

[18] [H Ballow], *A Treatise of Equity* (London, D Browne and J Schuckburgh, 1737).

[19] M Lobban, 'Mapping the Common Law: Some Lessons from History' [2014] *New Zealand Law Review* 21, 32.

None of the scholars was a professional academic, employed by (and teaching in) a university. Gilbert was a judge who rose to become Chief Baron of the Exchequer. Henry Thomas Colebrooke was a colonial administrator and independent scholar, a polymath with no legal training who was the founding father of Sanskrit scholarship in Europe. And Stephen Martin Leake was an independent legal scholar who after an early career at the London Bar retired to his family seat in Hertfordshire to write, and who is probably best known today for his work with Edward Bullen on pleading, which has survived into the modern era as *Bullen and Leake and Jacob's Precedents of Pleadings*.[20]

The contribution of this motley crew of pioneering contract scholars cannot be understood in isolation from the work of others active in the same period. Hence although Gilbert's work on contract, which was only recently published,[21] can lay claim to being the first systematic treatment of the subject in writing by a common lawyer, Ballow's 1737 *Treatise of Equity*[22] has been described as 'the first published English work on contract with any pretension to treat the subject on an abstract basis'.[23] As we have seen, the efforts of Gilbert and Ballow stand in contrast to the treatment of contract by the eighteenth-century institutional writers Wood[24] and Blackstone,[25] neither of whom spent much time discussing contracts, which both tied to notions of personal property. However, it is not clear how much should be read into this. Warren Swain plausibly argues that the cursory treatment of contract in these works was a reflection of their audiences, whose primary interests would have lain elsewhere, most obviously in the law of real property.[26] In any case, the publication of a slew of books on contract from 1790 onwards attests to the perceived significance of the subject by that time, and bolsters the argument that 'contract' or 'contracts' was conceived of by common lawyers as a legal category some time before 'tort' or 'torts'.[27] The two most important of the contract works of this period by English authors not considered in this volume are those of Powell (1790) and Chitty (1826), both adverted to previously.[28] (Details of the other works of this period can be found elsewhere.[29]) Powell's *Essay* has been described as 'a significant work but not a

[20] W Blair et al (eds), *Bullen and Leake and Jacob's Precedents of Pleadings*, 19th edn (London, Sweet & Maxwell, 2020).

[21] M Lobban (ed), *Jeffrey Gilbert on Property and Contract* (London, Selden Society, 2019).

[22] Ballow (n 18).

[23] DJ Ibbetson, *A Historical Introduction to the Law of Obligations* (Oxford, Oxford University Press, 1999) 218.

[24] T Wood, *An Institute of the Laws of England in their Natural Order* (London, B Lintot and R Williamson, 1720).

[25] Blackstone (n 16).

[26] Swain (n 15) 31–33.

[27] The first significant common law works on tort were F Hilliard, *The Law of Tort or Private Wrongs* (Boston, Little, Brown & Co, 1859) and T Addison, *A Treatise on the Law of Torts or Wrongs and their Remedies* (London, Stevens & Sons, 1860).

[28] Text to nn 12–13.

[29] See, eg, the list in J Gordley, *The Philosophical Origins of Modern Contract Doctrine* (Oxford, Clarendon Press, 1991) 254–55 (which includes American works). See also AWB Simpson, 'Innovation in Nineteenth Century Contract Law' (1975) 91 *LQR* 247, 253–54.

comprehensive one',[30] with a heavy weighting towards equity and to decisions before 1750, features that 'meant that he had more in common with someone like Ballow than the nineteenth century textbook writers'.[31] At the same time, however, his work gave 'some measure of conceptual unity to contracts as a subject'[32] while his emphasis on principles and his reliance on the natural lawyers and the centrality of 'mutual consent' presaged much of the work that followed. By contrast, Chitty's treatise of 1826 was a more comprehensive treatment of the subject, in which the author sought to 'extract principles from the authorities rather than attempting to set down individual decisions at any length', thereby enabling him 'to impose a strong external framework on the material'.[33] This approach bore fruit, as the treatise developed over time into the leading practitioners' work on the English law of contract.

In his chapter on Sir Jeffrey Gilbert in this volume (chapter two), Michael Lobban argues that his work on contract 'demonstrated the unity of the subject in a way which was not possible in the fragmentary treatment offered in abridgments and manuals of pleading',[34] and that he had a highly developed will theory of contractual obligation, which sought to reconcile 'a notion of contract based on the meeting of minds with the doctrine of consideration'.[35] This analysis has important implications for the familiar historical narrative according to which a will theory borrowed from continental jurisprudence was introduced into English law in the nineteenth century to provide an intellectual framework for the substantive legal rules that emerged as a result of the decline of trial by jury and changes in the rules on pleading. As Lobban says, the importance of Gilbert's work therefore lies not so much in its influence on subsequent developments – which was rather limited – as in the insight that it gives us 'into a lawyer's understanding of English contract law in the early eighteenth century'.[36] Not only can we observe in his work the influence of will theory before Pothier, but we can also see a clear appreciation of the distinction between form and substance well in advance of the nineteenth-century developments, as well as an emphasis on formal contracts, which were excluded from later works such as Chitty's.[37] More generally, the appeal of Gilbert's works (which extended far beyond contract) lies in their 'lucidity and system by comparison with the

[30] Swain (n 15) 148.

[31] *ibid*. For a discussion of Powell's work which situates it within the context of changes in law book publishing in the late eighteenth century, see TA Baloch, 'Law Booksellers and Printers as Agents of Unchange' [2007] *CLJ* 389, 415–18. According to Baloch (at 415), Powell's *Essay* was an example of a book which could be published in the light of those changes and 'perhaps would not have been before'.

[32] Waddams (n 17) 130.

[33] Swain (n 15) 178.

[34] Lobban, chapter two of this volume, p 54.

[35] *ibid* p 48. On Gilbert's analysis of consideration, see further, S Waddams, *Principle and Policy in Contract Law* (Cambridge, Cambridge University Press, 2011) 59–61.

[36] Lobban, chapter two of this volume, p 73.

[37] See Waddams (n 35) 62.

chaotic Abridgment format of merely collecting together cases on a particular point which went before'.[38]

All told, Gilbert has a good claim to having written 'the first serious work on [contract] in England'.[39] Nevertheless, his analysis had its limitations. His was a common law treatise which did not encompass the large swathes of contract law embodied in equity doctrine. And unlike later writers, such as Chitty and Leake, who sought to identify principles that explained the cases, Gilbert's work was little more than a commentary on the case law, which descended as it progressed into 'commonplacing of an "Abridgment" type'.[40] Finally, his idea of contracts as a transfer of rights was borrowed from Thomas Hobbes, and it is unclear to what extent this vision went beyond the transfer of property rights – though Lobban argues for an expansive reading – and hence to what extent, if at all, Gilbert's conception of contract extended beyond the attenuated Blackstonian idea of contract as primarily an adjunct of property.

Still, there is no doubt that, along with Ballow, Gilbert was a 'genuine pioneer', and it was not until Henry Thomas Colebrooke that 'this sort of project was attempted again'.[41] As Joanna McCunn demonstrates in her chapter on Colebrooke in this volume (chapter three), his attempt in his 1818 *Treatise on Obligations and Contracts*[42] was ultimately unsuccessful, but there is a great deal of interest in the story that she tells, and we can learn as much from his failure as we can from the successes of some of the other scholars considered in this book. The roots of that failure lay in the highly unorthodox approach that Colebrooke adopted, in which he eschewed common law method and the positive law as set out in the cases, and focused instead on abstract principles derived from a range of secondary sources, most of them civilian.[43] The result is that (for a common lawyer) 'perhaps the most striking feature of the *Treatise* is its almost total disregard for case law', with a mere 36 cases cited in the entire work, all of them derived from the earlier literature on contract.[44]

Colebrooke relied heavily on civilian writers, especially Pothier, but unlike other English scholars he did not even attempt to integrate the work of the civilians with common law sources, by using them to explain and systematise the case law. Instead, he simply set out the principles that he derived from these secondary sources, as if they had been handed down from on high, and regardless of their fit with the positive law.[45] The effect was 'to demand of his readers their

[38] M Macnair, 'Sir Jeffrey Gilbert and his Treatises' (1994) 15 *Journal of Legal History* 252, 258.

[39] Ibbetson (n 23) 216.

[40] Macnair (n 38) 258 (speaking of Gilbert's works in general).

[41] Swain (n 15) 276.

[42] HT Colebrooke, *Treatise on Obligations and Contracts* (London, Black, Kingsbury, Parbury and Allen, 1818).

[43] According to the breakdown of his sources by McCunn, chapter three of this volume, p 87, 70 per cent of them were civilian.

[44] *ibid*.

[45] Colebrooke's approach was grounded in the natural law belief that contract law was a universal set of principles derived from reason and common sense. Such thinking was pervasive in the late

assent to and understanding of' the complex conceptual claims being made, but 'without explanation of how they relate to practical consequences or to English law', and to make this demand 'on his own authority'.[46] McCunn also points out that, apart from its unusual methodology and dense style, Colebrooke's *Treatise* lacked originality, as he 'did not add anything new' to the texts from his sources, but 'simply condensed them and fused them together', so that in the entire work there 'are only a few points that he did not substantially derive from another writer'.[47] The result was 'a fantasy of contract law, based on the works of the natural lawyers and conjured up for the benefit of laymen with judicial postings in India'.[48] It is hardly surprising that a work 'which offered little usable guidance to the actual content of English law'[49] was a total flop in England itself. As for its intended audience in India, McCunn suggests that although such a work might have had some utility there, Colebrooke's was too difficult to read and use. It was in any case superseded by William Macpherson's more orthodox work of 1860[50] and rendered almost completely otiose by the passing of the Indian Contract Act 1872.

Despite its flaws, Colebrooke's *Treatise* should not be dismissed altogether.[51] According to McCunn, it 'had a clear, streamlined structure', which transcended local concerns with the forms of action and the common law/equity divide.[52] She also argues that much of his treatise prefigured later developments, and that his work paved the way for later nineteenth-century writers who sought to systematise English contract law, using concepts that he first introduced into the common law literature, such as the distinction between unilateral and bilateral contracts. He was, for example, the first English scholar to discuss mistake in any depth, and his consent-based analysis of mistake – inspired by Pothier – was subsequently adopted by other writers. It also seems likely that the failure of Colebrooke's work influenced later contract scholars, who avoided making the same mistakes by firmly rooting their discussion in the English case law, and by seeking to blend any principles borrowed from civilian sources with the domestic authorities.[53]

eighteenth and early nineteenth century: see M Lobban, 'Contract' in W Cornish et al, *The Oxford History of the Laws of England,* vol XII (Oxford, Oxford University Press, 2010) 301.

[46] S Waddams, 'The Authority of Treatises in English Law (1800–1936)' in M Godfrey (ed), *Law and Authority in British Legal History 1200–1900* (Cambridge, Cambridge University Press, 2016) 284–85.

[47] McCunn, chapter three of this volume, p 90.

[48] *ibid* p 100.

[49] Waddams (n 35) 9.

[50] W Macpherson, *Outlines of the Law of Contracts as Administered in the Courts of British India* (London, RC Lepage, 1860).

[51] See also Swain (n 15) 149: 'as the most theoretical work then in existence [Colebrooke's treatise] was an impressive achievement'.

[52] McCunn, chapter three of this volume, p 89.

[53] See Waddams (n 35) 10, referring to Chitty and Addison as examples of later writers who avoided the pitfalls of Colebrooke's approach.

One such scholar was Stephen Martin Leake, a transitional figure who served as a bridge between the early contract writers (such as Powell, Colebrooke and Chitty) and the great systematisers of the late nineteenth century, Anson and Pollock. In her chapter in this collection (chapter four), Catherine MacMillan argues that Leake was an ambitious jurist whose work on contract law 'was part of a larger and grander scheme to attempt to understand the whole of English law in a rational and systematic manner'.[54] By the time that his treatise *The Elements of the Law of Contracts*[55] was published in 1867, reforms to the pleading rules and the decline of jury trial meant that a raft of substantive questions of law were beginning to emerge from contract litigation. This created the conditions for a more scientific approach to the subject, which was congenial to a scholar who had studied mathematics at Cambridge.[56] As MacMillan shows,[57] Leake's work was a 'distinct break' from what had come before, and was highly original in two respects: first, in 'the reasoned use' of civilian writings 'as an analytical device to synthesise and analyse English law'; and second, in the organisation of the subject around a highly ordered[58] set of generally applicable rules and principles, such that he 'wrote of a law of contract, rather than laws of contracts'.[59] The result has been described by Swain as a 'new sort of contract treatise', which was more successful than its predecessors 'in presenting the law of contract as a single body of doctrine rather than an accumulation of individual types of contract'.[60] Moreover, because Leake had made an in-depth study of the cases on contract, he was able for the first time to extract from the English authorities principles of privity, acceptance, mistake and duress, impossibility of performance, damages and quasi-contract,[61] and to ground his pioneering analysis of subjects such as mistake firmly in the case law, as opposed to theory or the civilian literature.[62] This enabled him, for example, to reject Pothier's position on the uncommunicated withdrawal of an offer as inconsistent with

[54] MacMillan, chapter four of this volume, p 105. On his wider ambition, see C MacMillan, 'Stephen Martin Leake: A Victorian's View of the Common Law' (2011) 32 *Journal of Legal History* 3.

[55] SM Leake, *The Elements of the Law of Contracts* (London, Stevens & Sons, 1867).

[56] '[Leake's] vision was of a jurisprudence based on principle, of conceptions, rather than an accumulation of precedents': MacMillan (n 54) 6.

[57] MacMillan, chapter four of this volume, p 114.

[58] According to MacMillan (2011) (n 54) 8, '[t]he science of law Leake espoused was primarily one of order'.

[59] Hence he wrote in the preface to the second edition of his treatise that it was limited to the 'general Part' of contract law, 'the ground work common to all species of contracts': SM Leake, *An Elementary Digest of the Law of Contracts* (London, Stevens & Sons, 1878) ix (quoted by Lobban (n 45) 307).

[60] Swain (n 15) 202–203.

[61] On Leake's pioneering work on mistake, see C MacMillan, *Mistakes in Contract Law* (Oxford, Hart Publishing, 2010) ch 7. As she shows, it was Leake who first identified *Raffles v Wichelhaus* (1864) 2 H & C 906, 159 ER 375 and *Couturier v Hastie* (1865) 5 HLC 673, 10 ER 1065 as authorities on that subject. Leake also proposed a novel justification for the parol evidence rule, a version of which was later adopted by Corbin: see Waddams (n 35) 43–44.

[62] See Lobban (n 45) 471.

the cases and contrary to principle.[63] It also resulted in a work which, although limited to general principles, completely dwarfed Colebrooke's (which had come in at about 250 pages) at some 700 pages in its first edition and no less than 1,300 in its second.[64]

According to MacMillan, it was from Leake's 'meticulous efforts' that 'a modern conception of contract law, a law organised rationally around underlying principles, emerged'.[65] His treatise was also important 'because of the influence it had not only upon judges but also upon later English common law writers'.[66] And yet Leake's work has often been overlooked, and his reputation overshadowed by the likes of Chitty, Anson and Pollock. In her chapter, MacMillan puts forward various possible explanations for Leake's relative obscurity, including the fact that he was a somewhat isolated figure, far removed in rural Hertfordshire from both the great universities (though he examined the Bachelor of Civil Law degree at Oxford) and legal London, and so not well placed to market his work to either students or practitioners. It may also be attributable to the limits of Leake's 'scientific' method, which was primarily focused on organisation and order rather than conceptual analysis.[67] For all Leake's undoubted qualities as a contract scholar, therefore, his contribution to the discipline was soon eclipsed by the famous works of Anson and Pollock, although his treatise survived until the 1930s.[68]

B. Anson and Pollock

Unlike the early English contract writers, Anson and Pollock were academic jurists, who both held positions at the University of Oxford. In each case, their reputation as a contract scholar rests on a single text – ostensibly concerned with the 'principles' of contract law[69] – which ran to multiple editions under their pen.[70] Both clearly owed a debt of gratitude to Leake,[71] and it has been said that it was his 'systematisation of the common law of contract' which enabled

[63] See Waddams (n 35) 22–23.

[64] The scale of the second edition drew critical comment from Pollock: see Waddams (n 17) 142.

[65] MacMillan, chapter four of this volume, p 128.

[66] MacMillan (n 61) 123.

[67] See MacMillan (2011) (n 54) 20.

[68] The last edition was RRA Walker, *Principles of the Law of Contracts*, 8th edn (London, Stevens & Sons, 1931).

[69] This was no accident, but reflected the tradition of the treatise writers of the time, who 'inherited and claimed to express the belief that private law consisted essentially of a latent scheme of principles whose workings could be seen in and illustrated by the decisions of the courts': AWB Simpson, 'The Rise and Fall of the Legal Treatise: Legal Principles and the Forms of Legal Literature' (1981) 48 *University of Chicago Law Review* 632, 666. See also Waddams (n 35) 17.

[70] Pollock also wrote numerous shorter articles and notes on contract issues. Anson wrote very little else on private law.

[71] See MacMillan (2011) (n 54) 21.

them to construct their own treatises on the subject.[72] And yet they went far beyond Leake in constructing 'a theoretical and systematic framework of legal principle into which specific legal decisions could be fitted'.[73]

Sir Frederick Pollock's treatise on contract was published in 1876.[74] This was three years before Anson's,[75] and 11 years before Pollock's equally famous treatise on tort.[76] Writing after Pollock's death, Lord Wright commented that 'Leake's book was for practitioners, while Pollock's book was for students of principles and legal thinkers'.[77] More recently, it has been said that it was 'the first English book on contract law that could reasonably claim to be an academic work'.[78] Writing in the immediate aftermath of the Judicature Act 1873, Pollock succeeded in producing the first unified and coherent account of the English law of contract encompassing both common law and equity, an achievement highlighted in the title of his book. In his treatise he 'sought to present contract law in a scientific light', as 'a system of divisions or classifications arranged according to underlying principles'.[79] As James Gordley says in his chapter on Pollock in this volume (chapter six), the result was that his 'work shaped the way we still define such basic concepts as contract, consideration and consent', though it 'was also responsible for the problems we still face in using these concepts to understand the law of contract'.[80]

In seeking to systematise English contract law, Pollock relied heavily on civilian writers, and especially Savigny. Pollock's profound debt to Savigny was reflected in the close – but not slavish[81] – alignment of his treatise with the will theory; hence, he described a contract as 'before all things a transaction in which two or more persons consent',[82] and he was the first English writer fully to embrace the continental doctrine of 'intention to create legal relations'.[83] However, as time passed Pollock's references to Savigny and other continental sources dwindled,[84] perhaps out of concern that this might detract from the

[72] *ibid* 27–28.

[73] PS Atiyah, *The Rise and Fall of Freedom of Contract* (Oxford, Oxford University Press, 1979) 682.

[74] F Pollock, *Principles of Contract at Law and in Equity* (London, Stevens & Sons, 1876).

[75] W Anson, *Principles of the English Law of Contract* (Oxford, Clarendon Press, 1879).

[76] F Pollock, *The Law of Torts: A Treatise on the Principles of Obligations Arising from Civil Wrongs in the Common Law* (London, Stevens & Sons, 1887). Pollock's contribution to tort scholarship is critically examined in R Stevens, 'Professor Sir Frederick Pollock (1845–1937): Jurist as Mayfly' in *STL* (n 1).

[77] Lord Wright, 'In Memoriam: Sir Frederick Pollock, 1845–1937' (1937) 53 *LQR* 151, 154.

[78] S Waddams, 'Book Review' (2005) 55 *University of Toronto Law Journal* 1023, 1023. See also Gordley (n 29) 216 ('in England and the United States, contract theory never became truly systematic until the time of Pollock').

[79] MacMillan (n 61) 147. On Pollock's conception of law as a science, see *ibid* 145.

[80] Gordley, chapter six of this volume, p 149.

[81] See, eg, Pollock's rejection of Pothier's position on the uncommunicated withdrawal of an offer, discussed in Waddams (n 46) 285–87.

[82] Pollock (n 74) 1.

[83] Ibbetson (n 23) 233.

[84] See Gordley, chapter six of this volume, p 157.

appeal of his treatise as a work on the *English* law of contract. Furthermore, from the third edition of his work onwards there was a clear movement away from the subjectivism of the will theory towards a more objective approach of the kind that came to dominate twentieth-century common law scholarship, and which emphasised the reasonable expectations and reliance of the promisee.[85] This shift – which seems to have come about in part because of the influence of Holmes and Thomas Erskine Holland[86] – reflects a more general flexibility in Pollock's writing on contract, where he repeatedly showed that he was willing, albeit sometimes reluctantly, to change his views.[87] It also demonstrates that ultimately Pollock was a pragmatist willing to sacrifice doctrinal purity when it conflicted with the case law and what he saw as 'common sense' outcomes;[88] as his intellectual biographer Neil Duxbury has said, '[t]o claim, as Pollock did, that the common law is founded on reason, is not the same as claiming that it is rational, or even potentially rational'.[89] At the same time, the radical changes that were made to the introductory material in Pollock's book were not always carried through to the discussion of substantive issues in the remainder, and there was never a complete break from Savigny and the will theory.[90]

Sir William Anson's contribution to contract scholarship was very different from Pollock's. The prefaces to the first and sixth editions of his book make it clear that his primary motivation was to write a text suitable for students, particularly those who from 1877 onwards took a paper on 'Principles of the Law of Contract' in the School of Jurisprudence at Oxford.[91] As Robert Stevens emphasises in his chapter in this volume (chapter five), Anson was an effective and enthusiastic teacher, whose main interest lay in legal education. Although his book 'truly began the modern story of student law textbooks',[92] it lacked the scholarly ambition of Pollock's work. For a start, it was 'a small volume of 338 (relatively small) pages',[93] in which the somewhat scant references were put in marginal sidenotes rather than footnotes. This was because Anson 'sought to provide an outline of the principles of English contract law rather than an

[85] See Waddams (n 35) 50–53.

[86] Both OW Holmes, *The Common Law* (Boston, Little, Brown & Co, 1881) and TE Holland, *The Elements of Jurisprudence*, 2nd edn (Oxford, Clarendon Press, 1882) featured attacks on Savigny and the will theory. See further on Pollock's change of emphasis, MacMillan (n 61) 162–66.

[87] See, eg, his gradual coming to terms with the 'postal rule' (which he initially opposed), and his change of mind over the decision of the Court of Appeal in *Chandler v Webster* [1904] 1 KB 493 (CA), both traced by Waddams (n 35) at 30–31 and 142–44, respectively.

[88] N Duxbury, *Frederick Pollock and the English Juristic Tradition* (Oxford, Oxford University Press, 2004) 196. See the revealing quotation from the ninth edition of his contract treatise reproduced in *ibid* 214: 'Legal rules exist not for their own sake, but to further justice and convenience in the business of human life …'. *cf* Stevens (n 76), arguing that in his tort scholarship Pollock was inflexible and stubborn, and failed to adapt his treatise to take account of new developments.

[89] Duxbury (n 88) 282.

[90] See Swain (n 15) 205–206; MacMillan (n 61) 166–69 (discussing Pollock's treatment of mistake).

[91] See Anson (n 75) v; WR Anson, *Principles of the English Law of Contract*, 6th edn (Oxford, Clarendon Press, 1891) v.

[92] Stevens, chapter five of this volume, p 133.

[93] PS Atiyah, 'Book Review' (1981) 1 *LS* 100, 100.

exhaustive study'.[94] The book was also very derivative. The influence of Leake and especially Pollock was obvious and acknowledged,[95] and it seems clear that Anson could not have written his work without the benefit of their efforts.[96] And yet, '[p]ossibly because his ambition was more modest than Pollock's, Anson was more successful in realising it'.[97] Whereas the last edition of Pollock's treatise was published in 1950,[98] not only did Anson's textbook dominate the student market throughout the early twentieth century, but it continues to flourish today, the longest lasting student text in law in the anglophone world.[99]

Much of the appeal of Anson's book lay in its lucidity and directness,[100] which contrasted favourably with Pollock's somewhat ponderous and indirect style of expression.[101] He also 'took great care in the arrangement and proportion of his subject',[102] structuring his text around the chronology of a contract, which he traced through 'how a contract is made, what is needed to make it binding, what its effect is, how its terms are interpreted, and how it is discharged and comes to an end'.[103] This scheme was a brilliant innovation, with obvious pedagogical appeal, which has been imitated in countless other texts, such that 'it often seems as though much of the present shape of the law was actually created by Anson'.[104] Another explanation for the success of Anson's work was that it was less theoretical than Pollock's. He was 'not concerned about grandiose expositions of theory',[105] and although he also drew upon Savigny and other civilian jurists, he did so with a lighter touch than Pollock.

There was, however, a flipside to Anson's focus on brevity and clarity, which was that he frequently glossed over difficulties or over-simplified. Unlike Pollock, who was careful to hedge about his claims with qualifications where necessary, Anson strove to present the law in as straightforward a manner as possible, even when the true position was more complex.[106] He himself admitted that in seeking to make his work accessible to students he often ran 'the risk of seeming

[94] MacMillan (n 61) 170.

[95] Anson (n 75) vii.

[96] 'Anson's book was very closely based … on Pollock's': Waddams (n 17) 142.

[97] MacMillan (n 61) 170.

[98] PH Winfield, *Pollock's Principles of Contract*, 13th edn (London, Stevens & Sons, 1950).

[99] J Beatson et al, *Anson's Law of Contract*, 31st edn (Oxford, Oxford University Press, 2020).

[100] According to MP Furmston, 'Book Review' (1960) 23 *MLR* 206, 206, 'Sir William Anson's treatment combined accuracy and lucidity to a remarkable degree'.

[101] For an example of a 'convoluted assembly of qualified and counter-qualified double negatives' of Pollock's, see Waddams (n 35) 77. Contrast also the way that Pollock and Anson set out the principle that the adequacy of the consideration is not relevant (*ibid* 99–100). For trenchant criticism of Pollock's style, see Stevens (n 76) 75–76.

[102] MacMillan (n 61) 170.

[103] Atiyah (n 93) 100. As with most contract works of this era, remedies for breach were considered outwith the boundaries of the subject and not discussed.

[104] *ibid* 101. On the organisation of American contract works, see EA Farnsworth, 'Contracts Scholarship in the Age of Anthology' (1987) 85 *Michigan Law Review* 1406, 1434–37.

[105] MacMillan (n 61) 170.

[106] See, eg, Waddams (n 35) 78 (contrasting Pollock's 'cryptic and tentative' approach to issues of privity with Anson's 'plain and dogmatic' approach); and Duxbury (n 88) 202 (contrasting Anson's dogged assertion that all contracts must entail an offer and an acceptance with Pollock's more nuanced view).

to dogmatise',[107] and the absence of footnotes 'wholly precluded any secondary discussion of complexities, or any qualification' of the assertions made in the text.[108] And while Pollock demonstrated flexibility in moving away from the will theory over time, Anson stuck with it more doggedly,[109] so that a simplified form of the approach taken in Pollock's first edition was 'crystallised' in successive editions of Anson's work.[110] This is not of course to deny that Anson was capable of great sophistication and insight, and of substantially advancing the discussion of substantive questions.[111] Nevertheless, as Stevens says, in the end his 'contribution was of clarity, rather than of originality'.[112]

Both Anson and Pollock were in their own ways exceptionally influential scholars of contract law, with Pollock's influence more directly on the courts, and Anson's on the generations of law students for whom the study of contract law began (and, no doubt, often ended) with his textbook. But their joint impact was also greater than the sum of their individual contributions. The publication of the first editions of their works within three years of each other in the late 1870s marked the birth of the modern law of contract and gave it the distinctive shape and structure which it in large part retains to this day. In Atiyah's words:

> To put it at the lowest, it seems to me that these two academic giants are probably entitled to just as much of the credit for the creation of the general law of contract as all of the nineteenth century judges put together. The judges may have provided the bricks, but the design of the building was largely the work of the writers.[113]

C. Williston and Corbin

If Anson and Pollock are the 'academic giants' of English contract law, the equivalent figures in the United States are Williston and Corbin. For both men, the multi-volume treatise that bears their name was the crowning glory of an extraordinarily prolific and influential scholarly life focused mainly on

[107] Anson (n 75) vii.

[108] Waddams (n 17) 143–44.

[109] Hence the disagreement between the two on revocation of offers, where Anson's room for manoeuvre was limited by his insistence that in general simultaneous mutual assent was required for a contract to be formed: see Waddams (n 35) 26–28.

[110] Waddams (n 17) 144. This may in part be because Anson's other commitments prevented him from revising his work as thoroughly as he might otherwise have done: see MacMillan (n 61) 178.

[111] According to Atiyah, 'at times Anson's writing seems to have been almost prophetic' (Atiyah (n 93) 101, giving examples). See also B Coote (edited by R Bigwood), *Contract as Assumption: Essays on a Theme* (Oxford, Hart Publishing, 2010) 24 (crediting Anson with identifying 'the secret paradox' in cases where a promisor undertakes to do something which he or she was already obliged to do under a contract with a third party); and MacMillan (n 61) 212 (Anson's interpretation of *Smith v Hughes* (1871) LR 6 QB 597 'has become the modern treatment of the case').

[112] Stevens, chapter five of this volume, p 138.

[113] PS Atiyah, *Pragmatism and Theory in English Law* (London, Stevens & Sons, 1987) 173. See also Atiyah (n 73) 683 (it is to Anson and Pollock 'that we owe much of the power of the concepts of the law of contract').

contract law. Both were 'consolidators' in the sense in which we used that term in the introduction to *STL*, and they share many of the characteristics of the tort consolidators that we identified there: they were career academics; they are associated with canonical texts; their scholarly methodologies were relatively constant; they had a remarkable work ethic;[114] they were pragmatists who were sceptical of theory; and 'their influence came not … from a handful of "big ideas", but from the accumulated impact of their writings on a host of different topics, ranging across the entirety of the subject'.[115] It is also telling in this regard that the widely admired *Restatement (First) of the Law of Contracts*[116] – a classic example of scholarly 'consolidation' – was the result of a fruitful collaboration between the two men.

It is impossible to appreciate the contribution of Williston and Corbin to American contract scholarship without some sense of what came before them, though space constraints preclude a detailed discussion, which must therefore be sought elsewhere.[117] According to the American contract scholar Allan Farnsworth, '[c]ontracts scholarship was slow in coming to this side of the Atlantic' and in the early nineteenth century, 'American lawyers leaned heavily on English writers',[118] as evidenced by the publication of American editions of the books of (among others) Powell, Chitty and Leake. The first significant works on contract by Americans were the mid-century treatises of William Story[119] and Theophilus Parsons,[120] both of which were aimed primarily at practitioners. These were followed in 1871 by Langdell's casebook,[121] the first of a long line of such works that have dominated the student market in the

[114] Williston wrote in his autobiography that he consistently worked in the evenings, at weekends and even on vacation: S Williston, *Life and Law* (Boston, Little, Brown & Co, 1941) 303 (cited by AD Boyer, 'Samuel Williston's Struggle with Depression' (1994) 42 *Buffalo Law Review* 1, 39). He published his last law review article at the age of 88 (S Williston, 'The Law of Sales in the Proposed Uniform Commercial Code' (1950) 63 *Harvard Law Review* 561), some 62 years after his first. Corbin was 76 when the first edition of his treatise was published, and 89 when the second edition came out. According to Twining, much of Corbin's greatness 'lies in the consistency, patience and rigour with which he approached his chosen field of specialization': W Twining, *Karl Llewellyn and the Realist Movement*, 2nd edn (Cambridge, Cambridge University Press, 2012) 30.

[115] Goudkamp and Nolan (n 3) 23.

[116] *Restatement (First) of the Law of Contracts* (Philadelphia, American Law Institute, 1932). Grant Gilmore, admittedly prone to hyperbole, described the contracts *Restatement* as 'not only the best of the Restatements', but 'one of the great legal accomplishments of all time': G Gilmore, *The Death of Contract* (Columbus, Ohio State University Press, 1974) 59.

[117] For a very thorough account, on which the following text draws, see Farnsworth (n 104) 1407–24.

[118] *ibid* 1407.

[119] WW Story, *A Treatise on the Law of Contracts Not Under Seal* (Boston, Little, Brown & Co, 1844). William is not to be confused with his father Joseph, the great treatise writer.

[120] T Parsons, *The Law of Contracts* (Boston, Little, Brown & Co, 1853). This was a popular work, which 'supposedly … sold more copies than any other American treatise': LM Friedman, *A History of American Law*, 4th edn (New York, Oxford University Press, 2019) 608.

[121] CC Langdell, *A Selection of Cases on the Law of Contracts* (Boston, Little, Brown & Co, 1871). The second edition of this work was accompanied by an appendix consisting of short essays on the topics in its index, which was subsequently published separately as CC Langdell, *A Summary of the Law of Contracts* (Boston, Little, Brown & Co, 1880).

United States ever since.[122] A decade later, Holmes published *The Common Law*.[123] Though numbering less than a hundred pages, the three lectures devoted to contract in that book had a bigger impact on the subject than any previous work by an American author, most famously through Holmes's espousal of an objective theory of contract that stood in stark contrast to the will theory that had dominated English contract thinking up until that time. However, despite the gauntlet thrown down by Holmes, the next 40 years saw no significant new American books on contract,[124] and the tradition of reliance on English works continued, with multiple American editions of Pollock's treatise (including one by Williston in 1906) and of Anson's textbook (including three by Corbin, in 1919, 1924 and 1930), as well as the publication in 1891 of a bizarre book in which text from Leake's treatise was interspersed with cases from an English casebook modelled on Langdell's.[125]

The end of the 'lean years'[126] was marked by the publication of Samuel Williston's four-volume treatise in 1920.[127] That monumental work was preceded by a healthy stream of periodical literature on contract in the American law reviews, and full account must of course be taken of the contribution that Williston made to that literature when assessing his contract scholarship, as well as of his work as Reporter for the *Restatement (First)*.[128] But pride of place must go to the treatise. *Williston on Contracts* was a remarkable work, one of the four 'ultra-treatises'[129] which mark the pinnacle of the American tradition of treatise-writing, along with *Scott* on trusts,[130] *Wigmore* on evidence[131] and *Corbin* on contracts.[132] As Todd Rakoff says in his chapter on Williston in this volume (chapter seven), even though the treatise was clearly written for a professional audience of lawyers and judges, its contents amounted to much more than mere exposition. Williston used the space that the multi-volume format gave him to explore the history of the topic under discussion, to consider rival solutions to doctrinal problems, and to test the fit of those solutions with the law on

[122] See generally, Farnsworth (n 104).

[123] Holmes (n 86).

[124] The reasons for this are explored in Farnsworth (n 104) 1420–24, who argues that the most plausible explanation is the case method of teaching first adopted by Langdell at Harvard in 1870.

[125] W Keener, *Selections from Leake's Elements of the Law of Contracts and Finch's Cases on Contracts* (New York, Baker, Voorhis & Co, 1891). The casebook was GB Finch, *A Selection of Cases on the English Law of Contract* (Cambridge, Cambridge University Press, 1886). Unsurprisingly Keener's book was not successful and the experiment was not carried into further editions.

[126] Farnsworth (n 104) 1413.

[127] S Williston, *The Law of Contracts* (New York, Baker, Voorhis & Co, 1920).

[128] *Restatement (First) of the Law of Contracts* (n 116). He also wrote or edited numerous casebooks, and published treatises on commercial law topics, most notably sale of goods: S Williston, *The Law Governing Sales of Goods at Common Law and Under the Uniform Sales Act* (New York, Baker, Voorhis & Co, 1909).

[129] Simpson (n 69) 674.

[130] AW Scott, *The Law of Trusts* (Boston, Little, Brown & Co, 1939).

[131] JH Wigmore, *A Treatise on the System of Evidence in Trials at Common Law* (Boston, Little, Brown & Co, 1904).

[132] AL Corbin, *A Comprehensive Treatise on the Rules of Contract Law* (St Paul, West Publishing, 1950).

related topics and against 'his society's sense of justice',[133] with all this accompanied by extensive footnotes setting out the position in the different states of the union. Rakoff also argues that – unlike nineteenth-century English writers, such as Pollock – Williston did not generally reason deductively, drawing his conclusions from higher principles: his 'typical analysis does not proceed from a strong internal hierarchy of premises, such that many specific rules or doctrines proceed from a small number of strongly entrenched major propositions'.[134] This leads Rakoff to question the characterisation of Williston as a 'formalist' that pervades the existing literature on his scholarship, including the revisionist analysis of Mark Movsesian in his important article 'Rediscovering Williston'.[135]

Movsesian described Williston as a 'pragmatic-formalist' and argued that pragmatism was a central – perhaps *the* central – characteristic of his scholarship (as indeed it was for other private law consolidators of the early to mid-twentieth century, such as the tort scholars Sir Percy Winfield and William Prosser[136]). Hence Williston glossed the nineteenth-century conception of law as a 'science' by calling it a 'pragmatic science',[137] described his early Harvard colleagues (with apparent approval) as 'pragmatists' who 'felt themselves engaged in a practical profession',[138] and wrote in the preface to his treatise that he had 'endeavored to keep my discussions within the limits of practical usefulness'.[139] His pragmatism also manifested itself in a distaste for high theory. He had no truck with the will theorists and warmly embraced Holmes's rival objective approach to contractual obligation,[140] while more generally he cautioned against the academic tendency 'to get too far from the earth'.[141] Furthermore, practical considerations underlay Williston's commitment to keeping the law as simple, certain and comprehensible as possible. According to Allen Boyer – who connects this quest to Williston's struggle to reassert control over his mental health following bouts of depression – he 'held up simplicity and certainty as intrinsic values toward which the law should aspire', not for their own sake, but because this would result in clear rules that could be relied on without litigation.[142] Williston's quest for simplicity (and, concomitantly, for broad general rules across all contract types) was

[133] Rakoff, chapter seven of this volume, p 178.

[134] *ibid* p 189.

[135] ML Movsesian, 'Rediscovering Williston' (2005) 62 *Washington & Lee Law Review* 207.

[136] See Goudkamp and Nolan (n 3) 22, and the chapters on Winfield and Prosser in *STL* (n 1). Although Rakoff takes issue with the 'pragmatic' as well as the 'formalist' half of Movsesian's description, this is because Rakoff equates pragmatism with functionalism and efficiency, which we do not. By 'pragmatic' we mean sceptical of theory, abstraction and doctrinal 'purity', and focused instead on practical considerations and the real-world implications of legal rules.

[137] Williston, *Life and Law* (n 114) 202 (quoted by Movsesian (n 135) 231).

[138] S Williston, *Some Modern Tendencies in the Law* (New York, Baker, Voorhis & Co, 1929) 11 (quoted by Movsesian (n 135) 268).

[139] Williston (n 127) vol 1, iv (quoted by Rakoff, chapter seven of this volume, p 178).

[140] See Boyer (n 114) 25.

[141] S Williston, 'The Necessity of Idealism in Teaching Law' (1908) 2 *American Law School Review* 201, 203 (quoted by Movsesian (n 135) 233).

[142] Boyer (n 114) 23.

criticised by legal realists such as Walter Wheeler Cook, who argued in a review of the second edition of Williston's treatise that his methodology was underlain by 'an assumption that the legal universe is far simpler than the "realist" believes it to be',[143] and that the general, 'unified' law of contract portrayed by works such as Williston's was a myth. However, such criticism left Williston unmoved, and in his autobiography he attacked what he called 'the so-called functional approach', which 'if pushed to its limit' would require that 'a rule must be established for each separate state of facts', thereby returning contract law to a state of 'pre-Langdellian chaos'.[144]

Although some late twentieth-century legal historians painted a one-dimensional portrait of Williston as a reactionary classical formalist – in Morton Horwitz's words, 'a leading exemplar' of 'a legal ideology of formalism' that disguised 'gross disparities of bargaining power under a façade of neutral and formal rules of contract law'[145] – that caricature has since been attacked by other scholars, who have argued that Williston was a non-ideological conservative who shared some, though not all, of the concerns of the scholarly progressives of his era.[146] And although (as Rakoff emphasises) Williston's treatise was heavily focused on case law, and he showed little interest in the statutory regulation of contracts, that work and the *Restatement* did at least break the hold which English cases had hitherto had over the American contract literature.[147]

One of the progressives of Williston's era was Arthur Corbin, who himself produced an extraordinary six-volume treatise on contracts in 1950, towards the end of a career marked by a prolific output of law review articles and other publications, including a casebook of some 1,500 pages that was first published in 1921, and which ran to three editions.[148] In his chapter in this collection (chapter eight), Gregory Klass argues that for Corbin:

> [T]the task of both legal education and legal scholarship is not merely to transfer legal knowledge from teacher to student, author to reader, but to disabuse the student or the reader of their false sense of certainty about the law and to help them to see it as a contingent, evolving institution, one that builds on generalisations from past experience, but which must also attend to the changing demands of a social world.[149]

[143] WW Cook, 'Williston on Contracts' (1939) 33 *Illinois Law Review* 497, 504.

[144] The final phrase is Boyer's ((n 114) 43), not Williston's. We might take it to mean more generally the state of the subject prior to the late nineteenth-century system-builders.

[145] MJ Horwitz, *The Transformation of American Law 1780–1860* (Cambridge MA, Harvard University Press, 1977) 201. *cf* Friedman (n 120) 610, 711, who, although also hyperbolic ('volume after volume of a heavy void'; 'fully armored against the intrusion of any ethical, economic, or social ideas whatsoever'), does not make the same insinuation of ideologically driven duplicity.

[146] See Boyer (n 114) 23 ('There is … little which is reactionary about his philosophy'), 28; M Movsesian, 'Williston as Conservative-Pragmatist' (2007) 32 *Southern Illinois University Law Journal* 1.

[147] See Farnsworth (n 104) 1439–41.

[148] A Corbin, *Cases on the Law of Contracts* (St Paul, West Publishing, 1921).

[149] Klass, chapter eight of this volume, p 203.

Corbin was an avowed objectivist, describing the 'main underlying purpose' of contract law as 'the realization of reasonable expectations that have been induced by the making of a promise'.[150] He was also a pragmatist, whose non-elite mid-western background manifested itself in a modest and understated style that eschewed sweeping claims and grand theory,[151] as well as an insistence that the law must remain in step with the values and expectations of the community it serves.[152] But while Williston's pragmatism drove a quest for simplicity and certainty, Corbin's led him to embrace a certain degree of complexity and instability.[153] Hence Corbin's scepticism (highlighted by Klass[154]) about substantive definitions, as exemplified by his approach to consideration, which he argued was not a single definable concept, but an umbrella term embracing 'many doctrines serving different policies'.[155]

The question of whether Williston was a formalist finds an echo in the question of whether Corbin was a realist, which again admits of no simple answer. Corbin 'belonged to an in-between generation – he came after the Willistons and before the Llewellyns',[156] and so it is not surprising that he is difficult to pigeonhole. Although clearly he was a modernist who was very comfortable challenging convention and tradition, Kessler wrote after Corbin's death that he 'did not join the realist movement' and 'was rather critical of its tenets, and particularly of the position that decisions were not determined by rules and principles'.[157] At the same time, however, Corbin was clearly respected and even revered by leading realists,[158] shared their scepticism about legal certainty and abstract generalisations, and agreed with them that 'facts, not legal doctrines, play the major role in judicial decisions'.[159] Moreover, although he recognised the importance of legal rules, this was also true of all but the most extreme 'realists', and besides Corbin constantly emphasised that such rules were not immutable and eternal, but merely 'defeasible generalizations from past experience – working

[150] Corbin (n 132) § 1.

[151] Corbin 'had little interest in or use for abstract doctrine': G Gilmore, 'Friedrich Kessler' (1975) 84 *Yale Law Journal* 672, 674.

[152] See F Kessler, 'Arthur Linton Corbin – A Tribute' (1954) 64 *Yale Law Journal* 164, 168; MJ Horwitz, *The Transformation of American Law 1870–1960* (New York, Oxford University Press, 1992) 49 ('an earthy, pragmatic skepticism'). Corbin's no-nonsense attitude is reflected in his homely style, which is one of the attractions of his work: see, eg, AL Corbin, 'Discharge of Contracts' (1913) 22 *Yale Law Journal* 513, 519 ('If a man promises to dig a well yesterday, or to build a house on the sun, or to make a road to China on a straight line, no obligation is born').

[153] 'Professor Corbin refrains from making things clearer than they are': F Kessler, 'Arthur Linton Corbin' (1969) 78 *Yale Law Journal* 517, 523.

[154] Klass, chapter eight of this volume, pp 210–15.

[155] Kessler (n 153) 521.

[156] Gilmore (n 116) 60.

[157] Kessler (n 153) 519. See also G Gilmore, *The Ages of American Law* (New Haven, Yale University Press, 1977) 79: 'Corbin took no part in the Realist controversy'.

[158] See Gilmore (n 157) 79, and, for an example, see the praise heaped on Corbin by J Frank, 'Corbin on Contracts Volume Three' (1952) 61 *Yale Law Journal* 1109.

[159] HG Havighurst, 'Corbin on Contracts Volume Six' (1952) 61 *Yale Law Journal* 1139, 1139. This was reflected in the way that Corbin treated cases, which was quite different from, say, Williston: see Gilmore (n 157) 79–80.

rules in a constantly evolving social practice'.[160] Corbin's emphasis on the mutability of what he called 'tentative working rules'[161] reflected his belief that legal development was an evolutionary process, in which the ultimate test of theories, principles and rules was 'survival in conflict'.[162] And because this meant that legal change was inexorable, he believed that the creativity of the judges who made the law should be both acknowledged and celebrated.[163]

The extent of the contrast between Corbin and Williston is controversial. The historians who branded Williston a classical formalist tended to emphasise their differences, casting Corbin as a revolutionary figure instrumental in bringing down the edifice which Gilmore termed the 'Holmes-Williston' construct.[164] However, more recent scholarship – including the chapters on the two scholars in this volume – has challenged key assumptions underlying these claims, and in so doing cast doubt on the extent, though certainly not the existence, of the differences in their outlook and scholarship.[165] Perhaps the best we can do is to say that there is an element of Yin and Yang (or vice versa) to the relationship between Harvard's Williston and Yale's Corbin, and also to make the point that, regardless of those differences, these two greats of contract law scholarship clearly respected and liked each other.[166]

D. Kessler, Macneil and Atiyah

Williston and Corbin have sometimes been typecast as epitomes of two very different styles of contract scholarship, which we might label 'traditional' (or 'classical') and 'modern' (or 'realist'). Even if that is an over-simplification when applied to these two men, this dichotomy – or something like it – has some utility when it comes to other twentieth-century common law contract scholars. In particular, when we turn to consider the remaining jurists whose contributions are discussed in this volume, there would seem to be a fairly clear line between Kessler, Macneil and Atiyah, on the one hand (the 'modernists'), and Cheshire and Fifoot, Treitel and Coote (the 'traditionalists') on the other. As a result, in our view it makes sense to divide the remaining discussion of individual scholars in this chapter along this line, beginning with the modernists.

[160] Klass, chapter eight of this volume, p 207.

[161] AL Corbin, 'The Law and the Judges' (1914) 3 *Yale Review New Series* 234, 239.

[162] *ibid* 247. Corbin had studied science at the University of Kansas and been 'deeply impressed by the theory of evolution': Twining (n 114) 27.

[163] Hence 'Cardozo is his hero': Kessler (n 153) 520. For an analysis by Corbin of Cardozo's contract judgments, see AL Corbin, 'Mr Justice Cardozo and the Law of Contracts' (1939) 52 *Harvard Law Review* 408.

[164] See, eg, Gilmore (n 116) 57–58; LM Friedman, *American Law in the 20th Century* (New Haven, Yale University Press, 2002) 382 (calling Corbin 'the great anti-Williston').

[165] But *cf* Twining, chapter 15 of this volume, pp 393–94 (stressing the differences between the two).

[166] For compelling evidence in this regard, see AL Corbin, 'Samuel Williston' (1963) 76 *Harvard Law Review* 1327, 1329 (describing Williston as 'above all an affectionate and lovable elder brother').

One advantage of dividing up our discussion in this way is that we come next to Friedrich Kessler, whose greatest influence was Corbin,[167] and who embraced Corbin's vision of contract law as 'not a closed system of harmonious rules but an open system of social action rich in dynamic complexity and full of contradictions'.[168] Unlike the scholars considered thus far, Kessler's main contribution to contract scholarship came not through a single expository work encompassing the entire subject, but through a series of articles on distinct but related themes, as well as three editions of a casebook, which was co-authored with (variously) Malcolm Sharp, Grant Gilmore and Anthony Kronman.[169] Although the quantity of Kessler's writings on contract was modest by comparison with some of the other scholars considered here, his influence on the subject was immense. A highly original thinker, Kessler was adept at identifying and exploring in his work issues that would come to dominate contract law and scholarship in the decades that followed. Indeed, so prescient was he that many of his key ideas and insights acquired the air of orthodoxy within a relatively short space of time.[170]

Kessler's three most famous articles are the subject of close analysis in Hugh Collins's chapter on him in this volume (chapter ten), and his scholarly contribution has also been considered by Gilmore,[171] George Priest[172] and Christian Joerges.[173] Several common themes emerge from these studies. One is Kessler's emphasis on the relationship between contract law and freedom. By the time that he published his seminal article on 'Contracts of Adhesion' in the 1940s,[174] the ideal of freedom of contract had been substantially undermined by the development of monopolistic companies which used what Kessler called 'adhesion contracts' to impose their standard terms of business on their contracting partners.[175] Not only did Kessler identify the link between classical contract theory and *laissez-faire* economics, he also showed how the classical dogma of 'freedom of contract' had in fact become a tool of oppression in the hands of

[167] See Collins, chapter ten of this volume, p 255.

[168] F Kessler, 'Corbin on Contracts Volume One' (1952) 61 *Yale Law Journal* 1092, 1094.

[169] F Kessler and M Sharp, *Contracts: Cases and Materials* (New York, Prentice Hall, 1953). The later editions were published in 1970 and 1986.

[170] See Gilmore (n 151) 675.

[171] *ibid.*

[172] GL Priest, 'Contracts Then and Now: An Appreciation of Friedrich Kessler' (1995) 104 *Yale Law Journal* 2145.

[173] C Joerges, 'History as Non-History: Points of Divergence and Time Lags between Friedrich Kessler and German Jurisprudence' (1994) 42 *American Journal of Comparative Law* 163; C Joerges, 'Demos vs Ethnos in Private Law: Friedrich Kessler and his German Heritage' (1995) 104 *Yale Law Journal* 2137.

[174] F Kessler, 'Contracts of Adhesion – Some Thoughts About Freedom of Contract' (1943) 43 *Columbia Law Review* 629.

[175] Although this problem is now closely bound up with the idea of 'consumer protection', as Collins points out (chapter ten of this volume, p 262), Kessler did not focus on consumers as such in that article, which probably pre-dated the idea of consumers as a legal category. Moreover, Kessler's later work on vertical integration by contract concerned not consumers but franchisees: see F Kessler, 'Automobile Dealer Franchises: Vertical Integration by Contract' (1957) 66 *Yale Law Journal* 1135.

these monopolists, who could use it to impose 'a new feudal order' on 'a vast host of vassals'.[176] It is important to note that for Kessler this was not just a matter of *economic* exploitation, but a deeply *political* problem, in that the ability of the monopolist to dictate contract terms threatened an abuse of the legislative power inherent in the contractual form which he considered not only anti-democratic but positively fascistic.[177]

A second theme of these studies of Kessler is his radicalism, which is perhaps most apparent from his casebook, a work which marked a complete break from the traditional organisation of the subject,[178] included a series of entirely novel chapters on types of contract subject to high levels of regulation, and (in a quintessentially realist move) paired together cases that reached contradictory results on similar facts. Kessler's radicalism also manifested itself in the methodology of his seminal article on automobile franchises,[179] which anticipated the later empirical studies of Stewart Macaulay.

A final theme that threads through accounts of Kessler's scholarship is the influence of his training as a lawyer in Germany during the Weimar Republic. Unlike Treitel, who emigrated to England as a child to escape the Nazis, Kessler – whose wife was Jewish – travelled to the United States in 1934 as a fully qualified German academic, who had completed his doctorate and his 'habilitation' (both as it happens on American law). Kessler's civilian training made him more theoretically minded than other American modernists, such as Corbin and Macaulay, and may also explain his commitment to legal doctrine, albeit to the 'radically new doctrines' appropriate for the 'radically changed circumstances' in which he believed the modern law of contract was operating.[180] Furthermore, Kessler's roots enabled him to keep a foot in both the American and German scholarly camps throughout his career, and to bring a civilian perspective to bear on common law problems, most famously in his comparative analysis of 'culpa in contrahendo' and good faith,[181] the third of Kessler's articles – along with 'Contracts of Adhesion' and 'Automobile Franchises' – that Collins explores in his chapter.

Like Kessler, the work of Ian Macneil would not have been possible without the realist revolution in American legal thought. However, Macneil took contract scholarship in a very different direction, so much so that Gilmore

[176] Kessler (n 174) 640.

[177] According to Priest (n 172) 2147, 'Kessler concluded that modern contractual practice was the principal threat to contemporary political and economic freedom'.

[178] Chapter headings included 'Fairness of the Bargain and Equality. Exchange Justice' and 'Formalism in Our Law of Contracts'.

[179] Kessler (n 175).

[180] See Gilmore (n 151) 677; and for evidence, see Kessler (n 152) 165 (referring to the need for constant re-examination of concepts, doctrines, principles and institutions). Gilmore ((n 151) 681) observes that Kessler was unusual in his generation for having decisively rejected doctrinal orthodoxy but at the same time seeming 'never to have been tempted to go on to some form of antidoctrine as salvation'. He attributes this in part to Kessler's civilian training.

[181] F Kessler and E Fine, 'Culpa in Contrahendo, Bargaining in Good Faith, and Freedom of Contract: A Comparative Study' (1964) 77 *Harvard Law Review* 401.

categorised him (perhaps unfairly) as a 'New Conceptualist', who had 'forsaken the pluralism' of scholars such as Corbin, Llewellyn and Kessler.[182] Macneil was in any case a scholar of great complexity, and although he clearly rejected what he called the 'Willistonian' approach to contract, and accepted the allegations of doctrinal incoherence made against the classical model, he conceded that that model 'has been of enormous, and continues to be of substantial, value'.[183] He could also be highly critical of post-realist movements such as Posnerian economic analysis and critical legal studies.[184]

Before studying law, Macneil had majored in sociology, and his contract scholarship is markedly inter-disciplinary in character, with a consistent emphasis on 'the embeddedness of all contracts and contractual behaviour in ongoing social relations'.[185] His sociological/anthropological approach manifested itself in a central focus not on contract *law*, but on contract *itself*, which he defined broadly as 'the relations among parties to the process of projecting exchange into the future'.[186] Nowhere is this clearer than in his casebook, which exceeded even Kessler's for its radicalism, and which Macneil said was based on the 'fundamental assumption … that contract encompasses all human activities in which economic exchange is a factor', including marriage, corporate structures and collective bargaining.[187] The casebook was 'organised functionally',[188] and in the second edition the latter half of the work was structured around the concept of contract planning,[189] a concept Macneil had first explored in a 1975 article.[190] Too unorthodox to be widely adopted, the second edition of the casebook was not followed up with a third for over two decades, although in the meantime its structure was emulated in a more accessible work produced by Macaulay and his colleagues at the University of Wisconsin.[191]

Macneil is best known as the co-father (along with Macaulay) of 'relational contract theory', as set out in his case in numerous articles and his 1980

[182] Gilmore (n 157) 107–108, 147.

[183] D Campbell, 'Ian Macneil and the Relational Theory of Contract' in I Macneil (edited by D Campbell), *The Relational Theory of Contract: Selected Works of Ian Macneil* (London, Sweet & Maxwell, 2001) 8.

[184] On economic analysis, see IR Macneil, 'Efficient Breach: Circles in the Sky' (1982) 68 *Virginia Law Review* 947; and on critical legal studies, see Macneil (n 183) 302–303.

[185] Morgan, chapter 12 of this volume, p 299. The 'all' is important, as in Macneil's view even seemingly 'discrete' transactions take place within a web of social relations and (generally) a network of other contracts concerning the provision of credit and the like: see S Wheeler, 'Visions of Contract' (2017) 44 *Journal of Law and Society* S74, S85.

[186] IR Macneil, *The New Social Contract: An Inquiry into Modern Contractual Relations* (New Haven, Yale University Press, 1980) 4.

[187] IR Macneil, *Cases and Materials on Contracts: Exchange Transactions and Relationships* (Mineola, Foundation Press, 1971).

[188] J Feinman, 'The Reception of Ian Macneil's Work on Contract in the USA' in Macneil (n 183) 65.

[189] IR Macneil, *Contracts: Transactions and Relationships: Cases and Materials*, 2nd edn (Mineola, Foundation Press, 1978).

[190] IR Macneil, 'A Primer of Contract Planning' (1975) 48 *Southern California Law Review* 627.

[191] S Macaulay et al, *Contracts: Law in Action* (Charlottesville, Michie Co, 1995). The third edition of Macneil's casebook was IR Macneil and PJ Gudel, *Contracts: Exchange Transactions and Relations* (Mineola, Foundation Press, 2001).

monograph *The New Social Contract*,[192] a book which has generated a veritable flood of secondary literature and which is analysed in depth in Jonathan Morgan's chapter in this volume (chapter 12). A reviewer of the book summarised the central tenets of Macneil's relational theory as follows:

> [T]here are certain norms common to all contractual relations, that a concept of contractual relations based on the 'discrete transaction' cannot comprehend the range of contractual relations, or adequately utilise (weigh, balance) the shared norms, and consequently that we must start to construct a law … that is predicated upon the existence of the relational contract.[193]

It will be apparent from that synopsis that Macneil's work on relational contract was not especially legal in character. As Morgan says, he examined 'contracting practices and norms solely as *social* phenomena – to which contract law was at best incidental, at worst distorting'.[194] When coupled with his expansive definition of contract, this focus on the 'sociology of the contracting process'[195] gave Macneil's work an extraordinary breadth.[196] And while this seemed not to bother him, it did concern others, who questioned what the boundaries of his theory were, and why, for example, it was limited to 'future-looking' exchange relations.[197] Furthermore, the nature of Macneil's enterprise meant that (like the empirical work of Macaulay), it was primarily descriptive in character, and while he clearly believed that the reality he described had implications for contract doctrine, a recurrent criticism of Macneil is that he did not do more to identify what those implications were.[198] Another observation frequently made about Macneil's work is that it is complex and difficult to follow (at least for lawyers).[199] This has been said to 'mask the conceptual depth of his theoretical contribution',[200] and may in part explain why Macneil's ideas have so often been misunderstood, typically by assuming that he identified a distinct *category* of 'relational contracts', when in fact his theory posits that *all* contracts are

[192] Macneil (n 186).

[193] M Elliott, 'Book Review' (1981) 44 *MLR* 345, 346.

[194] Morgan, chapter 12 of this volume, p 300 (emphasis in original).

[195] Wheeler (n 185) S83.

[196] See J Feinman, 'Relational Contract Theory in Context' (2020) 94 *Northwestern University Law Review* 737, 741 (the theory encompasses 'an astonishingly wide range of transactions'). See also the summary of Macneil's social theory in Macneil (n 183) 46–53.

[197] Elliott (n 193) 347. See also at 351 (characterising Macneil's work as 'the promulgation of a new and all inclusive social theory'). As has been pointed out, 'relational analysis may be applied … to any social interaction in which reciprocity is the dominant element' (P Vincent-Jones, 'The Reception of Ian Macneil's Work on Contract in the UK' in Macneil (n 183) 73). *cf* the opposite criticism made by Twining, chapter 15 of this volume, p 400, that Macneil 'would have done better to root his vision in a broad … theory of social co-operation rather than a more restricted one of exchange'.

[198] See, eg, Elliott (n 193) 349; RE Barnett, 'Conflicting Visions: A Critique of Ian Macneil's Relational Theory of Contract' (1992) 78 *Virginia Law Review* 1175, 1190.

[199] See, eg, Elliott (n 193) 345; Feinman (n 196) 63 ('The style and complexity have put off many contract scholars, and certainly have prevented the work from being widely read by practising lawyers and judges').

[200] Wheeler (n 185) S86.

'relational', at least to some extent. Nevertheless, he must surely be the most important student of contract as a social phenomenon, and as a result is unquestionably a major figure in the history of the scholarship of contract law.

No criticisms could be made of the style of Patrick Atiyah, whose voluminous writings on contract law, history and theory are consistently engaging, and who 'eschewed complicated prose and obscure terminology'.[201] Like Kessler and Macneil, Atiyah was a post-realist contract scholar who rejected the classical tradition.[202] And although he was predominantly a scholar of English law, intellectually Atiyah was much closer to Kessler and Macneil than he was to the more traditional school of twentieth-century Commonwealth contract scholarship represented in this volume by Cheshire and Fifoot, Treitel and Coote.[203] This is apparent not only from Atiyah's fundamental beliefs about the nature of contract, but also from the opening chapter of his *An Introduction to the Law of Contract* ('*Introduction*'),[204] which focuses on contract as a social phenomenon, and from the profound inter-disciplinarity of his work, which ranges across law, economics, philosophy, political theory and history, and which, like Macneil's, is often only incidentally concerned with contract *law*.

Apart from Pollock, Atiyah is the only scholar considered in this volume who also featured in *STL*.[205] In the introduction to that book, we classified Atiyah as an 'iconoclast',[206] and, as James Goudkamp points out in his chapter on Atiyah in this volume (chapter 14), his work on contract was also characterised by an enthusiasm for challenging orthodoxy.[207] Drawing on the work of Fuller and Purdue,[208] Gilmore[209] and Horwitz,[210] Atiyah launched a multi-pronged attack on the idea of contract as a distinct legal category concerned with the enforcement of promises, in which the default remedy was and should be expectation-based. Instead, Atiyah argued, contractual liability was better understood as grounded on reliance and benefit, from which it followed that there was generally no justification for the enforcement of wholly executory contracts or for the award of expectation damages, and that the supposed boundary between contract on the one hand and tort and unjust enrichment

[201] Goudkamp, chapter 14 of this volume, p 375.

[202] On Atiyah's realist tendencies, see *ibid* p 378. See also Atiyah's more general works, such as Atiyah (n 113) and PS Atiyah and RS Summers, *Form and Substance in Anglo-American Law: A Comparative Study of Legal Reasoning, Legal Theory, and Legal Institutions* (Oxford, Clarendon Press, 1987).

[203] See, eg, PS Atiyah, 'Consideration: A Restatement' in his *Essays on Contract* (Oxford, Oxford University Press, 1986), the original version of which Atiyah says (at 179) was inspired by Corbin's work and which 'remains thoroughly Corbinian in intent'.

[204] PS Atiyah, *An Introduction to the Law of Contract* (Oxford, Clarendon Press, 1961) ch 1.

[205] J Goudkamp, 'Professor Patrick Atiyah (1931–2018)' in *STL* (n 1).

[206] Goudkamp and Nolan (n 3) 27–28.

[207] Goudkamp, chapter 14 of this volume, p 370.

[208] LL Fuller and WR Purdue, 'The Reliance Interest in Contract Damages' (1936–37) 46 *Yale Law Journal* 52, 373.

[209] Gilmore's *Death of Contract* (n 116) was the catalyst for *Rise and Fall*: see Goudkamp, chapter 14 of this volume, p 360.

[210] For Horwitz's influence on Atiyah, see Swain (n 15) 7, fn 36.

on the other was an illusion. This conception of contract – which Coote later labelled the 'reliance theory'[211] – underlay both the works of Atiyah explored in depth by Goudkamp, namely *The Rise and Fall of Freedom of Contract* ('*Rise and Fall*')[212] and *Promises, Morals, and Law* ('*PML*'),[213] as well as *Introduction* and the key periodical writings collected in his *Essays on Contract*.[214]

In his towering work of intellectual history, *Rise and Fall*, Atiyah sought to trace the modern history of the 'ideology' of freedom of contract, which he argued had flourished in the century from 1770 to 1870, but thereafter fallen into (seemingly terminal) decline. Atiyah associated that ideology with the classical model of contract law, and its 'decline and fall' with the disintegration of that model amidst a twentieth-century resurgence of reliance-based and benefit-based liabilities. Naturally, the connection between classical contract law and *laissez-faire* economics which Kessler had first identified pervaded this analysis.[215] The thesis put forward in *Rise and Fall* was subsequently bolstered in *PML* by a philosophical investigation of promises which led Atiyah to the radical conclusion that they were not in and of themselves a source of moral obligation. Although both works were widely acknowledged as significant achievements, the claims made in *Rise and Fall* and especially *PML* also met with a good deal of criticism,[216] and political and legal developments since the 1970s have cast significant doubt on the reliance theory and the supposed 'death of contract'.[217] As a result, it may be that Atiyah's more 'Corbinian' work on modern contract doctrine – as exemplified by the five editions of *Introduction* – will have more lasting influence than these two books. Nevertheless, Atiyah's scholarly range and dexterity, coupled with the sheer volume of consistently stimulating work which he has left behind him, undoubtedly make him one of the pre-eminent twentieth-century contract scholars of the common law world.

[211] Coote (n 111) 21–22. This is however somewhat misleading as it ignores the role played by ideas of benefit in the thinking of Atiyah and other adherents to the same analysis. Though less elegant, 'reliance/benefit theory' would therefore be a more accurate label.

[212] Atiyah (n 73).

[213] PS Atiyah, *Promises, Morals, and Law* (Oxford, Oxford University Press, 1981).

[214] PS Atiyah, *Essays on Contract* (Oxford, Oxford University Press, 1986).

[215] See, eg, Atiyah (n 73) 398.

[216] On *Rise and Fall*, see especially JH Baker, 'Book Review' (1980) 43 *MLR* 467 (the book is 'least convincing' in 'its legal aspect', where 'it shares some of the weaknesses of its American precursors'). On *PML*, see especially J Raz, 'Promises in Law and Morality' (1982) 95 *Harvard Law Review* 916, 938 ('an untenable view of promises'). Waddams has also pointed out ((n 35) 174) that Gilbert's treatise is inconsistent with some of the central claims that Atiyah made in *Rise and Fall* about the state of contract law in the eighteenth century. There are only passing references in *Rise and Fall* to Gilbert's work, which was not widely known about in the 1970s, although references had been made to it in Simpson (n 29).

[217] Politically, the rise of the 'New Right', heralded by the victory of the Conservatives under Margaret Thatcher in the UK general election of 1979 (the very year *Rise and Fall* was published). Legally, the resilience of contract as an autonomous source of obligation and of the boundaries separating it from unjust enrichment (a boundary reinforced by the publication of P Birks, *An Introduction to the Law of Restitution* (Oxford, Clarendon Press, 1985)) and tort (a boundary reinforced by the more restrictive approach taken by the English courts from the late 1980s to negligence claims for pure economic loss).

E. Cheshire and Fifoot, Treitel and Coote

The persistence of more traditional forms of doctrinal contract scholarship notwithstanding the challenges posed by the realists is demonstrated by the four scholars discussed next. It is no coincidence that all four were based in the Commonwealth, where the impact of realism, though still seismic, was less marked than in the US. Nor is it a coincidence that apparently Atiyah singled out the books written by Cheshire and Fifoot and Treitel for persistent criticism in his lectures at Oxford,[218] since the intellectual gulf between him and them was every bit as wide, if not wider, than that between Williston and Corbin.

Like Atiyah, Geoffrey Cheshire and Cecil Fifoot were Oxford dons who had a wide range of scholarly interests – indeed Cheshire is best known for his seminal studies of real property[219] and conflict of laws,[220] and Fifoot as a legal historian.[221] Their reputations as contract scholars rest almost entirely on their influential textbook *The Law of Contract* ('*Cheshire and Fifoot*'), a work first published in 1945,[222] and which has so far run to 17 editions. *Cheshire and Fifoot* was the first significant challenger to the dominance of *Anson* in the English student market[223] and clearly filled a gap.[224] It seems to have been the leading textbook for some time after it appeared on the scene,[225] and at least until the 1960s, when the competition stiffened with the revival of *Anson* by Anthony Guest[226] and the arrival of Treitel's *The Law of Contract*.[227]

[218] See Goudkamp, chapter 14 of this volume, p 358.

[219] GC Cheshire, *The Modern Law of Real Property* (London, Butterworth & Co, 1925).

[220] GC Cheshire, *Private International Law* (London, Butterworth & Co, 1935).

[221] See, eg, CHS Fifoot, *History and Sources of the Common Law: Tort and Contract* (London, Stevens & Sons, 1949).

[222] GC Cheshire and CHS Fifoot, *The Law of Contract* (London, Butterworth & Co, 1945). The authors also published a companion casebook, GC Cheshire and CHS Fifoot, *Cases on the Law of Contract* (London, Butterworth & Co, 1946), which ran to seven editions.

[223] J Salmond and PH Winfield, *Principles of the Law of Contract* (London, Sweet & Maxwell, 1927) clearly did not thrive and made it to only one further edition (J Salmond and J Williams, *Principles of the Law of Contract*, 2nd edn (London, Sweet & Maxwell, 1945)). The book was based on materials left by Sir John Salmond on his death in 1924. FH Lawson recounted being told by a German law professor that 'it did not read like an English law book at all, but like a book of German Pandekten, so clear and even was the flow of doctrinal statement': FH Lawson, 'Doctrinal Writing: A Foreign Element in English Law?' in E von Caemmerer et al (eds), *Ius Privatum Gentium: Festschrift für Max Rheinstein* (Tübingen, JCB Mohr, 1969) 202–203.

[224] See FH Lawson, 'Geoffrey Chevalier Cheshire, 1886–1978' (1980) 65 *Proceedings of the British Academy* 611, 623 (a book on contract 'was badly needed', as 'all the existing books had originally appeared a long time previously and later editions still betrayed older habits of thought').

[225] See Atiyah (n 73) 686 ('[*Cheshire and Fifoot*] largely replaced Anson as the leading students' work'); GH Treitel, 'Vicissitudes of an Academic Lawyer' (2019) 26 *Zeitschrift für Europäisches Privatrecht* 133, 151.

[226] AG Guest, *Anson's Law of Contract*, 21st edn (London, Stevens & Sons, 1959). Guest also revivified *Chitty on Contracts* and resurrected *Benjamin's Sale of Goods*.

[227] GH Treitel, *The Law of Contract* (London, Stevens & Sons, 1962).

The driving force behind *Cheshire and Fifoot* was clearly Cheshire,[228] although Fifoot's involvement doubtless explains the close attention to the historical development of the law and may also have brought to bear a more critical perspective. Cheshire's books were characterised by the building up of general propositions from the case law, which was incorporated into the text rather than being relegated to footnotes. His works were also admired for their elegant and clear style,[229] and the freshness of *Cheshire and Fifoot* was commended by reviewers.[230] The lucidity of the text may also be connected to the fact that the authors were well-established academics who had taught contract law for decades;[231] as Warren Swain says in his chapter in this volume (chapter nine), *Cheshire and Fifoot* 'was a work of mature reflection compiled after many years spent teaching the subject'.[232] For this and other reasons, the work was readily adaptable, as is shown by the success of the local editions which appeared in the 1960s in Australia[233] and New Zealand,[234] and – much later – in Singapore/Malaysia.[235]

Swain also makes the point that *Cheshire and Fifoot* was in the tradition of doctrinal English contract scholarship exemplified by the works of Pollock and Anson. In the preface to the first edition of the book the authors described one of their aims in publishing it as being to 'examine the principles underlying the English law of Contract',[236] a statement that nailed their colours firmly to the mast of the classical model, as did the structure of the work, which closely followed that of *Anson*. And while the reference to English law in that statement is unexceptionable – after all, it was a book about English law – the emphasis on it was echoed in the somewhat insular feel of *Cheshire and Fifoot*, which was sparing in its references to other jurisdictions. That insularity occasionally bubbled to the surface, as in the authors' claim that the idea of bargain was 'fundamental to the English conception of contract', with the result that

[228] See Lawson (n 224) 623.

[229] See, eg, the comment about Cheshire's *The Modern Law of Real Property* that its 'peculiar excellence … lies in its intelligibility not only to the swift but to the halt and lame': GDG Hall, 'Book Review' (1950) 13 *MLR* 402, 402.

[230] See, eg, D Hughes Parry, 'Book Review' (1949) 1 *Journal of the Society of Public Teachers of Law (New Series)* 301, 301 (review of second edition).

[231] Indeed, it seems likely that parts of the text were based on their lectures. There is a possible analogy here with another very successful textbook of the same era, Sir Percy Winfield's *Text-Book of the Law of Tort* (London, Sweet & Maxwell, 1937), the first edition of which was published when Winfield was in his late 50s. For the suggestion that the stylistic appeal of that work may have been connected to the experience of its author, see D Nolan, 'Professor Sir Percy Winfield (1878–1953)' in *STL* (n 1) 179–80.

[232] Swain, chapter nine of this volume, p 238.

[233] See JG Starke and PFP Higgins, *Cheshire and Fifoot's Law of Contract, Australian Edition* (Sydney, Butterworths, 1966) and subsequent editions.

[234] See JF Northey, *Cheshire and Fifoot's Law of Contract, New Zealand Edition* (Wellington, Butterworths, 1961) and subsequent editions.

[235] See ABL Phang, *Cheshire, Fifoot and Furmston's Law of Contract: Singapore and Malaysian Edition* (Singapore, Butterworths Asia, 1994) and subsequent editions.

[236] *Cheshire and Fifoot* (n 222) iii.

'An Englishman is liable, not because he has made a promise but because he has made a bargain'.[237] (This claim – which was presumably directed at the American tendency to define a contract as an enforceable *promise*, rather than an enforceable *agreement*[238] – was later described by Roscoe Pound as 'an example of the cult of local law for the sake of its localism which has been a feature of English institutional texts from the beginning'.[239]) Despite its conservatism, however, *Cheshire and Fifoot* – like Cheshire's other books – has been said to have 'introduced a new stage in the development of [an] important [branch] of English law by raising [its] literary treatment to a higher level and subjecting [it] to reasoned criticism'.[240] The book was eventually taken over by Michael Furmston, who was the sole author of nine editions, and whose name was added to its title in 1986.[241] As is typical of the more heavyweight style of student textbook, the work considerably expanded over time, almost doubling in length between the first and most recent editions.

That last mentioned characteristic has also been a feature of Sir Guenter Treitel's magisterial book on contract, the first edition of which was published in 1962. Indeed, Treitel's work – though still styled as a textbook – has expanded to such an extent (it now runs to over a thousand pages[242]) that it has become difficult to classify, since the level of detail and sophistication makes it particularly useful for practitioners, but also tends to put off all but the most committed and able of students.[243] In any case, regardless of its somewhat ambiguous audience, the niche that *Treitel* – since 2007 under the authorship of Edwin Peel – occupies in the now saturated market of contract law texts is an important one, and it stands as a testament to the immense contribution that its author made to the law of contract in England and beyond.

Like Kessler, Treitel was born in Germany and left that country for good in the 1930s to escape Nazi persecution. Unlike Kessler, however, Treitel made the trip to his new home in England as a boy, one of the thousands of Jewish children

[237] *ibid* 25.

[238] Perhaps it was also a dig at *Anson*, a work which defines a contract as an enforceable promise: see, eg, Beatson et al (n 99) 1–2.

[239] R Pound, *Jurisprudence* (St Paul, West Publishing, 1959) vol 3, 218. Pound's remark is quoted by Coote (n 111) 12.

[240] FH Lawson, P North revd, 'Cheshire, Geoffrey Chevalier (1886–1978)' in *Oxford Dictionary of National Biography*.

[241] MP Furmston, *Cheshire, Fifoot and Furmston's Law of Contract*, 11th edn (London, Butterworths, 1986). On Furmston's contribution to contract scholarship, see ABL Phang, 'Theory as Practice and Practice as Theory: The Integrated and Integral Contract Scholarship of Professor Michael Furmston' (2014) 31 *Journal of Contract Law* 12.

[242] The current edition is E Peel, *Treitel's The Law of Contract*, 15th edn (London, Sweet & Maxwell, 2020).

[243] This issue was raised as early as a review of the third edition, by which time the work already stretched to almost 900 pages. See B Coote, 'Book Review' (1971) 2 *Otago Law Review* 373, 375. See also ABL Phang, 'Giants of Contract Law – Some Personal Reflections' (2022) 2 *Singapore Law Journal* 1, 26–27.

who travelled on the famous 'Kindertransport'.[244] Treitel was later educated in the common law tradition at Oxford – where, other than a brief initial stint at the London School of Economics, he spent his entire academic career – and his connections with German law and scholarship were much weaker than Kessler's, though he did publish an important work on comparative contract law.[245] In contrast to Cheshire, Fifoot and Atiyah, Treitel's scholarly writings were almost all concerned with contract, either in general or in its application to specific commercial contexts, such as overseas sales and carriage of goods by sea.[246] In addition to his work on numerous editions of *Chitty on Contracts*, his writings on general contract law consisted of 11 editions of his textbook, six editions of a shorter expository work,[247] three monographs,[248] and a long list of shorter contributions in the form of articles, book chapters and casenotes.

As Andrew Burrows emphasises in his chapter on Treitel in this volume (chapter 11), he was a doctrinal legal scholar in the traditional mould, and his scholarly style stands in sharp contrast to that of his Oxford contemporary Atiyah.[249] Whereas Atiyah was an acerbic iconoclast fond of making sweeping and sometimes overstated claims about the law and its development, Treitel was measured and understated and his analysis 'rigorous, relentless and, above all, precise'.[250] Treitel's writings were characterised by a 'detailed and exhaustive but succinct and clear examination of doctrine',[251] in which general statements were typically qualified by a long list of exceptions so as to provide a coherent and comprehensive statement of the relevant law. He had little or no interest in theory, and generally took the law as he found it, with the result that his textbook was described by Coote, in a review of the third edition, as 'a rather conservative work'.[252] It would, however, be a mistake to paint Treitel as a died-in-the-wool formalist. (There are echoes of Williston here, especially in Treitel's emphasis on the internal coherence of legal rules, or in other words their consistency with each other.) As Treitel's last monograph – which was based on his 2001

[244] For the story of that journey and its aftermath, see GH Treitel, 'A German Childhood 1933–1942: Persecution and Escape' (2020) 28 *Zeitschrift für Europäisches Privatrecht* 591.

[245] GH Treitel, *Remedies for Breach of Contract: A Comparative Account* (Oxford, Clarendon Press, 1988). This was described as 'a masterly and weighty survey of an important topic': T Weir, 'Book Review' [1989] *CLJ* 152, 153.

[246] An exception is GH Treitel, 'Jane Austen and the Law' (1984) 100 *LQR* 549.

[247] GH Treitel, *An Outline of the Law of Contract* (London, Butterworths, 1975) and later editions.

[248] Treitel (n 245); GH Treitel, *Frustration and Force Majeure* (London, Sweet & Maxwell, 1994) and two further editions under his pen (see now E Peel, *Frustration and Force Majeure*, 4th edn (London, Sweet & Maxwell, 2021); GH Treitel, *Some Landmarks of Twentieth Century Contract Law* (Oxford, Clarendon Press, 2002).

[249] Sadly, after an early collaboration (PS Atiyah and GH Treitel, 'Misrepresentation Act 1967' (1967) 30 *MLR* 369), the two men fell out and their personal relationship was thereafter strained – or perhaps more accurately non-existent: see J Goudkamp, 'Patrick Atiyah 1931–2018' (2020) 19 *Biographical Memoirs of Fellows of the British Academy* 149, 174.

[250] Obituary, Sir Guenter Treitel QC, *The Times* (21 June 2019).

[251] F Reynolds, 'Guenter Treitel 1928–2019' (2020) 19 *Biographical Memoirs of Fellows of the British Academy* 129, 135.

[252] Coote (n 243) 375.

Clarendon lectures – shows, he was a scholar with a keen eye for the practical consequences and policy implications of legal rules.[253] And it is telling that when his textbook first appeared in the 1960s, it engaged much more thoroughly than its rivals with the statutory interventions that were beginning then to reshape aspects of the common law of contract.[254] Treitel was also far from insular, and regularly taught in US law schools, including alongside two of the co-authors of Kessler's casebook, Malcolm Sharp and Grant Gilmore, in Chicago.[255] Although this experience seems to have had little impact on Treitel's scholarly mindset (a realist he assuredly was not!), it did give him a good knowledge of American contract law, which was made manifest in his books on remedies and frustration, and which he could draw upon when discussing issues of English contract law.[256]

The final scholar considered in this collection is the New Zealander Brian Coote. Like Treitel, Coote was a doctrinal scholar who considered that 'a main purpose' of legal scholarship 'was assisting to improve the application of the law as actually practised'.[257] However, unlike Treitel, Coote never wrote a major work on contract law as a whole. Instead, his reputation rests on a combination of his early monograph on what he called 'exception clauses'[258] and a large body of journal articles on a broad range of contract topics, many of which were consolidated in three collections of his work that were published in the decade before he died.[259] Coote also made a major contribution to the development of contract law in New Zealand through his work for the Contracts and Commercial Law Reform Committee, which resulted in several important reforming statutes.[260]

In Coote's seminal book on exception clauses, he argued that these should not be understood as defences to a prima facie liability that arose independently of them – ie, as 'merely a shield to a claim for damages'[261] – but instead as setting

[253] See, eg, Treitel (2002) (n 248) 23, 38, 118–19. As a reviewer of Treitel's book on remedies observed, '[i]f the opinions and value-judgments seem hard to distinguish from the descriptions, that is because they are so reasonable and dispassionate as to seem equally objective': Weir (n 245) 153.

[254] See Burrows, chapter 11 of this volume, p 284. However, Treitel was sceptical about codification, which he thought would preserve the common law in aspic and inhibit beneficial developments: see Treitel (n 225) 165; Treitel (2002) (n 248) 4–9.

[255] Treitel (n 225) 155.

[256] See, eg, Treitel (2002) (n 248) 100–102, where he defends legislative reform of the third-party rule by drawing comparisons with the judicial reforms effected in the US.

[257] P Watts, 'Emeritus Professor Brain Coote, OBE, FRSNZ, Obituary' (2020) 36 *Journal of Contract Law* 1, 3.

[258] B Coote, *Exception Clauses: Some Aspects of the Law Relating to Exception Clauses for the Carriage, Bailment and Sale of Goods* (London, Sweet & Maxwell, 1964).

[259] Coote (n 111); B Coote (edited by JW Carter), *Contract as Assumption II: Formation, Performance and Enforcement* (Oxford, Hart Publishing, 2016); B Coote (edited by JW Carter and J Ren), *Coote on the New Zealand Contract Statutes* (Wellington, Thomson Reuters, 2017).

[260] On the New Zealand contract statutes, see W Swain, 'A Reputation for Boldness: Statutory Reform of Contract Law in New Zealand' in TT Arvind and J Steele (eds), *Contract Law and the Legislature: Autonomy, Expectations, and the Making of Legal Doctrine* (Oxford, Hart Publishing, 2020).

[261] Coote (n 111) 81.

out which obligations were being assumed by the promisor in the first place.[262] This conclusion followed from the central underlying themes of Coote's contract scholarship, which were that contract was a facilitative institution which enabled contract parties to assume legal obligations and concomitant liabilities, and that these were binding 'not because they have been imposed by law *ab extra*', but because the parties 'have themselves assumed them'.[263] According to Coote, these precepts did not stand in the way of extensive change to the classical law of contract, though whether it would or should so change depended in part on value judgments 'about such questions as whether and to what extent the law of contract should be used as an instrument for social or economic control' and the appropriate limits of paternalism.[264]

In a broad sense, therefore, Coote's was a value-neutral conception of contract, albeit with the caveat that the 'one characteristic essential to a contract is that it should be a means by which legal contractual liability can effectively be assumed by the party or parties to it'.[265] One consequence of Coote's theory was that he saw no point in looking for (alternative) justifications for the existence of contracts and contract law, such as 'upholding the institution of promising, or the sanctity of the human will, or protecting reasonable expectations'.[266] At the same time, however, the focus on the assumption, rather than the imposition, of obligation and the attendant potential liability did in his view have concrete implications for particular contract doctrines, including not only exception clauses, but also damages for breach (where he favoured a 'performance' measure[267]) and remoteness (where he argued that the extent of liability should depend on the degree to which the party in breach had assumed responsibility for the loss in question[268]).

Coote's discussion of specific issues like these was firmly within the Commonwealth doctrinal tradition, and his theory was premised on the belief (*pace* Atiyah[269]) that 'contract does, in an essential respect, differ from other forms of legal obligation'.[270] In his chapter on Coote in this volume (chapter 13), Stephen Waddams notes that in his valedictory lecture[271] he described himself

[262] It is interesting to consider whether Coote may have influenced, or been influenced by, Glanville Williams, who famously adopted an equivalent position in relation to the criminal law: see, eg, G Williams, 'Offences and Defences' (1982) 3 *LS* 233. Coote's time at Cambridge overlapped with that of Williams.

[263] Coote (n 111) 1.

[264] *ibid* 51.

[265] *ibid* 50.

[266] *ibid* 1. Coote subjects these sorts of theories to extended critique in B Coote, 'The Essence of Contract (Parts I and II)' (1988–89) 1 *Journal of Contract Law* 91, 183.

[267] B Coote, 'Contract Damages, *Ruxley*, and the Performance Interest' [1997] *CLJ* 537.

[268] B Coote, 'Contract as Assumption and Remoteness of Damage' (2010) 26 *Journal of Contract Law* 211.

[269] Text to nn 208–214.

[270] Coote (n 111) 10.

[271] B Coote, *Contract: An Underview – A Souvenir of a Valedictory Lecture* (Auckland, Legal Research Foundation, 1995).

as a formalist, albeit employing such a broad definition of formalism as to encompass many scholars who would no doubt reject that label.[272] Waddams is not convinced by the self-description and besides any such 'formalism' was clearly flexible and pragmatic. This is shown, inter alia, by Coote's writings on consideration,[273] and more generally by his view that it would be unrealistic to expect that internal self-consistency 'could ever be fully achieved in a system of judge-made law' – inconsistencies were inevitable at any given moment, since 'development and change are continuous'.[274] The fact that Coote was far from being a blinkered formalist is also demonstrated by his openness to insights from other disciplines[275] and by his close involvement with the sometimes radical statutory reform of New Zealand contract law.[276]

III. THEMES

In this final substantive part of the chapter we introduce a number of general themes that run through many of the other chapters of the book. These are: (1) civilian influences; (2) the relationship between England and the United States; (3) the relationship between England as 'metropole' and the colonies/Commonwealth; (4) the audiences of the scholars; and (5) the tension between a law of contract and a law of contracts.

A. Civilian Influences

The question of civilian influence on the common law of contract is a complex one which has been the subject of sustained analysis elsewhere.[277] In this brief discussion we merely highlight some aspects of that influence which come to the fore in the chapters that follow. We have already seen that the eighteenth- and nineteenth-century English writers on contract were heavily reliant on civilian scholarship, a reliance that 'was closely connected with the search for a principled, reasoned, ordered and "scientific" approach to law'.[278] Colebrooke was an extreme case in this regard, with the majority of his sources being continental in origin, and no attempt made to reconcile the claims derived from them with the English case law. By contrast, other early nineteenth-century writers

[272] Waddams, chapter 13 of this volume, pp 345–48. See also the defence of Coote's work in this respect by Rick Bigwood in Coote (n 111) vi–vii.

[273] See, eg, B Coote, 'Variations Sans Consideration' (2011) 27 *Journal of Contract Law* 185.

[274] Coote (n 111) 31.

[275] See B Coote, 'A Law Teacher Looks at His Trade' (1968) 6 *Alberta Law Review* 270, 279.

[276] On the influence of Coote's work on contract law throughout the Commonwealth, see ABL Phang, 'Contract as Assumption – The Scholarship and Influence of Professor Brian Coote' (2011) 27 *Journal of Contract Law* 247.

[277] A seminal discussion is Simpson (n 29).

[278] Waddams (n 17) 135.

tended to use civilian sources in a more limited or indirect fashion, borrowing from Pothier, for example, 'as and when they needed to explain developments in the case law'.[279] Later on, Pollock and Anson also employed civilian sources instrumentally to construct an overarching theoretical framework into which carefully curated English cases could be slotted. The difficulties to which this gave rise have been painstakingly exposed by legal historians such as Catherine MacMillan,[280] who observes:

> There was a selective borrowing or transplant of ideas inherent in this process, and the English treatise writers sought to impose these ideas upon an existing system of contract law but they struggled to relate the borrowed ideas to this law … The resulting body of law was often untidy, as principles were presented and expressed to have been established by cases which even a cursory examination revealed to be concerned with other matters. The process was not improved by inherent weaknesses in the borrowed theories of the civilians or by the fact that these theories were stripped from legal systems premised upon different rules and objectives than the common law.[281]

The central civilian figures in this now familiar story were the Frenchman Robert Joseph Pothier and the German Friedrich Carl von Savigny. As McCunn points out,[282] Pothier's *Traité des Obligations*[283] was the primary source for Colebrooke, who cited the Frenchman on average twice per page in his treatise. In his work of 1847, Addison also commended 'the elaborate and elegant works of Pothier',[284] and his influence continued to be felt throughout the remainder of the nineteenth century,[285] even if it faded somewhat towards the end.[286] The emphasis on general principles in Pothier's treatise, coupled with its plentiful examples, lucid style and clear structure, made him 'a useful guide',[287] who tended to be relied on 'in areas where English law lacked clarity or had little answer'.[288] The first English contract scholar to draw extensively on Savigny and his *System des heutigen römischen Rechts*[289] (published in the 1840s) was Leake. However, as we have seen Savigny's greatest impact came via Pollock, who described him as 'a man of true scientific genius',[290] and whose reverence for his work was such that he sometimes felt it necessary to cite it in the original

[279] Lobban (n 45) 303.
[280] MacMillan (n 61). See also Simpson (n 29); Gordley (n 29) ch 6; Ibbetson (n 23) ch 12.
[281] MacMillan (n 61) 4.
[282] McCunn, chapter three of this volume, p 87.
[283] RJ Pothier (translated by WD Evans), *A Treatise on the Law of Obligations or Contracts* (London, Butterworth, 1806).
[284] CG Addison, *A Treatise on the Law of Contracts and Rights and Liabilities Ex Contractu* (London, W Benning, 1847) vii (quoted by Waddams (n 17) 130).
[285] See Swain (n 15) 176 (Pothier cited more than 400 times in the English courts in the nineteenth century).
[286] See Waddams (n 35) 130.
[287] MacMillan (n 61) 106.
[288] *ibid* 104.
[289] FC von Savigny, *System des heutigen römischen Rechts* (Berlin, Veit und Comp, 1840–49).
[290] Pollock (n 74) 2 (fn) (quoted by Waddams (n 17) 133).

German on the ground that no literal translation was possible.[291] Pollock's use of a conceptual structure inspired by Savigny to construct an English doctrine of mistake is a classic example of civilian influence on the nineteenth-century common law of contract.[292] Nor should we overlook Savigny's influence on Anson, even if it was 'not nearly so pervasive as it was upon Pollock'.[293]

Although Pothier was admittedly a huge influence on early American contract law,[294] overall the impact of civilian writers on late nineteenth-century US contract scholarship was more muted – Holmes in particular warned against the dangers of importing legal concepts from the civilian tradition into common law analysis.[295] In any case, with the twentieth-century abandonment of the search for scientific principles, the appeal of civilian sources to common law contract scholars waned, and when modern English writers sought inspiration from abroad, they generally looked across the Atlantic rather than the Channel. As Brian Simpson rather caustically put it (writing in 1975):

> In contemporary treatises on English Contract law you will find little trace of this internationalism [*viz*, the earlier reliance on civilian writers] … such works as Anson (in its modern form), Cheshire and Fifoot, Treitel … and Atiyah … only occasionally relieve their insularity with references to other common law jurisdictions; they hardly ever step outside the common law world.[296]

Among the scholars considered in this volume, the most important exception to the late twentieth-century disinterest in civilian thinking and sources is Kessler, of whom Gilmore observed that his 'extraordinary achievement' as a legal emigré 'was to become a common lawyer without ceasing to be a civilian'.[297] We have already seen, for example, that aspects of Kessler's scholarship may have been attributable to his civilian training,[298] and it seems plausible to suppose that his path-breaking article on contracts of adhesion was influenced by German writings in the 1920s and 1930s on standard contract terms.[299] Kessler maintained strong intellectual connections with the country of his birth and published in German throughout his career.[300] He even wrote an article on the development of German contract scholarship in which he analysed the influence of Savigny.[301]

[291] See Waddams (n 17) 133–34.

[292] See MacMillan (n 61) ch 6.

[293] *ibid* 171.

[294] See JM Perillo, 'Robert J Pothier's Influence on the Common Law of Contract' (2005) 11 *Texas Wesleyan Law Review* 267, who points out (at 267–68) that one of 23 marble relief plaques in the chamber of the US House of Representatives depicting 'historical figures noted for their work in establishing the principles that underlie American law' is a portrait of Pothier.

[295] See MacMillan (n 61) 164. An exception was Langdell, who relied on Pothier even after his work (and civilian writings more generally) had fallen out of fashion in the US: see O'Gorman (n 11) 530–33.

[296] Simpson (n 29) 256.

[297] Gilmore (n 151) 673.

[298] See text to nn 180–81.

[299] See Joerges (1994) (n 173) 181.

[300] *ibid* 164.

[301] F Kessler, 'Some Thoughts on the Evolution of the German Law of Contracts – A Comparative Study: Part I' (1975) 22 *UCLA Law Review* 1066.

B. England and the United States

Apart from Coote, the scholars considered in this collection worked primarily in either England or the United States, and when it comes to contract scholarship the relationship between the two countries and their legal systems is a close but complex one. The same is of course true of tort scholarship, and this was a theme that we also explored in the introduction to *STL*.[302] We made the point there that the decline of the civil jury in most Commonwealth jurisdictions had accentuated the divide between tort scholarship in those systems and the US in the twentieth century. In contract, that distinction is less important, with the result that in this area the common ground between anglophone legal systems is greater.[303] However, some of the same fundamental differences are observable. One is the multi-jurisdictional nature of the American legal system,[304] which tends to drive scholars in a more theoretical or empirical direction,[305] with much of the most important doctrinal work being channelled into multi-volume treatises and *Restatements*, the scale of which is demanded by the complexity of the positive law across the various states. Another difference arises out of the American case method of teaching, which manifests itself in the plethora of student-oriented casebooks and the general absence of textbooks, or 'hornbooks'. One result of these two differences is that while the American scholars considered in this collection are best known for multi-volume treatises and/or law review articles, the reputations of English contract scholars have generally rested on multiple editions of the single-volume treatises (or more latterly textbooks) that bear their names: *Leake*, *Pollock*, *Anson*, *Cheshire and Fifoot* and *Treitel*. As the twentieth century wore on, these differences became more marked, and, when coupled with the greater impact of realism in the US, tended to manifest themselves in a widening gap between an American emphasis on what we earlier termed 'modernist' contract scholarship and the survival in the Commonwealth of more 'traditional' contract scholarship, albeit with many counter-examples on either side of the divide.

When it comes to the interactions between English contract scholars and American contract scholars, the story is one of ebb and flow. In the early days, the links were strong, but somewhat one-sided. There were American editions of the works of Powell and Chitty,[306] for example, but limited attention paid in England to American scholarship. In the era of Langdell, Holmes, Pollock and

[302] Goudkamp and Nolan (n 3) 33–34 (framed there as 'the US and the rest', ie, the US and the Commonwealth).

[303] Admittedly, Gilmore (n 116) 99–100 ascribes the formulation of so many issues as questions of law in the classical contract model to 'distrust of the role and function of the civil jury', but this claim is hard to square with the English experience.

[304] On this feature of the American legal landscape, see Twining, chapter 15 of this volume, pp 391–92.

[305] Although this tendency was more marked in the late twentieth century, it was also observable in the work of James Barr Ames, Langdell, and (to a lesser extent) Williston: see Lobban (n 45) 313.

[306] See Simpson (n 29) 253 (fn).

Anson, the connections remained important. The vast majority of the cases in Langdell's casebook were English,[307] for example, and the works of Pollock and Anson wielded 'great influence in the United States',[308] where (as we have seen) multiple American editions of those works were published.[309] As time passed, however, the relationship became more balanced, and dependence evolved into dialogue. The connections between Pollock and Holmes exemplify the transatlantic conversation that was taking place in the late nineteenth century on matters of contract law.[310] We have already seen that Pollock's move away from the will theory towards a more objective approach was almost certainly attributable in part to the work of Holmes, but the stream of influence was not one-way. After all, it was Pollock's definition of consideration that Holmes essentially adopted in *The Common Law*, and which eventually found its way into section 75 of the *Restatement (First)*.[311]

The dialogue continued to be a lively one well into the twentieth century, as is apparent from the publication in 1930 of an article by Corbin in the *Law Quarterly Review*, in which he argued that the English case law on trusts of a promise amounted to the equitable recognition of a third-party beneficiary rule.[312] In the late twentieth century, however, the personal connections between contract scholars on the two sides of the Atlantic weakened, although both Treitel and Atiyah regularly taught in the US, and – unusually for an English private lawyer – Atiyah regularly published articles in American law reviews.[313] In any case, by now the tide of influence had decisively turned, as is shown by, for example, the impact of Corbin and Gilmore on the thinking of Atiyah,[314] and by the fact that in recent times English and Commonwealth scholars have tended to respond to American contract scholarship, rather than the other way round.[315]

[307] Farnsworth (n 104) 1439.

[308] *ibid* 1413.

[309] Text to nn 124–25.

[310] For the details, see Kelley (n 10). For the wider transatlantic conversation on consideration, also involving Ames, Anson, Langdell and Williston, see Lobban (n 45) 380–82, 394–99. See too Lobban's account of a similar debate concerning offer and acceptance (*ibid* 346–48).

[311] See Gordley (n 29) 172–73.

[312] AL Corbin, 'Contracts for the Benefit of Third Persons' (1930) 46 *LQR* 12. See further, Treitel (2002) (n 248) 51–53.

[313] See Goudkamp, chapter 14 of this volume, pp 373–74, who emphasises Atiyah's particular interest in and admiration for American law and scholarship. Atiyah even co-authored with an American scholar a substantial comparative work on Anglo-American legal reasoning, theory and institutions: Atiyah and Summers (n 202).

[314] See nn 203, 209.

[315] This is particularly true in the case of the relational contract scholars Macneil and Macaulay: see, eg, the essays by Campbell and Vincent-Jones in Macneil (n 183); and D Campbell et al (eds), *Implicit Dimensions of Contract: Discrete, Relational and Network Contracts* (Oxford, Hart Publishing, 2003). But see also J Morgan, *Contract Law Minimalism: A Formalist Restatement of Commercial Contract Law* (Cambridge, Cambridge University Press, 2013), drawing on the work of the new formalists in the US.

C. 'Metropole' and Colonies/Commonwealth

We also touched in the introduction to *STL* on the relationship between England as metropole and her colonies and dominions (and later with the rest of the Commonwealth).[316] As in the case of tort, the British Empire and its aftermath pervades the story of the common law of contract and its scholarship. The tone was set by Addison, who described the law of contract as 'a universal law adapted to all times and races, and all places and circumstances'.[317] That that 'universal law' was *English* law was not really in any doubt. Some years after Addison's treatise was published, for example, a judge in a New Zealand contract case said that 'it would be a presumptuous thing in a colonial judge to over-rule the settled practice as laid down in the text books of England'.[318] It can readily be presumed that in the nineteenth century those 'text books' had yet greater influence in the British Empire than they did in the United States, even if the law itself was not as uniform as might be supposed.[319]

The idea of a 'universal law' of contract underlay Colebrooke's enterprise in writing a guide to it for colonial administrators in British India. When it came to contract law – unlike, say, family law and succession – few allowances were made for local custom and tradition, and Colebrooke simply assumed that the principles he derived from mostly civilian sources would provide a suitable framework for resolving commercial disputes between Indians. As McCunn points out, despite having an excellent knowledge of Hindu law, he cited few Indian sources, although he did seek to address practical issues that might arise in the Indian context, such as the existence of domestic slaves.[320] A similar approach was taken by William Macpherson when he wrote his *Outlines of the Law of Contracts as Administered in the Courts of British India*,[321] though he relied more on English texts than had Colebrooke, and incorporated into his analysis a selection of decisions of the Indian courts.[322] Macpherson went on to act as the secretary to the commission whose work culminated in the Indian Contract Act of 1872, legislation that was subsequently replicated in several former British colonies.[323] As the 1872 Act illustrates, 'the relationship between the West and its periphery was sometimes one of interaction, mutual influence,

[316] Goudkamp and Nolan (n 3) 34–35. See also J Goudkamp and J Murphy, 'Divergent Evolution in the Law of Torts: Jurisdictional Isolation, Jurisprudential Divergence and Explanatory Theories' in A Robertson and M Tilbury (eds), *The Common Law of Obligations: Divergence and Unity* (Oxford, Hart Publishing, 2015).

[317] Addison (n 284) v.

[318] Gresson J in *Re Maclean and MacAndrew* (Otago Daily Times, 27 May 1862) (quoted by W Swain, '"The Great Britain of the South": The Law of Contract in Early Colonial New Zealand' (2020) 60 *American Journal of Legal History* 30, 41).

[319] For a discussion of local variations in contract law observable in nineteenth-century New Zealand, see Swain (n 318).

[320] McCunn, chapter three of this volume, p 95.

[321] Macpherson (n 50).

[322] On Macpherson, see MacMillan (n 61) 108–12.

[323] See J Minattur, 'The Indian Contract Act: Its Wanderlust and Warmer Climes' [1972] *Journal of the Indian Law Institute* 107.

or independent (but parallel) development', and '[p]eripheries ... were often places of experimentation and innovation, including legal innovation'.[324] The phenomenon of reflection back from 'periphery' to 'metropole' is shown by the use which Pollock made of the 1872 Act when writing his treatise, in the preface to which he said that he had relied on it as 'a most instructive example of what can be done to consolidate and simplify English case-law'.[325]

After the nations of the Empire gained their independence, the symbiotic scholarly relationship between England and what was now the Commonwealth continued. Hence, for example, Atiyah first established himself as a contract scholar while working in the late 1950s at the University of Khartoum,[326] and he later worked for four years at the Australian National University, where his inaugural lecture concerned the doctrine of consideration.[327] Similarly, Macneil taught contract law at the University of East Africa in Dar es Salaam for two years – indeed his first book on contract was written to support his teaching there.[328] It is possible that Macneil's East African experience played a role in the development of his relational theory of contract, although, as Twining – who himself worked in both Khartoum (alongside Atiyah) and Dar es Salaam (before Macneil)[329] – points out,[330] he made little reference to it in his later work. Meanwhile, other Commonwealth countries such as Australia and New Zealand were slow to develop their own textbook tradition,[331] and there (and later in Singapore/Malaysia) the gap was filled in contract law by local editions of *Cheshire and Fifoot*.[332] Swain makes the point[333] that over time the authors of these homegrown editions became more assertive, so much so in the case of the New Zealand edition that it developed into a wholly independent work which is now the leading contract treatise in that country.[334] More recently, Coote had

[324] A Likhovski, 'The Intellectual History of Law' in MK Dubber and C Tomlins (eds), *The Oxford Handbook of Legal History* (Oxford, Oxford University Press, 2018) 154.

[325] Pollock (n 74) viii (quoted by Lobban (n 45) 307). So impressed was Pollock by the legislation that he included some of its provisions in appendices to his work. In later editions of his treatise, Pollock relied less on the 1872 Act, perhaps because of criticisms of it made by Holmes: see Kelley (n 10) 1723, fn 156.

[326] See further on Atiyah's time in Africa, Goudkamp, chapter 14 of this volume, pp 354–55.

[327] PS Atiyah, *Consideration in Contracts: A Fundamental Restatement* (Canberra, Australian National University Press, 1971).

[328] IR Macneil, *Contracts: Instruments for Social Co-operation – East Africa* (South Hackensack, Fred B Rothman, 1968).

[329] See W Twining, *Jurist in Context: A Memoir* (Cambridge, Cambridge University Press, 2019) chs 5–6.

[330] Twining, chapter 15 of this volume, pp 399–400.

[331] On the likely reasons for this in the Australian context, see Bartie (n 4) 28–29, who references the idea of a 'universal' common law, and the small numbers both of the law professors who would have written such books and of the law students who would have been the market for them. As for Canada, in an overview of contract and commercial law scholarship in common law Canada published in the 1980s, it was described as a 'young discipline', and the author listed English texts ahead of Canadian ones in a survey of 'key text sources in contracts': LE Trakman, 'Contract and Commercial Law Scholarship in Common Law Canada' (1985) 23 *Osgoode Hall Law Journal* 663.

[332] See text to nn 232–35.

[333] Swain, chapter nine of this volume, pp 245–47.

[334] See J Finn et al, *Burrows, Finn and Todd on the Law of Contract in New Zealand*, 7th edn (Wellington, LexisNexis, 2022).

a significant influence on English contract law from his base in Auckland, while at the same time spearheading legislative developments in his home jurisdiction that were later emulated in England and elsewhere.[335] As a result he 'helped to put New Zealand contract law and scholarship on the world map perhaps like no other New Zealand-based legal scholar in the twentieth century'.[336]

D. Audience

The intended audiences of the contract works of the scholars considered in this collection varied widely. They of course included legal practitioners, law students and legal academics, but they also extended in some instances to colonial administrators, businesspeople and even the educated public. In the case of some of the early English contract scholars, such as Addison and Chitty, there is no doubt that their primary audience was legal practitioners.[337] Colebrooke's intended readership is also clear, if unusual:[338] he wrote his treatise to provide a set of principles of contract law which could be used in the adjudication of disputes by judges in the courts of the East India Company. Gilbert's unpublished treatise is a more difficult case, as it is not obvious at whom it was directed (assuming that it was originally intended for publication). According to Michael Macnair, however, 'the analytic form and the character of the work as connected text' and the 'incompleteness of the coverage of the authorities' suggest that 'Gilbert was writing for a lay or student audience, rather than for a professional audience or himself'.[339]

The late nineteenth-century English writers show the importance of a scholar's intended audience for the nature and style of their work. Anson clearly wrote for the nascent student market, and as we have seen, this explains key features of his textbook, including its clear structure, its brevity and sparse references, and the lucid and simple way in which the law was set out. The first edition of the book was even published in a smaller format than other legal works, presumably so as to mark it out as a different kind of law book, intended for a different readership.[340] As AV Dicey later commented, '[t]he special virtue of the book lies in its precisely meeting the wants of a student who begins reading the law of contract'.[341] By contrast, as Anson himself observed, neither Leake nor Pollock 'wrote for beginners'.[342] Quite who they did write for is another matter. Lord Wright later said that 'Leake's book was for practitioners, while Pollock's book

[335] There is an interesting parallel between Coote and Sir John Salmond, who had a huge impact on the English law of tort from his base in New Zealand in the early twentieth century. On Salmond, see M Lunney, 'Professor Sir John Salmond (1862–1924): An Englishman Abroad' in *STL* (n 1).

[336] Rick Bigwood in Coote (n 111) vi.

[337] See Lobban (n 45) 302.

[338] See McCunn, chapter three of this volume, p 85.

[339] Macnair (n 38) 259.

[340] Waddams (n 17) 143.

[341] AV Dicey, 'Law-teaching, Oral and Written' in HH Henson (ed), *A Memoir of the Right Honourable Sir William Anson* (Oxford, Clarendon Press, 1920) 93 (quoted by MacMillan (n 61) 170).

[342] Anson (n 91) v.

was for students of principles and legal thinkers'.[343] That may have been an oversimplification in the case of Leake, since his intended readership is not clear, and may have changed over time. Commenting on the much enlarged second edition of Leake's treatise, Pollock said that 'one cannot help fearing that the gain to practitioners is a loss to students',[344] an observation that suggests that Leake's work was not originally perceived as a practitioner text,[345] even if later editions were presented in that way.[346] Furthermore, like Addison,[347] it is possible that Leake intended his treatise to be read not only by lawyers, but also by merchants and educated members of the public,[348] an ambition which we can safely assume was not realised. As for Pollock's own text, the vagueness of Lord Wright's remark about it nicely captures the ambiguity of its intended audience, which seems to have been both students and practitioners. That required a difficult balancing act, and while Pollock managed to pull it off during his lifetime, after his death his work came to be 'outflanked on the one side by Chitty (for practitioners) and on the other by Anson (for students)'.[349]

The intended readerships of the works of the twentieth-century contract scholars considered in this collection are generally obvious enough. The multi-volume treatises of Williston and Corbin were predominantly practitioner works,[350] though their erudition meant that they were drawn upon heavily by other scholars in the US and far beyond. The casebooks written by Corbin, Kessler and Macneil were equally clearly student works. The same was true of *Cheshire and Fifoot*, though, in a way typical of the leading English textbooks of its era,[351] it also came to be relied upon by practitioners and judges as a relatively concise and discursive treatment of the subject when compared with works such as *Chitty*. *Treitel* was also intended originally as a student text, although as we have seen it expanded considerably over time, and eventually settled in a rather ambivalent space somewhere between a student work and a practitioner work. Finally, the articles and monographs of scholars like Kessler, Macneil, Atiyah, Treitel and Coote were presumably intended primarily for an audience of fellow academics, although they found their way onto many student reading lists and, in the case of Treitel and Coote (and the more doctrinal work of Atiyah), they can also be understood as forms of what Burrows terms 'practical legal scholarship',[352] targeted in part at judges and other legal practitioners throughout the Commonwealth.

[343] Wright (n 77) 154.

[344] F Pollock, *Principles of Contract at Law and in Equity*, 3rd edn (London, Stevens & Sons, 1881) x (quoted by Waddams (n 17) 142).

[345] See also MacMillan (n 54), commenting (at 21) that while the style of Leake's work was 'initially thought more suitable to the student than the practitioner … it soon became clear that the work was of greater value to practitioners'.

[346] *ibid* 23.

[347] See MacMillan, chapter four of this volume, pp 113–14.

[348] On Leake's ambitions in this regard, see MacMillan (n 54) 11.

[349] Waddams (n 17) 142.

[350] On Williston's intended audience, see Movsesian (n 135) 267–68.

[351] See Goudkamp and Nolan (n 3) 36–37.

[352] Burrows, chapter 11 of this volume.

E. Contract and Contracts

Our final theme is the recurrent tension in common law contract scholarship between a law of *contract* and a law of *contracts*, or in other words between a conception of the relevant law as a unified body of generally applicable principles and a countervailing tendency to fragmentation along fault lines such as subject-matter and party identity.

Most of the early contract scholars, likely operating under civilian influence, structured their work either in whole or in part around types of contract, such as sale, lease and partnership – in England this was true of, for example, Chitty and Addison, and in the United States of Story and Parsons.[353] An exception is Colebrooke, whose published treatise was organised around general principles, though McCunn thinks it likely that his unpublished (and untraceable) second volume dealt with different types of contract – a compromise position latterly adopted by the editors of *Chitty*.[354] By contrast, the classical contract lawyers of the late nineteenth century sought to develop a general body of contract principles which were applicable across the board. In the words of Atiyah:

> The central idea that characterised [the works of the classical lawyers] was the *generality* of contract law, the fact that it could be stated at a high level of abstraction, and that the law applied indifferently to all kinds of contracts irrespective of the subject-matter.[355]

With the exceptions of Colebrooke and Macpherson – whose works were intended for a British Indian audience – Leake was the first English writer strictly to apply this idea, and to banish all discussion of particular contract types. He wrote in the preface to his treatise that it was exclusively concerned with 'the law of contracts in its general and abstract form, apart from its specific practical applications'.[356] The same approach was later taken by Pollock, Anson and the American Langdell. Note, however, that Leake still wrote of a 'law of *contracts*'. By contrast, Pollock took the ideal of an abstract general set of rules to its logical conclusion, and for the first time published a treatise on 'the law of *contract*'.[357] As Waddams has pointed out, this change of terminology was significant. The use of the singular lent 'itself more readily to a deductive approach' and suggested 'a high degree of conceptual unity', whereby 'one unified and

[353] See Horwitz (n 152) 12–13 (a typical mid-nineteenth-century American contract treatise 'contained separate chapters on the law of sales, insurance, negotiable instruments, agents, railroads, and so forth').

[354] See, eg, *Chitty on Contracts* (n 13), which has one volume on general principles and another on specific contracts.

[355] Atiyah (n 73) 400.

[356] Leake (n 55) v. In the preface to the second edition, Leake said that he had originally intended that edition to have a second part on specific contracts, but that he had subsequently abandoned the idea: Leake (n 59) ix.

[357] There is an obvious link in this respect with Pollock's tort scholarship, and especially his belief that there was a general principle of liability underlying the various individual torts: see Goudkamp and Nolan (n 3) 7–8.

coherent body of principles governs all contracts, whatever their nature'.[358] (Interestingly, however, while this usage – like its equivalent 'the law of tort' – became commonplace in England, and also Australia, Canada and New Zealand, it did not catch on in the US.)

The classical ideal of contract law as an abstract set of principles 'blind to details of subject matter and person'[359] was the subject of sustained attack in the twentieth century. First, it came to be perceived as part and parcel of an ideology of *laissez-faire* – according to Atiyah, when you eliminated the distinction between different types of contracts and contract parties you made it 'much harder to justify paternalist intervention which protects some parties against others'.[360] Second, the realists attacked it for divorcing the law from the complex reality of exchange transactions, which, they argued, could only properly be understood if full account were taken of the nature of the transaction and the parties to it. (This was what Llewellyn called 'narrow issue' thinking.[361]) And finally, increasing paternalism subjected the classical model to huge centrifugal pressures, as the interventions usually came in the form of legislation – or sometimes judicial implication of terms – that applied to particular contract types (housing, employment, credit, etc) or parties (such as consumers or employees). The result was that 'the law of contract shattered like a broken mirror, and splintered into subfields'.[362]

This fragmentation posed a challenge to contract law scholars of all persuasions, though their response to it generally depended on where they sat on the traditional/modernist (or classical/realist) spectrum. The traditionalists, such as Cheshire and Fifoot and Treitel, stayed true to the classical model of exposition established by Pollock and Anson by devoting all the chapters in their works to general principles. By contrast, the modernists tended to compromise by maintaining a primary focus on general matters (howsoever framed) but adding some discussion of particular contract types, as in Kessler's casebook.[363] One American scholar, Harold Havighurst, went further, and organised his casebook entirely around transaction types, but this proved too much for his intended readership to stomach, and the book was not a success.[364] That failed experiment serves as a useful reminder that there is an important link between the contract/contracts question and the question of audience. A combination of general discussion with analysis of specific types of contract is likely to be of

[358] Waddams (n 17) 141.
[359] LM Friedman, *Contract Law in America* (Madison, University of Wisconsin Press, 1965) 21.
[360] Atiyah (n 113) 170.
[361] See Twining (n 114) 137.
[362] Friedman (n 164) 384.
[363] For a qualified defence by a leading modernist of a generalised 'law of contracts', see IR Macneil, 'Whither Contracts?' (1969) 21 *Journal of Legal Education* 403.
[364] See Farnsworth (n 104) 1434. The work in question is H Havighurst, *Cases and Materials on the Law of Contracts* (Chicago, Callaghan, 1934). Havighurst acknowledged his debt to Leon Green, who had organised his casebook on torts according to the context in which the claim had arisen, rather than the usual conceptual categories. On Green, see J Steele, 'Professor Leon Green (1888–1979): Word Magic and the Regenerative Power of Law' in *STL* (n 1).

most use to a practising lawyer,[365] while a work organised entirely (or almost entirely) around general concepts is likely to be better suited to the classroom environment.

IV. CONCLUSION

In the introduction to *STL* we said that we thought it would be difficult after reading that book 'to escape the conclusion that scholars of tort law have played a significant role in the development' of that subject.[366] We have no doubt that readers of this volume will reach the same conclusion about scholars of contract law. In the case of tort, the existing literature on the influence of jurists on the law's development was somewhat limited (albeit with some significant exceptions). The position as regards contract is otherwise, and in this chapter we have drawn extensively on the relevant scholarship. Catharine MacMillan has, for example, argued that the English law of contractual mistake was essentially the product of scholars such as Leake, Pollock and Anson.[367] In her words, 'mistake as a legal doctrine was created by English theorists and not English judges'.[368] The influence of scholars on the development of contract law is also a pervasive theme of the work of David Ibbetson,[369] Michael Lobban[370] and Warren Swain[371] on the history of contract law in general, and of Stephen Waddams' book *Principle and Policy in Contract Law*.[372]

A reviewer of *STL* remarked of that collection that 'a central finding is the sheer range and diversity of forms' that scholarly influence over legal development can take,[373] a conclusion we believe can also be drawn from the current volume. And as we ourselves pointed out in the introduction to *STL*, that influence is generally subtle and indirect, and frequently imperceptible.[374] That is particularly true when it comes to arguably the most enduring channel for such influence, namely the mind of the law student.[375] As Atiyah has observed with regard to the English experience in particular:

> By the 1920s there were a large number of barristers and even judges whose first acquaintance with the law of contract had been obtained through the pages of Anson and Pollock; and there is a tradition that 'taught law is tough law'.[376]

[365] A point not lost on the editors of *Chitty*, or on Williston, who included in his treatise a volume on 'Particular Classes of Contracts': Williston (n 127) vol IV.

[366] Goudkamp and Nolan (n 3) 39.

[367] MacMillan (n 61).

[368] *ibid* 215. See also Swain (n 15) 229.

[369] Ibbetson (n 23) chs 11–13.

[370] Lobban (n 45).

[371] Swain (n 15).

[372] Waddams (n 35).

[373] Arvind (n 2) 114.

[374] Goudkamp and Nolan (n 3) 39–40.

[375] See McDonald (n 2) 485 ('[T]here can be no doubt of the indirect influence of academics and scholars on generations of students who go on to become lawyers, judges, parliamentarians and policymakers …').

[376] Atiyah (n 73) 685.

We hope that the chapters that follow will serve as a reminder of the significance of legal scholarship in the development of the common law. In England, it was the jurists – and not the judges – who really 'created' the modern law of contract, and gave it its distinctive shape and structure. Similarly, in the US it was scholars such as Langdell, Holmes, Williston and Corbin who fashioned the American common law of contract.[377] And this phenomenon of scholarly influence on contract law was repeated throughout the common law world, from the imprint left by Coote in his native New Zealand to the role that jurists played in the drafting of the Indian Contract Act. Nor of course did this phenomenon grind to a halt when the scholars who feature in this collection laid down their pens. For even if today's scholars of contract law have less scope than their predecessors to establish the basic parameters of the subject, their ability to shape the future development of contract law and to further understanding of contracts and contracting as legal, economic and social phenomena should not be in any doubt. But that is a story for another day.

[377] Of course, as Twining reminds us (chapter 15 of this volume, p 391), no such thing really exists, but, like many myths, the idea of an American common law of contract has such resonance that it has frequently shaped reality, in the form of the contract law of the individual states.

2

Sir Jeffrey Gilbert (1674–1726)

MICHAEL LOBBAN

IT IS GENERALLY accepted that English contract law was transformed in the nineteenth century, in particular under the influence of will theory. While in the eighteenth century, discussions of contract law centred on the different writs or forms of action used to bring contractual claims,[1] the nineteenth century saw a flourishing of treatises which sought to put the law on the foundation of clear principles.[2] The transformation of English contract law which this literary development reflected has been depicted in part as an intellectual story: that of the reception of ideas from the civilian tradition which, somewhat belatedly, allowed English lawyers to rethink the foundations of their law, and to use sharper tools to solve the problems which came before the courts. The reception of these rules went hand in hand with the reining in of the civil jury, as more questions of fact were turned into questions of law for judges to pronounce on, and for jurists to write about. Over a short period of time, according to the conventional story, the will theory gave rise to new doctrines which are now central to our idea of contract, including offer and acceptance and mistake and frustration.[3] While dominant, a will theory borrowed from civilian jurisprudence did not resolve English jurists' theoretical needs,[4] since doctrinal elegance was impeded by the need to accommodate English doctrines which did not fit the civilian model. 'The result was a mess'.[5]

[1] See, eg, J Gordley, *Foundations of Private Law* (Oxford, Oxford University Press, 2006) 288.

[2] The first published treatise explicitly devoted to contract was JJ Powell's *Essay upon the Law of Contracts and Agreements,* 2 vols (London, J Johnson and T Whieldon, 1790). The younger Joseph Chitty's *Practical Treatise of the Law of Contracts not under Seal* (London, S Sweet, 1826) written after the translation of Pothier into English, is generally seen as being much more theoretically informed than Powell. SM Leake's *The Elements of the Law of Contracts* (London, Stevens & Sons, 1867) and Frederick Pollock's *Principles of Contract at Law and Equity* (London, Stevens & Sons, 1876) compete for the claim of being the first 'principled' treatise of contract law, unbound to the old forms of action and seeking to bring together common law rules and equitable ones.

[3] See AWB Simpson, 'Innovation in Nineteenth Century Contract Law' (1975) 91 *LQR* 247. For the influence of continental jurists on the development of mistake, see further C MacMillan, *Mistakes in Contract Law* (Oxford, Hart Publishing, 2010).

[4] For Pollock's changes of view, see M Lobban, 'Introduction' in W Cornish et al, *The Oxford History of the Laws of England*, vol XII (Oxford, Oxford University Press, 2010) 308–12.

[5] DJ Ibbetson, A *Historical Introduction to the Law of Obligations* (Oxford, Oxford University Press, 1999) 221.

One doctrine which was not easy to explain in terms of will theory was that of consideration. If contract law was the product of the wills of two parties, both of whom could be shown to have intended to create legal relations, what need was there for consideration? As early as 1765, Lord Mansfield's King's Bench had suggested that where the parties' intention to be bound had been clearly evidenced in writing, it could not be seen as a *nudum pactum* for want of consideration: as he put it, 'the ancient notion about the want of consideration was for the sake of evidence only'.[6] Mansfield's attempts to by-pass the need for consideration failed, as later judges reiterated the centrality of consideration to the English law of contracts not under seal. When, at the high point of the influence of will theory in England, the House of Lords was given the opportunity to dislodge the doctrine of consideration in *Foakes v Beer*, it chose not to do so.[7] By then, consideration might have appeared to be like Holmes's 'clavicle in the cat' – one of those doctrines which 'survive in the law long after the use they once served is at an end and the reason for them has been forgotten'.[8] Instead, theorists now returned to look for theoretical explanations for the doctrine, some of which led jurists away from a will theory towards a bargain theory of contract.

More recently, there has been a recognition that jurists in the eighteenth century and earlier had already begun to think beyond the bounds of the forms of action, in terms of contractual obligations which derived from consent.[9] Historians of contract law have pointed to Sir Jeffrey Gilbert as the 'first English writer to provide a detailed treatment of the law of contract'.[10] They have drawn on his manuscript treatise on the law of contract, which has now been published in an edition by the Selden Society. An examination of Gilbert's work on contract allows us both to test how innovative the approach of the later treatise writers was; and to see how an earlier writer sought to reconcile a notion of contract based on the meeting of minds with the doctrine of consideration. Gilbert's work, which combined features of a modern, principled treatise with the old tradition of abridgments of cases, is also a bridge between an old and a new world: and this allows us to see in what ways he may have innovated.

Jeffrey Gilbert was born in Kent in 1674. He was admitted to the Inner Temple in 1692, and called to the Bar six years later. Little is known of Gilbert's life before 1714, although he appears to have practised regularly in both common law and chancery courts. Much more is known of his life after his promotion to the Irish Bench in 1714, as part of the purging of Tory judges in Ireland after the

[6] *Pillans v Van Mierop* (1765) 3 Burr 1663, 1669; 97 ER 1035, 1038.

[7] *Foakes v Beer* (1884) 9 App Cas 605 (HL). Given the chance to revisit this a century and a quarter later, the Supreme Court declined the opportunity: *MWB Business Exchange Centres v Rock Advertising Ltd* [2018] UKSC 24, [2019] AC 119.

[8] OW Holmes, *The Common Law* (Boston, Little, Brown & Co, 1881) 35.

[9] See W Swain, 'The Classical Model of Contract: The Product of a Revolution in Legal Thought?' (2010) 30 *LS* 513, 516–17; Ibbetson (n 5) ch 11. See also M Lobban, 'Mapping the Common Law: Some Lessons from History' (2014) 21 *New Zealand Law Review* 21.

[10] Swain (n 9) 517.

death of Queen Anne, and their replacement with Whigs. Thanks to the patronage of his friend Lord Chancellor William Cowper, Gilbert was appointed a justice of the King's Bench in Ireland in 1714 and became Chief Baron of the Irish Exchequer in the following year. Gilbert's time in Ireland was controversial, since he stood at the centre of a constitutional crisis, in which the Irish House of Lords disputed the British House of Lords' jurisdiction to hear an appeal from a decision of Gilbert's Exchequer. A loyal Court Whig, Gilbert felt himself bound by the body in Westminster, rather than that in Dublin, as a result of which the Irish Lords ordered his imprisonment as a 'betrayer of his Majesty's prerogative of judging cases in the High Court of Parliament in Ireland'.[11] Gilbert's stance did his career no harm at all, and on his return to England in 1722, he was made a Baron of the English Exchequer. An astute political operator, Gilbert also played a part in the downfall of Lord Chancellor Macclesfield, after being appointed in 1724 to head a committee to investigate the accounts of the Chancery masters. After briefly being one of the commissioners holding the Great Seal after Macclesfield's fall, he was appointed Chief Baron of the Exchequer in May 1726.

Gilbert died only five months after this appointment. His posthumous fame would rest not on his work on the Bench, but on the scholarly work he had done when at the Bar, in drafting a large number of manuscript treatises, many of which were posthumously published.[12] These treatises were parts of a large comprehensive overview of the law of England, which he never completed, and whose publication he forbade in his will. His wishes were circumvented by booksellers who obtained manuscript copies of various component parts which were in circulation. He is perhaps best known as author of the first treatise on the law of evidence, which went through four English editions in the eighteenth century before being considerably enlarged by Capel Lofft.[13] Another work which was regarded as pioneering was his *Law of Uses and Trusts*, first published in 1734 and reprinted in a second edition in 1741. Seventy years later, a new edition was

[11] The constitutional dispute was eventually settled in 1720 by a Declaratory Act (confirming the power to lie in Westminster). For details, see M Lobban (ed), *Jeffrey Gilbert on Property and Contract,* 2 vols (London, Selden Society, 2019) lxxi–lxxxiv and J Rudolph, *Common Law and Enlightenment in England, 1689–1750* (New York, Boydell Press, 2013) 233–45.

[12] AWB Simpson identifies Gilbert as one of only two proper treatise writers before Blackstone (the other being William Hawkins) (AWB Simpson, 'The Rise and Fall of the Legal Treatise: Legal Principles and the Forms of Legal Literature' (1981) 48 *University of Chicago Law Review* 632, 652–53). For Gilbert's wider project and life, see M Macnair, 'Sir Jeffrey Gilbert and his Treatises' (1994) 15 *Journal of Legal History* 252 and Lobban (n 11) xc–cix.

[13] G Gilbert, *The Law of Evidence* (London, Henry Lintot for W Owen, 1756). The treatise on *Evidence* comprised two parts, one on written and unwritten evidence, and the other on 'issues'. In Gilbert's original plan for a comprehensive treatise on English law, these two topics were to be dealt with separately in a projected part on the Law of Actions. This work was never completed but some of the material on issues found its way into his manuscript on contract, while material on evidence was put into separate manuscripts which did not deal with 'issues'. In the published treatise on *Evidence*, the two topics were united, with much of the material on issues which was used in the contract treatise being reproduced. For further detail, see Lobban (n 11) cxix–cxxi.

brought out by Edward Sugden, who opened his preface with the comment that '[f]ew works on legal subjects have been so universally referred to as Gilbert on Uses'.[14] Sudgen pointed out that the work was 'not finished for the public eye', and needed major editorial intervention.[15] However, in Sudgen's edition, it would continue to be cited in nineteenth-century cases. Gilbert's works on *Tenures*, and on the history and practice of various courts, including the Chancery, were also much in use in the eighteenth century.[16]

It was well known that a large proportion of Matthew Bacon's *Abridgment of the Law* was taken from Gilbert's manuscripts.[17] It is clear that Bacon also had access to Gilbert's manuscript treatise on contract. However, he did not reproduce it in the way that he did with much of Gilbert's other work.[18] Furthermore, in Bacon's hands, what Gilbert had treated as a unitary *genus* – contract – was fragmented into component entries which befitted an abridgment, including agreement, *assumpsit*, covenant and obligation. Consequently, the reader of Bacon would find the kind of fragmented, untheoretical view of the law of contract which historians associate with the eighteenth-century forms of action. At the same time, however, Bacon's definition of 'agreement' did in many ways distil the essence of Gilbert's argument:

> An agreement is the consent of two or more persons concurring, the one in parting with, and the other in receiving some right, property, or benefit; … that men should execute their agreements and perform their promises though made without writing or consideration, is enjoined by the law of nature; but in civil societies, and in ours in particular, circumstances are required which protect the weak, and those who are under the power of others; also provision is made against fraud and circumvention, and that no man should be injured in his property by the turn of an unwary expression.[19]

[14] Those who engaged with his work included FW Sanders, *An Essay on the Nature and Laws of Uses and Trusts* (London, E and R Brooke, 1791); W Cruise, *An Essay on Uses* (London, A Strahan for J Butterworth, 1795); J Fonblanque (ed), *A Treatise of Equity*, 2nd edn (London, W Clarke and Son, 1799).

[15] Sugden stated that he had looked through all the references: 'A great proportion of them required correction, and some were irrelevant … It was seldom that the cases were referred to by name, which rendered it a great labour to correct the references': ('Preface' in G Gilbert, *The Law of Uses and Trusts*, 3rd edn (London, W Reed, 1811) iv).

[16] On Gilbert as a historian, see also Rudolph (n 11) 259–64.

[17] For instance, both William Blackstone and Richard Wooddeson drew on the entry on leases in that *Abridgment*, and both assumed it to have been drawn from Gilbert's work. Blackstone stated that 'the subject is treated in a perspicuous and masterly manner': W Blackstone, *Commentaries on the Laws of England*, vol 2 (Oxford, Clarendon Press, 1768). *cf* R Wooddeson, *A Systematical View of the Laws of England*, vol 1 (London, Thomas Payne, 1792) 459n.

[18] Matthew Bacon drew selectively on Gilbert's discussion of contract: see for instance his treatment of *assumpsit* in M Bacon, *A New Abridgment of the Law*, vol 1 (London, E and R Nutt and R Gosling, 1736) 163ff, which uses some of Gilbert's material verbatim, but which puts the topics in a different order and also uses different examples.

[19] Where Gilbert's wording began 'contract is the act of two …', Bacon's began 'an agreement is the consent of two …' (Bacon (n 18) 67). In a side note, Bacon refers to the well-known derivation of 'agreement' out of *aggregatio* and *mentium* found in *Reniger v Fogossa* (1550) Plowd 1, 17; 75 ER 1, 27: this was not to be found in Gilbert.

Legal historians who have examined Gilbert's work have seen a more unified theory. Quoting a definition in Gilbert's manuscript almost identical to the first line in Bacon's passage quoted above,[20] they have identified in it a Hobbesian view of contractual liability generated by simple acts of will, foreshadowing the kind of theory developed in the nineteenth-century literature. At the same time, it has been argued that he muddied his theory by combining it with an orthodox common law description of consideration,[21] which left it unclear whether his view of contract was one to be explained by a will theory, or a bargain theory. It will be suggested in what follows that Gilbert had a more coherent theory than this suggests, and that his view of consideration – which echoed a position found in earlier writers – was compatible with his highly developed theory of the will.

I. EARLY MODERN CONCEPTIONS OF CONTRACT

The idea that there was a general category of contract of which *assumpsit*, debt and covenant were different forms was not new to Gilbert. Pleaders were familiar enough with the fact that contractual actions were different from tortious ones, and that the two could not be joined together in pleadings.[22] Law students were also familiar with the general word 'contract', which could be found in regular use in both case law[23] and treatise literature.[24] Furthermore, there were numerous definitions of contract, provided by jurists from the Elizabethan

[20] '[C]ontract is the act of two or more person concurring, the one in parting with and the other in receiving some property, right or benefit' (Lobban (n 11) 211, quoted in SM Waddams, *Principle and Policy in Contract Law: Competing or Complementary Concepts?* (Cambridge, Cambridge University Press, 2011) 59, 175; Swain (n 9) 517 and Ibbetson (n 5) 216).

[21] Ibbetson (n 5) 216–17; Swain (n 9) 517; Waddams (n 20) 60.

[22] The distinction can be seen in *Whyte v Rysden* (1625) Cro Car 20, 79 ER 623, where the plaintiff sued a defendant in tort, for damaging and detaining his horse in Exeter, having contracted for its hire in London. The objection to having the case tried at Exeter was overruled 'because the Tort is supposed to be done there and not at *London*, tho' the Contract was made in *London*': Anon, *The Law of Errors and Writs of Errors. Being a Treatise Wherein is Contained the Nature and End of the Writ of Error* (London, R & E Atkins, 1703) 160.

[23] For some random examples: *Dale v Copping* (1610) 1 Bulst 39, 80 ER 743 (on a promise by an infant to pay for his cure, 'this shall be taken as a contract'); *Winter v Foweracres* (1618) 2 Roll 39, 81 ER 645 ('a contract by parol upon good consideration is as strong as a covenant by deed'); *Rutter v Hebden* (1664) 1 Lev 147, 83 ER 341 ('Deceit brought for not marrying his daughter according to the agreement; and held well, for the contract is temporal'); *Gybbons v North* (1670) 1 Vent 75, 86 ER 53 ('a verbal contract cannot create a penalty'). See also *Tidcombe v Cholmley* (1701) Colles 166, 1 ER 232, with the pleadings set out in W Brown, *Praxis Almæ Curiæ Cancellariæ: The Third Part: A Collection of the Most Modern and Useful Precedents for Drawing Bills, Answers, and Demurrers*, vol 3 (London, JD and Robert Gibson, 1702) 341.

[24] Examples include Co Litt 145a ('if I contract with you to pay unto you 20 shillings, or a robe at the feast of Easter, after the feast you may bring an action of debt for the one or for the other'); G Duncombe, *Tryals per Pais: Or, the Law of England Concerning Juries by Nisi Prius, &c* (London, R and E Atkins for J Walthoe, 1702) 296 ('in an information upon an usurious contract by two, 'tis not sufficient to find a contract by one').

period onwards, which outlined what contracts were, and which discussed the role of assent and consideration in ways which would influence later jurists.

One definition which was frequently referred to came from William West's treatise on legal instruments, *Symboleography*, published in 1592.[25] In his discussion of 'covenants and agreements', he stated that 'A Covenant is the consent of two or more, in one selfe thing, to give, or to doe somewhat'.[26] There were two ways to consent in covenants. The first was 'true' consent, which was expressed by word or deed. '[W]e make choice with whom we will covenant', West explained: 'in a true consent our wills conjoin us'. The second kind of consent was feigned or fictitious consent, where the parties were by law 'deemed to consent, for the nature and reason of the business, which is between them both'.[27] It can be seen from this that the notion of the free will and consent was central to this Elizabethan concept of contracting; for West added that 'if there be any error or deceit in the consent or thing, for which the contract is entred into, that contract is either made altogether none, or of none effect'.[28] Similar notions that contracts were obligations generated by the agreement of two parties are to be found in other early modern legal sources, from Christopher St Germain's *Doctor and Student*[29] to William Sheppard's *Faithfull Councellor*.[30]

Besides agreement, early writers also stressed the centrality of consideration. For West, a cause or consideration was essential for an agreement to come into being. A promise without agreement – which he identified with the Roman notion of *policitatio* – was a *nudum pactum* breeding no obligation. As he put it, 'a promise is a covenant offered by one freely, which is of none effect in the law to produce an obligation if there be no cause why it should be done'.[31] On the other hand, 'a covenant or agreement which hath a cause, is termed a contract which is nothing else but an agreement with a lawful cause or consideration'.[32] West's definition proved popular, and was taken up (for instance) by John Cowell, who compressed it to the following formulation: 'Contract is a Covenant or Agreement with a lawful Consideration or Cause'.[33]

[25] W West, *The First Part of Symboleography* (London, Company of Stationers, 1610). This work opened with a discussion of 'the several natures of contracts and last wills' and obligations in law, which were defined in the Roman sense of a *vinculum iuris*.

[26] It was the consent of those who had both the natural capacity and the permission of law to do so (*ibid* s 4).

[27] *ibid* s 5.

[28] *ibid* s 11.

[29] C St Germain (edited by TFT Plucknett and JL Barton), *Doctor and Student* (London, Selden Society, 1974) 228: 'bargains and sales be called contracts, and be made by assent of the parties upon agreement' (spelling modernised).

[30] W Sheppard, *The Faithful Councellor: or the Marrow of the Law in English*, 2nd edn (London, RW for T Brewster, N Ekins and E Dod, 1653) 86–87: 'a Contract taken largely, is an agreement between two or more, concerning something to be done, whereby both parties are bound to each other, or one is bound to the other'.

[31] West (n 25) s 8.

[32] *ibid* s 10.

[33] J Cowell, 'Contract' in J Cowell, T Manley and W Kennet (eds), *The Interpreter: or Booke Containing the Signification of Words* (Cambridge, John Legate, 1607) (spelling modernised).

Such compressed definitions hardly explained the exact relationship between consideration and agreement. In dealing with the matter, West referred to St Germain's discussion of a *nudum pactum* in Chapter 24 of *Doctor and Student*. In the passage in question, the Doctor (who represents the civilian tradition) and the Student (who speaks for the common law) discuss whether one-sided promises are binding in conscience. On hearing that no action lay at common law on a bare promise, the Doctor asks whether English lawyers regard such promises as binding in conscience. He explains that in his tradition, although a promise did not bind in conscience if it 'be so naked that there is no manner of consideration why it should be made' – since there might be 'some error in the making of the promise' – it did bind if it was evident that the promisor really intended to be bound by his deliberate promise. One example where such an intention could safely be inferred was where a person promised a gift to a university or to a church.[34] The Doctor's argument rests on the idea that promises which are seriously intended should be enforced; and that canon law judges could see that at least some worthy promises must be taken to have been seriously intended.

This argument does not convince the Student. When the Doctor admits that a promise does not bind the conscience of a promisor who does not in fact intend to be bound, the Student points out that this means that a one-sided promise can never be enforced by a court, since it could never know the 'intent inward in the heart'.[35] It is for this reason that the court must look to consideration: a promise could only be enforced if the promisee 'have a charge by reason of the promise which he has also performed'. In the case of a promise to a university or a church 'where the party to whom the promise was made is bound to no new charge by reason of the promise made to him but as he was bound to before', no action could lie. The argument of this passage seems to be that, while the root of a contractual obligation is the intention to be bound, since it is impossible to know whether a person subjectively has such an intention, the court must look to the consideration for the promise, which requires some verifiable detriment suffered by the promisee. What is absent in this discussion is any mention of acceptance, which would ripen an offer into a contract. Instead, in a context where the language used is that of promises, the presence of consideration steps in to fulfil the function of a communicated acceptance to evidence the seriousness of intent.

For many later writers, consideration was not simply seen as evidence of a contractual intention, but as essential for a contractual exchange.[36] For example, having quoted the 'civilian' view that 'in all contracts … there must be

[34] St Germain (n 29) 229 (spelling modernised).

[35] *ibid* 230.

[36] Cowell's editors added explanatory material to flesh out the centrality of consideration. J Cowell, 'Contract' in J Cowell, T Manley and W Kennet (eds), *The Interpreter or Words and Terms used either in the Common or Statute Law of this Realm* (London, W Battersby, J Place, A & J Churchil, R Sare, 1701):

> if a Man make a Promise to me, That I shall have twenty Shillings, and that he will be Debtor to me thereof, and after I ask the twenty Shillings, and he will not deliver it; yet I shall never have an

something given in exchange', Blackstone argued that 'a consideration of some sort or other is absolutely necessary to the forming of a contract',[37] suggesting a distinct requirement beyond the agreement. Earlier in the century, Thomas Wood had also defined contract to be 'an agreement upon cause or consideration, ... something which consists in giving or doing by one of the parties, in pursuance of the agreement'. At the same time, Wood's own discussion is testament to the fact that there remained some theoretical uncertainty in regard to the relative role of agreement and consideration. For, as he explains, while some jurists 'fancy that it cannot be a contract unless it is *actus contra actum* ... I rather think it to be call'd a contract because after many debates the affair is contracted into an agreement between the parties'.[38] Wood's comments reflect the theoretical uncertainty – about the relative roles of agreement and consideration – which historians have sometimes attributed to Gilbert. In what follows, it will be argued that Gilbert had a more robust theory than is sometimes assumed, and that his view of the doctrine of consideration reflected the position of St Germain's Student more than that of Blackstone.

II. JEFFREY GILBERT'S CONCEPTION OF CONTRACT

In composing a treatise on contract, Gilbert demonstrated the unity of the subject in a way which was not possible in the fragmentary treatment offered in abridgments and manuals of pleading. His unitary conception is evident from the very structure of his projected grand treatise. His plan was to show first how property was acquired, and then how it was transferred. As he explained in his short theoretical *Treatise of the Law of Nature*:[39]

> If what a man has gotten by his lawful industry is properly his own, because he hath severed out of the wide common of nature for his own peculiar use, it follows that what a man hath thus gained he may part with to another, and this seems to have been the first foundation of contract.[40]

In his larger project to describe all of English law, Gilbert planned to explain the different ways in which property in land and chattels was acquired and transferred. The treatise on contract formed part of his wider discussion of personal property, whose rules he felt were rooted in a law of nature which could be

action to recover, because the Promise was no *Contract* but a bare Promise; and *ex nudo Pacto non oritur Actio*. But if any thing were given for the twenty Shillings, though it were but to the value of a Penny, then had it been a *Good Contract*.

[37] *Blackstone's Commentaries* (n 17) 444–45.

[38] T Wood, *A New Institute of the Imperial or Civil Law* (London, Richard Sare, 1704) 164–65.

[39] This treatise is part of the edition in Lobban (n 11).

[40] *ibid* 83. At the beginning of his discussion of contract, he describes it as the means 'whereby that propriety which was established among mankind by occupation and industry was conveyed from one man to another' (*ibid* 201).

figured out as a matter of theory. By contrast, he explained that the rules relating to the acquisition and transfer of real property derived from the feudal practices of the 'northern nations' which had settled in England, and had to be dealt with through a historical examination of those rules. Questions relating to the inheritance, devising or alienation of lands were to be dealt with in chapters which explained the feudal foundations of this law.[41]

Gilbert's conception of contract was based on a theory of the will. This is most clearly evident in his *Treatise of the Law of Nature*. In this work, he defines a contract as 'an act of the will made known by lawful significant signs that transfers my right to another, together with an act of his will concurring with mine to accept it'.[42] The notion that 'every contract is an act of the will'[43] runs through Gilbert's longer treatise on contract as well as in this shorter text. He stated that it was necessary to make contracts by 'certain and significant signs whereby his will may be made known, in as much as man's thoughts are the internal acts of the soul, which are not of themselves transparent and not to be discerned by any other'.[44] The fact that the will was communicated by speech and by writing allowed for two different kinds of contracting. The invention of speech first allowed people to contract with each other and to supply their mutual wants; the later invention of writing allowed them to 'preserve the acts and intentions of the mind long after they happened', which allowed the intention of the parties to be recollected more reliably than if it were left to the memory of witnesses.[45]

The fact that Gilbert routinely describes contracts as a means of transferring rights from one person to another may make it appear that he 'envisaged contract primarily as a means of transferring property',[46] rather than imposing obligations more broadly. His initial definition of a right, in the *Treatise of the Law of Nature*, certainly has a proprietary ring to it: '[r]ight is what a man hath power to exclude others from the use and command of by the rules of law'.[47] There are other indicators that he thought of rights in terms of property. According to Gilbert, in a state of nature, every man had a right to gather the

[41] Aspects of his treatment can be seen in G Gilbert, *A Treatise of Tenures in Two Parts* (London, E and R Nutt and R Gosling, 1730) and G Gilbert, *The Law of Devises, Revocations and Last Wills* (London, Henry Lintot, 1756). See also his manuscript chapter on 'Alienations' in Singleton MS 67, fo 92 (Arthur W Diamond Law Library, Columbia Law School) (part of which was reflected in the chapter on attornment in his treatise on *Tenures*). This chapter begins with:

> By the ancient feudal law the lord and tenant were so connected to each other by the ties of mutual benefit and services that the lord could not dispose of his own seignory without the consent and attornment of his tenants, nor could the tenant alien his lands without the consent of his lord.

[42] Lobban (n 11) 23.

[43] *ibid* 25.

[44] *ibid* 23.

[45] *ibid* 299.

[46] Waddams (n 20) 159.

[47] Lobban (n 11) 3; *cf* 14: 'a right *ex vi termini* is what a man may exclude others from and consequently defend to himself by the rules of law'.

fruits of the earth to preserve himself as well as a right to the products of his industry: 'And it is these rights which we call property'.[48] Having defined injustice as the violation of a right, and stating that there can be no injustice where there is no right, he writes, '[w]here there is no property, there is no injustice, for every property supposes a right'.[49] Discussing property, he also states that '[s]ince all right is gained by occupancy, the most significant and notorious sign of transferring right is the tradition or placing another in your own possession'.[50]

At the same time, it is also clear that Gilbert did not equate property with possession. A person wrongfully taking possession of my property 'gains no right, the former right is still in me'.[51] One could transfer a right by contract, without transferring possession, for '[a] man may transfer his right to commence at a day to come as well as presently'.[52] Different kinds of rights could also be granted in relation to property. Alluding to the kind of arrangements frequently found in family settlements, he noted:

> If A by one contract transfers a future right in any of his possessions to B and afterwards gives all the right which he has in the same possession to C, C has the present right subject to the claim of B at the time appointed. In like manner, if A grants his possession to B for a certain number of years and then grants all his right in such possession to C, then C shall have a reversion as the lawyers call it after the interest of B is determined. For C by the contract comes into the place of A.[53]

The right to property was transferred by acts of will. A man might therefore transfer property conditionally, depending 'upon uncertain events that are yet to come'.[54] In such cases, the contract had no force until the event occurred for 'my will to transfer right follows the event', and if the event never occurs 'there is no will of mine to transfer right and consequently no contract'.[55] Gilbert also discussed how rights which had been transferred could be resumed. One example was that of contracts with conditions subsequent. In such cases, 'my will to transfer right precedes the event of the condition' but 'my will to transfer right ceaseth' when the condition is broken and after that 'there is no contract but the right returns to me again'.[56] Equally, when a covenant is released, 'the release retransfers that right which the obligation caused'.[57]

Although Gilbert's initial definition of right has a proprietary ring to it, his description of it as a 'power to exclude others' may be read as embracing a wider range of rights than those relating to property. For instance, Gilbert speaks of

[48] *ibid* 18 (Proposition 2).
[49] *ibid* 21 (Proposition 13).
[50] *ibid* 31 (Proposition 37).
[51] *ibid* 19 (Proposition 5).
[52] *ibid* 24 (Proposition 8).
[53] *ibid* 27 (Proposition 19).
[54] *ibid* 28 (Proposition 27).
[55] *ibid* 29 (Proposition 28).
[56] *ibid* 29 (Proposition 29).
[57] *ibid* 26 (Proposition 17).

'my right of living'.[58] Explaining why contracts to 'do a thing impossible' are void, he states that 'every right supposes a power, which cannot be but on things in being or of the actions and modes of beings, as to run, fetch, carry etc'.[59] He makes it clear that people have rights to take certain actions. For instance, everyone in the state of nature 'hath a right to punish another for the injury received'.[60] Each person also had a right of judgement, since 'every man is judge of the means of his own preservation'.[61] Every man is the fittest judge of his own self-preservation, 'for since God has given to every man the power of discerning and choosing the means of his support, he wills the use of that power'. In this passage, Gilbert goes on to say that

> [a] man's judgment concerning the means of his own preservation ought to extend no farther than his own property, for if it extend beyond his own property, it is not a judgment concerning any right, for property and right are equivalent.[62]

However, it may be suggested that his concept of 'property' in this context might also embrace other rights which might legitimately be defended, such as life and limb.

Moreover, the theoretical treatise includes various examples of contractual obligations which do not entail the transfer of property. In general, 'whatever any man may lawfully do he may lawfully oblige himself to do'.[63] A man may 'oblige himself by contract to obey another'.[64] A party may also contract to ensure the performance of another contract:

> If A covenants to transfer any right to B and C covenants with B to see it executed and performed, C is bound by that covenant for C doth not here covenant to do any wrong to A because by the supposition A hath transferred his right and therefore this contract is obligatory.[65]

A man may oblige himself not to act:

> If A covenants with B not to assist C in any case, though B should kill C upon such a cause and occasion as to A seems unreasonable but to B reasonable, such a contract is obligatory, for what a man may lawfully do he may lawfully covenant to do.[66]

[58] *ibid* 41 (Proposition 19). At 27 (Proposition 20), he also makes it clear that a man cannot contract not to defend his own life against an aggressor who wishes to kill him. Since God's will is that mankind be preserved, 'no man hath power to take away his own life … and therefore can give no power over it to another, for no man can transfer that right to another which he hath not first in himself'.

[59] *ibid* 25 (Proposition 10).

[60] *ibid* 35 (Proposition 13).

[61] *ibid* 37 (Proposition 1); *cf* 21 (Proposition 15); 28 (Proposition 26).

[62] *ibid* 19 (Proposition 6).

[63] *ibid* 30 (Proposition 35). Equally, 'for things that appear possible at the time of the covenant, the party must be understood to design an obligation only to his utmost endeavour' (*ibid* 25 (Proposition 11)).

[64] *ibid* 38 (Proposition 8).

[65] *ibid* 28 (Proposition 24).

[66] *ibid* 28 (Proposition 22).

As these examples show, Gilbert understood that people may impose contractual obligations on themselves which involve no transfer of property, but generate rights in the promisee to some performance. The obligation comes from the acts of will, expressed by significant signs: '[i]n verbal contracts an obligation arises if the words can be proved seriously spoken and with an intention to perform'.[67] Furthermore, once the obligation of future performance is imposed by mutual acts of the will, it can only be discharged either by performance or by the same kind of exchange of will as that which generated the obligation. For (as he explains in the longer treatise on contract), '[a] man cannot bar an executory *assumpsit* made by himself by any revocation or countermand' before any steps are taken to perform the contract: 'since the will of both parties were required to the making of such contract, it cannot be discharged without the concurrence of them both'.[68]

Much of the content of the longer treatise was concerned with contracts which did not transfer property, but which generated obligations. Indeed, the very form of contract which Gilbert spent most time discussing in this treatise – the sealed bond – did not involve a transfer of property: it was 'a solemn contract [...] whereby the obligor acknowledges the receipt of the money and binds himself to the repayment'.[69] Its most common form was the penal bond with conditional defeasance, in which the bond was given as a security for the performance of a promise contained in the condition. Gilbert's illustrations of the kinds of conditions which might be included in such bonds showed a notion of contract far from the mere transfer of property, including such conditions as 'not to prosecute or continue a suit' or 'to make all such linen as [the obligee] should want during his living single'.[70]

Gilbert's conception of a contract as involving a transfer of rights was borrowed from Thomas Hobbes.[71] For Hobbes, it was essential to describe contracting in such terms, since it was only by way of an executed transfer of rights that people in the state of nature could give authority to the sovereign (whose presence would be necessary to uphold any executory contract). Unlike Hobbes, Gilbert was not interested in using the concept to explain how sovereign

[67] *ibid* 51 (Proposition 11).

[68] *ibid* 287, referring to *Hurford v Pile* (1618) Cro Jac 483, 79 ER 412; H Rolle, *Un Abridgment des Plusieurs Cases et Resolutions del Common Ley* (London, A Crooke et al, 1668) vol 1 32A pl 1, where a defendant agreed with the plaintiff that he would repay money due from a (third party) debtor who had been taken in execution, if the debtor was discharged by the plaintiff. Although the defendant told the plaintiff before the debtor was released that he would not 'stand to his promise'; the plaintiff released the debtor and recovered on the promise.

[69] Lobban (n 11) 310.

[70] *ibid* 412. Gilbert also considered the performance obligations in such conditions: 'If a man be obliged to repair a house or build a mill, he is excused if the obligee will not suffer him to do it, or if a stranger by the command of the obligee disturb him' for 'the condition become impossible by the act of the obligee and then he voluntarily recedes from the advantage and benefit which might accrue to him by the obligation' (*ibid* 343).

[71] See M Lobban, 'Thomas Hobbes and the Common Law' in D Dyzenhaus and T Poole (eds), *Thomas Hobbes and the Law* (Cambridge, Cambridge University Press, 2012).

authority was generated. For him, the notion explained the moment when the parties bound themselves to performance: it was the moment when one party gave a 'right' to another.[72] This language did nevertheless generate some problems for Gilbert's analysis. For the language implied that a right was something which the contracting party already possessed, rather than being something he might create, and that it could only be transferred once. This meant that if a man sold goods to one person, he could not sell them again to a second buyer: 'The first contract makes void the latter, because the first contract transfers all the right and consequently the second contract can pass nothing at all, and therefore doth not answer the definition of a contract'.[73]

In making this point, Gilbert argued that the second sale was a contract to do something impossible. It was consequently void; and since 'the right to the consideration [paid for it] remaineth still in the buyer', he could recover it.[74] This seemed to overlook the possibility that the seller might have generated a right in the buyer, for which he could be compensated in damages, even if he could not supply the specific thing. In fact, Gilbert had not overlooked it, for later in the same treatise, he says,

> If a man contract with another to pay him so many bushels of corn, he cannot before the arbitrator plead he hath it not and therefore it is impossible for him to pay it, for the very contracting supposes it possible, otherwise a man must make his own act in vain.[75]

In another passage, he suggests that the buyer might in some cases affirm a contract that initially appeared to be 'void':

> If a man as suppose A grants a field to B and afterwards grants it to C who is not acquainted to the other contract and then B releases to A, C is not bound to accept it, for the contract between A and C was at first void and passed no right to each other … though A may be held to the contract if C approves it before an indifferent arbitrator.[76]

As these passages show, Gilbert seemed himself to be aware that language of contracting as the transfer of a right to a thing was not particularly helpful in explaining the legal consequences of a seller intentionally promising to sell goods he no longer had. It was more easily explained if the right created by the mutual acts of will was the right to a performance, the failure to execute which could still be compensated.

[72] For a modern view of contractual transactions as transfers of rights, see P Benson, *Justice in Transactions: A Theory of Contract Law* (Cambridge MA, Harvard University Press, 2019).

[73] Lobban (n 11) 24 (Proposition 9).

[74] *ibid* 25 (Proposition 12).

[75] *ibid* 54 (Proposition 21). This would be contrary to Proposition 17, 'He that contracts in that he doth contract denies the action to be in vain, for it is against reason for a knowing man to do any thing in vain' (*ibid* 53).

[76] *ibid* 27 (Proposition 18).

III. CONTRACT FORMATION

Having set out his will theory, Gilbert explored its ramifications. The first question to consider was that of contractual capacity. In the shorter treatment in the *Treatise of the Law of Nature*, he argued that 'infants and madmen' had no capacity, for they had 'no power of deliberation and consequently they cannot have any will'.[77] Married women could not contract, since husband and wife were – for policy reasons which Gilbert explained – regarded as one person in law, and so 'must have one will which must be seated in the man'.[78] He also discussed the contractual capacity of corporations. Such bodies could enter into formal contracts in their corporate name; but no action lay against them on informal contracts, 'for a body that consists in agreement only can't take or pass any right but by solemn agreement'.[79]

How did those who had the necessary capacity manifest their will in making contracts? Modern contract law treatises habitually begin with an analysis of the formation of contracts via the exchange of offers and acceptances, through which a *consensus ad idem* is reached. Early modern writers in the civilian tradition also spoke in similar terms.[80] It is generally agreed that English jurists only began to articulate a doctrine of offer and acceptance in the early nineteenth century, when they came under the influence of civilian writers such as Robert-Joseph Pothier. This doctrine focused attention as much on the intentions of the offeree – on whose decision the coming into being of the obligation rests – as on those of the promisor.[81] Under the doctrine of offer and acceptance, rules could be generated which clarify when (and where) a contract comes into being, and whether and when a party making an offer can retract it.

The fact that this doctrine came to be articulated in nineteenth-century English legal treatises has been attributed not only to civilian influences, but also to the fact that courts were responding to problems arising from new forms of communication.[82] However, the fact that there were few rules on offer and

[77] *ibid* 49 (Proposition 1). This was repeated in the longer treatment (*ibid* 319), but he now added that 'most municipal laws' allowed infants to contract for necessaries, and to ratify their contracts when of full age.

[78] *ibid* 317.

[79] *ibid* 255.

[80] As Pufendorf put it, 'in all Obligations whatsoever, there is required the Consent of the Person to whom they are directed, or who obtains a Right by them; declaring (by himself or Deputy,) that he accepts the Obligation and the Right which it transfers to him': S von Pufendorf (translated by B Kennett), *Of the Law of Nature and Nations*, 2nd edn (Oxford, L Lichfield, 1710) 228.

[81] According to the civilian doctrine outlined by Pothier, an offer which has not been accepted – a mere pollicitation – generates no obligation; and it can be revoked at any time prior to an unequivocal acceptance by the offeree. Pothier's exposition of this was quoted by Chitty (n 2) 10.

[82] S Gardner, 'Trashing with Trollope: A Deconstruction of the Postal Rules in Contract' (1992) 12 *OJLS* 170. The cases most important for the development of this doctrine concerned informal contracts made by commercial parties dealing at a distance, or by investors entering into contracts to buy shares through the post: see *Cooke v Oxley* (1790) 3 TR 653, 100 ER 785; *Adams v Lindsell* (1818) 1 B & Ald 681, 106 ER 250; *Household Fire and Carriage Accident Insurance Company (Limited) v Grant* (1879) LR 4 Ex D 216 (CA).

acceptance to be found in treatises or case law before the nineteenth century should not lead us to assume that there was no notion hitherto that contracts were the product of offers which had been accepted. Families arranging the marriages of their children routinely negotiated over the settlements which would be made on the marriage, drawing up marriage articles which stipulated what each side would give, and then making formal settlements in consequence of such agreements. Equally, merchants had long traded over long distances, contracting for the sale and transportation of goods. These contracts were also put into formal documents, such as charterparties. The purpose of such formal contracts was to settle the question of what the parties had agreed to, and when, for it was meant to be embodied in a formal document, whose meaning could not be elucidated by a resort to parol evidence. In practice, there often remained room for disputes about whether an agreement had been reached,[83] but they tended to be raised in the Court of Chancery, when it was asked to decree specific performance of such agreements or to rectify formal contracts. In treatises focused on the common law side – such as Gilbert's on contract – such material tended to be omitted.

Gilbert's own analysis concentrated more on the person transferring a contractual right than on the person accepting it. Although he did insist that there had to be 'an act of [the recipient's] will concurring [...] to accept it',[84] his treatment of the need for acceptance was much thinner than was to be found in the works of the jurists on which he drew.[85] Gilbert clearly did not see much room for such questions to be raised when discussing either formal or informal contracts. Nonetheless, there are occasional passages where Gilbert reveals his thinking about how contractual intent is manifested in the process of contracting, both in formal ('written') contracts and informal ('verbal') contracts.

When it came to formal contracts, which on their face seemed to manifest complete agreement, the main plea used to question whether an agreement had been made was *non est factum*. In modern law, the plea of *non est factum* is associated with the extremely rare cases where parties seek to avoid contracts they have signed by claiming illiteracy or blindness.[86] Gilbert also included such arguments. He explained:

> when the person that delivered the deed is unlearned, and the deed is read and expounded to him in another sense than that which the deed really contains, then did not the party agree to the written deed, it is not the expression of his mind, nor to be accounted his deed.[87]

[83] The Statute of Frauds – which required many contracts to be evidenced in writing – allowed the courts to consider whether an exchange of letters had produced an agreement or not, or whether there had been such performance as to allow the court to infer (in effect) such as acceptance by performance as dislodged any presumption of fraud. See, eg, *Wankford v Fotherley* (1694) 2 Vern CC 322, 23 ER 807; *Parker v Serjeant* (1674) Rep temp Finch 146, 23 ER 80.

[84] Lobban (n 11) 23 (Definition).

[85] See T Hobbes (edited and translated by R Tuck and M Silverthorne), *On the Citizen* (Cambridge, Cambridge University Press, 1998) 37.

[86] See the brief treatment in E Peel, *Treitel's The Law of Contract*, 13th edn (London, Sweet and Maxwell, 2011) paras 8-086–8-083.

[87] Lobban (n 11) 429. For blindness, see 430.

However, the *non est factum* plea also allowed the court to look at more questions regarding when and whether the contract came into effect. To be valid, a formal deed had not only to be sealed, but also delivered. Gilbert traced this requirement to the policy of the 'northern nations' from whom the English derived much of their law, who 'thought there could not be a plainer act of reciprocal assent than this of a delivery'. Delivery, which was a sign of contractual intent on the part of the party seeking to bind himself, might be made not only by a physical act of tradition, but also by 'proper words that plainly express a design of putting the obligee in possession of the deed'. The words used could be significant. If an obligor flung a deed on a table, and said to the obligee, 'see that writing, take it as my deed', this constituted a delivery. However, if he sealed a deed and simply put it on a table, from which the obligee picked it up, it was not a delivery, 'because the laying it on the table is no act to put it in the possession of anybody'.[88]

The obligor's intentions also served to distinguish between a deed and an escrow. If a man handed over his deed to a third party, to deliver it to the obligee when certain conditions were performed, this was an escrow, and the deed was not binding until the conditions were in fact performed. If the third party (called the 'bailee' by Gilbert) delivered it before the conditions were performed, 'this is no deed because it wants the attestation of consent by delivery; for the bailee had no authority to deliver it otherwise than according to his commission and therefore his act is not to be imputed to the person whom he represents'.[89] Nor would this kind of deed be regarded as valid if the obligee either chanced upon it, or took it out of the possession of the bailee. By contrast, if the obligor delivered the deed to a third party 'for the use of' the obligee, then it could not be regarded as an escrow, since the wording showed that the bailee was to be regarded as the agent of the obligee rather than the obligor. Nor could the obligor deliver the deed as an escrow to the obligee himself, 'for when a deed is sealed and put in the possession of the party, there is the essential attestations of consent'. Although a man could put conditions into a bond, he could not add conditions when delivering it, which were not contained in the bond, unless by an escrow. Consequently, delivering a deed to the obligee, directly or via his agent, made the obligation complete, without any need to perform the conditions.

The rules relating to the delivery of deeds also revealed some points about when contracts came into being. Normally, this would not be a difficult question: it was when the deed was delivered. But what if a deed was delivered by someone without contractual capacity? Here, the rules varied. If a married woman sealed and delivered a bond while she was married, it was void, since she had no contractual capacity as a *feme covert*. However, if she delivered

[88] *ibid* 304, citing *Chamberlain v Stanton* (1588) 1 Leon 140, 74 ER 130, where the obligor successfully pleaded *non est factum*.

[89] Lobban (n 11) 307.

the same bond – without making a new seal – after becoming a *feme sole* (for instance after the death of her husband), it would then be valid, 'for the second delivery is an act of recognition of the seal, as well as putting it in possession of the party'.[90] Although she did not have to make a new seal, this would be a new contractual act. By contrast, if an infant delivered a bond, he could not give it new force by redelivering it when of age. Unlike the wife's first deed, which was void, the infant's was voidable, and so the second delivery could not make it a new contract, since the old one was still in being.[91] Gilbert also illustrated the effect of delivery on the question of when a deed took effect, by discussing the case of a parson who intended to sell an annuity, for which he needed the confirmation of his patron. In the case in question, the patron had sealed and delivered the confirmation before the grant had been made, but (since it was ineffective to confirm the grant) had redelivered the same deed afterwards. Here, the second delivery could not make the grant good: for although the first delivery was legally ineffective, it had all the 'essential attestations of consent', and so was in itself complete.[92]

When discussing delivery, Gilbert also made the point that the delivery of the deed had to be accepted: and that if it was rejected, this 'killed' the 'offer':

> If an obligation be made to A and delivered to B to the use of A and B tenders the obligation to A and A refuses it, the delivery has lost its force and the obligor may plead *non est factum*, because B cannot be presumed to be the attorney of and to act in his stead where he has expressly dissented from the deed; and since there is no concurrence of A, the delivery to him is void.[93]

As these examples show, there was scope in the law of formal contracts to raise questions about the time when the contractual obligation would come into being, and the manner in which it was brought about. The kinds of questions which medieval and early modern courts faced were clearly different from the kinds found in the nineteenth-century commercial law, but the analytical concepts which informed their resolution were not so distinct.

In contrast to formal contracts – or 'written contracts', as Gilbert dubbed them – verbal contracts were defined as

> the mutual act of two or more, transferring a right or benefit to each other in consideration of some benefit received where such contract is signified by words or any other signs other than the solemnities of signing and sealing required by the law.[94]

[90] *ibid* 305, following Rolle (n 68) vol 2, 26, 'Faits', pl 2.

[91] Unlike a wife, an infant could not plead *non est factum* to a deed which he had sealed and delivered, 'for if the contract be not absolutely void, there is such a deed in being'. He had to enter a special plea of infancy. Lobban (n 11) 319.

[92] Lobban (n 11) 306, following Rolle (n 68) vol 2, 26 'Faits', pl 9.

[93] Lobban (n 11) 305, citing *Whelpdale's Case* (1604) 5 Co Rep 119a, 119b; 77 ER 239, 241. In such cases, the obligor could plead *non est factum*.

[94] Lobban (n 11) 213. *cf* Baron Skinner in *Rann v Hughes* (1778) 7 TR 350a, 101 ER 1014: 'All contracts are, by the laws of England, distinguished into agreements by speciality and agreements by parol': the latter needed to be backed by consideration, the former did not.

Verbal contracts 'were the first and most natural way of contracting among mankind',[95] but as societies developed, written and solemn forms came to be used, since they could be more authentic indicators of the contractual will of the parties than was to be found in the memory of witnesses to the original words. In Gilbert's view, one could not safely take a contractual intention simply from words which had been spoken, since there was a danger that 'a man might be drawn into an obligation without any real intention by random words and ludicrous expression'.[96] It was for that reason that the courts looked to consideration. Although the quotation above suggests that Gilbert perceived the exchange of consideration as something distinct from the signs of contractual assent, his elaboration of the subject of verbal contracts suggests that they were not distinct: for it was the consideration which was itself the 'significant sign'.

Rather than speaking of offers and acceptances, he spoke of promises and consideration. In effect, the 'promise' took the place of an offer, and consideration took the place of acceptance. The promisor had to have the intention to contract with a particular promisee. With informal contracts, 'any words that shewed an intention to be obliged were obligatory if the consideration was sufficient; but if the words did not manifest such an intention, they would fail to create a promise, notwithstanding the consideration'.[97] To illustrate this point, Gilbert said that where one father told another (during discussions of a marriage between their children) that he would give £100 to the person who would marry his daughter, this did not generate a contractual promise, 'these words being only published at large and not spoke in forming of any contract'.[98]

Although an obligation might also be created where 'there were such receipt of money or goods as in law and justice required remuneration or recompense, whether any words passed between the parties or not', this did not mean that one had to pay for any unrequested benefits received. An unrequested benefit generated no obligation to recompense the person conferring the benefit, for if that were the case, one man could 'charge another by his own mere act without such parties ever expressing an intention to be obliged'.[99] The service received had to be requested for a promise to be raised on it. Thus, if a man declared in *assumpsit* for £20 money laid out to the use of the defendant, without saying it was at his request, this was ill, 'for it may be expended to the use of the defendant contrary to his desire, and then there is no consideration for such a promise'.[100]

This distinction explained the rule that a promise to pay in consideration of a service performed in the past was not good, unless there had been a preceding request for the performance; for 'the importunity at the time of receiving the benefit and the subsequent promise are signs sufficient to be obliged on the

[95] Lobban (n 11) 298.
[96] *ibid* 212; *cf* 215–16.
[97] *ibid* 252.
[98] *ibid* 252.
[99] *ibid* 214.
[100] *ibid* 216.

receipt of the benefit'. His comment that the subsequent promise was merely a valuation of 'such pains, property or benefits', which would otherwise be left to a jury, suggested that Gilbert thought that the contract was itself formed when the consideration requested was given: and not when the subsequent promise was made.[101] Why would the subsequent promise for an unrequested benefit not bind? According to Gilbert, it was because 'the subsequent promise stands alone and without consideration'. This was to see the provision of consideration as a response to a promise, as an acceptance is a response to an offer. In similar fashion, he argued that where the consideration given for the promise by the promisee was 'idle and insignificant', it was regarded as a nullity 'for there is a plain want of intention to be obliged'.[102]

Contracts could be entirely executory, resting on promises alone. In such cases

> each party hath his remedy by action, and there need be no performance of the *assumpsit* on one part, because the consideration doth arise out of the obligation of the mutual promises and not from the execution and performance of such promises; but such promises ought to be made at one and the same instant, otherwise at the time of the making they will be naked promises and without any consideration at all.[103]

This discussion sees the contract as coming into being at a single moment, with an exchange of promises which themselves constitute the consideration.[104] In practice – as the nineteenth- century case law showed – there might well be an interval in time between the first promise and the second promise (or the offer and acceptance), and there might be questions whether the promises 'mirrored' each other, or whether either had been revoked. In Gilbert's era, such questions were left to the jury to decide as matters of fact, which might be raised on fairly general pleadings, which did not set out the particular benefits or detriments, only the contract in general. In Gilbert's view, it was not necessary to go into detail on such matters, for as a matter of law, there was something of a presumption in favour of the contract. Where the contract was executory in whole or in part,

> the court will intend the act done or promise made to be either to the benefit of the defendant or to the prejudice of the plaintiff unless the contrary appear in the very promise itself … for a man's act in contracting is to be taken the strongest against him if it has the serious form of a contract.[105]

As has been seen, it was not simply formal deeds which had the 'serious form of a contract': informal contracts could just as easily be described in terms of acts of will.

[101] Explaining the rule, Gilbert argued that it was not just to request 'the pains, labour or property of another without returning a reasonable satisfaction', and the law supposed from the request that the party intended to pay (*ibid* 214).

[102] *ibid* 233.

[103] *ibid* 231.

[104] In such cases, it was 'the mere promise itself that gives me a remedy for such performance' (*ibid* 231).

[105] *ibid* 233.

IV. VITIATING FACTORS

Gilbert's will theory also required him to take into account factors which vitiated the contract. In his shorter theoretical discussion, he argued that fraud vitiated a contract, for those who were defrauded 'either know not what it is they part with or upon which terms, and without a precedent act of the understanding there is no will or consent at all'.[106] In the longer treatise, however, he pointed out that the common law offered only limited remedies in cases of fraud: 'contracts obtained by fraud, circumvention or surprise cannot be avoided at law, because the solemnities of contracting appear and the want of care and caution which is their fault cannot be alleged in discharge of such solemnities'.[107] To allow a party to claim to have agreed to something different from what was set out in a deed would be to allow a written contract to be varied by parol evidence; and 'it is down right madness to trifle with the solemnities of law and to pretend after the sealing that there was nothing seriously designed'.[108] Gilbert qualified this by adding that 'if there be any fraud in such solemn bargains the courts of equity allow a relief'; but this was not a jurisdiction he discussed in his common law treatise.[109] Nor did he address the effect of fraud on informal agreements: in such cases, a defrauded party could simply deny in an *assumpsit* that the contract declared on had been made; or he could sue in an action of deceit at common law. Since the first matter would be hidden in the jury's verdict, it did not generate law for Gilbert to discuss; and the latter was omitted altogether, perhaps because he did not regard it as a contractual matter.[110]

Gilbert spent more time discussing duress. Since this could be pleaded to avoid a deed, it generated more doctrine at common law.[111] As he explained, duress was

> such a circumstance which when shewn to the court will be a legal avoidance; because every contract must be the act and consent of the will, and such can't be where any compulsion is made use of, and by consequence such compulsion is a legal avoidance of such contract.[112]

[106] *ibid* 50 (Proposition 6). *cf* 25 (Proposition 14), 'where any man is deceived in the terms of his contract, the deceiver lets himself into possession of that property which is given in exchange without the consent of the owner'.

[107] *ibid* 208.

[108] *ibid* 212.

[109] As Bacon put it, 'It is clearly agreed, that the Court of Chancery had always an original jurisdiction in relieving against frauds, and that at this day it is the only court where matters of fraud are properly cognisable' (Bacon (n 18) vol 2, 610).

[110] *cf* Rolle (n 68) vol 1, 90.

[111] As Chitty put it, 'The old books abound with decisions relative to duress; but … a defence of this nature has now become of rare occurrence' (Chitty (n 2) 168).

[112] Lobban (n 11) 441.

Although evidence of duress could not be given under a plea of *non est factum* (since it *was* the deed of the party), it could be put in as a special plea. Not all duress vitiated a contract. As Gilbert explained,

> If A extorts a covenant from B by an unlawful fear or force, this doth not oblige … [but] if A contracts with B while under a fear or force that is just and lawful, or not arising in any manner from B, this contract is obligatory.[113]

This meant (for instance) that an obligation given by a man justly imprisoned for his delivery from gaol was valid, whereas one given by a man wrongfully imprisoned could be set aside for duress. Furthermore, the duress had to be exerted by the party obtaining the obligation, or at his bidding: a deed could not be avoided if the obligor had acted under duress from a stranger.

Gilbert did not deal in any detail with mistakes, though this was a familiar topic in civilian treatments of contract. In his short treatise, he dealt only incidentally with the matter, suggesting that mistakes of quality did not vitiate the sale of goods:

> if I mistake without any fraud in the buyer, the thing is sold irrecoverably, for the signs of transferring my right can be proved against me, but the want of knowledge of the nature of the thing sold or given in exchange cannot be proved for me, nay the presumption lies against me that I had a knowledge of the thing bought, since I take upon me to judge of the value of it.[114]

However, in the longer treatise on contract, he revealed that there were some occasions where a mistake might vitiate a contract, since it could be seen that the error was such that the parties' wills had not met. For instance, in some cases of mistaken identity, the plea of *non est factum* might be raised. As Gilbert explained, 'where a wrong party is sued, that bears the name of the obligor, he may plead *non est factum*, for then it is not any deed of his at all'.[115] However, if the obligor were sued on a deed by a person who had the same name as the obligee, he could not plead *non est factum*, having made the deed, but had to 'confess the truth of the deed, and avoid the special matter'.

Formal contracts could raise legal questions in relation to mistakes of identity in ways not done with informal contracts. Nevertheless, Gilbert did find some room to discuss other kinds of mistakes in informal contracts. As he explained, if there is an 'error in the consideration', a contract was not obligatory 'because there was plainly no intention to be obliged, nor no union of the mind in the same affair'. He illustrated this point with an example of a promise made in consideration of a forbearance to sue a third party. In such cases, he explained, the defendant only intended to be bound on the supposition that the third party was in fact liable at law or in equity, 'so that if that supposition fails, and J.S. never was indebted to the plaintiff, there was never any intention

[113] *ibid* 30 (Propositions 34, 35).
[114] *ibid* 50 (Proposition 6).
[115] *ibid* 433, citing *Dennis v St John* (1589) 1 Leon 322, 74 ER 293.

in the defendant to be bound'.[116] Gilbert also spoke of 'error in the consideration' when discussing a 1631 case, which held that a promise of forbearance to distrain unshocked corn could not be a good consideration for a promise, since such corn could not be distrained. Here, the consideration – the manifestation of contractual intent – rested on an error, that unshocked corn could be distrained.[117] By contrast, there was no mistake in the consideration where one man promised another that he would ensure that his sister – a married woman – kept her agreement to settle £100 on the man about to marry her daughter. For although a married woman could not at common law enter into any contract which might bind her husband's estate, she had made what was 'in common discourse called an agreement', and her brother had promised 'to see the thing done'. In this case, 'there is no error in the consideration', which meant that 'nothing can be alleged in behalf of [the brother] to shew that there was no real intention to perform it'.[118]

Many questions about the effect of fraud or mistake were not dealt with in Gilbert's treatise on contract, since it covered only questions of common law. He planned to deal with the Chancery and its remedies in a separate section on the courts. Some of this material was posthumously published, and in it a glimpse can be obtained of how that court would uphold genuine agreements and set aside or correct ones obtained by fraud or under mistakes. The fact that the Chancery looked for the true agreement can be seen from Gilbert's discussion of where that court ordered a specific performance of a parol agreement, which (under the Statute of Frauds) should have been in writing. If a defendant by his answer admitted that he had made a complete agreement, specific performance would be ordered, since the statute 'was designed to hinder fraudulent and surreptitious agreements, and not to vacate bargains that were fairly and honestly made'.[119] However, if the answer claimed the agreement was fraudulent or 'merely a communication of the terms to be further settled', it would not be decreed. If the answer showed the agreement was not complete, the plaintiff would lose on the pleadings; if his answer admitted that the contract was complete but claimed it was fraudulent, 'there the benefit of the plea is to be reserved to the hearing, because the fraud is still sub judice and in issue'.[120]

Gilbert also dealt in this treatise with some matters of rectification. One common problem for the Chancery in this era was how to deal with marriage

[116] Lobban (n 11) 218–19.

[117] *ibid* 221. He explained, that 'that cannot be taken for a pledge that cannot be returned in as good a plight as it was at the time of the taking'. He referred to *Morgan's case*, cited in *Reynolds v Prosser* (1656) Hardres 71, 73; 145 ER 386, 387.

[118] The case Gilbert digested here was one from 1639, where the Court held that 'this was an agreement, though of no effect in law' (*Marsh v Farrant* (1639) in Rolle (n 68) vol 1, 10, pl 3).

[119] G Gilbert, *The History and Practice of the High Court of Chancery* (London, Henry Lintot, 1758) 237; *cf Limondson v Sweed* (1711) Gilb Rep 35, 25 ER 25.

[120] Gilbert (n 119) 238.

settlements which differed from marriage articles drawn up prior to the execution of the settlement. Gilbert explained the rule thus:

> If an agreement be made before marriage by way of articles, and afterwards be formally drawn up before marriage by way of settlement, and anything is omitted, it is presumed *prima facie* to be waved, unless it can be proved to have been omitted by fraud or mistake; but if articles be made before marriage, and the marriage takes effect, and afterwards a settlement be made and any thing be omitted, there it cannot be presumed to be waived, because that cannot be after marriage.[121]

As he explained, the court could rectify mistakes so that the settlement would reflect what the parties had agreed.

He did not deal at length here with the relief Chancery gave where bonds had been obtained by fraud. However, he did note that if a man obtained a bond or covenant by fraud, and then assigned it over to a third person for a valuable consideration, that person could not recover on the bond: for to do so, he would have to sue in equity (since as an assignee he had no title in law), where the contract would not be held to be enforceable, 'because the bond or covenant being originally got by fraud, though the obligee or covenantee had obtained the solemnities of contracting'.[122] As these examples show, Gilbert was aware of various ways in which contractual consent would be vitiated. However, in a treatise summarising the main doctrines of the common law of his day, the treatment given of such questions was patchy.

V. CONSIDERATION

What role did consideration play in Gilbert's conception? In his *Treatise of the Law of Nature*, Gilbert said:

> No man transfers his own right to a stranger without benefit to himself, for since a man's own right is the means that subserves his own preservation, to transfer his right to a stranger without receiving some compensation is to destroy himself, contrary to the instinct of self preservation.[123]

Indeed, he argued that the very purpose of contracting was to allow people to exchange mutual benefits and engage in commerce. Nevertheless, he insisted at the same time that as a matter of theory – in the 'state of nature' – it was not essential to show that consideration had passed between the parties, in order to establish that a contract had been created. All that was necessary was that there had been a final deliberation of the will of both parties:

> As to the signs of transferring right, it is plain that a valuable consideration is not requisite to the validity of a contract in the judgment of the arbitrator. For where

[121] *ibid* 237. See also the illustrations at 254.
[122] *ibid* 286. The same rule did not apply in cases of land, where the fraudulent transfer did convey a legal title.
[123] Lobban (n 11) 23 (Proposition 3).

> an effect is, a cause must be supposed, whether it be known to us or no. If therefore a contract be shown to the arbitrator, he must suppose a valuable consideration whether that can be proved to him or not.[124]

If there were clear signs of consent, such as a written document or the handing over of goods, this was 'sufficient proof of a contract without valuable consideration appearing'. Since a person would only make a final determination of his will after he had satisfied himself of the benefit of so doing,[125] it could be presumed to have been made for a good consideration. Nor was it to be presumed that all contracts required an exchange. Discussing the use of solemn contracts in civil societies, Gilbert stated that they were 'so calculated as to give men time to be well aware and considerate what they are doing', so that if there was a formal contract made without any consideration, 'it is presumed to be a voluntary gift'.[126] Consideration in the form of an exchange was necessary only where there was uncertainty over whether the parties had exercised their will. This was the case of verbal contracts, for Gilbert argued that mere words could not be relied upon as demonstrating a final act of the will, since they 'are often thrown out at random'.[127] In such cases, the presence of consideration would be used to prove the existence of contractual intent, 'for no man transfers any right without benefit to himself and consequently there cannot be a right transferred on the one side that is a consideration given and no right transferred on the other'.[128]

Gilbert directly addressed the question 'whether a naked declaration of the mind is sufficient to alter propriety without any valuable consideration'.[129] More specifically, was a person in the state of nature obliged to keep his promise, before he had received what he had bargained for? Hobbes's answer to this question was that executory promises such as this could not bind in the state of nature: since there was no sovereign to enforce them, the promisor would be foolish if he performed his promise, simply trusting the other party to perform his part.[130] This was not a view Gilbert agreed with. He held that the promise was binding, before any recompense had been given, both for theoretical and practical reasons. To begin with, Gilbert argued that contracts made by the last deliberation of the will had to be kept as a matter of logic, since 'by contracting for some future action, the party wills it done, and by not doing it he wills it not done,

[124] *ibid* 51 (Proposition 8).
[125] *ibid* 52 (Proposition 12).
[126] *ibid* 207.
[127] *ibid* 51 (Proposition 11).
[128] *ibid* 51 (Proposition 9).
[129] *ibid* 206.
[130] In *De Cive* ('*On the Citizen*'), Hobbes argued that in the state of nature, agreements made by 'mutual trust' were 'invalid' if there was a just fear that the other party would not perform, for it was not reasonable to make anyone perform if the other party would not later perform his part: Hobbes (n 85) 37. In *Leviathan*, he described such contracts as void, since 'he who performeth first, does but betray himselfe to his enemy' (T Hobbes (edited by N Malcolm), *Leviathan* vol 2 (Oxford, Oxford University Press, 2012) 210).

which is to will a thing done and not done at the same time, which is a contradiction'.[131] On similar lines, he argued that

> He that contracts in that he doth contract denies the action to be in vain, for it is against reason for a knowing man do any thing in vain. He therefore that contracts in such a manner so as he thinks he is not bound to keep his contract at once thinks his contract a thing done in vain and not to be in vain, which is an absurdity.[132]

Gilbert also added that a breach of promise 'is a violation of the truth which is so necessary to be preserved among mankind'.[133] At the same time, he also gave practical arguments. In the state of nature, men had to be

> just to their words and promises, though they be without a valuable consideration, because otherwise there could be no intercourse or mutual society … if one person were not to trust the other without price actually paid, there could be no permutation.[134]

In modern international relations, where there was no superior state, princes would be tempted to break all their engagements on the ground that they had received no equivalent, if they did not feel bound by their promises.

In an inversion of the Hobbesian position, he therefore argued that in the state of nature, where there was no superior public judicature, 'all promises are equally obligatory'. However, with the institution of civil governments, a means was devised to protect people from being bound by 'the turn of an unwary expression'. One way of doing this was to provide for solemnities in contracts, which could be taken to be authentic expressions of the will, since 'every man is presumed to be in earnest when he contracts under the solemnities that the law has appointed'. The other means was consideration. A man's words were not to be taken to have been uttered in earnest if they were not put into solemn form; but the 'verbal bargain' was said to be complete if consideration was given

> because the fruit of another man's industry comes in place of his own and here can be no inlet to perjury, because the proprietor doth not part with his own without accepting of something in lieu of it from the other.[135]

Gilbert's views were set out in drafts which were not included in the version of the manuscript which Francis Hargrave acquired and which is now in the British Library; though it is evident from Bacon's summary (quoted above) that he, at least, had read them. In the Hargrave version – which is the one drawn on by the scholars who have most discussed Gilbert – his position was more equivocal on whether 'a naked declaration of the mind was sufficient to alter property'.

[131] Lobban (n 11) 24 (Proposition 5).
[132] *ibid* 53 (Proposition 17).
[133] *ibid* 207; *cf* 15 (Proposition 24).
[134] *ibid* 206.
[135] *ibid* 207–208.

He now set out two rival views. One of them 'very reasonably' argued that 'the duties of veracity oblige men to an exact and rigid fidelity in their words and promises'; the other held that 'the force of the engagement doth totally depend on the consideration'. Appearing now to sit on the fence, he stated that 'Our law hath held a middle between these extremes', holding men bound by solemn contracts (where 'the consideration shall be intended') but only holding verbal contracts binding in respect of the consideration.[136]

It is this passage which has led historians to hold that his treatment of consideration did not fit well with the will theory which seemed to inform his general definition; and that it in fact reflected an orthodox common law view of something given in exchange for a promise, which did not include 'any factor that evidenced seriousness of intention'.[137] However, on close examination, it appears that the language of intention did run through his treatment of consideration. Gilbert formulated the following rule: 'Where the solemnities of law are wanting to shew a serious intention of the parties, there the intent of the parties must be collected from the consideration'.[138]

As authority for this proposition, Gilbert cited St Germain's treatment, discussed above, in which the need for consideration is stressed because of the impossibility of knowing the subjective intentions hidden in any person's heart. Read thus, it can be seen that in Gilbert's view, the function of consideration was (to use Fuller's terms) both 'evidentiary' – to provide clear evidence of contractual intent – and 'cautionary' – to prevent parties from entering into contracts which were not seriously intended.[139] He did not see it as a vehicle to ensure that contracts would always contain mutual benefits, let alone an equality of exchange.

VI. CONCLUSION

Sir Jeffrey Gilbert left an important legacy in the large number of treatises which were published after his death, some of which – such as his treatise on the law of evidence – were particularly influential in defining new areas of study. His treatises were an important precursor to the golden era of the English legal treatise, which is often seen to have followed the publication of Blackstone's *Commentaries on the Laws of England*: they were an example of a form of

[136] *ibid* 211–12.

[137] Ibbetson (n 5) 237. Ibbetson further notes that Gilbert sets out the rule that a promise in consideration of natural love and affection would be ineffective, without explaining why an intention to be bound could not be inferred. However, this might be explained by the fact that the passage in question was inserted by an editor, rather than forming a part of Gilbert's original draft (see Lobban (n 11) 215, fn 10).

[138] Lobban (n 11) 217.

[139] LL Fuller, 'Consideration and Form' (1941) 41 *Columbia Law Review* 800.

literature which other lawyers could emulate, while also providing material on the basis of which others could develop their own works. Gilbert's treatise on contract, discussed here, cannot be claimed to have exerted the kind of influence on later scholars which his other works did. Unlike some of the works which were published, which were reproduced in multiple manuscript copies before their publication, the treatise on contract does not seem to have been copied and circulated in the same way. It is consequently difficult to trace any direct influence of Gilbert's treatise on contract on later writers; though (as has been seen) it is evident at least that Matthew Bacon had read it and was influenced by it in the discussion of contract included in his *A New Abridgment of the Law*.

Nonetheless, it remains an important work which should merit our attention, since it offers us an insight into a lawyer's understanding of English contract law in the early eighteenth century. Like the young lawyers who composed the first contract treatises to be published in the late eighteenth and early nineteenth centuries, Gilbert was aiming to summarise the law as it was understood in the profession, and to put it into a coherent rational framework. He was not seeking to change the law, but to explain it. This insight into early eighteenth-century law should also be of interest to modern lawyers for another reason. As with much of English private law, the shape of English contract law is the product of its history and many of its doctrines can only properly be made sense of by examining and understanding their history. In this endeavour, it is invaluable to make use of the insights of a philosophically minded historical jurist, who looked for the foundations of contract law beyond the categories of the forms of action.

Reading Gilbert not only shows us that eighteenth-century jurists had a conception of contract which in many ways looks strikingly modern. It might also offer insights into the function of some doctrines which contemporary jurists sometimes have difficulty explaining. For instance, jurists have long puzzled over how to explain the precise role and function of consideration.[140] Some modern jurists have sought to invigorate the doctrine, by elaborating theories which attribute to the doctrine a centrally important function in contract law.[141] Others, commenting on the elision in the case law of any notion that consideration need be something of objective value moving from the promisee,[142] have

[140] When late nineteenth-century jurists in Harvard and Oxford debated its role, they often provided definitions which seemed not to leave much of a distinct function for consideration. See, eg, the famous definition in Holmes (n 8) 265. See also JB Ames, 'Two Theories of Consideration' (1899) 13 *Harvard Law Review* 29; CC Langdell, 'Mutual Promises as a Consideration For Each Other' (1901) 14 *Harvard Law Review* 496.

[141] See, eg, Benson (n 72) 42: 'The requirement of consideration constitutes the contractual relation as such; consideration itself establishes and represents a particular kind of relation between the parties, thereby specifying the inner mechanism and core that animates the whole of contract law'. For a recent theory of consideration, see also J Lewinsohn, 'Paid on Both Sides: Quid Pro Quo Exchange and the Doctrine of Consideration' (2020) 129 *Yale Law Journal* 690.

[142] This is the effect of *Williams v Roffey Bros & Nicholls (Contractors) Ltd* [1991] 1 QB 1 (CA) in the field of contractual variation.

suggested that the law would be more coherent if the entire doctrine were abolished, allowing for the enforcement of gratuitous promises where they could be shown to have been seriously intended and obtained without fraud, duress or influence.[143] In exploring the question of whether consideration should continue to play a central role in the common law of contract or whether it is a doctrine which no longer has any function to perform, the insights into the doctrine of an early eighteenth-century jurist might prove surprisingly useful.

[143] See, eg, A Burrows, *Understanding the Law of Obligations* (Oxford, Oxford University Press, 1998) 197.

3

Henry Thomas Colebrooke (1765–1837)

JOANNA McCUNN*

I. INTRODUCTION

HENRY THOMAS COLEBROOKE was only incidentally a scholar of contract law. He was an East India Company official renowned as 'the founder and father of true Sanskrit scholarship in Europe'.[1] Despite his lack of formal, let alone legal, education, he rose to sit on the Company's highest court in Bengal and was accepted by the British as 'the foremost living authority on Hindu law'.[2] In his spare time, he researched and wrote obsessively about everything from algebra to zoology. Among his prodigious output was a slender treatise on contract law, which he self-published in his retirement and which soon slipped into obscurity.

Colebrooke's *Treatise on Obligations and Contracts* ('the *Treatise*')[3] slotted neatly into a series of contract law treatises that began to hit the English market in the late eighteenth century.[4] However, it was also a clear outlier. Colebrooke barely cited any English cases, instead stuffing his work with enigmatic references to 'P.F.' (the *Pandectes Françaises*), 'Menu' (the *Manusmṛiti*) or 'Vinn.' (Arnold Vinnius). Little of his elaborate discussion bore much close resemblance to contemporary English law, and so it is perhaps unsurprising that it failed

*I am grateful to colleagues who have offered their comments and suggestions, including the participants in the *Scholars of Contract Law* workshop and, in particular, Andrew Bell, Chathuni Jayathilaka, Antonia Layard, Michael Lobban, Catharine MacMillan and Lee McConnell.

[1] FM Müller, 'The Life of Henry Thomas Colebrooke' (1872) 136 *Edinburgh Review* 461, 462.

[2] R Rocher, 'Henry Thomas Colebrooke and the Marginalization of Indian Pandits' in B Kellner et al (eds), *Pramanakirtih: Papers Dedicated to Ernst Steinkellner on the Occasion of his 70th Birthday*, vol 2 (Vienna, Berger und Söhne, 2007) 742.

[3] HT Colebrooke, *Treatise on Obligations and Contracts* (London, Black, Kingsbury, Parbury and Allen, 1818).\

[4] DJ Ibbetson, *A Historical Introduction to the Law of Obligations* (Oxford, Oxford University Press, 1999) 220.

to make a lasting impact on contract law scholarship. The *Treatise* looks like an indulgent work of fanciful legal theorising – a curious occupation for this administrator and Sanskritist.

Appearances, however, are deceiving. The *Treatise* was in fact designed to meet a pressing practical need in British India, which lacked an established law of contract until 1872. It is also exactly the kind of work that one would expect from a man like Colebrooke, a scientifically-minded colonial official without legal training. As an outsider's attempt to review the state of contemporary European contract law, it sheds valuable light on the gulf between legal theory and practice in the early nineteenth century. It also illustrates the intimate relationship between the scholarship of that era and the British colonial enterprise. As one of the most unintentionally revealing legal works of its day, the *Treatise*, and its author, deserve closer attention from legal scholars than they have received to date.

II. BACKGROUND

A. Colebrooke and the East India Company

Colebrooke was born in 1765.[5] His father, Sir George Colebrooke, was a wealthy banker and the chairman of the East India Company.[6] When Colebrooke was 12 years old, his father was ruined; the family lost their home and moved to France in relative poverty.[7] Colebrooke did not attend school or university,[8] but obtained a post in the East India Company and set sail for Calcutta at the age of 17.[9]

The East India Company began life as a trading corporation, dependent on the goodwill of Indian rulers.[10] However, as the Mughal Empire collapsed, the Company became a major player in Indian politics.[11] In 1764, Company forces defeated the remaining Mughal armies to become the dominant power in north-east India.[12] The Mughal Emperor was reduced to a puppet ruler and was forced to grant the Company the *diwani*, the right to administer justice and collect revenue across Bengal, Bihar and Orissa.[13] The Company was much more interested in the latter than the former, viewing the provinces as 'a vast plantation

[5] TE Colebrooke, *The Life of H. T. Colebrooke* (London, Trübner & Co, 1873) 1.
[6] *ibid* 2.
[7] *ibid* 3; R Rocher and L Rocher, *The Making of Western Indology: Henry Thomas Colebrooke and the East India Company* (Abingdon, Routledge, 2012) 10.
[8] Colebrooke, *The Life of H. T. Colebrooke* (n 5) 5.
[9] *ibid*.
[10] R Travers, *Ideology and Empire in Eighteenth-Century India: The British in Bengal* (Cambridge, Cambridge University Press, 2007) 2.
[11] See generally W Dalrymple, *The Anarchy: The Relentless Rise of the East India Company* (London, Bloomsbury, 2020).
[12] *ibid* 201.
[13] *ibid* 207.

to be milked and exploited'.[14] The result was a terrible famine in which an estimated third of the population starved to death.[15]

The devastation of Bengal also led to a financial crisis in Europe. By 1783, when Colebrooke arrived in Calcutta, the Company had been forced to reform its administration.[16] To safeguard its revenue, the Company began to exercise its powers as *diwan* and to govern Bengal more directly.[17] Warren Hastings, the new Governor-General, emphasised continuity with the Mughal regime in order to avoid provoking unrest while the Company's hold on its territory was tenuous.[18] Under his leadership, the Company was transformed into an 'administrative service',[19] seeking to generate enough revenue to rule Bengal while securing a profit for investors.[20]

Colebrooke became a cog in this administrative apparatus. For a decade he shuffled around a series of lowly postings both in Calcutta and in the *mofussil*, rural Bengal. By 1793, he had been promoted to the position of revenue collector.[21] Alongside his official duties, he was studying hard: although Colebrooke had no formal education, he was a relentless autodidact. On his voyage out to India, he had kept a journal of astronomical observations;[22] later, short of books on another journey, he would ransack a surgeon's library and teach himself medicine.[23] He was particularly interested in mathematics and astronomy.[24] In order to investigate Hindu algebra, he learnt Sanskrit with the help of Indian scholars[25] and was soon reading widely in Hindu literature.[26]

Colebrooke's Sanskrit studies were not just a hobby. They were also useful for the colonial project; Orientalist scholarship was encouraged in order to legitimise Company rule.[27] Like other Company servants in India, Colebrooke had a 'dual basis' for studying Sanskrit: 'at one and the same time there was a scholarly curiosity to unlock the mysterious knowledge of the ancients, and an immediate practical necessity' to improve the government of Bengal.[28] Colebrooke was

[14] *ibid* 209.

[15] BS Cohn, *Colonialism and Its Forms of Knowledge: The British in India* (Princeton, Princeton University Press, 1996) 59.

[16] Dalrymple (n 11) 228–35. The famine occurred during Sir George Colebrooke's chairmanship and was partly responsible for his fall from fortune.

[17] Travers (n 10) 102–105.

[18] R Rocher, 'The Creation of Anglo-Hindu Law' in T Lubin, DR Davis Jr and JK Krishnan (eds), *Hinduism and Law: An Introduction* (Cambridge, Cambridge University Press, 2010).

[19] Dalrymple (n 11) 238.

[20] Cohn (n 15) 61.

[21] Rocher and Rocher (n 7) 15–22.

[22] Colebrooke, *The Life of H. T. Colebrooke* (n 5) 14.

[23] *ibid* 265.

[24] *ibid* 22.

[25] Rocher and Rocher (n 7) 21.

[26] *ibid* 23.

[27] S Ahmed, 'Orientalism and the Permanent Fix of War' in D Carey and L Festa (eds), *The Postcolonial Enlightenment: Eighteenth-Century Colonialism and Postcolonial Theory* (Oxford, Oxford University Press, 2013) 182.

[28] Cohn (n 15) 26.

fascinated by ancient Hindu texts: 'the Hindu', he wrote, 'is the most ancient nation of which we have valuable remains, and has been surpassed by none in refinement and civilization'.[29] However, he also took a practical view: there was 'a necessity' for the British to acquire 'exact information' about India, 'with the hope of facilitating ameliorations' in its condition.[30]

Leading this project was the Orientalist *ne plus ultra*, Sir William Jones, who declared that he would 'know India better than any other European ever knew it'.[31] Jones' studies had a major legal component; he was a lawyer who was appointed to the Supreme Court of Bengal in 1783.[32] Bengal at the time had two separate legal systems: the Supreme Court was a royal court, with jurisdiction primarily over British subjects in Calcutta,[33] while courts run by the Company as *diwan* administered law to Indians in the *mofussil*.[34] The Supreme Court was an English court and generally applied English law. However, it could also hear cases between Indian residents of Calcutta if they concerned inheritance or contract, and in such cases it applied the 'personal law' of the parties: Hindu law to Hindus, and Islamic law to Muslims.[35]

These personal laws were also applied by Company courts in the *mofussil*.[36] Hastings had rejected calls to introduce English law throughout the provinces,[37] arguing that Company rule must be adapted 'to the Manners and Understandings of the People'.[38] Jones agreed that this was 'obviously just': it would be 'the most grievous oppression' if Indians' sacred laws were 'superseded by a new system, of which they could have no knowledge'.[39] Thus, the Company courts were to apply Hindu or Islamic law in cases on 'inheritance, marriage, caste and other religious usages and institutions'; in other matters, including contract, the judge was simply to act in accordance with 'justice, equity and good conscience'.[40]

[29] Colebrooke, *The Life of H. T. Colebrooke* (n 5) 61.

[30] HT Colebrooke, 'A Discourse Read at a Meeting of the Royal Asiatic Society of Great Britain and Ireland, on the 15th of March, 1823', *Miscellaneous Essays*, vol 1, 2nd edn (London, Trübner & Co, 1873) 2.

[31] Quoted in EW Said, *Orientalism* (New York, Random House, 2014) 78.

[32] DJ Ibbetson, 'Sir William Jones and the Nature of Law' in A Burrows and A Rodger (eds), *Mapping the Law: Essays in Memory of Peter Birks* (Oxford, Oxford University Press, 2006) 621.

[33] WH Morley, *An Analytical Digest of All the Reported Cases Decided in the Supreme Courts of Judicature in India*, vol 1 (London, WH Allen, 1850) xiii–xxiii; *First Report of Her Majesty's Commissioners Appointed to Consider the Reform of the Judicial Establishments, Judicial Procedure, and Laws of India, &c* (London, Stationery Office, 1856) 188.

[34] Morley (n 33) xxxi–lxii; WAJ Archbold, *Outlines of Indian Constitutional History* (London, PS King & Son, 1926) 52–59.

[35] *First Report of Her Majesty's Commissioners* (n 33) 189; JDM Derrett, *Religion, Law and the State in India* (London, Faber and Faber, 1968) 236.

[36] Cohn (n 15) 26.

[37] Rocher (n 18) 78.

[38] Quoted in Cohn (n 15) 26.

[39] Quoted in HT Colebrooke, 'Preface to the Digest of Hindu Law on Contracts and Successions', *Miscellaneous Essays*, vol 1, 2nd edn (London, Trübner & Co, 1873) 461–62.

[40] MB Hooker, *Legal Pluralism: An Introduction to Colonial and Neo-Colonial Laws* (Oxford, Clarendon Press, 1975) 61; Derrett (n 35) 289.

This committed the British to learning Hindu law.[41] However, they were reluctant to rely on pandits, Hindu legal experts, for advice. Jones and his colleagues were suspicious of the pandits' integrity and accused them of counterfeiting law in exchange for bribes.[42] For Jones, the only solution was to translate Sanskrit legal texts into English. A first attempt at this had foundered: the *Code of Gentoo Laws* 1776 had to be orally rendered through Persian, and Jones complained that it was hopelessly inaccurate.[43] He duly learnt Sanskrit himself, and set about translating a wide range of Hindu literature.[44] He published the *Manusmṛiti* as the *Institutes of Hindu Law*[45] before starting work on a major project: the production of a digest of Hindu law, modelled on Justinian's Digest. This was to cover inheritance and contract law, as administered by the Supreme Court.[46] The sources would be compiled by pandits under Jones' supervision and he would translate the completed text.[47] This project was of vital importance to the colonial Government: it aimed to curb the power of the pandits and overwrite Hindu legal traditions with ones more familiar, and beneficial, to the British.[48]

However, the work seemed set for disaster when Jones died unexpectedly in 1794. The Bengal Government despaired of finding another translator until Colebrooke offered his services.[49] He was soon hard at work on the digest, translating texts that had been selected, arranged and annotated by the pandit Jagannātha Tarkapañcānana.[50] This was Colebrooke's first foray into the law, but he handled his materials with aplomb.[51] Some of his translations simply followed Jones' earlier work,[52] but he was able to evaluate the sources independently where Jones' interpretation conflicted with Jagannātha's commentary.[53] He worked so intensely that his friends, concerned for his health, resorted to 'breaking in upon his studies, and putting out his midnight lamp'.[54] The finished text was submitted at the end of 1796[55] and published in Calcutta and London as the *Digest of Hindu Law*.[56]

[41] Rocher (n 18) 79.
[42] *ibid* 81; Derrett (n 35) 243–44.
[43] Cohn (n 15) 27–28. 'Gentoo' was an early European term for Hindu.
[44] Ibbetson (n 32) 621.
[45] *ibid* 634–39.
[46] Colebrooke (n 39) 462–63.
[47] Rocher and Rocher (n 7) 34.
[48] J Majeed, *Ungoverned Imaginings: James Mill's The History of British India and Orientalism* (Oxford, Oxford University Press, 1992) 20; Ahmed (n 27) 199–201; MP Singh and N Kumar, *The Indian Legal System: An Enquiry* (Oxford, Oxford University Press, 2019) 14–15.
[49] Rocher and Rocher (n 7) 34.
[50] Colebrooke, *The Life of H. T. Colebrooke* (n 5) 74–75.
[51] Derrett (n 35) 248–49.
[52] Colebrooke (n 39) 473–74.
[53] See, eg, J Tercapanchánana (translated by HT Colebrooke), *A Digest of Hindu Law on Contracts and Successions*, vol 1 (London, J Debrett, 1801) 417, 442.
[54] Colebrooke, *The Life of H. T. Colebrooke* (n 5) 86.
[55] *ibid.*
[56] Rocher and Rocher (n 7) 37–38.

Colebrooke's translation was widely praised,[57] but the *Digest* itself was not a great success. One British critic described the compiler as 'semi-barbarous' and lacking 'European intelligence'.[58] Even Colebrooke was defensive, observing that Jagannātha's commentary was sometimes 'frivolous'[59] and disclaiming responsibility for its contents.[60] He continued to criticise Jagannātha's work in later life.[61] The problem was that the British conception of the *Digest* was fundamentally foreign to the Hindu legal tradition in which Jagannātha worked.[62] The British simply wanted to 'find out the rule of decision with the minimum of labour', and certainly without understanding the complexities of the pandits' method.[63] The end result pleased nobody, but, in seeking to impose their own 'scientific method' on Indian scholarship, Jones and Colebrooke had begun a process of reshaping Hindu law in a European mould.[64]

B. Colebrooke's Rise to Fame

Colebrooke's work on the *Digest* was a turning point in his career. In 1795, he was transferred from the Company's revenue branch to a judicial posting.[65] As a district magistrate, he now heard hundreds of cases every month in the Company courts.[66] He also continued to study widely: in 1797, he sent for works on dyeing, botany, chemistry, mathematics, physics and religion, as well as a telescope.[67] He built up a collection of Sanskrit manuscripts[68] and wrote papers about various aspects of Indian life.[69] In 1798, Colebrooke's judicial career was interrupted by an 'uncongenial' diplomatic mission.[70] However, he used the time to make observations on Indian geography and to publish even more papers. While his essays were 'dry' and 'clinical', Colebrooke was developing a reputation for 'thoroughness, precision, critical rigour and sobriety'.[71] He was praised

[57] *ibid* 37.
[58] Quoted in *ibid* 38.
[59] Colebrooke (n 39) 465.
[60] *ibid* 474.
[61] Colebrooke, *The Life of H. T. Colebrooke* (n 5) 224; HT Colebrooke, 'Preface to the Translation of Two Treatises on the Hindu Law of Inheritance', *Miscellaneous Essays*, vol 1, 2nd edn (London, Trübner & Co, 1873) 478.
[62] SN Mukherjee, *Sir William Jones: A Study in Eighteenth-Century British Attitudes to India* (Cambridge, Cambridge University Press, 1968) 140.
[63] Derrett (n 35) 247.
[64] S Ahmed, 'Notes from Babel: Towards a Colonial History of Comparative Literature' (2013) 39 *Critical Inquiry* 296, 321–22.
[65] Rocher and Rocher (n 7) 35.
[66] Colebrooke, *The Life of H. T. Colebrooke* (n 5) 82.
[67] *ibid* 92–93.
[68] Rocher and Rocher (n 7) 41.
[69] *ibid* 41–43.
[70] Colebrooke, *The Life of H. T. Colebrooke* (n 5) 109.
[71] Rocher and Rocher (n 7) 45, 202; see also Colebrooke, *The Life of H. T. Colebrooke* (n 5) 235.

for helping the Company learn 'the habits and prejudices of the natives', thereby furthering British interests in India.[72]

Colebrooke also continued his legal work. He employed pandits to compile a 'supplementary digest', which was to cover all Hindu civil, criminal and procedural law and remedy the perceived shortcomings of Jagannātha's Digest.[73] In 1800, unhappy with their work, he started to compile the legal texts himself.[74] This project would occupy him until the last decade of his life, but was never completed.[75] When his diplomatic posting ended in 1801, Colebrooke was appointed puisne judge of the *sadr diwani* and *nizamat adalat*s, the Company's superior courts of appeal on civil and criminal matters in Bengal.[76] This was a significant promotion, and came with an honorary position as Professor of Sanskrit and Hindu Law at Fort William College in Calcutta.[77] As we have seen, the Company courts were required to apply Hindu or Islamic law on certain 'religious' matters. Colebrooke was the only judge on the *sadr adalat*s who was an expert in Hindu law, and now bore much of the responsibility for their judgments.[78]

Under Colebrooke's influence, as both judge and translator, Hindu law was transformed.[79] He was even described by Orientalists as the 'legislator of India'.[80] Hastings had determined to apply authentic Indian laws, but Hindu law was fluid and diverse,[81] while the British needed clear, consistent rules that could easily be understood and enforced by Company judges.[82] The pandits struggled to supply such rules, frustrating British officials.[83] Orientalist scholars assumed that ancient Hindu law must have been corrupted by the pandits, and sought to 'rescue' the original codes.[84] The authority of the pandits was soon replaced by that of translated texts and precedents[85] – especially those produced by Colebrooke, who was accepted by the British as 'the foremost living authority on Hindu law'.[86] His advice was sought by British judges across India, and his opinions superseded those of the pandits, whose decrees he was now required to approve.[87] In 1850, one Anglo-Indian lawyer wrote that 'in any question of

[72] Rocher and Rocher (n 7) 45.
[73] *ibid* 46–48.
[74] *ibid* 48; Derrett (n 35) 251.
[75] Rocher and Rocher (n 7) 176.
[76] *ibid* 60.
[77] Colebrooke, *The Life of H. T. Colebrooke* (n 5) 191.
[78] Rocher and Rocher (n 7) 62.
[79] Rocher (n 2) 753.
[80] Müller (n 1) 482.
[81] DR Davis Jr, 'A Historical Overview of Hindu Law' in Lubin, Davis Jr and Krishnan (eds) (n 18) 18–19.
[82] Rocher (n 18) 82; Derrett (n 35) 250.
[83] Davis Jr (n 81) 26; Derrett (n 35) 249–50.
[84] Ahmed (n 27) 187–88; Cohn (n 15) 69.
[85] Rocher (n 18) 85; Derrett (n 35) 255.
[86] Rocher (n 2) 742.
[87] *ibid* 752–53.

Hindú law the word of the illustrious Henry Colebrooke is worth the exposition of a thousand Pandits'.[88]

The work of the *sadr adalats*, however, was not solely concerned with Indian law. It was not obligatory to apply the personal laws unless the case concerned a 'religious' matter.[89] Thus, in contract law cases, a Company judge was 'to a great extent without the guidance of any positive law beyond the rule that his decision shall be such as he deems to be in accordance with "justice, equity, and good conscience"'.[90] Some later lawyers recognised that this afforded 'but an indefinite foundation for a judicial system, especially considering that the Judges are not trained lawyers'[91] and that actions for debt or rent comprised the overwhelming majority of the Company courts' business.[92]

In Colebrooke's day, however, the position caused little concern. It was generally felt that most contract cases turned on their facts and did not need to be resolved using legal rules.[93] Colebrooke and his colleagues confidently identified the 'equitable' result in a wide range of contract cases without any reference to rules of law.[94] Indeed, contract law rules were seen as little more than applied common sense. Colebrooke wrote that, 'in the law of contracts, the rules of decision, observed in the jurisprudence of different countries, are in general dictated by reason and good sense; and rise naturally, though not always obviously, from plain maxims of equity and right'.[95] Sir Thomas Strange, a correspondent of Colebrooke's,[96] likewise explained that contract law rested 'upon principles so general, that they have been considered to belong to the law of nature, as manifested in the concurrent practice of civilized nations'.[97]

Colebrooke's active tenure as a judge lasted until 1807, when he was elevated to a seat on the Supreme Council of Bengal.[98] He now became 'the most prominent administrator-scholar in India', wielding broad legislative and executive powers[99] and admired for his 'profound and universal knowledge'.[100] He did not abandon his legal work entirely, but continued informally to advise the courts.[101]

[88] Morley (n 33) vii.

[89] Derrett (n 35) 234.

[90] *First Report of Her Majesty's Commissioners Appointed to Prepare a Body of Substantive Law for India, &c* (London, Stationery Office, 1866) 7.

[91] W Macpherson, *Outlines of the Law of Contracts, as Administered in the Courts of British India, Not Established by Royal Charter* (London, R C Lepage & Co, 1860) vii.

[92] *First Report of Her Majesty's Commissioners* (n 33) 197, 201.

[93] T Strange, *Elements of Hindu Law*, vol 1 (London, Butterworth & Son, 1825) xix; *First Report of Her Majesty's Commissioners* (n 33) 201.

[94] See, eg, WH Macnaghten, *Reports of Cases Determined in the Court of Sudder Dewanny Adawlut*, vol 1 (Calcutta, Sreenauth Banerjee and Brothers, 1867) 160, 189 and 192.

[95] Colebrooke, 'Preface to the Translation of Two Treatises on the Hindu Law of Inheritance' (n 61) 476.

[96] Colebrooke, *The Life of H. T. Colebrooke* (n 5) 280–81.

[97] Strange (n 93) 268. Hindu texts gave a similar impression, repeatedly admonishing that contract law rules could be 'inferred from common sense': see, eg, Tercapanchánana (n 53) 21, 450.

[98] Rocher and Rocher (n 7) 89–90.

[99] Colebrooke, *The Life of H. T. Colebrooke* (n 5) 282.

[100] Rocher and Rocher (n 7) 89.

[101] *ibid* 123.

He also published, in 1810, a translation of two treatises on Hindu inheritance law. This may have been his most influential work: not only did it form the basis of Anglo-Hindu inheritance law until 1956,[102] but the theory of regional schools of law proposed in its preface revolutionised British approaches to the Hindu tradition.[103]

Colebrooke continued to write at an astonishing rate, even during his tenure on the court. Between 1805 and 1816, he produced works on the Vedas, oxen, Jainism, the zodiac, frankincense, ancient inscriptions, Sanskrit prosody, the source of the Ganges, Hindu astronomy and camphor trees,[104] as well as reporting the first evidence that the Himalayas were the world's highest mountains.[105] Not all of his publications were successful, however. A Sanskrit grammar, aimed at beginners, was all but unusable: Colebrooke had 'measured the zeal and abilities of students by his own high standard', including a 'superabundance of rules' and omitting 'examples and illustrations'.[106]

Colebrooke also became increasingly prominent in Calcuttan society, serving as president of the Asiatic Society[107] and of Fort William College.[108] While he had earlier professed a 'dread of female attractions',[109] he fathered three children with at least one Indian woman in Calcutta[110] before marrying an English woman, Elizabeth Wilkinson, in 1810.[111] The couple had three sons before Elizabeth died only four years into the marriage.[112] By this time, Colebrooke was ready to leave India. His tenure on the Supreme Council had ended in 1812[113] and he had taken up an interim role as superintendent of the Calcutta Botanic Garden.[114] He resigned from the Company's service ten days after Elizabeth's death,[115] and sailed for England in 1814.[116]

Colebrooke had not lived in England since he was a child. However, he quickly plunged into London social life, joining a roster of learned societies[117] and helping to found the Athenaeum Club, the Astronomical Society, the Zoological Society and the Royal Asiatic Society.[118] He continued to write about India,

[102] *ibid* 112.
[103] Rocher (n 18) 84; Cohn (n 15) 73–74.
[104] Rocher and Rocher (n 7) 210–12.
[105] *ibid* 110–1.
[106] Colebrooke, *The Life of H. T. Colebrooke* (n 5) 205–206.
[107] Rocher and Rocher (n 7) 88.
[108] *ibid* 67.
[109] Colebrooke, *The Life of H. T. Colebrooke* (n 5) 45.
[110] Rocher and Rocher (n 7) 118–20. The circumstances are unknown, as it was standard practice in such cases not to record the mother's name on the birth certificate.
[111] Colebrooke, *The Life of H. T. Colebrooke* (n 5) 292–93.
[112] *ibid* 293.
[113] Rocher and Rocher (n 7) 125.
[114] *ibid* 127.
[115] *ibid* 129.
[116] *ibid* 130.
[117] *ibid* 148–55.
[118] *ibid* 151–63.

publishing works on Indian mathematics[119] and reporting on scientific research in Asia.[120] While he had been 'accidentally directed to antiquarian researches' in India, Colebrooke was now able to devote more of his time to his first love, science.[121] He installed a laboratory in his London apartments, collected minerals,[122] and theorised about the composition of the earth's core.[123] His mind teemed with projects, from the invention of a steam-powered plough[124] to the introduction of camels into South Africa.[125] He bought an estate at the Cape of Good Hope and remained a 'zealous advocate' of its wine despite consistent and heavy losses.[126] 'Easily attracted by inventions', he lost much of his fortune in speculations.[127]

In 1818, Colebrooke published the first volume of his *Treatise on Obligations and Contracts.*[128] Unlike his other works, this was privately printed; it was distributed by the Company's booksellers.[129] He made 'considerable progress' on a second volume[130] but never completed it.[131] For this Colebrooke blamed 'most vexatious proceedings in Chancery',[132] which had begun on the death of his older brother[133] and embroiled the family for over a decade.[134] By the time Colebrooke extricated himself, he no longer had 'health nor spirits for the undertaking'.[135] He was distracted by financial difficulties and family losses, including the deaths of two of his sons. By the end of the 1820s, ill health and failing eyesight had prevented him from working at all.[136] He died in 1837 at the age of 71.[137]

III. TREATISE ON OBLIGATIONS AND CONTRACTS

A. Project and Sources

The *Treatise on Obligations and Contracts* was Colebrooke's only legal work that was not exclusively about Hindu law. However, it was still fundamentally

119 Colebrooke, *The Life of H. T. Colebrooke* (n 5) 303.
120 Rocher and Rocher (n 7) 148–49.
121 Colebrooke, *The Life of H. T. Colebrooke* (n 5) 295.
122 *ibid* 296.
123 *ibid* 298.
124 Rocher and Rocher (n 7) 153.
125 Colebrooke, *The Life of H. T. Colebrooke* (n 5) 338.
126 *ibid* 330–31.
127 *ibid* 378–79.
128 Colebrooke (n 3).
129 Rocher and Rocher (n 7) 137.
130 Colebrooke, *The Life of H. T. Colebrooke* (n 5) 315.
131 *ibid* 345–46.
132 *ibid* 346.
133 Rocher and Rocher (n 7) 121–22.
134 *ibid* 132.
135 Colebrooke, *The Life of H. T. Colebrooke* (n 5) 346.
136 *ibid* 378–80; Rocher and Rocher (n 7) 179–85.
137 Colebrooke (n 5) 382.

concerned with law in India. The book itself includes no introductory material; this was intended to be published with the second volume.[138] Colebrooke's intentions, though, can be gleaned from a letter that he wrote to the directors of the East India Company in 1818. He explained that the work was 'the first part of a treatise designed for the instruction of the junior portion of the Hon[oura]ble Company's servants in the judicial department in India, and for the use of the Courts of Adawlut there'.[139]

Colebrooke was evidently dissatisfied with the state of contract law in the Company's courts, and sought to provide a basis for its improvement. There were no established sources of contract law in the *mofussil*; judges were simply referred to principles of 'justice, equity and good conscience'. Colebrooke's treatise was an attempt to concretise those principles by formulating 'an ideal law of contract'.[140] As we have seen, Colebrooke thought that contract law rules were similar 'in the jurisprudence of different countries', being 'in general dictated by reason and good sense'.[141] In this, Colebrooke was following the natural lawyers of the seventeenth and eighteenth centuries, whose ideas profoundly influenced his understanding of contract law.[142]

The key promise of natural law was that all legal rules could be expounded as a series of rational deductions from a few universal principles.[143] Schemes of law should therefore have a clear and logical structure,[144] and legal principles should be set out 'in a rational, coherent manner, as was appropriate to a science'.[145] Crucially, the works of the natural lawyers were not aimed at trained specialists but at laymen.[146] They were written with a clear, logical structure so that even readers without legal training would find them easy to follow.[147] Such works held an obvious attraction for Colebrooke, who had never trained as a lawyer.

Their methods would also have appealed, thanks to Colebrooke's interest in science and mathematics. Seventeenth- and eighteenth-century legal writers took an explicitly 'geometrical' approach to law, treating the process of legal reasoning as akin to mathematical deduction.[148] Scholars influenced by the natural

[138] Colebrooke (n 3) unpaginated introductory note.

[139] Quoted in Rocher and Rocher (n 7) 137.

[140] JDM Derrett, 'The Role of Roman Law and Continental Laws in India', *Essays in Classical and Modern Hindu Law*, vol 2 (Leiden, Brill, 1977) 662–63.

[141] Colebrooke, 'Preface to the Translation of Two Treatises on the Hindu Law of Inheritance' (n 61) 476.

[142] AWB Simpson, 'Innovation in Nineteenth Century Contract Law' (1975) 91 *LQR* 247, 255.

[143] NE Simmonds, *The Decline of Juridical Reason* (Manchester, Manchester University Press, 1984) 51.

[144] *ibid*.

[145] AWB Simpson, 'The Rise and Fall of the Legal Treatise: Legal Principles and the Forms of Legal Literature' (1981) 48 *University of Chicago Law Review* 632, 666.

[146] *ibid* 656; DJ Ibbetson, 'Natural Law and Common Law' (2001) 5 *Edinburgh Law Review* 4, 6.

[147] J Gordley, *The Philosophical Origins of Modern Contract Doctrine* (Oxford, Oxford University Press, 1993) 130.

[148] S Swaminathan, 'Mos Geometricus and the Common Law Mind: Interrogating Contract Theory' (2019) 82 *MLR* 46, 47–48; MH Hoeflich, 'Law & Geometry: Legal Science from Leibniz to Langdell' (1986) 20 *American Journal of Legal History* 95, 98–108. See, eg, S Pufendorf, *Of the Law of Nature and Nations* (Oxford, L Lichfield, 1703) 11–19 (1.2).

law tradition described law as a 'moral science' founded on 'first principles',[149] and compared their work with 'physical research'.[150] They aimed 'rationally [to] reorganise' contract law so that it would exemplify their prized virtues of order, logic and symmetry.[151] Their ideas came to dominate civilian legal discourse and were adopted by many English lawyers, including Colebrooke's predecessor Jones.[152]

Natural lawyers also concluded that the basic building blocks of law must be the same the world over.[153] 'Pure unsophisticated reason', wrote Jones, 'is the same in Italy as in England, in the mind of a Papinian and of a Blackstone'.[154] He lauded the 'striking uniformity among all nations … in those great and fundamental principles of law' that were 'deduced from natural reason'.[155] Roman law was often identified as a particularly fine source of these fundamental principles. For Jones, natural law principles were best illustrated in the works of the Roman jurists.[156] William David Evans also admired the 'intrinsic excellence' of Roman law, observing that, in 'this celebrated system, the mandates of authority bear a very small proportion to the deductions of reason'.[157]

During Colebrooke's time on the bench, he was required to administer civil law to European subjects in India.[158] He soon became a 'diligent and enthusiastic student of the civil law',[159] amassing a library of books on 'English and Civil Law'[160] and recommending 'elementary readings of civil law' to those embarking on careers in the Company.[161] Many of the civilian scholars whose works Colebrooke read were themselves natural lawyers, such as the German jurist Samuel von Pufendorf,[162] or had, like the Scottish writer John Erskine, been influenced by their works.[163] The *Treatise* was Colebrooke's attempt at 'alluring' other Company judges 'to that great fountain of jurisprudence'.[164] Its main

[149] WD Evans, 'Introduction' in RJ Pothier (translated by WD Evans), *A Treatise on the Law of Obligations or Contracts*, vol 1 (London, A Strahan, 1806), 35; JJ Powell, *Essay upon the Law of Contracts and Agreements*, vol 1 (London, J Johnson and T Whieldon, 1790) v.

[150] Evans (n 149) 53.

[151] Swaminathan (n 148) 48–52.

[152] See, eg, H Ballow, *A Treatise of Equity* (London, Nutt & Gosling, 1737) 1; W Jones, *An Essay on the Law of Bailments* (London, J Nichols, 1781) 123–24; Powell (n 149) iv–vi; Evans (n 149) 53.

[153] Simpson (n 145) 657.

[154] Jones (n 152) 14.

[155] W Jones, 'The Speeches of Isaeus in Causes Concerning the Law of Succession to Property in Athens', *The Collected Works of Sir WIlliam Jones*, vol IV (London, GG and J Robinson, 1799) 9.

[156] Ibbetson (n 32) 625.

[157] Evans (n 149) 46–47.

[158] Colebrooke, *The Life of H. T. Colebrooke* (n 5) 223; *First Report of Her Majesty's Commissioners* (n 90) 59.

[159] Colebrooke, *The Life of H. T. Colebrooke* (n 5) 191.

[160] *ibid* 223.

[161] Rocher and Rocher (n 7) 161; Colebrooke, *The Life of H. T. Colebrooke* (n 5) 280, fn 1.

[162] Ibbetson (n 146) 4–6.

[163] KGC Reid, 'Introduction' in J Erskine, *An Institute of the Law of Scotland* (Edinburgh, Edinburgh Legal Education Trust, 2014) xxx–xxxi.

[164] Colebrooke, *The Life of H. T. Colebrooke* (n 5) 279.

influence was the French writer Robert Joseph Pothier,[165] another disciple of natural law.[166]

Pothier's *Traité des obligations* (1761) was intended to 'provide a uniform body of general principles which could be applied across France',[167] just as Colebrooke's was for India. Evans translated it into English in 1806, but Pothier was admired in England even earlier:[168] Jones, for example, praised his 'luminous method' and 'clear manly style', adding that 'the greatest portion' of his analysis was 'law at Westminster as well as at Orleans'.[169] It is not clear when Colebrooke first became acquainted with Pothier's work, but he certainly read the French text as well as Evans' translation.[170] Thanks to Colebrooke's painstakingly thorough referencing, it is clear that Pothier was his primary source. Colebrooke referred to Pothier at an average rate of almost twice a page; in total, a fifth of his citations were to Pothier's works. Even the title of his treatise was derived from Evans' translation of Pothier.[171]

The civil law in general provided Colebrooke's main inspiration. Colebrooke's second largest source, comprising around a tenth of his references, was the French *Code Civil*, itself partly based on Pothier.[172] In fact, 42 per cent of Colebrooke's citations were to French texts. A further 28 per cent were to other civilian sources. Colebrooke was less impressed with the common law. He described it as 'law in disguise', which 'must be stripped of its technicalities before it could be made the subject of study'.[173] English sources made up only 28 per cent of Colebrooke's references, and the most significant was Evans' commentary on Pothier. Eustache-Nicholas Pigeau was cited more often than William Blackstone, and Denis Godefroy more frequently than Edward Coke. Aside from Evans, Colebrooke mainly resorted to a few other English treatise writers: John Joseph Powell, John Newland and Samuel Comyn.

To a common lawyer, perhaps the most striking feature of the *Treatise* is its almost total disregard for case law. Colebrooke made no attempt to survey the English case law systematically, citing only 36 cases across his 251 pages. These citations were all derived from the treatise literature, two-thirds of them from Evans' notes on Pothier, and Colebrooke was evidently unaware of relevant case law not mentioned in the treatises.[174] He was totally uninterested in the

[165] M Hogg, *Obligations: Law and Language* (Cambridge, Cambridge University Press, 2017) 38, 57.
[166] Gordley (n 147) 71; Swaminathan (n 148) 48.
[167] PS Atiyah, *The Rise and Fall of Freedom of Contract* (Oxford, Oxford University Press, 1979) 399.
[168] W Swain, 'The Common Law and the Code Civil: The Curious Case of the Law of Contract' in O Moréteau, A Masferrer and KA Modéer (eds), *Comparative Legal History* (Cheltenham, Edward Elgar, 2019) 385.
[169] Jones (n 152) 29.
[170] Colebrooke cited portions of the *Traitê* that were not translated by Evans: eg, Pothier's [240], cited at Colebrooke (n 3) 102; compare Pothier (n 149) 135.
[171] Hogg (n 165) 38, 57.
[172] Swain (n 168) 387.
[173] Colebrooke, *The Life of H. T. Colebrooke* (n 5) 280, fn 1.
[174] An example is given by W Swain, 'Without the Power to Drink or Contract' (2020) 24 *Edinburgh Law Review* 26, 37–38.

status of cases as authorities, often citing only the name of the judge whom he was quoting and no details of the case itself.[175] This is perhaps unsurprising: Colebrooke's key English sources offered him little encouragement to investigate the case law. Powell wrote that, if authorities took precedence over principle, 'the law must cease to be a rational and demonstrative science',[176] while Evans maintained that the conclusions of a scholarly writer were likely to be more accurate than those of a court.[177]

Colebrooke's treatise was certainly a poor guide to contemporary English law,[178] but that was by no means its purpose. Rather, Colebrooke's project was to identify universal principles of justice, equity and good conscience that could guide the application of contract law in the Indian *mofussil*. If anything, Colebrooke was surprisingly receptive to the common law. He had no quarrel with the substance of English law, only its method; he even praised the 'excellence of English jurisprudence' when compared with Dutch law in South Africa.[179] Colebrooke may also have been hoping that his treatise would find influence outside the narrow sphere of the Company's courts. Perhaps he sought to appeal to the judges of the Supreme Court of Bengal, who regularly applied English contract law.[180] He may even have hoped to find an audience in England itself, replicating Pothier's project in France; after all, he observed, progress made in British colonies could in time also secure 'the advancement of knowledge and improvement of arts at home'.[181]

B. Structure and Method

Colebrooke, then, based the *Treatise* on the writings of the natural lawyers and their followers. Unsurprisingly, its structure closely followed that of texts in this tradition, 'especially Pothier, by whose arrangement', Colebrooke's son noted, 'he was guided in his treatment of the subject'.[182] The *Treatise* was divided into four books. Book I did not, in fact, start in the same place as Pothier: Colebrooke began with a series of definitions and distinctions between different kinds of contract and obligation. Although many of these were taken from various sections of Pothier,[183] Colebrooke collected them together as introductory

[175] See, eg, Colebrooke (n 3) 65, 117, 196 and 219.
[176] Powell (n 149) vii.
[177] Evans (n 149) 76.
[178] S Waddams, 'Nineteenth-Century Treatises on English Contract Law' in A Fernandez and MD Dubber (eds), *Law Books in Action: Essays on the Anglo-American Legal Treatise* (Oxford, Hart Publishing, 2012) 131.
[179] Colebrooke, *The Life of H. T. Colebrooke* (n 5) 343.
[180] Derrett (n 140) 663.
[181] Colebrooke (n 30) 2.
[182] Colebrooke, *The Life of H. T. Colebrooke* (n 5) 279.
[183] In the first ten pages of the *Treatise*, Colebrooke took points from Pothier (n 149) 2–4, 71, 73, 103–107, 112, 130, 136, 144–45, 167 and 171.

material in a similar pattern to Erskine[184] and Pufendorf.[185] Colebrooke then picked up Pothier's structure. In Book II, he considered the essential elements of a contract (parties capable of contracting, a certain subject-matter, valid consent and so on), and discussed factors that would render a contract invalid, such as error, fraud and lesion. Book III turned to the interpretation and effect of contracts, examining different kinds of term, such as conditions and penalties, and different kinds of obligation. In Book IV, he dealt with the dissolution and extinction of obligations by performance, compromise, novation, rescission and so on. Unlike Pothier, Colebrooke did not include a final section on modes of proof.[186] Despite his title, he also made no attempt to cover systematically sources of obligations other than contract.

It can be seen that Colebrooke's treatise had a clear, streamlined structure. It was certainly vastly simpler than any English contract treatise then in existence. While common lawyers were already seeking to give contract law a more systematic structure,[187] the arrangement of their works was still distorted by the forms of action and the separation of law and equity. Colebrooke's treatise transcended these local concerns. The main flaw in its arrangement was that much of the Book II material on vitiating factors was repeated in the Book IV discussion of rescission.[188]

Colebrooke planned to supplement the *Treatise* with a second volume. The manuscript of this work has not been located; in 1871, Colebrooke's son sent it to Sir Raymond West, who was working at the Bombay High Court, and its subsequent fate is unclear.[189] We can therefore only guess regarding the second volume's contents. It seems likely, though, that it dealt with rules for particular kinds of contract, following the 'general part' of contract law in volume one. This was, after all, the structure of Pothier's works and of the *Code Civil*, Colebrooke's two major sources.

Not only the structure but also the contents of Colebrooke's work were very substantially derived from his principal sources. He provided an average of 8.6 citations per page of his treatise, but the bulk of these were to a few key texts. Three-fifths were to only five sources: Pothier's works, the *Code Civil*, Justinian's Digest, Erskine's *Institute*, and Evans' notes on Pothier. While Colebrooke referred to over 50 sources in total, two-fifths of these were only referenced once

[184] J Erskine, *An Institute of the Law of Scotland*, vol 2 (Edinburgh, John Bell, 1773) 411–15.

[185] Pufendorf (n 148) 201–205 (3.4.3-9).

[186] He intended to cover the Hindu law of evidence in his supplementary digest: Colebrooke, *The Life of H. T. Colebrooke* (n 5) 138.

[187] Gordley (n 147) 134.

[188] For example, there is discussion of married women's contracts in Colebrooke (n 3) 27–29 and 232–34.

[189] Rocher and Rocher (n 7) 138. Most of the Colebrooke family papers are not currently accessible to researchers, but Rosane Rocher has kindly confirmed that they do not include the second volume of the *Treatise* (email from Rosane Rocher to author, 10 May 2021). I have been unable to locate West's papers: they are not held by the Royal Asiatic Society, the British Library, or the University of Cambridge. It is possible that they remain in India. See also Simpson (n 142) 255, fn 32.

or twice. He certainly did not read all of his sources in full: for example, he only cited Charles Dumoulin when following a reference from Pothier.

Colebrooke approached his task like the compiler of a digest. His essential method was to extract key quotations from a variety of texts, paraphrase them, and bolt them together. His technique is clearly visible in the following excerpt from the *Treatise*:

> Intoxication, suspending reason, incapacitates a person for contracting, since it renders him incapable of consent. It suffices to render an engagement null, if the party was reduced to the state of not knowing what he did. For persons in a state of absolute drunkenness, and consequently deprived of the exercise of reason, cannot oblige themselves. A less degree of inebriety will not set aside an agreement, if no unfair advantage appear to have been taken. But, if the drunken man be brought into that situation by contrivance and management of the person who obtained the engagement from him, or any advantage be taken of him in the state of drunkenness, it is fraudulent.[190]

This can be compared with the following set of extracts from Colebrooke's sources:

> Drunkenness, when it goes so far as absolutely to destroy the reason, renders a person in this state, so long as it continues, incapable of contracting, since it renders him incapable of consent.[191]
>
> The Defendant may give in Evidence [to avoid a deed] that they made him sign it when he was so drunk, that he did not know what he did.[192]
>
> Persons, while in a state of absolute drunkenness, and consequently deprived of the exercise of reason, cannot oblige themselves; but a lesser degree of drunkenness, which only darkens reason, has not the effect of annulling the contract.[193]
>
> If … any advantage be taken of him, while he is in that situation, or if he is brought into it by the contrivance or management of the person, who obtained the deed from him, this would be fraudulent.[194]

Colebrooke did not add anything new to these texts from his sources; he simply condensed them and fused them together. In the whole *Treatise*, there are only a few points that he did not substantially derive from another writer. His project was not to produce original material, but to marshal an array of disparate sources into a largely coherent outline of contract law principles. Here, for example, he produced an amalgam of French, English and Scottish sources on the effects of intoxication on contracting.

[190] Colebrooke (n 3) 31–32.

[191] Pothier (n 149) 29.

[192] F Buller, *An Introduction to the Law Relative to Trials at Nisi Prius* (London, W Strahan and M Woodfall, 1772) 168.

[193] Erskine (n 184) 417.

[194] J Newland, *A Treatise on Contracts within the Jurisdiction of Courts of Equity* (London, J Butterworth, 1806) 365.

As well as extracting and arranging his texts, Colebrooke also pared them down to their essentials, discarding extraneous discussions, debates and illustrations.[195] His use of case law was limited to the extraction of key quotations; he generally ignored both the facts and any indication that the case had turned on them.[196] In one instance, for example, he treated a case as if it established a general rule, although Evans warned that its result was 'wholly referable to the construction' of the contract in question.[197] The resulting work is extremely concise: only 251 pages long, compared with Evans' 578-page translation of Pothier[198] or Powell's 749-page treatise.

Unfortunately, this approach also made the *Treatise* dry and difficult to read. Indeed, it was criticised by Colebrooke's contemporaries as 'too succinct' and 'wanting in practical examples'.[199] Colebrooke omitted illustrations or condensed them so brutally that they became positively unhelpful. Where Pothier discussed a custom of Orléans relating to interests in party walls,[200] Colebrooke referred gnomically to obligations 'between the owners of contiguous houses' without further explanation.[201] Similarly, Colebrooke classified conditions as casual, potestative or mixed, but defined them in purely abstract terms, omitting Pothier's helpful examples of each category.[202] As with Colebrooke's Sanskrit grammar, which contained too many rules and too few examples, it is hard to imagine that such a succinct work could be used by a complete beginner.

C. Common Law and Civil Law

In Colebrooke's view, contract law principles had two key features: they were similar 'in the jurisprudence of different countries' and were 'dictated by reason and good sense'.[203] His theory therefore ran into difficulties where different countries had different contract law rules. This was also a practical problem: his treatise would not be much use for Company judges if it set out a range of competing principles. Colebrooke's approach to law was that of an administrator, not a lawyer; he frequently displayed impatience with 'vain formality' and 'legal subtlety'.[204] His main concern, as it had been with Hindu law, was to provide a workable set of rules for courts in the *mofussil*, whether these accurately reflected an existing legal system or not. The treatment in his treatise,

[195] See, eg, Colebrooke (n 3) 158, where he disdains to discuss competing views in the literature.
[196] See, eg, the use of quotations from cases at *ibid* 51–52, 115, 161, 216 and 251.
[197] *ibid* 87; Pothier (n 149) 124, fn a.
[198] To this was added a 34-page biography of Pothier and a 66-page introduction.
[199] Colebrooke, *The Life of H. T. Colebrooke* (n 5) 279.
[200] Pothier (n 149) 73.
[201] Colebrooke (n 3) 9.
[202] *ibid* 11–12; Pothier (n 149) 112.
[203] Colebrooke, 'Preface to the Translation of Two Treatises on the Hindu Law of Inheritance' (n 61) 476.
[204] Colebrooke (n 3) 176, 197.

therefore, was Procrustean: the different principles of individual systems had to be made to look similar, so that all could be said to exemplify justice, equity and good conscience.

Colebrooke's task was made significantly easier by the scholars who preceded him. In particular, many of the English writers he drew on had already assimilated civilian materials into their treatises.[205] Thus, for example, he had no difficulty in formulating a basic definition of a contract as a 'voluntary agreement', since French, Roman, Scottish and English writers all agreed on this point.[206] Colebrooke provided definitions from Pothier and Erskine, both based on Justinian's Digest,[207] and from William Blackstone, who likely drew his definition from natural law sources.[208] Other English writers, like Powell, Evans and Comyn, had taken a similar approach.[209]

In general, the *Treatise* was most successful when Colebrooke could use existing scholarship to present a unified picture of contract law in this way. We have seen that he was able to blend common law and civilian sources on intoxication; this was thanks to Evans and Henry Ballow, who had already imported civilian theories on the topic to England.[210] Similarly, Colebrooke identified the civilian suspensive and resolutory conditions with the common law's conditions precedent and suspensive, an idea that he probably drew from Evans.[211]

Where the groundwork had not been laid by other writers, Colebrooke sometimes struggled to maintain a coherent narrative. For example, he had difficulty with mutual, onerous, synallagmatic, bilateral and reciprocal contracts; he took these concepts from a variety of sources, apparently on the incorrect assumption that they were all roughly synonymous.[212] At worst, he piled up inconsistent extracts from his sources without attempting to explain the relationship between them. In one confusing paragraph, he quoted both Powell's argument that a 'useless' contract was invalid and a passage from Evans that explicitly disagreed with Powell.[213]

In some cases, legal systems parted ways on a key doctrine, and Colebrooke had to bridge the gap between them. In the civil law, for instance, inequality of exchange, or lesion, could vitiate a contract, while in England, equity would grant relief only if the inequality were evidence of fraud.[214] Colebrooke generally adopted the English position, explaining that 'unreasonableness in a bargain,

[205] Gordley (n 147) 272.
[206] Colebrooke (n 3) 2.
[207] D.2.14.1.2.
[208] Gordley (n 147) 137.
[209] Simpson (n 142) 266.
[210] Swain (n 174) 35–36.
[211] Colebrooke (n 3) 10–11; Hogg (n 165) 91–92.
[212] Colebrooke (n 3) 9, 16; Hogg (n 165) 140–41, 235–36. Some of his confusion may have been caused by Evans' unhelpful translation: *ibid* 234–35.
[213] Colebrooke (n 3) 37; Powell (n 149) 231; Pothier (n 149) 81, fn a.
[214] Pothier (n 149) 23, fn a.

divested from fraud, mistake and oppression, is not a ground to set aside an agreement'.[215] However, he did not wholly purge his discussion of civilian influences, quoting Pothier's view that lesion alone could vitiate a contract.[216] His attempt to square the circle was the observation that both rules would lead to similar results in practice.[217]

Where his sources were clearly at odds, Colebrooke took more drastic steps to fit them together. A good example is his treatment of the doctrine of consideration, the common law's requirement of reciprocity in contracts, which did not exist in civilian systems.[218] English scholars had puzzled over this: some, like Jeffrey Gilbert, argued that consideration was simply evidence of a serious intention to contract,[219] while others portrayed consideration as equivalent to the civilian concept of *causa*, which concerned the parties' motives for contracting.[220] Still others followed Blackstone, who had misleadingly suggested that the civilians did have a doctrine of consideration.[221] All of these writers, however, maintained that a purely gratuitous promise could not be enforced at common law.[222]

Typically, Colebrooke followed his predecessors in seeking to align consideration with *causa*.[223] He explained that consideration was 'the mutual or reciprocal thing, which is the cause or motive of the engagement'.[224] Like Gilbert, he argued that 'the will of a party' was 'the essence of a voluntary agreement', and that consideration was only 'evidence of his will'.[225] However, he also went beyond his English sources and insisted that a gratuitous promise was enforceable, since liberality was a sufficient 'motive' to constitute consideration.[226] Here, he was following Pothier and adopting a thoroughly civilian concept of *causa*.[227] To make it appear that English law and civil law were as one on this point, Colebrooke even had to doctor his sources. For example, where Comyn identified 'a good and sufficient consideration or *quid pro quo*' as one ingredient

[215] Colebrooke (n 3) 57; see also 53, 55–56.
[216] *ibid* 54.
[217] *ibid* 56.
[218] Ibbetson (n 4) 236–37.
[219] *ibid* 237.
[220] Powell (n 149) 330; Pothier (n 149) 24; see Gordley (n 147) 137.
[221] W Blackstone, *Commentaries on the Laws of England*, vol 2 (Oxford, Oxford University Press, 2016) 300; S Comyn, *A Treatise of the Law Relative to Contracts and Agreements Not Under Seal* (London, J Butterworth, 1807) 8; see also Ibbetson (n 146) 16.
[222] Gordley (n 147) 138–39.
[223] Colebrooke (n 3) 38, 81.
[224] *ibid* 3; see also *ibid* 38.
[225] Colebrooke (n 3) 38.
[226] *ibid* 39.
[227] Pothier (n 149) 24. Colebrooke cited English sources as evidence that 'consanguinity and natural affection' were good consideration, but this applied only to consideration for raising a trust, and not to consideration for a contract: Colebrooke (n 3) 39. See Ibbetson (n 4) 206; AWB Simpson, *A History of the Common Law of Contract: The Rise of the Action of Assumpsit* (Oxford, Oxford University Press, 1975) 373.

of a contract,[228] Colebrooke replaced this with 'cause or consideration'.[229] This enabled him to elide Comyn's concept of contract and that in the French *Code Civil*.[230] Elsewhere, Colebrooke modified Erskine's definition of a contract, removing a reference to 'valuable consideration' and replacing it with, simply, 'consideration'.[231]

Colebrooke glossed over major disagreements between legal systems in order to present a coherent set of principles to his readers. However, he did not pretend that all contract laws were identical; indeed, he was scrupulous to point out local variations. For example, while 'infants, idiots, and insane persons' were 'by nature incapable of contracting', Colebrooke noted that other persons were 'by civil institutions rendered incapable of contracting', including married women and infants.[232] Their incapacity was 'not universal, nor the same in all systems of jurisprudence: but varies with the laws of different countries'. Thus, different legal systems had different ages of majority,[233] and granted more or less competence to married women.[234] Local sensibilities might also vary: contracts that were 'indecorous' in one country might be perfectly acceptable in others.[235]

It was commonplace for natural lawyers to distinguish between rules based on 'principles of universal application' and those with a 'local or temporary cause'.[236] Colebrooke's concern was to identify general principles of reason and equity, not to dictate the ways in which these were adapted to local conditions. Indeed, he was happy to offer a significant margin of appreciation for public policy concerns, and 'vigorous' in his defence of policy reasoning.[237] He observed, for example, that, 'upon the principle of national policy', catching bargains with heirs were 'treated as intrinsically corrupt, and repressed as radically pernicious',[238] while contracts in restraint of trade or marriage were also 'against the national and public policy'.[239] Colebrooke's sensitivity to such concerns likely reflected Company policy; as we have seen, the British sought to tailor their laws 'to the Manners and Understandings of the People' of India.[240] From Hindu law, too, Colebrooke would have learnt the importance of adapting universal legal principles to local custom and public sentiment.[241]

[228] Comyn (n 221) 2–3.
[229] Colebrooke (n 3) 20.
[230] *Code Civil*, art 1108. See also Pothier (n 149) 2.
[231] Colebrooke (n 3) 2; Erskine (n 184) 416. Erskine's definition is rather odd, given that consideration was not part of the Scots law of contract: Hogg (n 165) 286.
[232] Colebrooke (n 3) 26.
[233] *ibid*.
[234] *ibid* 28.
[235] *ibid* 33, 63.
[236] Evans (n 149) 41; see also *ibid* 37; Jones (n 155) 9–10.
[237] S Waddams, *Principle and Policy in Contract Law: Competing or Complementary Concepts?* (Cambridge, Cambridge University Press, 2011) 116.
[238] Colebrooke (n 3) 62.
[239] *ibid* 92.
[240] Cohn (n 15) 26.
[241] See, eg, Derrett (n 35) 89–90; Davis Jr (n 81) 19; A Michaels, 'The Practice of Classical Hindu Law' in Lubin, Davis Jr and Krishnan (eds) (n 18) 77.

D. Hindu Law

Perhaps the most 'remarkable' feature of the *Treatise* is that Colebrooke made hardly any use of Indian sources.[242] He cited Hindu law only 37 times, and legislation in Bengal twice: this amounted to only two per cent of his references. One later Anglo-Indian writer noted that the *Treatise* 'hardly comes within the class of works treating of Hindu law'.[243] Nonetheless, Colebrooke clearly wrote with an eye to his audience in India, including, for example, a correction to the *Digest of Hindu Law*.[244] On the rare occasions that he added his own commentary to the *Treatise*, it was couched in terms of 'equity'[245] or 'justice':[246] precisely the standards that Company judges were to apply.

The most striking evidence of Colebrooke's concern for Indian practice is his treatment of the law relating to slavery. For contemporary European writers, slavery was largely a theoretical concern, which was discussed in the context of ancient Rome[247] or, occasionally, distant colonies.[248] However, domestic slavery was widespread in India, and was thus a matter of everyday concern for Colebrooke. As an administrator, he was indifferent to Indian slavery, writing that it was 'marked with gentleness and indulgence'[249] and functioned as an important mechanism 'for the relief of the indigent'.[250] He evidently expected his readers to encounter enslaved people, and, unlike European writers,[251] discussed their limited capacity to hold property and make contracts.[252] He also went out of his way to identify enslaved people as the subject-matter of contracts. Where Pothier discussed the sale of an unascertained 'horse, furniture or pistols',[253] Colebrooke tweaked the illustration to 'a horse, a slave, a gun'.[254] The *Treatise* was clearly intended to address practical issues in India, even though it barely referred to Indian sources.

When Colebrooke did discuss Hindu law, it was often with a specific purpose: noting the similarities between Hindu and Roman law. Slavery, he observed, 'is recognised by the Hindu law, as by the Roman',[255] and 'in the Hindu law, as in the Roman jurisprudence, a slave has in general no property'.[256] Similarly, he

[242] Derrett (n 140) 663.
[243] Morley (n 33) ccxxvi.
[244] Colebrooke (n 3) 26.
[245] See, eg, *ibid* 99, 135, 176.
[246] See, eg, *ibid* 102, 191.
[247] A Watson, 'Seventeenth-Century Jurists, Roman Law, and the Law of Slavery' in P Finkelman (ed), *Slavery & the Law* (Madison, Madison House, 1997) 367.
[248] See, eg, Pothier (n 149) 232–33, 259, 552–53.
[249] Quoted in Rocher and Rocher (n 7) 97.
[250] Quoted in *ibid* 98. He even sought to mitigate penalties for slave-trading: *ibid*.
[251] See, eg, Pothier (n 149) 29–32; Pufendorf (n 148) 212–14 (3.5.3-5). Pothier referred to Roman law on the point: Pothier (n 149) 254.
[252] Colebrooke (n 3) 30–31, 230–32.
[253] Pothier (n 149) 167.
[254] Colebrooke (n 3) 110.
[255] *ibid* 26.
[256] *ibid* 232.

noted that 'by the Hindu as by the Roman law, heirs succeed to the obligations of ancestors',[257] and compared the Roman and Hindu nominate contracts.[258] In the latter, he was following Jones, who had introduced inappropriate Roman terminology into his translations of Hindu contract law texts.[259] Jones was keen to emphasise 'the general conformity between the Asiatick and European systems' of contract law,[260] and even suggested an Indian origin for Greek law, tentatively identifying the Hindu lawgiver Manu with Minos of Crete.[261] Later Anglo-Indian lawyers followed suit.[262]

It was a staple of contemporary Orientalist thought that India and Europe were part of a common, ancient civilisation.[263] In 1786, Jones had identified Sanskrit, Greek and Latin as members of a single Indo-European family of languages.[264] This sparked an obsessive search for other connections between Europe and India, as Orientalist scholars sought to locate Indian civilisation alongside ancient Greece and Rome.[265] While Europe had moved on since classical antiquity, however, India was thought to have degraded over time. Like his contemporaries, Colebrooke assumed that Indian culture was 'in an advanced state of degeneration',[266] writing that it had reached its 'utmost pinch of refinement' before 'the dawn of civilization in any other nation of which we have even the name in history'.[267]

The aim of these scholars was to recapture the purity of ancient Indian civilisation from later corruptions,[268] and so to shed light on the common origins of East and West. Europeans who discovered 'the wisdom of the ancients' in India were compared to Renaissance scholars recovering Greek and Roman thought.[269] Colebrooke, who compared ancient European and Indian mathematics, astronomy and philology,[270] was praised for 're-establish[ing] the spiritual brotherhood' of Europe and Asia.[271] Law, too, played a role in this enterprise; Colebrooke and others sought to recover the 'essence' of Hindu law from its 'earlier pure codes'.[272] By translating these texts, they were restoring 'not only the original Hindu law, but in a sense original law as such', common to ancient India, Greece and Rome.[273]

[257] *ibid* 25, 138.
[258] *ibid* 18.
[259] Ibbetson (n 32) 635–36.
[260] Jones (n 152) 116.
[261] W Jones (translator), *Institutes of Hindu Law: Or, the Ordinances of Menu* (London, J Sewell and J Debrett, 1796) viii–ix.
[262] See, eg, Strange (n 93) 280–82, 288, 304.
[263] Ahmed (n 27) 168.
[264] Majeed (n 48) 13.
[265] TR Metcalf, *Ideologies of the Raj* (Cambridge, Cambridge University Press, 2008) 14.
[266] Rocher and Rocher (n 7) 201.
[267] Colebrooke, *The Life of H. T. Colebrooke* (n 5) 61.
[268] Ahmed (n 27) 178, 188.
[269] Cohn (n 15) 46; Müller (n 1) 462–63.
[270] Müller (n 1) 467, 476, 483.
[271] *ibid* 463.
[272] Rocher (n 18) 80; Cohn (n 15) 69.
[273] Ahmed (n 27) 186.

Orientalists were deeply committed to identifying Hindu with Roman law, and this commitment left its trace in Colebrooke's treatise. However, Colebrooke was significantly more reliant on Roman than Hindu law: he cited ancient Roman sources over seven times more frequently than Hindu texts. The British, after all, thought very differently about modern Europe and modern India.[274] Roman law was not only admired for its own sake, but also because it gave 'law at this hour to the greatest part of Europe'.[275] Roman contract law had influenced contract law across Europe,[276] including in the 'scientific' systems that Colebrooke so admired. It was therefore worthy of forming the basis for Colebrooke's law of contract. Hindu law had little to offer in comparison, and Colebrooke barely attempted to integrate it into his scheme. Indian sources were only there to provide historical interest; they were so remarkably scarce because they were not intended to play a substantive role in the *Treatise*.

E. Reception

Colebrooke's treatise sought to identify universally valid principles of contract law for application in India and, perhaps, elsewhere. Its purpose, however, would not be realised: the *Treatise* was poorly received. Colebrooke was given 'very little encouragement' to produce the second volume, and even his son could praise the work only as 'a monument of the industry of the compiler'.[277] Subsequent assessments have struck a similar note: Michael Lobban writes that it 'never achieved significant influence', but stood testament to Colebrooke's 'keenness'.[278]

The *Treatise* was never widely adopted by Company judges in India. As a primer on basic contract law principles, it is difficult to imagine that it would not have improved the existing state of contract law in the *mofussil*. However, its difficulty appears to have been a stumbling block: JDM Derrett describes it as 'too strong a dose of what might, if it had been more gradually administered, have been a very healthful medicine'.[279] Colebrooke's son thought that 'the work is perhaps too succinct, and it is wanting in practical examples and illustrations'.[280] It was a difficult book to read and use: Colebrooke had stitched together a series of short texts without the explanations that would have helped untrained judges to parse them. Perhaps unsurprisingly, therefore, the *Treatise* was rarely used in the courts.[281] It was cited by a number of Anglo-Indian writers,

[274] Metcalf (n 265) 12.
[275] Colebrooke (n 39) 463 (quoting Jones).
[276] Evans (n 149) 46.
[277] Colebrooke, *The Life of H. T. Colebrooke* (n 5) 279.
[278] W Cornish et al, *The Oxford History of the Laws of England*, vol XII (Oxford, Oxford University Press, 2010) 301.
[279] Derrett (n 140) 663.
[280] Colebrooke, *The Life of H. T. Colebrooke* (n 5) 279.
[281] Derrett (n 140) 663, fn 10a.

but generally only for its insights on Hindu law.[282] Soon, it was largely forgotten. William Macpherson's 1860 treatise on contract law in the *mofussil* made use of Pothier, but not Colebrooke.[283] Colebrooke's son concluded in 1873 that the *Treatise* had 'met with little attention' in the Company's judicial branch.[284]

The *Treatise* seems to have fared even worse in England. Colebrooke was a complete outsider to English legal culture; he had not lived in the country since he was 12 years old, and his self-published book was unlikely to make a splash among insular English lawyers. Not only was it an unappealing read, but it also served no obvious function in the metropole. English lawyers were happy to pick and choose ideas from Pothier, a reputable French lawyer,[285] but Colebrooke was an unknown quantity from the colonies whose grasp of English law was shaky at best.[286] They were unlikely to take kindly to his attempts to lay down universal principles, especially where these conflicted with well-established authority.[287]

Colebrooke's work was also badly timed. By the end of the eighteenth century, the direct influence of natural law theories was in decline as a specifically English treatise literature began to blossom.[288] Many of these treatises were a skilful blend of English law and natural law ideas, which integrated existing common law rules into a natural law framework.[289] While they paid lip service to universal principles of reason, they were also faithful to the English authorities.[290] Their writers were not interested in creating a scientific system of contract law from scratch, but in gradually improving their existing legal traditions, using ideas from many sources.[291] These measured works gained more influence than Colebrooke's radical innovations, and their ideas soon filtered through to the courts.[292]

As English contract law developed throughout the nineteenth century, it also extended its influence in India. In 1860, Macpherson wrote that the contract law decisions of judges in the *mofussil* 'coincide in general with the rules of English Law',[293] while in 1867, Henry Maine observed that 'justice, equity and good conscience have of late years been much affected … by the English law of contract'.[294] Anglo-Indian law was soon in a sorry state, a 'motley amalgamation'

[282] See Strange (n 93) 272; Morley (n 33) ccxxvi; WH Macnaghten (edited by HH Wilson), *Principles of Hindu and Mohammadan Law* (London, Williams & Norgate, 1860) 136, 137–39, 142.

[283] Macpherson (n 91) xi.

[284] Colebrooke, *The Life of H. T. Colebrooke* (n 5) 279.

[285] Cornish et al (n 278) 303. See, eg, *Cox v Troy* (1822) 5 B & Ald 474, 480–81; 106 ER 1264, 1266.

[286] Hogg (n 165) 92.

[287] S Waddams, 'The Authority of Treatises in English Law (1800–1936)' in M Godfrey (ed), *Law and Authority in British Legal History, 1200–1900* (Cambridge, Cambridge University Press, 2016) 285.

[288] Ibbetson (n 146) 7; Simpson (n 145) 651–68.

[289] Ibbetson (n 32) 632; Swaminathan (n 148) 53.

[290] Ibbetson (n 146) 15.

[291] *ibid* 20.

[292] See generally Simpson (n 142); Ibbetson (n 4) 220–44.

[293] Macpherson (n 91) viii.

[294] Quoted in W Swain, 'Contract Codification and the English: Some Observations from the Indian Contract Act 1872' in J Devenney and MB Kenny (eds), *The Transformation of European Private*

of English and Hindu law.[295] Meanwhile, pressure was growing to introduce English law to India on a more formal basis.[296] This had been unthinkable when Colebrooke arrived in India, but it was now considered that it would 'promote the gradual progress of improvement in the state of the population'.[297] In Colebrooke's day, the British had sought to reconstruct Indian society and law on a European model, believing that these 'improvements' would be welcomed by Indians.[298] Following the 1857 Mutiny, however, the British despaired of their civilising mission[299] and began to argue that improved laws must be imposed on India by force.[300] Even officials who were sceptical of codification projects recognised that a wholesale importation of English law was better than its haphazard introduction by Company judges.[301]

In 1866, therefore, the Indian Law Commission proposed a codification of contract law for India, largely based on English law.[302] This was substantially enacted as the Indian Contract Act 1872.[303] As Colebrooke's son wrote, English contract law had undergone 'a great change' since the *Treatise* was composed; English lawyers could not have produced the 1872 Act during Colebrooke's legal career.[304] Like the *Treatise*, the Act boiled contract law down to basic principles that could easily be administered by untrained officials.[305] Unlike the *Treatise*, it did not make any claims to universal reason; it was simply a practical solution to the problems of imperial rule.[306]

The Act removed at a stroke the *Treatise*'s raison d'être.[307] Ironically, however, much of Colebrooke's treatise had prefigured the later development of English and Indian contract law. Throughout the nineteenth century, English lawyers had continued to borrow ideas from continental sources and to integrate them into the common law, often arriving at positions that Colebrooke had already reached. For example, Colebrooke was the first English writer to use

Law: Harmonisation, Consolidation, Codification or Chaos? (Cambridge, Cambridge University Press, 2013) 180; see also Derrett (n 35) 311.

295 K Mantena, *Alibis of Empire: Henry Maine and the Ends of Liberal Imperialism* (Princeton, Princeton University Press, 2010) 107–10.

296 Swain (n 294) 177.

297 *Second Report of Her Majesty's Commissioners Appointed to Consider the Reform of the Judicial Establishments, Judicial Procedure, and Laws of India, &c* (London, Stationery Office, 1856) 58.

298 Mantena (n 295) 2.

299 *ibid* 2–5.

300 *ibid* 41.

301 *ibid* 112.

302 *Second Report of Her Majesty's Commissioners Appointed to Prepare a Body of Substantive Law for India, &c* (London, Stationery Office, 1866). In 1858, Company rule in India had come to an end and sovereignty had been transferred to the British Crown.

303 See Swain (n 294) 186–89.

304 Colebrooke, *The Life of H. T. Colebrooke* (n 5) 280, fn 1; see also Mantena (n 295) 90.

305 Mantena (n 295) 93.

306 *ibid* 112.

307 It also put paid to West's plan to revive Colebrooke's unfinished second volume: Rocher and Rocher (n 7) 138.

the terminology of 'unilateral' and 'bilateral' contracts,[308] which subsequently became commonplace.[309] He referenced the civilian rules that would later form the basis of the English law on frustration[310] and damages,[311] as well as discussing an early version of intention to create legal relations.[312] Colebrooke's approach to mistake, duress and fraud was largely derived from Pothier.[313] So too was that of Macpherson, who helped to draft the Indian Contract Act 1872,[314] which, in turn, influenced the development of the law in England.[315]

Colebrooke's treatise, then, was too strong a dose of medicine for both Anglo-Indian and English lawyers. Difficult for laymen to use, and unattractive to common lawyers, it soon fell into disuse. However, its ideas would be independently developed by other writers in the century after its publication, with the result that it better reflected English contract law at the close of the nineteenth century than it did in 1818.

IV. COLEBROOKE AND CONTRACT LAW

What, then, can we make of Colebrooke as a scholar of contract law? His treatise is a motley collection of extracts from other works, paraphrased and sewn into a roughly coherent narrative. Colebrooke framed its contents as a set of universal principles based on reason. His marginal notes implied that they were recognised by writers from a variety of legal systems, but they were unmoored from any legal or historical context[316] and often sat uncomfortably together. The *Treatise* does not describe any real legal system; it is a fantasy of contract law, based on the works of the natural lawyers and conjured up for the benefit of laymen with judicial postings in India. Yet while Colebrooke's scheme may be startling to a lawyer, it was a thoroughly natural one for an eighteenth-century scholar-administrator to adopt. The twin threads running through Colebrooke's career were a love of science and a commitment to colonialism, and these were entwined in his contract law scholarship. Like Colebrooke's Sanskrit studies, his legal work was characterised by a 'mixture of scholarly curiosity and administrative convenience'.[317]

[308] Hogg (n 165) 140.
[309] *ibid* 141–45, 155–56.
[310] Colebrooke (n 3) 248–49; Simpson (n 142) 271.
[311] Colebrooke (n 3) 78; Simpson (n 142) 274–77.
[312] Colebrooke (n 3) 38; Simpson (n 142) 264.
[313] Ibbetson (n 4) 234; C MacMillan, *Mistakes in Contract Law* (Oxford, Hart Publishing, 2010) 108; W Swain, 'Reshaping Contractual Unfairness in England 1670–1900' (2014) 35 *Journal of Legal History* 120, 140; see Colebrooke (n 3) 46–54.
[314] Swain (n 294) 184; see Macpherson (n 91) xi.
[315] Ibbetson (n 4) 227, 235. Ibbetson suggests that Macpherson may have followed Colebrooke; it is possible that this is true, but he did not cite him as a source.
[316] There is a very uncharacteristic exception at Colebrooke (n 3) 152–53.
[317] Rocher and Rocher (n 7) 200.

First, Colebrooke was a scientist and mathematician, who joked that he even 'endeavoured to bring his thoughts to the form of equations'.[318] He was 'cool, analytical, composed, with the temperament of a jurist and mathematician'.[319] He had been encouraged to picture law as an idealised scientific system, the rules of which could be deduced from basic principles of reason. This was an appealing image, and it was so well-established in his sources that it likely never occurred to him that it was a mirage. Colebrooke was notoriously averse to speculative theorising; he worked 'carefully and honestly' and never allowed 'one word to escape his pen for which he has not chapter and verse'.[320] He diligently reviewed the treatise literature, and seems truly to have believed that he was expounding the principles of contract law that underlay all legal systems.

Colebrooke was not, however, a pure theoretician: he wrote 'from a sense of duty'.[321] As his son put it, he was 'a philosopher in action', who sought to 'treat political and social questions with the severity of scientific methods'.[322] During his career with the Company, his scholarship was always more or less directly concerned with improvements to the government of India.[323] He was entirely uninterested in subjects, like Hindu criminal law, that lacked practical relevance;[324] conversely, he retained his enthusiasm for even 'futile' mythology if it could shed light on a country's 'manners'.[325] While Jones wrote his *Essay on Bailments* as an intellectual exercise,[326] Colebrooke saw contract law as a matter 'bearing on the well-being of modern society'.[327] His treatise had an immediate practical purpose: identifying the principles of justice, equity and good conscience that underlay contract law, and so assisting Company judges to improve their administration of justice. His son described the work as 'a proof of his devotion to the public service to which he was attached'.[328]

These two sides of Colebrooke's character were brought together in his contract law scholarship. India was seen as an unruly backwater where Europeans could experiment with new ideas based on scientific reason.[329] Like many others, Colebrooke was committed to the 'improvement' of India[330] 'by diffusion of European science'.[331] He had already sought to impose a scientific

[318] Colebrooke, *The Life of H. T. Colebrooke* (n 5) 109.
[319] Rocher and Rocher (n 7) 202.
[320] Müller (n 1) 478–79.
[321] *ibid* 464.
[322] Colebrooke, *The Life of H. T. Colebrooke* (n 5) 109.
[323] Rocher and Rocher (n 7) 199.
[324] Colebrooke, *The Life of H. T. Colebrooke* (n 5) 275–76.
[325] Colebrooke (n 30) 4.
[326] Simpson (n 145) 660.
[327] Colebrooke, *The Life of H. T. Colebrooke* (n 5) 315.
[328] *ibid* 279.
[329] Mukherjee (n 62) 6; AL Stoler, 'Reason Aside: Reflections on Enlightenment and Empire' in G Huggan (ed), *The Oxford Handbook of Postcolonial Studies* (Oxford, Oxford University Press, 2013) 43.
[330] Colebrooke (n 30) 1–2.
[331] *ibid* 7.

method on Hindu law in order to rescue it from the pandits' corrupting interpretations and commentaries. The *Treatise* was likewise an attempt to improve Indian society by introducing a scientific, idealised system of contract law.

As he digested and amended his European sources, however, Colebrooke sought to improve not only Indian but also European law. This too could be 'law in disguise', its pure essence corrupted by technicalities.[332] Stephen Waddams describes Colebrooke's attitude to contract law as 'the approach of a grammarian seeking to discover an ancient and universal language, partly lost, partly corrupted by modern usages'.[333] With contract law as with Hindu law, Colebrooke aimed to reconstruct a perfect system from scattered and degraded evidence through the application of scientific method. Like his other work, his foray into contract law was a product of both his love of methodical intellectual pursuit and his drive to improve Indian and European society.

This combination was not unique to Colebrooke. For eighteenth-century European intellectuals, knowledge was to be dominated and improved in the same way as a subservient state. Samuel Johnson's aim in writing his dictionary, for example, was to conquer 'a new world … civilize part of the inhabitants, and make it easier for some other adventurer to proceed farther, to reduce them wholly to subjection, and settle them under laws'.[334] In his 'enthusiasm' for new knowledge, Colebrooke was compared to 'a traveller to the wastes of Africa or the ice-bound regions of the Pole'.[335] As Waddams observes, however, a contract lawyer was less like an explorer than a coloniser, who not only 'maps pre-existing territory, but also … assists in bringing about improvements'.[336] For Colebrooke, colonisation and contract law scholarship required similar skills: by bringing 'European science' to bear on a primitive and disorderly territory, he would civilise and improve it.

In both cases, too, Colebrooke's blind spots were the same. He was undoubtedly a diligent scholar with a scientific mind and painstaking habits. However, he evidently believed that his scientific methods could be applied to all fields of human knowledge. As a result, he sought to refine and improve both Hindu law and European contract law without a deep understanding of their methods. He relied on the most easily accessible sources, such as Sanskrit texts or English treatises, instead of mastering the true authorities, the pandits' learning and English case law. The result, in both cases, was a body of work that was well-suited to the 'exigencies of colonial rule':[337] it made legal knowledge easy for the Company to access and control, but at the cost of severing legal principles from the traditions in which they developed.[338]

[332] Colebrooke, *The Life of H. T. Colebrooke* (n 5) 280, fn 1.
[333] Waddams (n 287) 284.
[334] S Johnson, *The Plan of a Dictionary of the English Language* (London, J and P Knapton et al, 1747) 33.
[335] Müller (n 1) 464.
[336] Waddams (n 178) 142.
[337] Ahmed (n 27) 184.
[338] Compare Ahmed (n 64) 322.

Colebrooke's treatise was one of a kind; nothing similar was attempted by any later English writer.[339] It was a work very much of its time. Colebrooke's temperament was perfectly suited to the strain of contract law theory that prized scientific method above all. He sought to apply 'European science' to civilise both India and contract law in a project that fit snugly with other eighteenth-century intellectual obsessions. In devising a scheme of universal contract law principles for judges in India, Colebrooke took the promises of the natural lawyers seriously, but stumbled into a gulf between the rhetoric and reality of contract law in the early nineteenth century.

In many ways, Colebrooke's treatise was an impressive intellectual achievement. Like all of Colebrooke's work, it was erudite, methodical and thorough, and made uncompromising demands of the reader. Here, Colebrooke's son is speaking of his Sanskrit grammar, but could just as easily be describing the *Treatise*:

> Having reduced, as he hoped, to some method, the obscure, dispersed, and, what appeared in some cases, contradictory rules, which caused him to wander in an intricate labyrinth, he regarded all other labour as light in comparison. The absence of examples constituted the most serious objection to the work, as an elementary one; and there was something in the system which could not admit of the simplicity of arrangement at which he aimed.[340]

With contract law, too, Colebrooke sought to reduce obscure and contradictory rules 'to some method', but again encountered 'something in the system' that resisted his efforts. Colebrooke's natural law sources had led him to believe that the rationalisation of contract law would be both a simple and a practical project. In fact, neither turned out to be the case. Colebrooke's treatise was a valiant but doomed attempt to reduce the law of contract to a scientific system, and stands as a testament to the mania for improvement that gripped both the colonial officials and the contract law scholars of his day.

[339] Waddams (n 178) 132.
[340] Colebrooke, *The Life of H. T. Colebrooke* (n 5) 205.

4

Stephen Martin Leake (1826–1893)

CATHARINE MacMILLAN

MANY READERS OF this collection will wonder why an author most closely associated with civil procedure, as a co-author of *Bullen and Leake on Pleadings*, has been included in a study of scholars of contract law. This chapter examines Stephen Martin Leake's treatise on contract law and removes this wonder. Although Martin Leake has been largely overlooked in the development of contract law in nineteenth-century contract law treatises, he is an essential link between the older forms of contract literature and thought and how modern lawyers think and write about contract law. Martin Leake's work on contract law was a very distinct product of the reforming initiatives which prevailed in some quarters of the mid-Victorian Bar, most notably in the Middle Temple. Drawing upon his personal papers and unpublished manuscripts, it is argued that Martin Leake was a jurist with very high ambitions for the reform of legal education, of legal practice and as to the very substance of English contract law. His work on contract law was part of a larger and grander scheme to attempt to understand the whole of English law in a rational and scientific manner.[1]

There is an increasingly voluminous literature on how nineteenth-century treatise writers worked to develop and reform law.[2] It is clear that their work profoundly changed the course of contract law. The late Professor Simpson, in a series of articles, first stressed the importance of the treatise writers in effecting

[1] C MacMillan, 'Stephen Martin Leake: A Victorian's View of the Common Law' (2011) 32 *Journal of Legal History* 3 examines this wider ambition.

[2] The context in which nineteenth-century jurists undertook the development of contractual theory is explored by J Gordley, *The Philosophical Origins of Modern Contract Doctrine* (Oxford, Clarendon Press, 1991) chs 6–7; J Gordley, *The Jurists: A Critical History* (Oxford, Oxford University Press, 2013) ch 9; DJ Ibbetson, *A Historical Introduction to the Law of Obligations* (Oxford, Oxford University Press, 1999) chs 12–13; M Lobban, 'Contract' in W Cornish et al, *The Oxford History of the Laws of England*, vol XII (Oxford, Oxford University Press, 2010) 295–322; and S Waddams, 'What Were the Principles of Nineteenth-Century Contract Law?' in ADE Lewis et al (eds), *Law in the City: Proceedings of the Seventeenth British Legal History Conference, London, 2005* (Dublin, Four Courts Press, 2007).

innovation in the nineteenth century.[3] There has, however, been little sustained consideration of Martin Leake and his innovative contributions to the development of contract law. This is, no doubt, attributable to the otherwise obscure way in which this Victorian scholar lived and contributed to the academic debates of his day. As will be seen, the way in which he lived his life meant that he left little trace for later scholars. This chapter provides an explanation of how and why Martin Leake contributed to contract law scholarship. It is argued that he was instrumental in the creation of the modern form of contract law.

I. BIOGRAPHICAL DETAILS

Stephen Martin Leake was born in London in 1826. While his family, minor members of the landed gentry, was primarily associated with naval and military endeavours, Martin Leake himself belonged to a more cerebral branch. His father, Stephen Ralph Martin Leake, had held a position at Her Majesty's Treasury and his grandfather, John Martin Leake, had been a bencher at the Middle Temple.[4] Martin Leake was educated at Blackheath Preparatory School, then King's College School and went on to Cambridge in 1844 as a pensioner at St John's College. He took his BA in 1848, with the distinction of placing as the twentieth wrangler in the mathematical tripos. He was admitted to the Middle Temple later in the year and was called to the Bar in January 1853.[5] He likely chose the Middle Temple because of his grandfather, a senior member not only of this Inn but also at the Bar.[6] His choice of Inn is enormously significant in understanding all his later work.

Martin Leake joined the Hertfordshire and Essex Sessions and the Home Circuit but his early years of practice have left little record; it is quite possible that he had little by way of active practice.[7] He had been a student of the eminent special pleader, Edward Bullen. Whilst Bullen had been admitted to the Middle Temple, as a Catholic he was unable to take the oaths then necessary to be called to the Bar with the result that he practised at the outer Bar. It seems

[3] AWB Simpson, 'The Rise and Fall of the Legal Treatise: Legal Principles and the Forms of Legal Literature' (1981) 48 *University of Chicago Law Review* 632; and AWB Simpson 'Innovation in Nineteenth Century Contract Law' (1975) 91 *LQR* 247, reprinted in AWB Simpson, *Legal Theory and Legal History* (London and Ronceverte, Hambledon Press, 1987).

[4] HF MacGeagh and HAC Sturgess, *Register of Admissions to the Honourable Society of the Middle Temple*, vol II (London, Butterworths, 1949) 407.

[5] *ibid* 510.

[6] John Martin Leake had been admitted to the Middle Temple in 1790 and called to the Bar in 1797 (*ibid* 407). He died in 1862 the most senior barrister in England (Anon, 'Deaths' in *The Gentleman's Magazine and Historical Review* (1862) Jun 794).

[7] Leake's life was plagued with ill health and a career at the mid-Victorian Bar was difficult to establish; see generally D Duman, *The English and Colonial Bars* (London, Croom Helm, 1983) ch 3 and P Polden, 'The English Legal System' in W Cornish et al, *The Oxford History of the Laws of England*, vol XI (Oxford, Oxford University Press, 2010) 1047–54.

likely that Leake spent his time concerned with aspects of practice conducted outside the court, including pleadings, and often working cooperatively with Bullen. Together, in 1860, the two published the highly successful *Precedents of Pleading*.[8]

II. VICTORIAN LEGAL REFORMERS

This work on pleading was integral to the success of Martin Leake's work on contract law. Both these works, and Martin Leake himself, need to be placed in the often-forgotten context of the mid nineteenth-century common law. The Victorians were acutely aware that English common law and practice were in a shambolic state and over the course of the century proposals for the reform of the law, legal procedures, legal education and the legal professions abounded. Three areas of reform are particularly relevant to understanding Martin Leake's work on contract: the civil procedural reforms; the proposals for a changed legal education; and a growing desire on the part of English lawyers to place their substantive law on a scientific footing. The Middle Temple was often at the centre of these reforms and it was within his Inn that Martin Leake became imbued with this sense of reform.

The first major reform accomplished in English law was brought about in relation to civil procedure. The first half of the nineteenth century saw repeated Royal Commissions into the procedures of pleading as the process by which English litigants determined the nature of their dispute became increasingly cumbersome.[9] The first attempt to cure these deficiencies, the Hilary Term Rules of 1834, produced an arcane system of special pleading which frequently allowed litigants to succeed on the technicalities of a case rather than its merits. Reformers decried special pleading as 'the great and prominent evil of our present system' because it made 'the clearest right precarious, and the most dishonest pretension plausible'.[10] The system of special pleading, however, necessarily created a caste of experts, the special pleaders, upon whom the Bar relied. Bullen, an expert special pleader, effectively lost his craft by the reforms effected by the legislation recommended by three successive Royal Commissions, the Common Law Procedure Acts of 1852, 1854 and 1860. *Precedents of Pleading*, written with Martin Leake, was no doubt an attempt to make up for lost income.

[8] E Bullen and SM Leake, *Precedents of Pleadings in Actions in the Superior Courts of Common Law with Notes* (London, Stevens & Sons, 1860). The work, still considered important to barristers, is in its nineteenth edition: W Blair et al (eds), *Bullen & Leake & Jacob's Precedents of Pleadings*, 19th edn (London, Sweet & Maxwell, 2020).

[9] See C MacMillan, *Mistakes in Contract Law* (Oxford, Hart Publishing, 2010) 71–82 for a detailed discussion of these Commissions and their reforms and some of the impact that this had upon the development of substantive law.

[10] JG Phillimore, *Thoughts on Law Reform and the Law Review* (London, William Benning & Co, 1847) 3.

The extensive work necessary to write the treatise gave Martin Leake an excellent grasp of the substantive law and its interaction with the new procedures. In addition, Martin Leake would have been amongst the first to realise that as there would be no more use of the general issue in pleading in relation to contract disputes there would be a requirement to fill this gap with substantive law.[11]

The civil procedure reforms thus created the conditions necessary for English lawyers to begin to think about the substance of their laws. They were acutely conscious that the state of English law did not compare favourably with the jurisprudence of France, which had entered the nineteenth century with the new Code Civil nor Germany which was engaged in the long period of legal transformation which culminated in the *Bürgerliches Gesetzbuch*. In America, legal treatise writers were beginning to demonstrate how the common law could be analysed within legal literature. In England, however, a system organised by procedures rather than principles lacked the science Victorians embraced in other endeavours. This deficiency was even more apparent in light of the work of the English jurists Bentham and Austin. While it has long been recognised that the Middle Temple was at the centre of Victorian legal reform,[12] the role of Martin Leake in realising these reforms in relation to contract law has been overlooked. Two inter-related reforms were important to his work on contract law. The first was the reform of legal education; the second was the creation of a science of law.

By the mid-nineteenth century legal education in England was in a deplorable state. The Inns of Court had long since abandoned efforts at formal teaching and the subject was largely absent in English universities.[13] Mid-century Victorians saw the poor state of legal education as an impediment to a scientific understanding of law. Such an understanding was necessary not only to improve the existing state of the law but also to the proper function of the legislature in enacting law, to the functioning of the courts and to the administration of an ever-increasing empire with ever-increasing legal pluralism.[14] The need for a reform of legal education would have been all the more pressing given the increase in the number of barristers in the half century from 1835.[15]

[11] The point is recognised in *Precedents of Pleading* (1860) (n 8) 19–20, 267–74.

[12] R Cocks, 'The Middle Temple in the 19th Century' in RO Havery (ed), *History of the Middle Temple* (Oxford, Hart Publishing, 2011); R Cocks, 'That Exalted and Noble Science of Jurisprudence: The Recruitment of Jurists with Superior Qualifications by the Middle Temple in the Mid-Nineteenth Century' (1999) 20 *Journal of Legal History* 62; and R Cocks, *Foundations of the Modern Bar* (London, Sweet & Maxwell, 1983) ch 4.

[13] See, eg, J Baker, *Legal Education in London 1250–1850* (London, Selden Society, 2007) 15–44 and Polden (n 7) 1175–98.

[14] Select Committee on Legal Education, *Report from the Select Committee on Legal Education: Together with Minutes of Evidence, Appendix and Index* (HC 1846, 686) xxxii–xxxiv, xxxvii–xl.

[15] Cocks (2011) (n 12) indicates that the number of barristers in the Inns almost trebled during this period and that there was a sharp intake in admissions to the Middle Temple in the 1860s and 1870s: 304. With regard to practising barristers, though, the sharp increase at the beginning of the nineteenth century fell off from the mid-century, a result which had a negative impact on the prospects of junior barristers: Duman (n 7) 9.

At the forefront of the movement to improve legal education was that ardent and acerbic reformer, Richard Bethell, later Lord Westbury. Bethell led this reform movement from the Middle Temple, where he was the Chair of a 'Committee on Legal Education'.[16] The Committee's ambitions were great: students at the Middle Temple would undertake the organised study of general jurisprudence combined with civil law, by which they meant a modern Roman law. John Martin Leake, Martin Leake's grandfather, then one of the most senior men at the Bar and a bencher, supported these educational reforms.[17] Martin Leake himself was likely amongst those who attended the lectures brought about by these reforms. Combined with his university education, these lectures produced a man not only interested in jurisprudence and English law but also acutely conscious of the deficiencies of the forms of English legal education.[18]

As mid-century Victorians sought to reform their law, both in its application and in the jurisprudence which underlay it, they founded a number of societies with these objects in mind. These included Lord Brougham's Law Amendment Society in 1844,[19] the Juridical Society in 1855 and the National Association for the Promotion of Social Science in 1857. Martin Leake was involved with both these latter organisations, particularly the Juridical Society. The Juridical Society was a learned society of barristers concerned to advance the study and science of jurisprudence,[20] a study Bethell noted in his inaugural address as the Society's first president,[21] was particularly absent from the minds of English lawyers. Bethell identified a number of reasons for this absence: the practical division of law into different orders of common law, equity and civil law; the peculiarity of the English legal mind which was 'averse from the duty of extracting, consolidating, and arranging legal rules and principles';[22] the importance of cases as precedents rather than principles; an antipathy to the study of the Civil Law; and the want of a systematic legal education. The Society met regularly to hear and discuss papers given by ardent legal reformers and educators on a wide range of jurisprudential matters. A number of prominent law reformers associated with the Middle Temple including Bethell, Hugh (later Lord) Cairns, Henry Maine and John Phillimore were active in its work. Martin Leake had

[16] Cocks (1999) (n 12).

[17] 'A Calendar of the Inner Temple Records, vol IX 1836–1845' in CV Charlton (ed) (London, The Honourable Society of the Inner Temple, 2011) 1845.

[18] The poor state of legal education in England, particularly in comparison to that of Germany, is seen in the Report from the Select Committee on Legal Education (n 14). See also M Lobban, 'The Education of Lawyers' in Cornish et al (n 7).

[19] On the work of the Society, see generally M Lobban, 'Henry Brougham and Law Reform' (2000) 115 *The English Historical Review* 1184, 1205–206.

[20] Anon, 'The Juridical Society' (1857) 3 *Law Magazine & Law Review Quarterly Journal of Jurisprudence* 3rd series 1.

[21] R Bethell, 'Inaugural Address' in *Papers Read Before the Juridical Society 1855–1858* (London, V&R Stevens & GS Norton, 1858).

[22] *ibid* 5.

more than a passing interest in the Society, delivering papers to the Society, three of which were published,[23] and serving on the Council for a period of time.

During this early period in his career, Martin Leake delivered a paper before the National Association for the Promotion of Social Science Glasgow congress in 1860.[24] The subject of his paper, 'On the Formal Science of Law', taken together with an unpublished manuscript of a lecture given to the Juridical Society, 'On the State of the Science of Law in England'[25] indicate the objectives he sought to fulfill in his contract treatise. Martin Leake's thoughts on a science of law were formed with reference to the work of John Austin.[26] Martin Leake was concerned to cultivate a 'purely formal science of law, with the view of establishing a systematic arrangement of the body of law upon a sound and scientific basis' and that the most effective and practical manner of achieving this was 'to point out some of the elementary principles on which such science depends'.[27] There were many reasons why attention had to be paid to the science of English law. While the 'genius of the English law is distinctively to invest science with an outward invisible form',[28] the want of a 'definite and tangible scientific shape'[29] was severely felt, particularly amongst students of law. Many of these students arrived at their legal studies with university learning only to view the learning and wisdom of the law with an awe and amazement 'produced by phenomena the causes of which are secret and incomprehensible'.[30] The result of years of laborious studies left them lawyers with an instinctive rather than scientific knowledge of the law.

Martin Leake was critical of most works concerned with English law, particularly those 'who expended lifelong but lifeless labour in making abridgements catalogues of law'.[31] Students needed to learn law in a manner other than through alphabetical listings. What Martin Leake advocated was the deduction of a scheme of law from the sources of law itself: 'a scientific system consists in the union of all the different parts of a subject into a single, which, embracing all the parts, at the same time assigns to each its fitting place relating to the rest'.[32]

[23] SM Leake, 'The Principles of Legislation Involved in the Statute of Frauds, as it Affects the Law of Contracts' in *Papers Read Before the Juridical Society 1855–1858* (n 21) 271–92; SM Leake, 'On Some Points in the Theory of the Law of Property' in *Papers Read Before the Juridical Society 1855–1858* (n 21) 531–54; and SM Leake, 'The Taxation of Suitors' in *Papers Read Before the Juridical Society 1858–1863*, vol II (London, V&R Stevens & GS Norton, 1863) 385.

[24] SM Leake, 'On the Formal Science of Law' in GW Hastings (ed), *Transactions of the National Association for the Promotion of Social Science 1860* (London, John W Parker, Son & Bourne, 1861) 155–61.

[25] Hertfordshire Archives and Local Studies Library (HA) file DE/MI/86743. The manuscript is entitled 'On the State of the Science of Law', undated it bears the annotation 'Read before the Juridical Soc.'. The manuscript is numbered and further references in this chapter adopt this pagination.

[26] MacMillan (n 1) 5–7 contains a discussion of this Austinian influence.

[27] Leake (n 24) 155.

[28] 'On the State of the Science of Law' (n 25) 3.

[29] *ibid* 4.

[30] *ibid* 6.

[31] *ibid* 26.

[32] *ibid* 43.

Such a scientific system had advantages beyond the learning of law by legal students for it enabled law to become 'a subject of personal instruction'[33] for members of the public. Those in important stations in society ought not to be solely dependent upon legal professionals for their knowledge of the law. In addition, a scientific ordering of law allowed the legal system to progress over time and to accommodate use and practice as changes occurred. Martin Leake had ambitions far greater than a scientific system of contract law. Influenced by the work of Austin, Martin Leake regarded a scheme of individual duties assembled according to their inherent nature and relations as integral to the determination of the nature and authority of law.[34]

III. MARTIN LEAKE'S *ELEMENTS OF THE LAW OF CONTRACTS*

Having completed the first edition of *Precedents of Pleading*, Martin Leake turned his attention in the early 1860s to deducing the principles of English contract law,[35] in an effort to give effect to the scientific scheme of law he called for. While Austin inspired him, Austin's own lectures had ended without consideration of contracts, probably because Austin himself realised the impossibility of reconciling his command theory with such rights.[36] The work of Martin Leake is important as an attempt to implement some of Austin's ideas in a detailed study of specific subject areas of the common law. In writing his contract treatise, Martin Leake relied little on Austin's jurisprudence but found his notion of rights a useful beginning to the study of contract law. With reference to the recently published second edition of Austin's *Province of Jurisprudence*,[37] Martin Leake began with a division between Rights to Things (*jura in rem*) and Rights against a Person (*jura in personam*). A *jus in personam*, where the owner of a right was entitled to some act or performance of another, consisted of two forms of rights – rights arising *ex contractu* and those arising *ex delicto*. Adopting Austin's classification, derived itself from Roman law, Leake accepted that rights arising *ex contractu* or *quasi ex contractu* were 'original and independent sources' and thus classed as primary rights.[38] Rights *ex contractu* were, in English law, 'rights arising from contract', a term

> used to indicate not only the bond of law arising between and connecting the two parties to the contract, but also, as occasion requires, the right on the one side and the legal duty or liability on the other, which are comprised in the contract.[39]

[33] *ibid* 50.

[34] *ibid* 48–49.

[35] Amongst his surviving papers are early drafts and notes related to his Contract Law treatise. Martin Leake recycled paper by writing on the reverse of paper used for other purposes and these early notes contain the drafts of pleadings with dates of 1861 and 1862 (HA file DE/MI/86743).

[36] M Lobban, *A History of the Philosophy of Law in the Common Law World, 1600–1900* (Dordecht, Springer, 2007) 182–86.

[37] J Austin, *The Province of Jurisprudence Determined*, 2nd edn (London, John Murray, 1861).

[38] SM Leake, *The Elements of the Law of Contracts* (London, Stevens and Sons, 1867) 4.

[39] *ibid* 5.

Austin was not the only English jurist Martin Leake drew upon, for he made reference to both Blackstone and Maine among his sources. Austin, however, had the most significant impact in Martin Leake's work as he provided a demonstration of how the law could be mapped within a coherent structure around a form of conceptual analysis.

Martin Leake reinforced these conceptions with the work of civilian jurists in this endeavour, initially by von Savigny's *System of Modern Roman Law*[40] and later by the pandectists Mackeldey and Warnkoenig.[41] Pothier's *Treatise on the Law of Obligations*[42] was also consulted, as were the Roman Digest and *Code of Justinian*.[43] He admired Roman law for its scientific system although he thought it deficient as it made no consideration of the duty of man in society.[44] The study of Roman law and the work of civilian jurists was not an unusual event for English lawyers at that time. What set Martin Leake apart, though, was his detailed and careful study of English case law and his attempt to organise this law conceptually without unduly distorting what the cases had decided. Such a detailed study was painstaking in the extreme and undertaken only by men with considerable amounts of time.[45] Time, though, was what Martin Leake had.

While Anson later wrote that Martin Leake withdrew from London life because of increasing deafness,[46] the real reason was that he suffered from what was probably depression and anxiety, for which he treated himself with opium.[47] Although the observation was not published, one obituarist identified as Martin Leake's only fault that 'he was too sensitive, too delicate minded, too retiring'.[48] With his father's death in 1865, Martin Leake's inheritance allowed him to withdraw from further practice and to retreat to the family seat in Hertfordshire. There he completed *The Elements of the Law of Contracts*.[49] Martin Leake remained in Hertfordshire for the rest of his life, along with his wife Isabel, a barrister's daughter, and an ever-increasing number of children. In his unpublished writings on 'General and Special Duties', Martin Leake was of the firm view that women could not participate in government and its constitution because of 'their physical organization and their intellectual inferiority'.[50]

[40] FC von Savigny, *System des heutigen Römischen Rechts* (Berlin, Veit und Comp, 1840).

[41] These somewhat unusual choices likely arose because Mackeldey existed in a French translation: J Beving (translator), *Manuel de droit romain, contenant la théorie des Institutes, précédée d'une introduction à l'étude du droit romain* (Brussels, Société typographique belge, 1841); and LA Warnkoenig, *Commentarii Juris Romani Privati*, vol 1 (Liège, Apud J Desoer, 1825) 125–29 was in Latin.

[42] RJ Pothier, *Traité d'Obligations* (Paris, Derube, 1761).

[43] Martin Leake owned a copy of J Ortolan, *Explication Historique des Institutes de Justinien* (1827) and appears to have relied upon it in his understanding of Roman Law.

[44] 'On the State of the Science of Law' (n 25) 16–17.

[45] A similar effort was undertaken by Edward Fry with regard to his *A Treatise on the Specific Performance of Contracts*; see also C MacMillan, 'Sir Edward Fry: Law, Science and Religion' (2020) 41 *Journal of Legal History* 122.

[46] WRA [probably Sir William Reynell Anson], 'Stephen Martin Leake' (1894) 10 *LQR* 1.

[47] A Clayton, *Martin-Leake Double VC* (London, Pen & Sword Books, 1994) 21.

[48] *ibid* 22.

[49] Leake (n 38).

[50] 'General and Special Public Duties', HA file DE/MI/86743.

This view seems not to have been a barrier to allow Isabel to undertake the management of his life and those of their eight children. The overriding direction he left for his executors as to his burial was to 'do as wife wishes'.[51]

Martin Leake's impact on contract law is understood only by surveying the then state of treatises in this area. While there were numerous treatises on different types of contracts,[52] there were only two principal treatises[53] dealing with contract law as a whole.[54] The first was Addison's *A Treatise on the Law of Contracts*[55] and the second was Chitty's *A Treatise on the Law of Contracts*.[56] Both were tired works which then existed in their fifth and seventh editions respectively; both were ponderous in length and both approached their subject by means of a mass of ill-considered details. Chitty had written the first edition of his treatise in 1826 as he realised that the rapid and varied expansion of commerce had created an abundance of new contractually based disputes. He wrote with the avowed object of selecting those contract cases which were 'of common occurrence in business, and are consequently of the highest practical utility'.[57] While Chitty was concerned to elucidate the principle upon which the individual decisions he wrote of were based, it was not until his second edition, written with an eye to Pothier's *Treatise on Obligations*, that he sought to write a treatise on 'the principles of the Law of Contracts' which was simultaneously 'a useful Nisi Prius book'.[58] Chitty's work was, in truth, always aimed at practitioners rather than students. There was little consideration of 'principles' as such and a great deal of emphasis upon particular forms of contracts and its composition consisted of an ever-enlarging accretion of case law.

In writing his treatise, Addison expressed an even grander ambition than Chitty, writing not only for lawyers but also for the mercantile men who needed a knowledge of the obligations they assumed and also for those who sought

[51] HA file DE/MI 86336.

[52] Examples of which can be found in: C Blackburn, *A Treatise on the Effect of the Contract of Sale* (London, W Benning, 1845); JB Byles, *A Practical Treatise of the Law of Bills of Exchange* (London, S Sweet, 1834); C Abbott, *A Treatise of the Law Relative to Merchant Ships and Seamen* (London, Butterworth, 1802).

[53] JW Smith, *The Law of Contracts* (London, W Benning & Co, 1847) provided a shorter exposition of Contract Law. The work had been based upon Smith's lectures to students at the Law Institution and although intended as an exposition of Contract Law principles, the work was not only outdated but also suffered from the approach of examining the subject organised around forms and types of contracts.

[54] See especially W Swain, *The Law of Contract 1670–1870* (Cambridge, Cambridge University Press, 2015) ch 8 for a discussion of the treatises involved in the development of a modern contract law.

[55] CG Addison, *A Treatise on the Law of Contracts*, 5th edn (London, V&R Stevens, Sons and Haynes, 1862).

[56] J Chitty, Jun (edited by JA Russell), *A Treatise on the Law of Contracts*, 7th edn (London, H Sweet, 1863).

[57] J Chitty, Jun, *A Practical Treatise on the Law of Contracts, Not under Seal and Upon The Usual Defences to Actions thereon* (London, H Sweet, 1826) iv.

[58] J Chitty, Jun, *A Practical Treatise on the Law of Contracts, Not under Seal and Upon The Usual Defences to Actions thereon*, 2nd edn (London, H Sweet, 1834) iii.

to understand the law as a part of a liberal education.[59] He endeavoured to base contract law upon 'broad and general principles of universal law', aligning English cases with 'the great body of the Roman law'.[60] His division of contract law into a long series of chapters, each almost exclusively concerned with different types of contracts in the style of an abridgement, worked to prevent his ambition rather than to realise it. This ironic result was not lost on his contemporaries.[61]

In addition to these treatises there was also a work now long out of style, *Smith's Leading Cases*.[62] The work brought together what the editors viewed as 'leading cases' in the law, with each establishing a point or principle of real practical importance. The report of each case was reproduced in its entirety and this was, in turn, followed by a series of editorial observations that were drawn about the importance of the case. For students the collection was intended as a simplified method of reading cases rather than relying upon commentaries and abridgements; for practitioners, it was intended as a portable collection of cases to be carried into court and on the circuit. While its popularity was no doubt driven by the lack of any real alternative, the modern reader is inclined to agree with Dicey's description of it as a literary monstrosity 'in which pile after pile of notes is laid so to speak in layer after layer on the top of some case, worthless in itself, and entirely crushed under the weight of superincumbent comment'.[63]

A. The Innovation of *Elements*

Martin Leake's *Elements of the Law of Contracts* was a distinct break from what had come before in the writing of contract law treatises. It marked a new approach to the consideration and analysis of contract law, an approach which came to dominate the exposition of the subject in England in later centuries. There was nothing new in examining or analysing English contract law with reference to the work of civilian or Roman law jurists. The publication by the Selden Society of Jeffrey Gilbert's manuscript *Treatise on Contract and Property*, and the accompanying introduction by Professor Lobban,[64] clearly reveals that some jurists had begun to conceive of 'a coherent theory of contract as the product of the will'[65] before the nineteenth century. Gilbert's work, however, still

[59] CG Addison, *A Treatise on the Law of Contracts and Rights and Liabilities Ex Contractu* (London, W Benning & Co, 1847) iii–iv.

[60] *ibid* iv. Roman law was to form the greatest of the influences upon Addison's conceptions of contract.

[61] Anon, 'Addison's Treatise on Contracts' (1847) 6 *Law Magazine or Quarterly Review of Jurisprudence* 210.

[62] JW Smith (edited by FP Maude and TE Chitty), *A Selection of Leading Cases on Various Branches of the Law*, 5th edn (London, Maxwell, 1862).

[63] AV Dicey, *Can English Law be Taught at the Universities?* (London, Macmillan & Co, 1883) 25.

[64] M Lobban (ed), *Jeffrey Gilbert on Property and Contract* (London, Selden Society, 2019).

[65] *ibid* cliii (referring to *Gilbert's Treatise on Contract and Property*). See also Lobban, chapter two of this volume.

retained many features of earlier forms of legal literature and he did not deal with general concepts of law;[66] for these reasons Lobban has described the treatise as a 'staging post'[67] in the writing of contract treatises.

Martin Leake's treatise, in contrast, forms the beginning of a modern approach to contract writing. Two elements of Martin Leake's efforts were highly original and laid the basis for this modern approach. The first was the conscientious care he took to ensuring that when incorporating civilian jurisprudence that he represented English law as it was and not as he thought it ought to be or how it could be reinterpreted to fit civilian jurisprudence. There is a reasoned use of the civilian jurisprudence as an analytical device to synthesise and analyse English law. Such a result is attributable to his reading of civilian jurists and of English case law; the surviving records of his library provide a good indication of what he read in both these areas.[68]

The second level of originality was even more significant and it lay in the very approach he devised. Martin Leake, through a meticulous study of English case law, arrived at the 'elementary rules and principles of the law of contracts'[69] and he organised his subject around these rules and principles rather than their application to particular kinds of contracts. Martin Leake wrote of a law of contract, rather than laws of contracts. His education as a mathematician is evident in the logical approach he took to his work. Indeed, as thrift attended all his actions, some of his manuscripts were written on the reverse side of his mathematical notes from university.

Within contract law Martin Leake defined each topic by its nature and provided an order in his chapters set by the formation and development of a contract. He began with Chapter I, concerned with the formation of contracts, followed by II, the parties to a contract, before proceeding to consider in Chapter III the matter of contracts. This led him to two important chapters concerned with the discharge of contracts and then the damages payable upon breach of contract. The treatise concluded with the important subject of the assignment of contracts. Each chapter was, in turn, divided into sections and sub-sections. These operated to identify each particular subject conceptually and demonstrate its relationship to the related components. In this sense, Martin Leake had achieved a scientific system of law through a Linnean system of classification. This classification was achieved on the basis of a conceptual analysis of the relevant principles. This was a marked difference from the often haphazard manner in which earlier treatises veered from procedures to general discussions to long expositions concerned with particular kinds of contracts or discussions of cases. Martin Leake's analysis and order was both rational and novel. In devising it he rejected the approach of existing authors who employed what Dicey termed the

[66] Lobban (n 64) cliv.
[67] *ibid* cliii.
[68] 'A catalogue of Valuable Law Books, Including the Library of the late S Martin Leake, Esq', HA file DE/MI/86752.
[69] Leake (n 38) v.

'unmeaningness' of existing classification in which division was substituted for definition and in which divisions possessed 'absolute uninstructiveness'.[70]

In addition to the classifications presented in logical scheme of principles, *Elements of the Law of Contract* was written with a great clarity of exposition. Brevity and concision made the work readable. At points, Martin Leake coined phrases which continue to have a conceptual resonance: 'agreement consists in two persons being of the same mind concerning the matter agreed upon'[71] is one such example. So, too, was the direct manner in which he informed his readers that such an agreement could only be judged by the outward expressions of an individual.[72] It is evident from his written style that he still harboured the ambition that law could be rendered intelligible to the general reader.

B. The New Elements of *Elements*

In his treatise, Martin Leake made certain refinements to the case law, construing judicial statements capable of more than one meaning in a definite manner or interpreting statements to create a positive duty. In so doing, he became the first treatise writer to write of matters which are now accepted as orthodox within English contract law. It was Martin Leake, in considering the necessity of agreement to contractual validity, who first insisted that for a contract to be formed acceptance had to be communicated.[73] Similarly, Martin Leake's interpretation of the 1861 decision of *Tweddle v Atkinson*[74] served to establish the rule that only a party to a contract could sue upon it. As Professor Ibbetson has observed, reports of the case display confusion as to whether the Court of Queen's Bench refused the action of the plaintiff because he was not a party to the contract or because he had not provided any consideration.[75] Martin Leake explained the case as one based on the ground that the plaintiff was not a party to the contract.

Martin Leake included a chapter in which he considered three situations which might render an agreement void in certain conditions. Treatise writers had long examined one of these, fraud, but Martin Leake's treatise was novel in that it was the first to provide an examination of the doctrines of duress and mistake. He provided a detailed consideration of duress. Where a party 'was induced to consent by fear and intimidation, imposed by the violence or threats

[70] Dicey (n 63) 13. Dicey coined the terms with reference to Smith's *Law of Contracts* but his criticism applies equally to other contract treatises.

[71] Leake (n 38) 8.

[72] *ibid*.

[73] *ibid* 8, 13; Michael Lobban observes that the case upon which the proposition was based does not entirely support the proposition (M Lobban, 'Contract' in W Cornish et al, *The Oxford History of the Laws of England*, vol XII (Oxford, Oxford University Press, 2010) 338).

[74] *Tweddle v Atkinson* (1861) 1 B & S 393, 121 ER 762.

[75] DJ Ibbetson, 'English Law before 1900' in J Hallebeek and H Dondorp (eds), *Contracts for a Third-Party Beneficiary: A Historical and Comparative Account* (Leiden, Brill, 2008) 113.

of the other party, he may avoid the agreement'.[76] The ambit in which duress operated to vitiate an agreement was a narrow one, though, consisting of actual violence to the person or in threats of violence to the person. The reader of Addison's treatise looked for the topic in vain;[77] Chitty's readers were informed that parol evidence could be admitted to prove duress before being told 80 pages later that this was a defence of little application in the nineteenth century.[78]

Analysis of the other doctrine he introduced to English contract treatises, mistake, was even more detailed.[79] Mistake, he explained, arose through the ignorance or misconception of some matter by which the agreement apparently made was not the agreement intended to be made or which would not have been made but for the mistake. Mistake could be of one party alone or both parties; the consequences of the mistake depended upon the particular circumstances in which it arose. Where a mistake operated it avoided the contract although the strict rule of the common law was 'tempered' by the doctrines and practices of the Courts of Equity where mistake was a defence to an action for specific performance, a ground to reform (rectify) a contract or 'set aside the mistaken agreement'.[80] Intriguingly, while Martin Leake's explanation of mistake was obviously derived from the civilians, he supported his principles with English cases rather than the writings of continental jurists. And his approach was greatly influenced by the procedural aspects of pleading mistake. He was at pains to point out, for example, that the Common Law Procedures Act 1854 allowed a party to set up a mistake in an agreement as courts of law could now allow equitable grounds in some instances. In these efforts it was Leake who kept *Raffles v Wichelhaus*[81] from its well-deserved obscurity when he employed it as an example in his discussion of mistake.[82] The case was really an example of a series of clever pleadings on the part of Wichelhaus's counsel; the case first came to Martin Leake's attention in relation to these pleadings.[83]

The subject of damages was one generally avoided by nineteenth century contract treatise writers.[84] Although acknowledging that the right of action for damages is regulated by the 'Law of Procedure', Martin Leake considered

[76] Leake (n 38) 205.

[77] A brief paragraph concerned with duress was added to the end of a chapter on illegal, immoral and fraudulent contracts in the next edition (LW Cave, *Addison on the Law of Contracts*, 6th edn (London, Stevens and Sons, 1838) 911).

[78] Chitty (n 58) 107, 189.

[79] A more detailed assessment of his role in the development of the doctrine of mistake is in MacMillan (n 9) ch 5.

[80] Leake (n 38) 174.

[81] *Raffles v Wichelhaus* (1864) 2 H & C 906, 159 ER 375.

[82] Professor Simpson misattributed this role to Judah Benjamin and overlooked Martin Leake (AWB Simpson, 'The Beauty of Obscurity: Raffles v Wichelhaus and Busch (1864)' in AWB Simpson, *Leading Cases in the Common Law* (Oxford, Clarendon Press, 1995)).

[83] MacMillan (n 9) 186–90.

[84] Pollock, for example, never could bring himself to include a chapter in his treatise and it fell to Winfield to include it in the 12th edition of 1946: PH Winfield, *Pollock's Principles of Contract*, 12th edn (London, Stevens, 1946). With regard to the nineteenth-century treatment of damages, see Swain (n 54) 197–200.

the topic because the measurement of damages was conducted according to general rules and principles of law. As Professor Swain has observed,[85] in doing so Martin Leake was the first to provide a modern formulation of the measure of damages, that

> the general damage is commonly described as the loss sustained by the plaintiff from the non-performance of the contract; the benefit which the plaintiff would have received if the contract had been kept is the measure of damages if the contract is broken.[86]

He then quoted the now commonly applied formula of Baron Parke in *Robinson v Harman*[87] that the damages awarded for a breach of contract are awarded on an expectation measure. Chitty's readers, in contrast, would have found the case buried in a footnote to a more specific proposition concerned with a breach of a contract to sell land.[88] Martin Leake also observed that there were certain losses, such as disappointment or annoyance to feelings, which could not be awarded as damages for a breach of contract. A contract for marriage was an exception to this limitation, though.[89] His treatment of the subject was thought to be of 'great value' by contemporaries.[90] It is also strikingly modern in its approach.

Elements of the Law of Contract was also the first major work on contract to consider quasi-contract or, as Martin Leake termed it, 'contracts implied by law'. He was concerned to consider why the common law might give relief in instances where there was no contract between the parties. He considered the subject in relation to different kinds of contracts which arose by their different modes of formation. One of these, simple contracts, could be further divided between those which arose from the agreement of the parties and those which arose independently of agreement as a contract implied in law.[91] While other treatise writers wrote of implied contracts[92] their examinations consisted largely of catalogues of cases in which relief had been given on the basis of an implied contract or an implied term in a contract. Indeed, so little scrutiny did they give to the matter that their works exhibited confusion between contracts implied by law and terms implied by law. Martin Leake clearly distinguished implied terms from implied contracts[93] and was then concerned to explain both the relation of the implied contracts to contract and also why the law created such liability. He evidently began his considerations from the work of Austin and Maine[94] and with reference to the French *Code Civil*. As Professor Lobban

[85] Swain (n 54) 199.
[86] Leake (n 38) 565.
[87] *Robinson v Harman* (1848) 1 Ex 850, 154 ER 363.
[88] Chitty (n 56) 285, fn l. The case is misnamed *Robinson v Hardman*.
[89] Leake (n 38) 565–66.
[90] Anon, 'Review: *The Elements of the Law of Contracts*' (1867) *Law Journal* 138, 170.
[91] Leake (n 38) 7.
[92] Chitty (n 56) 55–62; Addison (n 55) 17–37.
[93] Leake (n 38) 11–12, 39.
[94] *ibid* 7, fn a.

has observed, neither Austin nor Maine was terribly helpful in the examination of this subject.[95] Probably for this reason Martin Leake expanded his research to include Pothier, Mackeldey and Warnkoenig.[96] Significantly, he also approached this question from the perspective of a pleader and the importance of the action of *assumpsit* before the enactment of the Common Law Procedure Act 1852. Martin Leake thus made clear that contracts implied by law, and thus protected by the same form of action, *assumpsit*, were not contracts at all for their existence depended upon the 'pure fiction' of a promise to pay a debt imposed by law.[97] The principle underlying legal intervention in these cases of implied contracts was the prevention of unjust enrichment:

> The transactions between two parties, other than agreement, which give rise to contracts, may be described generally as importing that some undue pecuniary inequality exists in the one party relatively to the other which justice and equity require should be compensated, and upon which the law operates by creating a debt to the amount of the required compensation.[98]

While Martin Leake made little of this analysis in his ensuing discussion of the cases,[99] it marked a tentative development. It was not, though, one largely followed by later nineteenth century treatise writers and quasi-contract was not a treatise subject for any English jurist.[100] Had it become so the development of the law of obligations would have run a different course.

Contemporaries greeted the publication of *Elements of the Law of Contracts* in largely positive terms. As the *Law Times* observed, while the law of contracts was well served with treatises, Martin Leake made a valuable contribution in treating the subject 'in a more scientific form than is usually seen in English law books'.[101] The treatment of the subject by means of the exposition of clear principles, logically ordered and indicating the cases upon which the principles were based, was particularly valued. While it was accepted that the practitioner would benefit by a reminder of the principles of the cases, it was thought that it would be 'an excellent work for the law student'.[102] The reviewer for *The Law Journal* agreed with this assessment: 'this is a work of the highest order of merit, compendious not prolix, hitting the happy means between the abstract and the concrete method of treating law'.[103] His attempt to bring order to the chaos of the cases by means of distinct principles was particularly applauded. Only the *Law Magazine's* reviewer thought that the work had fallen short of the goal of

[95] Lobban (n 2) 568.
[96] Leake (n 38) 39.
[97] *ibid.*
[98] *ibid.*
[99] Neither in this first edition nor in his subsequent two editions.
[100] Possibly prompted by Martin Leake, Anson did include a brief appendix on the relation between contract and quasi contract (WR Anson, *Principles of the English Law of Contract* (Oxford, Clarendon Press, 1879) 321–27).
[101] Anon, '*The Elements of the Law of Contracts*' (1867) 42 *Law Times* 430.
[102] *ibid.*
[103] Anon (n 90) 169.

enunciating English contract law as a series of principles.[104] The appreciation of the utility of the treatise by fellow lawyers can be seen, though, in the fact that a lawyer as experienced, and versed in the civil law, as Judah Benjamin wrote his *Treatise on the Law of Sale of Personal Property*[105] the following year using Martin Leake as an authoritative source on the English law of contract.

IV. THE DIGEST OF LAW

The last edition of *Precedents of Pleading* that Martin Leake worked on was the third, published in 1868. While the volume continued (and continues) to be published, Martin Leake turned his attentions to other areas. It has been noted at the outset that two of his principal reforming objectives in writing *Elements of the Law of Contracts* were to facilitate legal education and to reform the way English lawyers thought about their law. For the rest of his life he now dedicated his efforts to a third objective: the codification of English law. The second edition of his contract treatise attempted to effect this objective. In tandem with calls for the reform of the administration of justice were calls to reform the substance of English law through codification.[106] Martin Leake's unique role in this regard was his attempts to translate the reformers' objectives into a practical reality. A Digest of Law Commission was formed within a year of the Commission of the Administration of Justice and was charged with the duty of inquiring into the expediency of a Digest of Law and how best to achieve this object.[107] Once again, Lord Westbury was at the centre of this reform, although his age and the difficult nature of his relationship with other commissioners were greatly to limit his effectiveness. A Digest was recognised as the best preparation for any future codification of English law.[108] The Digest of Law Commission decided, accordingly, to organise a portion of English law as a digest and held a competition to select authors to prepare digests on bills of exchange, mortgages and easements.[109] Martin Leake, unsuccessfully, submitted a proposal to prepare a digest on bills of exchange.[110]

[104] Anon, '*The Elements of the Law of Contracts*' (1867) 23 *Law Magazine & Review Monthly Journal of Jurisprudence, 3rd series* 162, 163.

[105] JP Benjamin, *A Treatise on the Law of Sale of Personal Property: with References to the American Decisions and to the French Code and Civil Law* (London, Henry Sweet, 1868).

[106] See WM Best, 'Codification of the Laws of England' in *Papers Read Before the Juridical Society 1855–1858* (London, V&R Stevens & GS Norton, 1858) 209; FV Hawkins, 'Digests and Codes, with Reference to Law Reform' (1866) 11 *The Jurist New Series* 29; JF Macqueen et al, 'What Would be the Best Mode of Reducing the Law of England to a Compendious Form?' (1866) 12 *The Jurist New Series* 402; and FS Reilly, 'A Code or a Digest?' (1873) 2 *Law Magazine & Review Monthly Journal of Jurisprudence, 4th series* 420.

[107] Law Commission, *First Report of the Digest of Law Commission* (C (1st series), 3849) (1867) 3.

[108] *ibid* 6.

[109] *The Times* (3 December 1867) 9.

[110] SM Leake, *A Scheme of a Digest of Law: with a Specimen Digest of the Law of Bills of Exchange* (London, JE Taylor, 1868).

The official attempt to digest English law failed before the sample digests were completed. The prohibitive expense of digesting cases was to mean that the common law was to remain uncodified.[111] An unintended effect of this attempt, though, was that it left the creation of digests to private efforts.[112] Martin Leake was at the forefront of these private efforts and set about preparing a Digest of the Law of Property.[113] He had already advocated the importance of a code before the Juridical Society 'for the enlightenment and use of the public'[114] and he now argued that if a 'Digest were to obtain the sanction of habitual use, the transition to a Code would be little more than a matter of form'.[115] For his overall classificatory scheme, Martin Leake relied upon Austin's division between primary law and secondary law, and, also derived from Austin's use of Roman law, for a division of substantive law into a 'law of persons' and a 'law of things'. A uniform order of titles within the Digest was necessary to make the Digest consistent within its parts and to make the titles auxiliary to one another. Once the logical order of the titles had been settled upon, these could then be filled with every rule and principle of English case law, excluding only those which were obsolete or cases which turned upon their own facts. His plan, he revealed, was 'peculiarly applicable' to those areas of law such as contract or property in which the same principles recur with only a varied application.[116] He recognised that while a code required the sanction of public authority, a code or a digest had to contain the same material 'and for the same purpose, namely, that the law may be readily accessible to all'.[117] The development of a digest was a wide field of inquiry in which private exertions could assist.[118]

Martin Leake set about providing these private exertions with his publications on the law of property.[119] With regard to contract, he published in 1878 what amounted to a second edition of his treatise, now retitled as *An Elementary Digest of the Law of Contracts*.[120] Together with his treatise on land law he intended for these to be two titles in a comprehensive Digest of Law which would advance the progress of a public digest or code which would, in turn, solve so many of the difficulties experienced in the promulgation and administration of the law.[121]

[111] As one of the commissioners observed, the expense of digesting the common law proved prohibitive: Reilly (n 106) 426.

[112] The dissolution of the Commission inspired the production of *Halsbury's Laws of England*: see GW Wickersham, 'The American Law Institute and the Projected Restatement of the Common Law in America' (1927) 43 *LQR* 451, 453–54.

[113] SM Leake, *An Elementary Digest of the Law of Property in Land* (London, Stevens & Sons, 1874) and SM Leake, *A Digest of The Law of Uses and Profits in Land* (London, Stevens & Sons, 1888).

[114] 'On the State of the Science of Law' (n 25) 51.

[115] Leake (n 110) 7.

[116] *ibid* 6–7.

[117] Leake (1874) (n 113) vi.

[118] *ibid*.

[119] *ibid* and Leake (1888) (n 113).

[120] SM Leake, *An Elementary Digest of the Law of Contracts* (London, Stevens & Sons, 1878).

[121] *ibid* vii–viii.

Martin Leake's original classifications of his contract treatise were retained, and in this sense his original objective of a natural and logical division of the subject was met. In the *Digest of the Law of Contracts* he sought, in creating a digest, to provide a much more comprehensive account of the case law and to produce a greater arrangement of sub-divisions within his earlier classifications. This second work, as a digest, was a much lengthier affair: 1344 pages in comparison with the earlier 700. In addition to the greater number of cases covered, he expanded his treatment of the law in relation to the capacity of persons, implied contracts, the statute of frauds and the discharge of contracts. Some of his subjects had become more nuanced as a result of legal developments in the previous decade, such as mistake and illegality.

The performance of contracts for the sale of goods was given a more extended treatment, largely because of the greater significance of the subject following the publication of Benjamin's treatise on sale.[122]

In other areas, Martin Leake added new subjects. He provided a new section on the construction of contracts and a much more extensive consideration of the capacity of contracting parties. The enactment of the Judicature Acts brought other changes and he now sought to provide a more comprehensive account of the equitable aspects of contract law. A section on undue influence was added to his consideration of duress and he now considered the jurisdiction of a court of equity to set aside agreements which had been induced by undue influence or pressure. The greatest change to the treatise, though was a much more extended and comprehensive part on 'Remedies for Breach of Contract' in place of 'Damages'. Here he became the first treatise writer to write of damages and the equitable relief of specific performance and injunctions in the same consideration. To his account of remedies he included a discussion on interest and a more extended examination of liquidated damages and penalties.

While the *Digest of the Law of Contracts* was met with critical approval,[123] it failed to realise Martin Leake's ambition of establishing the basis upon which a larger Digest of Law could be established. The size and the complexity of the *Digest of the Law of Contracts* meant that it was largely used by practitioners, rather than the students for whom he had originally written.[124] Martin Leake wrote a third edition of his contract treatise which he entitled *A Digest of Principles of the Law of Contracts*.[125] He wrote now explicitly for practitioners, his wider ambitions in legal education and digests now abandoned. Indeed, Martin Leake probably wrote this work solely for the profit he thought it would generate. By 1891 not only was his health failing but his financial situation had

[122] Benjamin (n 105).

[123] Anon, 'Mr Leake on Contracts' (1879) 14 *Law Journal* 322.

[124] A point observed by Frederick Pollock in his *Principles of Contract*, 3rd edn (London, Stevens & Sons, 1881) x–xi in a subtle preferment of his own contract treatise and that of his colleague, Anson, for student use.

[125] SM Leake, *A Digest of Principles of the Law of Contracts*, 3rd edn (London, Stevens & Sons, 1892).

deteriorated significantly as a result of an unfortunate investment in a company run by his brother.[126] There is marked difference in this third edition as all of the larger jurisprudential reforms he had proposed in the earlier editions were abandoned. While Martin Leake carefully updated the law, he removed his introductory chapter in which he had sought to set contract within a larger jurisprudential framework. And so, too, he removed most of the references to civilians throughout the work. Martin Leake died the year after this third edition of his contract treatise was published; his widow, with minor children to support, sold the copyright in his works to the publishers for £575.[127] Five further editions of *Principles of the Law of Contracts* were published, the final one in 1931.[128] Within England it had become a treatise for practitioners; and one not that different from the revised later editions of *Chitty*. The change in *Chitty*, though, had been brought by the example of Martin Leake's work.

V. THE EFFECT OF MARTIN LEAKE'S *LAW OF CONTRACTS*

What was the effect of Martin Leake's *Law of Contracts*? As has been noted, his hope of spurring the production of a comprehensive Digest or Code of the common law has never been realised. Further, it would appear that his work was never used to any large extent by English law students as a means of understanding contract law. Examiners are slow to change their reading and when his work appeared it was observed that it was 'a very useful production' for students 'but as the examiners have fixed on Chitty on Contracts … it will be better to have that work'.[129] When he changed his approach in his second edition to a digest, his work ceased to be the short reference students require and at a point when a new author, Sir William Anson, wrote a contract treatise far better adapted to student needs.[130] That Anson was a university tutor in the subject gave him a practical advantage in the successive, and frequent, editions of his shorter treatise that Martin Leake could never achieve.

Martin Leake's new scientific approach was to have appeal on the other side of the Atlantic. In Canada, his work on contract law does appear to have been used to teach students law.[131] One Canadian lawyer even prepared a synopsis of the principles in *Leake on Contract*, combined with those in *Benjamin on Sales*, for use by law students.[132] Canadian lawyers found the work useful in

[126] Clayton (n 47) 21. As Clayton recounts, Martin Leake struggled to provide a suitable education for his six sons. Neither of his daughters were sent to school.

[127] HA, file DE/M1/86637.

[128] RRA Walker, *Principles of the Law of Contracts/ by the Late S Martin Leake*, 8th edn (London, Stevens, 1931).

[129] Anon, 'Contracts' (1867) 7 *Law Students' Examination Chronicle* xlviii.

[130] Anson (n 100).

[131] The complaint was raised that a member of the Law Society had taken *Leake on Contracts* out of the library and retained it for months: Anon, 'Law Society' (1878) 14 *Canadian Law Journal* 235.

[132] TM Higgins, *An Analysis of Leake on Contracts and Benjamin on Sales* (Toronto, The Carswell Company, 1893).

their practice; at least one edition appeared in which notes on the Canadian law had been added.[133] In the United States, the book was clearly consulted and a selection of Leake's principles were added as commentary to *Finch's Cases on Contracts* to provide a textbook for students.[134] This unusual English offering of cases provided a competitor at Columbia University to Langdell's Harvard casebook.[135]

Where Martin Leake did succeed was in creating a scientific system of contract law, one that established a systematic arrangement of the body of contract law upon the elementary principles of the subject. With an eye to the civilians for jurisprudence and for structure, Martin Leake wrote a logical law of contract developed around the principles of the subject and set out in their natural order. In doing this he paid particular care to the decided cases. This was the only way in which a scientific system would prevail within an English legal environment. It was through his patient efforts that English contract law ceased to be written in treatises which resembled the old abridgments or commentaries. As one contemporary wrote '"Leake on Contracts" is an excellent example of what a legal treatise ought to be'.[136]

The revolution effected by his work can best be seen in the two contract treatises written after Martin Leake's treatise. Neither of these bore much resemblance to what had come before Leake's treatise, although both bore a great deal of resemblance to his treatise. The first was Frederick Pollock's *Principles of Contract at Law and in Equity*[137] in 1876 and the second was Sir William Anson's *Principles of the English Law of Contract* in 1879. Both authors were enormously indebted to Martin Leake's work. As their titles indicated, they wrote a law of contract and not of contracts, an enormous shift from the efforts of treatise writers such as Addison, Chitty and Smith. Pollock and Anson organised their subject, with varying degrees of success in Pollock's case, around the principles of English contract law. While they made a much greater use of civilian jurists than Martin Leake, their ability to create a structure of English contract principles was dependent upon Martin Leake's work. Anson's ability to create a 'logical and consistent' law of contracts, one with 'an ordered and luminous statement of the principles which govern the contractual relation',[138] was dependent upon Martin Leake's initial exposition and ordering of a system

[133] AE Randall, *The Law of Contracts/ by the Late S. Martin Leake, Including Notes on the Canadian Law by Hon Mr Justice Russell*, 6th edn (Toronto, Canada Law Book Company, 1912).

[134] WA Keener, *Selections from Leake's Elements of the Law of Contracts and Finch's Cases on Contracts* (New York, Baker, Voorhis & Co, 1891); *Selections from Leake's Elements of the Law of Contracts and Finch's Cases on Contracts*, 2 vols (New York, Baker, Voorhis & Co, 1895).

[135] EA Farnsworth, 'Contracts Scholarship in the Age of the Anthology' (1987) 85 *Michigan Law Review* 1406, 1414–15.

[136] Anon, 'Reviews: Leake on Contracts' (1892) 27 *Law Journal* 561. In the view of an American Reviewer, Leake was 'one of the best of the modern authors of legal treatises in England' (Anon, 'Keener's Selections on Contracts' (1892) 26 *American Law Review* 321).

[137] F Pollock, *Principles of Contract at Law and in Equity* (London, Stevens & Sons, 1876).

[138] JMI, 'Principles of the English Law of Contract' (1893) 5 *Juridical Review* 362.

of principles. This is not to say that these were agreed, or even particularly well-defined principles, of contract law[139] but simply that a means of conceiving contract law in a framework of principles emerged. Both gave consideration to the 'new' doctrines Martin Leake had written of, such as mistake and duress.

Anson acknowledged in the preface to his first edition that he had not only made frequent references to Martin Leake's work but also that it 'must needs enter largely into the composition of a work such as mine professes to be'.[140] In Anson's fifth edition he observed that his own writing was greatly helped by the work of Martin Leake and Pollock but that, of the two, Martin Leake dealt with the subject exhaustively and 'that I got most information from Mr. Leake'. In writing Martin Leake's obituary he emphasised that 'his book on Contract, which appeared in 1867, was in its first edition the most scientific treatise on this branch of the law'.[141] As Anson explained:

> To say that books are stored with knowledge, and that this knowledge is well arranged, may not seem to say very much. But those who know the mass of detail which, in some sort of arrangement, goes to make up a legal treatise; those who have wandered in the wilderness of ill-compatcted learning of which so many text-books consist; still more, those who have tried for themselves to select and arrange the material for a work on any great department of our law, will appreciate, to the full, the happy combination of learning and method displayed in the writings of Mr. Leake.[142]

The frequent references to Martin Leake's work in the first edition of his *Principles of Contract* indicate that Pollock wrote with a copy of Martin Leake's work to hand. In a typical Pollock manner, though, it was not until page 326 that he acknowledged Martin Leake as 'a writer entitled to great respect'.[143] In the preface to his third edition, Pollock described Leake's *Digest of the Elements of the Law of Contracts* as an 'excellent book' with 'value as a comprehensive book of reference'.[144] Pollock, though, was suspicious of Austin and Martin Leake was probably too close to Austinian jurisprudence to laud.

The very success of the contract treatises of Pollock and Anson, particularly as part of the new Oxford law faculty, served to eclipse Leake's contract treatise. Professor Sugarman has argued that the main intellectual task of the early classical law dons was the ordering of the chaos of case law through the identification of underlying principles. This intellectual task was undertaken to provide professional legitimacy to these new university law scholars.[145] While Leake was

[139] See S Waddams, 'What Were the Principles of Nineteenth-Century Contract Law?' in A Lewis et al (eds), *Law in the City* (Dublin, Four Courts Press, 2007).

[140] Anson (n 100) vii.

[141] WRA (n 46) 3.

[142] *ibid*.

[143] Anson (n 100) 326; 'a most accurate lawyer' (F Pollock, *Principles of the Law of Contract*, 8th edn (London, Stevens & Sons, 1911) 199). A similar compliment is again paid towards the end of his life in F Pollock, 'Our Jubilee' (1935) 51 *LQR* 5.

[144] Pollock (n 124) x.

[145] D Sugarman, 'Legal Theory, the Common Law Mind and the Making of the Textbook Tradition' in W Twining (ed), *Legal Theory and Common Law* (Oxford, Basil Blackwell, 1986) 29–30.

certainly acquainted with these dons, for he was a law examiner at Oxford, he was not integrated into this new clique. In short, it is not a surprise that Dicey, in his influential inaugural lecture of 1883, applauds the contract writing efforts of Anson and Pollock but omits to mention Martin Leake.[146] What these and other efforts from these new university legal scholars did was to obscure the painstaking efforts of Martin Leake in the organisation of English contract law by principles devised through methods of conceptual analysis.

Finally, in evaluating his work, it is important to observe that the law reports indicate that practitioners used his contract treatise. It is cited in the law reports, often in response to judicial questions. This indicates that counsel carried the volume, as a form of small portable library, into court as a reference source.[147] Judicial references to his work were favourable.[148]

VI. CONCLUSIONS

Why has the importance of Martin Leake's work on contract remained so obscure and overlooked? There are a number of reasons for this relative obscurity. The first is that it takes time to persuade lawyers to consult other works once they have become familiar with a particular author and approach. Modern readers are aghast at the organisation and approach of an Addison or a Chitty, but those are the volumes and the approaches with which Victorian lawyers and judges were familiar. And for a barrister, a volume with a multiplicity of cases, to be carried into court as a small portable library, is of more use that one which sets out succinct principles at the cost of the case compendium. As we have seen, it also appears that examiners and barristers were slow to recommend Martin Leake as an introductory text. The second is that within a dozen years of his first edition, Pollock and Anson emerged with treatises based on this same concept of a scientific system of principles rather than an accretion of decided cases. Anson came to dominate the law student market and Pollock the practitioner market. In some ways, Martin Leake's very success in writing a treatise in this scientific and principled way became a weakness when others emulated the novelty of his effort.

The third reason is that Anson and Pollock were simply more effective in how their work was disseminated and how they promoted the new role of the university legal scholar. Martin Leake, it must be remembered, remained in the Hertfordshire countryside and suffering from then undiagnosed mental health issues. It seems most unlikely that he was either desirous or capable

[146] Dicey (n 63).

[147] See, eg, *Hirschfeld v The London, Brighton, and South Coast Railway Co* (1876) 2 QBD 1 (QBD) 4; *Hamlyn v Betteley* (1880) 5 CPD 327 (CPD) 329; *Ward v The National Bank of New Zealand Ltd* (1883) 8 App Cas 755 (PC) 757; *Colonial Insurance Co of New Zealand v Adelaide Marine Insurance Co* (1886) 12 App Cas 128 (PC) 130; and *Earl of Sheffield v London Joint Stock Bank Ltd* (1886) 34 Ch D 95 (CA) 104.

[148] *Moule v Garrett* (1872) LR 7 Ex 101, 104 (Cockburn CJ); *Byrne & Co v Leon Van Tienhoven & Co* (1880) 5 CPD 344 (CPD) 347 (Lindley J); *Thorn v City Rice Mills* (1889) 40 Ch D 357 (Ch D) 360 (North J).

of promoting his work in the ways that Anson and Pollock, both Oxford law professors at a critical stage in the development of English legal education, were able to promote their work and their views. Martin Leake's personal papers indicate that sales of the third edition of his work were not proceeding as well as sales of the second edition.[149] Given that his treatise now had rivals in its scientific, principled approach this is unsurprising. Pollock, as Professor Duxbury has observed, 'was centrally placed among the legal aristocracy'[150] of his day. The dedication of his *Principles of Contract* to Lord Lindley was indicative of the status he held within this legal community and the attention his work on contract law gained.[151] While *Principles of Contract* was the work of a young man, Pollock came to be enormously influential as a treatise writer, and as the editor of the Law Reports and the *Law Quarterly Review*. Martin Leake was an independent scholar insufficiently established to leave a legacy to rival Pollock's.

Anson was not as central a figure to the aristocracy of legal scholarship in his day, but he was an important intellectual figure. As an active member of the Oxford law faculty, he tutored in contract and regularly revised his treatise on the subject. His was a treatise more readily accessible to students – less encumbered with the cases necessary for a digest and providing a host of simple examples to illustrate the principles advanced. A textbook, moreover, has a powerful legacy in shaping the minds of those new to a subject.

By the end of the nineteenth century law had come to be taught in universities. Legal treatises were no longer the preserve of young barristers keen to establish themselves at the Bar. It is not surprising, then, that in the development of legal literature at this time the work of Anson and Pollock, the Oxford academics, was lauded within these new circles. When Dicey delivered his inaugural lecture 'Can English Law be Taught at the Universities' in 1883 it is unsurprising that he praised the efforts of Anson and Pollock, not Leake:

> If youthful learners are capable of gratitude there must surely be a large class of students who render daily thanks to Sir William Anson and Professor Pollock for having delivered them from the burden of Addison's ponderous confusion, and from the useless toil imposed by the attempt to understand the futile subtleties of J.W. Smith.[152]

It served Dicey's own ends to advance Pollock and Anson as the treatise writers who had first mastered the principles of English contract law.[153]

In short, the dominance of Anson and Pollock in the writing of English treatises and the conception of English contract law worked to obscure Martin

[149] HA, file DE/M1/86750.

[150] N Duxbury, *Frederick Pollock and the English Juristic Tradition* (Oxford, Oxford University Press, 2004) 20.

[151] *ibid* 188–89.

[152] Dicey (n 63) 23.

[153] *ibid* 14.

Leake's work on contract. This has persisted into the modern era. Holdsworth's identification of Pollock's work on contract and tort as 'the first books in which the principles of these branches of law were treated in a manner which was both scientific and literary'[154] was a view which was followed with little critical examination by later authors.[155] It is unlikely, though, that either man would have written contract treatises as they did without the example set by Martin Leake.

An examination of Martin Leake's life, and the era in which he lived, reveals, in one sense, a failed set of grand ambitions about the development of a particularly English jurisprudence. In another sense, though, Martin Leake's scholarship in contract law was a resounding success. He demonstrated a method by which Austinian jurisprudence could be put to use in understanding the common law. His treatise was clearly a factor in improving the study of law. It was from his pen that some of the first doctrines of modern contract law emerged. Most importantly, though, it was from his meticulous efforts that a modern conception of contract law, a law organised rationally around underlying principles, emerged. Martin Leake's science of contract law changed the way contract scholars viewed law. It is for this reason that he truly belongs amongst the scholars of contract law.

[154] W Holdsworth, *Some Makers of English Law: The Tagore Lectures, 1937–1938* (Cambridge, Cambridge University Press, 1938) 285.

[155] See, eg, HD Hazeltine, 'Sir Frederick Pollock, Bart, 1845–1937' (1949) 35 *Proceedings of the British Academy* 233; CHS Fifoot, *English Law and Its Background* (London, G Bell & Sons, 1932); and Lord Wright, 'In Memoriam: Right Hon. Sir Frederick Pollock, Bart, KC, DCL 1845–1937' (1937) 53 *LQR* 151. The result has been unduly to emphasise the originality of Pollock's scholarship: see, eg, Duxbury (n 150) 188–89.

5

Professor Sir William Anson (1843–1914)

ROBERT STEVENS

'I never liked the law nor do I now'.
William Anson, Autobiographical Fragment.[1]

'Education cannot secure success in life, but it can go a long way to make life interesting'.
William Anson, speech on the second reading of the 1902 Education Bill.

'No class of literature is more evanescent than the legal textbook'.
William Anson, obituary notice for Stephen Martin Leake.[2]

I. THE LIFE

A. Background

Anson's life was more interesting than his scholarship. In this, at least, he resembled the earlier contract lawyer Judah P Benjamin.[3]

William Reynell Anson was born in 1843, the eldest son of Sir John William Hamilton Anson and his wife Elizabeth. His father died in 1873 in a railway accident, and William inherited the baronetcy. He was educated at Eton, from where he went to Balliol to study classics, obtaining first classes in Moderations and Finals. In 1867 (after a failed first attempt in 1866) he was elected to a Fellowship at All Souls, then a different institution from the one it is today.

[1] Extracted in HH Henson (ed), *A Memoir of the Right Hon Sir William Anson* (Oxford, Clarendon Press, 1920) 18.

[2] (1894) 10 *LQR* 2, 3.

[3] Judah P Benjamin QC (1811–1884), Secretary of State for the Confederacy (1862–1865), English barrister and original author of *Benjamin's Sale of Goods*.

The All Souls Fellowship then, as now, carried with it no obligations and he departed Oxford for practice. He was called to the Bar in 1869 and was the pupil of Alfred Thesiger,[4] whose kindness and energy had a profound impact upon him: 'I have known no man whom I love better or reverence more'.[5] His practice on the Northern Circuit was undistinguished, and he considered leaving, only to be dissuaded by Thesiger.

Fortunately, his life was changed by his election to the Vinerian Readership in English Law at Oxford in 1874, in succession to Thomas Erskine Holland[6] who had held the post only briefly. He attained this without at that point any discernible achievement in the field, based upon his promise and appearing clever.[7] Although this post carried with it no residency requirement, he quit practice and returned to All Souls. Which he never left again.

B. Oxford

Prior to the 1860s, and for many years thereafter, All Souls was not a place of high academic achievement. This was a result of the bulk of its Fellows being 'Founders' Kin'. The young Anson was a reformer, but not a radical one. He was one of two representatives of the College involved in drawing up new statutes for its future. These changes required Fellowships to be either for seven years or for life, and also increased the obligations of the College to promote University education, changes disliked by the older Fellows. After this task was complete, the post of Warden became vacant in 1881. He was elected, aged 38, defeating Ernald Lane, the candidate for the conservatives (who subsequently became the Dean of Rochester). Anson was the first layman to serve as the College's Head of House. *The Times* described the College at the time as combining 'the pleasures and amenities of a well-found country house, the easy luxury of a Pall Mall club, and something, at least, though not too much, of the atmosphere of a learned society'.[8] He was to serve as Warden for the remaining 33 years of his life.

Within Oxford more generally he was to play a prominent role, a member of Council from 1884 to 1899, and an active member of many University Boards. In these roles he seems to have been an ameliorative, effective and moderate figure. He was, as so often with Heads of House, a 'College man', successfully

[4] Alfred Thesiger (1838–1880) was made a Lord Justice of Appeal in 1877, aged 39, dying in 1880 aged 42. His most famous judgments are *Household Fire and Carriage Accident Insurance Company Ltd v Grant* (1879) LR 4 Ex D 216 (CA) (the 'postal rule') and *Sturges v Bridgman* (1879) LR 11 Ch D 852 (CA) (no defence of 'coming to the nuisance').

[5] Henson (n 1) 19.

[6] Thomas Erskine Holland (1835–1926), Chichele Chair of International Law and Diplomacy (1874–1910). Holland is probably remembered today, if at all, for his work in jurisprudence rather than international law.

[7] This system of appointments was still in place in Oxford in the early 1990s for which I am personally grateful.

[8] *The Times* (4 November 1881).

opposing for example the creation of Faculty boards with the power to create 'University lectureships' for inter-Collegiate teaching.[9]

Outside of the University, he was chancellor of the diocese of Oxford (1899–1912), a fellow of Eton, chairman of the council of Oxford House in Bethnal Green,[10] trustee of the British Museum and the National Portrait Gallery, and chairman of Oxfordshire quarter sessions (1894–1914). He was elected a Fellow of the British Academy in 1902.

In 1898 he became Vice-Chancellor of the University. At that time, the post was filled by Heads of House by order of seniority. Others ahead of him in the queue had turned down the role. Anson, typically, took it on out of a sense of duty. However, he resigned the post after a few months to become one of the two MPs for the University,[11] which seat he held unopposed for 15 years until his death.

C. Law

Anson was one of the small group of men (the others being James Bryce,[12] AV Dicey,[13] Henry Maine,[14] Erwin Grueber,[15] Kenelm Digby[16] and TE Holland) that led, from around 1872 onwards, to the revival, or probably more accurately the birth, of the serious study and teaching of law at the University of Oxford. From the perspective of their impact upon the University, Anson was 'perhaps the most important figure'.[17] The lifetime achievements of this class dwarf those of any comparable collection of academic lawyers at Oxford before or since.

[9] J Howarth, 'The Edwardian Reform Movement' in MG Brock and MC Curthoys (eds), *The History of the University of Oxford: Vol VII: Nineteenth Century Oxford, Part 2* (Oxford, Oxford University Press, 2000) 837.

[10] Oxford House is a charity, established in 1884, originally set up for students and graduates of Keble College to work as volunteers to alleviate the impact of urban poverty: www.oxfordhouse.org/oxford_house_history. Anson's sister, Elizabeth, was one of the founders in 1889 of an equivalent women's refuge, St Margaret's House also in Bethnal Green: www.stmargaretshouse.org.uk.

[11] University seats for Oxford and Cambridge had been created in 1603 by James I. The voters were graduates of the Universities, whether they were resident or not. The anomaly of double representation through University seats was only finally removed in 1950.

[12] James Bryce (1838–1920), Fellow of Oriel (1862–1889), Regius Professor of Civil Law, Oxford (1870–1893), Liberal MP for South Aberdeen (1885–1907), President of the Board of Trade (1894–1895), Chief Secretary for Ireland (1905–1907), Ambassador to the United States (1907–1913); from 1914 Viscount Bryce of Dechmount. Bryce, alongside Holland, was responsible for the creation of a separate Law School, the reform of the BCL and DCL degrees, and the creation of a separate Law Board.

[13] AV Dicey (1835–1922), Vinerian Professor of English Law (1882–1909).

[14] Henry Maine (1822–1888), Fellow of Trinity Hall (1844–1861), Regius Professor of Civil Law, Cambridge (1847–1954), Council of India (1861–1869), Corpus Professor of Jurisprudence (1869–1877), Master of Trinity Hall (1877–1887), Whewell Professor of International Law (1877).

[15] Erwin Grueber (1846–1933), Reader in Roman Law, University of Oxford (1881–1893), Professor, University of Munich (1893–1933).

[16] Kenelm Digby (1836–1916), Fellow of Corpus Christi (1864–1868), Vinerian Reader in English and Civil Law (1868–1874), Permanent Under Secretary of State at the Home Office (1895–1903).

[17] B Nicholas, 'Jurisprudence' in Brock and Curthoys (n 9) 391.

After this group, the study of law in Oxford (and elsewhere) entered into a period of relative decline, from which it only really began to recover in the 1950s. Their great collective failure was that they did not succeed in training or inspiring a generation to come after them. The most able continued to choose to study classics not law,[18] and the number of judges to have studied law was negligible.

Under Anson, All Souls became ever more important for the study of law in Oxford. The Chichele Chair of Public International Law had already been created in 1859, but under Anson, the Regius and Vinerian chairs became permanently attached to the College, and the College created Readerships in English Law (1906), Roman Law (1908) and a lectureship in Private International Law (1910). This was in a period when almost all other colleges had no law fellows. Those fellows elsewhere who taught law held the post in some other capacity, such as Bursar.

On his election as Warden, Anson gave up the teaching of law for Balliol. All Souls was then, as now, a College composed of Fellows, but until 1925 it did have four undergraduate Bible Clerks. Since they were in danger of being left in isolation, Anson made a bargain whereby they would be treated as members of Trinity (particularly for purposes of sports) in return for which he would act as a tutor for Trinity's lawyers.[19] So, in 1886 he resumed teaching for Trinity College which he continued until 1898 and his election as Vice-Chancellor of the University. He provided tutorials for ten or 12 hours each week, and organised other teaching for the men. This was, at the time, very unusual. Most College teaching was done by undistinguished College lecturers who had little connection with those holding University posts. Anson seems to have thoroughly enjoyed the teaching of men in tutorials. He did it because he loved it. Indeed, he offered help to those from other Colleges who approached him.[20] He expressed profound regret at having to give up the role.[21]

He produced, and had printed, for his students a small book of light comic verse: *Ballads en Termes de la ley*[22] (he also published anonymously a number of poems in the *Oxford Magazine*). These were intended as an aide memoir for the students. A flavour of the standard of this poetry can be given.

> There are rules about breach of contract which try the legal brain,
> Yet I think I can state them clearly if your patience will stand the strain;
> For I've got it down in my note-book, in characters fair and large,
> Every breach is a cause of action, though it may not be a discharge.[23]

[18] See the plaintive valedictory lecture of J Bryce, *Legal Studies in the University of Oxford: A Valedictory Lecture Delivered Before the University, June 10, 1893* (London, Macmillan, 1893).

[19] FH Lawson, *The Oxford Law School 1850–1965* (Oxford, Clarendon Press, 1968) 76.

[20] MC Curthoys, 'The Colleges in the New Era' in Brock and Curthoys (n 9) 135.

[21] Henson (n 1).

[22] Published posthumously in 1914.

[23] 'The Ballad of the Discharge of Contract by Breach'.

Or

> Mrs Carlill is bring her action,
> And the Company surely must break;
> Yet the jurist may feel satisfaction,
> Such a fine leading case it will make.
> It's a case that quite bristles with points,
> With points that excite and enthral,
> For she's a litigious woman,
> And its's a Carbolic Smoke ball;
> Oh, she's a litigious woman,
> And it's a Carbolic Smoke ball.[24]

Whatever we think of the quality of these lines, they do enable us to have some feel for Anson the man. He was not a pompous, overly-serious, individual. Rather, he was genuinely interested in the education of the young and liked other people. Dicey's verdict was that he was 'the best teacher of English Law to be found in Oxford'.[25] The affection others had for him is apparent from the pages of the memoir published after his death by a number of those who had known him.[26] A good person for an Oxford College to have as a Head of House, or for a student to have as a tutor.

His last pupil, from 1912 onwards, was the Prince of Wales, later briefly Edward VIII, whom he instructed in the English Constitution for an hour a week. As a young man he had turned down the opportunity to act as a tutor for Kaiser Wilhelm II.[27]

The teaching of law in Oxford and elsewhere at the end of the nineteenth century was made more difficult by the absence of any textbooks. Law only became a separate School from history in 1872. Indeed, it was the historians, not the lawyers, who had insisted upon the separation. In 1875 Digby published his *History of the Law of Real Property*,[28] but this was as its title suggests a history book, reflecting the fact that in that era the focus was on teaching the history of the various areas of law. The book that truly began the modern story of student law textbooks was Anson's *Principles of the English Law of Contract and of Agency in its Relation to Contract*[29] published in 1879. This book, followed a year later by Holland's *Elements of Jurisprudence*,[30] demonstrated that law itself was capable of being taught at a University level.

[24] 'The Ballad of General Offers'.
[25] Henson (n 1) 86.
[26] *ibid.*
[27] *ibid* 38.
[28] KE Digby, *An Introduction To The History Of The Law Of Real Property* (Oxford, Clarendon Press, 1875).
[29] W Anson, *Principles of the English Law of Contract and of Agency in its Relation to Contract* (Oxford, Clarendon Press, 1879).
[30] Holland's book, and W Markby, *Elements of Law* (Oxford, Clarendon Press, 1871), ranged much more widely into the discussion of substantive law than a work of legal theory would today,

Contract had been introduced as a subject on to the Oxford law syllabus in 1877, and Anson was trying to meet the needs of his students. Contract law was at that time the only subject of the modern common law covered, the other subjects being jurisprudence, Roman law, international law, and the histories of constitutional law and that of real property. The law of torts was not introduced as a paper until 1905, nearly 30 years later, probably reflecting, and adding to, the relative disorder in which that area was and still is. The first usable textbook on torts did not appear until Salmond's in 1907. Criminal law had to wait until 1930 before being examined.

In 1884 Anson met in the rooms of Sir William Markby[31] with Bryce, Holland and Sir Frederick Pollock, where they agreed to launch the *Law Quarterly Review* with Pollock as editor. Anson sat on the editorial board, but personally contributed little to the journal (indeed, he published very little beyond his books).

D. All Souls

In the 1850s, All Souls consisted of a Warden and 40 Fellows, none of whom was under any obligation to perform any educational function, and many of whom were non-resident. Around a third were clerics. Many were the sons of peers or baronets. With no students, Fellows were recruited from other Colleges, and Anson was part of a group of men from Balliol who were eventually to change its character.

In 1852 a Royal Commission had recommended that 24 of the College's fellowships should be suspended, to be replaced by four professors funded by the money so saved.[32] The College objected, and this led to the compromise creation of two professors, and the abolition of ten fellowships. More importantly, in 1857 the 'Founders' Kin' privilege was abolished, and a condition of future fellowships that they had either won a University prize or obtained a first class in Moderations or Finals was imposed. This was to transform All Souls from being an embarrassment into being a place of academic excellence. Anson was one of the early beneficiaries of this change.

In the 1870s, the University of Oxford was increasingly subject to political scrutiny. The income of the Colleges (as today) dwarfed that of the University itself. This led to the Selborne Commission, which in turn resulted in the setting up of a Common University Fund, out of which the Colleges subsidised the University. All Souls, although at that time not a particularly wealthy College,

and in a world without student textbooks on criminal law or the law of torts, were consequently more important.

[31] Sir William Markby (1829–1914), Judge of the Calcutta High Court (1866–1878), Reader in Indian Law (1878–1890).

[32] Oxford University Commission, *Report of Her Majesty's Commissioners appointed to inquire into the State, Discipline, Studies and Revenues of the University and Colleges of Oxford* (C 1428, 1852).

had (as today) no students to drain its resources, and was required to support chairs and readerships for the University.

Although it was not Anson who transformed the finances of All Souls, which was to happen later in the twentieth century, he was a competent administrator, and personally a generous benefactor to the College. In 1882 the College had new Statutes, which fell to him to implement. Prize fellowships for life were abolished, replaced by seven-year fellowships. Non-stipendiary 'distinguished' fellowships were introduced, and once a prize fellowship had expired, those with whom it was thought useful to keep a connection were given £50 annually as a retainer. This kept an association for those who became distinguished, primarily in the law and politics. This is recognisably the system in place today.

By 1883, around one third of the College's funds were being diverted for University purposes. The agricultural depression of the 1880s and onwards hit All Souls (as other Colleges) hard, but fortunately the College owned land in London that was ripe for re-development, which occurred under Anson's period as Warden. By the time of the war, and Anson's death, the College's finances were on a secure footing.

Over time the number of clerics declined, but the social exclusivity of All Souls continued, with more peers and baronets than elsewhere. Between 1870 and 1914, 20 of the Fellowship had become MPs, including the Warden himself.

The current character and composition of All Souls, for good or ill, with the emphasis on law, history and politics, and a semi-detached connection with University education, is Anson's greatest legacy. He was the College's second founder. The College's chapel has a life-sized monument to him. Without him, more radical reform may well have been imposed from outside.

E. Women

Although considered a liberal Head of House, and in his younger days he was certainly a reformer, the admission of women to the University, and allowing them to sit examinations, put Anson on the side of the status quo. (He was also an opponent of women's suffrage.)[33] Two institutions for women's education, outside of the University, Lady Margaret and Somerville Halls, had been founded in 1879, and Anson had been one of those who had helped raise money for buildings for the former. However, women were not at that point permitted to sit University examinations. In 1884 Anson opposed the (successful) votes to allow women to sit a narrow range of the examinations open to men. Women were only allowed to sit for Jurisprudence in 1890. However, allowing the sitting of exams still did not permit women to graduate and so be awarded a degree. In 1896 Anson chaired a committee opposed to admitting women to

[33] Henson (n 1) 214.

the University, resulting in a pamphlet ironically entitled *The Due Recognition of Women by the University* with essays devoted to preserving Oxford as a sanctuary for men. The women's Halls remained private institutions unrecognised by the University until 1910. It was not until 1920 that women were finally allowed to graduate, but a cap limiting the number admitted remained in place until 1957. Anson was not opposed to the education of women at a university *per se* but believed it should be done separately, at a different institution, from that of men. Many male academics at Oxford still believed this, of course, well into the 1980s. The first woman to be elected a Fellow of All Souls was appointed in 1981.

F. Politics

Anson had stood, unsuccessfully, for election in 1880 as a Liberal candidate in West Staffordshire, but even at that point he was no follower of Gladstone, but of the more conservative Lord Hartington. In his election address he expressed his opposition to Home Rule for Ireland. In his politics he was always more Unionist than Liberal.

When in 1898 one of the two University seats fell open, he had at first resisted becoming an MP on the basis that he was now too old to make any mark in politics. Indeed, his weak speaking voice, which may also account for his lack of success at the Bar, entailed that he was not a prominent figure.[34]

He served from 1902 as Parliamentary Secretary to the Board of Education, in the Conservative government of Arthur Balfour, and took charge of seeing the Education Bill of 1902 (which he had no responsibility for drafting) through the Commons.[35] He resigned, with the Balfour government, in 1905, and after the large Liberal victory of 1906 spoke for the opposition against subsequent Liberal government education measures. He opposed both the Finance Act (1909–1910) and the Parliament Act (1911).[36] In the coronation honours of June 1911, he was recognised with membership of the Privy Council.

In a letter to *The Times* of 31 March 1914, a few months before his death, on the issue of Home Rule he came close to calling for armed resistance:

> It is idle to compare the resistance of Ulster to a strike, and if we compare the position of Ulster with that of the American Colonies, the case of Ulster is infinitely stronger.
>
> If the Covenanters meet the treatment which I have described with armed resistance, I for one believe with a conviction which no results of a Referendum or a General Election can alter, that they are justified in their resistance.

[34] 'Memoir and Appreciation' *The Times* (5 June 1914).

[35] The Education Act 1902 provided state funds for Church of England primary schools, was unpopular amongst Noncomformists, led to civil disobedience, and was partially responsible for the Liberal landslide of 1906.

[36] Removing the power of the House of Lords to block money Bills and reducing the maximum duration of Parliament from seven to five years.

> ...
>
> No Parliament is entitled to transfer a free, loyal, and law-abiding community from one form of government to another against its will.

II. THE BOOK

A. Introduction

Outside of his textbooks, Anson published relatively little.[37]

Anson's contract textbook, *Principles of the English Law of Contract*, started as an introductory primer for students, drawing heavily upon Leake's practitioners' text and Pollock's earlier book. Anson himself attributed Leake as having been the greater influence.[38] It has hardly ever been cited by a court because it is not a book aimed at practitioners.[39] (This may be a slightly unfair benchmark, as during Anson's life there was a convention against the citation of living writers.)The book's success led to US editions. Arthur L Corbin edited the third, fourth and fifth editions of the book for that market.[40] This editing work primarily involved removal of the English statutes and the addition of some US case law.

Anson himself produced the first 11 English editions of his book, handing over the editing of the 12th in 1910 to Maurice Gwyer, an All Souls Fellow.[41] Gwyer then edited five editions until its 16th in 1923. It was then taken over by James Leslie Brierly,[42] yet another Fellow of All Souls, who edited it until the 20th

[37] On private law: W Anson, 'Some Notes on Terminology in Contract' (1891) 7 *LQR* 337 (a trivial piece on judicial language); W Anson, 'Derry v Peek in the House of Lords' (1890) 6 *LQR* 72 (a casenote); W Anson, 'Assignment of Choses in Action' (1901) 17 *LQR* 90 (a misconceived piece criticising Jenks' views on the role of consideration in assignment); '*Carlisle and Cumberland Banking Co v Bragg*' (1912) 28 *LQR* 190 (a casenote). On public law: W Anson, 'Mr Pike on the House of Lords' (1895) 11 *LQR* 86 (review article); W Anson, 'The Government of Ireland Bill and the Sovereignty of Parliament' (1886) 2 *LQR* 427 (on the construction of a Bill never to be enacted); W Anson, 'Parliament and the British Constitution' (1912) 12 *Columbia Law Review* 674 (criticising Jenks' defence of the Parliament Act 1911).

[38] 'Preface' in W Anson, *Principles of the English Law of Contract*, 6th edn (Oxford, Clarendon Press, 1891).

[39] Although see *Trident General Insurance Co Ltd v McNiece Bros Pty Ltd* (1988) 165 CLR 107 (HCA) where Deane J makes use of Anson's statement that privity of contract is axiomatic to obligations based upon agreement.

[40] Published in 1919, 1924, and 1930 respectively.

[41] Maurice Gwyer (1878–1952), Vice-Chancellor of University of Delhi (1928–1950), Chief Justice of India (1937–1943), Fellow of All Souls (1902–1916).

[42] James Leslie Brierly (1881–1955), Fellow of Trinity College, Oxford (1913–1920), Professor of the University of Manchester (1920–1922), Chichele Professor of International Law (1922–1947). He edited *Anson* with JC Miles (1870–1963), Fellow of Merton for three editions from the 17th in 1929 before carrying on the work alone. Miles and Brierly were responsible for the casebook, JC Miles et al, *Cases Illustrating General Principles of the Law of Contract* (Oxford, Clarendon Press, 1923), said to have been 'begun in the lifetime of the late Sir William Anson and with his approval in the hope that it might prove a useful companion volume to his book'. The book is

edition in 1950. It was not until the 21st edition,[43] produced by Anthony Guest[44] in 1959, that the direct connection with Anson and All Souls was broken.

His contribution was of clarity, rather than of originality. Over the editions it filled out, until by the time of his death, it could be said to be a treatise. This expansion had its downsides, and Dicey recommended that the beginner search out the first edition before attempting the last. Dicey's verdict was also that Anson's contract text showed his qualities as a teacher, whereas his two-volume text on *The Law and Custom of the Constitution* (1886 and 1892) revealed his qualities as a scholar.[45] The survival of the former, and the demise of the latter, may in part be attributable to these different qualities. A clear exposition of the standard position can be carried forward by subsequent authors, whereas a more distinctive and innovative work will die with its creator. Originality is not always a virtue in writing about law. The same phenomenon was to occur in relation to Dicey's own work, where his innovative *Introduction to the Study of the Law of the Constitution*[46] had no new editions after his death, whereas his *A Digest of the Law of England With Reference to the Conflict of Laws*[47] is today the standard exhaustive practitioners' treatment (although, like Anson, little trace of his own words remain in the text). However, Dicey's work on the constitution is often cited and referred to, unlike Anson's. The explanation seems to be that Dicey stated his views on topics such as parliamentary sovereignty and the rule of law with a vividness that the more careful and qualified Anson did not employ. In his own preface, Anson stated that 'He [ie, Dicey] has done the work of an artist. I have tried to do the work of a surveyor'.

The different longevity of these books also demonstrates the need for a market (in Anson's case students, in Dicey's practitioners) regardless of the quality of the work. Perhaps it also shows how far and fast public law has changed when compared with private law, so that books from the past are of historical interest only in the former field, with new editions being relatively otiose. One of the remarkable features of reading old editions of Anson's contract book today is that so many of the cases he is employing should be familiar to students today. This may be contrasted with a book from even 50 years ago on the law of torts, which appears to us now to be an echo from a different world.

one of extracts, with no commentary. There had been earlier casebooks, but none in England has achieved the status of CC Langdell's *Selection of Cases on the Law of Contract* (Boston, Little, Brown & Co, 1871).

[43] The subject of a ludicrously unfair review by Michael Furmston (1933–2020) (1960) 23 *MLR* 206, subsequently, from 1965, the editor of *Cheshire and Fifoot's Law of Contract*.

[44] Anthony Guest (1930–), Professor, King's College London, formerly Fellow of University College, Oxford.

[45] The last edition of the first volume on Parliament by Gwyer appeared in 1922. The Scottish constitutional lawyer Arthur Berridale Keith (1879–1944) produced the fourth and last edition of the second volume on government in 1935.

[46] AV Dicey, *Introduction to the Study of the Law of the Constitution* (London, Macmillan, 1885).

[47] AV Dicey, *A Digest of the Law of England With Reference to the Conflict of Laws* (London, Stevens & Sons, 1896).

B. The Writing

Anson's text is distinguished by homely examples ('If *A* promises to paint a portrait of *X* and *X* promises to pay £100 if *M* approves the likeness – this is a contract for the sale of a chattel, the payment to depend upon a condition';[48] 'A man gets into a public omnibus at one end of Oxford Street and is carried to the other, the presence of the omnibus is a constant offer by its proprietors of such services … and the man who accepts those services promises by his acceptance to pay the fare at the end of the journey'[49]). This accessibility and simplicity does not, however, entail the dumbing down of the form that modern publishers insist upon in treating law students as infants. There are no boxes, arrows, different fonts or (heaven help us) cartoons to distract the reader. There is a lot of detail.

The writing is pithy. An example might be this defence of the postal rule.

> If *X* sends an offer to *A* by messenger with request for a written answer by bearer, is it *A's* fault of the letter of acceptance is stolen from the bearer's pocket? If *X* has asked for a verbal answer and the messenger who is to say 'yes' is struck with paralysis on the way home, it would seem unreasonable to say no contract has been made.[50]

This is writing as advocacy, regardless of whether we are convinced. This defence of the postal rule is also typical of the approach of the author. The point of the book is not to critique the results reached by the judges. We do not hear very much about the unfair results for consumers, employees, or other vulnerable parties the application of some of these rules may have. The approach is, generally, to describe and justify, not to criticise. That said, in discussing Lord Mansfield's view that in commercial contracts writing should suffice as a substitute for consideration, he acknowledged:

> The logical completeness of our law of contract as it stands at present is apt to make us think that its rules are inevitable and must have existed from all time. To such an impression the views set forth by Lord Mansfield in 1765 are a useful corrective.[51]

Absent the authority of Mansfield however, there is little acknowledgment that criticism could be made of the law as it is.

There is more history in the book than would usually be expected today. We learn how the action of trespass on the case came to be applied to breach of contract, and how assumpsit was applied by a fiction to claims *quasi ex contractu*. In later editions, there is less on the Sale of Goods Act than the importance of that statute warrants, but that is no less true of more modern texts with even less excuse.

[48] W Anson, *Principles of the English Law of Contract*, 10th edn (Oxford, Clarendon Press, 1903) 18.
[49] *ibid* 19. This seems to be a misunderstanding of how London buses worked. The passenger had to pay the conductor before reaching his destination. Anson probably never travelled on one.
[50] *ibid* 33.
[51] *ibid* 118.

C. Scope

The content of the work contains, from today's perspective, some curious inclusions and omissions.

Included are chapters on agency and assignment, now usually thought too difficult for the beginner and so cast into outer darkness (or into rag-bag books and courses called 'Commercial Law' or 'Advanced Obligations' (*sic*)). This provides one explanation for why, today, the current edition still discusses agency and assignment (albeit somewhat cursorily, omitting discussion of issues that Anson had included such as assignment by operation of law). There is a chapter on the evidential rules for the proof of a contract, that nowadays no book on contract specifically would include.

More interestingly, excluded is any discussion of the quantification of the obligation to pay damages upon breach, or any consideration of court orders. In this respect he followed other works, such as Pollock, to whose book Winfield subsequently added a brief chapter on 'Remedies for Breach of Contract' in the 12th and last edition after Pollock's death.

Anson's reasons for these exclusions, although unfashionable today, were rigorously logical. He saw his book as concerned with when legal obligations are created by agreement: contract. The legal obligations created by breach of contract (the obligation to pay damages) arises for a different reason: wrongdoing. Such obligations are 'precisely similar in kind to that which arises upon a delict'.[52] Obligation arising from court orders (injunctions, specific performance) are 'imposed upon the parties *ab extra*'. The court creates a new obligation, which may reflect a pre-existing contractual obligation, but may not (most obviously when a case is wrongly decided). In both of these cases (the obligation to pay damages, the obligation to comply with court orders compelling performance), the obligation is not arising from the agreement itself, although an agreement may (of course) be a condition of these other obligations arising. They did not therefore belong in the book.

Anson's book therefore covered the contractual relation from beginning (agreement) to end (discharge) but it did not go on to consider its afterlife or successor obligations.

Corbin, in producing his one-volume edition of his treatise aimed at students,[53] culled from his eight-volume general work, also excluded the same material, presumably reflecting what he had been teaching at Yale. (Corbin's 'abbreviated' text is still over 1,200 pages long. Whatever his other qualities, concision was not one.) In the US editions of *Anson*, Corbin had included a very brief section on remedies, omitting by far and away the most common court order in contract disputes, the action for the agreed sum, a curious invisibility in US law that continues to this day.

[52] *ibid* 8.
[53] AL Corbin, *Corbin on Contracts* (St Paul, West Publishing, 1952).

For black-hearted practical litigation lawyers, taught through the case law method, this exclusion of 'remedies' seems inexplicable. After all, it might be said, what matters at the end of a legal dispute is the order, whether for damages, the agreed sum, specific performance, or an injunction, that a court gives. Why leave out the entire point of the matter?

From the perspective of a transactions lawyer, this realist perspective is not very real at all. Most commercial parties to contracts, at least when solvent, *want* to perform them. Far more significant to them is the reputational damage of non-performance than any possible remedial order a court may award against them. The parties want to know what their obligations are in order to perform them. The disaster scenario of litigation that gets all the way to a court order being made, the world litigation lawyers (and judges) live in, is the exceptional case.

In the United States the 'realist' perspective that what really matters are court orders is reflected in Lon Fuller's casebook, *Basic Contract Law*,[54] which starts with the law of remedies. The greatest (indeed only) film dedicated to the teaching of contract law, *The Paper Chase* (1973), commences with a student (Timothy Bottoms) being humiliated at Harvard by Professor Charles Kingsfield (John Houseman) for the failure to read the first case assigned. That case is *Hawkins v McGee*[55] ('the hairy hand' case on damages at the start of Fuller's book) which reflects the experience of John Jay Osborn Jr, the author of the novel on which the film is based, showing how the contract course was being taught in the late 1960s.

Similarly in England today, although it would be very unusual to consider remedies at the outset, no book (or course) would follow Anson (and Pollock) in excluding remedies altogether.

However, there was not only logic but pedagogical sense behind the earlier approach. In principle it would make sense to have separate books and courses on the quantification of damages for wrongdoing, and on the distinct issue of when courts will make orders. Some of the issues raised in relation to these matters are specific to the contractual context, but many are not. One example is the common erroneous belief that the principle governing the quantification of damages for wrongdoing differs between breach of contract ('the expectation measure'), torts ('the reliance measure') and equitable wrongdoing (who knows?) when in fact it is identical (an obligation to put the plaintiff in as close to the position as if the wrong had not occurred as can be obtained through the payment of money). It is not obviously correct that we are wiser than our predecessors.

By contrast, Anson includes discussion of voluntarily assumed obligations that are not contractual because they are not supported by consideration,

[54] LL Fuller, *Basic Contract Law* (St Paul, West Publishing, 1947).
[55] *Hawkins v McGee* 146 A 641 (NH 1929).

exemplified in his day by *Wilkinson v Coverdale*[56] and today by *Hedley Byrne & Co Ltd v Heller & Partners Ltd*.[57] Discussion of these rules makes more sense within a book on contract than torts, as they have very little family relation to the law concerning car accidents, false imprisonment, and the like.

The book covers neither the conditions of certainty nor that of 'intention to create legal relations'. The explanation as to why not is that both of these rules concern the enforceability of a contract, and not its validity. Anson was concerned with the latter, and not the former. Later English books were to put 'intention to create legal relations' upfront as a condition of there being a contract. By contrast, the rule has never been thought to apply in the United States, Corbin considering it 'erroneous',[58] although his objection to it was based upon the misconception that it concerned the actual subjective intentions of the parties, as opposed to whether as a matter of construction the meaning of the agreement was to create legal obligations.

Anson also includes a brief section on *quasi-contract*, such as the obligations created by a judgment debt, claims for contribution by one of several co-debtors who has paid the entirety of a debt, or the mistaken payment of a sum of money not owing. However he makes it quite clear that these claims are not contractual, and that they are included because of their historical relation to claims based upon agreement.

D. Theory

Anson is careful to distinguish obligations arising from agreement from those that do not. This emphasis on contracts being enforceable *agreements*[59] (ie, dependent upon an offer and an acceptance) may be contrasted with the current edition, which instead places the emphasis on contract being the law of *promises* (a wider category than agreement) whilst failing to specify when, absent an agreement, a contract arises.

He followed Pollock in paying lip service to Savigny's 'will' theory of contract law, the idea the obligation was created by a meeting of the parties' minds.[60] He also followed Pollock in implausibly defining promise to mean agreement, so as to accord with this theory. Savigny's Vulcan mind-meld theory was adopted *faute de mieux*.

[56] *Wilkinson v Coverdale* (1793) 1 Esp 75, 170 ER 284.

[57] *Hedley Byrne & Co Ltd v Heller & Partners Ltd* [1964] AC 465 (HL).

[58] Corbin (n 53) 34.

[59] See also E Peel, *Treitel's The Law of Contract*, 15th edn (London, Sweet & Maxwell, 2020) 1.

[60] See also *Haynes v Haynes* (1861) 1 DR & SM 426, 432; 62 ER 425, 445: 'when both parties will the same thing, and each communicated his will to the other, with a mutual engagement to carry it into effect, then (and not until then) an agreement or contract between the two is constituted' (Kindersley VC).

TE Holland in his *Elements of Jurisprudence* criticised Savigny's theory in the following way:

> Must there be, as Savigny puts it, 'a union of several wills to a single whole and undivided will'? Or should we rather say that here more even than elsewhere, the law looks, not at the will itself, but at the will as voluntarily manifested? When the law enforces contracts, it does so to prevent disappointment of well-founded expectations, which although they usually arise from expressions truly representing intention, yet may occasionally arise otherwise.
>
> If, for instance, one of the parties to a contract enters into it, and induces the other party to enter into it, resolved all the while not to perform his part under it, the contract will surely be good nevertheless.[61]

Although in one edition Anson tried to respond to Holland's objections, by arguing that the law necessarily adopted a fiction by barring the proof of the contrary intention, in subsequent editions he confined the discussion to a brief footnote.[62] It seems likely that it was Holland's objections, in combination with those of Holmes, that led to Pollock down-playing Savigny's theory. In later editions of his own work Holland acknowledged this shift when he said:

> This view opposed as it is to the current authority of Sir F Pollock and Sir W Anson was originally put forward with some diffidence. It is now restated with more confidence, since English friends who were at first decidedly opposed to it are converts to its truth.[63]

As a matter of judicial authority of course, Holland's view had been earlier authoritatively stated by Blackburn J in *Smith v Hughes*[64] in 1871.

Corbin adopted the same 'induced expectations' view as Holland in his definition: 'That portion of the field of law that is classified and described as the law of contracts attempts the realization of reasonable expectation that have been induced by the making of a promise'.[65]

Holland's influence upon Corbin is clear in his early work.[66]

By the penultimate edition of his own book, Holland had adopted a *proto*-reliance theory to explain the objective approach.

> The question in these case should always be: was the expression of one party such as should fairly have induced the other to act upon it? If so but not otherwise, it is in the interests of society that the loss should fall upon the other.[67]

[61] TE Holland, *Elements of Jurisprudence*, 2nd edn (Oxford, Clarendon Press, 1882) 194–95.

[62] W Anson, *Principles of the English Law of Contract*, 2nd edn (Oxford, Clarendon Press, 1882) 9–13.

[63] TE Holland, *Elements of Jurisprudence*, 12th edn (Oxford, Clarendon Press, 1917) 261.

[64] *Smith v Hughes* (1871) LR 6 QB 597 (QBD).

[65] Corbin (n 53) 2.

[66] AL Corbin, 'Offer and Acceptance' (1917) 3 *Yale Law Journal* 169, 205.

[67] Holland (n 63) 265.

And so the stage was already set before the First World War, for the later twentieth century debate between two blind men, will and reliance theorists, as to who it was who could really see.

In practice Anson did not let the (implausible) will theory get in the way of his account of the law. He had no difficulty, for example, in defending privity of contract as axiomatic on the basis that agreement-based rights could only be acquired by those who are a party to the agreement, regardless of what may have been intended by the various parties as a matter of psychological fact.

OW Holmes's theory that what matters, and matters only, is whether or not a court will make an order against a particular defendant was given satisfactory short shrift: 'I cannot think it desirable to push legal analysis so far as to disregard altogether the aspect in which men view their business transactions'.[68]

Because the theoretical basis of contractual obligations gives Anson such little concern, such consideration as he does give the issue is not allowed to get in the way of accurately stating the positive law. The doctrine of consideration is simply and clearly stated, with the relevant exceptions (eg, negotiable instruments, the undertaking of a gratuitous service although not enforceable as a contract does give rise to liability for harm through a failure to use due care) simply listed. No attempt is made to justify these and other rules as a matter of principle.

E. Substance

Reading Anson today, what is most striking is how much he gets right. It might be thought that this is because, being first, he wrote the book upon which all others are based, shaping the understanding of the law of modern readers. Other contemporary writers are however much easier to criticise.

The chapter on assignment is unfortunately weak, reflecting a more general failure to understand the nature of equitable rights, and why equity could permit 'assignment' when the common law could not. This leads to a more general failure to understand that statutory assignment (which involves a transfer of rights) differs fundamentally from equitable assignment (which is closer to a trust, which involves no transfer). These different forms of 'assignment' then give rise to different rules (eg, does the debtor need to have notice? Is there a formality requirement? Is consideration necessary? Are multiple assignments possible?). It is probably too harsh to criticise Anson for these failures however as so few modern writers seem aware of the justification for the differences. Perhaps the failure of Anson just carries on into other works.

Similarly, the chapter on 'discharge by breach' too often runs together the issues of when one party's obligation to perform is conditional with the question

[68] Anson (n 48) 9.

of breach of contract. The difficulties of separating out the different senses of condition, and what it is we mean by 'discharge for breach', have bedevilled subsequent English contract writers, which has lacked its Corbin who took a more principled approach to the different ideas. Perhaps it is here where the decision to exclude remedies altogether from consideration has had its worst consequence.

F. Legacy

Until the publication of Cheshire and Fifoot's text in 1945, the only serious competition to Anson was Pollock's far less readable work.[69] The first edition of *Treitel* appeared in 1962. (The preface to the first edition of *Treitel* justifies the book's existence on the basis that it gives more consideration to the cases concerning carriage of goods by sea than did previous work.[70] It is unfortunately impossible to imagine any new contract text today seeking to explain itself in a similar way.)

Today the English market is completely different, indeed saturated with medium sized textbooks aimed at students.[71] These are often produced in frequent new editions in order to stop students 'wasting' their money on the marginally different older second-hand editions, something legal publishers can justify because of the small changes that occur because of new case law.

One reason for this development is economic. A lot more students now study law each year. Contract is a compulsory subject for purposes of qualification. A successful student text will make money. A single publisher, in an attempt to grab as much of the market for itself as it can, today lists the publication of 15 contract texts, including nutshells and works of cases and commentaries. Few, if any of these books, would ever be cited in court or used by a practitioner. Books

[69] AT Carter (1861–1946), Student of Christ Church (1886–1926), had produced *Elements of the Law of Contract* (1902), which was clear and nicely written but the equivalent of a modern day 'nutshell'. It went through seven editions, the last in 1931. FH Lawson, in his otherwise institution promoting volume, *The Oxford Law School 1850–1965* states that Carter was a 'sinister and ambiguous figure' ((n 19) 106). He 'developed the habit of systematically neglecting all his pupils except the very few who, for some reason or other, interested him … Many stories were once current about his malicious wit, commonly directed against helpless butts'. 'Obituary' *The Times* (31 July 1946), although much more positive, is entirely consistent with this verdict.

[70] GH Treitel, *The Law of Contract* (London, Stevens & Sons, 1962).

[71] N Andrews, *Contract Law*, 2nd edn (Cambridge, Cambridge University Press, 2015); TT Arvind, *Contract Law*, 2nd edn (Oxford, Oxford University Press, 2019); M Chen-Wishart, *Contract Law*, 6th edn (Oxford, Oxford University Press, 2018); PS Davies, *JC Smith's The Law of Contract*, 3rd edn (Oxford, Oxford University Press, 2021); E Macdonald and R Atkins, *Koffman & Macdonald's Law of Contract*, 9th edn (Oxford, Oxford University Press, 2018); E McKendrick, *Contract Law*, 13th edn (Oxford, Oxford University Press, 2019); R Merkin and S Saintier, *Poole's Textbook on Contract Law*, 15th edn (Oxford, Oxford University Press, 2021); J O'Sullivan, *O'Sullivan & Hilliard's The Law of Contract*, 9th edn (Oxford, Oxford University Press, 2020); R Stone and J Devenney, *The Modern Law of Contract*, 13th edn (London, Routledge, 2019). This list could be added to by including 'nutshell' guides.

such as these are also rarely the subject of serious reviews in journals, so it is hard for students to tell which are good and which are not. There is a market failure here, with the good lost amidst the bad. Few of us who are interested in the law of contract will ever read these books from cover to cover, so that what is good in them will not be known to a wider audience.

It is interesting to contrast the market in the United States, where student textbooks, such as Anson, are almost unknown today. Instead, there are lengthy treatises (by Corbin and Farnsworth), the *Restatement*, casebooks (with considerable commentary) and 'nutshells'.

When I first studied law, more than 30 years ago, I was banned from using *Anson*, which was considered insufficiently detailed. We were permitted to use *Treitel*, with the only acceptable alternative being *Chitty*. Few students would follow such restrictions today. However, modern day students could do worse than start, as Dicey advised, with the first edition of *Anson*, and then proceed to read the subsequent statutes and cases to work out what has happened over the last 140 years. Studying law is about acquiring the strengths of a skilled lawyer, and you can only achieve that by reading the primary legal materials. Reading a digested account by an academic might enable you to pass an exam, but it will not help you gain intellectual muscle mass.

III. CONCLUSION

Even at this distance, and whatever his flaws, William Anson is easy to like. Without dedicated people, institutions such as the University of Oxford, its Law Faculty and All Souls, would not thrive. He had a genuine love of teaching, which he did on a voluntary basis.

That his name lives on, at least in England, through the textbook that carries his name, is a result of his being a pioneer. Other books (such as Pollock's) are now no longer read. This is partly the result of the clarity, which created a brand name based upon quality, that it made commercial sense to keep alive. It is also attributable to Anson's handing over the production of the text to Gwyer during his lifetime and allowing the latter to change it as he saw fit. After Pollock's death, his words were treated by his subsequent editors as unalterable Holy Writ speeding the books into history. Senior living authors are often far more precious about their work than was Anson.

It is also partially just luck. If Professor Anthony Guest, after a gap of nine years, had not produced a new edition in 1959 it seems unlikely that it would have been revived. There was an even longer gap between the last edition produced by Guest, the 26th, in 1984, and the 27th by Sir Jack Beatson in 1998. The current 31st edition has the most impressive list of authors of almost any student text.[72] It may be wondered how many student textbooks in any

[72] In addition to Beatson, Lord Burrows and Professor John Cartwright.

discipline are still being published so many years after the first.[73] However, none of Anson's original text survives in the current edition.

Those of us who think we might achieve immortality through our scholarship alone should learn a lesson from Anson's life. The Anson Reading Room in All Souls is named after him because of his service, not his brilliance. He influenced more people through his teaching and friendship than any of us can by a dozen articles in leading journals. There are probably more extant portraits of him than for anybody else in this volume.

Anson 'was a short, rather neat man, clear-headed, witty and always considerate'.[74] A lifelong bachelor, his sisters Elizabeth, Florence and Gertrude lived with him in the Warden's lodgings, acting as hostesses for all his long tenure. In June 1914 Anson died at All Souls, with his surviving sisters by his side. He is buried in Holywell cemetery.

[73] Within law, there are older practitioners' texts still being updated (eg, JF Archbold, *Archbold Criminal Pleading, Evidence and Practice*, (London, Pheney, Sweet and Millikin, 1822)). Outside law, H Gray, *Gray's Anatomy*, (London, JW Parker & Son, 1858); S Standing (ed), *Gray's Anatomy*, 42nd edn (Elsevier, 2020) has a longer history of being updated as a student text.

[74] Sir George Clark, quoted by Lawson (n 19) 78.

6

Professor Sir Frederick Pollock (1845–1937)

JAMES GORDLEY

I. INTRODUCTION

IN THE EIGHTEENTH century, literature on the common law of contract amounted to little more than a few pages in Blackstone's *Commentaries on the Laws of England* and the reports of decided cases.[1] The decided cases themselves did not concern what we call contract law but the scope of the common law writs of covenant and assumpsit. The common lawyers systematised their law in the nineteenth century, drawing extensively on continental authors.[2] Sir Frederick Pollock played a key role. As he acknowledged, he borrowed from the great German jurist Friedrich Carl von Savigny, who tried to explain the Roman law still in force in much of Germany by a small number of carefully defined concepts. Pollock tried to do the same for the common law. His work shaped the way we still define such basic concepts as contract, consideration and consent. It was also responsible for the problems we still face in using these concepts to understand the law of contract. Some of these problems arise because of the difficulty reconciling them with the common law cases. Others arise from the very attempt to explain law by a small number of carefully defined concepts.

Pollock was educated at Eton and Trinity College, Cambridge, and called to the Bar by Lincoln's Inn in May 1871. His grandfather, Sir Jonathan Frederick Pollock, had been Lord Chief Baron of the Exchequer. His cousin, Lord Hanworth, formerly Sir Ernest Murray Pollock, was Master of the Rolls. He seemed destined for legal practice, which he found he did not like. If he had then been offered the chance of 'returning to Cambridge and the classics',

[1] AWB Simpson, 'Innovation in Nineteenth Century Contract Law' (1975) 91 *LQR* 247, 250–51.
[2] J Gordley, *The Jurists: A Critical History* (Oxford, Oxford University Press, 2013) 204–12.

he said that 'it might have been hard to resist'.[3] Then, as his biographer Neil Duxbury described, his life was changed through the influence of three men with whom he worked closely.[4] One was Nathaniel Linley, a fellow practitioner who had written a *Treatise on the Law of Partnership*,[5] from whom Pollock said, 'I learnt that law is neither a trade nor a solemn jugglery but a science'.[6] The second was James Shaw Willes, a Justice of Common Pleas, whom he described to his friend Oliver Wendell Holmes as 'a man of profound learning in the law ... whose knowledge is radiant and kindles answering fire'.[7] The third was James Bryce, a fellow barrister who shared his love of mountaineering, who advised him to study Roman law by reading the works of Savigny, which he did with enthusiasm.[8] Pollock maintained close relations all his life with practising lawyers. He was Editor-in-Chief of the Law Reports from 1895 to 1935. In his academic work, however, he drew on Savigny and an extensive knowledge of the decided cases to present the common law of property, tort and contract as a science which explained the law by carefully defined concepts.

Before the nineteenth century, common lawyers thought in terms of writs rather than categories such as contracts or torts. To obtain relief, the plaintiff needed to bring his case within the appropriate writ. The writs were originally established to determine which cases could be heard in the king's courts. A plaintiff whose case did not fall within a writ might be deserving of relief but he should seek it elsewhere: for example, in a manorial court, ecclesiastical court, admiralty court or merchants' court. The scope of each writ was determined by a constellation of cases decided by common law judges. There was no law of contract, tort and property as we think of them today. There were writs of covenant, assumpsit, trespass in assault and battery, trespass to land (*quare clausem fregit*), trespass to chattels (*de bonis asporatis*), ejectment, and so forth. In the nineteenth century, common lawyers began to develop a systematic body of doctrine to explain the scope of these writs. They drew on civil law. A leading role was played by treatise writers and the foremost among them was Pollock.

He wrote one of the first systematic treatises on the law of torts. In civil law, the defendant was liable for fault: he acted intentionally or negligently.

[3] F Pollock, *For My Grandson: Remembrances of an Ancient Victorian* (London, Murray, 1933) 161–62, quoted in N Duxbury, *Frederick Pollock and the English Juristic Tradition* (Oxford, Oxford University Press, 2004) 21.

[4] Duxbury (n 3) 21–23.

[5] N Lindley, *A Treatise on the Law of Partnership Including its Application to Joint-Stock and other Companies* (London, William Maxwell, 1860).

[6] Pollock (n 3) quoted in Duxbury (n 3) 22.

[7] F Pollock, *Treatise on the Law of Torts: A Treatise on the Principles of Obligations Arising from Civil Wrongs in the Common Law* (London, Stevens & Sons, 1887) vii, quoted in Duxbury (n 3) 22.

[8] Duxbury (n 3) 23.

At common law, a plaintiff suing for trespass did not allege that the defendant was at fault, and there were only a few reported cases in which the defendant pled that because he was not at fault he was not liable. In those cases, the remarks of the judges are confusing and apparently contradictory. Some said that the defendant was not liable if he had done his best,[9] some said that he was,[10] and some said he could escape liability if his conduct was the product of 'unavoidable necessity'.[11] As CHS Fifoot said, '"[f]ault," "inevitable accident," "negligence" are words used indiscriminately without reflection and almost without meaning'.[12]

Pollock claimed that liability for 'personal wrongs' as in battery, assault, false imprisonment, slander and libel, liability is imposed 'generally speaking' when the wrong is 'wilful or wanton'. 'Either the act is intended to do harm, or, being an act evidently likely to cause harm, it is done with reckless indifference to what may befall by reason of it'.[13] In contrast, in torts such as nuisance and negligence, the defendant is generally held liable for 'negligence', that is 'for a failure to observe due care and caution'.[14] In these respects, 'the Roman conception of delict agrees very well with the conception that appears really to underlie the English law of tort'.[15] Powell's approach was seconded in 1891, in *Stanley v Powell*,[16] when the Court held that the absence of negligence was a defence in an action of trespass.

[9] See, eg, *The Thorns Case* (1466) YB 6 Edw 4, Mich fol 7 pl 18 (Choke CJ: 'As to what has been said that they [thorns] fell ipso invito [on another's land], this is not a good plea; but he should have said that he could not do it in any other manner or that he did all that was in his power to keep them out'); *Mitten v Faudrye* (1626) Pop 161, 161–62; 79 ER 1259, 1260 (excusing the defendant because he 'did his best endeavor'); *Wakeman v Robinson* (1823) 1 Bing 213, 215; 130 ER 86, 87 (Dallas CJ: 'If the accident happened entirely without default on the part of the defendant or blame imputable to him, the action does not lie …').

[10] See, eg, *The Thorns Case* (n 9) (Littleton J: 'If a man suffers damage, it is right that he be recompensed'); *Bessey v Olliot* (1682) YB 34 Car 2, Raym Sir T 467, 467 (Sir Thomas Raymond: 'In all civil acts the law doth not so much regard the intent of the actor as the loss and damage of the party suffering …'); *Leame v Bray* (1803) 3 East 593, 600; 102 ER 724, 727 (Grose J: '[I]f the injury be done by the act of the party himself at the time or he be the immediate cause of it, though it happen accidentally or by misfortune, yet he is answerable in trespass').

[11] *Dickenson v Watson* (1682) T Jones 205, 205; 84 ER 1218, 1219 (holding that the defendant who had shot the plaintiff and pleaded accident was not excused 'for in trespass the defendant shall not be excused without unavoidable necessity').

[12] CHS Fifoot, *History and Sources of the Common Law: Tort and Contract* (London, Stevens & Sons, 1949) 191 speaking of *Weaver v Ward* (1616) Hobart 134, 134; 80 ER 284, 284, in which the Court said that the defendant was liable even though he was not at fault but he would not be if he were 'utterly without fault', if the accident were 'inevitable', and if he 'had committed no negligence to give occasion to the hurt'.

[13] F Pollock, *The Law of Torts: A Treatise on the Principles of Obligations Arising from Civil Wrongs in the Common Law*, 8th edn (London, Stevens & Sons, 1908) 9.

[14] *ibid* 11, 18.

[15] *ibid* 17.

[16] *Stanley v Powell* [1891] 1 QB 86 (QBD).

In property law, a basic civil law distinction is between ownership and possession. In nineteenth century Germany, there was an famous debate between Savigny and Rudolf von Jhering as to why possession was protected since, by definition, ownership is a right and possession is not.[17] In granting writs of ejectment, the English courts had never been clear about whether they were protecting ownership or possession until the Court of Queen's Bench decided *Asher v Whitlock* in 1865.[18] In that case, the Court allowed a prior possessor to recover land to which it was clear he did not have title. In a series of prior cases, the courts had allowed the possessor to recover, saying that the plaintiff's prior possession was evidence of title.[19]

Pollock resolved the dispute between Savigny and Jhering by saying that possession 'is a kind of title'.[20] '[W]e treat the actual possessor not only as legal possessor but as owner, as against everyone who cannot show a better right …'.[21] Pollock believed that his solution best explained both Roman law and common law.[22] Contemporary English treatises use Pollock's theory to explain the common law. The common law has 'no such concept as absolute title'.[23] The owner has a right that is good against all the world and the possessor has a right that is good against everyone except the true owner.[24]

At common law, a plaintiff could recover for a broken promise in covenant, if the promise had been made under seal, or in assumpsit, if it had consideration. There was no principle or definition fixing the meaning of promise or consideration.

[17] FC von Savigny, *Das Recht des Besitzes Eine Zivilistische Abhandlung*, 7th edn, (Aaalen, Scientia Verlag, 1990), § 6; Rudolf Jhering, *Ueber den Grund des Besitzschutzes*, 2nd edn (Jena, Mauke, 1869) 45–46, 54–55.

[18] *Asher v Whitlock* (1865) 1 LR 1 QB.

[19] The principle was laid down by Lord Holt at the end of the 17th century. He said that 20 years of possession raised a presumption that the plaintiff had title. *Stokes v Berry* (1699) 2 Salk 421, 91 ER 366. In 1777, Lord Mansfield repeated Holt's rule but paradoxically allowed a plaintiff to recover who could not prove possession for that length of time: *Denn ex dem Tarzwell v Barnard* (1777) Cowp 595, 98 ER 1259. In 1829, in *Doe dem Hughes v Dyeball*, the plaintiff won by proving that after he had been in possession a year and that the 'defendant had forcibly taken possession': *Doe dem Hughes v Dyeball* (1829) M & M 345, 173 ER 1184. The Court did not explain whether he won because he had possession or because possession was regarded as evidence of title. In 1841, a jury was instructed that it could find that the plaintiff had title since he had been in possession, although for less than 20 years: *Doe dem Humphrey v Martin* (1841) Carr & M 32, 174 ER 395.

[20] F Pollock and RS Wright, *An Essay on Possession in the Common Law* (Oxford, Clarendon Press, 1888) 19. Pollock wrote Parts I and II and Wright wrote Part III.

[21] F Pollock, *A First Book of Jurisprudence for Students of the Common Law* (London, Macmillan, 1896) 172.

[22] *ibid* 179.

[23] R Megarry and W Wade, *The Law of Real Property*, 6th edn by C Harpum (London, Sweet & Maxwell, 2000) para 3–122.

[24] B McFarlane, *The Structure of Property Law* (Oxford, Hart Publishing, 2008) para 1.4; FH Lawson and B Rudden, *The Law of Property*, 3rd edn (Oxford, Oxford University Press, 2002) 65.

An increasing number of treatise writers regarded these writs as constituting a common law of contract. The first treatise on the common law of contract was written by John J Powell in 1790,[25] followed by William Taylor (1849),[26] and, in the United States, by Samuel Comyn (1809),[27] William Wentworth Story (1851)[28] and Theophilus Parsons (1860).[29] One of the first truly systematic treatises was written by Stephen Leake in 1867.[30] One task of the treatise writers was to explain the meaning of promise and consideration.

In Pollock's treatise on contract, published in 1876,[31] contract law acquired a form that is familiar to us. He borrowed extensively from continental jurists and principally, as he said himself, from Savigny. Pollock's object was to use the ideas that he borrowed to explain the common law of contracts as it was to be found in the decisions of English courts. He achieved a synthesis which was less doctrinaire that that of Savigny and more sophisticated than earlier common law writers.

II. PROMISE

At common law, promises could be enforced in covenant or assumpsit. As Brian Simpson noted, the conception of promise was one-sided: what mattered was whether a promise had been made and then broken. It became two-sided in the nineteenth century: contract required the assent of two or more parties.[32]

Pollock played a leading role in this transformation. He began the later editions of his treatise by stating crisply: 'Every agreement and promise enforceable by law is a contract'.[33] An 'agreement' is 'an act in the law whereby two or more parties declare their consent as to any act or thing to be done or forborne by some or one of those persons for the use of others'.[34] A 'promise' is '[t]he declaration of any person of his intention to do or forbear anything at the request or for the use of another'.[35]

[25] JJ Powell, *Essay upon the Law of Contracts* (London, J Johnson and T Whieldon, 1790).

[26] WJ Taylor, *A Treatise on the Differences between the Law of England and Scotland Relating to Contracts* (Edinburgh, T & T Clark, 1849).

[27] S Comyn, *A Treatise of the Law Relative to Contracts and Agreements Not Under Seal* (Flatbush, Isaac Riley, 1809).

[28] WW Story, *A Treatise on the Law of Contracts* (Boston, Little, Brown & Co, 1851).

[29] T Parsons, *The Law of Contracts*, 4th edn (Boston, Little, Brown & Co, 1860).

[30] SM Leake, *Elements of the Law of Contract* (London, Stevens & Sons, 1867).

[31] F Pollock, *Principles of Contract at Law and in Equity, Being a Treatise on the General Principles Concerning the Validity of Agreements, with a Special View to the Comparison of Law and Equity, and with References to the Indian Contract Act, and Occasionally to Roman, American, and Continental Law* (London, Stevens & Sons, 1876).

[32] Simpson (n 1).

[33] F Pollock, *Principles of Contract: Being a Treatise on the General Principles Concerning the Validity of Agreements in the Law of England*, 4th edn (London, Stevens & Sons, 1885) 1.

[34] *ibid.*

[35] *ibid.*

The reason Pollock spoke of 'agreement and promise', rather than merely 'agreement', was to bring promises that were enforceable in covenant within his definition of contract. 'Under English law, promises are binding even without mutual assent if they are made under seal'. 'In practice,' however, mutual consent or 'proposal and acceptance' are 'the normal and most important elements' of 'the general conception of contract'.[36]

We still define contract in much the same way. According to Edwin Peel, 'A contract is an agreement giving rise to obligations which are enforced or recognised by law'.[37] '[A]n agreement is made when one party accepts an offer made by the other'.[38] 'An offer is an expression of willingness to contract on specified terms, made with the intention that it shall become binding as soon as it is accepted by the person to whom it is addressed'.[39]

According to the *Restatement (Second) of the Law of Contracts* of the American Law Institute: 'A contract is a promise or a set of promises for the breach of which the law gives a remedy, or the performance of which the law in some way recognises as a duty'.[40] 'A promise is a manifestation of intention to act or refrain from acting in a specified way, so made as to justify a promisee in understanding that a commitment has been made'.[41] 'An agreement is a manifestation of mutual assent on the part of two or more persons'.[42]

Peel and the *Restatement (Second)* explain, at a later point, that promises under seal are binding without an acceptance.[43] That much survives of what Simpson called the 'one-sided' conception of contract.

The two-sided conception was a child of civil law. Roman law, as has often been noted, did not have a law of contract, but rather a law of particular contracts, or, more accurately, a law of particular agreements (*pacta, conventiones*). 'Elegantly', according to Ulpian, Pedius said that 'there is no contract, no obligation, that does not have within in an agreement (*conventio*) whether it is formed *re* or *verbis*'[44] by delivery or by words. Even *stipulatio*, which was a formal contract obligating only the promisor, was formed when he answered the question 'Do you promise such-and-such?' when asked by the promisee. Texts dealing with a one-sided promise concerned the peculiarly Roman institution of *pollicitatio*. A citizen would promise to make a gift or confer some benefit on a city. The promise was enforceable without an acceptance.[45]

[36] *ibid* 9.

[37] E Peel, *Treitel's The Law of Contract*, 15th edn (London, Sweet & Maxwell, 2020) para 1-001.

[38] *ibid* para 2-001.

[39] *ibid* para 2-002.

[40] *Restatement (Second) of the Law of Contracts* (Philadelphia, American Law Institute, 1981) § 1.

[41] *ibid* § 2(a1).

[42] *ibid* § 3.

[43] Peel (n 37) para 3-172 (adding that therefore '[t]he binding force of such a promise does not depend on contract at all'); *Restatement (Second) of the Law of Contracts* (n 40) § 95(2) (a promise under seal is binding even if the promisee does not 'manifest assent' as long as the 'document' is 'delivered').

[44] D.2.14.1.3.

[45] D.50.12.3.

Before Pollock wrote, Leake had tried less successfully to marry the one-sided conception of the common law writs to the two-sided conception of the Roman *pacta*. He began with the Roman principle that an obligation (*obligatio*) arises from a *pactum*, which he translated as 'agreement'. 'Agreement', he said, 'consists of two persons being of the same mind concerning the matter agreed upon'.[46] He then defined 'promise' to require mutual assent:

> In an agreement as the source of a legal contract, the matter agreed upon must import that one party shall be bound to the other in some act or performance which the latter shall have a legal right to enforce. The signification of the intent to do some act, or observe some particular course of conduct, made by one party to the other, *and accepted by him*, for the purpose of creating a right to its accomplishment is called a promise.[47]

His definition passed into the India Contract Act of 1872, which provided:

> a) When one person signifies to another his willingness to do or to abstain from doing anything, with a view to obtaining the assent of that other to such act or abstinence, he is said to make a proposal.
>
> b) When the person to whom the proposal is made signifies his assent thereto, the proposal is said to be accepted. A proposal when accepted becomes a promise ....

His attempt to define promise in terms of agreement was forced. Pollock pointed out that 'a promise, in the ordinary sense of the word, must be made before there is any acceptance of it by the person to whom it is made ...'.[48] Moreover, it did not fit English law in which a promise made under seal is binding without mutual consent. 'Certainly', Pollock said,

> this doctrine is of an archaic and technical kind, resting as it does more on the formal character of a deed than on any principle of general application; and possibly, or more than possibly, its expediency is doubtful. But it is a settled part of the law of England.[49]

According to Neil Duxbury, the exception for promises under seal illustrates Pollock's 'reluctance to embrace generalizations'.[50] It illustrates the difficulties of remaining consistent while fitting the one-sided conception of the traditional common law to the two-sided conception Pollock took from continental authors.

[46] Leake (n 30) 8.
[47] *ibid* 9 (emphasis in the original).
[48] Pollock (n 33) 6.
[49] *ibid*.
[50] Duxbury (n 3) 201–202.

In the first edition of his work, Pollock acknowledged that he was breaking new ground. He began by observing that '[i]t is somewhat curious that no such thing as a satisfactory definition of Contract is to be found in any of our books'.[51] He was frank about the source of his own definition. He was borrowing from Savigny.

> Considering the amount of coincidence (if not more than coincidence) between English and Roman law in the main principles of Contract, I have felt justified in making a pretty free use of the Roman law for purposes of illustration and analogy. … On points of Roman law (and to a considerable extent, indeed, on the principles it has in common with our own), I have consulted and generally followed Savigny's great work.[52]

For Savigny, a basic concept was that of a *Willenserklärung*, a declaration of will or intention. A declaration of will directed to producing legal consequences is a *Rechtsgeschäft*[53] – a word that has no English equivalent but is often translated as a 'legal transaction' or 'act in law'. A *Vertrag*, which Pollock translated as 'agreement in its widest sense',[54] is constituted by the declarations of intention of more than one party. Their declarations must match each other (*übereinstimmen*).[55] Pollock said, paraphrasing Savigny, the 'intention of the parties' is 'directed to legal consequences; and … those consequences must be such as to confer rights or impose duties on the parties themselves'.[56] He quoted Savigny in a footnote: '*in diesem, der Wille auf ein Rechtsverhältniss als Zweck gerichtet ist, in jenen Fällen auf andere Zwecke*' – 'in these, the will is directed as its purpose to a legal relationship, and in those to other purposes'. Pollock acknowledged that 'the want of an English equivalent for *Rechtsverhältniss* has made some circumlocution unavoidable in the text.'[57]

For Pollock, these concepts had to be adapted to fit the promises enforceable in covenant and assumpsit. As he noted, *Vertrag* or 'agreement' included '[n]ot only contract, but every sort of conveyance'.[58] Pollock explained that in Roman law, an agreement (*pactum*) could create an obligation (*obligatio*). 'A promise accordingly is an agreement which produces an obligation'.[59] He noted:

> The distinction is this: the case of a contract something remains to be done by one or by each of the parties, which the other has or will have a right to call upon him to do. Now, in the language of Roman law (which is often adopted by our own, but perhaps cannot strictly be called part of it), there is a technical and appropriate name for this

[51] Pollock (n 31) 1.
[52] *ibid* viii.
[53] FC von Savigny, *System des heutigen Römischen Recht*, vol 3 (Berlin, Veit und comp, 1840) § 104.
[54] Pollock (n 31) 1, citing *ibid* § 140.
[55] Savigny (n 53) § 104.
[56] Pollock (n 31) 2.
[57] *ibid* 2 fn a.
[58] *ibid* 3.
[59] *ibid* 5.

> state of things. When one man has a peculiar right (i.e., not a merely public right, or a right incident to ownership or a permanent family relation) to control another man's actions by calling upon him to do or forbear some particular thing, there is said to be an obligation between them.[60]

He quoted Savigny's definition of an *obligatorischer Vertrag* as 'the union of more than one party in a concordant declaration of will through which an obligation is to arise'.[61] Admittedly, in English law, that definition would not work in the case of a promise made under seal which need not be accepted. But that was a peculiarity of English law.

After the second edition, however, although acknowledging his debt to Savigny, Pollock de-emphasised it. He no longer explained Savigny's ideas at length and quoted him only occasionally. He found English equivalents, and venerable ones, for terms such as *Rechtsgeschäft*. An agreement must be 'in our old English phrase, an act in law', that is, it must be 'capable of having legal effects'.[62]

> [T]he word *use* is familiar in English law-books from early times in such a connection as this; and I think it mostly if not always imports the creation of a personal claim, *Forderung* as the German writers call it, on the part of him for whose use a thing is said to be done.[63]

As we have seen, Pollock adapted Savigny's definitions to English law. His work resembled that of Savigny in another respect as well. Savigny explained contract law by identifying such basic concepts as will and declaration and using them to define legal institutions such as contract. His method is often called *Begriffsjurisprudenz*, the jurisprudence of concepts. The definitions were supposed to explain Roman law, and they were to be accepted only if they could do so. Yet the aim was a system of concepts, definitions and logical inferences from these definitions that resembled mathematics. 'In every triangle', Savigny said, 'there are certain given features from the relations of which all the rest are deducible .... In like manner, every part of our law has points by which the rest may be given: these may be termed leading axioms'.[64] The difficulty is that 'to distinguish them, and to deduce from them the internal connection … is one of the most difficult problems of jurisprudence. Indeed, it is peculiarly this that gives our work a scientific character'.[65]

[60] *ibid.*

[61] *ibid* 5, fn b: '*vereinigung Mehrerer zu einer übereinstimmenden Willenserklärung, wodurch unter ihnen eine Obligation entstehen soll*' citing FC von Savigny, *Das Obligationenrecht als Theil des heutigen römischen Rechts*, vol 2 (Berlin, Veit und comp, 1853) 7–8.

[62] Pollock (n 33) 2.

[63] *ibid* 2.

[64] FC von Savigny, *Vom Beruf unsrer Zeit für Gesetzgebung und Rechtswissenschaft* (Heidelberg, JCB Mohr, 1840) 38.

[65] *ibid.*

Rudolf Jhering attacked the jurisprudence of concepts because it neglected the purposes which the law serves. He described 'purpose' as 'the creator of the entire law …; there is no legal rule which does not owe its origin to a purpose'.[66] Yet a method based on logical inferences from definitions had no more use for purposes in law than that method did in mathematics. The same criticism was made by Pollock's American friend, Oliver Wendell Holmes, who denied that legal questions cannot be 'settled deductively, or once for all'.[67] He criticised those who think 'that the only force in the development of law is logic', 'that a given system, ours, for instance, can be worked out like mathematics from some general axioms of conduct'.[68]

Although Pollock greatly admired Savigny, he was less confident about the degree to which legal questions could be settled deductively. Definitions were helpful but imperfect. He began the later editions of his treatise by stating:

> Our first business is to separate and analyze the elements which, generally speaking, concur in the formation of a contract. A series of statements in the form of definitions, though necessarily imperfect, may help to clear the way.[69]

As we have seen, he was perfectly willing to amend Savigny's definitions to fit in the action of covenant in which a promise did not need to be part of an agreement. Even if that rule is 'archaic and technical', 'it is a settled part of the law of England'.[70]

Nevertheless, like Savigny, he explained contracts by defining. Savigny wished to show that his formulations fit Roman law. Pollock wished to show that his own fit the English cases. Neither explained legal institutions such as contract in terms of purposes. As Pollock described the task of jurists, '[t]heir business is to learn and know, so far as is needful for their affairs, what rules the State does undertake to enforce or administer, whatever the real or professed reasons for these rules may be'.[71]

We can see this contrast by comparing Pollock's and Savigny's account of promise and agreement with that of Hugo Grotius (1583–1645), whose work was still widely read in the early nineteenth century, or that of the philosopher-jurist John Austin (1790–1859). They both tried to explain why, in principle, a promise needs to be accepted.

According to Grotius, a promise is binding if the promisor intended to transfer the right to demand performance to the promise. If so, he made a 'perfect' promise.[72] Grotius anticipated 'transfer theories' of contract like those of Peter

[66] R von Jhering (translated by I Husa), *Der Zweck im Recht* (Boston, The Boston Book Company, 1913) liv.

[67] OW Holmes Jr, 'The Path of the Law' in OW Holmes Jr, *Collected Legal Papers* (New York, Harcourt, Brace & Co, 1920) 182.

[68] *ibid* 180.

[69] Pollock (n 33) 1.

[70] *ibid* 6.

[71] F Pollock, *A First Book of Jurisprudence for Students of the Common Law* (London, Macmillan, 1896) 26–27.

[72] H Grotius, *De iure belli ac pacis libri tres* (1688) II.xi.4.

Benson.[73] Indeed, Benson cited Grotius.[74] Grotius concluded that because a perfect promise transfers a right, it cannot be binding without the promisee's consent any more than a transfer of property without the consent of the transferee.[75]

According to Austin,

> a convention *naturally* raises in the mind of the promisee … an *expectation* that its object will be accomplished: and to the expectation naturally raised by the convention, he as naturally shapes his conduct. … To prevent disappointments of such expectations, is therefore a main object of the legal and moral rules whose direct and appropriate purpose is the enforcement of pacts and agreements.[76]

An acceptance is necessary because 'unless the existence of the expectation were signified by the promisee, the promising party would not be appraised of its existence, although the proffered promise had actually raised it'.[77] Austin anticipated contemporary contracts theorists who explain why promises are enforceable in terms of expectation and reliance.

Although Grotius and Austin explained the need for mutual assent by giving a larger account of why promises should be binding, Pollock did not. Like Savigny, he defined contract in terms of an agreement and agreement in terms of mutual assent. No further justification was needed than that these definitions were coherent and, for Pollock, they explained English law, as for Savigny, they explained Roman law. It could be said of them, as it has been of other nineteenth-century jurists, '[t]he contract is obligatory simply because it is the contract'.[78]

It is striking that Pollock was satisfied with Savigny's definition even though, he, like Austin, recognised that contracts are enforced 'to establish a positive sanction for the expectation of good faith which has grown up' between the parties, and that

> [h]e who has given a promise is bound to him who excepts it, not merely because he has expressed a certain intention, but because he has so expressed himself as to entitle the other party to rely on his acting in certain way.[79]

[73] P Benson, *Justice in Transactions: A Theory of Contract Law* (Cambridge MA, Harvard University Press, 2019) 8. See SV Shiffrin, 'Promising, Intimate Relationships, and Conventionalism' (2008) 117 *Philosophy Review* 481, 507, 516; A Ripstein, *Force and Freedom: Kant's Legal and Political Philosophy* (Cambridge MA, Harvard University Press, 2009) 109. The phrase 'transfer theory' is from H Dagan and M Heller, *The Choice Theory of Contracts* (Cambridge, Cambridge University Press, 2017) 33.

[74] Benson (n 73) 10.

[75] Grotius (n 72) II.xi.1.3–4.

[76] J Austin, *The Province of Jurisprudence Determined*, vol 1 (Miami, 2017) (Kindle edn) loc. 7090 135–36.

[77] *ibid* locs. 7122–30, 136.

[78] E Gounot, *Le Principe de l'autonomie e la volonté en droit privé: contribution à l'étude critique de l'individualisme juridique* (Paris, A Rousseau, 1912) 129, quoted in V Ranouil, *L'Autonomie de la volonté: naissance et évolution d'un concept* (Paris, Presses universitaires de France, 1980) 72, fn 31.

[79] Pollock (n 33) vii.

He objected that if, as Holmes thought 'the promise in a contract were held to be [either to] perform or pay damages … it would not answer to the reasonable expectations of promisees'.[80] On the basis of such statements, Arthur Goodhart concluded that Pollock never subscribed to a will theory,[81] although we have seen how close his definition of contract was to Savigny's. Having observed that these statements were made after Pollock's first edition, Duxbury concluded that 'Pollock lost his initial enthusiasm for [a will] theory',[82] although Pollock continued to define contract in the same way. What they indicate is that Pollock was perfectly comfortable recognising that a contract serves such purposes while defining contract without regard to them. That is the conceptualist approach to which Jhering objected. As we will see later, Pollock flatly rejected the claim that a promise should be enforced simply because the promisee had relied upon it.

III. CONSIDERATION

A promise was enforceable in covenant if it was made under seal. Since the sixteenth century, a promise was enforceable in assumpsit if it had 'consideration'. As John Dawson noted,

> 'Consideration' was only one of the words employed to precipitate the vague sensation that it was necessary to stop somewhere. … [T]he term 'consideration' on its first appearance merely expressed obscurely the feeling that there should be some sufficient reason, ground or motive that would justify enforcement of a promise.[83]

A promise to exchange had consideration. Some promises were enforced by drawing a tendentious analogy to promises to exchange. For example, in *Sturlyn v Albany*, the plaintiff had leased to a third party who had granted his estate to the defendant. The plaintiff asked the defendant to pay the rent which he promised to do if the plaintiff would show him a deed proving the rent was due. The showing of the deed was said to be consideration for the paying of the rent. The Court said, 'when a thing is done, be it never so small, this is a sufficient consideration to ground an action'.[84] Sometimes consideration was found for promises that were not part or a bargain or exchange in any ordinary sense: for example, a promise to give money to a prospective son-in-law upon his marriage,

[80] Letter to OW Holmes, Jr (13 June 1927) in MD Howe (ed), *Holmes-Pollock Letters, The Correspondence of Mr Justice Holmes and Sir Frederick Pollock, 1874–1932*, vol 2 (Cambridge MA, Harvard University Press, 1961) 200–201. Similarly, Letter to OW Holmes, Jr (29 November 1928) *ibid* 232–33 ('For my part, I stick to the promisee's reasonable expectations …').

[81] AJ Goodhart, 'Introduction' in F Pollock, *Jurisprudence and Legal Essays* (London, Macmillan, 1961) x–xi.

[82] Duxbury (n 3) 195.

[83] JP Dawson and WB Harvey, *Contract and Contract Remedies: Cases and Materials* (Brooklyn, Foundation Press, 1959) 540.

[84] *Sturlyn v Albany* (1587) Cro Eliz 67, 78 ER 327.

or to return an object loaned or deposited with the promisor. In these cases, the only alternatives for the common law courts would be to refuse to enforce such promises, or to require that they be made under seal. The first alternative was unfair, and the second was unrealistic, since one can hardly imagine that a prospective son-in-law or a person who was doing another a favour gratuitously would ask for a seal.

Nevertheless, beginning with William Blackstone,[85] common law treatise writers identified the 'consideration' necessary for an action to lie in assumpsit with the civil law concept of *causa*. Powell[86] and Taylor[87] did so in England, and, in the United States, Comyn,[88] WW Story[89] and Parsons.[90] As Simpson said, the common lawyers seemed to regard consideration as a local version of the doctrine of *causa*.[91]

The French jurist Robert Pothier explained that a contract might have either of two *causes* (*causae*). One *cause* for which one party contracts 'is that which the other party gives him or obligates himself to give him'. The other is 'the liberality which one party wishes to exercise towards the other'.[92] Contracts with the first kind of *cause* are contracts of mutual interest (*contrats intéresses de part et d'autre*); those with the second kind are 'contracts to do good' (*contrats de bienfaisance*).[93] Contracts of mutual interest require 'equality so that one of the parties is injured if he gives more than he receives'.[94] In principle, 'the injury (*lézion*) that a parties suffers … is sufficient in itself to render such contracts invalid (*viteux*) although the law does not remedy every injury'.[95]

The common law treatise writers identified consideration with the *causa* of an exchange, or, in Pothier's words, a 'contract of mutual interest'. As Blackstone said, 'consideration is something mutual, reciprocal – something given in exchange'.[96] If a contract with consideration was an exchange and enforceable in assumpsit, it seemed to follow that gratuitous contracts were enforceable in covenant if they were made under seal. Thus there was a parallel to civil law. Contracts of 'mutual interest' were enforceable without a formality. In civil law, promises to give away money or property required the formality of notarisation.

[85] W Blackstone, *Commentaries on the Laws of England*, vol 2 (Oxford, Clarendon Press, 1766) 444–46.
[86] Powell (n 25) 331.
[87] Taylor (n 26) 16.
[88] Comyn (n 27) 2.
[89] Story (n 28) 431, fn 1.
[90] Parsons (n 29) 355.
[91] Simpson (n 1) 262.
[92] R Pothier, *Traité des obligations* (Paris, Debure, 1761) § 41.
[93] *ibid*.
[94] *ibid* § 33.
[95] *ibid*.
[96] Blackstone (n 85) 444.

Pollock described covenant as a remedy to enforce gratuitous promises and assumpsit as one to enforce contracts of exchange. 'An informal and gratuitous promise, however strong may be the motives or even the moral duty on which it is founded, is not enforced by English courts of justice at all'.[97] To be enforceable, such a promise required a formality: the seal. In contrast, a promise is enforceable in assumpsit where '[a]n act or forbearance of the one party, present or promised, is the price for which the promise of the other party is bought, and the promise thus given for value is enforceable'.[98] The 'act or forbearance, present or promised' is the consideration.

Pollock then faced the problem of how consideration could be equated with bargain or exchange when English courts had found consideration in transactions that were not bargains or exchanges in any ordinary sense. He ingeniously redefined bargain or exchange so that his definition would fit these cases as well.

According to Pollock,

> Consideration means not so much that one party profited as that the other abandons some legal right in the present, or limits his legal freedom of action in the future, as an inducement for the act or promise of the first.[99]
>
> [I]t is enough that … the party giving it does thereby undertake some burden, or lose something which in contemplation of law may have value.[100]

For Pothier, as we have seen, contracts 'of mutual interest' required 'equality so that one party is injured in that one of the parties is injured if he gives more than he receives …'.[101] Pollock derived his definition of exchange from the opposite principle. He cited Thomas Hobbes: 'The value of all things contracted for is measured by the appetite of the contractors, and therefore the just value is that which they be contended to give'.[102] This 'idea', he said, 'is characteristic not only in English positive law but in the English school of jurisprudence and politics'.[103] The rule that a court will not 'enter into an inquiry as to the adequacy of consideration is reached "by a deduction" from this principle'.[104] 'And the legal rule is long-standing and illustrated by many cases'. He quoted the passage cited above from *Sturlyn v Albany*.[105] 'The principle of all these cases may be summed up in the statement made in so many words by the judges in more than one of them, that the promisor got all that he bargained for'.[106]

[97] Pollock (n 33) 168.
[98] *ibid* 167.
[99] *ibid.*
[100] *ibid.*
[101] Pothier (n 92) § 33.
[102] Pollock (n 33) 172; citing T Hobbes, *Leviathan* (Cambridge, Cambridge University Press, 1935) I.xv 102.
[103] Pollock (n 33) 172.
[104] *ibid.*
[105] *Sturlyn* (n 84).
[106] Pollock (n 33) 174.

His definition enabled him to classify transactions as exchanges in which 'the promisor got all that he bargained for' even though the transaction was not an exchange in the ordinary sense. 'Marrying the promisor's daughter at his request is put as a good consideration' for a promise to pay money to the promisee after the marriage takes place.[107] For Pollock, the marriage was 'the price of the promise' and 'all that [the promisor] bargained for'.[108]

Promises to care for and return objects gratuitously loaned were also bargains. Pollock cited *Bainbridge v Firmstone*,[109] which held that '[i]f a man who owns two boilers allows another to weigh them, this is a good consideration for that other's promise to give them up after such weighing in as good condition as before'.[110]

So were promises to care for and return objects gratuitously deposited with the promisor. In *Coggs v Bernard*,[111] a porter was held liable for damaging a cask of rum which he had promised gratuitously to carry to the owner's lodgings. According to Pollock, in such a case

> the bailor parts with present legal control of the goods; and this is so far a detriment to him, though it may be no benefit to the bailee, and the bailee's taking possession of the goods if for the bailors use and convenience.[112]

In support of his definition, Pollock also cited cases which were bargains in the ordinary sense. The courts had said that it was enough that a party had all that he bargained for or that the adequacy of consideration did not matter. In those cases, however, the problem the courts were addressing was that the promisor seemed to have received nothing of value from the promisee although he had actually obtained the very benefit that he was seeking.

In *Lawes v Purser*,[113] the defendant agreed to pay the plaintiff 20s a ton for the use of an invention for processing manure. The plaintiff was supposed to license him a patent on the process. The defendant did use the process but the patent proved to be void. The plaintiff's counsel argued that

> the defendants have enjoyed the benefit of the plaintiff's permission to use the patent right .... Their situation is analogous to that of a person who has actually occupied land by permission of another; such occupier must pay the rent to the party who let him in, though the title to the land be in a third person.[114]

Coleridge J observed that 'he who has, in fact, enjoyed a consideration by permission of another must pay for it'.[115] Wightman J held that there was

[107] Pollock (n 31) 151–52.
[108] *ibid.*
[109] *Bainbridge v Firmstone* (1838) 8 Ad & El 743, 112 ER 1019.
[110] Pollock (n 31) 154.
[111] *Coggs v Bernard* (1703) 2 Ld Raym 909, 92 ER 107.
[112] Pollock (n 33) 173.
[113] *Lawes v Purser* (1856) 6 El & Bl 930, 119 ER 1110.
[114] *ibid* 931.
[115] *ibid* 934 (Coleridge J).

consideration because 'the defendants had, in fact, all they bargained for'.[116] Pollock summarised the case by saying that 'a license by a patentee to use the patented invention is a good consideration though the patent should turn out to be invalid'.[117] The patent, however, was not the benefit the defendant sought. He obtained the benefit he sought even though the patent was invalid.

In *Westlake v Adams*,[118] the parties had not complied with statutory provisions which, the promisor claimed, were necessary for his promise to be enforceable. In response to an advertisement, a father apprenticed his son to a wood carver who asked for £40 in return. The father persuaded a charitable society to pay the word carver £20, and, without telling the society that he was doing so, wrote an IOU to the wood carver for the remaining £20. After the boy finished his apprenticeship, the father refused to pay. The Court held that the promise was not a fraud on the charitable society, and that the father must pay despite a statute that said all sums payable for an apprenticeship must be mentioned in the indenture. Pollock described the case as one in which 'the execution of a deed, though invalid for want of statutory requisites, [has] been held good consideration'.[119] On the previous page, Pollock had quoted a remark made by one of the judges in this case: it is an 'elementary principle that the law will not enter into an inquiry as to the adequacy of consideration'.[120]

In *Cheale v Kenward*,[121] the plaintiff promised to transfer stock to the defendant which he had purchased for £50 which he had not yet paid. The defendant assumed the duty to pay for the stock. The plaintiff argued that therefore he had not promised to transfer anything of value. The Chancellor observed, '[w]hether the stock would be valuable or valueless at the time of the agreement no one could tell. Their value was merely speculative … But … the Defendant was willing to take the chances of the speculation'.[122] '[T]he shares might ultimately turn out to be worth more than the amount due upon them, and, at all events, the possibility of their being valuable would be sufficient to constitute an agreement to transfer them a good consideration'.[123]

English and American jurists still define consideration in the same way as Pollock. According to Peel and Treitel,

> The doctrine is based on the idea of reciprocity: 'something of value in the eye of the law' must be given for a promise in order to make it enforceable as a contract. An informal gratuitous promise therefore does not amount to a contract.[124]

[116] *ibid* 935 (Wightman J).
[117] Pollock (n 33) 173.
[118] *Westlake v Adams* (1858) 5 CBNS 248, 141 ER 99.
[119] As he observed, however, 'the justice of the decision was very plain: … the apprentice had in fact served his time, so that the benefit of the consideration had been fully enjoyed' (Pollock (n 33) 173). By his definition the justice of the decision should not have mattered.
[120] *ibid* 172.
[121] *Cheale v Kenward* (1858) 3 De G & J 27, 44 ER 1179.
[122] *ibid* De G & J 30–31; ER 1180.
[123] *ibid* De G & J 31; ER 1180.
[124] Peel (n 37) para 3-002.

According to Peel and Treitel, 'some value' must be given for a promise although 'the courts do not, in general, ask whether adequate value has been given'.[125] 'Some value' seems to have meant to Peel and Treitel only as much as it did to Pollock. Like Pollock, they cited *Bainbridge v Firmstone* in which allowing the promisee to weigh the promisor's boilers was held to be consideration for a promise to look after them and give them back.[126] In explaining *Coggs v Bernard*, they acknowledged a problem that Pollock did not. The Court held that in entrusting a porter with a cask of spirits was consideration for his promise to look after it. Peel and Treitel noted that 'parting with possession is hardly a detriment' to the promisee.[127]

In the United States, Pollock's definition was accepted enthusiastically by his friend Oliver Wendell Holmes.[128] Holmes' admirer Samuel Williston wrote it into the *Restatement (First) of the Law of Contracts*[129] for which he served as Reporter, whence it passed into the *Restatement (Second)*:

> To constitute consideration, a performance or return promise must be bargained for. A performance or return promise is bargained for if it is sought by the promisee in exchange for that promise.[130]
>
> ...
>
> If the requirement of consideration is met, there is no additional requirement of equivalence in the values exchanged ...[131]

Yet, in the United States, there has been doubt, since the early twentieth century, as to whether this definition can explain the cases that Pollock formulated it to explain. Beginning in 1856 in *Hammersley v De Biel*,[132] courts sometimes said that a promisor was bound because he had made a 'representation' on which the promisee had 'acted'. 'The principal class of cases', Pollock noted, were promises to those about to marry. He believed that such promises had consideration. They did not support the doctrine of 'making representations good'.[133] Williston disagreed.[134] He cited such cases in support of a

[125] *ibid* para 3-013.

[126] *ibid* para 3-004.

[127] *ibid* para 3-169.

[128] OW Holmes Jr, *The Common Law* (Boston, Little, Brown & Co, 1881) 193–94. See Letter from OW Holmes to F Pollock (17 June 1880) in Howe (n 80) 14–15. As Duxbury noted, Holmes was commenting on the first edition of Pollock's treatise which he had just received: Duxbury (n 3) 209. Consequently, although his formula was clarified in later editions, one cannot say that '[i]n the first two editions' he had not 'offered a definition of his own. ... Consideration remained a black hole': *ibid* 206.

[129] *Restatement (First) of the Law of Contracts* (Philadelphia, American Law Institute, 1932) § 75.

[130] *Restatement (Second) of the Law of Contracts* (n 40) § 71.

[131] *ibid* § 79.

[132] *Hammersley v De Biel* (1845) 12 Cl & F 45, 62, 88; 8 ER 1312, 1320, 1331.

[133] Pollock (n 33) 692–700.

[134] However, the disagreement was not expressed in his edition of Pollock's treatise although he did note that this doctrine could explain certain American cases that Pollock's formula for consideration could not: F Pollock (edited by GH Wald and S Williston), *Principles of Contract at Law and in Equity*, 7th English edn, 3rd American edn (New York, Baker, Voorhis & Co, 1906) 650, fn 1.

new doctrine,[135] promissory reliance, which he wrote into the *Restatement (First)*[136] with the support of Arthur Corbin. A promise without consideration is enforceable if the promisee changed his position in reliance on it. Corbin had arrived at this principle at almost the same time but by a different route. In his 1919 edition of Anson's *Principles of the Law of Contract*, he claimed that when courts find consideration they are sometimes holding the promisor liable because of 'subsequent facts consisting of acts in reliance on the promise'.[137] Although he did not say so expressly, he seems to have been thinking of the cases in which courts had found consideration for gratuitous loans and deposits of property.[138] The lender relied on the borrower's promise to look after and return the object loaned. The owner of the case relied on the porter's promise to look after and return it.

So, in the United States, Pollock's formulation survives even though the cases it was meant to explain are now explained differently. It is doubtful, however, that the doctrine of promissory reliance really does explain these results. A person who marries is not relying on a parent's promise of money if he would have married only for love. The *Restatement (Second)* provides that 'a marriage settlement is binding … without proof that the promise induced action or forbearance'.[139] Presumably, to recover under that provision, the plaintiff need not claim he married for money. Similarly, a borrower must repay a loan even if the lender had not relied on his promise to do so. Bassiano would have to repay the money he borrowed from Antonio, the merchant of Venice, even if Antonio never expected him to do so, and made the loan because he preferred to lose his money rather than his friend. Presumably, the porter in *Coggs v Bernard* would have to look after and return the cask entrusted to him, even if the owner had to entrust it to someone, and he were the only porter in sight.

[135] S Williston and G Thompson, *A Treatise on the Law of Contracts*, vol 1 (New York, Baker, Voorhis & Co, 1937) § 139.

[136] *Restatement (First) of the Law of Contracts* (n 129) § 90.

[137] WR Anson (edited by AL Corbin), *Principles of the Law of Contract with a Chapter on the Law of Agency*, 14th English edn, 3rd American edn (New York, Banks Law Publishing Co, 1919) § 118, fn 3. He had come close to this position a year earlier when he disapproved a statement by Holmes that '[i]t is not enough that the promise induces the detriment or that the detriment induces the promise if the other half is wanting' (*Wisconsin & Mich RR v Powers* 191 US 379, 386 (1903)). Corbin said that '[t]here are all too many decisions enforcing a promise where the only consideration was some expected action in reliance upon it for us to adopt [this statement] without reserve' (AL Corbin, 'Does a Pre-Existing Duty Defeat Consideration? – Recent Noteworthy Decisions' (1918) 27 *Yale Law Journal* 362, 368).

[138] In the text Corbin was editing, Anson had listed them as exceptions to the normal requirements of consideration (Anson (n 137) §§ 122, 133–35). In contrast, Williston, while uncomfortable with these cases, seems to have thought that they could be explained as instances of genuine consideration or else as tort actions (Williston and Thompson (n 135) § 138).

[139] *Restatement (Second) of the Law of Contracts* (n 40) § 90(2).

IV. ASSENT

Before the nineteenth century, as Simpson noted, courts had said little about the effect of mistake on consent.[140] In civil law, the doctrine of mistake went back to Ulpian. He said: 'It is obvious that there must be consent in contracts of sale. Therefore a sale is invalid if there is dissent as to the fact of sale or the price or any other matter'. He said that when copper is sold for gold (*aes pro auro*), consent is absent because they differ in 'substance' (*substantia*). When wine which has soured is sold for wine, there is consent because 'the *ousia* [a Greek word meaning essence] is pretty much the same'.[141]

'Substance' had many meanings in Greek philosophy but it is clear that Ulpian had no definite philosophical meaning in mind.[142] He was groping for a word that vaguely indicated a difference in kind and could explain cases like copper sold for gold. The late scholastics later attached a more definite meaning to it by drawing on Aristotelian distinction between substance and accidents.[143] An echo is to be found in Pothier although by the time he wrote, the philosophical significance of that distinction may have been largely forgotten:

> Error annuls an agreement not only when it falls on the thing itself but also when it falls on the quality of the thing that the contracting parties had principally in view and which constitute the substance of the thing .... It is otherwise when the error falls only on some accidental quality of the thing.[144]

Pollock said:

> The whole topic [of mistake] is surrounded with a great deal of confusion in our books, though on the whole of a verbal kind, and more embarrassing to students than to practitioners. Exactly the same kind of confusion prevailed in the civil law (whence indeed at some of it at least has passed on to our own) until Savigny cleared it up in the masterly essay which forms the Appendix to the third volume of his System. The principles there established by him have been fully adopted by later writers. They appear to be in the main applicable to the law of England, and we shall accordingly be guided by them.[145]

According to Savigny[146] (and Pollock),[147] in and of itself, a mistake has no influence on the validity of a contract. For Duxbury, that statement shows

[140] Simpson (n 1) 265–69. On how little was said in the early 19th century, see J Gordley, *The Philosophical Origins of Modern Contract Doctrine* (Oxford, Oxford University Press, 1991) 144–45.

[141] D.18.1.9.pr.

[142] No Greek philosopher would have said, as Ulpian did, that whether the *ousia* is the same depends on whether the wine soured into vinegar (it does) or was prepared as vinegar (it does not).

[143] Gordley (n 140) 88–90.

[144] Pothier (n 92) § 18.

[145] Pollock (n 31) 357.

[146] Savigny (n 53) § 114.

[147] Pollock (n 31) 356, fn a, 357–58.

that Pollock 'believed that contract doctrine presented problems of liability too complex to be resolved by a will theory'.[148] It shows instead that Pollock agreed with Savigny who did have a will theory, as Duxbury acknowledged.[149] By definition, a contract is constituted by the declaration of will or intent (*Willenserklärungen*) of two or more parties. The declarations must be in accord (*Übereinstimmung*) with each other and with the will that they purport to declare. Relief is given when they are not in accord: a party declared something other than what he meant, or the declaration of one party does not match that of another.[150] Doubtless, the mismatch is due to a mistake of some sort. But the reason for giving relief is not the mistake itself. It is absence of an element that is necessary, by definition, for a contract to be formed.

Sometimes, the declaration of will or intention of one party does not match the declaration of the other. For Pollock as for Savigny, there is no contract. Pollock explained in his first edition, 'the question whether the parties really meant the same thing cannot arise, for they have not even said the same thing'.[151] At the beginning of his treatise, he said that 'the parties must be assured by mutual communication that a common intention exists, that they mean the same thing in the same sense'.[152]

Pollock then discussed two cases in which a contract was not formed because there was no 'common intention'. 'First, it may happen that each party meant something, it may be a perfectly well understood and definite thing, but not the same thing which the other meant. Thus their minds never met, as is not uncommonly said …'.[153] The declarations matched but not the will of the parties. For Savigny, that was why, according to Ulpian, there was no contract when one party meant to sell one field and the other party meant to buy another.[154] Pollock's illustration was *Raffles v Wichelhaus*,[155] 'a sale of 125 bales of Surat cotton, to arrive ex "Peerless" from Bombay'.

> The defendants meant a ship called the 'Peerless' that sailed from Bombay in October, and … the plaintiff offered to deliver, not any cotton that arrived by that ship, but cotton that arrived by a different ship also called the 'Peerless' and that sailed to Bombay in December.[156]

'Next', Pollock said,

> it may happen that there does exist a common intention, which however is founded on an assumption made by both parties as to some matter of fact essential to the

[148] Duxbury (n 3) 198.
[149] *ibid* 192.
[150] Savigny (n 53) § 135.
[151] Pollock (n 31) 371.
[152] *ibid* 3–4.
[153] *ibid* 373.
[154] Savigny (n 53) § 135.
[155] *Raffles v Wichelhaus* (1864) 2 Hurl & C 906, 159 ER 375.
[156] Pollock (n 33) 429.

> agreement. ... Here there is in some sense an agreement: but it is nullified in its inception by the nullity of the thing agreed upon. And it seems hardly too artificial to say that there is no real agreement. ... In both sets of cases we may say that the agreement is nullified by fundamental error.[157]

Explaining this type of case was very difficult for Pollock as for Savigny.

As an illustration, they both referred to Ulpian's sale of copper for gold. According to Savigny, the reason that sale is void is that some properties of an object are bound up with its identity. These are properties by which a thing is classified as a thing of a certain type 'according to concepts dominant in actual commerce'.[158] If a party declared his will to contract for an object that he mistakenly believed to have such a property, his will did not match his declaration.[159] Similarly, Pollock said that

> some attribute which the thing in truth has not may be a material part of the description by which the thing was contracted for. If this is so, the thing as it really is, namely without that quality, is not that to which the common intention of the parties was directed, and the agreement is void.[160]

Citing Savigny, Pollock said that the characteristic must be 'such that according to the ordinary course of dealing and use of language the difference made by the absence of the quality wrongly supposed to exist amounts to a difference in kind'.[161]

In this way, the idea that some characteristics are 'essential' inasmuch as their presence or absence constitutes a difference in kind, crept back into the law governing mistake despite the efforts of Savigny and Pollock to keep it out. In *Kennedy v Panama New Zealand & Australian Royal Mail Co*,[162] the Court denied relief because there was no 'difference in substance' when the shareholder purchased stock in the company falsely believing it had a valuable contract with the Government. In its decision, according to Pollock, '[t]he rule governing this whole class of cases is fully explained',[163] adding that 'it is an important part of the doctrine, both in our own law and in the civil law (d), that the difference in substance must be complete'.[164] Nevertheless, for Savigny and for Pollock, the explanation was supposed to be that for relief to be given for an error in a characteristic of an object, in the minds of the parties, the characteristic must constitute a difference in the thing's identity. If an object lacked that characteristic, it was not the object that the parties intended.

[157] *ibid* 373.
[158] Savigny (n 53) § 137.
[159] *ibid*.
[160] Pollock (n 31) 393.
[161] *ibid* 393, fn b citing Savigny (n 53) § 137.
[162] *Kennedy v Panama New Zealand & Australian Royal Mail Co* (1867) LR 2 QB 580.
[163] Pollock (n 31) 386.
[164] *ibid*.

Some nineteenth-century German jurists objected that Savigny's solution contradicted his own principles.[165] If the significance of a characteristic to a party did not matter, its significance according to 'commercially dominant concepts' should not matter either. Windscheid accepted Savigny's solution despite the difficulty because, he admitted, he could not think of any other way to explain the Roman text concerning copper sold as gold.[166] A version of it passed into § 119(2) of the German Civil Code which provides: 'A mistake over those characteristics of a person or a thing that are regarded as essential in commerce counts as an error in the declaration'.

Remarkably, although Pollock claimed to accept Savigny's account of the effect of mistake, he presented two others alongside it which are not only different but conflicting.

In one, the reason that relief is given is not because there is an absence of consent, but because the mistake concerns an assumption on which the agreement was made. 'There does exist a common intention, which however is founded on an assumption made by both parties as to some matter of fact essential to the agreement'.[167]

> In this case the common intention must stand or fall with the assumption on which it is founded. If that assumption is on wrong, the intention of the parties is from the outset incapable of taking effect. But for their common error it would never have been formed, and it is treated as non-existent. Here there is in some sense an agreement: but it is nullified in its inception by the nullity of the thing agreed upon. And it seems hardly too artificial to say that there is no real agreement. The result is the same as if the parties had made an agreement expressly conditional on the existence at the time of the supposed state of facts: which state of facts not existing, the agreement destroys itself.[168]

In the other account, the mistake must be mutual. '[T]he error must be common to both parties'.[169] Pollock was following a suggestion made by Cockburn CJ in *Smith v Hughes* that for relief to be given, both parties must be mistaken.[170] Pollock claimed that the mistake was mutual in Ulpian's case of 'copper sold for gold', the error was common to both parties.

> What does *pro auro*, as for gold, imply as here used? It implies that the buyer thinks he is buying, and the seller that he is selling, a golden vessel: and further, that the

[165] E Bekker, 'Zur Lehre von der Willenserklärung: Einfluss von Zwang und Irrthum' (review of A Schliemann, *Die Lehre vom Zwange*) (1861) 3 *Kritische Vierteljahresschrift für Gesetzgebung und Rechtswissenschaft* 180, 188–89; A Renaud, 'Zur Lehre von Einflusse des Irrthums in der Sache auf die Gültigkeit der Kaufverträge mit Rücksicht auf v. Savigny: Der *error in substantia*'' (1846) 28 *Archiv für die Civilistische Praxis* 247, 247–54; M Hesse, 'Ein Revision der Lehre von Irrthum' (1877) 15 *Iherings Jahrbücher für die Dogmatik des heutigen römischen und deutschen Privatrechts* 101.

[166] B Windscheid, *Lehrbuch des Pandektenrechts*, vol 1, 7th edn (Frankfurt, Literarische Anstalt Rütten & Loening, 1871) § 76a.

[167] Pollock (n 31) 373.

[168] *ibid.*

[169] *ibid* 373, 393.

[170] *Smith v Hughes* (1871) LR 6 QB 597, 603, cited by *ibid* 395, fn b.

> object present to the minds of both parties as that in which they are trafficking – the object of their common intention – is, not merely this specific vessel, but this specific vessel, being golden. Then, and not otherwise, the sale is void.[171]

He concluded:

> Accordingly, when the law is stated to be that 'a party is not bound to accept and pay for chattels, unless they are really such as the vendor professed to sell, and the vendee intended to buy' the condition is not alternative but strictly conjunctive. A sale is not void merely because the vendor professed to sell, or the vendee intended to buy, something of a different kind. It must be shown that the object was in fact neither such as the vendor professed to sell nor such as the vendee intended to buy. And so in the case supposed the sale will not be invalidated by the mistake of the buyer alone, if he thinks he is buying gold.[172]

Citing Savigny,[173] he acknowledged that

> [t]he somewhat refined distinction here taken does not seem to exist in the civil law … according to whom it makes no difference whether there be on the part of the vendor ignorance, passive knowledge, or even actual fraud: the sale being wholly void in any case.[174]

Indeed, by Savigny's reasoning, it could not matter whether the error was common to both parties. He maintained that a party is mistaken about the identity of the thing contracted for if he is mistaken about a property by which a thing is classified as a thing of a certain type 'according to concepts dominant in actual commerce'. If he believes an object to be gold when it is copper, he does not intend to buy or sell that thing. Contracts are made by mutual intent – by the declaration of will of two or more parties. There is no mutual consent as long as one party does not intend to be bound.

Pollock's solutions are still with us and, with them, the difficulties both of understanding them and of reconciling them. Peel and Treitel drew the same distinction as to whether a characteristic of an object as to which the parties are mistaken, in their minds, concerned its identity.

> The cases and examples concerning mistake as to quality cannot be perfectly reconciled, but there is a principle that runs through them. A thing has many qualities. A car may be black, old, fast, and so forth. For any particular purpose one or more of these qualities may be uppermost in the mind of the persons dealing with the thing. Some particular quality may be so important to them that they actually use it to *identify* the thing. If the thing lacks that quality, it is suggested that the parties have made a fundamental mistake, even though they have not mistaken one thing for another, or made a mistake as to the existence of a thing.[175]

171 Pollock (n 31) 393.
172 *ibid* 394–95.
173 Savigny (n 53) 293.
174 Pollock (n 31) 395, fn b.
175 Peel (n 37) para 8-020.

Yet Peel and Treitel introduced the issue of mistake by drawing distinctions, like those of Pollock, between whether the parties intended different things or made a mistaken assumption, and whether one party was mistaken or both.

> Mistake negatives consent when it puts the parties at cross-purposes so as to prevent them from reaching mutual agreement, e.g., because they intend to contract about different things. The cases in this category are often referred to as cases of unilateral mistake .... Mistake nullifies consent where the parties reach an agreement which is based on a fundamental mistaken assumption made by both of them ...[176]

In the United States, Oliver Wendell Holmes and Samuel Williston adopted an 'objective' theory of contract, in part, because they did not think it possible, as Pollock had, to explain relief by an absence of assent. Holmes noted, '[i]t is commonly said that the failure of a contract in such a case is due to the fact of a difference in kind between the actual subject-matter and that to which the intention of the parties was directed'.[177] He claimed that the real reason for relief was that the parties' words and acts referred to different things, or there was no object to which these words or acts referred. In such cases, according to Williston, 'the acts of apparent assent, when their real meaning is discovered, do not in truth indicate assent'.[178] Holmes's illustration was a hypothetical case in which 'A agreed to buy, and B agreed to sell, "these barrels of mackerel", and ... the barrels in question turn out to contain salt'. The contract was void, Holmes said, because the words are contradictory: 'these "barrels" are not "mackerel" but "salt"'.[179] What if the parties had said 'these barrels', falsely believing but not saying that they contained mackerel? Holmes answered with a phrase he used more than once: 'The distinctions of the law are founded on experience, not on logic'.[180] In other words, Holmes's distinction was not founded on logic.

Perhaps for that reason, Williston, inconsistently, tried to find another solution. He adopted two suggestions made by Pollock. In his treatise, Willison said that a contract is voidable when both parties were mistaken as to a 'fundamental assumption'.[181] It also had to be 'mutual'. Williston did not try to reconcile those conclusions with his objective theory. Nevertheless, they passed in the *Restatement (First)* and thence into the *Restatement (Second)*. According to the *First Restatement*, for relief to be given the mistake must be 'mutual', and the parties must be mistaken 'as to a fact assumed by them as the basis on which they entered into the transaction'.[182] According to the *Restatement (Second)*, the

[176] *ibid* para 8-001.
[177] Holmes (n 128) 310.
[178] Williston and Thompson (n 135) § 20.
[179] Holmes (n 128) 310–11.
[180] *ibid* 312.
[181] Williston and Thompson (n 135) § 1544.
[182] *Restatement (First) of the Law of Contracts* (n 129) § 502.

mistake must be 'mutual', and it must concern 'a basic assumption on which the contract was made'.[183]

It is still not clear why relief should be given only if a mistake is mutual. If, as Pollock thought, a contract requires mutual assent, the assent of only one party is not enough. If, as Williston thought, a contract does not require assent, it is not clear why mutual mistake should matter.

Nor is it clear what a basic assumption might be. According to a comment in the *Restatement (Second)*, '[t]he parties may have had such a 'basic assumption' even though they were not conscious of alternatives'. Moreover, even an assumption of crucial importance to a party may not be 'basic': for example, 'market conditions and the financial situation of the parties are ordinarily not such assumptions …'.[184] So we arrive at the curious rule that the parties must have made an assumption, although they may not consciously assume anything, and that the assumption may not be 'basic' even if it is crucial.

V. CONCLUSION

To a greater extent than we like to admit, we are today where Pollock left us. We still define contract as a promise or agreement that the law will enforce. Yet there is no generally accepted explanation of why the law should enforce a promise or agreement. We still use a version of his formula to determine when contract has consideration. We do so even though we recognise that this formula was devised to explain cases that it really does not explain. We still say that a promise or agreement requires consent. Yet we have no generally accepted doctrine that explains what the parties must know in order to consent.

Biologists speak of 'punctuated evolution'. A species appears abruptly, remains relatively unchanged for eons, and then is transmuted into a new species. Pollock and a few like-minded common law jurists transformed the law of contract in a very short period of time. Its central doctrines, and the problems they bring with them, then remained the same for one-and-a-half centuries.

[183] *Restatement (Second) of the Law of Contracts* (n 40) § 152(1).
[184] *ibid* § 152, cmt b.

7

Professor Samuel Williston (1861–1963)

TODD D RAKOFF*

SAMUEL WILLISTON WAS born on 24 September 1861,[1] in Cambridge, Massachusetts, where he grew up. He matriculated at Harvard College in 1878.[2] After graduating, he worked for a few years as a private secretary and then as a teacher at a boarding school near Philadelphia.[3] He enrolled at Harvard Law School in 1885, when the case method of study was already well established, and graduated after three years, having been on the first board of editors of the *Harvard Law Review*.[4] He clerked for Justice Horace Gray of the US Supreme Court, and then began practicing in Boston.[5] In his first year of practice he was offered an assistant professorship at Harvard, and for several years thereafter he taught while also devoting considerable time to practicing.[6] He became a full professor in 1895.[7] He remained on the faculty until 1938, and remained intellectually active even after that.[8] He died in 1963, 101 years old. *Time* magazine, probably the preeminent news magazine of the era, ran an obituary that referred to him as 'A Yankee Socrates'.[9]

Williston was, by all accounts, a fine teacher. Judge Learned Hand, an early student, said of him, '[W]hile this Socrates of ours never coerced our assent, like his prototype he did not let us alone until we had peered into the corners

* My thanks to the other authors for their helpful comments during the online workshops that led up to this volume, and to Harvard Law School librarian Deanna Barmakian for her excellent research assistance.

1 S Williston, *Life and Law* (Boston, Little Brown & Co, 1940) 3.
2 *ibid* 36.
3 *ibid* 56–70.
4 *ibid* 71, 83.
5 *ibid* 87.
6 *ibid* 107, 129.
7 *ibid* 141.
8 E Griswold, 'Samuel Williston – 1861–1963' (1963) 76 *Harvard Law Review* 1324, 1325.
9 *Time* (1 March 1963).

of our minds, and had in some measure discovered the litter they contained'.[10] Karl Llewellyn – a 'realist' professor and not himself on the Harvard faculty – described Williston (in 1930) as 'probably the most widely beloved teacher of law in this country'.[11] In a memorial tribute, in 1963, former Supreme Court Justice Felix Frankfurter – a former student (and colleague) of Williston's – wrote that 'of all the teachers in any branch of learning I have seen in action or have talked with, Samuel Williston can be most aptly described as an artist of the first order'.[12]

What might be considered Williston's first article on the law of contracts, a slim review of Keener's 'A Treatise on The Law of Quasi-Contracts', appeared in 1893.[13] His last substantial article, a critique of 'The Law of Sales in the Proposed Uniform Commercial Code', was published in 1949.[14] In between, his professional work on the law of contracts can be divided into three categories. First, he drafted several statutes for the Commissioners on Uniform State Laws, most notably the Uniform Sales Act, recommended for enactment by the Commissioners in 1906 and (by Williston's count) enacted in 37 jurisdictions before it was overtaken by the Uniform Commercial Code.[15] Second, he wrote many articles regarding particular wrinkles in the law of contracts and, more comprehensively, published in 1920 a 3,000-plus-page-long treatise, *The Law of Contracts* (always called *Williston on Contracts* and generally referred to as 'the Treatise' in this chapter).[16] Third, he was the reporter for the *Restatement (First) of the Law of Contracts*, which was drafted, critiqued, and redrafted during the 1920s, and finally promulgated by the American Law Institute in 1932. (Throughout the period he also edited and revised a classroom casebook on contracts, the direct successor to Langdell's paradigm-establishing one.)

If one wants to get to the heart of Williston's thinking, it is best to focus on the second category – the articles and especially the Treatise. It is the articles and Treatise that are pure Williston. By contrast, the Sales Act, although of

[10] L Hand, 'Foreword' in Williston (n 1) ix.

[11] KN Llewellyn, 'Note Review of Williston, Some Modern Tendencies in the Law (1929)' (1930) 16 *ABA Journal* 809.

[12] F Frankfurter, 'Samuel Williston: An Inadequate Tribute to a Beloved Teacher' (1963) 76 *Harvard Law Review* 1321, 1322.

[13] S Williston, 'Book Review' (1893) 7 *Harvard Law Review* 245. Williston also helped prepare the 8th edition of *Parsons on Contracts*, which also appeared in 1893. By his own account, he was not allowed to make any major changes in what he considered a book both out of date and not of the first quality (Williston (n 1) 136–37).

[14] S Williston, 'The Law of Sales in the Proposed Uniform Commercial Code' (1949) 63 *Harvard Law Review* 561.

[15] *ibid* 563–65.

[16] S Williston, *The Law of Contracts*. (The publication date is not entirely clear. The four basic volumes all claim a 1920 copyright, and the work is normally catalogued using that date. Williston himself said that 'The book was published in 1919 in four volumes' (Williston (n 1) 264). A fifth volume, entitled 'Forms' and prepared by Clarence Lewis, bears both a copyright and publication date of 1922.)

undoubted practical importance, was by Williston's own account patterned on the English Sale of Goods Act so that there would be cross-country uniformity.[17] And the *Restatement of the Law of Contracts*, also of undoubted importance and innumerable citations, was in the end the product of the American Law Institute and the result of many hands, including importantly Arthur Corbin as Special Adviser. Moreover, the form of the *Restatement* made it more assertive than illuminating. As a critical review of the *Restatement*, written by the Dean of the Yale Law School, put it, citing many cases from its early years:

> It does not seem too much to say that while the courts cite the restatement, they quote, discuss and follow Williston. One cannot read these cases without seeing the demonstration that the courts, *for the difficult points*, need and look to discussion and analysis, not formal statement.[18]

Williston's articles were mostly short (at least compared with today's fare) and to the point. They bore titles such as 'Consideration in Bilateral Contracts'[19] and 'Mutual Assent in the Formation of Contracts'.[20] By and large they self-presented as attempts to fit together bits and pieces of the law into doctrinal lines of cases. At least in retrospect, they read as drafts of various parts of the Treatise. The Treatise[21] itself is divided into 55 chapters, ranging from 'Chapter I: Definition of Terms' to 'Chapter LV: Statute of Limitations'; the intervening chapters are mostly denominated doctrinally, such as 'Chapter V: Acceptance of Offers'. These chapters, in turn, are divided into numerous sub-parts, whose titles also raise doctrinal issues. Thus, Chapter V leads off with '§ 64: Necessity of acceptance', continues in '§ 66: Intention to accept is unimportant except as expressed', passes on to '§ 73: Acceptance must comply with the terms of the offer', and goes on to some more specialised topics, such as '§ 91: When silence and inaction may amount to assent'. A typical page consists of text and copious footnotes, split in any which way, but overall perhaps coming out 60 per cent text, 40 per cent footnotes; the footnotes themselves consist largely of straight case citations.

Williston wrote for a professional audience, comprising attorneys and judges whose minds were already used to viewing the law as arising from the outcome

[17] Williston (n 14) 563–64.

[18] CE Clark, 'The Restatement of the Law of Contracts' (1933) 42 *Yale Law Journal* 643, 662 (emphasis in the original).

[19] S Williston, 'Consideration in Bilateral Contracts' (1914) 27 *Harvard Law Review* 503.

[20] S Williston, 'Mutual Assent in the Formation of Contracts' (1919–1920) 14 *Illinois Law Review* 85.

[21] When I talk about 'the Treatise', I mean the original, early 20s, version (S Williston, *The Law of Contracts* (New York, Baker, Voorhis & Co, 1920). A second edition of *Williston on Contracts* appeared seriatim in the 1930s. Williston prepared part of it, and had final approval over any new material, but the bulk of the work of revision was done by George Thomson, professor of law at Cornell (Williston (n 1) 266). In 1950, Williston wrote that '[m]y treatises on *Sales* and on *Contracts* belong wholly to the publishers' (Williston (n 14) 561, fn 1). A third edition of the Treatise, revised by Walter Jaeger, first appeared in 1957; a fourth edition, revised by Richard Lord, first appeared in 1990.

of controversies, and used to tackling cases in a doctrinal manner.[22] But if a work of scholarship is best identified by the question it tries to answer, it would be a mistake to view *Williston on Contracts* as an effort to give a simple answer to the question, 'what is the law?' on a particular topic, supported by citations that could be copied into a brief. Most of the section-by-section discussions are much richer than that. Williston talks about the history of the issue; Williston spends the time to delineate contesting solutions to doctrinal questions; Williston tells readers which view has the support of a majority of jurisdictions, though he often advocates for the minority view; Williston tests the fit of possible solutions for a particular issue with the decided doctrines on adjacent issues; Williston tests the possible doctrines against what he understands to be the existing practice and the likely intentions of typical parties; and Williston also tests the possible solutions against his society's sense of justice. Williston himself perhaps thought of his discussions as being the proper way to answer the question 'What is the law?' on any topic, taking a satisfactory answer to be what a thoughtful and skilled judge would decide, or what a knowledgeable practitioner would forecast such a judge would do. In the Preface to the Treatise he writes:

> I make no apology for devoting some space to legal analysis and criticism. Coke speaks of himself as 'knowing for certain that the law is unknowen to him that knoweth not the reason thereof;' and in the modern welter of decisions on both sides of many questions, the learned Chief Justice would not be likely to change his mind were his lot cast in the twentieth century. But I have endeavored to keep my discussions within the limits of practical usefulness …[23]

Or perhaps Williston thought that he was entitled to express his own views on topics he had worked on for years. Or perhaps he was just following in writing the patterns he had developed as a teacher using the case method to probe for underlying rationales. Whichever the case may be, one is reading an analysis of a social practice, a legal institution, written from the inside by someone who wants to support it and put it into a good light, rather than try to debunk it.

The fourth edition of *Williston on Contracts* is available on the Westlaw database, and is apparently continuously kept up to date, at least as regards case citations. It seems to track the original in its general organisation, but, not surprisingly after a century, the text is often different. No effort seems to be made to tell readers when they are reading Williston's own words. To this reader, at least, the current version seems to lack the 'voice' of the original, the sense that one was listening to a particular, authoritative scholar who wanted to convince the reader of the good sense of what he said, rather than simply reciting a bland statement of 'the law'.

[22] The nature of the intended audience is also shown by Volume V of the Treatise as sold by the publisher, entitled 'Forms' and prepared by Clarence M Lewis. This contains form after form for possible contracts of all sorts – 600 plus pages of them. In the Introduction to the volume, Williston wrote: 'It was early recognised in planning for the TREATISE ON THE LAW OF CONTRACTS which I have written, that it was desirable, if not essential, that a book of forms should form a part of the undertaking. I did not think it desirable, however, that I should personally undertake this part of the work' (The Treatise (n 21) i).

[23] The Treatise (n 21) iii–iv.

If one accepts that goal, the Treatise is, in my view, really very good. It brings together a lot of what there is to say about doctrinal issues in contracts, and relates these points sensibly to each other. It does, often, discuss the law as debatable and dependent on an assessment of where the balance of considerations lies, rather than simply asserting an outcome as, too often, the *Restatement* would do. In short, it is not by accident that Williston's writing on contracts became *Williston on Contracts*, an authoritative statement of contract law in the United States for the last 100 years. To put the matter most simply, per Westlaw '*Williston on Contracts*' was cited in cases 975 times up to 1929, and, in the original and succeeding editions, over 1,000 times in each succeeding decade up to the present.[24] To put the matter more complexly, here's Peter Benson of the University of Toronto:

> Williston's *A Treatise on the Law of Contracts* represents the most systematically and carefully worked-out presentation of the legal point of view that culminates several decades of intensive and highly sophisticated efforts by such masters of the common law as Pollock, Holmes, Langdell, Ames, Holdsworth, Salmond, and Leake, to bring order and internal consistency to the law of contract. These writers, and Williston in particular, were remarkably successful in achieving this aim.[25]

But this success has not pleased everyone. There has been criticism of Williston's approach from the day the Treatise was published until the present. Of course, being criticised a century later is also testimony, if only backhandedly so, to the importance of the work.[26] But the criticisms must be investigated.

These criticisms fall into three groups.[27] The first is: the Treatise lacks theoretical grounding. The second is: the Treatise is too formal to serve its basic purpose of helping to resolve disputes fairly and usefully. The third is: the Treatise is, purposefully or not, part of a programme to hide behind an

[24] It is, of course, very difficult to determine exactly how much influence on the law this large number of citations actually signals. For example, shortly after the Treatise appeared it was three-times cited in Cardozo's famous opinion in *Jacob & Youngs, Inc v Kent* 129 NE 889 (NY 1921), which in turn becomes the leading opinion on the question of what constitutes substantial performance in a construction contract, and what its legal effect shall be. All three citations are to §§ 841 or 842 of the Treatise, dealing with substantial performance, and they include a quotation from Williston: 'In the nature of the case precise boundaries are impossible' – which is the thrust of Cardozo's opinion. But, of course, Cardozo cites other authorities, and writes a wonderful explication of the rule in his own voice, too. Yet again, the opinion, despite its later acceptance as a leading case, was decided on a 4–3 vote, and the authority of Williston may have mattered in reaching the result. Query: do these citations stand for a substantial influence, continued in the hundreds of cases in which *Jacob & Youngs Inc v Kent* is itself cited, whether Williston's name appears or not, or do they stand for a nice embellishment on what would have happened anyway?

[25] P Benson, 'Introduction' in P Benson (ed), *The Theory of Contract Law: New Essays* (Cambridge, Cambridge University Press, 2001) 2.

[26] The reception of Williston up until 2005 is canvassed in ML Movsesian, 'Rediscovering Williston' (2005) 62 *Washington & Lee Law Review* 207, 208–13.

[27] I am putting to one side minor critiques, made in some of the reviews of the Treatise, on the order of: Williston's use of language wanders a bit and is not consistent, or Williston misinterprets a specified line of precedent.

abstract description of apparently fair doctrine, forces that perpetuate social and economic inequality.

First, then, the claim that the Treatise is untheoretical. Williston, it might be said, presents no philosophical treatment of the obligation of promises or of contractual freedom – he produces no economic analysis of the efficiency of enforcing contracts or of its welfare effects – and he offers no sociological analysis of the trust it requires or of the solidarity it produces. Or, as Lon Fuller put the point in a review of the second edition, Williston 'believes that there exists in the cases "a law of contracts", and that it must be sufficiently simple and consistent with itself to be capable of intelligible statement', but what is needed – said Fuller – is 'a philosophic examination of basic premises'.[28] As to this criticism, I think that Williston would simply enter a demurrer. And there are some who would sustain it, who see the excellence of the Treatise to lie exactly in its 'caseness', its matter of 'factness'.[29] Whichever side of the issue one is on, the truth that the Treatise is not theoretical in any of the ways we speak of legal theory today cannot be contested. But the fact that there are valuable things that Williston does not do, does not mean he does not do valuable things.

The second criticism – that the Treatise is too formal to accomplish the very things it is meant to do – cuts much deeper, if it is true. It is important, in considering this range of issues, to distinguish the concept of 'doctrinal' from the concept of 'formal'. *Williston on Contracts* is undoubtedly doctrinal. Indeed, one might say that it is unabashedly doctrinal, in the sense, as already suggested, that it is the culmination of a scholarly project carried out by many writers over many years to take bits and pieces of case law that are highly situational – such as who is responsible if a telegram has been mis-transcribed, or what is the effect of the unknown death of a contracting party just as the deal is about to be finally struck – and combine the bits into more general categories. As to this effort as a whole, one may well have multiple, and somewhat contradictory, responses. One might think that without doctrine – without creating some categories of what counts as being like what else, and what counts as being different – there can be no equality before the law. (Even the abstract, totally equal, stock characters 'A' and 'B' of the *Restatement* – one might say, especially these stock characters – exist not 'naturally', but as a result of the legal imagination.) One might also think that any set of categories that is used will tilt discussions in one way or another. (If we make contracting into a process of 'offer' and 'acceptance', we are making it more transactional in appearance than it may well be in fact.[30])

[28] See, eg, LL Fuller, 'Williston on Contracts, Revised Edition' (1939) 18 *North Carolina Law Review* 1, 13–14. To the same effect, see Benson (n 25) 2–3.

[29] See BA Black, 'Some Contract History: About Samuel Williston' in DW Hamilton and AL Brophy (eds), *Transformations in American Legal History II 299–300* (Cambridge MA, Harvard University Press, 2010) (what motivated Williston was 'his own investment in honesty, candor, and fairness').

[30] See I Macneil, 'The Many Futures of Contracts' (1974) 47 *Southern California Law Review* 691 (theory of relational contract) (discussed by Morgan, chapter 12 of this volume).

This tension is unresolvable; and in any case Williston did not try, at least as far as I know, to resolve it. What he thinks, I believe, is that he is using categories that are already present in the legal culture he is speaking to and about,[31] but of course, like any situated critic, he is also refining them.

This unresolvable tension inherent in any use of doctrine is different from the question of whether the particular doctrine used is, or is not, formal. Formality is a feature of a doctrine that is a matter of degree, more or less. It depends on the substance of the doctrine, and how it is meant to be used. To illustrate, consider § 90 of the *Restatement (First) of the Law of Contracts*:

> A promise which the promisor should reasonably expect to induce action or forbearance of a definite and substantial character on the part of the promisee and which does induce such action or forbearance is binding if injustice can be avoided only by enforcement of the promise.[32]

This clearly functions the way doctrines do: it focuses the inquiry on a few, specified points; it makes some evidence relevant, and some irrelevant; it helps determine the final legal result. It is a substitute for the most central doctrine of contract law, the doctrine of consideration. But it contains parts that vary widely as to their formality. The words 'of a definite and substantial character' increase the formality of the 'action or forbearance' necessary to trigger the provision,[33] while 'if injustice can be avoided only by enforcement' is about as informal as can be.

In the context of the response to *Williston on Contracts*, sparked as it was by the rise of legal 'realism' in American legal scholarship, there are at least three different (albeit connected) claims that might be included in the proposition that a legal argument or legal doctrine is 'too formal'. First, it might mean that the offered analysis is too deductive, that the components of the argument are arranged in a hierarchical order and the lower points (such as what count as the operative facts) are erroneously thought to be logically entailed from the higher ones. A claim that there is a sharp distinction between the law of contracts and the law of quasi-contracts, and that the major rules of contract law can be derived from this distinction, would be an example of this kind of formality. Second, it might mean that, however the operative elements of the doctrines are derived, they are overly broad: they encompass too many situations that are in fact meaningfully different, and try to treat all of them as if they were the

[31] For example, Williston rejects adopting in any strict way Hohfeld's very precise linguistic analysis of legal categories because of its unnaturalness to those who use the law. See S Williston, *Some Modern Tendencies in the Law* (New York, Baker, Voorhis & Co, 1929) 130–39. In a somewhat more argumentative posture, he also critiques Llewellyn's statement of the virtues of legal realism for its 'belief in the desirability of grouping legal situations in narrower categories than has been customary' as a posture that 'substitutes precedent for reason' (Williston (n 1) 213).

[32] *Restatement (First) of the Law of Contracts* (Philadelphia, American Law Institute, 1932) § 90.

[33] Correspondingly, when the 'definite and substantial' requirement was dropped in the *Restatement (Second) of the Law of Contracts* (Philadelphia, American Law Institute, 1981) § 90, the provision became less formal.

same thing. The idea that all contracts begin with an 'offer', and that offers are all meaningfully the same (that is, are subject to the same rules of acceptance) whether made in business or socially, whether written or oral, whether to a specific individual or to everyone, would be an example of formality of this type. Third, it might mean that the operative facts for the application of the proposed doctrines are meant to be easily and overtly ascertainable, dependent only on the 'form' of what occurred (and, procedurally speaking, easily determined by the judge rather than the jury). Making the interpretation of a contract depend on whether it is incorporated in a signed writing, stating specific terms, rather than depending on the process by which agreement was reached and the intentions of the parties thereto, is to be formal in this sense.[34] 'Too formal' in the view of the critics.

Of course, all law – at least any legal decision that goes beyond Max Weber's ideal-type of Kadi justice – is to some degree formal. The question of whether the Treatise is 'too' formal is self-evidently a matter of degree. Undoubtedly it sets out (as stated in its first page) 'to treat the subject of contracts as a whole, and to show the wide range of application of its principles'.[35] And clearly Williston cared a lot about the formality of particular doctrines, because he cared about whether doctrine was usable, and usable not only by judges but by those who had to predict what the judges might say. But those were not the only things he cared about. To evaluate the question of degree, we need to look more particularly at what the Treatise says.

It is true that, at times, Williston resolves an issue with an offhanded and simple remark that seems inadequate for the complexity of the question at hand. 'It is a necessary requirement in the nature of things that an agreement in order to be binding must be sufficiently definite to enable a court to fix an exact meaning upon it'[36] is one example. 'It is a consequence of the rule that unsealed promises without consideration are not binding, that offers unless under seal or given for consideration may be revoked at any time prior to the creation of a contract by acceptance'[37] is another. But he can just as straightforwardly reject

[34] Regarding claims that *Williston on Contracts* is too formal in one or the other of the specified senses, see, eg, H Dagan and M Heller, *The Choice Theory of Contracts* (Cambridge, Cambridge University Press, 2017) 7–9 (Williston too trans-substantive); F Kessler, 'Review of Volume One of Corbin on Contracts' (1952) 61 *Yale Law Journal* 1093 (*Williston on Contracts* 'tried to restore the lost unity of the law of contracts; Corbin on Contracts avoids the trap'); M Horwitz, *The Transformation of American Law 1780–1860* (Cambridge MA, Harvard University Press, 1977) 200–201 (objective theory a formalism that disguises social reality); G Gilmore, *The Death of Contract* (Columbus, Ohio State University Press, 1974) 32–34, 42–44 (Williston as too deductive); at 57–60 (Corbin interested in facts, Williston not); WW Cook, 'Williston on Contracts [2d ed.]' (1938–39) 33 *Illinois Law Review* 497, 505ff (Williston wrongly assumes doctrinal unity of socially different situations). For general discussions of claim that Williston was formal or too formal, see AD Boyer, 'Samuel Williston's Struggle with Depression' (1994) 42 *Buffalo Law Review* 1 and Movsesian (n 26).

[35] Williston, 'Preface' in the Treatise (n 21) iii.

[36] *ibid* § 37.

[37] *ibid* § 55.

technical, doctrinal logic when it seems to him to be wrong. 'Whatever may be the apparent technical difficulties, it is obvious that justice requires some remedy to be given'.[38] And it is also true that he can state simply, propositions of considerable sophistication:

> Only on the supposition that every act or word in the formation of a contract can have but one possible sense can interpretation lose its importance. Even on this supposition interpretation still is a logical necessity … the law must decide in any litigation on a contract referring by name to Blackacre that the word is applicable to some particular piece of land.[39]

To get an understanding of what Williston's jurisprudence in practice amounted to, we will have to go beyond quotation of adventitious remarks and look at his fuller discussions.

We can begin with a topic which continues to be controversial in American law: the proper way to interpret written agreements.[40] The most 'formal' view of this matter would start by assuming that words and texts have a plain meaning which should be directly enforced by a court, and only where the text is mired in ambiguity should the court go on to consider evidence beyond the document's face to help determine its meaning. The polar opposite view would assume that words are always used contextually, and the court must hear evidence, both of usages and of the intentions of the particular parties, before it can determine what the agreement means.

Williston adopts the second point of view for what he terms 'informal' agreements – oral agreements, or those for which such writing as there might be was not meant to be a full statement of the deal. In that case, a party is bound only by 'the sense in which the party who used the words in question should reasonably have apprehended that the other party would understand them', and if these senses materially differed between the parties, there would be no contract.[41] Written contracts, however, are different. 'Formal and written contracts may exist though parties attach different meanings to the language' because the parties 'have assented to the writing as the adequate expression of the things to which they agree'.[42]

Even accepting this focus on the written text, however, there is still interpretive work to be done. Williston, borrowing from Wigmore, lists four possible standards of interpretation.[43] On the assumption that the assent is to the writing, Williston excludes as not relevant any 'individual' meaning or a peculiar,

[38] *ibid* § 357 (regarding the need to give a remedy directly to the named beneficiary of a life insurance policy).

[39] *ibid* § 601.

[40] Compare *Trident Center v Connecticut General Life Ins Co* 847 F2d 564 (9th Cir 1988) with *Pacific Gas and Electric Co v GW Thomas Drayage & Rigging Co* 442 P2d 641 (Cal 1968).

[41] The Treatise (n 21) § 605.

[42] *ibid* § 606.

[43] *ibid* § 603.

secret 'mutual' meaning. That leaves us to interpret using '[t]he standard of the community, or *popular* standard, meaning the common and normal sense of words; [or] the *local* standard, including the special usages of a religious sect, a body of traders, an alien population, of a local dialect'.[44] The proper answer, says Williston, 'is the local standard; that is, the natural meaning of the writing to parties of the kind who contracted at the time and place where the contract was made, and with such circumstances as surrounded its making'.[45] He asserts that this follows both from the 'weight of authority and on principle', but as he makes no effort to prove the weight of authority, and indeed acknowledges that the cases are mixed, it is the 'on principle' argument that carries the burden.[46] We should choose the local standard, he says, because it is very likely the meaning the other party to the deal would ascribe to the agreed words, but is not subject to the uncertainties of proof that use of a purely individual, or idiosyncratic mutual standard would entail. '[A] reasonable degree of certainty is attained if words are construed according to a standard not peculiar to the parties, but customary among persons of their kind under the existing circumstances'.[47]

Williston goes on to embrace the corollary that there is no need to show that the 'normal' or 'popular' meaning of contractual language is ambiguous, before evidence of the 'local' standard – usages or circumstances – can be shown, even though courts often assert the contrary.[48] 'The only kind of evidence … likely to cause difficulty', he says, 'is that relating to previous negotiations between the parties, especially if these negotiations lead to the formation of the subsequent written contract in question'.[49] Here, of course, we run smack into the parol evidence rule. Williston's solution is the logical one on his analysis: the parties' negotiations may not be used to show their actual intent, but may be used, even without proof of ambiguity, 'to prove that the parties were dealing in regard to a matter or to secure an object, or under circumstances where local usage would give a particular meaning to the language'.[50]

How formal is all of this? Clearly Williston's approach to written contracts embraces both elements of form and pieces of context. Our evaluation will look

[44] *ibid* (Williston quoting *Wigmore on Evidence* § 2461) (emphasis in original).

[45] *ibid* § 607. (We should incidentally note, and credit, Williston (and Wigmore) for adopting such a capacious point of view regarding local usages at a time when the foreign-born population of the United States was very high and xenophobia was rampant.)

[46] *ibid*.

[47] *ibid* § 608. Williston does allow that 'in case of deeds of conveyance, or of negotiable instruments, which are relied upon not simply by the parties to them, but by others, the normal rather than the local standard may be defensible' (*ibid*).

[48] *ibid* § 629; see also § 650: '[I]t is often said also that usage is admissible to explain what is doubtful but never to contradict what is plain. If this statement means that usage is not admitted to contradict a meaning apparently plain if proof of the usage were excluded (and this is what the statement seems naturally to mean), it is inconsistent with many decisions and wrong on principle'.

[49] *ibid* § 630.

[50] *ibid*.

very different if we imagine the supposed alternative to be a legal regime that tells judges to look only at the face of a document and enforce its apparent, ordinary – 'plain' – meaning, or instead imagine a legal regime that tells judges to admit and use any evidence, whether of negotiations or otherwise, that is relevant to determining what the intentions of the parties in fact were. Williston asserts that his in-between position has case support, but it would seem that the existence and general use of the parol evidence rule in American contract law would make the first of these comparative regimes closer to being the standard than the second. If so, it would seem that Williston is propounding rules that are less formal than their likely alternatives. He recognises the difficulties of proof inherent in purely subjective modes of interpretation, but what he advocates makes interpretation more contextual – more dependent on proof – than one might expect from a supposed 'formalist'.

Another good example of Williston's modulated approach in action is his chapter on duress.[51] It begins with a quick summary of the older, more restricted doctrines of undue influence as well as of duress, coalescing in a broader modern law under the latter term. He then addresses what he considers the general feature of duress cases to be: that consent was coerced. Here he flirts with 'freedom of will' language (hard to apply since duress operates by influencing a choice, not by preventing one) but ultimately settles on a somewhat more operational basic rule for finding duress: 'the consent of the party seeking to avoid the transaction was coerced. That is, that he was actually induced by the duress or undue influence to give his consent and would not have done so otherwise'.[52]

Williston then turns to a contested point: whether the standard just stated contains an 'objective' element. Here, shorn of numerous citations in footnotes, is what he has to say:

> The statements in the early books assert that in order to constitute duress by threats the threats in question must be such as to put a brave man in fear. Later, the standard of courage was somewhat reduced, but it was said that duress must consist of something sufficient to overcome the will of a person of ordinary firmness, and the rule in this latter form with more or less qualification is frequently repeated in modern cases, though in many of the cases which repeat the formula, the question was not really involved. The tendency of the modern cases, and undoubtedly the correct rule is that any unlawful threats which do in fact overcome the will of the person threatened, and induce him to do an act which he would not otherwise have done, and which he was not bound to do, constitute duress. The age, sex, capacity, relation of the parties and all the attendant circumstances must be considered. This follows the analogy of the modern doctrine of fraud which tends to disregard the question whether misrepresentations were such as would have deceived a reasonable person, and confines the question to whether the misrepresentations were intended to deceive and did so.[53]

[51] *ibid* §§ 1601ff.
[52] *ibid* § 1604.
[53] *ibid* § 1605.

It would be hard to say that this passage is formal, let alone 'too formal'. There are two lines of cases, both recent, from which a choice must be made. In so far as we are given a reason for why one of them is 'undoubtedly' correct, it is not deductive logic, but an analogy (to fraud) that supplies the premise. More clearly, Williston rejects, rather than accepts, a 'reasonable person' test that might be operationalised with somewhat hard edges, that might develop into a series of rules based on precedent, and whose effect, accordingly, might be predictable, or at least easily determined in pre-trial motions. To the contrary: the 'relation of the parties' matters and 'all the attendant circumstances must be considered'.

Much of the rest of the chapter about duress addresses particular examples of the general idea that '[t]he pressure must be wrongful'.[54] Some examples Williston states as straightforward rules:

> a threat to bring [legal] action is not such duress as to justify rescission of a transaction induced thereby ... provided the threat is made in good faith; that is, in the belief that a possible cause of action exists.[55]

However, even these are often contextual at least in part:

> Even a threat of ordinary litigation may be made under such circumstances as to render the threat wrongful as a means of coercion ....Thus, where one of the parties is in such a position as to be easily dominated by the other, or is old and weak-minded, a transaction induced by such a threat may be avoided.[56]

This same pattern of stating a dominant rule, but allowing for an occasional exception based on the interaction of the parties, appears in Williston's discussion under the section heading: 'Neither persuasion nor pressure of circumstances is duress'.[57]

> Nor is it duress or undue influence when a party is constrained to enter into a transaction by force of circumstances for which the other party is not responsible. But it seems clear that if such circumstances were known and advantage taken of them by the other party a degree of pressure which would not ordinarily amount to duress, might have such coercive effect as to invalidate a transaction.[58]

One could, of course, write an entire corpus about the limits of what 'the other party', singly or as a class, 'is not responsible' for. In the first sentence of this passage, Williston restates without discussion (but with citations) a fundamental common-law point of view: we are responsible for what we ourselves, individually, do. And he seems to accept that what we do – ie, action – can be easily, one might say naturally, separated from what we do not do – ie, inaction.

[54] *ibid* § 1606.
[55] *ibid*.
[56] *ibid* § 1607.
[57] *ibid* § 1608.
[58] *ibid*.

Given the flux of actual existence, this seems to be a formal cut-off both in an epistemological sense and in the courtroom sense of furnishing a basis for a motion to dismiss. Yet Williston waivers in the second sentence, and says that taking advantage of known outside pressures might count, too. As he provides no citations for that claim, but says it 'seems clear', we are left with the sense that the doctrine is more porous than it seems. Perhaps Williston's innate sense of fairness is showing.

Overall, then, the Treatise's discussion of duress seems to mix formal and more contextual elements: the pressure must be wrongful, and it must be the cause of the actual decision made; general social conditions not caused by the other party are not taken into account; but the party under pressure need not resist the pressure to a 'reasonable person' standard; and if baleful extrinsic circumstances were known and taken advantage of, the transaction might be invalid. As in the case of interpretation, Williston's actual treatment of duress seems more modulated than the attribution 'formalist' might suggest.

As a final example of the range of considerations Williston deemed relevant to solving a legal question, we can look at his discussion of the implied term in real estate contracts concerning the point in time when the risks of ownership transfer from the vendor to the vendee. Williston opens by saying that the question of an implied 'obligation of the buyer to perform his promise to pay the price in spite of the destruction or deterioration of the premises subsequent to the formation of the contract involves a fundamental question of contractual liability'.[59] He then, in a section entitled 'Risk generally thrown upon the purchaser', states the law briskly:

> Since the decision of *Paine v Meller* it has not been doubted in England that the purchaser is not excused from fulfilling his promise to purchase by any accidental injury to the property. It is not surprising that the English law has had a marked effect upon the decisions in the United States. A majority of the American courts which have dealt with the subject have, either in *dicta* or decisions, indicated their assent to Lord Eldon's view though not always without qualification. But there is, nevertheless, a strong dissent.[60]

The right rule, however, as stated in the title to a section that appears some 19 pages later, is that the 'Risk should pass to the purchaser on transfer of possession and not before'.[61]

In the intervening sections Williston makes the following points:

- The equity maxims used to justify the English rule have no persuasive power.[62] ('When, therefore, it is said that equity regards one who has a contract right to property in the future as the immediate owner of it, it is in effect said

[59] *ibid* § 928.
[60] *ibid.*
[61] *ibid* § 940. (In fact, the argument goes on even after the conclusion is stated.)
[62] *ibid* § 929.

that equity regards two things which are inherently different as the same. Only the hoary age and frequent repetition of the maxim prevents a general recognition of its absurdity.')

- While there are many rules which follow the idea of equitable ownership[63] (for example: 'The vendee can call for a conveyance of the property from a donee.'[64]), there are many rules that do not[65] (for example: 'The vendor in possession is liable for taxes.').[66] In so far as these differences reflect a split between law and equity, there is no reason for making that distinction.[67]
- The English rule originated before the law for sales of goods shifted to viewing the promises in bilateral agreements as mutually dependent; the rule shifting the risk of loss to the vendee is a historical hangover inconsistent with this more modern approach.[68]
- If the date of transfer of possession is stipulated by the agreement to be different from the date of transfer of title, the intentions of the parties are mostly clearly revealed by the date of transfer of possession.[69]
- The argument that 'as the vendee gets the benefit of any chance improvement of the property, he should therefore suffer the chance loss' is unpersuasive; 'there are practically no chance improvements analogous to chance destruction'.[70]
- 'The practical advantages of leaving the risk with the vendor until transfer of possession are obvious'. 'It is wiser to have the party in possession of property care for it at his peril, rather than at the peril of another'. In addition, the vendor is normally insured at the time of the making of the contract, and the vendee relies on this insurance.[71]
- And finally, the equity rule does not follow the approach taken in analogous, purely contractual, cases regarding excuse for acts of God, such as *Taylor v Caldwell*.[72]

What are we to make of this argument, other than that it is long and very rich?[73] Much of the argument is not fundamentally doctrinal. It is factual – the likelihood of chance improvements is small; and it is situational – it is the person

[63] *ibid* § 930.
[64] *ibid*.
[65] *ibid*.
[66] *ibid* § 937.
[67] *ibid* § 934.
[68] *ibid* § 933.
[69] *ibid* § 940.
[70] *ibid* § 941.
[71] *ibid* § 942.
[72] *ibid* § 943.
[73] And indeed, longer than just presented, for Williston also discusses the matter as it was treated in Roman Law (*ibid* §§ 947ff) and as then currently treated in what he calls 'continental law' (*ibid* §§ 951ff).

in possession who can take practical precautions to preserve the property. If we imagine the 'realist' Karl Llewellyn analysing the problem as a matter of 'situation-sense', these are points he, too, would make.[74] And in so far as the argument is doctrinal, it is not very formal. The reference to the probable 'intention of the parties' at one point might be thought to be a very abstract – and perhaps fictitious – way of handling who bears the risk of loss here. But by and large the doctrinal points are not made deductively; rather than being seen as conclusions drawn from higher principles, doctrines are rather tested for fit with each other.[75] Indeed, in some sense even the argument against equity is also based on an assertion of fact over form. Williston sets the stage for his discussion with an attack on oft-employed equity maxims such as, 'Equity regards as done what is agreed to be done'. And this attack is fundamentally an assertion by Williston (not the courts) as to what is the fact: 'It can hardly be denied that present ownership is a different thing from future ownership. However certain it may be that in the future one will become the owner of property, it is a different thing from owning it now'.[76]

Let us return to the general question: Is *Williston on Contracts* 'too formal'? As already stated, this question seems to include claims that it is mistakenly deductive, that it unites under single analyses situations that are in fact very disparate and meaningfully different, and that it overly differentiates rules by looking at superficial differences that are only matters of form.

To start, Williston's typical analysis does not proceed from a strong internal hierarchy of premises, such that many specific rules or doctrines proceed from a small number of strongly entrenched major propositions. The logic of the Treatise is not, generally speaking, formal in that sense. True, Williston often says that a rule is right not merely as a matter of precedent, but also 'on principle'. But the principle is often left unstated, and it is not clear that he is referring to the same principle from example to example. Indeed, the analyses are rather unsystematic; the considerations that Williston brings to bear in answering one question are not the same as he uses for the next. Sometimes, for example, he worries about the functional impact of what he discusses, and sometimes he does not. No doubt what he presents is a form of reasoning, but it is not a deductive form. Rather, it is jigsaw puzzle reasoning: choosing from among the pieces that might fit a particular space that piece whose edges match the constraints set by the other parts of the puzzle. It is a search for coherence.

[74] See T Rakoff, 'Implied Terms: Of "Default Rules" and "Situation Sense"' in J Beatson and D Friedmann (eds), *Good Faith and Fault in Contract Law* (Oxford, Clarendon Press, 1995).

[75] Moreover, the historical point about contract law having elsewhere moved to seeing mutual promises as interdependent, is, in Williston's view, fundamentally a proposition about what is the fair way to understand how people relate to each other – a proposition that replaced a formalist contention that the promises of each party are independent unless stated to be mutually conditioned (The Treatise (n 21) § 813).

[76] *ibid* § 929.

It is true, however, that each piece of the puzzle is viewed primarily as an element of doctrine: how does this rule of offer and acceptance law match up with this element of the doctrine of consideration? As already said, Williston is definitely a doctrinalist; his questions are asked and answered in doctrinal categories. How far the contents of his doctrines are formal, however, is a debatable question. Duress, defined in terms of a particular decision that would not have been taken but for some pressure emanating from the other party, is both a wide-sweeping and relatively specific approach. But when it must also be a wrongful pressure, and that wrongfulness depends on the characteristics of the actual person subject to the pressure (rather than on those of the 'reasonable person'), it is much less formally realisable. Similarly, while it overstates the matter to say that Williston totally divides written from oral contracts, that is the basic thrust of what he says,[77] and while we can imagine borderline cases, that is a straightforward difference of form. When he goes on to say that written contracts should be interpreted according to local usage, that that usage is subject to proof, not merely of trade usages, but linguistic group by linguistic group, and that that proof can, in some cases at least, include the previous conversations between the parties, the idea that he is expounding a simple rule, easily implemented, flat across many factual circumstances, is harder to maintain. Finally, we should note that, as to the legally constructed performance terms added to contracts concerning matters not specified by the parties, Williston departs from doctrinal formulations and substitutes situationally defined categories. The implied term for when risk of loss passes in a real estate contract, discussed above, is an example taken from Book V of the Treatise – 'Particular Classes of Contracts' – which, in addition to 'Contracts for the Sale of Land', also includes chapters, among others, on 'Contracts for the Sale of Personal Property', 'Contracts of Employment and Contracts to Marry', 'Contracts of Bailment and of Innkeepers', and so forth. (In all, this part of the Treatise runs for 572 pages.) And his reasoning, as we have seen, matches that more contextual approach.

In an excellent article published in 2005, 'Rediscovering Williston',[78] Professor Mark Movsesian responded to what he described as 'the conventional wisdom [that] has lumped Williston together with the great villains of contemporary jurisprudence, the classical formalists'.[79] This account of Williston, he said, 'presents an incomplete and distorted picture of his jurisprudence ... Williston's work has more balance and nuance, and shows more continuity with contemporary contracts scholarship, than we commonly suppose'.[80] In particular,

[77] Williston includes within his category of 'formal' contracts not just contracts overtly meant to state the whole deal, but also contracts with memoranda in writing to satisfy the Statute of Frauds (*ibid* § 604).

[78] Movsesian (n 26).

[79] *ibid* 210.

[80] *ibid* 213.

Movsesian said that 'Williston is a formalist ... But his jurisprudence is not essentialist ... Rather, Williston advocates formalism on pragmatic grounds. For him, formalism's appeal lies in the fact that it promotes the important everyday benefits of simplicity, predictability, and comprehensibility'.[81]

I have no doubt that Professor Movsesian is looking at the same Williston as I am: Williston clearly 'has more balance and nuance' than is ordinarily understood. But I think I would not call Williston a pragmatic formalist. His logic, as I have already said, seems to me less deductive than the label 'formalist' suggests. Moreover, while there is no doubt that Williston sometimes espouses the value of easily operated rules, he also easily overrides that value. Finally, when he overrides formal values he often does so in terms of values that are not easily described as 'pragmatic', if by that we mean to denominate (as does the modern scholarship that Movsesian refers to) functional values. Williston, as I see it, often relies on a deep sense of justice, if we understand justice to be fairness in the interpersonal sense.[82] That seems apparent to me, for example, in his advocacy of a 'local' rather than 'popular' standard for the interpretation of written contracts: the eschewed popular (or common meaning) standard is – in a world of organisations based on written documents, as was probably already the world of the 1920s – the more efficient standard, although the less fair.

What Williston does not seem to rely on, however, is a sense of justice in what we might call a sociological sense, that is, justice in light of socially structured imbalances of power.[83] This brings us to the charge that (to use Morton Horwitz's framing of it) 'Williston was a leading exemplar' of 'a legal ideology of formalism ... that could ... disguise gross disparities of bargaining power under a façade of neutral and formal rules of contract law'.[84] And that, in turn, brings us to the cusp of the Constitutional debate raging at the same time that *Williston on Contracts* was written.

[81] *ibid* 213–14.

[82] This is also the view espoused in Black (n 29).

[83] When social hierarchy does enter the analysis, Williston's instinct is to convert it into the interactions of individuals. For example, in his treatment of duress, already discussed, Williston says that '[t]he age, sex, capacity, relation of the parties and all the attendant circumstances must be considered'. This formulation implicitly treats hierarchies of age and sex as a matter of the personal 'relation of the parties'. In discussing the question of who has to perform first, employer or employee, Williston is more forthright (The Treatise (n 21) § 830):

> The employee must render the service before the payment for it is due. In the nature of things there is no reason why this should be true, but usage is inveterate that the employee shall trust the employer for compensation rather than the employer pay first and trust the employee for the performance of his undertaking; and parties must be understood to contract with reference to the usage. Perhaps the origin both of the usage and of the law is that the employers have been in a position to establish both.

But having made this, for him, unusual observation, he then just accepts this apparent class-favouring rule without further comment.

[84] Horwitz (n 34) 201.

From roughly the turn of the nineteenth to the twentieth century, to the middle of the Great Depression, the Supreme Court of the United States pursued a vigorous programme of protecting 'freedom of contract'. The rights of parties to make deals and have them enforced, it said, was part of the 'liberty' that is protected against unwarranted governmental interference by the due process clauses of the Constitution. Broadly stated, governments could restrict contractual rights in pursuit of the general welfare, but they could not realign those rights between classes of parties; social forces as they played out through the common law of contracts had to be left alone. *Lochner v New York*, decided in 1905,[85] symbolises the era. There, the Court struck down a New York state statute limiting the working hours of bakers to 60 hours a week. The Court rejected the state's claim that being a baker was a dangerous occupation, and asserted more broadly, in the words of Justice Peckham, that the statute unduly restricted the freedom not only of the employer, but also of the employee:

> There is no reasonable ground for interfering with the liberty of person or the right of free contract, by determining the hours of labor, in the occupation of a baker. There is no contention that bakers as a class are not equal in intelligence and capacity to men in other trade or manual occupations, or that they are not able to assert their rights and care for themselves without the protecting arm of the state, interfering with their independence of judgment and of action. They are in no sense wards of the state.[86]

Or, as this abstract equality was rephrased in the *Adair* case, shortly thereafter, '[o]f course, the liberty of contract relating to labor includes both parties to it. The one has as much right to purchase as the other to sell labor'.[87]

Contemporaneous with his Treatise, Williston in 1921 published an article called 'Freedom of Contract'.[88] In it, he discussed both the proposition that the force of contracts was based on the will of the parties, the 'meeting of the minds', and the proposition that human freedom depended on unrestricted enforcement of the deals that parties made, 'laissez-faire'. He considered both of these doctrines to be nineteenth-century exaggerations. And he thought them wrong in principle. As to the importance of private agreement, he wrote:

> Obvious as it is that contractual liability, like all other liability, is based on rules of law, and that the rules of law imposing liability of every kind are based on policy, and that policy may often require a man to be held on what he has justified the adverse party to suppose he would do rather than on what he actually intended to do, the point was not clearly observed while the extreme theory of the necessity of a meeting of minds was held.[89]

[85] *Lochner v New York* 198 US 45 (1905).
[86] *ibid* 57.
[87] *Adair v US* 208 US 161, 174 (1908).
[88] S Williston, 'Freedom of Contract' (1921) 6 *Cornell Law Quarterly* 365.
[89] *ibid* 368.

Among his examples of very well-established legal doctrines not based on the intention of the parties, he discussed the judicial refusal to enforce agreed-on penal damage clauses and the allowance of an excuse, in bilateral contracts, upon the opposite party's substantial failure to perform, even if no such condition had been specified.

As to the role of legislatures as limited by the due process clauses of the US Constitution (as interpreted in *Lochner*) to matters of 'safety, health, morals and general welfare of the public', he wrote:

> This statement need not be quarreled with, but its general language affords wide opportunity for difference of application. If the words 'health, morals and general welfare' are liberally construed and due weight given to the opinion on those matters of the legislature which enacted a law, as compared with the individual opinions of the judges who pass upon its constitutionality, sufficient scope is allowed for reasonable social experiment, but in the very case from which the passage which I have quoted was taken, the United States Supreme Court, upholding the New York Court of Appeals, paid scant respect to the opinion of the New York legislature that a limitation of working hours in bakeries to ten hours would promote health, morals and general welfare, and held the statute unconstitutional.[90]

After identifying many cases in which the courts had stuck down legislation, especially legislation favourable to employees, Williston then said that there had been a 'slow turning of the tide' on employment (and other) legislation, including limitations of hours and the fixing of minimum wages.[91] 'Observation of results has proved that unlimited freedom of contract … does not necessarily lead to public or individual welfare and that the only ultimate test of proper limitations is that provided by experience', he wrote.[92] This is not the fiery attack on the Supreme Court's doctrine that others, like Roscoe Pound, had written. ('Why then do courts persist in the fallacy? Why do so many of them force upon legislation an academic theory of equality in the face of practical conditions of inequality?'[93]) But anyone who reads the article will conclude that Williston favoured the new tide he spied; he may not have been in favour of every act he mentioned, but overall he thought the statutes were beneficial, that they indeed represented the triumph of paying more attention to concrete social experience than to abstract theory. In the straightforward political sense – progressive legislation, up or down – this cannot be considered a conservative point of view.[94]

[90] *ibid* 376.

[91] *ibid* 377. Many of the cases Williston cites upheld statutes that limited their protection to women and children. He remarks: 'if women may be protected for their own good and that of the public from selling their labor on such terms and conditions as may be agreed upon with their employers, there is no reason why men should not be. Women are citizen as well as men, and if women's freedom of contract may be restricted to such a degree as circumstances make reasonable, it follows that men's freedom also may be' (*ibid* 378).

[92] *ibid* 374.

[93] R Pound, 'Liberty of Contract' (1908–1909) 18 *Yale Law Journal* 454.

[94] However, the trend of history, we might note, moved more slowly than Williston expected. In 1923, the US Supreme Court struck down a minimum wage law protecting women (*Adkins v Children's Hospital* 261 US 525 (1923)) and in 1936 again struck down one protecting women and

But we cannot leave this article quite so soon. Its thrust is that there is no concept of 'freedom of contract' that makes contract law different in kind from other types of law; it is all a question of policy based on experience. At the same time, Williston's Treatise treats contract law as a relatively determinate subject with boundaries. Some of these boundaries are doctrinal, as in the separation between contract and restitution (or quasi-contract) that surfaces now and again. But the most striking boundary lies in the materials he overwhelming uses: judicial cases.

Now, it cannot be said that the Treatise ignores the existence of statutes. It mentions their existence (often only in some states, named or unnamed) in many of its doctrinal sections, perhaps as much as a warning to practitioner-users as anything else.[95] For a few topics – regarding a married woman's ability to contract, or the possible separate obligations of joint debtors – the statutes are cited state by state, and briefly explicated.[96] There is substantial discussion in one such instance, regarding statutes abolishing the common law effects of the seal – which Williston criticises because he thinks the legal system needs some way to make gratuitous promises binding.[97] But by and large the attitude of the Treatise to particular statutes of this pointedly doctrinal sort, that they may change the law in particular aspects but do not affect the general thrust of the analysis, is exemplified by their treatment in the Index volume, where there is a several-hundred-pages table of cases, but no table of statutes.

There are, however, three parts of the Treatise that are heavily statutory: the chapter on Statutes of Limitations;[98] several chapters on the Statute of Frauds;[99] and the parts of the Treatise devoted to 'Particular Classes of Contracts' that concern the rules set out in various uniform acts, notably the Uniform Sales Act.[100] Yet these, too, are divorced from the thrust of the Treatise as a whole. Statutes of Limitations provisions are treated, perhaps not surprisingly, as stating fundamentally procedural rules rather than rules going to the meaning of

minors (*Morehead v New York ex rel Tipaldo* 298 US 587 (1936)). 'Freedom of contract', wrote Justice Butler, 'is the general rule and restraint the exception' (*ibid* 610–11). A law fixing minimum wages for women and minors was then upheld in 1937 (*West Coast Hotel Co v Parrish* 300 US 379 (1937)). But it was still a debatable question what would happen when the federal Fair Labor Standards Act (FLSA) of 1938, setting minimum wages more generally, came before the Court. See RL Stern and RS Smethurst, 'How the Supreme Court May View the Fair Labor Standards Act' (1939) 6 *Law and Contemporary Problems* 431. The FLSA was sustained in 1941 (*US v Darby* 312 US 100 (1941)), the Court decreeing that 'it is no longer open to question that the fixing of a minimum wage is within the legislative power and that the bare fact of its exercise is not a denial of due process' (*ibid* 125).

[95] See, eg, the Treatise (n 21) § 230, mentioning statutes regarding the effect of infancy; §§ 365–66, mentioning statutes affecting recoveries by third-party beneficiaries.

[96] *ibid* §§ 268–69, regarding a married woman's ability to contract; § 336, regarding the separate obligations of joint debtors.

[97] *ibid* §§ 218–19.

[98] *ibid* §§ 2001–44.

[99] *ibid* §§ 448–600.

[100] *ibid* §§ 955–1011.

contractual liability as a whole.[101] The Statute of Frauds is seen through the same lens: 'it seems better to call the rule of the statute one of remedial procedure, somewhat analogous to the rule of the Statute of Limitations'.[102] The Sales Act is, of course, more than that. It could perhaps have been used to establish a point of view regarding the common law of contracts as a whole.[103] But Williston does not do that. His discussion elsewhere of the general law of warranty of quality, for example, relies on common-law case law – including older common-law case law regarding the sale of goods – but does not refer to or cite the Sales Act.[104] Perhaps this is because Williston understands the Sales Act itself as codifying the common law.[105] But, whatever the reason, the title of the chapter that includes consideration of the Sales Act – 'Particular Classes of Contracts' – seems to reflect the limited purpose to which it is discussed.

The relationship between statutes and common law reappears in an article Williston published in 1942.[106] Here he listed '[t]he objects that an ideal system of private law should seek to attain' as follows:

1. Tribunals that are independent, unbiased and learned.
2. Tribunals that are not autocratic and are sympathetic with the *mores* of the community.
3. The law should afford a prompt and conclusive settlement of disputes.
4. Each party to a litigation should have a reasonable opportunity to present evidence and argument in support of his claim.
5. The rules governing the disposition of cases and adjustment of rights should be fair and just and logically coherent in their general application.
6. The result in each litigation should be fair and just as between the parties to it.
7. Freedom of contract and individual initiative should be permitted.
8. The rights and duties of individuals should be so adjusted as to promote social welfare.
9. The rules should have stability, so that individuals may safely rely on past precedents in determining their rights and duties and in predicting the outcome of litigation.[107]

Assuming that the sequence of criteria is intentional, it is striking that, in pursuing the 'ideal system of private law', Williston begins with tribunals deciding

[101] *ibid* § 2002.
[102] *ibid* § 527.
[103] For example, the Uniform Commercial Code, Article II, the successor to the Sales Act, has been relied on to establish the existence of 'unconscionability' as part of the common law. See *Williams v Walker-Thomas Furniture Co* 350 F 2d 445 (DC Cir 1965).
[104] The Treatise (n 21) §§ 1505–1506.
[105] *ibid* § 982.
[106] S Williston, 'Fashions in Law with Illustrations from the Law of Contracts' (1942) 21 *Texas Law Review* 119.
[107] *ibid* 119–20.

individual disputes. The issues we have just discussed regarding 'freedom of contract', and the proper role of the legislature in articulating 'social welfare', do not appear until steps 7 and 8. Through point 6 we appear to be in a litigative procedural frame. Yet by that time the system is already enjoined to reach, in litigation, a 'fair and just' result. What has made that possible? Steps 1 to 5 describe a system of procedural fairness and tribunals that apply rules that are 'fair and just and logically coherent'. And the prerequisite to this is judges who are not 'autocratic' but rather, from the start, 'are sympathetic with the *mores* of the community'.

Williston was not – neither in the 1921 article on 'Freedom of Contract', nor in the 1942 article we are now discussing – opposed to legislation in general. But the question is, how did he see it interacting with the common law of contracts. The answer, I think, is that he saw statutes (and ensuing administrative implementation) as changing the outcomes of cases, but not as changing the fundamental bases of common law thinking except in their slow impact on the culture in general. As he saw it, statutes, primarily, were about the pursuit of social welfare, and the common law, primarily, was a continuation of the mores of the society to reach just outcomes between parties, ie, the 'private law'. This, of course, was not a unique view; indeed, one might say that it was implicit in the doctrine of substantive due process we just discussed. That doctrine said that statutes needed to be justified, and justified on the basis of being in pursuit of the general welfare. For otherwise they might just be grabs by those with political power. The common law set the background rules against which statutes were compared, because the common law was conceived to be non-ideological, or perhaps just the way we were.

Speaking more broadly, Williston, I think, understood the common law not politically, but as a deeply cultural event. Like culture in general, it was not rationalised from one particular point of view, but rather combined various normative and practical elements in various ways. The judge was expected to be wise in the sense of being able to discover and articulate the values actually at play in any controversy. Having done that, the judge was expected to correct those mores so they were 'fair and just and logically coherent', and then apply the culturally correct, but thoughtful, answer to the situation before him. Done properly, a judicial decision was an exemplar of the culture, and correspondingly a signpost to the standards of justice it contained.

And the role of a treatise writer vis-à-vis the body of law and social interactions that he was trying to systematise?[108] He was meant to understand the customs and mores of the society, but not be limited to them. He was to be more active than an anthropological 'participant observer', but he was not meant to be a 'social engineer' designing institutions or rules abstractly for general

[108] I am speaking here based on Williston's lecture entitled 'The Work of Teachers of Law Affecting Its Development', but in my terms, not Williston's. The lecture comprises Ch III of Williston (n 31) 107–58.

advantage, without regard to what had gone before. Nor was he meant to be what might be called a 'philosophical engineer', insisting that the whole body of law be seen from a single point of view. Like a judge, he was, I think, meant to be 'wise', understanding the various social forces and values at stake, able to differentiate the main thrusts from the qualifications or aberrations, and careful about upsetting existing compromises among values or points of view, but yet not prohibited from recommending changes.[109]

One might take this point of view regarding judges and scholars as being inherently conservative in a cultural sense, although how it would play out in terms of the distribution of power or advantage in a society would depend on the concrete norms at stake. And one must also take into consideration Williston's willingness to accept, even advocate for, a departure from existing doctrine to be made by legislation even when he thought judges should not open up the case law that far.[110] This again – depending on the concrete political distribution of forces – might, or might not, make his approach conservative.

Regardless of the political slant, the result of this point of view, systematically applied, is to wall off statutory developments, except those that tinker with specific doctrines, from informing a parallel development in common law thinking. Take, for example, the question of a legislatively established minimum wage. Assuming it is accepted by the legal system, as it ultimately was in the United States, what does it stand for? Williston, in the 1921 article, describes 'minimum wage laws' as laws 'forbidding employment under ordinary circumstances for less than an amount fixed as the minimum upon which life may be decently and reasonably supported'.[111] That is a fair, one might even say favourable, description. But it is a description – perhaps influenced by the Supreme Court's doctrine – phrased in terms of general social welfare. If we instead framed the statute in terms that made it continuous with the transactional justice of the common law, it would look different. If we said, for example, that minimum wage laws represent a refusal to enforce private wage arrangements for less than the statutorily specified minimum, because they were presumptively entered into under duress, we would be making a very different claim. We would be recognising that being poor in a market society, lacking skills valued by the marketplace and lacking the capital needed to work independently, constitutes being under duress when deciding to accept an offer of employment at a very low wage.[112]

[109] *cf* his view of *stare decisis* ('It is also easy to pay too great respect to the rule of *stare decisis* by failing to overrule a previous decision that no longer commends itself to the court') (Williston (n 31) 85–86).

[110] For example, in the Treatise he suggests that the problem posed by foreseeable reliance on, but not yet acceptance of, an offer for a unilateral contract – the crossing-the-Brooklyn-Bridge problem – cannot be solved within the case law, but is ripe for legislative resolution (The Treatise (n 21) § 60, 60a). The *Restatement (First) of the Law of Contracts* (n 32), for better or worse, did stipulate a solution in § 45.

[111] Williston (n 88) 377.

[112] We could then substitute for the contract rate the minimum wage in satisfaction of a restitutionary claim for the fair value of work done.

Williston, as we have seen, says that the general (although perhaps occasionally qualified) rule is that the 'force of circumstances for which the other party is not responsible' does not constitute duress. But if we treated the now-common passage of minimum-wage laws as relevant to the general common-law doctrine, we would open up the entire question, submerged in the Treatise, of whether social circumstances not caused by the opposing party can be treated as creating legally effective duress.[113]

More broadly yet, we can ask whether it is possible, in the present day with its plethora of statutes and administrative agencies, to continue the treatise tradition at all. *Williston on Contracts*, for example, has a fine section on fraud that is reformist in tone, especially as regards the requirement of intention to deceive, and reaching the following crescendo:

> The real issue is no less than this: When a defendant has induced another to act by representations false in fact though not dishonestly made, and damage has directly resulted from the action taken, who should bear the loss?
>
> In considering which doctrine is the better, consideration should be given chiefly to two things. First: logical consistency with itself in all parts of the law governing misrepresentation. Secondly: the inherent justice of the rule proposed. That the law of misrepresentation as laid down in Derry v. Peek [requiring scienter] is hopelessly inconsistent with the law governing misrepresentation when relied on as the basis of warranty or estoppel can hardly be denied …
>
> The inherent justice of the severer rule of liability which in some cases at least holds a speaker liable for damages for false representation, though his intentions were innocent and his statements honestly intended, is equally clear. However honest his state of mind, he has induced another to act, and damage has been thereby caused …[114]

Willison goes on to consider the (usually mixed) cases on various aspects of the proposed doctrine, and possible qualifications in particular circumstances.

But if we wanted to know the law today as to the general question of what has to be shown to establish liability of some sort for misrepresentation, where would we turn? For the question directly at issue in *Derry v Peek*[115] – the need (or not) to prove scienter in fraud actions concerning securities offerings, we would go to the Securities Act of 1933 and maybe the Securities Exchange Act of 1934, and the regulations thereunder, as well as to their interpretation by the Securities and Exchange Commission and by the courts. For questions concerning the boundaries of the law of misrepresentation more broadly, we would need to look at the Federal Trade Commission Act and its regulations; at the Food and Drug Act and its regulations; at the Federal Truth-in-Lending Act and its regulations;

[113] The *Restatement (Second)* fudges this issue by making an offer coming from an opposing party potentially a threat, which seems perhaps doctrinally useful but contrary to the ordinary understanding of the terms. (See the *Restatement (Second) of the Law of Contracts* (n 33) § 176 and comment a).

[114] The Treatise (n 21) § 1510.

[115] *Derry v Peek* (1889) LR 14 App Cas 337 (HL).

at the Dodd-Frank Act and its regulations; at various state consumer protection statutes and their accompanying regulations; and on and on. And we would not find consistent results – not consistent as to what constitutes a representation; not consistent as to scienter; not consistent as to the need to show reliance by recipients of the misrepresentation; not consistent as to possible remedies; and so forth. There would be a residue of situations as to which only the common law of fraud applies, but in terms of social impact, that residue would be small.

The explanation for this state of affairs is obvious: each of these departures from the common law is based on a statute, each of these statutes covers only part of the possible universe, and the requirements of each statute reflect, at least in part, the particular political constellation of its passage. The predominant approach to these statutes in the American legal culture is, unsurprisingly, to treat each of them as establishing a unique body of law. In courts, and in the scholarly literature, the questions that are addressed are: What did Congress mean when it said such-and-such, and how do we tell what Congress meant?; and, if an administrative agency is involved, what did the agency say, and how much deference do we give to the agency? Unless there is clear evidence that one statute was based on another, it would be considered wrong, in such a universe, to cite from the way misrepresentation is treated in one of these regimes to the way it is treated in another. Whether one could repeat the work of the great common law treatise builders, and, taking the various statutory embodiments of a core doctrine such as fraud as raw material, proceed to organise them into intelligible categories and principles, is unknown: no one, to my knowledge, has tried. There has been no attempt to build a general meta-theory that would justify one departure from the common law in this statute, and a different departure in that statute.[116] There are of course books organising the law of particular practice areas, such as securities law. But the law is segmented; there is no claim that there is a general doctrine.[117]

In a fine article, Brian Simpson has traced the history of legal treatises in the Anglo-American world, which, he said, culminated in four 'ultimate treatises'. Listed chronologically, they were: *Wigmore on Evidence*, *Williston on Contracts*, *Scott on Trusts* and *Corbin on Contracts*.[118] But, he said, writing

[116] Perhaps not surprisingly, the current, online fourth edition of *Williston on Contracts*, ch 69, appears to state the law of fraud solely based on its common law embodiment. This leads to statements such as: 'No legal wrong is caused by false and fraudulent representations unless they induce action in reliance upon them' § 69:32 (Westlaw, 26/6/2021). Assessment of the accuracy of this statement depends on quibbling about the words 'legal wrong'; rather than pursuing that argument, perhaps it suffices to say that it is quite clear that, to take one example, the Federal Trade Commission can and does determine that an advertisement is 'deceptive' under its governing statute if it has the 'capacity to deceive' customers, without showing that anyone has actually relied on the advertisement. The consequence is a 'cease and desist' order that takes the advertisement – which might have been constructed at considerable cost – out of circulation.

[117] On this segmented situation in general, see TD Rakoff, 'The Shape of the Law in The American Administrative State' (1992) 11 *Tel-Aviv University Studies In Law* 9.

[118] AWB Simpson, 'The Rise and Fall of the Legal Treatise' (1981) 48 *University of Chicago Law Review* 632, 674.

in 1981, the 'treatise-writing tradition' in America had 'declined rather markedly'.[119] In Simpson's view, this was primarily a result of the 'realist movement' that 'involved a skepticism and even a cynicism about the significance of legal doctrine in the determination of cases'.[120] To me, that sounds rather 1980-ish; it is my impression that predictions of the demise of doctrine, common around that time, have turned out to be wrong. At the least, courts still cite doctrine, and contracts professors, online, frame questions to each other in doctrinal terms; perhaps everyone is playing a deep game, but, while doctrine is surely not everything, I doubt it is nothing. The much bigger challenge to Williston's treatise, or to the treatise tradition in general, is that it is meant to organise common law decisions, and most of the law, even most of the law of contracts, is statutory.

In this changed universe, *Williston on Contracts* is still very significant as a historical landmark. Many of the statutes I have just mentioned are best understood as departures from the common law in particular ways rather than as *sui generis* law-making efforts, and you cannot analyse a departure without knowing where you started. But, for the practitioner or the professor, relying on Williston today as describing the law – which, after all, was its original purpose – would be a risky business.

[119] *ibid* 676–77.
[120] *ibid* 677.

8

Professor Arthur Linton Corbin (1874–1967)

GREGORY KLASS*

I. INTRODUCTION

THE STORIES US legal scholars tell about themselves often involve revolution against the existing order. The Legal Realists revolted against Langdell's Formalism; the Critical Legal Studies movement rejected the quietism of Legal Process Theory and exposed the limits of the then dominant liberal rights discourse; Critical Race scholars, in turn, took the Critical Legal Studies scholars down a notch; and coming from a very different direction, early practitioners of Law and Economics uprooted traditional, muddied understandings of the common law, replacing them with clear-headed analysis of incentive effects and social welfare.

In *The Death of Contract*, Grant Gilmore depicts Arthur Linton Corbin as the hero of just such a story. Corbin was 'a non-establishment revolutionary', who set out to overturn the classical theory of contract built by Christopher Columbus Langdell, Oliver Wendell Holmes and Samuel Williston.[1] On Gilmore's reading, Corbin belongs to the vanguard of Legal Realism, leading the charge against a doctrinaire, formalist and stultified approach to the law of contracts.

* This chapter benefitted very much from the comments of other contributors to this volume and my colleague Daniel Ernst, and from the extraordinary research services of the Georgetown Law Library. I am especially grateful to William Twining and Guido Calabresi, each of whom shared in conversation recollections of encounters with Corbin.

[1] G Gilmore, *The Death of Contract* (Columbus, Ohio State University Press, 1974) 60. Or more fulsomely: 'resituated in time, Corbin's attack on the prevailing orthodoxy assumes revolutionary proportions' *ibid* 58; see also 55–85. Gilmore had been a student of Corbin, and Corbin recommended him to Robert Braucher for work on the second *Restatement*. Letter from AL Corbin to R Braucher (2 November 1959) in JM Perillo, 'Twelve Letters From Arthur L. Corbin to Robert Braucher' (1993) 50 *Washington and Lee Law Review* 755, 761.

Gilmore's story does not fit all that we know about Corbin.[2] Although Jerome Frank and Karl Llewellyn included Corbin on their list of Legal Realists,[3] Corbin rejected the label, explaining in a letter to Llewellyn that '[t]here are too many self-styled "Realists" whose eyes were opened and yet saw nothing'.[4] Nor was the relationship between Williston and Corbin a battle between old guard and new. Corbin's review of the first edition of Williston's treatise, though not uncritical, lauded its breadth and attention to detail. Ten years later, Williston invited Corbin to work with him on the *Restatement (First) of the Law of Contracts*, producing a work that bears clear marks of each.[5] At the time of Williston's death, Corbin wrote that Williston was to him 'above all an affectionate and lovable elder brother'.[6]

The stories Corbin told about himself were of a different type. Rather than struggle against existing orthodoxies, Corbin describes a personal path of discovery and transformation. In Corbin's story, the hero overcomes a naïve longing for legal certainty and comes to a clearheaded understanding of the law's contingency, complexity and growth. It is the story that Benjamin Cardozo tells in a passage from his 1921 Storrs Lecture, which Corbin was fond of quoting:

> I was much troubled in spirit, in my first years upon the bench, to find how trackless was the ocean upon which I had embarked. I sought for certainty, and I was oppressed and disheartened when I found that the quest for it was futile. I was trying to reach land, the solid land of fixed and settled rules, the paradise of a justice that would declare itself by tokens plainer and more commanding than its pale and glimmering reflections in my own vacillating mind and conscience. I found, with the voyagers of Browning's Paracelsus that the real heaven was always beyond. As the years have gone by, and I have reflected more and more upon the nature of the judicial process, I have become reconciled to the uncertainty, because I have grown to see it as inevitable. I have grown to see that the process in its highest reaches is not discovery but creation; and that the doubts and misgivings, the hopes and fears, are part of the travail of

[2] Daniel Klau dismantles Gilmore's telling of the relationship in a student note, D Klau, 'What Price Certainty? Corbin, Williston, and the Restatement of Contracts' (1990) 70 *Boston University Law Review* 511.

[3] Frank and Llewellyn listed Corbin 'as figures of central stimulus in the new ferment' KN Llewellyn, 'Some Realism about Realism' (1931) 44 *Harvard Law Review* 1222, 1226, fn 18.

[4] Letter from AL Corbin to KN Llewellyn (1 December 1960), quoted in L Kalman, *Legal Realism at Yale: 1927–1960* (Chapel Hill, University of North Carolina Press, 1986) 241, fn 83.

[5] Williston wrote of his work on the *Restatement*:

> My greatest indebtedness was to Arthur Corbin. His mastery of the law of contracts was only equalled by his generosity in contributing his best efforts to a work that for the most part would pass under another's name. He had moreover made a special study of terminology, and his keen eye for ambiguities and inexactness of expression saved me in many slippery places. His friendship and that of the Director [William Draper Lewis] and Professor Thompson remain major benefits to me of my work with the Institute. For a part of the *Restatement of Contracts* Arthur Corbin assumed the position of reporter and I acted as one of the advisers.

S Williston, *Life and Law: An Autobiography* (Boston, Little, Brown & Co, 1940) 312.

[6] AL Corbin, 'Samuel Williston' (1963) 76 *Harvard Law Review* 1327, 1329.

> mind, the pangs of death and the pangs of birth, in which principles that have served their day expire, and new principles are born.[7]

Corbin's and Cardozo's stories follow the plot of Plato's Allegory of the Cave: a journey from darkness into light, from illusion to truth.

Nor is this a journey that the protagonist takes alone. Socrates introduces the Allegory of the Cave as 'an image of our nature in its education and want of education'.[8] Similarly for Corbin the task of both legal education and legal scholarship is not merely to transfer legal knowledge from teacher to student, author to reader, but to disabuse the student or the reader of their false sense of certainty about the law and to help them to see it as a contingent, evolving institution, one that builds on generalisations from past experience, but which must also attend to the changing demands of a social world.

This Socratic approach accounts for what is so distinctive about *Corbin on Contracts: A Comprehensive Treatise on the Working Rules of Contract Law*.[9] The multi-volume treatise seeks not only to instruct the reader in the law of contract, but also on how to think about the law of contract and the common law generally. Like any treatise on the common law, *Corbin on Contracts* synthesises vast numbers of judicial decisions and stakes out and defends distinctive positions on doctrinal questions. But when read as a whole, the treatise provides not so much a unified theory of contract law – though there are hints of one – as it does a theory of common law reasoning and the reasons for having a common law.

II. BIOGRAPHY

Arthur Linton Corbin was born on a Kansas farm in 1874, as he observed, 'only nine years after the death of Abraham Lincoln'.[10] He died in New Haven, Connecticut in 1967, the year of the Summer of Love and two years before Neil Armstrong stepped onto the Moon.

Corbin's grandmother, Anna Sumner Corbin, immigrated from Connecticut to Kansas as a widow with four sons in 1857. The family was part of the Kansas free state, anti-slavery movement, and were friends with the abolitionist John

[7] B Cardozo, *The Nature of the Judicial Process* (New Haven, Yale University Press, 1921) 166–67. One might wonder whether Cardozo lifted the metaphor from Corbin, who wrote in 1914 (AL Corbin, 'The Law and The Judges' (1914) 3 *The Yale Review New Series* 234, 237):

> In law, as in other phases of life, we find ourselves swimming blindly in a sea of particular instances, straining to make safe landing on the shore of some absolute and unvarying rule. We have hundreds of approximations to such rule; but let us not deceive ourselves into thinking that our doctors of law have reached that firm foundation, any more than have our doctors of divinity or doctors of science.

[8] Plato (translated by A Bloom), *The Republic* (New York, Basic Books, 1968) 514a.

[9] AL Corbin, *Corbin on Contracts: A Comprehensive Treatise on the Working Rules of Contract Law*, 2nd edn (St Paul, West Publishing, 1963).

[10] AL Corbin, 'Sixty-Eight Years at Law' (1964) 13 *University of Kansas Law Review* 183, 183.

Brown. Anna's eldest son and Arthur's father, Myron, took part in actions led by Brown, and then fought in the Civil War as a member of the 12th Kansas Infantry Regiment. After the war, Myron married Elizabeth Linton and worked the family farm in Linn County, where Arthur was born. Myron and Elizabeth were committed to education, with Elizabeth teaching in the county schools. When Arthur was 14, the family moved to Lawrence for the sake of the children's schooling. Years later, Corbin told Fredrich Kessler he walked the 75 miles from Linn to Lawrence in bare feet.[11]

Corbin received his undergraduate degree from the University of Kansas in 1894, taught high school in Kansas for three years, then in 1897 entered Yale Law School, graduating in two.[12] Corbin had been encouraged to come to Yale by his older sister, Alberta, who was a PhD candidate at the university.[13] After receiving his law degree, Corbin spent four years practicing law in the small mining town of Cripple Creek, Colorado.[14] In 1903 he returned to Yale Law as its first full-time faculty member. In that role Corbin was instrumental in transforming Yale from something like a trade school, in which most of the faculty were practicing attorneys, into an academic institution.[15] Especially notable were Corbin's roles in the hiring of Wesley Newcomb Hohfeld and Walter Wheeler Cook as professors, and the appointment of Thomas Swan as Dean.[16] Between 1923 and 1932, Corbin worked closely with Samuel Williston on the American Law Institute's *Restatement of the Law of Contracts*. Although the project involved the work of a committee, Williston wrote that his greatest indebtedness in the project was to Corbin,[17] and Corbin is listed as Reporter for the chapter on Remedies.[18] Corbin remained a member of the Yale Law faculty until his compulsory retirement in 1943, at age 68. He published the first edition of *Corbin on Contracts* seven years later in 1950, the second edition in 1963, and continued to add substantive updates for several years after. Starting in 1959, Corbin involved himself informally in the drafting of the *Restatement (Second) of the Law of Contracts*, commenting in letters to the Reporter both on the project as a whole and on draft chapters.[19] The evidence we have suggests, however, that Corbin's

[11] RH Jerry II, 'Arthur L. Corbin: His Kansas Connection' (1984) 32 *Kansas Law Review* 753, 753–54.

[12] Corbin (n 10) 183–84.

[13] Jerry (n 11) 758. Alberta later returned to Lawrence to teach German at the University of Kansas, where she eventually became the Dean of Women. Corbin Hall on the university campus is named after Alberta (*ibid*).

[14] Corbin (n 10) 185.

[15] *ibid*.

[16] F Kessler, 'Arthur Linton Corbin' (1969) 78 *Yale Law Journal* 517, 518.

[17] Williston (n 5).

[18] 'Introduction' in *Restatement (First) of the Law of Contracts* (Philadelphia, American Law Institute, 1932) vii, x.

[19] See Perillo (n 1). According to the *Yale Law Journal's* bibliography of Corbin's publications, at the beginning of the process Corbin sent to the American Law Institute a draft complete revision of the *Restatement (First)*: 'Bibliography of the Published Writings of Arthur Linton Corbin' (1964) 27 *Yale Law Journal* 311, 322–23. Corbin himself reported that he spent 'the better part of eighteen

influence on the *Restatement (Second)* lay more in his vast body of scholarship than in the suggestions he made during the process. Although Corbin left behind a large number of published works, the Yale Law Library appears to have lost his papers.[20]

III. TEACHING

Corbin never engaged directly with the major theorists of his day. Late in life he wrote of his early years that '[t]o me, Austin was merely a *name*', and 'in my early teaching years I knew nothing of Roscoe Pound except that he talked of "sociological jurisprudence"'.[21] As William Twining has observed, Corbin's theory of law emerged not from engagement with the works of other theorists, but from a felt need to address a practical problem: the gap between the 'primitive and barely articulated assumptions of judges, practitioners, and laymen' and the law's actual operation, particularly in judicial decisions.[22] Corbin sought to bridge that gap first as a teacher, and later in his scholarship.

When Corbin was a law student, the Yale Law Faculty employed the 'Yale System', which relied primarily on textbooks, recitations, and lectures, using cases only as illustrations.[23] At the age of 85, Corbin described his legal education at Yale as traditional, rote and 'not too arduous':

> The reason ... was that the teaching was chiefly by lecture and textbook. In each course a few specially selected case reports were added, but these were always chosen as illustrations of the 'rules' and principles that were handed out. These cases were always excellent and interesting, but we were never required to study and discuss a group of cases, to pass an immature judgment with respect to conflicting decisions or inharmonious reasoning. In the cases that we studied, the court's decision was always 'right.' *Ipse dixit*.[24]

In the same biographical reflection, Corbin did not celebrate his own accomplishments as a student. Although Robinson's *Elementary Law* 'was indeed pretty dull reading, ... we were docile enough and lazy enough to be willing to

months in making [a] one-man revision of practically the entire *Restatement*, including sections, commentary, and illustrations': Corbin (n 10) 187. Corbin's draft has apparently been lost: Perillo (n 1) 755.

[20] SD Gerber, 'An Ivy League Mystery: The Lost Papers of Arthur Linton Corbin' (2002) 53 *South Carolina Law Review* 605, 607. In response to an enquiry from the Georgetown Law Library, the Yale Law Library confirmed in March 2021 that it still has almost nothing from Corbin in its archives.

[21] Letter from AL Corbin to W Twining (October 1965), quoted in W Twining, *Karl Llewellyn and the Realist Movement*, 2nd edn (Cambridge, Cambridge University Press, 2012) 29, 450.

[22] Twining (n 21) 29.

[23] FC Hicks, *Yale Law School: 1869–1894* (New Haven, Yale University Press, 1937) 34.

[24] Corbin (n 10) 184.

be "told" the law'.[25] Corbin was equally self-effacing about his four years of practice in Cripple Creek immediately after graduation.

> Some of the pleadings I drew in my few civil cases plainly exhibited my lack of training in the analysis of the factual problems involved and in the construction and application of legal 'rules' and principles. Fortunately, most of my legal opponents were equally incompetent.[26]

One might guess that these comments are the false modesty of a highly accomplished octogenarian. But reading Corbin broadly gives one the sense that his humility was also a midwestern habit of mind. In any case, Corbin clearly distinguished himself enough at Yale[27] that, after four years of non-elite practice in a backwater Colorado mining town, he was invited to join the faculty.

Corbin reported that when he began teaching law, he found it impossible to implement the Yale System. 'Mere verbally repeated "rules" created no excitement and aroused no interesting discussions'.[28] Nor, however, did he switch to the approach Langdell had introduced at Harvard 30 years earlier, which required students to derive fundamental legal principles from a highly curated collection of judicial decisions.[29] Corbin instead asked his students to grapple with the facts, reasons and doctrines expressed in the opinions, with the goal of disabusing the students of a naïve sense of legal certainty. '[The student] soon realizes the inadequacy of his basis for an independent judgment and the extent of the labor that looms before him. It is no wonder that after a few months the student is in a maze of uncertainty'.[30] In the process, student and instructor each:

> discovers that his own basis for an independent judgment is inadequate, that it is true that 'no two cases are alike,' that the 'rules' and 'principles' laid down by judges and

[25] *ibid*. Robinson's book is a summary of Blackstone's *Commentaries on the Laws of England*. Robinson explains his approach in the preface (WC Robinson, *Elementary Law* (Boston, Little, Brown & Co, 1882) vi):

> Regarding this treatise as a manual for the use of students, the author has adopted a style as didactic and concise as possible. Nearly every sentences is intended to be an answer to a question, and to embody some maxim, principle, or definition. Illustrations, as well as explanations, have generally been omitted, the student having access to such aids in the text-books to which he is consistently referred. Conjectures, and expressions of private opinions, have also been scrupulously avoided, and the beaten track of authority has been followed, as nearly as the author could himself discern it.

[26] Corbin (n 10) 185. Corbin was even more blunt in a letter to Llewellyn: 'the pleadings I drew in four years of practice were a scandal and a crime': letter from AL Corbin to KN Llewellyn (1 December 1960), quoted in Twining (n 21) 28.

[27] According to a newspaper report, Corbin received the Jewell Prize for the best annual examination in the senior class: *The Morning Journal-Courier* (27 June 1899) 3.

[28] Corbin (n 10) 185.

[29] See CC Langdell, *A Selection of Cases on the Law of Contracts* (Boston, Little, Brown & Co, 1871) viii:

> Law, considered as a science, consists of certain principles or doctrines. To have such a mastery of these as to be able to apply them with constant facility and certainty to the ever-tangled skein of human affairs, is what constitutes a true lawyer; and hence to acquire that mastery should be the business of every earnest student of law.

[30] Corbin (n 10) 185.

> by the text writers are variable and conflicting, and … that the rules and principles are in a constant state of evolutionary change.[31]

In 1908, Corbin formally recommended that the Yale faculty abandon the Yale System and switch to the case method of teaching. By 1916 the case method was widely used at the school.[32]

Corbin's critical approach in the classroom sought to turn his students not into sceptics, but into pragmatic empiricists. He wrote to Karl Llewellyn that in the late 1920s he had to 'fight for life as a law teacher' when his students were falling under the sway of a trio of young Realists at Yale, 'all three telling these beginners that there is "no law," only separate cases … and all three (however green behind the ears) telling it with explosive, atomic power'.[33] Throughout his career Corbin distanced himself from both the sceptical and the reductionist strains of Legal Realism, and especially the claim that judicial decisions were not guided by rules and principles.[34] Corbin explained that the goal of his critical pedagogy was to teach students a modest empiricism:

> Throughout my teaching career, my efforts were directed at inducing and compelling my students to acquire a background and a method of analysis that would enable them to form and to maintain opinions and generalizations of their own. The judicial opinions and the 'great books' of the past are an essential part of that background … are the base from which we take the next step forward.[35]

Corbin sought to teach his students not only that the law was made not discovered, but also that legal rules are best understood as defeasible generalisations from past experience – working rules in a constantly evolving social practice.

Corbin's most famous student was Karl Llewellyn. Llewellyn entered Yale Law School in 1915 and remained there during the First World War, unable to fight with the US forces due to his participation on the German side early in the war.[36] The Yale Law student body was at the time about half its usual size, and Llewellyn stood out among his peers. Corbin later reported that he and Llewellyn 'working hand-in-hand' together wrote half the comments and case notes in the 1918–19 *Yale Law Journal*, for which Llewellyn served as Editor-in-Chief.[37] This was the beginning of a friendship that would last until Llewellyn's death in 1962. Llewellyn and his wife Soia Mentschikoff both called Corbin 'Dad', and Corbin signed letters to Llewellyn the same.[38] The friendship between Corbin and Llewellyn was built on a sympathy of ideas, and no

[31] *ibid* 186.

[32] TW Swan, 'Professor Arthur L. Corbin Creator of the Present-Day Yale Law School' (1964) 74 *Yale Law Journal* 207, 208.

[33] Letter from AL Corbin to KN Llewellyn (1 December 1960), quoted in Kalman (n 4) 107.

[34] See Kessler (n 16) 519 (describing Corbin's relationship with the Realists at Yale).

[35] AL Corbin, 'Principles of Law and their Evolution' (1954) 64 *Yale Law Journal* 161, 162.

[36] Twining (n 21) 95, 535–43.

[37] AL Corbin, 'A Tribute to Karl Llewellyn' (1962) 71 *Yale Law Journal* 806, 806.

[38] See, eg, Letter from AL Corbin to R Braucher (2 November 1959) in Perillo (n 1) 760, 764; Gerber (n 20) 629, 635.

intellectual biography of Llewellyn would be complete without a discussion of his relationship to Corbin.[39]

In his farewell address to the Yale Law faculty, Corbin described law professors as 'the midwives who start the infant lawyer and jurist on his way'.[40] Corbin's pedagogy was Socratic in the original sense of the term. In the *Theaetetus*, Socrates elicits from his young interlocutor various definitions of 'knowledge', only to find each inadequate – 'all of which our midwife's skill pronounces to be mere wind eggs and not worth the rearing'.[41] Socrates's goal was not to turn his students into sceptics or Sophists. It was to instill in them a form of modesty, both with respect to their own knowledge and with respect to the nature and grounds of knowledge generally:

> Then supposing you should ever henceforth try to conceive afresh, Theaetetus, if you succeed, your embryo thoughts will be the better as a consequences of today's scrutiny, and if you remain barren, you will be gentler and more agreeable to your companions, having the good sense not to fancy you know what you do not know.

I know of no evidence that Corbin read Plato deeply. But his farewell reference to Socratic midwifery nicely captures his own pedagogy. One encounters the same approach in *Corbin on Contracts*.

IV. CONCEPTUAL ANALYSIS

If Corbin was sometimes mistaken for a Legal Realist, it is perhaps because he was a modernist: an early twentieth-century thinker who did not feel bound by traditional modes of legal argument and analysis, and who sought for a new, clear-eyed approach to the law. The first step in that approach was to diagnose various forms of confusion embedded in legal language and to develop a new, more transparent vocabulary.

Corbin was in this respect in step with his time. Starting at the beginning of the twentieth century, Anglo-American philosophy took what Richard Rorty describes as a 'linguistic turn', premised on 'the view that philosophical problems are problems which may be solved, or dissolved, either by reforming language, or by understanding more about the language we presently use'.[42] The goal was to

[39] See Twining (n 21) 95–97.

[40] AL Corbin, 'Farewell of Arthur Corbin to the Yale Law School Faculty' in G Calabresi, *The Future of Law and Economics: Essays in Reform and Recollection* (New Haven, Yale University Press, 2016) 173, 175. See Plato (translated by FM Cornford), *Theaetetus* in E Hamilton and H Cairns (eds), *The Collected Dialogues of Plato* (New York, Pantheon, 1961) 150b–51d (in which Socrates compares his skills in teaching youth to that of a midwife). In the next sentence, Corbin describes law professors as 'the gadflies that sting judges into better action'. See Plato, *Apology* in *ibid* 30e–31a (in which Socrates compares himself to a gadfly).

[41] Plato, *Theaetetus* (n 40) 210b.

[42] RM Rorty, 'Introduction: Metaphilosophical Difficulties' in RM Rorty (ed), *Linguistic Philosophy, The Linguistic Turn: Recent Essays in Philosophical Method* (Chicago, University of Chicago Press, 1967) 3.

escape the intellectual traps our everyday language lays for us, or as Wittgenstein put it, to show the fly the way out of the fly bottle.[43] Felix S Cohen described this approach to legal scholarship in his 1935 'Transcendental Nonsense and the Functional Approach'. Invoking Frege, Russell, Wittgenstein and other early analytic philosophers, as well as the American Pragmatists, Cohen argued that legal reasoning is too often misled by the 'vivid fictions and metaphors of traditional jurisprudence', whereas it should be attending to 'the social forces which mold the law and the social ideals by which the law is judged'.[44]

Although Cohen provided one of the clearest descriptions of the new analytic approach, the founding document appeared some 22 years earlier in Wesley Newcomb Hohfeld's 'Some Fundamental Legal Conceptions as Applied in Judicial Reasoning'.[45] Hohfeld's analytic schemas were not novel; he drew from a range of earlier theorists.[46] But Hohfeld's concise analysis of abstract legal concepts appeared at the right time and place, and his conceptual schema was widely used and discussed in early twentieth-century US legal scholarship.

Corbin was an important early champion of Hohfeld and his system. It was Corbin who recommended 'Fundamental Legal Conceptions' for publication in the *Yale Law Journal*,[47] and it was Corbin who facilitated bringing Hohfeld to Yale law faculty. In 1919, a year after Hohfeld's untimely death, Corbin published a short summary of Hohfeld's system for students,[48] and he reprinted Hohfeld's table of jural relations in the introduction in his 1919 edition of Anson.[49] The next year, in an address to the annual meeting of the American Association of Law Schools, Corbin provided something like a deduction of Hohfeld's jural relations, together with a detailed defence against critics.[50] Corbin reported later in life that Williston asked him to assist him on the *Restatement* project

[43] L Wittgenstein (translated by GEM Anscombe), *Philosophical Investigations* (Oxford, Blackwell, 1953) § 309.

[44] FS Cohen, 'Transcendental Nonsense and the Functional Approach' (1935) 35 *Columbia Law Review* 809, 812.

[45] WN Hohfeld, 'Some Fundamental Legal Conceptions as Applied in Judicial Reasoning' (1913) 23 *Yale Law Journal* 16. One finds this approach even earlier in Hohfeld's writings. In 1909, for example, Hohfeld provided the following account of corporate personhood (WN Hohfeld, 'Nature of Stockholders' Individual Liability for Corporation Debts (pt. 1)' (1909) 9 *Columbia Law Review* 285, 290, fn 14):

> In reality when we say that the so-called legal or juristic person has rights or that it has contracted, we mean nothing more than what must ultimately be explained by describing the capacities, powers, rights, privileges (or liberties), disabilities, duties and liabilities, etc., of the natural persons concerned or of some of such persons.

[46] The Yale Law Library has a copy of John Austin's *Lectures on Jurisprudence* with annotations that Hohfeld made as an undergraduate.

[47] AL Corbin, 'Foreword' in WN Hohfeld, *Fundamental Legal Conceptions as Applied in Judicial Reasoning* (New Haven, Yale University Press, 1964) vii.

[48] AL Corbin, 'Legal Analysis and Terminology' (1919) 29 *Yale Law Journal* 163.

[49] WR Anson (edited by AL Corbin), *Principles of the Law of Contract with a Chapter on the Law of Agency*, 3rd American edn (New York, Banks Law, 1919) vi.

[50] AL Corbin, 'Terminology and Classification in Fundamental Jural Relations' (1921) 4 *American Law School Review* 607, reprinted with alterations in AL Corbin, 'Jural Relations and Their Classification' (1921) 30 *Yale Law Journal* 226.

because Williston wanted to ensure that the work would be consistent with Hohfeld's analysis.[51]

Hohfeld's system is purely analytic. It aims to identify basic legal concepts, to use them to diagnose conceptual confusions, and to develop a technical vocabulary that avoids such confusions going forward. The goal is to clear the ground for substantive legal argument, not to provide the materials for it. As Corbin put the point:

> It solves no problem or social or juristic policy, but it does much to define and clarify the issue that is in dispute and thus enables the mind to concentrate on the interests and policies that are involved, and increases the probability of sound conclusion.[52]

Although Corbin's attraction to conceptual analysis predated his first encounter with Hohfeld,[53] Hohfeld's work provided a powerful toolkit. Throughout his writings, Corbin deploys Hohfeld's categories to identify conceptual confusion and clarify legal questions. Two examples illustrate: Corbin's definition of 'contract' and Corbin's approach to the consideration doctrine.

In his 1910 article, 'Waiver of Tort and Suit in Assumpsit', Corbin advances a fairly standard definition of 'contract': 'The great distinctive feature of these transactions is the *agreement* of the parties, the mutual assent, the meeting of the minds. This *agreement* is the origin of the obligation attached by the law and called contractual'.[54] Only seven years later, and four years after Hohfeld published 'Fundamental Legal Conceptions', one finds Corbin rejecting such substantive definitions. In 'Offer and Acceptance, and Some of the Resulting Legal Relations' (a Hohfeldian title if there ever was one), Corbin instead distinguishes various meanings that, depending on context, 'contract' might have:

> The term contract has been used without much discrimination to refer to three different things: (1) the series of operative acts of the parties expressing their assent and resulting in new legal relations; (2) the physical document executed by the parties as an operative fact in itself and as the lasting evidence of their having performed the necessary operative acts; (3) the relations resulting from the operative acts, consisting

[51] Corbin (n 47) xii.

[52] *ibid* xi.

[53] In the same year in which Hohfeld published 'Fundamental Legal Conceptions', Corbin published 'Discharge of Contracts' (1913) 22 *Yale Law Journal* 513. This short article maps the logical space created by two distinctions: Thomas Holland's differentiation of primary from secondary obligations, TE Holland, *The Elements of Jurisprudence*, 10th edn (Oxford, Oxford University Press 1906) 141–42, and the analytic difference between conditions precedent and conditions subsequent – between conditions on the existence of an obligation and obligations that are conditional in structure. Corbin's article appeared in May, Hohfeld's in November.

[54] AL Corbin, 'Waiver of Tort and Suit in Assumpsit' (1910) 19 *Yale Law Journal* 221, 222. The definition is the first I find articulated in Corbin's writings, and recalls Anson's: 'Contract is that form of agreement which directly contemplates and creates an obligation: the contractual obligation is that form of obligation that springs from agreement' (WR Anson (edited by E Huffcut), *Principles of the English Law of Contract and of Agency in Its Relation to Contract*, 8th edn and 1st American edn (New York, Banks & Bros, 1896) 2).

> of a right or right *in personam* and the corresponding duties, accompanied by certain powers, privileges and immunities.[55]

There are two things to note about this passage, which reappears only slightly modified in *Corbin on Contracts*.[56] First, the analysis is pure Hohfeld. The list of jural relations under the third meaning of 'contract' – legal rights, duties, powers, privileges, immunities – is drawn directly from the most famous section of 'Fundamental Legal Relations'. To understand contract law, one must attend not only to duty to perform, but to the full range of jural relations that pertain to contractual relationships, from the power to make an offer to a party's immunity against modifications without consent to the secondary duty to pay damages after breach. Corbin's distinction between the first and third meanings of 'contract' is equally Hohfeldian, reprising the latter's distinction between operative acts and the legal relations to which they give rise.[57] Thus Hohfeld observes: 'One moment ["contract"] may mean the agreement of the parties; and then, with a rapid and unexpected shift, the writer or speaker may use the term to indicate the contractual obligation created by law as a result of the agreement'.[58] Finally, Corbin's description of contractual writings, the second meaning of 'contract', incorporates Hohfeld's distinction between operative facts, which by themselves suffice to effect a legal change, and evidential facts, which are legally relevant only in so far as they are evidence of other facts, operative or evidential.[59]

The second thing to note is that Corbin's approach is, like Hohfeld's categories, purely analytic. Corbin's multipart definition does not describe the acts that give rise to contracts, the types of writings that memorialise those acts, or the jural relations they generate. Instead, it identifies the logical structure of any contractual transaction: operative acts by the parties, sometimes including a writing, that produce a change in their jural relations.

In his treatise, Corbin observes that courts and scholars commonly provide more substantive definitions of 'contract'. Williston and the *Restatement (First)* define 'contract' as a promise or a set of promises whose breach gives rise to

[55] AL Corbin, 'Offer and Acceptance, and Some of the Resulting Legal Relations' (1917) 26 *Yale Law Journal* 169, 169.

[56] Corbin (n 9) vol 1, § 3.

[57] Hohfeld (n 45) 20–25.

[58] *ibid* 25.

[59] *ibid* 25–28. Hohfeld attributes his distinction between operative and evidential facts to Thayer (*ibid* 25, fn 393) (quoting JB Thayer, *A Preliminary Treatise on Evidence* (Boston, Little, Brown & Co, 1898) 393). In fact, Hohfeld's conception of operative facts is broader than Thayer's, which derives from Heinrich Brunner's distinction between *carta* and *notitia* (H Brunner, 'Carta und Notitia: ein Beitrag zur Rechtsgeschichte der germansichen Urkunde' (1877) in K Rauch (ed), *Abhandlung zur Rechtgeschichte: gesammeltes Aufsätze von Heinrich Brunner* (Weimar, Herman Bölhaus Nachfolger, 1931) 458). Brunner and Thayer apply the distinction only to juristic acts, ie, exercises of a legal power. Hohfeld appears to apply it to any act with a legal effect, such as the commission of an assault (Hohfeld (n 45) 26).

a legal remedy;[60] Anson defines 'contract' as a legally enforceable agreement (the definition Corbin had once advocated);[61] and the Uniform Commercial Code defines 'contract' as the total obligations which result from such an agreement.[62] Corbin identifies two problems with such substantive definitions. First, they are incomplete. Each names an operative fact – promise or agreement – that itself requires definition and further description. Second and more significantly, substantive definitions tend to import an 'inarticulate major premise' as to which acts should suffice to generate a contractual obligation.[63] There is, however, no reason to expect the rules governing formation to be so simple that they can be captured in a single definition. '[T]o determine whether a "contract" has been made and what are the resulting legal relations is a matter for the entire treatise, not for an introductory chapter. Instead of simplicity and uniformity, we shall find complexity and variation'.[64] Substantive definitions might at times be necessary to clarify how one is using a word. But they should never be understood as more than 'working definitions', to be revised as needed and discarded when they cease to capture the rule. And at the outset, it is preferable to define 'contract' in terms of its structural features – voluntary acts effecting a change in the actors' jural relations to one another – rather than by the nature of those acts or the substance of the relations.

One encounters the same analytic approach in Corbin's discussions of consideration. In his 1920 review of Williston's treatise, Corbin praises Williston's treatment of the doctrine. Williston does not posit a single definition of 'consideration', but canvasses the history of the doctrine, proposes two separate definitions, one for unilateral contracts and one for bilateral contracts, then discusses a number of exceptional cases, including agreements under seal, promissory estoppel, promises by a discharged bankrupt and a promise to pay a debt barred by the statute of limitations.[65] Corbin considers this treatment admirable in that '[i]t shows clearly that in fact the courts enforce many promises for

[60] S Williston, *The Law of Contracts*, vol 1 (New York, Baker, Voorhis & Co, 1920) § 1.

[61] Anson (n 54) 2.

[62] *Restatement (First) of the Law of Contracts* (n 18) § 1.

[63] Corbin (n 9) vol 1 § 3.

[64] *ibid*. Interestingly, Williston makes a parallel point in the first edition of his treatise. After defining 'contract' as a promise or set of promises to which the law attaches legal obligation, he writes(Williston (n 60) vol 1, § 1.):

> This definition may seem somewhat unsatisfactory since it is necessary subsequently to define the circumstances under which the law does in fact attach legal obligation to promises, but in order to make a definition which should state these circumstances it would be necessary to compress the whole law of formation of contracts into a sentence, which is impossible.

One might say that Corbin's definition merely goes to the next level of abstraction.

[65] Williston (n 60) vol 1, §§ 102 ('Definition of valid consideration in a unilateral contract'), 103f ('Final definition of valid consideration in bilateral contracts'), 109 and 139; and vol 1A, §§ 158, 160–78.

which there was no agreed equivalent given in exchange'.[66] He draws, however, a distinctly non-Willistonian conclusion:

> The complexity of the result and the many admissions that conflict exists and that certain very large classes of cases must be regarded as 'exceptional' indicate that in many twilight zones the court must trust to instinct rather than to definition or 'theory' or 'established principle.' The effect of this is that the doctrine of consideration (or its manifold substitutes) approaches the similarly nebulous doctrine of *causa* in the Roman Law.[67]

In the end, Williston's sensitivity to the diversity of situations and holdings within the case law undermines his own attempt to provide simple substantive definitions of 'consideration'.

The chapter on consideration in *Corbin on Contracts* opens not with a definition, but with a question: Is a definition of 'consideration' practicable?[68] Corbin answers it by telling of his own journey through case law. Reading through recent judicial opinions has left him

> assured that the reasons for enforcing informal promises are many, that the doctrine of consideration is many doctrines, that no definition can rightly be set up as the one and only correct definition, and that the law of contract is an evolutionary product that has changed with the time and circumstances and that must ever consider to so change.[69]

The only fixed, generic definition one can give of 'consideration' is therefore empty and analytic:

> [W]hen the statement is made that no informal promise is to be enforceable if it is without consideration, it must be understood as a statement that no informal promise is enforceable unless it is accompanied by one of those factors that have been held, more or less generally, to be sufficient to make a promise enforceable.[70]

'Consideration', for Corbin, refers to whatever reasons the law recognises for enforcing an informal promise or agreement. Such a definition is pure tautology. But this is how it should be. Substantive definitions risk producing legal arguments that avoid the issue.

This is not to say that substantive definitions of legal terms are always wrongheaded. Definition is not destiny, as Williston's multi-layered discussion of the consideration doctrine illustrates. Corbin does not therefore fault Williston for adopting a substantive definition. 'Having made a choice and warned his readers thereof, with his reasons, he can be further required only to be consistent'.[71]

[66] AL Corbin, 'Review of Samuel Williston, *The Law of Contracts*: Vol I' (1920) 29 *Yale Law Journal* 943, 944.

[67] *ibid*.

[68] Corbin (n 9) vol 1, § 109.

[69] *ibid* § 109.

[70] *ibid* § 110.

[71] Corbin (n 66) 493 (discussing Williston's definition of 'contract').

But Williston's attachment to first principles tends to lead his own analysis astray. Substantive definitions are problematic when one seeks in them answers to hard legal questions.

Corbin finds an example in Williston's early treatment of an offeror's power to revoke. The issue is a familiar one: when an offeree can accept by performance only, empowering the offeror to revoke any time before acceptance – here right up to the completion of performance – risks unfairness. The offeree might accomplish almost everything requested, and then due to a revocation receive nothing in return. Williston admits the 'obvious injustice' of such an outcome,[72] but argues that the consideration requirement demands it. '[A]ny other result involves either a violation of recognized principles of contract, or the invention of new ones', for the offeror cannot be 'bound by a promise for which he has not received, and may never receive, the consideration requested'.[73]

In his 1920 review, Corbin provides two responses. First, Corbin deploys Hohfeld's categories to diagnose a confusion in the argument. The offeror who cannot revoke his offer is not yet under a duty. Irrevocability is not a duty but a disability: the offeror does not have the power to extinguish the offeree's power of acceptance.[74] The duty to perform comes into existence only if and when the offer is accepted. If consideration is the *sine qua non* of contractual duties, a rule that the beginning of acceptance by performance renders the offer irrevocable does not violate the consideration doctrine.

But conceptual clarity does not of itself answer the question. Corbin's second response is that the existing doctrine of consideration is not a straightjacket. If irrevocability upon the beginning of an acceptance by performance requires the invention of new principles, courts should invent them. 'The history of the law consists chiefly in the destruction and modification of old theory by new practice'.[75] Here Corbin was prescient. Section 45 of the *Restatement (First)* provides that the beginning of acceptance by performance binds the offeror to perform conditional on completion of performance.[76] The comments identify two independent grounds: part performance provides sufficient consideration for a subsidiary, implied promise not to revoke, and the offeree's justifiable reliance can suffice to make the offer binding.[77]

For Corbin, substantive definitions of legal terms should be treated always as 'working definitions', and statements of legal rules as 'working rules', subject to revision and possible rejection based on new evidence, experience and examples. This explains why Corbin could sign on to the *Restatement (First's)* treatment of the consideration doctrine. The *Restatement* provides a simple, substantive

[72] Williston (n 60) vol 1, § 60.

[73] *ibid* §§ 60, 101. Williston's analysis tracks Langdell's: see CC Langdell, *Summary of the Law of Contracts*, 2nd edn (Boston, Little, Brown & Co, 1880) 240–41.

[74] Corbin (n 66) 944.

[75] *ibid.*

[76] *Restatement (First) of the Law of Contracts* (n 18) § 45.

[77] *ibid* cmt b.

definition of 'consideration',[78] but then goes on to identify a long list of exceptions to the consideration requirement.[79] Whether one defines 'consideration' narrowly and then allows exceptions to the requirement, or broadly as any facts that support legal enforcement, the key is to remain open to the many grounds for enforcement at work in contract law.[80]

V. THEORY OF THE COMMON LAW

If analytic clarity is for Corbin the path out of the Cave, it is not the end of the journey. 'Rules of law are not constructed by mere analysis and mere logic'.[81] Conceptual analysis tells us neither what the law is nor what it should be. Whereas the Legal Realists who addressed those questions tended either to fall into rule scepticism, typified in the quip that a court's decision might best be explained by what the judge ate for breakfast,[82] or to fall back on one or another of the emergent social sciences,[83] Corbin describes and defends a distinctive form of common law judicial reasoning, one that both recognises the law's contingency and affirms its rational basis:

> Having thus been freed from illusion and delusion, the study most be continued until it demonstrates that useful working rules and definitions can be found and stated; that such rules and definitions, if well constructed, are useful guides to justice even though they are not absolute and eternal.[84]

In Corbin's farewell letter to the Yale Law Faculty, written when he was still in the middle of writing the first edition of his treatise, Corbin defends the modesty of this approach:

> I believe that there is greater hope, of human welfare and happiness, if we are conscious of our limitations, if we abandon the quest for absolutes, if we confess that justice is wholly relative and human, and if we erect our temple of peace upon a foundation, made as stable as we can by a neat balancing of interests, determined by as careful and complete a study of human experience as possible.[85]

The core idea reappears in the subtitle Corbin chose for his magnum opus: 'A Comprehensive Treatise on the Working Rules of Contract Law'.

[78] *ibid* §§ 19, 75.
[79] *ibid* §§ 85–94 and 535.
[80] Corbin makes essentially this point in Corbin (n 9) vol 1, § 116.
[81] Corbin, 'Jural Relations and Their Classification' (n 50) 237.
[82] See D Priel, 'Law Is What the Judge Had for Breakfast: A Brief History of an Unpalatable Idea' (2020) 68 *Buffalo Law Review* 899.
[83] See N Duxbury, *Patterns of American Jurisprudence* (Oxford, Oxford University Press, 1995) 79–97; Twining (n 21) 41–55, 60–67.
[84] Corbin (n 9) vol 1, § 109 (discussing the definition of 'consideration').
[85] Corbin (n 40) 174–75. Calabresi states without explanation that the letter was written in 1941 (*ibid* 10) though Corbin retired from the Yale Law Faculty in 1943.

Corbin's theory of the common law can be restated in five interlocking claims: the work of the common law judge is empirical; sound judicial decisions draw from multiple sources; the law should, and generally does, reflect existing social values or mores; because social structures and mores change over time, the law too must evolve; consequently, legal rules and principles should be understood to be 'working rules', subject to revision and even wholesale rejection should the need arise.[86]

For Corbin, common law judicial reasoning is not deduction from facts and rules to case outcomes. Precedent and principle do not sufficiently constrain judicial decision-making for that to be so. '[H]owever "well-settled" the rules may be, their application to life is always uncertain .... In all cases the judge must construct his own major premise'.[87] The judicial process requires instead a form of inductive reasoning, one that begins with the facts and decisions of past cases and ends with a judgment as to the best resolution of the case at Bar. In 1954, Corbin told a story about a lunch he had around 1920 with some of the young Legal Realists on the Yale faculty. When they posed the question, 'Do you think there is such a thing as a legal principle?', Corbin allowed that legal principles are not things 'handed down from on high', but maintained:

> [T]hat there are useful generalizations based on long human experience; that although no two cases are ever exactly alike, there are groups of cases that have much in common; that by careful and imaginative analysis and comparison of these cases it is possible to construct general rules, doctrines, principles, which are of great value in directing and predicting future human and judicial action in similar cases.[88]

The idea of 'imaginative analysis' is key. Judicial empiricism, for Corbin, is not mere scientific induction. It does not count past factual scenarios, *rationes decidendi* and case outcomes to identify a majority rule.[89] It is the imaginative projection of a proposed ruling onto past facts and decisions, as well as future cases, as a means of testing ruling and the rule in a wide range of instances against the balance of reasons and the judgments of oneself and others.

To say that judging is an inductive process using imaginative projection is not yet to provide an account of how judges do or should decide cases or establish

[86] Corbin's theory of the common law is very close to Cardozo's as described by John Goldberg in 'Community and the Common Law Judge: Reconstructing Cardozo's Theoretical Writings' (1990) 65 *New York University Law Review* 1324. A systematic comparison of the two, while beyond the scope of this chapter, would be an interesting project.

[87] Corbin (n 7) 239.

[88] Corbin (n 35) 162.

[89] The above sentence describes one of the approaches taken by the Reporters for the American Law Institute's *Restatement of the Law of Consumer Contracts*: See O Bar-Gill, O Ben-Shahar and F Marotta-Wurgler, 'Searching for the Common Law: The Quantitative Approach of the Restatement of Consumer Contracts' (2017) 84 *University of Chicago Law Review* 7. I critically examine that approach in G Klass, 'Empiricism and Privacy Policies in the Restatement of Consumer Contract Law' (2019) 36 *Yale Journal on Regulation* 45.

rules. It is here that one finds Corbin's pluralism. The sources of individual judicial decisions are, and should be, manifold:

> The rules come from all possible sources – from constitutions and statutes; from the decisions of other judges; from legal writers, ancient and modern, in this and in other countries; from books of religion and morality; from the general principles of right and wrong in which the judge was trained from his youth up; from the rules of action customarily followed in the community, lately referred to by Lord Chancellor Haldane as *Sittlichkeit*; from the judge's own practice and interest and desire. The judge, if honest, lays down either a rule that has been approved or acquiesced in by the community in the past, or a rule to which he believes the community will in the future give approval and acquiescence.[90]

Pluralism of this type entails a high degree of judicial discretion. No matter how much a judge claims that the law compels the result in a case, in fact the judge always has a choice in both outcome and reason. If established legal rules are manipulable and the sources of judicial judgment are multiple, then there is no one correct outcome to the novel case.

The check on judicial decisions, for Corbin, lies not in the existing law or the principles that organise it, but in the community's sense of justice. Although the individual judicial decision has multiple sources, one among them provides the ultimate criterion of correctness: *Sittlichkeit*, or social mores. Here one sees the influence on Corbin's thinking of Yale sociologist William Graham Sumner and Sumner's student Albert Galloway Keller.[91] And though Corbin reported he was unfamiliar with Roscoe Pound's work when he began teaching,[92] one also hears echoes of Pound's 1907 call for a sociological jurisprudence:

> In all cases of divergence between the standard of the common law and the standard of the public, it goes without saying that the latter will prevail in the end. Sooner or later what public opinion demands will be recognized and enforced by the courts.[93]

Like Pound, Corbin posits that correspondence between law and social mores is both desirable and inevitable. The law should be an expression of community values, and a legal rule that offends community values will not endure. If the

[90] Corbin (n 7) 240.

[91] A former student recalled that Corbin made frequent reference in his Contracts course to Sumner's *Folkways*, which 'served as a constant reminder that the law is a part of changing civilization and that the history of law is the history of man and society' (D Arant, 'Professor Arthur L. Corbin' (1964) 74 *Yale Law Journal* 212, 214). See WG Sumner, *Folkways, A Study Of The Sociological Importance Of Usages, Manners, Customs, Mores And Morals* (Boston, Athenæum Press, 1906). And whereas several scholars have traced Karl Llewellyn's sociological jurisprudence to German sources, Corbin attributed it in part to the influence during Llewellyn's undergraduate years at Yale of Sumner and Keller (Corbin (n 37) 806; see J Whitman, 'Note: Commercial Law and the American Folk: A Note on Llewellyn's German Sources for the Uniform Commercial Code' (1987) 97 *Yale Law Journal* 156; JE Grise, M Gelter and R Whitman, 'Rudolf von Jhering's Influence on Karl Llewellyn' (2012) 48 *Tulsa Law Review* 93).

[92] See n 21.

[93] R Pound, 'The Need for a Sociological Jurisprudence' (1907) 19 *Green Bag* 607, 615.

judge 'constructs and applies a rule that is in conflict with the interests and desires and customs of the many, … [t]he man-mountain will quake, and the house of logic that the judge built will come tumbling about his ears'.[94]

As the conditions of social life and social values change over time, the law therefore should and will evolve with them. Here the common law's particularistic approach is of special value. Legal reform should not be outsourced to economists, sociologists, moral philosophers or other high theorists.

> Ardent reformers and confident legislators often believe that they are wise enough to generalize for the future; but experience indicates that the best way to turn mores into law is to do it piecemeal by the 'molecular motion' of the courts.[95]

The driving force behind progress in the law is not theory or sweeping legislative change, but the hard case: the case in which the existing legal rule is out of step with the community's sense of justice:

> When a stated rule of law works injustice in a particular case; that is, would determine it contrary to the 'settled conventions of the community,' the rule is pretty certain either to be denied outright or to be undermined by a fiction or a specious distinction.[96]

As in natural evolution, the common law achieves progress not by design, but through a process of variation and selection.

Consequently, the law is at all times a mix of both the old and the new. 'There will always be two large fields of legal uncertainty – the field of the obsolete and the dying, and the field of the new born and growing'.[97] Here we return to Corbin's insistence that legal rules be understood always as mere working rules:

> Those of lesser wisdom and more self-conceit will state their doctrines as absolutes and eternal. A law that is composed of tentative, working rules is indeed a human law; but it is also a natural law – it is as 'natural' as rain, as 'natural' as birth and death.[98]

This understanding of the common law accounts for Corbin's consistent enthusiasm for the American Law Institute's *Restatement* project. The *Restatements* for Corbin were not attempts to identify the fundamental principles of contract law, which would involve a return to a formalism, a refusal to admit the variety and contingency of legal rules. Rather, they were empirical undertakings. In 1929, while the committee was still working

[94] Corbin (n 7) 250.

[95] AL Corbin, 'The Restatement of the Common Law by the American Law Institute' (1929) 15 *Iowa Law Review* 19, 28.

[96] AL Corbin, 'Hard Cases Make Good Law' (1923) 33 *Yale Law Journal* 78, 78 (citation omitted).

[97] Corbin (n 7) 243.

[98] Corbin (n 35) 163.

on the *Restatement (First) of the Law of Contracts*, Corbin described the *Restatements* project:

> The work of the Institute is an attempt to state anew what the practices and customs of this great and seething community now are, as they are evidenced by innumerable instances of judicial action at the pin-points of strain and conflict. It is an attempt to demonstrate and to state in words the uniformities (the rules) that are to be found in those innumerable instances and to make a selection and a recommendation from among competing rules and practices. It is an attempt to analyze and classify and define, at a time when such reorganization work appears to be loudly demanded, and thus supply a guiding hand to those who may desire guidance in directing the strong arm of the state.[99]

The great advantage of the *Restatement* form is that it is nonbinding on courts. A civil code represents the final statement of an authoritative body, ossifying the law and inviting textual analysis and argument from definition. Civil codes reify and stultify. Because a *Restatement* is not binding, it should not 'become the basis of extended commentaries or the subject of textual interpretation'.[100] Nor should it 'operate to limit the development of the law in accordance with changing conditions, practices, and mores'.[101] Rather than a statement of fundamental legal principles or rules, a properly formed *Restatement* contains a concise depiction of the working rules at one stage of the law's evolution, thereby providing legal practitioners the materials they need for those rules' refinement, modification and even possible rejection.

The major elements of Corbin's theory of the common law appear as early as his 1914 essay, 'The Law and the Judges'. Fifty years later, the 1964 Pocket Supplement to *Corbin on Contracts* summarised and reaffirmed the same vision:

> A study of the appellate court decisions can never decrease in value or interest, for the reason that they constitute the living evidence of the continuing evolutionary process of our judicial system, both in the statement of its 'working rules,' and as to its success or failure in the administration of 'justice.' Such a study necessarily demonstrates the possibility of constructing reasonably definite 'working rules' to serve as guides to the lawyer in giving advice to his client and to the courts in reaching and justifying a decision. These rules can never be absolute and eternal; as 'guides' they cannot be infallible; but if well constructed they can be useful. At the same time confusion and injustice are the sure result of the uncritical repetition of verbal formulas handed down from the past. A worded rule is of little value apart from the facts to which it is applied; and the very existence of a 'rule' depends upon the sum-total of its applications. With the expansion of population, the changes in social, economic and physical conditions, and the variations in the prevailing notions of men as to justice and morality (the *mores* of the time), all 'rules of law,' constitutional,

[99] Corbin (n 95) 38.
[100] *ibid.*
[101] *ibid.*

> statutory and judge-made, must likewise change. Certainty is an illusion, and the illusion of certainty is the mother of injustice and turmoil.[102]

Corbin was not a philosopher. From his earliest writings to the last, he does not make the case for the above theory of the common law so much as pronounce it. And the theory is open to obvious criticisms. Although Corbin acknowledges that individual judges often issue rulings based on confusion or corruption, he assumes that the great judge has access both to the wisdom embodied in past decisions and to the community's present sense of justice. Corbin also largely ignores the role of wealth, class, race and politics in determining who gets on the bench, which arguments make it into court, and which legal rules are likely to survive. It is not that Corbin neglects such factors entirely. The Preface to *Corbin on Contracts* allows that '[it] cannot be said that the law operates uniformly with respect to the promises of the rich and the poor, the employer and the employee'.[103] But mostly Corbin draws his picture of the common law cathedral from within. As arguably befits a treatise author, Corbin takes the perspective of a cautious believer. Although he was happy to knock down false idols, he had no desire to tear down the church.

VI. REASONABLE EXPECTATIONS AND CONTRACT INTERPRETATION

Corbin's regular reflections on judicial practice, the nature of the common law, and the relation of law to society are among the most distinctive features of *Corbin on Contracts*. In the Preface to the first edition, Corbin acknowledges and explains his penchant for theorising:

> A general treatise on some one special branch of law, even though that branch is as broad and inclusive as the law of contracts, may be thought not to be the place for a discussion of general theories of jurisprudence. But one who prepares a treatise on any branch of the law cannot avoid applying theories of jurisprudence.[104]

That said, it would be negligent in a chapter devoted to Corbin not to pay a bit more attention to what he had to say about the law of contracts. This section discusses two aspects of Corbin's approach to contract law: his quiet attachment to the reliance theory and his account of contract interpretation.

Fourteen years before Lon Fuller's 'The Reliance Interest in Contract Damages',[105] one finds Corbin asserting, in an explanation of the objective approach to contract interpretation, that the goal of contract law is not

[102] Quoted in Corbin (n 10) 188.
[103] Corbin (n 9) vol 1, § 2.
[104] AL Corbin, *Corbin on Contracts: A Comprehensive Treatise on the Working Rules of Contract Law* (St Paul, West Publishing, 1950) iv.
[105] LL Fuller and WR Perdue Jr, 'The Reliance Interest in Contract Damages: 1' (1936) 46 *Yale Law Journal* 52.

to realise the probable intentions of the parties, but 'to secure the fulfilment of the promisee's reasonable expectations as induced by the promisor's act'.[106] Despite Corbin's aversion to high theory, *Corbin on Contracts* opens with the same claim:

> That portion of the field of law that is classified and described as the law of contracts attempts the realization of reasonable expectations that have been induced by the making of a promise. Doubtless this is not the only purpose by which men have been motivated in creating the law of contracts; but it is believed to be the main underlying purpose, and it is believed that an understanding of many of the existing rules and a determination of their effectiveness require a lively consciousness of this underling purpose.[107]

It is this reasonable expectations thesis that Gilmore emphasises in *The Death of Contract*, arguing that Corbin was responsible for section 90 of the *Restatement (First)* (recognising promissory estoppel), thereby planting the seed of reliance-based liability that would grow to destroy the exchange theory of Holmes, Langdell and Williston. Although the story Gilmore tells does not square with the evidence, it is notable that Corbin chose to open his treatise with this broad assertion about the basic purpose of contract law.

Corbin does not treat the reasonable expectation thesis as a first principle from which to deduce legal rules. Perhaps the most charitable reading of it, given Corbin's methodological commitments, is as an empirical generalisation, based on his reading of a vast number of judicial decisions. That said, one finds him articulating the thesis as early as 1917, long before there was reason to defer to his knowledge of the case law. And the thesis sometimes plays a substantive role in *Corbin on Contracts*, nudging the analysis in a particular direction. It shows up, for example, in Corbin's argument that consideration does not serve as evidence of the parties' intent to be bound, but is 'evidence that the expectation of performance was reasonable and that refusal to enforce would not satisfy the community'.[108] And Corbin devotes an entire chapter to 'Reliance on a Promise as Ground for Enforcement'.[109] The thesis also plays a central role in Corbin's highly influential account of contract interpretation.

Corbin's understanding of interpretation bears the mark of Hohfeld. To interpret the meaning of parties' words and actions is to determine the character of an operative act, an act that effects a legal change. Interpretation does not specify the act's legal effects: the resulting change in the parties' legal duties and other jural relations. For that we require a separate rule. Corbin translates this

[106] Corbin (n 55) 205.
[107] Corbin (n 9) vol 1, § 1.
[108] *ibid* vol 3, § 534.
[109] *ibid* 'Reliance on a Promise as Ground for Enforcement', vol 1A, ch 8, §§ 193–209.

Hohfeldian point into Francis Lieber's distinction between interpretation and construction. As Corbin draws the distinction:

> By 'interpretation of language' we determine what ideas that language induces in other persons. By 'construction of the contract,' as the term will be used here, we determine its legal operation – its effect upon the action of courts and administrative officials. If we make this distinction, then the construction of a contract starts with the interpretation of its language but does not end with it; while the process of interpretation stops wholly short of a determination of the legal relations of the parties.[110]

Interpretation, whether done by a judge or a jury, is on this understanding a purely factual enquiry, one that precedes and provides the materials for determining the parties' legal relations according to one or more rules of construction.[111]

Corbin's account of the nature of contract interpretation rests on two additional premises. The first concerns the nature of meaning and its relation to context, and can be found in one of the best-known passages in *Corbin on Contracts*:

> [I]t can hardly be insisted on too often or too vigorously that language at its best is always a defective and uncertain instrument, that words do not define themselves, that terms and sentences in a contract, a deed, or a will do not apply themselves to external objects and performances, that the meaning of such terms and sentences consists of the ideas that they induce in the mind of some individual person who uses or hears or reads them, and that seldom in a litigated case do the words of a contract convey one identical meaning to two contracting parties or to third persons. Therefore, it is invariably necessary, before a court can give any meaning to the words of a contract and can select one meaning rather than other possible ones as the basis for the determination of rights and other legal effects, that extrinsic evidence shall be heard to make the court aware of the 'surrounding circumstances,' including the persons, objects, and events to which the words can be applied and which caused the words to be used.[112]

Corbin was no philosopher of language, and the above passage suggests a relatively naïve conception of meaning: the meaning of words or sentences 'consist of the ideas they induce in the mind', be it the mind of a speaker, hearer, reader

[110] *ibid* vol 3, § 534. For more on Corbin's distinctive understanding of the interpretation-construction distinction, see G Klass, 'Contracts, Constitutions, and Getting the Interpretation-Construction Distinction Right' (2020) 18 *Georgetown Journal of Law and Public Policy* 13, 19–21; LA Cunningham, 'Hermeneutics and Contract Default Rules: An Essay on Lieber and Corbin' (1995) 16 *Cardozo Law Review* 2225.

[111] Corbin (n 9) vol 3, § 554. The same idea can be found in Corbin's discussion of offers (*ibid* vol 1, § 11):

> There are two kinds of questions that are presented to the courts for their solution. First. What were the facts that occurred or existed? This question must be answered by making a historical investigation, by receiving oral testimony and other evidence, and drawing inferences therefrom. Secondly. What is the legal operation and effect of the facts that are found to have existed.

[112] *ibid* vol 3, § 536.

or someone else. One can, of course, define 'meaning' however one wishes. And perhaps this is how courts approach interpretation in contracts cases. But few if any philosophers of language would agree with the above as a general account of meaning. There are many ways to interpret the meaning of a word, sentence or speech act that have nothing to do with the ideas they elicit in a particular speaker, hearer or other person.[113]

Still, this is the conception of meaning Corbin advances, and it has two important implications for his account of interpretation. First, context always matters. 'No language, however, fully and carefully "integrated," applies itself to the persons and objects and performances involved'.[114] Because the ideas a speech act induces always depend in part on context, one cannot identify meaning (in Corbin's sense) without considering the circumstances of use. Second, the same words might induce different ideas in separate occasions of their use, and might induce different ideas in separate individuals on a single occasion of their use. Consequently, words and speech acts commonly have multiple meanings, any of which can legitimately be said to be their meaning.

Because a single speech act can have different meanings for different persons, we need a rule to determine which meaning governs. 'In every case of interpretation, even though the contract is "integrated," the first question is: Whose meaning and understanding is it to which it is the purpose of the law to give legal effect'.[115] Unlike interpretation, this is a legal question. If interpretation identifies the various meanings a speech act has, we need a rule of construction to specify which of those meanings is legally operative.

It is here that the reasonable expectation thesis makes an overt appearance, forming the second premise of Corbin's theory of meaning. In the case of a will or a sealed document on which no one has yet relied, it is the testator's or promisor's meaning that governs. But that is not the rule of construction for contractual agreements. When the parties to an agreement attach different meanings to the words one or both use, one reasonable and the other unreasonable, it is the reasonable meaning that governs. Corbin finds the explanation for this rule in reasonable expectations thesis:

> The foregoing result is reached because, as our system of contract law has grown, one of its chief purposes is to secure the realization of expectations reasonably induced by the expressions of agreement, when this can be done without running counter to other expectations and understandings that were also reasonably induced.[116]

[113] For a good overview, see J Speaks, 'Theories of Meaning' in EN Zalta (ed), *The Stanford Encyclopedia of Philosophy* (Spring 2021), available at http://plato.stanford.edu/archives/spr2021/entries/meaning/.

[114] Corbin (n 9) vol 3, § 538.

[115] *ibid* § 537.

[116] *ibid.*

In short, the objective theory of interpretation, for Corbin, flows from the reasonable expectation thesis. If A and B attach different meanings to their agreement, A's unreasonable and B's reasonable, B's must govern:

> It is not the meaning that A gave; or the meaning that a normal user of English would have given; or the meaning that the court may hastily think is 'plain and clear.' … [All these] are merely steps in the evidential search for B's meaning and A's reason to know it; no one of them is the one that must prevail.[117]

Because the goal of contract law is to protect parties' reasonable expectations, the only meanings that matter are the ones that one or both parties actually attached to their agreement.

Corbin maintains that the above holds true without regard to whether the words at issue appear in an integrated writing. If the legally salient meaning of words lies in the ideas they induce in one or both parties, and if those ideas always depend on context, then context is always relevant to interpreting a writing. Williston had argued that when parties agree to an integrated writing, they typically agree to be bound by the words' plain meaning, without regard to whether that meaning corresponds to their individual understandings.[118] Corbin rejects this account of integration. 'It is true that in such cases, the parties are found to have assented to the written words as the definitive operative expression of their minds. This is an assent to those words, not to any particular meaning of them'.[119] Here again Corbin recurs not to judicial decisions but to principle:

> A court exists for the purpose of doing justice to the parties before it, and should not be misled into doing something else by some third person's definition of a word even though the contracting parties both assented to a writing containing it.[120]

Corbin's influence on the *Restatement (Second's)* sections on contract interpretation is unmistakable. Section 202 provides as the first rule in aid of interpretation that '[w]ords and other conduct are interpreted in the light of all the circumstances, and if the principal purpose of the parties is ascertainable it is given great weight'.[121] The comments to sections 201 and 202 read as though they had been lifted directly from *Corbin on Contracts*. 'Words are used as conventional symbols of mental states'.[122] '[T]he context of words and other conduct is seldom exactly the same for two different people'.[123] 'The objective of interpretation in the general law of contracts is to carry out the understanding of the parties rather than to impose obligations on them contrary to their understanding'.[124]

[117] *ibid*.
[118] Williston (n 60) vol 2, § 607.
[119] Corbin (n 9) vol 3, § 539.
[120] *ibid* § 539.
[121] *Restatement (Second) of the Law of Contracts* (Philadelphia, American Law Institute, 1982) § 202(1).
[122] *ibid* § 201, cmt a.
[123] *ibid* § 201, cmt b.
[124] *ibid* § 201, cmt c.

'The meaning of words and other symbols commonly depends on their context'.[125] And whereas the *Restatement (First)* suggested a separate rule for the interpretation of integrated writings, the *Restatement (Second)* advocates a single rule for all contractual communications.[126] Again the explanatory comment could have been written by Corbin. 'It is sometimes said that extrinsic evidence cannot change the plain meaning of a writing, but meaning can almost never be plain except in context'.[127]

Viewed from the distance of several decades, Corbin's approach to contract interpretation exhibits significant blind spots. One is Corbin's conception of the meaning as 'the ideas that "contractual acts" induce in the mind of some individual person who uses or hears or reads them'.[128] I have suggested that, given Corbin's broader commitments, this claim is most charitably read as an empirical generalisation regarding how courts in fact interpret contractual agreements. Thousands of judicial decisions, however, have articulated and applied a different conception of meaning, embodied in the so-called plain meaning rule:

> [W]hen parties set down their agreement in a clear, complete document, … [e]vidence outside the four corners of the document as to what was really intended but unstated or misstated is generally inadmissible to add to or vary the writing.[129]

Plain meaning, on this conception, is the meaning reasonably attached to the words of a writing stripped of much of the evidence of the context surrounding its original use.

Corbin's response is to deny that language ever has a plain meaning. 'A study of many cases shows that however "plain and clear" may be our chosen definition of the term "integrated", its application to the facts of any particular case may be very far from "plain and clear".'[130] But the appellate cases that make up the bulk of Corbin's evidence hardly provide a representative sample. And Corbin's claim about the inherent ambiguity of language draws on his narrow definition of 'meaning'. The fact that words in a writing can induce different ideas in different persons and in different contexts does not entail that they do not have a conventional meaning discoverable without that added context. To respond that that conventional meaning does not count as 'meaning' in the relevant sense is to fall back on precisely the sort of argument from definition that Corbin elsewhere rejects.

[125] *ibid* § 202, cmt b.

[126] *Restatement (First) of the Law of Contracts* (n 18) §§ 230, 232; *Restatement (Second) of Contracts* (n 121) §§ 202, cmt b, 212(1) ('The interpretation of an integrated agreement is directed to the meaning of the terms of the writing or writings in the light of the circumstances, in accordance with the rules stated in this chapter').

[127] *ibid* § 212, cmt b.

[128] Corbin (n 9) vol 3, § 536.

[129] *WWW Associates, Inc v Giancontieri* 566 NE 2d 639 (NY 1990).

[130] Corbin (n 9) vol 3, § 539.

In addition to his narrow definition of meaning, Corbin's account of interpretation assumes a narrow conception of the act of contracting. Corbin understands contractual agreements as, first and foremost, agreements about what one or both shall do, to which the law happens to attach legal effects, not as juristic acts, in which the parties decide for themselves what their legal relationship will be.[131] One can see this naturalised picture of contractual agreements in Corbin's account of integration. The parties' agreement to integrate a writing is not, for Corbin, an agreement that the writing will have a particular legal effect: that it shall serve as the sole legal evidence of the terms contained in it. It is simply an agreement that all prior agreements shall by discharged or merged into the present one.[132] This is why Corbin can so confidently claim that an integration is an assent to the words in a writing, 'not to any particular meaning of them'.[133] Because integration is not a juristic act, there is no reason to think that the parties understand their words in anything but their everyday meanings.

Accordingly, Corbin rarely, if ever, considers the impact that one or another legal rule might have on parties' understandings or behaviour. Contract interpretation should track parties' everyday understandings and expectations, not seek to shape them. But some parties contract in the law's shadow; their expectations and actions are shaped by the law. In such transactions, it is by no means obvious that a party's assent to the words in an integrated writing is not also an assent to whatever meaning a court might give those words. This was precisely Williston's point: when sophisticated parties contract in a jurisdiction that employs a plain meaning rule, each reasonably expects to be bound by the plain meaning of their integrated writing – whether or not it corresponds to their individual understandings. Sometimes assent to a writing might well be assent to a meaning of the words in it that neither party holds.

Finally, Corbin never asks what rule of interpretation parties, at the time of contracting, are likely to prefer. The role of courts in contracts cases, on Corbin's theory, is strictly backward looking: to protect the parties' reasonable expectations and do justice between them. It is not obvious, however, that this is what parties want. Justice is often expensive, and it can be difficult to predict what courts will consider a just outcome in any given case. Parties might prefer to be bound by a meaning that is cheaper to discover, easier to predict, and more difficult to manipulate – even if it does not always correspond to their individual understandings.

In short, Corbin's account of interpretation is premised on his claim that the primary purpose of contract law is to protect parties' reasonable expectations.

[131] I discuss these different views of contractual agreements in G Klass, 'Three Pictures of Contract: Duty, Power and Compound Rule' (2008) 83 *New York University Law Review* 1726.

[132] Corbin (n 9) vol 3, § 574.

[133] *ibid* § 539.

My own view is that the claim is not wrong, but incomplete. Contract law additionally serves to enable exchange transactions between parties who do not otherwise trust one another, to guide parties to efficient and socially valued forms of interaction through default and mandatory rules, and often to realise parties' legal intentions.

It is difficult to fault Corbin for failing to integrate these aspects of contract law into his thinking. When *Corbin on Contracts* first appeared in 1950, the will theory, Langdell's formalism, and Holmes's dogmatic division between law and morality were all within living memory. And it was still ten years before the appearance of Ronald Coase's 'The Problem of Social Cost',[134] not to mention the subsequent rise of law and economics. If arguments from party incentives and expectations, from the value of predictability, and from the minimisation of litigation costs today seem obvious, it is because legal scholars have now been applying economic analysis and game theory to contractual transactions for more than 50 years. Corbin would not be surprised by any of this, given his own understanding of the law as in a constant state of flux. In short, Corbin's approach to contract law was of its time.

VII. CONCLUSION

Although this chapter has focused on the broad strokes of Corbin's work, Corbin spent most of his time as a scholar attending to the fine lines drawn in judicial opinions. The theory of the common law that Corbin published in 1914, after only ten years in the academy, is almost identical to the theory he articulated in 1954 and then again in 1964.[135] Having arrived early at his own view of the common law, Corbin spent most of his scholarly life focusing on the case law and on the construction of his treatise. When Corbin was in his 80s, he could still be found in the Yale Law Library reading room poring over recent judicial opinions. Guido Calabresi, who was a student at the time, reports the light there was so poor that Corbin would bring his own reading lamp and, refusing offers of help from students, would crawl under the table to plug it in himself.[136] And as William Twining recalls in his Afterword to this volume, when he interviewed Corbin at his home nearly a decade later, Corbin had a box full of index cards sitting next to his armchair. Corbin was still taking notes on the appellate opinions for the supplements to his great treatise.[137] It was this passion for the actual, often messy work of courts, combined with analytic clarity and a clear-eyed vision of an evolutionary logic to the common law, that gives *Corbin on Contracts* its authority and accounts for its influence.

[134] RH Coase, 'The Problem of Social Cost' (1960) 3 *Journal of Law and Economics* 1.
[135] Corbin (n 7); Corbin (n 35); Corbin (n 10) 188.
[136] Author's conversation with G Calabresi (25 May 2021).
[137] See Twining's chapter 15 of this volume, text to n 20.

9

Professor Geoffrey Cheshire (1886–1978) and Cecil Fifoot (1899–1975)

WARREN SWAIN

Don clerical, Don ordinary,
Don self-absorbed and solitary;
Don here-and-there, Don epileptic;
Don puffed and empty, Don dyspeptic;
Don middle-class, Don sycophantic,
Don dull, Don brutish, Don pedantic;
Don hypocritical, Don bad,
Don furtive, Don three-quarters mad;[1]

TODAY, GEOFFREY CHEVALIER CHESHIRE and Cecil Herbert Stuart Fifoot seem to us to be figures from another world. After all, they were born during the reign of Queen Victoria. Both men were involved in a particular academic milieu, termed by Noel Annan as a 'golden-age'.[2] Designations of golden ages run the risk of caricature but it is not too fanciful to regard the inter-war period as a continuation of the nineteenth-century university – captured by Evelyn Waugh's description of Oxford in the 1920s as 'still a city of aquatint'.[3] In 1912, the year Cheshire was elected to a Fellowship at Exeter College, the number of law teachers in England and Wales was tiny.[4] Although

[1] H Belloc, *Verses* (London, Duckworth & Co, 1910).

[2] N Annan, *The Dons: Mentors, Eccentrics and Geniuses* (London, Harper Collins, 2000) 136. Care, of course, needs to be taken with this sort of generalisation which is only likely to fit with a certain section of Oxford society. For one element of Oxford between the wars, see L Mitchell, *Maurice Bowra: A Life* (Oxford, Oxford University Press, 2009) 151–77.

[3] E Waugh, *Brideshead Revisited* (London, Penguin, 1962) 23.

[4] It has been estimated that there were around 100 law teachers in 1908 – the Inns of Court and the Law Society are included in that figure. The vast majority of academic lawyers were in Oxford, Cambridge and London (F Cownie and R Cocks, *'A Great and Noble Occupation!' The History of the Society of Legal Scholars* (Oxford, Hart Publishing, 2009) 3–4).

a few of those teaching law at the time were serious scholars, most were not.[5] Law had only existed as a separate Jurisprudence School at Oxford since 1872.[6] It can be argued that only comparatively recently has the subject been consistently taken seriously as an academic discipline in England. Amongst some dons in nineteenth-century Oxford, Jurisprudence enjoyed the same poor standing which media studies does in the popular imagination today. These attitudes persisted until the 1950s when, in Brian Simpson's account, law emerged as a proper academic enterprise in Oxford.[7] Even then and for quite a long time afterwards, most legal research in Britain was what might be called 'black-letter' or 'expository'. This began to change in the 1970s partly because some legal academics in England and Wales became interested in ideas from the United States, including the Critical Legal Studies and Law and Society movements.[8] Since that time, legal scholarship has become more varied – although that does not necessarily mean that it has become particularly perceptive or more worthwhile.[9]

Cheshire and Fifoot were within an older tradition of legal writers who saw their role as providing exposition. Yet neither man was a narrow specialist. Even by the standards of the time, Cheshire had wide interests which went beyond the confines of one narrow legal discipline. He is perhaps best remembered today as an early pioneer of private international law rather than as a writer on contract law. Fifoot retains his reputation through his writings on legal history. This was a time when academic lawyers with broad concerns within the legal discipline were common. These days they hardly exist at all.

Cheshire and Fifoot's treatise on contract law, *The Law of Contracts*[10] (hereinafter referred to as *Cheshire and Fifoot*) was first published in 1945 but in some respects it resembled books on the law of contract published during the late nineteenth century when legal treatises were the dominant form of legal literature.[11] It was one of the last new books of this genre – although new

[5] A minority of nineteenth-century law professors like Frederic Maitland would be significant figures in any era.

[6] B Nicholas, 'Jurisprudence' in MG Brock and MC Curthoys, *The History of the University of Oxford: Volume VII: Nineteenth-Century Oxford, Part 2* (Oxford, Oxford University Press, 2000) 385, 389–96.

[7] AWB Simpson, *Reflections on the Concept of Law* (Oxford, Oxford University Press, 2011).

[8] W Twining, *Blackstone's Tower: The English Law School* (London, Sweet & Maxwell, 1994) 141–46.

[9] Some judges, particularly in the United States, have been critical of the modern direction of legal scholarship: see HT Edwards, 'The Growing Disjunction between Legal Education and the Legal Profession' (1991–92) 91 *Michigan Law Review* 34; B Gardner, 'Interviews with United States Supreme Court Justices: Chief Justice John G Roberts Jr' (2010) 13 *Scribes Journal of Legal Writing* 5, 37 ('What the academy is doing, as far as I can tell, is largely of no use or interest to people who actually practice law'). It is perhaps best not to contemplate too carefully the value of large amounts of legal scholarship that is now produced. For a more optimistic view, see A Burrows, 'Challenges for Private Law in the 21st Century' in K Barker et al (eds), *Private Law in the 21st Century* (Oxford, Hart Publishing, 2017) 32–40.

[10] GC Cheshire and CHS Fifoot, *The Law of Contracts* (London, Butterworth, 1945).

[11] AWB Simpson, 'The Rise and Fall of the Legal Treatise: Legal Principles and the Forms of Legal Literature' (1981) 48 *University of Chicago Law Review* 632; W Swain, 'The Legal Treatise and the History of the Common Law' [2014] *Queensland Legal Year Book* 132.

editions of earlier works continue to appear with some regularity.[12] The volume was important for another reason. Editions of *Cheshire and Fifoot* appeared in New Zealand and then in Australia during the 1960s. These editions provide valuable insight into the state of the law of contract in those jurisdictions; they trace the declining influence of the English law of contract.

I. GC CHESHIRE: A BRIEF BIOGRAPHY

Geoffrey Chevalier Cheshire was born in 1886.[13] His father was a solicitor and Registrar of Northwich County Court. Cheshire matriculated in Jurisprudence at Merton College, in 1905. Merton, one of the oldest and wealthiest colleges,[14] had by then quickly established a reputation in Law. FE Smith, the future Lord Chancellor Lord Birkenhead, was elected to a Law Fellowship in 1896.[15] His replacement as Law Fellow, JC (later Sir John) Miles, taught Cheshire. Miles who had no great claims as a legal scholar would become Warden of Merton in 1936.[16] After reading for the BCL, Cheshire lectured for a few years at University College of Wales, Aberystwyth. In 1911, he was called to the Bar at Lincoln's Inn, although he never seems to have practised. He subsequently returned to his old college as a stipendiary lecturer in 1911 before being elected a Tutorial Fellow at Exeter College the following year. Following the outbreak of the First World War, Cheshire obtained an army commission and spent the last few years of the War in the Royal Flying Corps in a balloon reconnaissance unit.[17] During the War, Cheshire married Primrose Barstow and they went on to have two sons, one of whom was the well-known Second World War pilot and philanthropist, Leonard.[18] After the War, Cheshire returned to Exeter College, where from 1919 to 1933 he was also Bursar.[19]

[12] It was not quite the last major book in this tradition. A later work appeared in 1962, GH Treitel, *The Law of Contract* (London, Stevens & Sons, 1962). For a discussion of Professor Treitel, see Burrows, chapter 11 of this volume.

[13] For more detailed biographical information, see FH Lawson, 'Geoffrey Chevalier Cheshire 1886–1978' (1980) 65 *Proceedings of the British Academy* 610; FH Lawson, P North revd, 'Cheshire, Geoffrey Chevalier (1886–1978)' in *Oxford Dictionary of National Biography*.

[14] On Merton at the time, see GH Martin and JRL Highfield, *A History of Merton College* (Oxford, Oxford University Press, 1997) 325–29.

[15] J Campbell, *FE Smith First Earl of Birkenhead* (London, Jonathan Cape, 1983) 65–85. EA Knox and AA Prankerd had previously taught the subject for the college (FH Lawson, *The Oxford Law School 1850–1965* (Oxford, Clarendon Press, 1968) 51–52, 80–81, 254).

[16] Miles produced a casebook on contract law, J Miles, *Cases Illustrating General Principles of the Law of Contract* (Oxford, Clarendon Press, 1923). This was designed as a companion to Anson's contract treatise but consisted of little more than extracts from decisions without commentary.

[17] Balloon reconnaissance was used to assist artillery battalions. It was dangerous work.

[18] R Morris, *Cheshire: The Biography of Leonard Cheshire, VC, OM* (London, Penguin, 2000). Leonard also read Jurisprudence at Merton like his father.

[19] The arrangement whereby a Tutorial Fellow was also Bursar was not uncommon at the time and was a useful extra source of income for the Fellow concerned.

Hanbury remembered attending Cheshire's lectures:

> To demonstrate Cheshire's outstanding abilities as a lecturer, one need only recall his lectures on Future Estates in Real Property, which he delivered in Exeter in Michaelmas Term, 1920. The hour he chose was 9 a.m., the winter was cold, and some of his auditors had a long way to come; yet his class was larger at the end than at the beginning.[20]

Cheshire's dry sense of humour was no doubt a factor in his popularity with undergraduates. One of his sons recalled how Cheshire confused more than one visiting scholar by telling them he was thinking of writing a legal textbook, *The Rights of Dogs*.[21] Following the death of Sir William Holdsworth in 1944, Cheshire was elected as the Vinerian Chair of English Law which is based at All Souls.[22] He retired from Oxford in 1949. For a further decade following formal retirement he taught Property Law and Conflict of Laws at the Council for Legal Education. While the focus of this volume is on contract scholarship, Cheshire wrote on many diverse topics. This is unsurprising given that Tutorial Fellows of his vintage were expected to teach a range of subjects.[23] Most of his published writing on contract law came towards the end of his career. One early article considered the tort of unlawful molestation;[24] his first major work, however, concerned real property. After many decades of delay,[25] a series of statutes had finally reformed English real property law in the mid-1920s.[26] Cheshire's, *The Modern Law of Real Property*,[27] came at an opportune time and quickly established itself as the leading work on the new legislation.[28] Cheshire was able to use his connections to steal a march on other authors. Miles's friendship with FF Liddell, the draftsman of the legislation, meant that he was able to receive advanced copies of the Bills as work progressed on drafting.[29] As Cheshire explained in the preface, '[d]espite the short time available, I felt that something was required, before the new era dawned in January, 1926, to enable students to envisage a legal system which is, in many respects, widely different from that described in existing books'.[30] Under the title *Cheshire and Burn's Modern Law of Real Property*,[31] this work remains in press.

[20] HG Hanbury, *The Vinerian Chair and Legal Education* (Oxford, Basil Blackwell, 1958) 242.
[21] Morris (n 18) 7.
[22] Hanbury (n 20) 242–43.
[23] To some extent this is still true of course in both Oxford and Cambridge.
[24] GC Cheshire, 'Unlawful Molestation' (1923) 39 *LQR* 193.
[25] This story is documented in detail in JS Anderson, *Lawyers and The Making of English Land Law 1832–1940* (Oxford, Oxford University Press, 1992).
[26] Law of Property Act 1925; Land Registration Act 1925; Land Charges Act 1925; Settled Land Act 1925.
[27] GC Cheshire, *The Modern Law of Real Property* (London, Butterworth, 1925).
[28] This book also generated a steady income (Morris (n 18) 5). Professor Beale was told in the 1970s that Cheshire made the then enormous sum of £17,000 a year in royalties from his books.
[29] Anderson (n 25) 312.
[30] Cheshire (n 27) vi.
[31] EH Burn and J Cartwright (eds), *Cheshire and Burn's Modern Law of Real Property* (Oxford, Oxford University Press, 2011).

Cheshire became All Souls Lecturer in Private International Law in 1922. In 1935, he published *Private International Law*.[32] Although private international law had been an interest of the prominent jurist AV Dicey, it had not yet become a mainstream area of study.[33] In a *Law Quarterly Review* article coinciding with the publication of his treatise, Cheshire gave an overview of the subject in which he observed:

> It is true that of all the main branches of English jurisprudence Private International Law can claim the most recent birth; it is true that the events which call it into operation could scarcely occur with frequency until the peace that succeeded the Napoleonic wars ushered in the industrial age and fostered the growth of international trade and travel; it is true that no book was published on the subject in England until 1858; but nevertheless a perusal of the authorities shows that the main principles had been established and the lines of future development laid down before the first issue of this Journal in 1885.[34]

One reviewer, having noted the need for a new treatment of the subject, praised Cheshire's willingness to criticise orthodox opinion.[35] Cheshire would return to the subject of private international law over the following decades.[36]

II. CHS FIFOOT: A BRIEF BIOGRAPHY

Cecil Fifoot was born in Wales in 1899.[37] Commissioned in the Royal Field Artillery in the First World War, he was wounded and left partially deaf. After the War, Fifoot went up to Exeter College which brought him into contact with Cheshire. Having graduated in Jurisprudence, he was called to the Bar by the Middle Temple in 1922. Unlike Cheshire, Fifoot practised law full time for a couple of years. While in practice in South Wales he married a Norwegian, Hjördis Baars.[38] After a short time, he returned to Oxford in 1924 as a Tutorial

[32] GC Cheshire, *Private International Law* (Oxford, Clarendon Press, 1935). The work is still in print, P Torremans et al, *Cheshire, North & Fawcett Private International Law* (Oxford, Oxford University Press, 2017).

[33] AV Dicey, *A Digest of the Law of England with Reference to the Conflict of Laws* (London, Sweet & Maxwell, 1908). In addition to Dicey's treatise there was a second earlier work: J Westlake, *A Treatise on Private International Law* (London, W Maxwell, 1858) but this was of course dated.

[34] GC Cheshire, 'Private International Law' (1935) 51 *LQR* 76.

[35] (1935) *Journal of the Society of Public Teachers of Law* 65. The same point was made by others; another reviewer referred to 'constructive criticism', see (1935) 16 *British Yearbook of International Law* 218. In the preface, Cheshire (n 32) vii, Cheshire spoke of 'a spirit of constructive criticism'.

[36] A Mendelssohn-Bartholdy and GC Cheshire (eds), *Renvoi in Modern English Law* (Oxford, Clarendon Press, 1937); GC Cheshire, *The English Private International Law of Husband and Wife* (London, Martinus Nijhoff Publishers, 1963).

[37] For a more detailed biography, see GC Cheshire, 'Fifoot, Cecil Herbert Stuart, 1899–1975' (1976) 61 *Proceedings of the British Academy* 428.

[38] They had a son Richard Fifoot who became the Bodleian's Librarian.

Fellow at Hertford College. In addition to tutorials, he also undertook various college offices including Bursar and Dean. Hertford at the time was not a wealthy or glamourous college. Its new foundation had occurred less than a century earlier. Evelyn Waugh, who had been a Hertford undergraduate in the 1920s, described his college as 'a respectable but rather dreary little college' to which he added 'there was no scholar of importance among the dons'.[39]

Edward Burn, later a Student at Christ Church, and author of editions of Cheshire's work on real property, described Fifoot's teaching style:

> He immediately established a rapport with his audience. A thin stooping figure, he looked as he lectured if he were defying us not to listen to him. None could defy him. Authoritative and learned he sparkled with humour. We listened and chuckled with him, and so the more readily transcribed into our notebooks the apt phrases which illustrated his argument.[40]

Anne Smart, an undergraduate in the 1950s, remembered Fifoot's lectures too: '[he] had no difficulty in filling to capacity the Hall at Hertford College on a Saturday morning'.[41] A correspondent to *The Times*, writing after Fifoot's death, recalled that he used to say to his classes: 'I am trying not only to put the law in a nutshell but to keep it there'.[42] Although he may have been a good lecturer, some of the descriptions of him suggest a rather aloof and even prickly personality. He was described by an undergraduate as 'quite brilliant, cold, but cheerful and efficient'.[43] Fifoot was one of the few Hertford Fellows of the era who was married. As a result, he lived out of college, which may offer part of the explanation for this less than warm description of his personality. However, there was probably more to it. Cheshire commented that Fifoot did not

> take kindly to criticism. Once he had reached a conclusion after much thought, to persuade him that he might possibly be mistaken was a task not lightly to be undertaken. The discussion might engender a certain heat at times, perhaps a trace of arrogance, but however stormy the argument might have been he never harboured the slightest resentment.[44]

[39] E Waugh, *A Little Learning* (London, Penguin, 1983) 164. His father was of a different view, pointing out in a letter to his son that the scholarships at Hertford were larger than other colleges (Letter from Arthur Waugh to Evelyn Waugh (15 December 1921) in A Waugh and A Bell (eds), *The Complete Works of Evelyn Waugh, vol 30, Personal Writings 1903–1921: Precocious Waughs* (Oxford, Oxford University Press, 2017)).

[40] Cheshire (n 37) 431.

[41] A Smart, 'Reading Roman Law with Edward Burn' in J Getzler (ed), *Rationalising Property, Equity and Trusts: Essays in Honour of Edward Burn* (Oxford, Oxford University Press, 2003) 324, 326.

[42] *The Times* (27 March 1975).

[43] A Goudie (ed), *Seven Hundred Years of an Oxford College: Hertford College, 1284–1984* (Oxford, Hertford College, 1999) 83.

[44] Cheshire (n 37) 434. Fifoot's failure to be elected to the Vinerian Chair in succession to Cheshire, which he might reasonably have expected, may also have contributed to his gloom. I am grateful to Professor Reynolds for this information.

Cheshire also observed that '[i]t would be an exaggeration to describe him as an optimist. Like many others, he took a grim view of the world in general and particularly of England'. His pessimism, however, proved to be a useful characteristic when it came to winning bets against other members of the Senior Common Room during the Second World War.[45]

Fifoot wrote several books on English legal history. The broadest ranging of these was *English Law and its Background*.[46] One obituarist described this as 'a short light hearted book ... which already showed his highly individual style, and still remains the most interesting short account of English legal history for the layman or the beginner in law'.[47] A second book, *Lord Mansfield,*[48] had been, until relatively recently, the standard legal biography of the Chief Justice.[49] In that book, he had a good deal to say about mid-eighteenth century contract law. His main thesis was that he saw a distinction between the way that Lord Mansfield developed commercial law and contract law. The former, he argued, was much more influenced by the needs of merchants than the latter. In fact there is no need to draw the line so sharply.[50] There are also points of detail on which it is possible to take issue with Fifoot's analysis, particularly the suggestion that Lord Mansfield had intended to develop a principle of 'moral obligation'. The better interpretation, however, may be that it was simply an attempt by the common law to encroach into the jurisdiction of the Court of Chancery.[51]

Having produced a volume of Maitland's letters for the Selden Society,[52] Fifoot went on to write a short biography of England's greatest legal historian.[53] More than perhaps any of his other books, the biography of Maitland gives a very good sense of Fifoot's authorial voice which was spare, clear and concise. There is the occasional flash of wit of a donnish sort[54] and some unexpected emotional insight.[55] A few years before his death, Fifoot also delivered a

[45] The wager book still sits in the Senior Common Room of Hertford College – a selection of wartime bets can be found in Goudie (n 43) 105–106.

[46] CHS Fifoot, *English Law and its Background* (London, C Bell & Sons, 1932).

[47] *The Times* (7 February 1975) reproduced in the Hertford College magazine. I am grateful to the Hertford College Archivist, Dr Lucy Rutherford, for sending me a copy of the magazine.

[48] CHS Fifoot, *Lord Mansfield* (Oxford, Oxford University Press, 1936).

[49] This has been superseded by J Oldham, *The Mansfield Manuscripts and the Growth of English Law in the Eighteenth Century*, 2 vols (Chapel Hill, University of North Carolina Press, 1992) and NS Poser, *Lord Mansfield: Justice in the Age of Reason* (Montreal and Kingston, McGill-Queen's University Press, 2013).

[50] W Swain, *The Law of Contract 1670–1870* (Cambridge, Cambridge University Press, 2015) 42–106.

[51] Fifoot (n 48) 137; W Swain, 'The Changing Nature of the Doctrine of Consideration 1750–1850' (2005) 26 *Journal of Legal History* 55, 62–65.

[52] CHS Fifoot, *Letters of FW Maitland* (London, Selden Society, 1965).

[53] CHS Fifoot, *Frederic William Maitland: A Life* (Cambridge MA, Harvard University Press, 1971).

[54] See, eg, *ibid* 13 ('pamphlets, even when relieved by *jeux d'esprit*, are not a satisfying diet for middle age').

[55] Fifoot is particularly good on Maitland's decision to leave the Bar. He of course spoke from personal experience on this issue.

lecture on Pollock and Maitland's *The History of English Law Before the Time of Edward I*,[56] which was then published as a pamphlet.[57] Fifoot was also one of the first scholars to consider the influence of jurists on legal development. He chose the nineteenth century as the subject of the Hamlyn Lecture in 1959. His *Judge and Jurist in the Reign of Queen Victoria*[58] is an example of what some have called 'conservative' legal history.[59] The idea that individuals shaped the development of the law was unfashionable for decades but recently has come back into favour.[60] Fifoot's central thesis was that there was a large gap between the law as promoted by jurists and the law applied by judges.[61] The lectures were given using material planned for a larger book on the subject of judges and jurists; the book was unfortunately never written.[62]

III. WRITING ON CONTRACT LAW IN ADDITION TO *CHESHIRE AND FIFOOT*

In 1928 Cheshire became the general editor of the nineteenth edition of *Stephen's Commentaries on the Law of England*.[63] This work was in the same tradition as Sir William Blackstone's *Commentaries on the Laws of England*.[64] The first edition appeared in four volumes between 1841 and 1845.[65] Cheshire replaced a long-standing editor, Edward Jenks, and set about remodelling the commentaries. In the preface he wrote, 'This edition of Stephen's Commentaries has been entirely rearranged and rewritten'.[66] Although the overall work was reduced in size, the sections on contract and tort were expanded.[67] Volume three on contract and tort was the first collaboration between Cheshire and Fifoot. Fifoot contributed the historical introduction, the section on agency and co-authored the part on tort law together with Cheshire and CK Allen.[68] The general contract part

[56] F Pollock and FW Maitland, *The History of English Law Before the Time of Edward I* (Cambridge, Cambridge University Press, 1895).

[57] CHS Fifoot, *Pollock and Maitland* (Glasgow, University of Glasgow, 1971).

[58] CHS Fifoot, *Judge and Jurist in the Reign of Queen Victoria* (London, Sweet & Maxwell, 1959).

[59] M Horwitz, 'The Conservative Tradition in the Writing of American Legal History' (1973) 17 *American Journal of Legal History* 251.

[60] See, eg, the Legal Biography Project at LSE: www.lse.ac.uk/law/legal-biography-project.

[61] The relationship between jurists and judges continues to cause debate: RA Posner, *Divergent Paths: The Academy and the Judiciary* (Cambridge, MA, Harvard University Press, 2016).

[62] Cheshire (n 37) 432.

[63] GC Cheshire et al (eds), *Stephen's Commentaries on the Laws of England* (London, Butterworth, 1928).

[64] Published in the 1760s.

[65] HJ Stephen, *New Commentaries on the Laws of England (Partly Founded on Blackstone)* (London, Butterworth, 1841–45).

[66] Cheshire et al (n 63) v.

[67] *ibid* vi.

[68] ET Williams, T Honoré revd, 'Allen, Sir Carleton Kemp (1887–1966)' in *Oxford Dictionary of National Biography*, 23 September 2004. Allen is best known for his CK Allen, *Law in the Making* (Oxford, Oxford University Press, 1927) which went on to appear in seven editions.

was written by CK Allen. Much of the material in the historical introduction would be reused in *Cheshire and Fifoot*.

Stephen's Commentaries aside, neither man wrote very much about modern contract law beyond *Cheshire and Fifoot*. The subject nevertheless did intersect with their other interests. Cheshire would consider contract law as applied in private international law.[69] He also wrote a little on English contract law. In the *Law Quarterly Review*, he considered 'the proverbially difficult' subject of mistake of fact.[70] This article would later go on to form the basis of the relevant section in *Cheshire and Fifoot*. Fifoot's main contribution to contract scholarship, aside from *Cheshire and Fifoot*, was found in his *History and Sources of the Common Law*.[71] This volume collected printed historical sources on contract and tort to which Fifoot added a commentary. The primary audience were students. Fifoot believed that it was important for law students to understand where the modern law had come from through primary sources.[72] The introductory commentaries at the beginning of each chapter, arranged by form of action, is still perfectly serviceable today as an introduction to the history of contract and tort. As a collection of materials, however, it has since been superseded by *Baker and Milsom Sources of English Legal History*[73] which contains manuscript as well as printed sources.

In the late 1940s, in a jointly written and extensive casenote,[74] Cheshire and Fifoot would consider the controversial decision of Denning J in *Central London Property Trust v High Trees House Ltd*.[75] The authors were supportive of this departure from orthodoxy which they argued was based on 'a slim but sufficient catena of authority'.[76] The article provided an opportunity to analyse the rule in *Pinnel's Case*,[77] also known as the rule in *Foakes v Beer*.[78] The authors were uneasy with the established position that the acceptance of a lower sum could not amount to satisfaction of, and good consideration for, a larger debt. Their comments also illustrate their methodology as writers. They trace the history of the exclusory rule and the precedents which underpinned Denning J's attempt to circumvent some of its effects. This led them into a discussion of the rules of

[69] JHC Morris and GC Cheshire, 'The Proper Law of a Contract in the Conflict of Laws' (1940) 56 *LQR* 320.

[70] GC Cheshire, 'Mistake as Affecting Contractual Consent' (1944) 60 *LQR* 175.

[71] CHS Fifoot, *History and Sources of the Common Law: Tort and Contract* (London, Stevens & Sons, 1949).

[72] Cheshire (n 37) 432.

[73] J Baker (ed), *Baker and Milsom Sources of English Legal History*, 2nd edn (Oxford, Oxford University Press, 2010).

[74] GC Cheshire and CHS Fifoot, 'Central London Property Trust Ltd. v. High Trees House Ltd' (1947) 63 *LQR* 283.

[75] *Central London Property Trust v High Trees House Ltd* [1947] KB 130 (KBD).

[76] Cheshire and Fifoot (n 74) 288.

[77] *Pinnel's Case* (1602) 5 Co Rep 117a, 77 ER 237.

[78] *Foakes v Beer* (1884) 9 App Cas 605 (HL).

waiver and the role of Equity. Their whole approach was premised on the idea that the law of contract had some internal logic and that within the doctrine of precedent, there was an answer that made sense. This meant that although the House of Lords before 1966 did not have the power to not overturn its own decision in *Foakes v Beer*, Denning J's solution was presented as a valuable way of blunting the impact of a rule that they disliked. Given the later celebrity of Lord Denning, it is perhaps unsurprising that the decision has attracted such a lot of attention since. However, back in 1947, Denning J was just another newly appointed High Court judge. Here, the personal connection shared between Denning J and Cheshire was significant. It was Cheshire who used his position to promote the cause of his friend, Denning.[79] It was by no means inevitable that *High Trees* would become such a prominent authority. Without this push, it might have suffered the same fate of another first instance judgment a year earlier which had also bypassed *Foakes v Beer* but just as quickly had been forgotten about.[80] The wider point is that Cheshire and Fifoot were willing to criticise the status quo but ultimately had faith in the common law to come up with pragmatic solutions.

IV. *THE LAW OF CONTRACT* WITHIN AN INTELLECTUAL TRADITION

By the time that the first edition of *The Law of Contract* appeared in 1945,[81] both authors were secure in their reputations. Cheshire held the Vinerian Chair, and Fifoot was the All Souls Reader in English Law. Their treatise was a work of mature reflection compiled after many years spent teaching the subject. In the preface to their treatise, the authors set out a statement of their aims that is worth quoting in full:

> We profess to examine the principles underlying the English law of Contract, to indicate the difficulties which surround their application, to illustrate them from the accidents of litigation and the practices of life, and, where such a course seems profitable, to justify or excuse their vagaries by reference to their history.[82]

The emphasis on 'principles underlying the English law of Contract' puts *Cheshire and Fifoot* within the nineteenth-century classical contract tradition.[83]

[79] Lord Denning, *The Discipline of Law* (London, Butterworths, 1979) 200; Lord Denning, *The Family Story* (London, Butterworths, 1981) 78.

[80] *Buttery v Pickard* (1946) 62 TLR 241 (KBD) was noted by PV Baker (1947) 63 *LQR* 278 but otherwise disappeared into obscurity. Interestingly, *High Trees* did not appear in the All England Law Reports until 1956.

[81] Cheshire and Fifoot (n 10).

[82] *ibid* iii.

[83] S Waddams, 'What *Were* the Principles of Nineteenth-Century Contract Law?' in A Lewis et al (eds), *Law in the City: Proceedings of the Seventeenth British Legal History Conference* (Dublin, Four Courts Press, 2007) 305–18.

One of the leading treatise writers of that earlier time, Sir William Anson, explained in the preface to his *Principles of the Law of Contract* that:

> The main object with which I have set out has been to delineate the general principles which govern the contractual relation from its beginning to its end. I have tried to show how a contract is made, what is needed to make it binding, what its effect is, how its terms are interpreted, and how it is discharged and comes to an end.[84]

Anson was not the first writer to try to place the law of contract within a methodical structure. As far back as the early eighteenth-century, Jeffrey Gilbert had attempted to construct some sort of rationale framework for the law of contract.[85] Over a century and a half, various other writers tried to do the same.[86] Over time, these works became more comprehensive and more highly developed as well as lengthy. Most of these writers were influenced to varying degrees by Robert Joseph Pothier's idea that contracts were formed by a meeting of wills.[87]

By the time that *Cheshire and Fifoot* came along, there were three main competitor works, all of which had begun life in the nineteenth century. A possible twentieth century rival by Sir John Salmond was published posthumously[88] and only ran to two editions. The first edition was edited by Percy Winfield in 1927 and the second edition had James Williams as editor and appeared in 1945.[89] Reviewing the book in 1946, Denning, wrote that, 'the book cannot be pronounced a good one' and compared the work unfavourably with *Cheshire and Fifoot*, which he reviewed at the same time and described as 'a good book'.[90]

The first of the nineteenth century treatises by Joseph Chitty appeared in 1826.[91] A nineteenth edition was published just before the Second World War.[92] From the beginning, Chitty's treatise was aimed at legal practitioners and over

[84] WR Anson, *Principles of the Law of Contract* (Oxford, Clarendon Press, 1879) v.

[85] His work has only recently been published, see M Lobban (ed), *Jeffrey Gilbert on Property and Contract*, vol 1 (London, Selden Society, 2019) cliii.

[86] As well as those mentioned elsewhere in the text, these include H Ballow, *A Treatise of Equity* (London, E & R Nutt, 1737); JJ Powell, *Essay Upon the Law of Contracts and Agreements*, 2 vols (London, J Johnson, 1790); HT Colebrooke, *Treatise on Obligations and Contracts* (London, Black, Kingsbury, Parbury and Allen, 1818); SM Leake, *The Elements of the Law of Contracts* (London, Stevens & Sons, 1867).

[87] Pothier appeared in an English translation in 1806: RJ Pothier (translated by W Evans), *A Treatise on the Law of Obligations or Contracts*, 2 vols (London, A Strahan, 1806).

[88] I am grateful to Professor Hugh Collins for drawing this book to my attention. For some details of this work, see A Frame, *Salmond: Southern Jurist* (Wellington, Victoria University Press, 1995) 236–37.

[89] PH Winfield, *Principles of the Law of Contract by the late Sir John Salmond and Percy H Winfield* (London, Sweet & Maxwell, 1927); J Williams, *Principles of the Law of Contract by the late Sir John Salmond and James Williams*, 2nd edn (London, Sweet & Maxwell, 1945).

[90] (1946) 62 *LQR* 190, 191.

[91] J Chitty, *A Practical Treatise on the Law of Contracts not Under Seal* (London, S Sweet, 1826).

[92] C Odgers (ed), *Chitty's Treatise on the Law of Contract*, 19th edn (London, Sweet & Maxwell, 1937).

time it had grown in length and contained a mass of authority. The second treatise, written by Sir William Anson, was designed for law students and was the closest in its conception to *Cheshire and Fifoot*. Anson's approach as a writer was made clear in a letter that he enclosed in with a copy of his treatise to his friend, Thesiger LJ, where he admitted: 'Writing as I have done for students and beginners I have ventured on a definitiveness of statement as to the results of cases which would have been presumptuous in a book of practice'.[93]

The nineteenth edition of Anson's book, edited by James Brierly, and which appeared in the same year as *Cheshire and Fifoot*[94] was beginning to show its age. Cheshire and Fifoot made the perceptive point that while Anson's book 'has directed the steps, not only of the present authors, but of generations of pupils', the 'mode of treatment, apposite sixty years ago, may be thought out of focus with present needs'.[95] Sitting mid-way between these two treatises, a third, by Sir Frederick Pollock, could be read by practitioners or law students. *Principles of Contract at Law and in Equity*[96] offered a more complex and nuanced analysis than the two other works. However, at its centre was a tension between Pollock's theoretical framework and the law as it was applied by the courts.[97] When it came to Pollock's treatise, Cheshire and Fifoot claimed rather oddly that it was not comprehensive – which is perhaps not the most obvious of its faults. The final edition written by Pollock was published in 1921.[98] The editor of the eleventh edition which appeared in 1942, Sir Percy Winfield, was himself a distinguished jurist.[99] This was a large work of over 600 pages of text. Unlike Anson's treatise, it had nearly reached the end of its life. The final thirteenth edition was published in 1950, three years before Winfield's death.

Cheshire and Fifoot owed a great deal to these earlier authors, especially Anson, as they themselves recognise. Their own treatise was hardly novel in its conception. The pattern of writing about contract law was already well established. The most important feature of this tradition was the way that contract law was presented as a single body of legal doctrine rather than as an accumulation of rules which attached to different forms of action or different types of contract. While this gave the subject much-needed coherence – in contrast for example to the law of tort[100] – it involved several assumptions. For

[93] The letter dated 20 March 1879 is reproduced in S Waddams, *Principle and Policy in Contract Law* (Cambridge, Cambridge University Press, 2011) 212.

[94] JL Brierly (ed), *Anson's Law of Contract: Principles of the English Law of Contract*, 19th edn (Oxford, Clarendon Press, 1945).

[95] Cheshire and Fifoot (n 10) (preface).

[96] F Pollock, *Principles of Contract at Law and in Equity* (London, Stevens & Son, 1876).

[97] N Duxbury, *Frederick Pollock and the English Juristic Tradition* (Oxford, Oxford University Press, 2004) 196.

[98] F Pollock, *Principles of Contract at Law and in Equity*, 9th edn (London, Stevens & Sons, 1921).

[99] PH Winfield, *Pollock's Principles of Contract*, 11th edn (London, Stevens & Sons, 1942).

[100] The literature on tort law in the nineteenth century was rather sparse in contrast to that on contract and of the English writers only Pollock made a serious attempt to provide a level of intellectual coherence to the subject: F Pollock, *The Law of Torts: A Treatise on the Principles*

example, it was premised on the idea that contracts are the product of negotiation between two roughly equal parties which then produces an agreement. There were a number of issues with this paradigm not least of which was that by the nineteenth century, standard form contracting had become commonplace.[101] Cheshire and Fifoot did not diverge from this pattern.

Because treatises in the classical tradition are premised on the core concept of an agreement, they always begin with an examination of the nature of agreement and the doctrine of offer and acceptance. In traditional fashion, *Cheshire and Fifoot* emphasised the centrality of agreement: 'The idea of mutual assent, however elusive in practice, was at the root of contract'.[102] The standard arrangement was also followed with offer and acceptance, consideration, intention to create legal relations, content of a contract, enforceability, vitiating factors, capacity, privity, discharge and remedies. A final chapter considered quasi-contract. This structure was relatively similar to the way that Anson ordered his material in his first edition. This ordering of the material is still reflected in modern treatises that are part of this tradition.[103] Quasi-contract has gradually disappeared from contract treatises with the emergence of a distinct legal doctrine of unjust enrichment or restitution.[104]

One feature of *Cheshire and Fifoot* distinguishes the work from the other contract treatises. The history of contract features much more prominently. The first edition contained a 17-page overview on the history of the subject. History intruded at other points as well. The topic of consideration is prefaced with a historical introduction,[105] as is the Statute of Frauds.[106] This approach is not entirely unusual, but the extent to which history featured was novel and is notable for reflecting Fifoot's strong belief that the modern law needed to be understood in its historical context. It remains a feature of the book in later editions. From the ninth edition, after Fifoot's death, the historical introduction was re-written by the leading legal historian, AWB Simpson.[107]

of Obligations Arising from Civil Wrongs in the Common Law (London, Stevens & Sons, 1887). For a critique of Pollock's tort scholarship, see R Stevens, 'Professor Sir Frederick Pollock (1845–1937): Jurist as Mayfly' in J Goudkamp and D Nolan (eds), *Scholars of Tort Law* (Oxford, Hart Publishing, 2019).

[101] Horse sales were an early example of standard form contracting, see W Swain, 'Horse Sales: the Problem of Consumer Contracts from a Historical Perspective' in J Devenney and M Kenny (eds), *European Consumer Protection: Theory and Practice* (Cambridge, Cambridge University Press, 2012) 297. For other examples, see R Cranston, 'The Rise and Rise of Standard Form Contracts: International Commodity Sales 1800–1970' in R Cranston et al (eds), *Commercial Law Challenges in the Twenty First Century* (Stockholm, Iustus Forlag, 2001).

[102] Cheshire and Fifoot (n 10) 19.

[103] In the modern edition of *Anson* for example, J Beatson et al, *Anson's Law of Contract*, 31st edn (Oxford, Oxford University Press, 2020).

[104] This process began in 1966 with R Goff and G Jones, *The Law of Restitution* (London, Sweet & Maxwell, 1966).

[105] Cheshire and Fifoot (n 10) 42–44.

[106] *ibid* 106–109.

[107] MP Furmston, *Cheshire and Fifoot's Law of Contract*, 9th edn (London, Butterworths, 1976).

V. *THE LAW OF CONTRACTS*: DESCRIPTION AND CRITIQUE

It might be expected that *Cheshire and Fifoot* would contain an accurate description of the law of contract in 1945. It was up-to-date with the analysis of the case law which never feels so excessive that it weighs the book down. Rather, the focus is on the most important authorities.[108] There is some reference to academic writing as well.[109] But it also provided a critique of various aspects of contract doctrine, albeit by modern standards, a rather cautious one. Nevertheless, it was still a step forward from the previous generation of contract scholars. Of the nineteenth-century writers, Pollock, more than his contemporaries, went beyond pure description and drew parallels elsewhere including with Equity and the Indian Contract Act 1872. There was also some critical comment, for example, in relation to the rule in *Foakes v Beer*.[110] Although the fact of his criticism was usual, Pollock was no radical. He often found himself conflicted. In private correspondence, he was prepared to criticise the doctrine of consideration. In a letter to Goodhart, he would declare that 'I see no defence for the doctrine as it stands'.[111] However, none of these criticisms made their way onto the public pages of his treatise.

By the time that *Cheshire and Fifoot* appeared there was at least some appetite for reforming contract law. The Law Revision Committee had published a report in which it had recommended major reforms of consideration.[112] Lord Wright, who chaired the Committee, had earlier concluded that consideration 'is a mere incumbrance'.[113] He argued that it could be replaced by simply asking if a contract was intended. The Committee stopped short of such a radical measure. Instead, it accepted that consideration should be retained but made several proposals for modification of the existing law. These deliberations provided the backdrop for Cheshire and Fifoot to consider the current state of the doctrine of consideration. Their discussion also reflects the way that they thought about contract law and law reform.

Cheshire and Fifoot were not radicals. Tearing everything up and starting over was incompatible with the importance that they placed on the history

[108] By way of contrast see the comments by Lord Burrows on Professor Treitel in chapter 11 of this volume. Dr Jonathan Morgan has made the useful observation to me in correspondence that the suitability of *Cheshire and Fifoot* for students may have unfairly damaged its reputation as a serious work in contrast to Treitel's book, which is a less useful work for law students.

[109] The reference to academic commentary was picked up by Denning in his book review (Denning (n 90) 191). It is notable that the academic authorities referred to are a surprisingly eclectic mix for the period, including Canadian and American writers, which went beyond men like Ames and Story, see, eg, Cheshire and Fifoot (n 10) 33, 37.

[110] *Foakes v Beer* (n 78).

[111] Duxbury (n 97) 204.

[112] Law Revision Committee, *Sixth Interim Report (Statute of Frauds and the Doctrine of Consideration)* (Cmd 5449, 1937).

[113] Lord Wright, 'Ought the Doctrine of Consideration to be Abolished from the Common Law?' (1936) 49 *Harvard Law Review* 1225, 1251.

of contract law. Instead, they preferred to accept the status quo and argue for minor improvements. Their first response to those who criticised the doctrine of consideration was to defend it: 'once it is concluded that the English law seeks to enforce not promises but bargains, the element of mutuality, which is the essence of consideration, becomes intelligible and appropriate'.[114] It was also argued that in practice, consideration caused few problems because the requirement was almost always satisfied in business transactions.[115] The proposal of the Law Revision Committee to allow writing to be treated as equivalent to consideration was also criticised as amounting to 'a strange confusion of thought'. They were probably correct in the theory that the Committee ultimately 'lacked the courage of their convictions' and, as a result, were forced into an unhappy compromise between retaining the current law and abandoning consideration as had been advocated for by Lord Wright.[116]

Some of the more modest Committee proposals met a more favourable reception from Cheshire and Fifoot. Their reaction to the suggestion to abolish the rule in *Foakes v Beer* was that it 'would certainly bring the law into accord with business practice',[117] recognising that it could only be changed by statute. In their note on *Central London Property Trust v High Trees House Ltd*,[118] they concluded that 'the sting of the rule ... may justly be said to have been drawn',[119] albeit noting that estoppel could only be raised by way of a defence. The marginal note to the second edition of *Cheshire and Fifoot* summed up their analysis of the decision: 'new way of escape suggested'. Having then conceded that there was little prospect of legislative intervention, they would conclude that 'whilst the rule cannot now be abolished by judicial action, it may still be neutralised by the exercise of a beneficent ingenuity'.[120] They explained further that 'while it cannot directly negative the rule in Foakes v Beer, can at least neutralise its results'. All of this shows their great faith in the common law method which was made quite explicit in the remark that '[i]n this, as in other problems of English law, an accumulation of experience is necessary before a final solution can be reached'.[121] The same philosophy was implicit in the publication of a companion casebook to *Cheshire and Fifoot*.[122] In this volume, the cases are left to speak for themselves without any exposition or critical commentary. This approach is out of step with more modern casebooks.[123]

[114] Cheshire and Fifoot (n 10) 72.
[115] *ibid.*
[116] *ibid.*
[117] *ibid* 73.
[118] *Central London Property Trust v High Trees House Ltd* (n 75).
[119] Cheshire and Fifoot (n 74) 289.
[120] CG Cheshire and CHS Fifoot, *The Law of Contract*, 2nd edn (London, Butterworth, 1949) 69.
[121] *ibid* 70.
[122] CG Cheshire and CHS Fifoot, *Cases on the Law of Contract* (London, Butterworth, 1946). The last edition appeared in 1977 (MP Furmston, *Cheshire and Fifoot's Cases on the Law of Contract*, 7th edn (London, Butterworths, 1977)).
[123] Including one co-authored by Furmston: HG Beale et al, *Contract: Cases and Materials* (London, Butterworths, 1985).

Michael Furmston joined Cheshire and Fifoot as a co-author on the eighth edition in 1972. The work remained an Oxford enterprise – at the time Furmston was a Fellow of Cheshire's own college.[124] Furmston took over as the sole author on the ninth edition in 1976.[125] By the tenth edition, both of the original authors had died. Yet as Furmston made clear in the preface to the tenth edition in 1981, 'in content and style *Cheshire and Fifoot* remains predominantly theirs'.[126] Today, it remains a conservative work; a point that can be illustrated by the way the topic of quasi-contracts was only omitted from the 15th edition in 2006 – over a decade after the recognition of unjust enrichment as a distinct body of law in England.[127] History continues to play an important part in the work; indeed the historical introduction was rewritten for the current 17th edition.[128] The fact that since its conception *Cheshire and Fifoot* has remained largely unchanged is not necessarily a weakness, especially given the work's iconic status in England and overseas.

VI. OVERSEAS EDITIONS OF *CHESHIRE AND FIFOOT*

Cheshire and Fifoot soon began to be cited in the High Court of Australia.[129] Yet Australian judges did not necessarily accept its analysis uncritically. In *Coulls v Bagot's Executor & Trustee Co Ltd*,[130] Windeyer J said he disagreed with the idea (new in the sixth edition) that the rule that consideration move from the promisee and the rule that only those who are parties to a contract could bring a claim were the same rule.[131] A few years later, however, the same judge praised the work in a different context.[132] *Cheshire and Fifoot* was also cited by the Supreme Court of New Zealand.[133] In the early 1960s, as the former British colonies began to develop their distinctive legal traditions, homegrown editions of *Cheshire and Fifoot* began to appear.[134] This development reflects the iconic status that the book had already acquired by then, but perhaps

[124] Furmston was subsequently a Pro-Vice Chancellor, Dean and Professor at the University of Bristol and Dean and Professor at Singapore Management University.

[125] MP Furmston, *Cheshire and Fifoot's Law of Contract*, 9th edn (London, Butterworths, 1976).

[126] MP Furmston, *Cheshire and Fifoot's Law of Contract*, 10th edn (London, Butterworths, 1981) v.

[127] MP Furmston, *Cheshire, Fifoot & Furmston's Law of Contract*, 15th edn (Oxford, Oxford University Press, 2006) v. The House of Lords recognised unjust enrichment in *Lipkin Gorman v Karpnale Ltd* [1991] 2 AC 548 (HL).

[128] MP Furmston, *Cheshire, Fifoot & Furmston's Law of Contract*, 17th edn (Oxford, Oxford University Press, 2017). This section is now written by Professor David Ibbetson.

[129] *Steele v Tardiani* (1946) 72 CLR 386 (HCA) 402 (Dixon J).

[130] *Coulls v Bagot's Executor & Trustee Co Ltd* (1967) 119 CLR 460 (HCA).

[131] *ibid* 494; see also CG Cheshire and CHS Fifoot, *The Law of Contract*, 6th edn (London, Butterworths, 1964) 65.

[132] *Placer Development Ltd v Commonwealth* (1969) 121 CLR 353 (HCA) 366.

[133] *Angelo v Kean Clarke Brothers* [1950] NZLR 1 (SC) 6 (Finlay J).

[134] New Zealand and Australian editions were joined much later on by a Singapore/Malaysia version: A Phang, *Cheshire, Fifoot and Furmston's Law of Contract*, 2nd edn (Singapore, Butterworths, 1998).

more prosaically, the fact that the then publisher, Butterworths, had overseas divisions. *Cheshire and Fifoot* also had the advantage that it could be adapted fairly easily to local circumstances. These overseas versions not only preserved the English legal tradition but were also critical in challenging it. By providing an authoritative account of contract law, these editions provided a basis for reassessing the place of English law in these jurisdictions. In New Zealand in the decades that followed, the Contract and Commercial Law Reform Committee set about creating a series of statutes. By the 1980s, much of the country's contract law was contained in statute.[135] In Australia, outside of the confines of the Trade Practices Act 1974, statute played a more marginal role. Within the Federal system, an authoritative statement of precedent was nevertheless important in providing a platform for the High Court in the 1980s to push more aggressively Australian contract law in a new direction.

The first of the overseas editions of *Cheshire and Fifoot* appeared in New Zealand in 1961. Its editor was the legendary Auckland Law Faculty Dean, Professor John Frederick 'Jack' Northey.[136] Northey summed up in the preface precisely why a New Zealand edition was so important:

> New Zealand lawyers have been denied access for far too long to a comprehensive text-book on the New Zealand Law of Contract. They have been obliged to make use of books published in the United Kingdom containing few references to New Zealand and Commonwealth decisions. It was therefore necessary to supplement the English texts and to discover the New Zealand statutory provisions corresponding to those discussed in the text.[137]

The New Zealand version of *Cheshire and Fifoot* would eventually evolve from 1997 into *Burrows, Finn and Todd on the Law of Contract in New Zealand*,[138] where it remains the pre-eminent contract treatise in the jurisdiction. It is difficult to understate the value of the New Zealand edition in providing a definitive statement of the law in the years just before the Contract and Commercial Law Reform Committee began work on the contract statutes. It inevitably raised the profile of New Zealand decisions and helped the law in that jurisdiction to find its voice.

[135] For this process see: W Swain, 'Who Pays for the Grog? The Contractual and Commercial Law Reform Committee, Law Reform in New Zealand' (2019) 25 *New Zealand Business Law Quarterly* 17–29; W Swain, 'A Reputation For Boldness: Statutory Reform of Contract Law in New Zealand' in J Steele and TT Arvind (eds), *Contract Law and the Legislature* (Oxford, Hart Publishing, 2020) 107–24.

[136] Northey was Dean of the Auckland Law Faculty for nearly 20 years (B Coote, *Learned in the Law: The Auckland Law School 1883–2008* (Auckland, Legal Research Foundation, 2009) 72).

[137] JF Northey, *Cheshire and Fifoot's Law of Contract, New Zealand Edition* (Wellington, Butterworths, 1961) v.

[138] In the current edition: J Finn et al, *Burrows, Finn and Todd on the Law of Contract in New Zealand*, 6th edn (Wellington, LexisNexis, 2018).

The situation across the Tasman was much the same. An Australian edition of *Cheshire and Fifoot* was published in 1966.[139] It soon began to be referred to by the High Court.[140] Like Northey, Starke and Higgins were at pains to stress the local character of the law of contract:

> The Australian law of contract, although largely founded upon the English law, is in a number of important respects not identical with it. It is true that so far as common law principles are expressed or reflected in English case-law, Australian judges treat the English decisions with respect, and if not as binding, at least as having persuasive authority. Yet even here, one finds tides or currents of Australian judge-made contract law moving sometimes in a different direction.[141]

As it developed, the Australian editions came to be more critical of long-established English doctrines. By the 1980s, the High Court began to promote a more characteristically Australian law of contract.[142] As a result, it was necessary to change the whole ethos and organisation of the Australian edition of Cheshire and Fifoot from the sixth edition.[143] Very tellingly the historical introduction now appears at the back alongside a section on Australian history.[144] Estoppel[145] and the principle of unconscionability more broadly[146] are much more central to contract law in Australia than in England and this began to be reflected in the treatise.[147] For the past few decades, the Australian editions have criticised long-standing English contract doctrine. Some judges have picked up on this. For example in the leading modern authority on privity of contract, *Trident General Insurance Co Ltd v McNiece Bros Pty Ltd*,[148] Toohey J, who favoured an exception to the rule for contracts of insurance, drew on a passage in the Australian *Cheshire and Fifoot*,[149] which described the trust instrument as a

[139] JG Starke and PFP Higgins, *Cheshire and Fifoot's Law of Contract* (Sydney, Butterworths, 1966).

[140] *Thomas National Transport (Melbourne) Pty Ltd v May & Baker (Australia) Pty Ltd* (1966) 115 CLR 353 (HCA) 375 (Windeyer J).

[141] Starke and Higgins (n 139) 5.

[142] For an introduction to these developments, see JW Carter and A Stewart, 'Commerce and Conscience: The High Court's Developing View of Contract' (1993) 23 *University of Western Australia Law Review* 49.

[143] JG Starke et al, *Cheshire and Fifoot's Law of Contract*, 6th edn (Sydney, Butterworths, 1992).

[144] NC Seddon and RA Bigwood, *Cheshire & Fifoot's Law of Contract*, 11th edn (Sydney, Lexis Nexis, 2017). In contrast, in New Zealand the current edition of *Burrows, Finn and Todd* contains a historical introduction at the start of the book although it does now contain a brief discussion of the New Zealand history.

[145] Following *Waltons Stores (Interstate) Ltd v Maher* (1988) 164 CLR 387 (HCA). For the development of this doctrine, see A Stewart et al, *Contract Law: Principles and Context* (Cambridge, Cambridge University Press, 2019) 118–32.

[146] Unconscionability is reflected in various Australian contract doctrines, most obviously in the rules relating to relief from unconscionable bargains, see Stewart et al (n 145) 380.

[147] Starke et al (n 143) 152–68, 422–35.

[148] *Trident General Insurance Co Ltd v McNiece Bros Pty Ltd* (1988) 165 CLR 107 (HCA) 169.

[149] JG Starke et al, *Cheshire and Fifoot's Law of Contract*, 5th edn (Sydney, Butterworths, 1988) para 1535.

'disappointing and unreliable' solution to privity. On other occasions, an idea promoted in *Cheshire and Fifoot* gained less support. In *Butcher v Lachlan Elder Realty*,[150] Kirby J in his dissent referred to a passage in *Cheshire and Fifoot* which suggested that an exemption clause was of no effect in the face of a claim under section 52 of the Trade Practice Act 1974.[151] The same judge, once again dissenting in *Koompahtoo Local Aboriginal Land Council v Sanpine*,[152] referred to the Australian *Cheshire and Fifoot* which stated there was no third 'intermediate' category of terms alongside conditions and warranties.[153] The majority on both occasions disagreed.

VII. *CHESHIRE AND FIFOOT* IN THE ENGLISH COURTS

In 1963, nearly two decades after it was first published, Megaw J described *Cheshire and Fifoot* as 'a well-known textbook'.[154] He would use the same description again a decade later.[155] At the time there was still a convention against citing a living author. The convention was never an absolute one[156] and after the Second World War, it began to break down. Citation of living authors was still relatively uncommon in the 1950s. But by the 1970s, the practice was more frequent.[157] By the late 1940s, *Cheshire and Fifoot* had begun to be cited by counsel in the course of argument in the House of Lords.[158] Into the 1950s and 1960s, the work was sometimes referred to in argument by itself[159] or alongside other authoritative works like *Anson* or *Chitty*.[160] References to *Cheshire and Fifoot* by counsel in reported cases increased in the 1960s.[161]

[150] *Butcher v Lachlan Elder Realty* Pty Ltd [2007] HCA 61; (2007) 233 CLR 115.

[151] *ibid* 657, which refers to NC Seddon and MP Ellinghaus, *Cheshire and Fifoot's Law of Contract*, 8th edn (Sydney, Butterworths, 1997) 591–92.

[152] *Koompahtoo Local Aboriginal Land Council v Sanpine* Pty Ltd (2007) 233 CLR 115 (HCA).

[153] *ibid* 158, which refers to NC Seddon and MP Ellinghaus, *Cheshire and Fifoot's Law of Contract*, 9th edn (Sydney, Butterworths, 2008) 1032.

[154] *Edwards v Skyways Ltd* [1964] 1 WLR 349 (QBD) 366.

[155] *Lewis v Averay* [1972] 1 QB 198 (CA) 209.

[156] For detailed discussion of the convention and its application see, N Duxbury, *Jurists and Judges: An Essay on Influence* (Oxford, Hart Publishing, 2001) 62–84; S Waddams, 'The Authority of Treatises in English Law' in M Godfrey (ed), *Law and Authority in British Legal History 1200–1900* (Cambridge, Cambridge University Press, 2016).

[157] Duxbury *ibid* 81; A Paterson, *The Law Lords* (London, Macmillan, 1982) 16.

[158] *Comptoir D'Achat et de Vente du Boerenbond Belge SA v Luis de Ridder* Lda *(The Julia)* [1948] AC 293 (HL) 305; *Hill v William Hill (Park Lane Ltd)* [1949] AC 530 (HL).

[159] *Mason v Clarke* [1955] AC 778 (HL) 783; *Shamia v Joory* [1958] 1 QB 448 (QBD) 455; *Port Line Ltd v Ben Line Steamers Ltd* [1958] 2 QB 146 (QBD) 155.

[160] *Bell House Ltd v City Wall Properties Ltd* [1966] 1 QB 207 (QBD) 212 (*Anson*); *Burnett v Westminster Bank* [1966] 1 QB 742 (QBD) 754 (*Anson*); *Frisby v BBC* [1967] Ch 932 (Ch D) 935 (*Chitty*); *Rondel v Worsley* [1969] 1 AC 191 (HL) 212 (*Chitty*).

[161] In addition to those cases otherwise cited: *Muskham Finance Ltd v Howard* [1963] 1 QB 904 (CA) 909; *Rookes v Barnard* [1964] AC 1129 (HL) 1140; *Car and Universal Finance Co Ltd v Caldwell* [1965] 1 QB 525 (CA) 546; *Suisse Atlantique Société d'Armement Martitime SA v NV Rotterdamsche Kolen Centrale (The Silvretta)* [1967] 1 AC 361 (HL) 375; *Teheran-Europe Co Ltd v ST Belton (Tractors) Ltd* [1968] 2 QB 545 (CA) 548.

It was rarer for *Cheshire and Fifoot* to be cited by judges at least to begin with – but this may just reflect the wider practice of the time. One judge who did cite the work from the early 1950s was Lord Denning.[162] Given his friendship with Cheshire, this is perhaps unsurprising. He also cited Fifoot's historical work.[163] By the 1960s, *Cheshire and Fifoot* became to be cited more widely in judgments, and on occasion, quite lengthy passages were quoted.[164] Although containing some critical comment, *Cheshire and Fifoot* did not challenge the status quo. In this respect, it was not unlike the approach of the vast majority of appellant judges of the era. In turn, *Cheshire and Fifoot* was usually aligned with a judicial opinion.[165] The nature of the work meant that it was particularly well suited to be used as an authoritative description of areas of contract doctrine as a reliable statement of the law of contract at a given time.[166] An example of this can be found in a speech of Lord Wilberforce from the late 1960s in *Esso Petroleum Co Ltd v Harper's Garage (Stourport) Ltd*[167] when he used *Cheshire and Fifoot* to make the point that contracts in restraint of trade could be listed and classified. In this respect, *Cheshire and Fifoot* was very much in the same category as much longer established works like *Chitty* and *Anson* which it was sometimes cited alongside.[168] From the late 1960s, a number of appellant judges in addition to Lord Denning began to use *Cheshire and Fifoot* to state orthodoxy in their judgments. The treatise was also particularly popular with Sachs LJ, born the year after Fifoot, and an Oxford graduate,[169] who in the course of one judgment, explained that the law was 'compactly and accurately stated' in *Cheshire and Fifoot*.[170] On occasion, judges would raise the work in the course of argument for much the same purpose.[171]

Into the 1970s, *Cheshire and Fifoot* continued to fulfil the role as a reliable statement of the current law of contract.[172] In *Wickman Machine Tool Sales*

[162] *Bennett v Bennett* [1952] 1 KB 249 (CA) 260.

[163] *Southport Corp v Esso Petroleum Ltd* [1954] 2 QB 182 (CA) 196.

[164] *Beswick v Beswick* [1966] Ch 538 (CA) 550; *Rodriguez v RJ Parker* [1967] 1 QB 116 (QBD) 133; *Tote Investors v Smoker* [1968] 1 QB 509 (CA) 517; *Gallie v Lee* [1969] 2 Ch 17 (CA) 31.

[165] A good example can be found in the judgment of Sellers LJ in *Ingram v Little* [1961] 1 QB 3 (CA) 54. For other examples not otherwise mentioned, see *Jones v Padavatton* [1969] 1 WLR 328 (CA) 331.

[166] For a contrary argument that the work is wrong, see *Eastern Distributors Ltd v Goldring* [1957] 2 QB 600 (CA) 603.

[167] *Esso Petroleum Co Ltd v Harper's Garage (Stourport) Ltd* [1968] AC 269 (HL) 337.

[168] *Bell House Ltd v City Wall Properties Ltd* [1966] 1 QB 207 (QBD) 220 (*Anson*).

[169] Lord Roskill, 'Sachs, Sir Eric Leopold Otho (1898–1979)' in *Oxford Dictionary of National Biography*.

[170] *Bolton v Mahadeva* [1972] 1 WLR 1009 (CA) 1015. For other examples from this judge, see *Connell v Motor Insurers' Bureau* [1969] 2 QB 494 (CA) 505; *Decro-Wall International SA v Practitioners in Marketing Ltd* [1971] 1 WLR 361 (CA) 374.

[171] *Empresa Cubanna de Fletes v Lagonisi Shipping Co Ltd* [1971] 1 QB 488 (CA) 498 (Phillimore LJ).

[172] Other examples include: *Holwell Securities Ltd v Hughes* [1974] 1 WLR 155 (CA) 161 (Lawton LJ); *Lloyds Bank v Bundy* [1975] QB 326 (CA) 333 (Lord Denning MR); *Esso Petroleum Co Ltd v Mardon* [1976] QB 801 (CA) 826 (Ormrod LJ); *Barton v Armstrong* [1976] AC 104 (HL) 119 (Lord Cross); *Owen v Tate* [1976] QB 402 (CA) 413 (Stephenson LJ).

Ltd v L Schuler AG,[173] the leading decision on contractual interpretation, Lord Simon referred to *Cheshire and Fifoot* alongside *Anson* and *Halsbury's Laws of England*.[174] The same judge referred to *Cheshire and Fifoot* again in *Banning v Wright*,[175] and even engaged with the substance of the work when he remarked that 'This tends to suggest that Cheshire and Fifoot are right, that there is no essential juridical difference between waiver and variation'.[176]

Cheshire and Fifoot was in the hands of a new author from 1976 but it continued to be cited by judges in much the same way as before – as a definitive statement of the current law of contract.[177] This also made it a useful resource for counsel. In *Levison v Patent Steam Carpet Cleaning Co Ltd*,[178] when Michael Beloff referred to a majority of academic option, he cited *Cheshire and Fifoot* alongside several other works including *Chitty* and *Treitel*.[179] Given Lord Denning's admiration for *Cheshire and Fifoot*, there was some tactical sense in referring to them on this occasion.[180] Beloff lost the appeal for other reasons, but the case provides as good an illustration of the way that *Cheshire and Fifoot* had quickly become a repository of largely orthodox opinion which appellate judges felt comfortable in relying on for analysis.[181] When Lord Hailsham concluded that the question of whether leases could be frustrated was not settled by authority but had to be decided on principle, one important source for reaching that conclusion was *Cheshire and Fifoot*.[182] The treatise continues to be cited in England into modern times.[183]

VIII. THE ROLE OF *CHESHIRE AND FIFOOT*

It is one thing for a legal writer to be cited or even quoted and quite another to be influential on the outcome of the decision. Citation should not necessarily be equated with influence.[184] Lord Denning was unusual amongst appellate

[173] *L Schuler AG v Wickman Machine Tool Sales Ltd v L Schuler AG* [1974] AC 235 (HL).
[174] *ibid* 240.
[175] *Banning v Wright* [1972] 1 WLR 972 (HL).
[176] *ibid* 991.
[177] *Shell (UK) Ltd v Lostock Garage Ltd* [1976] 1 WLR 1187 (CA) 1202 (Lord Denning MR).
[178] *Levison v Patent Steam Carpet Cleaning Co Ltd* [1978] QB 69 (CA).
[179] *ibid* 75.
[180] Beloff was not alone in seeing the attraction of reference to *Cheshire and Fifoot* when appearing before Lord Denning (*H Parsons (Livestock) Ltd v Uttley Ingham & Co Ltd* [1978] QB 791 (CA) 794).
[181] *Gibson v Manchester City Council* [1979] 1 WLR 294 (HL) 302 (Lord Edmund-Davis); *Alec Lobb (Garages) Ltd v Total Oil (Great Britain) Ltd* [1985] 1 WLR 173 (CA) 191 (Waller LJ); *Lombard North Central plc v Butterworth* [1987] QB 527 (CA) 536 (Mustill LJ).
[182] *National Carriers Ltd v Panalpina (Northern) Ltd* [1981] AC 675 (HL) 690.
[183] Examples include: *XX v Whittington Hospital NHS Trust* [2018] EWCA Civ 2832, [2021] AC 275 [62]; *Simantob v Shavleyan* [2019] EWCA Civ 1105 [48] (Simon LJ); *Sunrise Brokers LLP v Rodgers* [2014] EWCA Civ 1373, [2015] ICR 272, 292 (Longmore LJ).
[184] Duxbury (n 156) 82–84.

judges of his generation in being prepared to admit that he was influenced by academic commentary.[185] While some academic writers have undoubtedly influenced the development of the law, it is fair to say that the impact of legal scholarship is somewhat sporadic.[186] A few elements of the process of influence can be illustrated with reference to Lord Denning. In *Associated Japanese Bank (International) Ltd v Crédit du Nord SA*,[187] Steyn J suggested that Lord Denning's analysis of *Bell v Lever Brothers Ltd*[188] in *Magee v Pennine Insurance Co Ltd*[189] was influenced by *Cheshire and Fifoot*. Cheshire and Fifoot had consistently argued for a narrow interpretation of *Bell v Lever Brothers Ltd*[190] in which common law mistake could only vitiate a contract where it concerned the existence of the subject-matter of the contract. There is a pleasing symmetry in the way in which Cheshire and Fifoot used a decision of Lord Denning in *Solle v Butcher*[191] to support their analysis.[192] They seized on the fact that Lord Denning took a very narrow view of *Bell v Lever Brothers Ltd* when he explained that a contract should only be set aside for mistake when there was a 'failure of some condition on which the existence of the contract depends, or for fraud, or on some equitable ground'.[193] On this view, a common mistake, even a fundamental one, was not sufficient at law to vitiate a contract. It would be necessary to resort to Equity in such cases. The narrow view of *Bell v Lever Brothers Ltd* and the existence of a separate doctrine of equitable mistake however now seem very doubtful following *Great Peace Shipping Ltd v Tsarvliris Salvage (International) Ltd*.[194]

The debate around the doctrine of mistake, if nothing else, demonstrates that the impact of judges, even one as important as Lord Denning, as well as legal writers, is often transitory. *Cheshire and Fifoot* has achieved the standing that it has partly because it is 75 years old. But there is more to it than that. Over three-quarters of a century, it has only had one author in addition to the original two.[195] This means that while the current edition is not identical to the first edition (it is much longer for a start), it retains much of the character of

[185] Paterson (n 157) 18.

[186] For a more optimistic view, see Lord Rodger, 'Judges and Academics in the United Kingdom' (2010) 29 *University of Queensland Law Journal* 29; J Beatson, 'Legal Academics: Forgotten Players or Interlopers?' in A Burrows et al (eds), *Judge and Jurist: Essays in Memory of Lord Rodger of Earlsferry* (Oxford, Oxford University Press, 2013).

[187] *Associated Japanese Bank (International) Ltd v Crédit du Nord SA* [1989] 1 WLR 255 (QBD) 267.

[188] *Bell v Lever Brothers Ltd* [1932] AC 161 (HL).

[189] *Magee v Pennine Insurance Co Ltd* [1969] 2 QB 507 (CA).

[190] *Bell* (n 188).

[191] *Solle v Butcher* [1950] 1 KB 671 (CA).

[192] GH Cheshire and CHS Fifoot, *The Law of Contract*, 3rd edn (London, Butterworths, 1952) 180.

[193] *Solle* (n 191) 691.

[194] *Great Peace Shipping Ltd v Tsarvliris Salvage (International) Ltd* [2002] EWCA Civ 1407, [2003] QB 679.

[195] Following the death of Professor Furmston in 2020, any new edition will have a new author.

the first edition.[196] A cursory glance at the table of contents shows that. The only major differences are the exclusion of the chapter on quasi-contract and the inclusion of a chapter 'Some Factors Affecting Modern Contract' which considers some contextual factors (such as EU law, consumer law, globalisation and human rights) which would not have been relevant in 1945. This gives the work a sense of stability and continuity which, when combined with clear exposition, explains its popularity. In an area like contract law in which legal doctrine develops relatively slowly, these qualities may explain why the work has endured so long. At the same time, the treatise has proved to be adaptable. The Australian edition especially is quite different from its English counterpart. Nonetheless, these various editions in different jurisdictions over time still have a common thread which can be traced back to the contract treatises of the late nineteenth century.

[196] The main text excluding the front matter and the index is 435 pages. The current 17th edition is 817 pages long.

10

Professor Friedrich Kessler (1901–1998)

HUGH COLLINS*

THE SELECTION OF Friedrich Kessler as the subject of this chapter springs from a recognition of his distinctive approach to contract law and his influence on my own work. He was trained in detailed doctrinal comparisons between civil and common law systems, but he added to those skills two further dimensions. He was one of the pioneers of viewing the law of contract from the perspective of sociological and empirical studies of the functioning of markets in a capitalist society. He was also a leading exponent of the application to the law of contract of approaches to the common law and legal reasoning associated with American Legal Realism. Unlike formalist textbook writers, Kessler favoured the view that judicial decisions are always specific to the particular facts of a case, not determined by formal legal rules, but rather produced by weighing competing principles and consequences for social policy, and that the best judgments represent a quest for justice and fairness.

I. ÉMIGRÉ BAGGAGE

When Friedrich (Fritz) Kessler arrived at Yale Law School on 12 October 1934 to take up his Rockefeller Foundation Fellowship, we can be sure that he brought with him some heavy baggage. I am not only referring to the fact that he was accompanied by his second wife, Eva, and their two daughters, Maria and Inge. This transatlantic voyage was not an ordinary trip. As a Jew living in Germany, Eva faced persecution. The Nazi party had seized power the year before and had used the law and brute force to attack all their opponents. Fortunately, the Kessler family could escape to America to start a new life, so they must have taken as much as they could carry with them.

* I am grateful for helpful comments from participants at the seminar where a draft of this chapter was presented and Nick Sage.

Adding to the weight of that luggage, there would have been a trunk of Kessler's law books, for surely no aspiring law professor could be parted from such vital possessions. Kessler had just reached the stage in his career when he could apply for a tenured professorship. He was born in Hechingen, Germany, 25 August 1901, the son of Wilhelm and Helene (Krueger) Kessler. His stern father was a judge and army officer. Fritz was educated at universities in Tübingen, Munich, where he was a student of Max Weber in a course called *Rechtssoziologie* (legal sociology), and in Marburg (a family tradition), before his years in Berlin between 1926 and 1934. He became a research member of the newly created Kaiser Wilhelm Institute for Foreign and International Law (later to become the Max Planck Institute in Hamburg), working under its magisterial Director Ernst Rabel, a scholar credited as the founding father of systematic study of comparative law in Germany.[1] Both Kessler's doctoral dissertation[2] and his habilitation[3] concerned US law and comparisons with German law. The habilitation, a book-length learned text necessary to become a professor of law in Germany, was focussed on a comparison of negligence liability in tort. He became a *Privatdozent* (lecturer) at the *Handelshochschule* (the school of commerce in Berlin) from 1931–34.

On arrival at Yale, Kessler pursued those doctrinal comparative studies, publishing in quick succession four major articles concerning topics in comparative commercial and financial law.[4] At Yale he was an Instructor and Assistant Professor. Between 1938 and 1947, he was recruited by the University of Chicago Law School as an Associate Professor and then full Professor. He became a US citizen in 1942. In 1947, as a result of the persuasion of Dean Sturges over a bottle of Jack Daniels,[5] he returned to Yale as Justus Hotchkiss and then Sterling Professor of law, until his retirement in 1970. Having always been devoted to teaching, from 1970–78, Kessler taught actively on a post-retirement or 'visiting' appointment basis at Boalt Hall, Berkeley, California. He died in Berkeley aged 96 in 1998.

The Yale law school that Kessler joined in 1934 was the hotbed of American Legal Realism.[6] Kessler was clearly attracted to both the 'pragmatic

[1] S Grundmann and K Riesenhuber (eds), *Private Law Development in Context: German Private Law and Scholarship in the 20th Century* (Cambridge, Intersentia, 2018) 107.

[2] F Kessler, *Uniform State Laws in den Vereinigten Staaten-Das Recht der Eheschliessung* (1927) 1 *Zeitschrift fur Auslandisches und Internationales Privatrecht* 185, 886.

[3] F Kessler, *Die Fahrlassigkeit Im Nordamerikanischen Deliktsrecht Unter Vergleichender Berucksichtigung des Englishchen und des Deutschen Rechts* (Berlin, de Gruyter, 1932).

[4] F Kessler, 'The American Securities Act and Its Foreign Counterparts: A Comparative Study' (1935) 44 *Yale Law Journal* 1133; F Kessler, EH Levi and EE Ferguson, 'Some Aspects of Payment by Negotiable Instrument: A Comparative Study' (1936) 45 *Yale Law Journal* 1373; F Kessler, 'Commercial Arbitration in Civil Law Countries' (1937) 1 *Arbitration Journal* 277; F Kessler, 'Forged Indorsements' (1938) 47 *Yale Law Journal* 863. See 'select bibliography' of works by F Kessler at (1995) 104 *Yale Law Journal* 2153.

[5] JK McNulty, 'A Student's Tribute to Fritz Kessler' (1995) 104 *Yale Law Journal* 2133.

[6] L Kalman, *Legal Realism at Yale, 1927–1960* (Chapel Hill, University of North Carolina Press, 1986).

instrumentalist' approach to legal reasoning that was being advanced in teaching and new casebooks,[7] and the innovative empirical studies of the workings of the legal system under the leadership of Dean Clark.[8] During his years at Yale, Kessler no doubt learned much from many colleagues and co-authors in the field of contract law such as Grant Gilmore, but Fritz is reported[9] as acknowledging that the greatest influence was his senior colleague Arthur Corbin, author of the magisterial eight volume account of the law of contract.[10] Indeed, as far as I can discern, Kessler never doubted the general approach and framework of the law of contract presented by Corbin, including its more controversial aspects such as regarding the doctrine of promissory estoppel as functionally equivalent to and of equal importance as the doctrine of consideration.[11]

All those family possessions and law books constituted a substantial burden on the migration from Germany to the USA, yet the heaviest baggage that Kessler carried with him was surely in his head. Like many of his contemporary German scholars, he was horrified by the political and legal developments in Germany under Nazi rule. Shortly before the family had left Germany, the Government had passed legislation in the spring of 1934 that effectively dismissed all non-Aryans and other political enemies from universities.[12] Kessler wondered whether the use of law as an instrument of savage oppression by fascist dictators in Europe was in some way supported or at least not prevented by views about the nature of law. He explored this anxiety in two extraordinarily erudite articles in which he drew upon ancient and modern philosophy, contemporary political commentary, and a thorough appreciation of the field of jurisprudence.[13]

In response to the shocking fact that Hitler had seized power lawfully, Kessler expressed the worry that the philosophy of legal positivism had somehow opened the way to the translation of might into right through its doctrine that the existence of authoritative law was a matter of fact or power, not dependent on the moral qualities of the law itself. He drew attention to the neglected rival

[7] RS Summers, *Instrumentalism and American Legal Theory* (Ithaca, Cornell University Press, 1982).

[8] JH Schlegel, 'American Legal Realism and Empirical Social Science: From the Yale Experience' (1979) 28 *Buffalo Law Review* 459.

[9] McNulty (n 5) 2135.

[10] AL Corbin, *A Comprehensive Treatise on The Rules of Contract Law,* vols 1–8 (St Paul, West Publishing, 1950); see the review by F Kessler, 'Corbin on Contracts Volume One' (1952) 61 *Yale Law Journal* 1093.

[11] Several works indicate that he was a loyal 'Corbinista': F Kessler, 'Arthur Linton Corbin 1874–1967' (1967) *Yale Law Reporter* 30–31 (memorial to Professor Corbin, approved by the Yale Law School faculty on 6 June 1967); F Kessler, 'Arthur Linton Corbin–A Tribute' (1954) 64 *Yale Law Journal* 164.

[12] Gesetz zur Wiederherstellung des Berufsbeamtentums, 1933 Reichsgesetzblatt [RGBl]; see also C Joerges, 'Demos vs. Ethnos in Private Law: Friedrich Kessler and His German Heritage' (1995) 104 *Yale Law Journal* 2137, 2140.

[13] F Kessler, 'Theoretic Bases of Law' (1941) 9 *University of Chicago Law Review* 98; F Kessler, 'Natural Law, Justice and Democracy—Some Reflections on Three Types of Thinking about Law and Justice' (1944) 19 *Tulane Law Review* 32.

tradition of natural law, mentioning with approval lectures by Fuller about the inner morality of law.[14] Drawing on the writings of St Thomas Aquinas, Kessler concluded that 'Positive law, to be just, must meet three requirements: it must serve the common good, its burdens must be distributed according to proportionate equality, and finally, it must be issued by a legislator within the bounds of his authority'.[15] As well as that tentative exploration of the ideas of natural law, Kessler also wanted to bring to his understanding of the nature of law and the crisis in Germany his knowledge of sociology, history and social theory. This task relied on one last heavy piece of baggage in the trunks of the Kessler family – the heaviest book of all.

We can infer that Kessler brought with him his collection of the works of Max Weber in German. My evidence is that he frequently placed references to his German copy of what was subsequently translated as *Economy and Society* in footnotes in his articles and quite often as the first footnote.[16] In many ways, Weber provided Kessler with the intellectual framework for all that came afterwards. One of the key themes in Weber's sociology of law was that capitalism as an economic system required predictable and reliable market exchanges, which could only be achieved by a formally rational system of law, as found in the newly minted German civil code. Kessler was only too aware from his doctoral studies and his early years at Yale that the common law was anything but the formally rational system that Weber had envisaged. Kessler observed that, in the common law, 'The fact that rule was competing with counter-rule and exception and that a legal science was very slow in developing' and the fact that the law was irrational and full of gaps was used by business to its advantage.[17] Kessler asked himself, how could capitalism thrive in America with the chaos of the common law? His answer was that until capitalism in America reached its maturity, it could forgo a formally rational legal system. He explained developments in American legal thought such as legal formalism in the late nineteenth century and the *Restatements* of the American Law Institute as premature and misguided attempts to bring rationality to the system.

> What the analytical jurists failed to realize was their 'legalistic' approach, bent as it was upon building up a rational and harmonious legal system (formal rationality),

[14] LL Fuller, *The Law in Quest of Itself* (Chicago, Northwestern University Press, 1940), a series of lectures given at Chicago when Kessler worked there, and cited in Kessler (1941) (n 13) 104.

[15] Kessler (1944) (n 13) 57.

[16] See, eg, Kessler (1941) (n 13) 99, fn 1, which reads: 'Max Weber, Rechtssoziologie, in 2 Wirtschaft und Gesellschaft 496 et seq., 3 Grundriss der Sozialoekonomik (2d ed. 1925)'; *cf* F Kessler, 'Contracts of Adhesion – Some Thoughts about Freedom of Contract' (1943) 43 *Columbia Law Review* 629, 629, fn 1. Weber's work was not fully translated into English until it appeared as M Weber (translated by G Roth and C Wittich), *Economy and Society* (Berkeley, University of Berkeley Press, 1978), but his work on law was available earlier to an English-speaking audience thanks to M Rheinstein, *Max Weber on Law in Economy and Society* (Cambridge MA, Harvard University Press, 1954).

[17] Kessler (1944) (n 13) 49.

> inevitably forced them into higher and higher, and therefore lifeless, abstractions, the more the increasing instability of the underlying social system led to conflicting decisions and theories.[18]

In contrast, the more recent work of American Legal Realists had demonstrated that:

> preoccupation with efforts at making the law consistent and predictable (at a high level of abstraction) may afford an easy escape from a more important task: namely, of constantly testing out the desirability, efficiency and fairness of inherited legal rules and institutions in terms of the present needs of society.[19] … For the founders of liberal positivism, the enemy of free enterprise and liberalism was an all-powerful state. A liberal economic system, as they assumed, would maintain and even improve the moral, political and legal institutions of society. The founders of liberalism did not have the vision to foresee that the capitalistic system has within itself forces which, if unchecked, will inevitably change a free enterprise system into monopoly capitalism and a liberal democracy into a pluralistic society which knows nothing but divided loyalties.[20]

Kessler concluded that in such a divided society, a democratic system of government that requires a pragmatic consensus and inclusion of minority viewpoints can no longer function and that the rule of positive law can no longer guarantee liberty. In these passages, Kessler endorsed American Legal Realism as providing not only an accurate description of how the common law functioned, but also as a necessary part of a framework of ideas linked to natural law that could support democracy and social justice. Of course, Kessler was not alone among German scholars in questioning whether legal positivism and other ruling ideas about law had contributed to the catastrophe of National Socialism.[21] Where he seems to have diverged from his German contemporaries, particularly Franz Böhm and the ordo-liberal search for a rigid economic constitution,[22] was to emphasise the dangers of legal formalism and abstract concepts as distractions from the need to ensure social justice and an empowered democracy.

After the Second World War and the restoration of democracy and the rule of law in Europe, Kessler ceased to publish such anxious philosophical reflections. Instead, he became famous rather for his work in contract law, commercial law and the law of tort. He is probably best known among US lawyers for his book *Contracts: Cases and Materials*, first published with Professor Malcolm

[18] *ibid* 50.

[19] *ibid* 52

[20] *ibid* 52–53. Kessler's idiosyncratic concept of 'liberal positivism' seems to be a synthesis of political ideas that starts with Hobbes and Locke, but is developed by Bentham, Adam Smith and other liberal political philosophers.

[21] The most influential was G Radbruch, 'Gesetzliches Unrecht und Ubergesetzliches Recht' (1946) 1 *Suddeutsche Juristen-Zeitung* 105.

[22] E Mestmäcker, 'Franz Böhm' in Grundmann and Riesenhuber (n 1) 125. It is perhaps for this reason that Kessler's writings appear to have had no influence in the German debates: Joerges (n 12) 2141–42.

Sharp of Chicago (1953), later with Professor Grant Gilmore of Yale (1970) and a third edition with Gilmore and Professor Anthony Kronman of Yale (1986).[23] This assessment of his contract law scholarship only has space to mention a few aspects of that popular student book comprising text and cases.

One feature of that casebook that puzzles and confuses students is the pairing of cases together that apparently reach opposite results on very similar facts. This pairing reveals the underlying American Legal Realist approach to legal studies: the details of the facts are always important, abstract principles do not decide concrete cases, and judges rely more on instrumental considerations than the formal rules. For instance, the casebook pairs the well-known case of *Sherwood v Walker*,[24] with *Wood v Boynton*.[25] *Sherwood v Walker* concerned a sale of a cow where, unbeknown to both parties, the supposed barren cow was with calf and therefore worth at least $800, not the sale price of $80. Ordering a retrial, the Court insisted that if the mistake was mutual, it was a fundamental mistake that vitiated the contract. In *Wood v Boynton*, in contrast, a small stone was sold to a jeweller for $1; it turned out to be an uncut diamond worth $1,000. Although the Court held that neither party knew the stone was a diamond, the contract was upheld. The paired and apparently contradictory cases are followed by seven pages of commentary and comparison with other cases, including the intriguing thought: 'The plaintiff in *Sherwood* was a banker; would it have made a difference if he had been a butcher?'[26] These comparisons serve the purpose of, first, provoking reflections on whether the character of the parties influences the result, and second, whether ultimately the court relies on a judgment about fairness to decide the issue.

Indeed, a recurrent feature of the casebook is the emphasis that it places on fairness in contract law. Kessler wanted to explain to students that the task of a common law judge in the law of contract was not only to protect the predictability of contracts as a facilitative engine of market exchange, but also to use the law as a vital mechanism to protect against misuse of freedom of contract, a mission that he summed up as 'the idea of justice in exchange'.[27] Whilst acknowledging the influence of this textbook among law students and myself,[28] in this necessarily brief and selective assessment of his published work on the law of contract, I will concentrate rather on what I personally regard as his three most innovative law review articles, which were, aside from the second edition

[23] F Kessler, G Gilmore and AT Kronman, *Contracts: Cases and Materials*, 3rd edn (Boston, Little, Brown & Co, 1986). The preface explains that Gilmore died shortly after beginning work on the third edition, so that it was written by Kessler and Kronman: xxix.

[24] *Sherwood v Walker* 33 NW 919 (Mich 1887).

[25] *Wood v Boynton* 25 NW 42 (Wis 1885).

[26] Kessler, Gilmore and Kronman (n 23) 892.

[27] *ibid*, the title of ch 4, 533. *cf* F Kessler and G Gilmore, *Contracts: Cases and Materials,* 2nd edn (Boston, Little, Brown & Co, 1970) 440, where the heading of ch 5 is 'Fairness of the Bargain and Equality. Exchange Justice'.

[28] I note, for instance, the use of the phrase 'the justice of exchange', in H Collins, *The Law of Contract* (London, Weidenfeld and Nicholson, 1986) 8.

of his casebook with Gilmore, his work that had the greatest influence on my own writings.

II. CONTRACTS OF ADHESION

In 1943, Kessler set out his views on contract law in general in what is his most highly cited signature piece: 'Contracts of Adhesion – Some Thoughts about Freedom of Contract'.[29] In barely 14 pages he launched an attack on what he believed was the dysfunctional common law of contract. The essay commenced with an understanding, inspired by Weber, of how the law of contract provides an essential mechanism for the intense division of labour in modern capitalist societies. He acknowledged that the move away from a limited range of fixed contract types to a general law of contract that permitted freedom to choose the terms of contracts was essential and inevitable for the further intensification of the division of labour. But he pointed out that what this necessary freedom of contract entailed was the conferral on parties to contracts of the power to legislate the rules for contractual undertakings. For Kessler, therefore, the principle of freedom of contract was not so much a moral principle that respected freedom of the individual as a legal institution necessitated by a society that relied heavily on markets for its system of ordering.

Kessler then introduced his claim that the development of mass production and mass distribution in the capitalist economy in the twentieth century made a 'new type of contract inevitable – the standardised mass contract'.[30] He explained the attraction of these mass contracts largely in terms of risk. Most clearly these contracts can contain exclusion clauses that take care of risks that are hard to calculate and quantify. Furthermore, the standard form contract reduces legal risks such as the chance that judges or juries might be swayed by their emotions. Kessler accepted that the reduction of costs achieved by standard form contracts benefitted everyone in terms of reduced prices. Kessler added, however, that large businesses with strong bargaining power can impose their terms on weaker parties who are frequently not in a position to shop around, either because the supplier has a degree of monopoly power or because all suppliers use the same terms. Kessler observed that very often the weaker party submits to terms that will only be communicated in full later on. Finally, Kessler noted how standardised contracts were used as a device to build up 'industrial empires'[31] by regulating the distribution of goods all the way down to the consumer.

[29] Kessler (1943) (n 16).
[30] *ibid* 631.
[31] *ibid* 632.

Turning to the law, Kessler described how the courts had responded to the development of standard form contracts. He noted that the judges refused to abandon the elementary rules of contract law that granted freedom of contract to those seeking to impose their standard form contracts on others. What judges did instead with a view to helping the victims of unfair terms in standard form contracts, as he illustrated, was to use a mixture of techniques of interpretation of contract terms to assist the weaker party and to develop alternative remedies in tort law. He noted that these devices such as interpretation 'contra proferentem' generated considerable uncertainty in the law, because contract terms were held not to mean what they reasonably might be understood to mean. This uncertainty had forced legislatures to intervene in many instances.

Kessler concluded that 'the pious myth that the law of contract is of one cloth has stood in the path of progress'.[32] He asked: 'can the unity of the law of contracts be maintained in the face of the increasing use of contracts of adhesion?'[33] He acknowledged that the task of building up a 'multiple system of contract law is eminently difficult', especially since it was hard to define the category of contracts of adhesion.

> In dealing with standardized contracts courts have to determine what the weaker contracting party could legitimately expect by way of services according to the enterpriser's 'calling', and to what extent the stronger party disappointed reasonable expectations based on a typical life situation.[34]

Kessler argued that judges could achieve this task through techniques such as implied terms. What stopped judges from performing this task, according to Kessler, was their emotional attitude towards freedom of contract. Judges convince themselves that fidelity to freedom of contract will achieve certainty and is morally right, whereas Kessler took the view that in fact the judges' approach often generated unpredictability and injustice. He insisted, however, that the common law of contract has the flexibility to achieve justice:

> the elasticity of the common law, with rule and counter-rule constantly competing, makes it possible for courts to follow the dictates of 'social desirability'. Whatever one may think about the possibility of separating the 'law that is' from the 'law that ought to be', this much is certain: In the development of the common law the ideal tends constantly to become the practice.[35]

In his closing peroration, Kessler returned to his sociology of capitalism. He argued that 'in the happy days of capitalism'[36] freedom of contract for everyone provided a route to greater wealth and social justice based on fair exchanges, but now the powerful 'industrial and commercial overlords' could 'impose a new

[32] *ibid* 634.
[33] *ibid* 636.
[34] *ibid* 637. Kessler draws on the concept of life situation from KN Llewellyn, 'Review' (1939) 52 *Harvard Law Review* 700, 704.
[35] Kessler (1943) (n 16) 638.
[36] *ibid* 641.

feudal order of their own making upon a vast host of vassals'[37] simply by imposing their standard form contracts on every transaction. As a result, contract law based upon the misleading ideal of freedom of contract was being used to destroy competitive capitalism, and the law or private legislation contained in the terms of the contract escaped any state control or accountability. In short, big business was imposing an authoritarian system of control, without democratic accountability, through the device of standard form contracts. The legal ideology that believed unquestioningly in the value of freedom of contract and the necessary unity of general contract law was blind to the use that contracts were now being put in some contexts to undermine competitive markets and to support undemocratic oligarchies.

Although Kessler's article on contracts of adhesion is much cited, it is also frequently criticised and even dismissed as irrelevant. In order to identify Kessler's achievement in this chapter properly, it is worth briefly assessing some of these criticisms.

One frequent criticism, which is made for instance by Professor Rakoff, is that Kessler failed to distinguish between standard form contracts and contracts of adhesion.[38] It is evident that not all standard form contracts are imposed by large businesses on smaller ones and consumers; they often apply between small businesses of equal bargaining power or are used by businesses without any kind of monopoly power. This criticism of Kessler seems to me unfair. In his article, Kessler cited many earlier studies of standard form contracts and showed how the practice developed historically.[39] He recognised how standard form contracts can helpfully manage risks and reduce costs for all business in competitive markets. Kessler's point was rather that large businesses, with strong bargaining power, can use their contracts to regulate their whole business sector, both the supply chain and the distribution chain, in a way that primarily serves their own interests in assured profits. This law-making process, masquerading as freely agreed contracts, was unregulated and was not democratically accountable. Harking back to Kessler's nightmares about what happened in Nazi Germany, he was warning that this kind of oligarchical rule poses a threat not only to competitive markets but ultimately to democracy and the constitution itself.

Today, many may regard these concerns about the demise of capitalism and democracy as exaggerated. But we should not forget that commencing shortly after Kessler wrote his piece, in advanced industrial societies there was a considerable increase in business regulation and much stiffer competition laws were developed. Today, a large company like Microsoft that tries to rule its market sector by imposing contracts on its distribution chain runs into legal barriers

[37] *ibid* 640.

[38] T Rakoff, 'Contracts of Adhesion: An Essay in Reconstruction' (1983) 96 *Harvard Law Review* 1174, 1218.

[39] Kessler (1943) (n 16) 631.

such as competition laws that prevent anti-competitive market domination.[40] The criticism that Kessler ignored the beneficial use of standard form contracts between equal bargaining parties is mistaken, though certainly his focus was on a particular misuse of standard form contracts by large businesses. It is noticeable, indeed, that Rakoff, having made the criticism that Kessler had not properly appreciated the range of uses of standard form contracts, concluded his discussion by in a sense voicing the opposite conclusion: 'Once it is recognized that contracts of adhesion arise from the matrix of organizational hierarchy, the argument for enforcement of form terms as a recognition of "freedom of contract" in its usual sense is unsupportable.'[41] That was exactly Kessler's point except that by 'organisational hierarchy' he included production and distribution chains, as well as relations within a single corporation.

It is true, however, that to modern eyes, Kessler did not address what is regarded as the main context in which contracts of adhesion are misused, namely those imposed on consumers by retailers. Modern discussions of the problems presented by standard form contracts perceive their source to lie almost entirely in informational asymmetries between a business and a consumer. The consumer does not know or understand what is in the small print of the retailer's standard form contract, with the consequence that consumers do not make optimal decisions. The solutions proposed by exponents of this kind of analysis based on the economics of information usually require more information, or better targeted information, or more transparent and comprehensible information in order to address this bargaining weakness of consumers. Kessler did not consider these issues about the economics of information. Indeed, at the time he wrote this article, I doubt that the idea of a consumer as a legal category existed. Moreover, the use of standard form contracts may not have been so omnipresent in retail markets as it became by the 1970s, perhaps being confined in the 1940s to contracts with insurance companies, banks and other types of transactions where the allocation of the risk was a core part of the transaction: the contract was the 'thing' that was being bought.[42]

It will be recalled that Kessler's own proposed remedy for the misuse of contracts of adhesion was to develop a separate branch of law from general contract law to regulate them because the ordinary law of contract was far too wedded to the idea of freedom of contract. What happened in fact in the USA, in line with proposals originally advanced by Llewellyn,[43] has been that judges have acquired the power to invalidate unfair terms in contracts in individual

[40] Case T-201/04 *Microsoft Corp v Commission* (2007) ECR II-03601.

[41] Rakoff (n 38) 1237.

[42] A Leff, 'Contract as Thing' (1970) 19 *American Law Review* 131; WD Slawson, 'Standard Form Contracts and Democratic Control of Lawmaking Power' (1971) 84 *Harvard Law Review* 529.

[43] KN Llewellyn, *The Common Law Tradition* (Boston, Little, Brown & Co, 1960) 370.

cases and retrospectively on the ground that the term violates the principle of good faith, or is unconscionable, or unreasonable, or some other loose test of fairness. Another approach to the problem of unfair terms in standard form contracts has been to use an administrative mechanism to prevent unfair terms from entering the market in the first place, which is the main strategy in the law of the European Union.[44] But Kessler's proposal for two laws of contract, though supported by some scholars such as Rakoff, has proved hard to implement. The reasons for the failure of Kessler's proposal seem to me to be twofold. First, Kessler did not spell out in detail how judges could use implied terms and standards set by normal and reasonable commercial practice to override freedom of contract. Second, a judge would need a clear rule to determine into which class any contract should fall, so that there would be no doubt whether or not the special law applicable to adhesion contracts should apply. But the only sharp line that legislatures have been able to draw has been between consumer contracts and contracts between two businesses. The special law can then apply to consumer contracts, though that fails to address Kessler's main concern that it was large businesses that were using contracts of adhesion to control whole market sectors. Rakoff's own proposal of where to draw the line using seven criteria is useful,[45] though it would throw up many hard borderline cases. These criteria would also not require special treatment for franchise and distributorship agreements, which were types of contract at the heart of Kessler's concerns about contracts of adhesion, and which were the subject of his next innovative article to be considered.

III. VERTICAL INTEGRATION BY CONTRACT

In 1957 Kessler published his article entitled: 'Automobile Franchises: Vertical Integration by Contract.'[46] This article is important, in my view, for two main reasons. One concerns the methodology of the piece, and the other its original insights into the legal construction of the business model that has subsequently been called 'networks' or 'hybrids'. The article is interesting as well because it provides a detailed study of a commercially important contract, the franchised distributorships granted by American automobile manufacturers, which are contracts of adhesion *par excellence*.

[44] Council Directive 93/13/EEC of 5 April 1993 on unfair terms in consumer contracts [1993] OJ L95/29.

[45] Rakoff (n 38) 1176–80. Criteria 7 and probably 6 would not be satisfied.

[46] F Kessler, 'Automobile Dealer Franchises: Vertical Integration by Contract' (1957) 66 *Yale Law Journal* 1135.

A. Methodology

The first reason for regarding this article as remarkable is that I cannot think of an earlier work about the law of contract that so clearly merits the label of socio-legal studies. This article appeared before the celebrated work of Stewart Macaulay in the 1960s,[47] for instance, and it draws on much more empirical material than the Legal Realists who wrote about contract law. The article began with a wealth of empirical information about the system of retail selling of cars in the USA through franchised distributorships. Kessler then provided a thorough examination of the detailed standard form franchise contracts of the five big automobile manufacturers as they evolved in the course of the first half of the twentieth century. This analysis was used to demonstrate the enormous economic power of these manufacturers over the whole supply chain. Finally, the article analysed legislative attempts to regulate these franchise agreements, concluding with a close and critical assessment of the federal statute: the Automobile Dealers Day in Court Act of 1956. Of course, there had been previous legal analyses of these franchise agreements. There had also been extensive assessment of these distributorships in the business and economic literature. Moreover, there had been official investigations of this business model with a view to determining whether or not these franchises violated anti-trust laws. Kessler drew on all these non-legal materials and combined them with a sharp appreciation of the precise, though shifting drafting of contracts and the crafting of judicial opinions in this highly litigated field. He examined the formulation of the legislation, which included a duty placed on the manufacturers to perform and only terminate the contract in good faith. Finally, he speculated about how damages might be calculated for breach of this duty of good faith. He brought together seemingly effortlessly this diverse body of material, both the empirical context of the transactions and their consequences for society and the law.

This socio-legal methodology has many benefits. My idiosyncratic pleasure with the article is often found in the footnotes. The centrepiece of the article is a close term by term investigation of the content of these standard form contracts and a consideration of why the lawyers drafted the contracts in the way they did. Consider, for instance, footnote 110,[48] which is a reference to the decision in 1930 of the federal Court of Appeals 4th Circuit in *Chevrolet Motor Co v Gladding*.[49] In that note, Kessler explained that the 1926 version of the Chevrolet franchise agreement conferred on the manufacturer the right to terminate the contract upon ten days' notice if the dealer did not exclusively represent the manufacturer

[47] D Campbell (ed), *Stewart Macaulay: Selected Works* (Cham, Springer, 2020) 133; see especially S Macaulay, 'Changing a Continuing Relationship between a Large Corporation and Those Who Deal With It: Automobile Manufacturers, Their Dealers, and the Legal System', part 1 (1965) *Wisconsin Law Review* 483, part 2 (1965) *Wisconsin Law Review* 740.

[48] Kessler (n 46) 1151.

[49] *Chevrolet Motor Co v Gladding* 42 F 2d 440 (4th Cir 1930).

and upon 60 days' notice if 'any question arose which threatened the mutually satisfactory business relationship'. Chevrolet had terminated the contract on giving ten days' notice for violation of the exclusive representation provision. The jury held that the provision had not been breached, so Chevrolet was in breach of contract for failing to deliver the cars that had been ordered by the dealer for the rest of the year. Furthermore, the Court decided that Chevrolet could not exercise its discretionary powers under the contract, such as the power to decline to meet orders for cars, in an arbitrary way. Kessler recounted how in response to this decision, General Motors altered their standard form contract and followed Ford by making the contract terminable 'at will'. Because that provision might not fully insulate them against claims that the power of termination had been exercised arbitrarily, General Motors subsequently reduced all their franchises to fixed-term one-year agreements, so that they would simply expire without the manufacturer having to make a decision at all.

As fascinating as that discussion of the evolution of the standard form contracts that construct the franchise relation proves, the socio-legal analysis becomes even more remarkable in the closing pages of the article. Here Kessler analysed the new federal legislation, the Automobile Dealers Day in Court Act. He made a number of technical legal points, but then offered an interpretation of what good faith means in the statute. His contention was that the statute was supposed to correspond to existing good practice in the standard form contracts used by the manufacturers. The purpose of the statute was therefore to reinforce business norms and customary practices, not to impose new standards. In relation to termination clauses, for instance, Kessler explained that the good faith standard had been understood in the industry, both in the terms of the express terms in contracts and in actual practice, as requiring cause to be shown for termination of contracts and that prior to any termination the manufacturer should warn and consult the franchisee of their reasons for dissatisfaction and give the dealer a fair opportunity to remedy the situation.[50] Kessler argued that the meaning of good faith under the statute should reinforce those practices, though in addition it should ensure that the reason given for termination should be one that amounts to a substantial violation of the franchise contract, considered as a whole. Kessler warned, however, that the standardised contracts were based on lengthy experience of what is critical for successful performance of the franchise, so that if the contract identified a particular type of reason for termination as substantial, a court should interfere only with extreme caution. He did not want to protect the dealer against competitive pressures, because that would be achieved mostly at the consumer's expense.[51] In this way, Kessler drew on his knowledge of the content of the standard form contracts and normal business practice to guide the courts in determining the meaning of good faith.

[50] Kessler (n 46) 1182.
[51] *ibid* 1189.

He certainly did not suggest that the courts should tightly control the manufacturers, but rather supported a balanced approach that reflected the pattern of good practice in the industry. He summed this up by saying that the success of the good faith provision will 'depend on the ability of the judiciary to apply the statute in a manner which accords the dealer a greater degree of independence without destroying manufacturer and consumer interests in an efficient dealership system'.[52]

B. Networks

The second reason for selecting this article has been hinted at already. This was Kessler's most thorough investigation of how contract law constructs and sustains the social order and markets of a capitalist society. In this particular article, he attempted to explain and illustrate how contract law could be used to create industrial empires and systems of economic control and governance that were powerful enough to rival those of governments themselves. The phenomenon of the economic and political power exercised by the managers of huge corporations was widely acknowledged. What was not appreciated as much was that power could be exercised not only through the internal hierarchical structure of corporations, but also through contracts that achieved something equivalent to, but not the same as, a vertically integrated organisation. By means of such contracts, a hub organisation such as the automobile manufacturer could exercise complete control over its supply chain and distribution network without integrating supplier and distributors into its corporate organisation. This control could be achieved through standard form contracts or contracts of adhesion. In recent decades, considerable theoretical work has gone into two main issues with regard to these networks or hybrid organisations.[53]

One line of enquiry has focussed on what efficiency advantages might be obtained by opting for a network rather than a vertically integrated organisation such as a single company or a parent company with subsidiaries. Perhaps the most accepted explanation of the competitive advantages of networks over integrated organisations is that networks are better at innovation and responding to changes in the market than single organisations. Kessler spotted this point, though not exactly in these terms, when he observed that the

[52] *ibid* 1179.

[53] C Joerges (ed), *Franchising and the Law: Theoretical and Comparative Approaches in Europe and the United States* (Baden-Baden, Nomos, 1991); GK Hadfield, 'Problematic Relations: Franchising and the Law of Incomplete Relations' (1990) 42 *Stanford Law Review* 927; M Amstutz and G Teubner (eds), *Networks: Legal Issues of Multilateral Co-operation* (Oxford, Hart Publishing, 2009); G Teubner and H Collins, *Networks as Connected Contracts* (Oxford, Hart Publishing, 2011); S Grundmann, F Cafaggi and G Vettori (eds), *The Organizational Contract: From Exchange to Long-term Network Cooperation in European Contract Law* (Farnham, Ashgate, 2013).

independent distributors could adjust their marketing techniques to local conditions quickly and effectively, which produces greater sales than a nationwide campaign conducted by the manufacturer. The general point about innovation as a competitive advantage over vertical integration is, however, broader. If an independent dealer comes up with a great marketing scheme for its locality, the franchisor can spot this competitive advantage and diffuse this information or idea throughout its network. Networks may have superior qualities concerning innovation to organisations because the independent franchisees may be able to avoid the 'group think' of single organisations.

A second line of enquiry about networks is of greater interest to Kessler and other lawyers. Networks can be labelled a system of 'organised irresponsibility'. This label highlights the point that the hub organisation such as the automobile manufacturer can insulate itself against risks and legal liabilities by avoiding the legal form of an integrated organisation. In his article, Kessler noted briefly that the avoidance of liability was the main reason for the invention of the franchise system for dealerships in the first place in about 1910.[54] Initially, the manufacturers had sold their cars through agents. Under this agency arrangement, the manufacturer entered into direct contractual relations with consumers, thereby exposing it to the risk of having to pay compensation for defective products, late delivery and misrepresentations. By transforming dealers into independent businesses, purchasers of cars had no direct contractual relation with the manufacturer, which made it much harder for consumers to bring a direct claim against the manufacturer.[55] The manufacturer could also minimise or eliminate other kinds of risks, such as the possibility that the conduct of one dealer might harm the business of another. Admittedly, resale price maintenance became harder within the network form of organisation because the contracts had the potential to violate anti-trust (competition) laws, but manufacturers succeeded in fending off many attacks on anti-competitive practices within franchises.[56]

At the same time as minimising legal risks, through these franchise arrangements the automobile manufacturers managed to obtain complete control over the dealers, perhaps even greater control than over agents to whom certain duties of loyalty might be owed. Although that degree of control was eventually achieved by the detailed standard form contracts that dictated how dealers should conduct their franchises, Kessler's analysis alerted me for the first time

[54] Kessler (n 46) 1140–41.

[55] Until a direct action for negligence causing personal injury was permitted in *MacPherson v Buick Motor Co* 111 NE 1050 (NY 1916). A contractual action against the manufacturer, which also invalidated disclaimers, only became possible after *Henningsen v Bloomfield Motors Inc* 161 A 2d 69 (NJ 1960), a decision in which Kessler's 'Contracts of Adhesion' was cited.

[56] Kessler (n 46) 1145 on elimination of resale price maintenance, which was caused by the application of the Sherman Antitrust Act 1890 to analogous cases: 1158.

to the point that where there is strong inequality of bargaining power, in fact there is no need for a long-term contractual relation at all. A manufacturer with strong bargaining power can simply indicate the terms on which it will do business with dealerships in the future, but make no commitment at all about whether or not any business will be undertaken. If the dealers want cars to sell in their shops, they have to do what they are told and be grateful for what they are given. In the absence of any commitments to supply or order cars, there appeared to be no contractual relation between the manufacturer and the dealership at all on the ground of lack of 'consideration' or, as the courts sometimes said, 'lack of mutuality'. Any complaints by dealers were met by the successful defence that there had been no breach of contract by the manufacturer because in the absence of mutuality or consideration there was no long-term franchise contract at all.[57]

In the longer term, however, binding standard form contracts became the legal framework for franchises, because distributors achieved considerable bargaining power themselves from their expertise and investments in retail outlets and goodwill from servicing customers' needs. As we have noted already, however, in the 1930s and 1940s these contracts were one-sided adhesion contracts that granted considerable power to the automobile manufacturers. Not only did they demand that the distributor should market their own products exclusively, but also the terms granted rights to terminate the contract for minor breaches or for no cause at all. The contract would be couched in terminology that conferred a discretionary power on the manufacturers, so that if there was a requirement of cause for termination, the manufacturer would claim to be the exclusive judge of whether or not there was a cause. It is true that by the 1940s exclusive dealing clauses appeared to be illegal under competition law,[58] but Kessler noted that the removal of those clauses in the contracts did not change the practice of exclusive dealing one jot. He speculated on the basis of evidence from decided cases that manufacturers simply threatened to discontinue the franchise if a dealer tried to market a competitor's product, which produced the desired result.[59] Exercising coercion of that kind was apparently not regarded by the courts as unlawful or contrary to anti-trust law.[60] It was this virtual absence of any control over abuses of a dominant market position that eventually led to the legislative reform in state statutes and then ultimately the Federal Day in Court Act.

[57] The same argument is used today in relation to various kinds of casual and precarious work relationships, where employers insist they have not promised to offer any work and that therefore there can be no consideration or mutuality to constitute a contract of any kind, with the consequence that such zero-hours workers have no employment law rights whatsoever: see, eg, *Carmichael v National Power Plc* [1999] 1 WLR 2042.

[58] Clayton Antitrust Act of 1914, s 3; *Standard Oil Co v United States (Standard Stations)* 337 US 293 (1949) (tied 'gas stations').

[59] See, eg, *United States v General Motors Corp* 121 F 2d 376, 398 (7th Cir), certiorari denied, 314 US 618 (1941).

[60] *United States v JI Case Co* 101 F Supp 856 (D Minn 1951); Kessler (n 46) 1163–64. Actual terminations of distributorships were also not regarded as abuses under competition law: 1165–67.

Finally, Kessler reflected on the implications of the role that the law of contract had played in the development of the franchise system and its conferral of power without responsibility on automobile manufacturers. He noted, as one might expect, how the courts in the USA insisted that freedom of contract should apply and that, in the absence of duress at the time of entry into the contract, the bargain was binding. According to the courts, if the dealers did not bargain for terms that protected them against abuses or required good faith in termination, they only had themselves to blame.[61] Kessler criticised this stance as 'unrealistic'.

> While a franchise may originate as the product of free bargaining inasmuch as a prospective dealer can stay out of the automobile merchandising business altogether, it becomes a glaring example of a contract of adhesion at the time of renewal when the dealer has invested heavily in the business. Should the franchise be cancelled, or not renewed, the dealer must wind up his business with a great financial loss; he will also lose whatever benefits of good will he has gained.[62]

In this passage, Kessler identified the source of inequality of bargaining power primarily in the sunk investments of the dealer in the franchise that makes compliance with the manufacturer's instructions, whether or not warranted under the contract, essential. Furthermore, because of these sunk investments, the manufacturer has an assured market in its dealers, so that it could offload models of cars that prove unpopular onto the dealers even though they do not want them.[63]

IV. A DUTY TO BARGAIN IN GOOD FAITH?

In 1964, Kessler published his article: 'Culpa in Contrahendo, Bargaining in Good Faith, and Freedom of Contract: A Comparative Study'.[64] This article was a return to his early training under Rabel in Berlin in systematic comparative law. As well as having the benefit of 30 years of teaching contract law at Yale, on this occasion, he had a co-author: his research assistant, Edith Fine.[65] In my view, this article is one of the classics of comparative contract law, in

[61] Kessler (n 46) 1155–56.

[62] *ibid* 1156.

[63] *ibid* 1140.

[64] F Kessler and EW Fine, 'Culpa in Contrahendo, Bargaining in Good Faith, and Freedom of Contract: A Comparative Study' (1964) 77 *Harvard Law Review* 401.

[65] For a biography, see EW Fine, 'Associate Justice Memorial' 40 Mass App Ct 1135 (1996). Fine was Kessler's paid research assistant, but was generously credited with equal authorship. What Edith Fine brought to the research project is unclear, though certainly she was an impressive lawyer. After her undergraduate degree she worked as a secretary and then, when Harvard Law School opened its doors to women, she managed to gain admission, one of only five women in her graduating class of 1957. She enjoyed a varied and outstanding legal career which culminated in nearly two decades on the Massachusetts Court of Appeals. She took the position of research assistant to Kessler while her husband was a medical student at Yale and they started a family.

which Kessler drew, to great advantage, on his vast knowledge of both the common law and civil law systems. As the subject of this article is the duty to bargain in good faith, it might be thought that Kessler was an advocate for this controversial doctrine. But that would be untrue. On the contrary, he frequently rejected broad statements of duties to bargain in good faith.

> Occasionally, the thesis has been advanced that once parties have entered into negotiations for a contract neither party can break them off 'arbitrarily' without compensating the other party for his reliance damages. Case law and literature, on the whole, however, have had the good sense to reject this idea.[66]

Instead of supporting a broad duty to bargain in good faith, he preferred what might be called, to borrow a well-known phrase, 'piecemeal solutions in response to demonstrated problems of unfairness'.[67] What makes Kessler's account so perceptive, in my view, is that he explained that the recognised problems for which piecemeal solutions are required are generated in part by the formal logic of the law itself.

Let me illustrate this point by briefly discussing the topic of unilateral mistake. The question is what should happen where one party enters into a contract on the basis of a serious mistake, such that if that party had known the truth about the facts, that mistaken party would not have entered into the contract at all. Kessler explained that civil law jurisdictions, with their broad support for a subjective will theory of contract, were driven to the conclusion that the mistaken party should be able to avoid the contract because consent was vitiated by the mistake, whereas the common law, with its objective approach to consent, would normally conclude that the contract was binding, as in *Smith v Hughes*.[68] Then Kessler observed that those all or nothing solutions of the subjective and objective approaches to consent inevitably prove unappealing once one adds further details to the facts. For instance, should it make a difference that one party was aware of the other's mistake, or at least ought to have been aware of it? Or should it make a difference that one party induced the other's mistake by making a negligent or innocent misrepresentation? Kessler explained how the idea of '*culpa in contrahendo*' was developed in German law, most famously by Rudolph von Jhering,[69] to address those additional complexities by supporting the conclusion that, although the contract might be vitiated for lack of consent owing to the unilateral mistake, both parties might owe duties to compensate the other for losses incurred as a result of any fault that may have caused or contributed to the vitiating unilateral mistake. Similarly, Kessler explained that common law had the opposite problem: given that the

[66] Kessler and Fine (n 64) 412.

[67] *Interfoto Picture Library Ltd v Stiletto Visual Programmes Ltd* [1989] QB 433 (CA) 439 (Bingham LJ).

[68] *Smith v Hughes* (1871) LR 6 QB 597 (CA).

[69] R von Jhering, 'Culpa in contrahendo, oder Schadensersatz bei nichtigen oder nicht zur Perfektion gelangten Verträgen' (1861) 4 *Jahrbücher Für dei Dogmatik des Heutigen Römischen und Deutschen Privatrechts* 1.

contract was apparently binding on the mistaken party, how could relief be given when these additional facts were included? Typical solutions included an extremely broad equitable doctrine of rescission for innocent misrepresentation,[70] a refusal to order specific performance,[71] or the finding that there was no binding contract if the offeree must have known that there was a mistake in the formulation of the offer.[72] In Kessler's account, we observe how different legal systems start with different premises, but then through various devices tailored to the particular legal framework of analysis produce similar outcomes in hard cases.

In demonstrating how the general rules require exceptions and modifications to accommodate the complexity and nuances of the fact situations, Kessler was not advocating any particular approach to the issue of pre-contractual bargaining duties. Yet he is clearly encouraging the belief that there is nothing surprising or untoward about the development of such doctrines or exceptions if they address problems generated by the formalism of contract law itself. He could see nothing wrong, for instance, in the use of equitable estoppel to create an exception to a requirement that a contract must be evidenced in writing in appropriate circumstances such as where the promisor had intimated that formalities would be unnecessary or that they would shortly be forthcoming.[73] If the requirement of formality was being used to obtain an inequitable advantage from a promisee who had reasonably relied on the informal agreement, the use of equitable estoppel was justified. Although not advocating a general doctrine of a duty to bargain in good faith or to refrain from fault during the bargaining process, Kessler presented the need for adjustments to general rules in a compelling way that was integral to the process of legal reasoning and he therefore sought to remove any doubts about the need for piecemeal solutions to injustices arising during the bargaining process.

The article is also fascinating to my mind for the way that it brings together a wide range of legal doctrines in the common law that are not usually seen as having a unified structure or even a common thread. When lawyers think about topics such as the duty to bargain in good faith, they might focus on matters such as misrepresentation, duties of disclosure and protection from abrupt withdrawal from negotiations for a contract. While Kessler's article addressed those topics, the landscape he drew was far broader. Once the problem that the law has to address is characterised as the application by the common law

[70] See, eg, *Redgrave v Hurd* (1881) LR 20 Ch D 1 (CA); *Smith v Land and House Property Corp* (1884) LR 28 Ch D 7 (CA).

[71] See, eg, *Tamplin v James* (1880) LR 15 Ch D 215 (CA).

[72] See, eg, *Hartog v Colin & Shields* [1939] 3 All ER 566 (KBD); *Scriven Brothers & Co v Hindley & Co* [1913] 3 KB 564 (KBD).

[73] Kessler and Fine (n 64) 415. In similar circumstances, German law uses the doctrine of *culpa in contrahendo* to cure the lack of formality and make the informal contract legally enforceable, which may go further than the remedies available for proprietary estoppel under English common law.

of an objective test of consent to all issues concerned with the formation of binding contractual obligations (or the exact opposite rule in civil law countries), many other topics that are generally regarded as fitting into completely different parts of the law of contract suddenly become central to the topic of the duty to bargain in good faith or, more precisely, fault during the bargaining process. One perhaps surprising example discussed by Kessler, for instance, is the postal acceptance rule. Once the objective test of consent is interpreted to mean that a postal acceptance concludes the contract, the law has to address occasional cases where the rule seems to work injustice. Such a case might be where the letter of acceptance was incorrectly addressed as a result of carelessness; another instance might be where the offeree had heard facts from which it could be inferred that the offer had been withdrawn prior to posting the letter of acceptance. From Kessler's point of view, the postal acceptance rule and its exceptions was just another typical example of piecemeal solutions that address problems arising during the bargaining process for which the formalism of the objective test of consent proves to be a blunt instrument of justice.

As I have said, Kessler's essay did not take a clear position on whether the common law should recognise a general duty to bargain in good faith. From his perspective, that misunderstands the problem that the law needs to solve. The difficulties that need to be addressed are generated to a considerable extent by the formalism of the general rules of the law of contract. What the law needs to do is construct piecemeal solutions rather than another general rule. But what standard of justice should trigger the search for an exception to the general rules? Kessler noted in his essay both Jhering's use of the concept of fault and the promiscuous use of concepts of good faith with a wide variety of meanings by other German scholars, but he did not clearly choose between them. When I read his article, however, it seemed clear to me that the unifying thread for the piecemeal solutions was a perception that fault by one party disentitled it from relying on the general rule. In my own work, therefore, I adopted the position that a broad concept of fault operates in the common law, as in the law of innocent misrepresentation, not merely a requirement of good faith in the sense of honesty in fact.[74] As for the topics that are generally discussed these days under the heading of a duty to bargain in good faith, as Kessler makes clear, there is generally no fault in the required sense in withdrawing from negotiations without warning or in failing to disclose material information. However, there may be special situations where, because of the dealings between the parties and their relationship, justice requires an exception to be made. In my view, Kessler's main point was that the courts should not stand on their formalist high horse and refuse to construct such exceptions, because it was their rigid following of over-inclusive rules that had created the difficulty or injustice in the first place.

[74] See, eg, H Collins, *The Law of Contract*, 4th edn (Cambridge, Cambridge University Press, 2013) ch 10: 'The Duty to Negotiate with Care' 179.

Views among scholars differ about the value and purpose of comparative law. It is possible to question what advantage is to be obtained from merely stating the rules of a variety of legal systems and noting that they have similarities and differences. Some progress was made by the functionalists, who set out to demonstrate that despite the differences in legal concepts between legal systems, they end up reaching similar conclusions. There must be a suspicion, however, that there tends to be an inherent bias in functionalist accounts that encourages them to dismiss variations in outcomes between legal systems as of minor significance in order to maintain the functionalist thesis. My own, perhaps chauvinistic view, is that the most important purpose served by comparative law studies is that they help one to understand one's own legal system better.[75] From this perspective, Kessler's article on bargaining in good faith is a standout achievement. Although we learn a great deal about many European legal systems and their functional similarities in the course of the article, its point is ultimately about how to make sense of the common law. The insight of Kessler's article is that the common law does not need an independent duty to bargain in good faith, but it does need rules to redress various kinds of fault during the bargaining process that induce parties to enter contracts where it appears unjust or unfair to hold them to their contract.

V. THE SIGNIFICANCE OF KESSLER'S SCHOLARSHIP

I have written several books about the law of contract. They reveal, I realise belatedly, a greater intellectual debt to Kessler than I appreciated at the time. My only excuse for this is that his perspectives had often so deeply embedded themselves in my understanding of the law of contract that I was unaware of their influence most of the time. The core idea of his articles on contracts of adhesion and franchising is that we need to understand the social and economic practice fully including how these contracts function in practice before we can successfully regulate them. This is also the starting-point of both *Regulating Contracts*[76] and *Networks*.[77] Those books and my first textbook *The Law of Contract* also used social theory to understand the role of the law of contract in constructing and shaping the market order at the heart of modern society.[78] This approach drew on the work of Marx, Weber and legal scholars who had in their turn developed those analyses of the structures of capitalist society such as Otto Kahn-Freund and, of course, Friedrich Kessler, for the purpose of understanding the general structures of the law.[79]

[75] H Collins, 'Methods and Aims of Comparative Contract Law' (1991) 11 *OJLS* 396.
[76] H Collins, *Regulating Contracts* (Oxford, Oxford University Press, 1999).
[77] Teubner and Collins (n 53).
[78] Collins (n 28).
[79] O Kahn-Freund, 'Introduction' in K Renner (ed), *The Institutions of Private Law and Their Social Functions* (London, Routledge, 1949).

My textbook also embraced the perspective of American Critical Legal Studies, which doubted the accuracy of traditional doctrinal accounts of the law for two reasons. The first reason was that the standard accounts of the law typically suppressed cases that were perceived as anomalous, so that significant tensions and even contradictions in the legal reasoning of judges and legal scholars almost disappeared from sight. The second ground for doubting traditional accounts of the law of contract was that they tended to privilege analyses of the law that appeared to support a neo-liberal view of a market society, in which freedom of contract was the cardinal principle because it was both morally compelling and welfare maximising. This aspect of the methodology encouraged a search for suppressed principle in those cases that were forgotten or dismissed as mistakes. Judgments where Lord Denning MR rescued the gullible from those seeking to take advantage of them were not in this book treated as anomalies but rather as representing important counter-principles in themselves. On this approach, for instance, it was possible to gather together a wide variety of discordant decisions and doctrines to reveal that the repeated denial by judges that they were concerned with ensuring fairness between the parties to contracts was for the most part misleading rhetoric. No doubt that anti-libertarian stance was the main reason that in his review of the book Tony Weir recommended that it should be burned.[80]

Reading my textbook again after many years, I can detect the influence of Kessler both in its general approach and in much of the detail. His American Legal Realist perspective, with its emphasis on the common law being comprised of competing principles, was not far removed from the Critical Legal Studies perspective that I used. The difference, if there was one, concerned the ambition to discover principles that could compete with the neo-liberal traditional account of contract law that privileged freedom of contract and wealth maximisation. Although that ambition was not evident in most of Kessler's publications, it was certainly at the forefront of his article on contracts of adhesion and lies behind his concern about vertical integration by contract. What might Kessler have thought of my textbook?

As it happens, I may know the answer to that question. On 30 October 1989, some three years after publication of my textbook, Kessler wrote to me in Brasenose College, Oxford, from Berkeley. His spidery handwriting is not easy to decipher, so there are gaps in my comprehension, but this is what I can make out:

> Dear Professor Collins
>
> It was by sheer accident that I discovered your Contracts. It is a beautiful book. … immediately and I have finished it. Now I am reading it for the second time and I am … moved when finding occasional references to my work. Our Casebook has appeared in [? a third edition]. I am responsible for about half of the book. Should

[80] T Weir, 'H Collins, *The Law of Contract*' (1986) 45 *CLJ* 503.

> you be interested in the book, let me know and I will arrange with our publishers to get you a copy.
>
> I am sure you do not expect me to agree with everything in your book. I am more of an old fashioned liberal (…). But this has not dampened my pleasure. Nor does Tony Weir change my mind ….
>
> *Apropos Sherwood v Walker* we do not know the final outcome (New trial!).
>
> With my thanks for the book
>
> I remain faithfully yours
>
> Fritz Kessler
>
> It is now almost 40 years ago that I had dinner in your College with Lawson and Kahn-Freund who was an old friend. I took a class with … Weber.

I am extremely pleased to have this opportunity to acknowledge my substantial debt to Fritz Kessler's work. I hope that I have encouraged others to appreciate the significance of his most innovative articles for the history of legal scholarship about the law of contract.

11

Professor Sir Guenter Treitel (1928–2019)

ANDREW BURROWS

I. INTRODUCTION

SIR GUENTER TREITEL died at the age of 90 on 14 June 2019. As a law student at Oxford in the 1970s, I used his textbook on *The Law of Contract* (then in its fourth edition) and I attended his contract lectures (including no fewer than 16 lectures on the doctrine of frustration!). During my five years as a Law Commissioner in the 1990s, he was a great help to me on the project that led to the Contracts (Rights of Third Parties) Act 1999. I still have the beautifully hand-written letters, running to many pages and containing scores of specific points (there were 83 in one letter), in which, at my request, he commented on the Law Commission's draft report and the draft bill. During the last decade of his life, I saw and chatted with him on a regular basis – usually at lunch once a week – at All Souls College. He was by then an Emeritus Fellow having previously been the Vinerian Professor of English Law and a Professorial Fellow at the college. I gave one of the tributes at his memorial service in which I described him as '*the* world authority on the English law of contract in all its glory'.

It follows from my close association with Guenter that it is not entirely straightforward for me to offer an objective analysis of his work as a scholar of contract law. Nevertheless, in what follows I have tried to put our friendship largely to one side and to review his contribution as dispassionately as possible.

II. HIS EARLY YEARS

Although one can isolate Guenter's work from his early life, it is appropriate to offer a brief description of those extraordinary years, as a Jewish boy growing up in, and fleeing in the nick of time from, Nazi Germany. This is not least because, inevitably, they deeply affected and shaped everything Guenter later did in his life. He told the story in a gripping lecture to the Oxford Chabab Society in September 2012[1] and it is set out in more detail in an article published posthumously entitled 'A German Childhood 1933–1942: Persecution and Escape'.[2]

Guenter's first personal experience of anti-Semitism came in 1935, when the Nuremberg laws were passed formally reducing Jews to second-class citizenship. At the age of seven, he was expelled from state school simply because he was Jewish. Suddenly, his previous non-Jewish friends spurned him and, on one occasion, beat him up on the stairs of his apartment building where they also lived. Later on, at parks and other places, not least the playground at the back of the Berlin zoo which had been a refuge for Jewish friends to play in, away from verbal and physical persecution on the streets, signs appeared saying 'Jews not welcome'. Matters became worse in 1938. His uncle, who had fought for the Germans in the First World War and was decorated with the Iron Cross, was taken away for a period in a concentration camp and emerged emaciated and with what Guenter described as a 'hunted look' in his eyes.[3]

This led the Treitel family to try to leave Germany. Another uncle had married and was living in England and, shortly after the horrors of *Kristallnacht*, this meant that, with a great deal of difficulty, Guenter and his brother were found places on the famous *Kindertransport* out of Germany in March 1939 heading for a sponsor in England. On the train out of Berlin, Guenter was interrogated to make sure he was not carrying more than one mark or any gold. Guenter remembered being worried that he would be hauled off the train when he realised that he had not disclosed that his fountain pen had a gold nib. On arrival at the port at Hamburg, he described the relief at embarking on the ship to leave Germany. 'The relief that I felt when walking up the gangplank is indescribable; I had felt nothing like it before nor have I experienced anything similar since.'[4] On arrival at Southampton, having left wintry cold Berlin, he could not fail to appreciate the symbolism because 'the air was mild, it was obviously Spring, the sun was shining and the daffodils were out'.[5]

Guenter was of the view that, had he stayed in Germany, and had he been lucky enough to survive, he would have followed his father into the legal profession and would have had a far less satisfying life than he had enjoyed as an academic lawyer in England. In a moving finale to his lecture to the Chabab Society, he asked which words from Shakespeare might be said to sum up his life given those dark early years. His answer was six words from 'As You Like It' (Act 2 Scene 1): 'Sweet are the uses of adversity'.

[1] GH Treitel, 'Lecture to the Oxford Chabab Society' (September 2012), available at https://vimeo.com/48474737.

[2] GH Treitel, 'A German Childhood 1933–1942: Persecution and Escape' (2020) 28 *Zeitschrift fur Europaisches Privatrecht* 591 (with forewords by Reinhard Zimmermann and Birke Häcker).

[3] *ibid* 601.

[4] *ibid* 609.

[5] *ibid* 610.

III. FOUR CATEGORIES OF PUBLICATIONS

In considering the range of Treitel's scholarship, it is helpful at the outset to divide his publications into four categories. Of these, it is clear that, as with most of the tort scholars considered in *Scholars of Tort Law*,[6] his greatest influence has been through the many editions of his textbook.

So the first category simply and solely comprises Treitel's textbook, *The Law of Contract*. The first edition was published in 1962 and, under Treitel's authorship, it ran to 11 editions (the 11th edition being published in 2003). It then became *Treitel on Contract* by Professor Edwin Peel for the 12th edition in 2007 and is now, under Peel's continued authorship, in its 15th edition (published in 2020). This textbook is Treitel's most famous and important work and epitomises his style of scholarship. It will therefore be the main focus of this chapter.

However, it is worth noting that, alongside that major textbook, Treitel also produced a shorter textbook – conceived as making the law of contract accessible to non-law students, for example those studying business degrees – entitled *An Outline of the Law of Contract*. The first edition of this shorter book was published in 1970 and ran to six editions, the last being in 2004. Close examination shows that this book represents, in effect, a concise summary of *The Law of Contract* with the same basic rules and exceptions highlighted but with many of the details omitted. It is a remarkably clear and succinct account of the law of contract – and occasionally the relative lack of detail means that the exposition is clearer than in the main work – but, in terms of assessing the features of Treitel's scholarship, it adds very little, if anything, to what we can glean from the main book.

The second category of publications contains Treitel's contributions to two major practitioner works, both in the *Common Law Library Series*: *Chitty on Contracts* and *Benjamin's Sale of Goods*. These are included as a separate category because Treitel's labours on these books continued, off and on, for almost all his academic life and he was deeply committed to them. He was an editor for 50 years of the former (between 1968 and 2018) and an editor of the latter for 40 years. Also worthy of mention in this category, as it is probably more accurately viewed as being a work for practitioners rather than being an academic monograph, is *Carver on Bills of Lading* (first edition in 2001 and running to a third edition in 2011). Co-authored with Professor Francis Reynolds, this comprises a completely rewritten version of the original work by Carver. Also falling within this category was Treitel's very first foray into book authorship which took the form of writing afresh four chapters (none of which was directly focussed on contract law) in the seventh edition (published in 1961) of *Dicey on the Conflict of Laws*. As *Dicey, Morris and Collins on the Conflict of Laws* (now in its 15th edition, 2018), this remains the leading practitioner work on English private

[6] J Goudkamp and D Nolan (eds), *Scholars of Tort Law* (Oxford, Hart Publishing, 2019).

international law (although Treitel's subsequent decision to focus on contract law meant that his contribution to this book was limited to that one edition). Treitel also wrote the general chapter on contract in *English Private Law* (first edition, edited by Peter Birks, in 1998).[7]

A third category comprises Treitel's academic monographs. There were three of these. The first was *Remedies for Breach of Contract: A Comparative Account* (1988) which built upon his much earlier contribution to the *International Encyclopaedia of Comparative Law* (1976, edited by Arthur Von Mehren) and examined remedies for breach across Anglo-American, French and German law. The second was *Frustration and Force Majeure* (1994) which ranged across Anglo-American law and was the culmination of Treitel's deep fascination (as I recall from his student lectures) with that area of contract law and with the history behind some of the cases, such as the burning down of the Sussex Music Hall in 1861 resulting in the leading case of *Taylor v Caldwell*.[8] Finally, there was his 2002 book, containing the three Clarendon Lectures he gave in Oxford in 2001–2002, *Some Landmarks of Twentieth Century Contract Law*. He here examined, in depth, agreements to vary contracts, the battle over privity, and types of contractual term.

The final category of Treitel's publications contains his articles, essays and case-notes. There was a steady flow of these throughout his career. In my view, the five most important are as follows:

i. **'Specific Performance in the Sale of Goods' [1966] Journal of Business Law 211**
   This article is particularly important for recognising what Treitel labelled 'commercial uniqueness'. In deciding whether specific performance should be ordered of a contract for the sale of goods, Treitel argued that the courts have accepted that, in addition to physically unique goods, which cannot be replaced by using an award of damages to purchase substitute goods, there are commercially unique goods. These are goods which cannot easily be replaced in the market, for example, petrol at a time of an acute shortage of petrol or heavy machinery which will take many months to re-manufacture. As damages are inadequate, specific performance of the obligation to deliver such commercially unique goods is therefore appropriate.
ii. **'Consideration: A Critical Analysis of Professor Atiyah's Fundamental Restatement' (1976) 50 Australian Law Journal 439**
   This was a long article written in direct response to an attack on the conventional understanding of the doctrine of consideration by Patrick Atiyah,

[7] He remained as author for that chapter for the second edition in 2007 (edited by Andrew Burrows) before handing over the chapter to Ewan McKendrick for the third edition in 2013 (also edited by Andrew Burrows).

[8] *Taylor v Caldwell* (1863) 3 B & S 826, 112 ER 309.

Consideration in Contracts: A Fundamental Restatement (1971).[9] Atiyah and Treitel were, for several years, academic rivals in Oxford. Their style and approach to scholarship could not have been more different. Treitel was concerned with the accurate detail of the law and had no real interest in sweeping broad theories. Atiyah, in contrast, saw the law as reflecting important overall policies and intellectual or social trends. In this essay, Treitel rejected Atiyah's heretical central argument that consideration means nothing more than a good reason for enforcing a promise. Rather he argued that the conventional understanding of consideration as a requested benefit or detriment is accurate albeit with some exceptions and with reliance on 'invented consideration'. For Treitel this reflected accurately the law as understood and applied by the judges. To argue, as Atiyah had done, that the better interpretation was that that was all a myth was anathema to Treitel.

iii. **'Doctrine and Discretion in the Law of Contract' (his inaugural lecture as Vinerian Professor in 1980, published by Oxford, Clarendon Press, 1981)**
Given Treitel's love of detailed clarity in the law of contract, it is not surprising that he was against the trend in some legislation affecting contracts – in particular the Unfair Contract Terms Act 1977 – to confer wide-ranging discretions on judges, for example to determine whether an exclusion clause was a fair and reasonable one to have been included. Wherever possible, he thought that rules were preferable to discretions albeit that he allowed for considerable flexibility by recognising numerous exceptions to the rules.

iv. **'Fault in the Common Law of Contract' in M Bos and I Brownlie (eds), Liber Amicorum for the Rt Hon Lord Wilberforce (Oxford, Clarendon Press, 1987) Ch 11**
One of the most overlooked areas of English contract law is the standard of liability. While there is a tendency to assume that the contractual standard is one of strict liability, in many areas (for example, the contractual duties owed by a professional to its client) that is inaccurate and the correct standard is one of reasonable care albeit that this is all subject to whatever precise terms are agreed by the parties. In this illuminating essay, Treitel looks in detail at this question that has both practical and theoretical importance.

v. **'Damages for Breach of a CIF Contract' [1988] Lloyd's Maritime and Commercial Law Quarterly 457**
In many respects, this is my favourite of Treitel's articles. It deals with the fiendishly difficult and technical question of when 'market loss damages' are available for the breach of a cif contract. Treitel argued that, as the authorities were slowly but surely showing, and as logic dictated, such

[9] PS Atiyah, *Consideration in Contracts: A Fundamental Restatement* (Canberra, Australian National University Press, 1971).

damages are available only where there is a 'double breach'. That is, where neither the documents nor the goods are in conformity with the contract. The article shows off all Treitel's best qualities of clear and rigorous analysis of the cases however detailed and difficult the subject-matter may be.

IV. SOME GENERAL POINTS ABOUT TREITEL'S PUBLISHED WORK

In looking across those four categories, three general points about Treitel's body of published work should be stressed.

First, his work was almost entirely concerned with the law of contract. With the exceptions of his earliest writings (eg on the conflict of laws) and a light-hearted excursus in his 1984 article in the *Law Quarterly Review* into law and literature (through his examination of the legal problems in the works of his beloved Jane Austen),[10] he was really only concerned to write about the law of contract (including relevant restitutionary remedies). In addition to his unrivalled knowledge and understanding of the general principles of contract law, he had a specialist expertise in relation to international contracts for the sale of goods (eg cif and fob contracts). In this respect, his four chapters in *Benjamin's Sale of Goods* and his chapters in *Carver on Bills of Lading* comprise some of his most original and brilliant work albeit that their drilling down into the very fine details of the case law and statutes may not be to everyone's taste. They were once described to me by one expert and former colleague of Treitel as engaged in looking at how many angels there are on a pinhead.

Second, despite being German (he retained a slight Germanic accent throughout his life), Treitel was largely concerned with writing on the English law of contract. While well capable of producing important comparative work, as shown by his comparative law book on remedies for breach of contract, he was primarily fascinated by the English law of contract, especially the case law. Perhaps surprisingly, he showed relatively little interest in the general law of contract in civil law jurisdictions, including Germany.

Third, using the helpful classification of tort scholars put forward by Goudkamp and Nolan in *Scholars of Tort Law*, Treitel was indisputably a 'consolidator'.[11] His scholarship falls squarely within what one may describe as 'black-letter law' or 'practical legal scholarship' (also often referred to as 'doctrinal legal scholarship').[12] It examines in great depth and detail what the judges

[10] GH Treitel, 'Jane Austen and the Law' (1984) 100 *LQR* 549.

[11] J Goudkamp and D Nolan, 'Pioneers, Consolidators and Iconoclasts: The Story of Tort Scholarship' in Goudkamp and Nolan (n 6).

[12] *cf* Todd Rakoff's analysis in chapter seven of this volume of Williston as 'unabashedly doctrinal'. I have steered clear of the further debate, wonderfully explored by Rakoff in relation to Williston, as to whether Treitel was a formalist and what precisely is meant by that term. But certainly my perception is that Williston was a more creative and wide-ranging doctrinal scholar than Treitel.

have laid down in past cases and what precisely are the effect of statutes. His work engages hardly at all with other academic writing. And, in particular, he showed no interest in grand overarching theories, such as moral rights reasoning or economic analysis. Working out, and explaining as clearly and succinctly as possible, the sophisticated patterns of the common law were what inspired him. Perhaps not surprisingly therefore even his writing aimed at students appealed to practitioners and judges. Indeed, as successive editions of his textbook on Contract became longer and more detailed, it may be that judges and practitioners became his primary readership and admired his work the most.

V. TREITEL'S PRINCIPAL WORK: *THE LAW OF CONTRACT*

As I have indicated, it is indisputable that Treitel's most famous work and the one for which he will most be remembered is his textbook, *The Law of Contract*. This section focuses on a number of aspects of that work. We begin by examining the ways in which his textbook was different to others. We shall then move on to draw out in some detail the particular type of practical legal scholarship that the book epitomises.

A. How Did Treitel's Textbook Differ from Others?

By the time in the late 1950s when Treitel was considering writing his textbook, there were two other main student textbooks on the English law of contract: *Anson's Law of Contract* and *Cheshire and Fifoot's Law of Contract*. The first edition of the former by William Anson had been published in 1879. The first 11 editions (the 11th edition being published in 1906) were written by Anson himself but thereafter other authors took over. The 21st edition published in 1959 was written by JL Brierly. *Cheshire and Fifoot* had first appeared in 1945 and there were fourth and fifth editions, by the original authors, in 1956 and 1960. By this stage, *Pollock's Principles of Contract* was fading away with the last ever edition (the 12th edition in 1946) being edited by Winfield (who, it is of interest to note, used brackets to indicate his amendments from Pollock's text). Like today, *Chitty on Contracts*, albeit superbly edited by a new team put together by the general editor John Morris in 1961 (including, for example, Tom later Lord Bingham), was aimed at practitioners and not students.

It would seem clear, therefore, that in the late 1950s Treitel looked at *Anson* and *Cheshire and Fifoot* and decided that there was room for another student text. The preface to the first edition of his book published in 1962 indicates that he thought the existing texts were somewhat old-fashioned and had an excessive focus on contracts for the sale of goods rather than the full range of commercial life. He also recognised that his book included more detail – and in that sense he was hinting at a higher level of sophistication – than the other student texts.

He explained his motivation in the following way:

> [M]y choice of subject was to a large extent governed by the fact that I was not entirely satisfied with the treatment of it, admirable though it was, in other books on English contract law. Their emphasis on one particular contract (ie sale of goods) seemed to me to be hard to justify when much of the development of the subject had taken place in cases concerned with other aspects of commercial practice. The analysis in the existing books of developments in the courts also seemed to me to do less than justice to the sophistication with which the judiciary had handled these developments. In retrospect, I would say that I hoped to raise the level of academic discourse in the subject. I did not put it to myself in quite this way; but (consciously or not) that was what I tried to do in the 40 years and 11 editions of the book that followed its original publication in 1962.[13]

Although Treitel's view that the other books tended to focus too much on contracts for the sale of goods is puzzling (because that does not appear to be a particular feature of those books), it is clear that he was concerned to examine the judges' reasoning in more depth than the other student books. He also included many more cases so that what he was providing was a more complete picture of the common law of contract than that contained in those other texts. He also refused to shy away from complexity so that his book examined topics that were not addressed at all in the other books (a classic example being his chapter on 'plurality of parties').

Another distinctive feature of his book, although not mentioned by him, was the full and careful attention he paid to statutes. A table of statutes had first been included in *Anson on Contract* in the 19th edition in 1945. Right from the start, Treitel was concerned to give statutes the central importance they merited and he integrated common law and statute in describing and understanding the law of contract. Although Treitel's first love was the common law, he had unrivalled skills in being able to work with statutes and to make them comprehensible. His ability to explore the scope and application of statutes was just as great a feature of his work as was his attention to the detailed reasoning of the judges in areas of pure common law.

B. Black-Letter Law/Practical Legal Scholarship

While conscious that his work was so described, Treitel did not like the academic derision that often lay behind the term 'black-letter law', especially in the United States academy. He explained that he stopped his lecturing visits to Charlottesville, Virginia, despite continuing invitations:

> [B]ecause at that time the Law and Economics movement held sway in the Law School there with an almost religious fervour; and my apostacy in that regard did

[13] GH Treitel, 'Vicissitudes of an Academic Lawyer' (2019) 26 *Zeitschrift für Europäisches Privatrecht* 133, 152.

> not go down well with its high priests. ... I began to be perturbed at the lack of tolerance which was increasingly evident in some leading American Law schools of failure to adhere to this or that theory which was perceived as being the only one in which academic discourse was to be conducted ... I was also perturbed by the criticism, from adherents of such schools of thought, of so-called 'black letter law'. This concept seemed to me to be a sort of Aunt Sally – an invention of the critics which was easy enough to demolish but which bore no relation to reality. I had long been convinced that the common law was a highly sophisticated instrument which, in its practical application, was totally different from the 'black letter law' invented by such critics.[14]

While I think it is a better strategy to defend 'black-letter law' rather than seeking to deny its existence, one can easily avoid the unwelcome baggage that may go with the label by referring instead to 'practical legal scholarship'. And there is no doubt that Treitel's textbook did epitomise practical legal scholarship or, more precisely, a particular type of practical legal scholarship. In understanding Treitel's contribution, it is an important exercise to try to identify in detail the precise approach to, and style of, practical legal scholarship that Treitel's textbook adopted.

C. The Features of Treitel's Brand of Practical Legal Scholarship

In considering this, I would suggest that there are ten important features of Treitel's form of practical legal scholarship as exhibited by his textbook (and I here go no further than the last edition of the book for which he was responsible, ie the 11th edition in 2003).

i. Detailed Clarity, Comprehensivity and Complete Accuracy

The writing in Treitel's textbook is very precise and succinct with not a word wasted. The clarity of thought and mastery of the subject-matter shines through. Although that makes it readable, it is a slow read precisely because so much careful analytical thinking is packed into the account. When I was a student in the 1970s, I bought all three of the recommended textbooks, *Anson*, *Cheshire and Fifoot* and *Treitel* and found all three very useful. But there is no doubt that, for a student, Treitel was the most difficult of the three (tutors tended to say that only the best students should use it) albeit that it had great merits, including its comprehensivity and complete accuracy.

[14] *ibid* 168. I was very pleased to read Todd Rakoff's comment, at p 200 in chapter seven of this volume, indicating that, contrary to what is often thought, doctrine is not dead in the USA: 'At the least, courts still cite doctrine, and contracts professors, online, frame questions to each other in doctrinal terms; perhaps everyone is playing a deep game, but, while doctrine is surely not everything, I doubt it is nothing.'

ii. Internal Coherence not Deep Theories

Treitel's explanations of the law were closely tied to the reasoning of the judges and, to the extent that they went beyond that, they were rooted in history and the pursuit of internal coherence. What I mean by the latter may be illustrated by the following example. In discussing the reasons for the benefit aspect of the doctrine of privity (whereby a third party has no right to enforce a contract to which it is not a party), Treitel wrote this:

> A system of law which does not give a gratuitous promisee a right to enforce the promise is not likely to give this right to a gratuitous beneficiary who is not even a promisee. The doctrines of privity and consideration, though not identical, are intimately connected. This connection helps to explain the development of the doctrine of privity.[15]

However, underlying deep theories, whether, for example, economic analysis or moral reasoning, find no place in his account. Nor do ideas such as the tension between market individualism and consumer welfare. Rather, the law is presented as a sophisticated but autonomous body of rules driven by logic and practicality.

iii. Rules and Exceptions

To produce a coherent account across such a wide area, one technique is to focus on the key cases and principles and to leave out complications. That was very much *not* Treitel's approach. His technique to produce coherence was one of articulating general rules followed by potentially numerous qualifications or exceptions to them. We see this from the very first page of his textbook. A contract we are told is 'an agreement giving rise to obligations which are enforced or recognised by law'. However we are then informed that there are qualifications that need to be made to this, such as the objective approach to agreement and the implication of terms by law. In Chapter two, it is stated that agreements are usually made by offer and acceptance, but in some cases this 'analysis is impossible or highly artificial'.[16] A principal exception given is multipartite agreements as in *The Satanita*.[17] Similarly, in relation to consideration, the doctrine and its application are set out at length. But then we come to a section headed 'Special Cases' which refers to either clear exceptions to the need for consideration (such as letters of credit) or where particularly careful reasoning is required in order to decide that there is consideration (as in relation to unilateral contracts, for example).

[15] GH Treitel, *The Law of Contract*, 11th edn (London, Sweet & Maxwell, 2003) 588.
[16] *ibid* 47 (footnote omitted).
[17] *The Satanita* [1895] P 248 (CA), affd *sub nom Clarke v Dunraven* [1897] AC 59 (HL).

iv. Limited Criticism

Although there are criticisms of the case law and indications of solutions and reforms, they are relatively rare and are quickly and lightly and often tentatively offered. An example is Treitel's comments on the case of *Dickinson v Dodds*,[18] which laid down the rule that withdrawal of an offer may be communicated to the offeree by a third party and need not be by the offeror.

> The rule that communication of withdrawal need not come from the offeror can be a regrettable source of uncertainty. It puts on the offeree the possibly difficult task of deciding whether his source of information is reliable, and it may also make it hard for him to tell exactly when the offer was withdrawn. … Certainty would be promoted if the rule were that the withdrawal must be communicated by the offeror, as well as to the offeree.[19]

In relation to 'invented consideration' Treitel wrote: 'The courts have not been very consistent in the exercise of this discretion and its existence is a source of considerable uncertainty in this branch of the law.'[20] He is perhaps somewhat less reticent in his criticism of statutes. For example, he wrote of the Law Reform (Frustrated Contracts) Act 1943, 'contracts for the sale of goods should have been wholly excluded from the operation of the Act of 1943. Their partial exclusion does not satisfy the requirements of either convenience or justice'.[21]

v. Almost Exclusive Reliance on Primary Sources

There is very little reference to academic work. Although there are some references in footnotes, there is virtually no examination in the text (with the exception of the views of, for example, law reform bodies) of particular academic views, and certainly no attempt to engage directly with them by discussing in the text their strengths and weaknesses. What one has, therefore, is almost complete reliance on primary sources, whether cases or statutes. In a similar vein, there is surprisingly little use made of hypothetical examples – a very common academic technique – to test out what the law is. The impression given is that the case law is so rich that, when fully unearthed, one will find all the examples one needs.

vi. Richness of Detail

The wealth of information contained within the book is breathtaking. It is plain that the research behind it has been painstaking. It follows that one can almost always find some help if one is stuck on a point. Just to give one example, some years ago I was puzzled as to what is meant by a deed poll. I mentioned this to

[18] *Dickinson v Dodds* (1876) 2 Ch D 463 (CA).
[19] Treitel (n 15) 42.
[20] *ibid* 71.
[21] *ibid* 919.

Guenter over lunch. He explained the position to me and said that I would find this in his book. Sure enough the distinction between deeds inter partes and deed polls was carefully explained, albeit somewhat hidden away under a subsection on the Law of Property Act 1925, s 56, which itself fell under the wider heading of statutory exceptions to the privity doctrine.[22]

vii. Loss of Big Picture?

The big danger of trying to present all the details of the law is that one loses sight of the bigger picture. More specifically, in reading Treitel's account, it would be difficult for many students to work out which should be regarded as the leading cases and which are relatively subsidiary. There are so many cases – some of them obscure – referred to in the text, let alone in the footnotes, that it can be difficult to detect which are the ones that really need to be focussed on. Here I think lies the weakness of *Treitel* as a student text compared to *Anson* and *Cheshire and Fifoot* (a weakness that was not so apparent in the first edition but became ever more problematic in later editions). Those texts would not only tend to exclude material that is marginal and complex but would also tend to highlight the leading cases more prominently by discussing them in greater detail. A classic example of this was Treitel's account of the famous case of *Central London Property Trust Ltd v High Trees House Ltd*.[23] The wider significance of that case was lost within the details of Treitel's discussion of common law and equitable waiver and forbearance and even the label of promissory estoppel was not used by him. The idea that the doctrine of promissory estoppel posed a major threat to the doctrine of consideration becomes lost in his exposition.

viii. Lack of Interest in Taxonomy

A further feature of Treitel's work is that he was not especially interested in taxonomy and structure. In the preface to his first edition, he clarified that he

[22] *ibid* 669 (now para 14–131). I was made acutely conscious of Treitel's thoroughness when he emailed me a few years ago saying that he was having difficulty locating the judgment of the Court of Appeal, given by Vos LJ, in a case called *Nextia* which had been referred to in a subsequent Court of Appeal decision. 'Andrew', he wrote, 'you're good at finding cases on the internet. Could you find a copy of Vos LJ's judgment for me?' So I duly investigated and discovered that, unusually, Vos LJ had ordered that his judgment should be restricted to the parties and should not be made public. Presumably the later Court of Appeal had then been given the judgment by one of the parties. So I reported back to Guenter, thinking that I would be putting his mind at rest, that as there was no public record of the decision he could safely ignore it. But that was not good enough for Guenter. A week later, I walked into lunch and he gave me a beaming smile and raised his thumbs. 'I've got that *Nextia* case' he said. 'Somehow Professor Beale managed to get hold of it for me'. 'Did it say anything of interest?' I asked him. 'Oh no', he said, 'nothing of interest at all' but added, triumphantly, 'but now I know it said nothing of interest at all'.

[23] *Central London Property Trust Ltd v High Trees House Ltd* [1947] KB 130 (KBD).

was departing from what he saw as the problematic division of the subject into Parts. 'I have abandoned the traditional division of the subject into "parts" as this seemed to raise more problems than it solved.' This is surprising because, given Treitel's tight analytical mind, one might have expected that a clear structure, set out in Parts, would have appealed to him. But ultimately it appears that he was concerned that this would unnecessarily constrain his practical analysis. Moreover, he was no doubt conscious that judges had not found it necessary to refer to any particular taxonomy. As it was, he set out in general terms how the book fitted together at the end of his first chapter where he explained that

> the law of contract is concerned with the circumstances in which agreements are legally binding [and thus] it deals mainly with the two questions of agreement and legal enforceability. …
>
> [There are also] the rules relating to plurality, privity, assignment, transfer of liabilities and agency [which] determine who is bound by, and entitled to the benefit of, an agreement. The rules relating to remedies assume the existence of an enforceable agreement, and deal with the precise methods of enforcing it. These methods are in principle determined by law [rather than by the agreement].[24]

However, it was clear that, for Treitel, the structure and taxonomy of contract law was of less importance than making sure that one covered the law that was within, *or directly relevant to*, the law of contract. Contract was, in this sense, a contextual rather than a conceptual category. We see this most clearly in his treatment of restitution. Restitutionary remedies are dealt with throughout in relation to various ineffective contracts (such as void, voidable or illegal contracts) and are discussed in detail in the chapter on remedies for breach of contract. There is no recognition that, for example, the restitution of money for total failure of consideration, following termination of the contract for breach, does not obviously fall within Treitel's description of the relevant remedies as being concerned to *enforce* the contract (ie that it is not a remedy *for* breach of contract). In general, his treatment of restitution shows little recognition or acceptance of there being a law of unjust enrichment that, conceptually, should be distinguished from the law of contract.

ix. Eccentricities

While a great strength of Treitel's work was its accuracy and careful attention to detail, there were a few unhelpful eccentricities or peculiarities in his description or analysis of the law. I shall briefly give six examples. First, he had a chapter headed 'standard form contracts' which almost entirely comprised an examination of exemption clauses. The heading 'standard form contracts' (rather than

[24] GH Treitel, *The Law of Contract* (London, Stevens, 1966) 5–6. This passage was retained, subject to minor modifications, in the eleventh edition: Treitel (n 15) 6.

'exemption clauses') does not fit well with the sequence of chapters because plainly most of the rules of contract – and hence the other chapters of the book – apply equally to standard form contracts as to other contracts. Moreover, there can be exemption clauses outside standard form contracts. Second, there was virtually no discussion at all of the interpretation of contracts. This most important aspect of contract law – on which whole books have been written – was confined (with the exception of exemption clauses) to just one paragraph under the parole evidence rule.[25] Although it is true that English academics generally did not wake up to the importance of interpretation until the discussion by Lord Hoffmann in *Investors Compensation Scheme Ltd v West Bromwich Building Society*[26] – and there was a similar neglect in *Anson* and *Cheshire and Fifoot* – there were discussions in other books and one might have expected Treitel to have seen the huge practical importance of this topic. Third, he preferred the terminology of 'rescission' for breach and persisted with it, long after it had become clear that the more accurate and less confusing terminology was 'termination' (or 'discharge') for breach. Fourth, he adopted a very difficult approach to mistake at common law which drew an impossible distinction between mistake nullifying consent and mistake negativing consent. Fifth, he persisted with a notion of 'fundamental terms'[27] even after it had become clear that there are only three types of term – conditions, warranties and innominate terms – and that 'fundamental breach' is a rule of construction and is not a rule of law. Sixth, some of his analysis of the law on damages is confusing and unhelpful. It is clear that, looking back at the first four editions, he was suddenly influenced in writing the fourth edition by having read Fuller and Perdue, 'The Reliance Interest in Contract Damages'.[28] But the consequent inclusion of a new section on 'compensation for what?' is highly misleading in treating reliance damages and, even worse, an award of restitution as if they protect valid interests within the law of contract when the truth of the matter is that damages for breach of contract are solely concerned to put the claimant into as good a position as if the contract had been performed.[29] This may be regarded as the only obvious example of Treitel placing excessive reliance on an academic article and being led astray by so doing! But he was also uncharacteristically loose in other aspects of the application of the compensatory principle: hence his support, for example, for the minority judges in *Golden Strait Corp v Nippon Yusen*

[25] Treitel (n 15) 197.

[26] *Investors Compensation Scheme Ltd v West Bromwich Building Society* [1998] 1 WLR 896 (HL).

[27] See also GH Treitel, *Some Landmarks of Twentieth Century Contract Law* (Oxford, Oxford University Press, 2002) ch 3.

[28] LL Fuller and WR Perdue, 'The Reliance Interest in Contract Damages' (1936) 46 *Yale Law Journal* 52.

[29] See A Burrows, 'Comparing Compensatory Damages in Tort and Contract: Some Problematic Issues' in S Degeling, J Edelman and J Goudkamp (eds), *Torts in Commercial Law* (Pyrmont NSW, Thomson Reuters, 2011) 367, 385–90.

Kubishika Kaisha, The Golden Victory[30] (who, indeed, relied on his flawed case-note on the Court of Appeal's decision).[31]

x. New Editions

Treitel took a particular approach to new editions. It was made clear in various prefaces that the new edition was not merely an updating exercise of including new material, but gave him the opportunity to put forward his own new thinking. He explained his approach as follows:

> [A] considerable amount of rewriting and what might be called reconceptualisation was required for each of these new editions as I had set my face against the commonly held view that a new edition of a legal text involved no more than a process of 'updating'.[32]

Very commonly, as he made clear in the various prefaces, about a quarter of the text was new in each edition. This was all very well and to be applauded. However, because he was so anxious to be comprehensive, and because of the explosion in law reporting, successive editions of *Treitel* became ever longer and more difficult. The arrival on the market of superb shorter books on contract meant inevitably that students tended to turn away from *Treitel* and it has tended to become seen as a practitioner work and a reference work for students rather than as a student text.

VI. MERITS OF PRACTICAL LEGAL SCHOLARSHIP

The features explored above mark out Treitel's particular brand of practical legal scholarship. I anticipate that, for some in the legal academy, his work will be regarded as being of marginal importance and may even be dismissed as largely irrelevant, old-fashioned and dull. The modern trend is to regard true legal scholarship as being theoretical rather than practical and as being concerned not with the details of the law but with the deep level principles and policies that, looking in from the outside, may be said to underlie the law. The intended readership is increasingly fellow academics alone and not also practitioners and judges. The research and study of law is increasingly seen, within law schools, as divorced from law as a practical discipline and as being a non-autonomous branch of, for example, the social sciences. Careful analysis of the details of the case law and statutes is, increasingly, not the modern name of the game in our law schools. In my view, this idea that practical legal scholarship is not true legal

[30] *Golden Strait Corp v Nippon Yusen Kubishika Kaisha, The Golden Victory* [2007] UKHL 12, [2007] 2 AC 353.

[31] GH Treitel, 'Assessment of Damages for Wrongful Repudiation' (2007) 123 *LQR* 9.

[32] Treitel (n 13) 159.

scholarship or has less value than deep theoretical accounts of the law urgently needs to be dispelled.

I have elsewhere put forward a detailed defence of practical legal scholarship against the modern trend in many law schools of dismissing it as being of limited worth.[33] Professor Jane Stapleton has similarly called for the importance of this form of scholarship to be recognised.[34] Since joining the Supreme Court, my appreciation of the importance of such scholarship has, if anything, been strengthened. I do not wish to repeat all of what I have said elsewhere on this topic but, in defending Treitel's work, I shall here make three brief points in defence of practical legal scholarship.

First, practical legal scholarship matters because that is the style of scholarship that is used by, and is relevant to, judges and practitioners in deciding cases in the English courts. The judges want to hear legal argument, based on precedent, in order to arrive at an answer to the factual question before them that not only satisfies their intuitions, but is also justified according to legal rules and principles. Law as applied in the courts is a system of practical reasoning focused on providing answers to factual disputes. In light of that, there seems to be every good reason why legal research should apply the same techniques. If the English courts are not using, for example, economic analysis, or insights from sociology or deep philosophical theory in deciding cases – and clearly they are not – it is hard to see why one should regard those as primary tools of analysis. Surely, at least in the first instance, it is justifiable to analyse a case using the language and approach adopted by those arguing and deciding the case. This is not to deny that other approaches may be interesting and relevant. But that they should be seen as a substitute for – or as somehow more important than – practical legal reasoning seems perverse. As Lord Rodger wrote:

> [O]ne has to wonder whether it is altogether satisfactory for academic writers to go direct to the more theoretical aspects of a subject without ever really engaging with the nitty-gritty of how it actually operates in practice.[35]

In other words, studying law first and foremost requires that one truly knows and understands the details of the law; and one acquires that knowledge and understanding by practical legal reasoning.

Second, it may of course be that those who criticise the practical legal scholars, or seek to downgrade their status, do so because they find the autonomous study of law boring and unchallenging. Some find grand, high-level theories, even if removed from practicality, far more interesting than picking through fine working detail. I have heard it said that practical legal scholarship amounts to

[33] A Burrows, 'Challenges for Private Law in the 21st Century' in K Barker, K Fairweather and R Grantham (eds), *Private Law in the 21st Century* (Oxford, Hart Publishing, 2017) 29, 32–40.

[34] J Stapleton, *Three Essays on Torts* (Oxford, Oxford University Press, 2020).

[35] A Rodger, 'Judges and Academics in the United Kingdom' (2010) 29 *University of Queensland Law Journal* 29, 36.

nothing more than mindless description that could be carried out by anyone with half a brain. The clever ones are those who develop the grand theories. For someone who finds the details of the law endlessly fascinating and, in many respects, extremely complex – so that to obtain a true understanding of the concepts and principles is very challenging – it is hard to see how all this can be regarded as either easy or dull.

Third, I am not suggesting that practical legal reasoning is the only form of analysis worthy of pursuit by legal academics. Different forms of analysis, and critiques, of the law plainly have a role to play. So, for example, I applaud the work of those engaged in socio-legal studies, just as I do the work of great figures of jurisprudence. Ideally all law students, while not sacrificing the core focus on doctrine, should have some exposure to legal history, sociological theories of law, philosophical reasoning and economic analysis. Indeed, there is indisputably a very difficult question for every practical legal scholar as to how deep a theory one needs to have in order to make sense of the law, while remaining intelligible to those who have to decide and argue about particular facts. I have friends who are professional philosophers who seem to think that almost everything that any lawyer says in so-called legal reasoning is hopelessly superficial. However, my essential point is that, precisely because law (unlike philosophy) is a practical subject, practical legal reasoning and scholarship should remain at the core of legal research and training, such that it would be quite wrong for that type of reasoning to be relegated to the side-lines. At our core, legal academics must be able to talk the language of, and interact with, those who are practising law, whether as barristers, solicitors, judges or legislative drafters. Yet, in many law schools, it is that doctrinal core that is under attack.

In my view, therefore, Treitel's work as a practical legal scholar has been, and remains, of great and central importance in our understanding of the English law of contract. In general terms, his sort of scholarship – practical legal scholarship – needs to recover its place at the heart of our law schools.

Having said all that, there are three aspects of Treitel's particular and extreme brand of practical legal scholarship that I would not seek to defend. On the contrary, these seem to me to be serious weaknesses in his scholarship.

First, Treitel's almost exclusive focus on the primary sources – the cases and statutes – means that in some ways his work diminishes the role of the practical legal scholar. The advocate in the appellate court and law students alike can gain greater understanding from what legal academics, engaged in practical legal scholarship, have to say about the cases and statutes. Not to engage seriously with those debates is to rob the reader of potentially important insights. True it is that Treitel would look carefully at law reform proposals of, for example, the Law Commission. But he barely devoted any time looking at the writings of academics.

Second, and linked to the first criticism, is that Treitel's work may lead one into the false impression that practical legal scholarship tends to shy clear of criticisms of the law and is not a creative form of reasoning. In general, that is a false perception as shown by the vigorous debates among practical legal scholars about the merits of the latest case. Take, for example, the law of unjust enrichment. No one could seriously suggest that practical legal scholarship in that area does not involve criticism of the law.

Third, as I have already indicated, Treitel's obsessive concern with collecting all relevant cases became counter-productive in leading to a loss of clarity in seeing the bigger picture. What the appellate courts (as well as law students) need from practical legal scholars is help in seeing a particular case in its wider context. The bigger picture is essential in order for the law to develop coherently. Legal academics are in a strong position to provide that bigger picture but, to do so, they need to cut through some of the detail. Treitel's incisive mind sometimes allowed him to do so. But too often his account is so rooted in the mass of cases that one may struggle to see the wood for the trees.

VII. CONCLUSION

I consider myself very fortunate to have come to know Guenter well during our time together as Fellows at All Souls. Prior to then I had admired his work. However, when I came to know him better, it was his general knowledge and wit and laughter that became almost as important. His many anecdotes, carefully and precisely told, made him a sparkling companion.

Guenter's life and work were forever shaped by his escape from Germany in 1939. Looking back on those early years, and the kindness shown to him on arrival in England, meant that Guenter believed that he owed a huge debt to this country. Although one may debate the strengths and weaknesses of his particular brand of practical legal scholarship, there is no doubt in my mind that one can truly say of the man and his work that his repayment was sweet indeed.

12

Professor Ian Roderick Macneil (1929–2010)

JONATHAN MORGAN*

PROFESSOR IAN MACNEIL, The Macneil of Barra, led an extraordinary life – both as man and scholar. How many contract lawyers have combined their academic duties with hereditary chieftainship of a Scottish clan? How many clan chieftains have established themselves as leading theorists of the law of contract? (Or indeed how many contract scholars, come to that?) Macneil seems a biographer's dream.

However, an intellectual biography of Ian Macneil provides a forbidding task. He is widely acknowledged as the father of relational contract theory – or at least its co-parent, with Stewart Macaulay (born 1931). The relational theory has established itself as the main rival to mainstream traditional (or 'classical') thinking about the law of contract over the past half century. At this point, consensus runs out. Writing about relational theory, and especially Macneil's place within it, raises a number of overlapping difficulties. First, relational contract is a diverse school of opinions, united mainly by its opposition to traditional contract law.[1] To attempt a comprehensive account of its multifaceted development would exceed this chapter's scope. Second, Macneil's prolific scholarship is, to say the least, challenging for contract lawyers to understand. Third, and surely not unrelatedly, Macneil was disappointed by his theory's reception.

Paradoxically then, Macneil was one of the most significant contract scholars in the post-war period – and yet his achievement is ambiguous, even doubtful. This chapter attempts to resolve the paradox. Macneil wrote extensively about contractual relations, their social basis and normative structure. His research focused less squarely on contract *law*, as most lawyers would understand it. The work of drawing out the implications for contract doctrine has fallen to others. Perhaps unsurprisingly, it has not proven straightforward.

* I am indebted to David Campbell, Rory Macneil and William Twining.

[1] See, eg, D Kimel, 'The Choice of Paradigm for Theory of Contract: Reflections on the Relational Model' (2007) 27 *OJLS* 233.

Also unsurprising is the widespread resistance to Macneil's relational contract theory. Macneil deliberately set out to challenge centuries of (in his view mistaken) thought about the nature of contracting – a philosophy exemplified by traditional contract law. It is difficult to overturn such deeply embedded views. Macneil was fully conscious of the scale of the task. While he succeeded in establishing a serious rival, it is yet to supplant established notions of contract law.

Why not? For Macneil (and his many followers), lawyers' hostility to relational theory must stem from several rather unattractive factors: legal conservatism, intellectual incuriosity, and free-market ideology. Such attitudes have undoubtedly played a part. Yet we suggest that this is not the entire story. Classical contract law has gained a reasoned defence as the appropriate basis for a significant subset of contractual activity – that involving sophisticated commercial parties. Of course though, the perceived requirement to *justify* traditional contract law flows directly from Macneil's challenge to it. Its correctness can no longer just be assumed.

Moreover, even stout defenders of the traditional approach admit it struggles when applied to relational contracts of the kind to which Macneil tirelessly directed scholarly attention. Important developments in English law may best be explained by the influence of Relational Theory. Macneil's ultimate legacy is a law of contract more diverse and better understood.

I. THE LIFE OF IAN MACNEIL

Ian Roderick Macneil was born in New York on 20 June 1929.[2] He received his BA at the University of Vermont. After serving in the US army during the Korean War (although not seeing active combat), Macneil completed his studies at Harvard Law School (JD 1955). He clerked for the Chief Judge of the Court of Appeals (First Circuit) in New Hampshire, followed by three years of legal practice there. Macneil began his academic career at Cornell University in Ithaca, NY (1959–80). He was also a visiting professor at the University of East Africa, Dar-es-Salaam (1965–67), where he wrote his first contract casebook.[3] (There were other visiting positions at Duke, Virginia, Oxford, and finally Edinburgh.) In 1980 Macneil moved to Northwestern University, Chicago, as John Henry

[2] See IR Macneil, 'Biographical Statement' in IR Macneil (edited by D Campbell), *The Relational Theory of Contract: Selected Works of Ian Macneil* (London, Sweet & Maxwell, 2001); 'Obituary: Ian Macneil, Clan Chief and Lawyer' *The Scotsman* (Edinburgh, 19 February 2010); R Macneil, 'Preface' in D Campbell et al (eds), *Changing Concepts of Contract* (London, Palgrave Macmillan, 2013).

[3] IR Macneil, *Contracts: Instruments for Social Co-operation – East Africa* (South Hackensack, Fred B Rothman, 1968). See also chapter 15 of this volume by William Twining – a near contemporary of Macneil's in Dar-es-Salaam.

Wigmore Professor of Law, until his retirement. (David Ruder, a former Dean at Northwestern, described Macneil as a 'warm, empathetic and forthright person' whom students 'greatly admired' – despite his 'reputation as a tough teacher'.)[4]

Macneil's father, Robert Lister Macneil, a descendant of the hereditary clan chiefs of Barra in the Outer Hebrides, bought the Southern part of the island in 1937 (Ian Macneil attended Castlebay Primary School there in 1938–39). Macneil succeeded as the 46th Chief of the Clan Macneil upon his father's death in 1970, becoming (in his own words) 'an active proprietor of a Hebridean crofting estate' and 'member of the Barra community – to the limited extent possible for anybody not born there'. Following retirement from Northwestern, Macneil was proud that his family had 'largely repatriated ourselves from North America to Scotland' – albeit he lived mostly in Edinburgh, not on Barra. In 2004 Macneil donated his 9,000 acres of crofts to the Scottish Government, for the benefit of the Barra community (an earlier attempt apparently faltered because he was locally considered a good landlord).[5] Macneil had already transferred the ancestral seat, Kisimul Castle, restored by his father,[6] to the care of Historic Scotland on a 1,000 year lease at the rent of £1 and a bottle of whisky annually (specifically Talisker, with the right reserved to vary the producer). The islanders held Macneil in well-deserved affection – for his commitment to Barra and his genial personality. Upon Macneil's death in Edinburgh on 16 February 2010, the MP for the Western Isles paid tribute to his service to the Barra community, his campaign to retain Barra's vital air transport links, and 'considered submissions on the [Scottish Parliament] Crofting Bill'. He was succeeded as Chief of the Clan Macneil of Barra by his elder son, Rory.

It is impossible to overstate how glamorous this sounds. (Most contract lawyers would be lucky to serve on the college gardens committee, never mind administering a large crofting estate in the Outer Hebrides.) It is also impossible to resist linking Macneil's unusual life story with his contract scholarship. For he (tentatively) did so himself: 'The rich social complexities of his life probably contributed to Macneil's escape from the narrow ruts of classical and neoclassical contract into the openness of relational contract'.[7]

It can also be noted that in later years Macneil had an extensive practice as an arbitrator which took him 'out of the Ivory Legal Tower'.[8] Arbitration was his second main scholarly interest.[9] Did this experience influence Macneil's view of contract law? Plausibly, it may have done. But 'arbitration' covers a

[4] PV Tremmel, 'Obituary: Ian R Macneil' (*Northwestern*, 17 February 2010), available at www.northwestern.edu/newscenter/stories/2010/02/macneil.html.

[5] See 'Islands Gifted to Residents' (*BBC News*, 5 September 2003), available at http://news.bbc.co.uk/1/hi/scotland/3083024.stm; *cf* Macneil (2013) (n 2) xvi–xvii.

[6] RL Macneil, *Castle in the Sea* (Glasgow, Collins, 1964).

[7] Macneil (2001) (n 2) xiii.

[8] *ibid* xiii.

[9] IR Macneil et al, *Federal Arbitration Law* (Boston, Little, Brown & Co, 1994).

wide range of activity. An arbitration may be the close (albeit private) equivalent of court-based adjudication, as in (say) English shipping arbitrations. Or it could be sharply different in approach, like the European tradition of the '*amiable compositeur*'. Of course the difficulty is in finding out directly just how particular arbitrations work, given their confidentiality (itself a central attraction of dispute settlement outside the courts). At any rate Macneil himself seemed rather equivocal. He once declared: 'I am not a devoted promoter of arbitration'.[10] Consistent with his approach to contract relations, Macneil suggested it would be 'fruitful' for the legal system to take a more 'conciliatory' approach to dispute resolution.[11] But he seemed sceptical about arbitration enthusiasts' claims that, among other advantages, arbitration reduces conflict levels and thereby preserves relationships.[12] 'Conciliatory' dispute-resolution is harder than it sounds. Can conciliation be compelled? As Macneil noted, the 'large administrative bureaucracies' created under the National Labor Relations Act (US) have proved 'only marginally effective in forcing good faith bargaining on recalcitrant employers and unions'.[13] Given these remarks, it seems unlikely that Macneil's experience of arbitration drove his contract theory. They were surely complementary interests, but 'alternative dispute resolution' does not provide easy solutions to the problems of regulating 'relational contracting'.

II. MACNEIL'S SCHOLARLY WRITING

Macneil wrote extensively about contract for three decades (c.1960–1990), with more sporadic publications thereafter. An almost complete bibliography appears in the selection of Macneil's papers edited by David Campbell.[14] (Macneil published little following this 2001 collection.)[15] His earlier works include general reflections about contract law and legal education.[16] Three editions of a singular student contract casebook appeared in different iterations, at wide intervals.[17] There were also analyses of various specific doctrines, such as agreed

[10] IR Macneil, *American Arbitration Law: Reformation, Nationalization, Internationalization* (New York, Oxford University Press, 1992) ix.

[11] IR Macneil, *Contracts: Exchange Transactions and Relations: Cases and Materials*, 2nd edn (Mineola, NY, Foundation Press, 1978) 175.

[12] *ibid* 1110.

[13] Macneil (n 10) 6.

[14] Campbell (2001) (n 2) 387–90.

[15] *cf* IR Macneil, 'Reflections on Relational Contract Theory after a Neo-classical Seminar' in D Campbell et al (eds), *Implicit Dimensions of Contract: Discrete, Relational, and Network Contracts* (Oxford, Hart Publishing, 2003). The history of Hebridean offshore castles was Macneil's last scholarly preoccupation from 2004 until his death: Macneil (2013) (n 2) xix–xx.

[16] See, eg, IR Macneil, 'The Master of Arts in Law' (1965) 17 *Journal of Legal Education* 423; IR Macneil, 'Whither Contracts?' (1969) 21 *Journal of Legal Education* 403.

[17] Macneil (n 3) (a precursor); IR Macneil, *Contracts: Exchange Transactions and Relations* (Mineola, Foundation Press, 1971); Macneil (n 11); IR Macneil and PJ Gudel, *Contracts: Exchange Transactions and Relations* (Mineola, Foundation Press, 2001).

remedies and the formation of contracts.[18] But the bulk of Macneil's scholarly output sought to uncover the relational nature of contracts and contracting. Relational contract was certainly the focus of Macneil's mature scholarship, and his most influential scholarly legacy.

Macneil's seminal publication was a lengthy article in 1974, 'The Many Futures of Contracts'.[19] It was followed by several other extended articles about relational contracting over the following ten years.[20] In 1979 Macneil gave the Julius Rosenthal lectures at Northwestern University, published as *The New Social Contract: An Inquiry into Modern Contractual Relations*.[21] There were also critical appraisals of the nascent and influential economic analysis of law.[22] Later in his career, Macneil tended to respond to criticisms and (as he perceived them) misunderstandings of relational contract theory, rather than advancing new primary claims.[23]

Throughout this large body of work, Macneil emphasised the embeddedness of all contracts and contractual behaviour in ongoing social relations. His campaign has proved hugely influential. It is no doubt clichéd to identify a 'paradigm shift' but Macneil's work fits Kuhn's original definition for an intellectual revolution. After Macneil, scholars return to 'normal science' (which is for lawyers, one supposes, doctrinal scholarship) within the parameters of the new relational paradigm.[24] Perhaps the comparison is inexact, for significant disagreement remains about what the new 'ordinary scholarship' should look like, even assuming that Macneil's relational paradigm is accepted. It may be one of those revolutions when it is still too early to say what its effects will be.[25]

[18] IR Macneil, 'Power of Contract and Agreed remedies' (1962) 47 *Cornell Law Quarterly* 495; Macneil's contributions to RB Schlesinger, *Formation of Contracts: A Study of the Common Core of Legal Systems* (London, Stevens & Sons, 1968).

[19] IR Macneil, 'The Many Futures of Contracts' (1974) 47 *Southern California Law Review* 691.

[20] See, eg, IR Macneil, 'A Primer of Contract Planning' (1975) 48 *Southern California Law Review* 627; IR Macneil, 'Contracts: Adjustment of Long-Term Economic Relations under Classical, Neoclassical, and Relational Contract Law' (1978) 72 *Northwestern University Law Review* 854; IR Macneil, 'Values in Contract: Internal and External' (1983) 78 *Northwestern University Law Review* 340.

[21] IR Macneil, *The New Social Contract: An Inquiry into Modern Contractual Relations* (New Haven, Yale University Press, 1980).

[22] See, eg, IR Macneil, 'Efficient Breach of Contract: Circles in the Sky' (1982) 68 *Virginia Law Review* 947.

[23] See, eg, IR Macneil, 'Relational Contracts: What We Do and Do Not Know' (1985) *Wisconsin Law Review* 483; IR Macneil, 'Contracting Worlds and Essential Contract Theory' (2000) 9 *Social & Legal Studies* 431; IR Macneil, 'Relational Contract Theory: Challenges and Queries' (2000) 94 *Northwestern University Law Review* 877.

[24] T Kuhn, *The Structure of Scientific Revolutions* (Chicago, University of Chicago Press, 1962).

[25] Disappointingly, Zhou Enlai's famous 1972 remark about France probably referred to the Parisian student demonstrations of 1968, not the Revolution of 1789.

III. INFLUENCES ON MACNEIL

Macneil was a contract scholar of his time and place – mid-twentieth century America – only more so. He fully shared the contemporary scepticism about legal doctrine that can conveniently be called 'Realism'. Macneil's scholarly interest in doctrinal law declined after the early years of his career. The great assault on the 'classical' rule-bound law of contract had, after all, already taken place. Corbin's treatise is seen as the pinnacle of realist-doctrinal thought (if that is not a contradiction).[26] Retrospectively, Macneil singled out Lon Fuller's intellectual influence: '[Fuller's] half-escape from classical and neo-classical contract law begged for something more'.[27]

Karl Llewellyn, although outside the present volume, also deserves mention – not just for his Realist contract scholarship, but as the driving force behind the sales provisions of the Uniform Commercial Code. Llewellyn put into action his faith in open-textured rules and 'situation sense' – specifically, the need for courts to enforce commercial customs and practices existing beyond the formal legal rules. Macneil took Llewellyn's project to its logical conclusion perhaps, examining contracting practices and norms solely as *social* phenomena – to which contract law was at best incidental, at worst distorting.

As that remark suggests, Macneil's attitude toward contract law was sceptical and his relationship with black-letter scholarship fraught. That is true of all the Realists to some degree. Stewart Macaulay, although surely sympathetic to Llewellyn's approach, noted the 'messy' results of his 'Grand Style' adjudication and the considerable demands it places on courts: 'Article 2 of the U.C.C. often reads as if Llewellyn, its drafter, expected it to be applied by judges such as Cardozo and Learned Hand'.[28] (While English lawyers might remain confident of their senior judiciary's uniform quality, they are not all Mansfields, Scruttons or Hoffmanns.)

Macneil, though, had less faith in the potential for common law heroism than these predecessors. Corbin, for example, preferred the piecemeal reshaping of the common law through 'molecular movements' to any sweeping general theory; and praised the value of appellate decisions as 'the living evidence of the continuing evolutionary process of our judicial system'.[29] Macneil was more sceptical, although did not reject the study of judicial decisions altogether. (William Twining thinks this equivocation typical of the 'deeply conflicted' lawyers

[26] Corbin rejected the 'Realist' label which Grant Gilmore later attached to him. Corbin believed that rules and principles were both possible and desirable. However, Corbin's Treatise emphasised the complexity, malleability and fallibility of contract doctrines. See Klass, chapter eight of this volume, p 202.

[27] Macneil (2001) (n 2) xiii.

[28] S Macaulay, 'Relational Contracts Floating on a Sea of Custom? Thoughts About the Ideas of Ian Macneil and Lisa Bernstein' (2000) 94 *Northwestern University Law Review* 775, 803.

[29] See Klass, chapter eight of this volume, p 219.

who revolt against formalism in their scholarship, while remaining broadly traditional in their teaching.)[30] Thus, Macneil felt constrained to structure his student casebooks around appellate opinions, if only because of 'the presently prevailing aims of the first-year [law] curriculum'.[31] He accepted that the facts of disputes provided students with valuable 'vicarious experience'.[32] Macneil also suggested, rather wonderfully, that judges' opinions are virtually unique as a record of *reasoned* decision-making in human affairs, and well worth studying.[33] Despite this, the common law of contract had serious flaws. First, its mistaken intellectual premises (as extensively chronicled in Macneil's ground-breaking research). Second, the inherent limits of rules produced by *litigation* – arising from *failed* relationships. This misleads lawyers. It is extraordinarily hard to remember that most contracts are *performed*, flexibly and co-operatively, when consuming an 'exclusive diet of appellate cases … [ie] post-mortem reviews of defunct relations'.[34] Litigation distorts every living contractual relationship – like a laboratory scientist drying out a jellyfish in order to examine it.[35] Small wonder that 'Realist' or not, Macneil's mature research engaged little with contract doctrine, and even his student casebook went as far as he thought he could in presenting other kinds of materials, for example extensively quoting industry-standard contract terms to correct the lawyer's impoverished and pathological focus on disputes.

IV. MACNEIL'S INFLUENCE

The body of this chapter will consider, in some detail, Macneil's relational theory and its scholarly impact. Nonetheless, readers may welcome a provisional summary of Macneil's influence.

His legacy is curiously divisive. While (American) contract scholars universally acclaim Macneil's importance, there is considerable disagreement about his theory's implications for the law of contract. Macneil's work on relational contracting has been described (admiringly) as 'both prolific and distinctive'.[36] A jaundiced critic might suspect prolixity and obscurity. Macneil's writing can undeniably be difficult for doctrinal lawyers to understand. His method and concerns seem more sociological than strictly legal. Notwithstanding his extensive scholarship, Macneil did not spell out the consequences for contract doctrine. The reticence seems deliberate. Macneil's earlier work shows that he

[30] See Twining, chapter 15 of this volume, pp 379–80.
[31] Macneil (n 11) xix.
[32] *ibid* 56.
[33] Macneil (1965) (n 16) (compare Twining's discussion of Llewellyn's views).
[34] Macneil (n 11) 54–56.
[35] Macneil (1969) (n 16).
[36] WC Whitford, 'Ian Macneil's Contribution to Contracts Scholarship' (1985) *Wisconsin Law Review* 545.

was entirely capable of writing first rate, critical doctrinal scholarship – in the mould of a Corbin (or modern English style, Atiyah) rather than a Williston (or Treitel). But Macneil later wrote of the 'immense frustration' he felt about his participation in a comparative study of offer and acceptance.[37] The 'final straw' was a wasted summer (1964) failing to extract coherent common law principles about 'agreements to agree'. Macneil decided this was a 'fool's errand' because the reality of contract relations is incompatible with the sharp, decisive moment of agreement presupposed by the classical law.[38] Macneil thereafter expounded 'reality', in conscious opposition to contract law's ('non-existent') paradigm of 'discrete' transactions.

Macneil's disillusion with doctrinal scholarship generates difficulties for contract lawyers. Their concern *is* with legal doctrine. How precisely should the law respond to the challenge thrown down by Macneil's relational theory? To simplify, some lawyers infer that the law of contract should enforce relational norms – concerning itself with the governance and preservation of contractual relations rather than just resolving disputes. However, others argue that contract law is by its nature an institution for the resolution of disputes – or at least works better as such than as a relationship-preservation mechanism. This school of thought (sometimes labelled 'neo-formalist') is more cautious about Macneil's implications for legal doctrine. It holds that notwithstanding Macneil's revelatory account of real-world contracting, contract law should maintain its traditional form. (It should, in Macneil's language, remain 'discrete'.) Moreover, that is what contracting parties want and expect contract law to do.

Robert Scott is one of the leading 'neo-formalists'. In a symposium about Macneil's work, Scott wrote:

> The debate that divides the academics who think about these questions is not over the nature of *contract* as an institution. We are all relationalists now. In that sense Macneil and Macaulay have swept the field. Contract, we now know, is complex and subjective and synthetic in every sense of those terms. The debate, rather, is over the proper nature of *contract law*. All contracts are relational, complex and subjective. But contract law, whether we like it or not, is none of those things. Contract law is formal, simple, and (returning to Macneil's terminology) *classical*.[39]

In the same symposium, Richard Speidel (a leading champion of relational contract) dismissed this as '[n]onsense' – because those (like Scott) 'advocating the virulent strain of the new formalists are neither realists nor relationalists and the sooner we say so the better'.[40]

[37] Macneil (2001) (n 2) xiii, referring to Schlesinger (n 18).

[38] *ibid* xiii.

[39] RE Scott, 'The Case for Formalism in Relational Contract' (2000) 94 *Northwestern University Law Review* 847, 852 (emphasis in original). (For Macaulay, see section IX below.)

[40] RE Speidel, 'The Characteristics and Challenges of Relational Contracts' (2000) 94 *Northwestern University Law Review* 823, 845, fn 86.

While the semantics of the word 'relationists' are unimportant, the underlying disagreement is significant. How should contract law respond to changing ideas about the nature of contracting – ie about the practice that contract law exists to regulate and support? It is a truism of commercial law that it strives to uphold the expectations and practices of actors in the commercial world. Given this well-accepted role, Macneil's theory seems to have dramatic implications. If Macneil has transformed our understanding of commercial relations, must not contract law be transformed to accord with the new understanding? That seems the obvious implication of the relational theory. Many scholars have accordingly sought to analyse its disruptive impact upon the law of contract (eg, in England, David Campbell, Hugh Collins and Catherine Mitchell). The rejoinder (eg Scott's) alleges that this over-simplifies the relation between contract law and contract practice. The law need not always mirror practice. In Scott's view, contract *law* may better support relational contracts by being studiedly 'non-relational'. Each side has strong arguments. No consensus has emerged. This essay's concern is not to decide who is *right* about Macneil's lessons for the law of contract. Rather to emphasise Macneil's intellectual legacy: a debate about contract law's essential nature and its relation with real-world practice.

We turn next to Macneil's relational theory and its influence. Having outlined the 'Essential Theory' we suggest its difficult reception stems in part from Macneil's failure to spell out the implications for legal doctrine. Other scholars have drawn doctrinal lessons from the relational theory, but controversy persists. Problematic questions include the extent to which (or the occasions on which) contract law should enforce duties of trust and co-operation (ie 'solidarity' or good faith); when it should prioritise implicit expectations and norms over express written terms; and when it should enforce agreements outside the conventional *commercial* sphere. We also outline Macneil's theory's corroboration from field studies of contractors' attitudes and behaviour. Stewart Macaulay, the pioneer of such empirical research, is therefore regarded as the co-founder of relational contract, alongside Macneil. But as for Macneil's theory, even accepting the descriptive accuracy of Macaulay's accounts of real-world contracting practice, the question remains about their true implications for contract law.

A closing section examines reasons for resistance to relational theory. At the end of his career, Macneil expressed disappointment about contract lawyers' reluctance to accept it. But at the very least, his achievement has been to require traditionally-minded lawyers to *justify and defend* contract law's 'discrete' approach. It would be supremely complacent to assume that contract law's traditional approach must always be the right one, having read Macneil's critique.

V. MACNEIL'S 'ESSENTIAL CONTRACT THEORY'

Macneil latterly referred to his approach as 'Essential Contract Theory' (to distinguish it from relational contract more generally). It defies ready summary.

However, some themes of Macneil's theory and his modus operandi can be indicated.

The central point is that *all contracts are made and performed within a framework of broader social relations*. Properly to understand the social phenomenon of contracting and exchange, this must be grasped. The social context surrounding any strict legal obligations generated by the agreement cannot be ignored.

It is relatively easy to see the importance of relationships within complex long-term contracts. In these, a high degree of co-operation and flexibility is needed to bring the parties' joint aims to successful fruition. Such co-operation evolves as the parties work closely together, sharing information and adjusting their working patterns, during ongoing performance. (The corollary is that much of that relationship is not *and cannot be* planned in any detail by a formal agreement at the outset of the relationship.) Such complex contracts are as important as they are common.

Yet even so-called 'discrete' contracts are equally embedded in social relations. The classic example is a one-off sale of a generic commodity (ie something readily priced). The very fact that the parties are exchanging by mutual agreement – as opposed to (say) one of them seizing the other's property – depends on and presupposes a number of social conditions obtaining.[41] The parties must be able to communicate to persuade each other to enter into reciprocal co-operation. A peaceable social order must be in place, to prevent parties simply taking what they want by force.

We habitually neglect these social preconditions for supposedly 'discrete' exchange because we literally take them for granted. Macneil noted about sales – the epitome of the discrete transaction – that lawyers can analyse such transactions in isolation only because we already understand the social context for sales.[42] He regretted that

> behavioral aspects [of contract] are phenomenally easy for most people to overlook. They tend to be taken for granted, taken as given, taken as unimportant, taken as if they were somehow bestowed by nature, taken as free goods – you name it.[43]

A fully 'discrete' contract is in fact the exception rather than the norm. A homely example is shopping in a supermarket. The customer's visit could be viewed in isolation – a one-off transaction, simultaneously made and performed through payment at the checkout. Yet given the likelihood (and immense commercial desirability) of repeat custom, such an isolated analysis would omit much. Supermarkets go to considerable lengths to develop and retain customer loyalty, eg through reward schemes or exchanging undesired goods (beyond the remedies

[41] See, eg, Macneil (1983) (n 20) 344.
[42] Macneil (1985) (n 23) 483.
[43] IR Macneil, 'Relational Contract Theory: Challenges and Queries' (2000) 94 *Northwestern University Law Review* 877, 887 (adding: 'Nowhere is this more true than in the Queen of the Social Sciences, Economics').

provided by law). Macneil noted that while the purchase of shares is often given as a paradigmatic example of a 'discrete' transaction, this is misleading. Stock markets are highly regulated by law, and ongoing relations between brokers and firms are important context for a supposedly isolated sale.

So Macneil emphasised that all contracts must be understood as embedded in wider social relations. He accepted however, that the degree of that embeddedness does vary. There is a spectrum from more 'relational' to more 'discrete' transactions. This emerges clearly from Macneil's consideration of the norms underlying contractual behaviour.[44]

Macneil set out a list of norms that are common to and 'essential to *any* behavior we might be willing to call contractual'.[45] The final catalogue of these was:

> (1) role integrity (requiring consistency, involving internal conflict, and being inherently complex), (2) reciprocity (simply stated as the principle of getting something back for something given), (3) implementation of planning, (4) effectuation of consent, (5) flexibility, (6) contractual solidarity, (7) the restitution, reliance, and expectation interests (the 'linking norms'), (8) creation and restraint of power (the 'power norm'), (9) propriety of means, and (10) harmonization with the social matrix.[46]

Of these Macneil called special attention to *reciprocity* and *solidarity* ('the first among equals in exchange relations').[47] Reciprocity is (no less) the key to resolving an inescapable tension of human existence. People are both entirely selfish and entirely social, at the same time. Thus human behaviour is irretrievably 'irrational' (indeed, Macneil says, 'schizophrenic'). Reciprocity, ie receiving something in exchange for something given, 'neatly releases, or at least eases, the tension'. While exchange can be immediate or simultaneous, in practice many exchanges take place in the future or on an ongoing basis. This is the domain of contract – an exchange of *promises* (promises being a way to project reciprocity forward across time). To make such future projection possible there must be solidarity – ie 'a belief in being able to depend on another'. (In other words, 'solidarity' here connotes trust.) Solidarity is both necessary for exchange, but also grows out of it. As Macneil said: '[The] demands of [social] solidarity are built into exchange itself; the very ways by which people engage in exchange are principal ways of building solidarity. Nor is it possible to continue exchanging without building solidarity'.[48]

[44] See, eg, Macneil (1983) (n 20) 346–66.
[45] *ibid* 346 (emphasis in original).
[46] *ibid* 347 (footnotes omitted); *cf* the list of merely five 'broad principles of contract law' in Macneil (n 19) 808–809; and see for discussion IR Macneil, *The New Social Contract* (New Haven, Yale University Press, 1980) 40–59 (with 'propriety of means' there omitted as a separate category).
[47] IR Macneil, 'Political Exchange as Relational Contract' in Campbell (2001) (n 2) 119.
[48] *ibid* 118–19.

Some of the ten common norms are particularly prominent in 'discrete' contracts and others in more 'relational' contracts. The ideal discrete transaction would isolate the particular exchange from all other relations between the parties, governed exclusively by what was expressly agreed at the outset. The dominant norms here are planning and consent. The contract would ideally plan the transaction exhaustively, dealing with all future questions of performance (or adaptation of performance, or non-performance). The future course of the contract would be mapped out at the initial moment of agreement. (This model is of course familiar to contract lawyers.) Such 'sharply articulated exchange planning' requires that obligations must be monetised, measured and defined with precision, eliminating the need for co-operation or sharing the benefits and burdens of the emerging transaction.[49] Macneil accepted the value of the 'focusing norm' at the core of discrete contracts: 'It enables people to deal precisely with one thing at a time – to keep their eyes on the ball – a vital factor in much human endeavour'.[50] However, the discrete approach comes at a cost. It requires:

> the sacrifice of relational values of many kinds [such as the preservation of the parties' relationship], because it focuses sharply on money and other easy-to-quantify subjects of exchange … and it uses precise promise as a touchstone … [The] intensification of the planning and consent norms in discrete transactions affects the other common contract norms, often drastically.[51]

Macneil uses the term 'presentiation' to describe anticipation of the contract's future at its outset (ie bringing the future into the present). 'Presentiation' is a condition of and indeed another word for that process of planning (we could note that 'presentiation', a baffling term that has not caught on, illustrates the difficulty in much of Macneil's writing). Macneil argued that 'presentiation', although theoretically central to classical contract law, is impossible in practice. Even the simplest transactions 'go far beyond the capacity of bounded rationality to encompass everything in one grand moment of consent' (let alone in complex relationships – imagine 'trying to draft in 1960 a specific contract with the United States Government to put a man on the moon in 1970!').[52] Defining obligations exclusively by the initial agreement is an unobtainable ideal. Every contract must always contain an unplanned part (a gap that contains, at best, an anticipation of future co-operation when unforeseeable contingencies arise). The actual performance of every contract always involves subtle adjustment of it – the fleshing out of inevitably vague standards.[53]

[49] IR Macneil, 'The Many Futures of Contracts' (1974) 47 *Southern California Law Review* 691, 795–96.

[50] Macneil (1980) (n 46) 63.

[51] Macneil (1983) (n 20) 360, 361.

[52] Macneil (1980) (n 46) 62, 47.

[53] Macneil (n 11) 890.

Only legal doctrine provides the 'reservoir of clear, precise content' necessary to fill the gaps that inevitably arise.[54] But only through an 'imaginative array of fictions' can the law's rules be brought into 'the realm of [the parties'] consent'.[55] Macneil accepted that some degree of consent is fundamental to contract, distinguishing contractual from tortious obligations. (He remarked that only consent's complete elimination through bureaucratic central planning could produce 'the death of contract'.)[56] But in complex contracts, Macneil observed that consent is very much less complete than lawyers suppose. It plays 'no more than a triggering role', ie choice at the outset to enter 'a relationship which will involve much else' (imagine an employee starting a new job).[57] Although consent in this attenuated sense remains the hallmark of contract, to postulate consent to 'the full scope of complex planning' for all the details of performance and contingencies (as the law does) was 'downright silly'.

Macneil insisted repeatedly that no contract can be entirely 'discrete': there is '*no such thing* in real life as a discrete transaction'.[58] Full ex ante planning is impossible. The other norms can never be eliminated entirely:

> understanding even heavily transactional [discrete] contracts requires recognition of the factors external to the [express] promise fragment of the transaction ... a full recognition that contracts consist of a variety of components, of which truly communicated promise ... is but one coequal component, and not always even that.[59]

This is even more obvious for more 'relational' transactions. (Macneil once said that 'Relational contract law is so all-pervasive that one feels almost foolish in giving examples' before offering the following from the employment field alone: 'workmen's compensation, numerous antidiscrimination laws, social security taxation and benefits, ... workplace regulations, wage and hours legislation. All of these are relational contract law'.)[60]

Macneil declared his goal was simply descriptive: 'it did not occur to me consciously that I might be developing a theory. Rather, I was simply exploring and trying to make sense of reality, the reality of what people are actually *doing* in the real-life world of exchange'.[61] His sources of that 'reality' appear, to the average contract lawyer, astonishingly wide –almost comically eclectic.[62] As Macneil summed it up:

> [my] exploration has delved into many areas: animal behavior, primitive human behavior, feudal society, England and Scotland from the sixteenth to the eighteenth

[54] Macneil (1980) (n 46) 62.

[55] *ibid* 49; on this *cf* RE Barnett, 'Conflicting Visions: A Critique of Ian Macneil's Relational Theory of Contract' (1992) 78 *Virginia Law Review* 1175.

[56] Macneil (1980) (n 46) 50.

[57] *ibid.*

[58] Macneil (n 43) 896 (emphasis in original).

[59] Macneil (n 49) 734.

[60] Macneil (n 43) 897.

[61] *ibid* 879 (emphasis in original).

[62] Has any other contract lawyer reflected on the altruism of the soldier ant, dying to save its colony? (*cf* Macneil (n 49) 799).

> century, modern East Africa, traditional and modern Polish marriages, political exchange behavior, countless areas of modem socioeconomic life, and even Utopia.[63]

Such a remarkable range of human activity shows that Macneil practised what he preached when he warned that true comprehension:

> exceed[s] the capacities of neoclassical contract law scholars. They must become something else – anthropologists, sociologists, economists, political theorists, and philosophers – to do reasonable justice to the issues raised by contractual relations. Exchange and planning, the basic areas of expertise of the contracts scholar, have now become just two of the many factors in a complete social organism.[64]

(In fact, lawyers were not alone in their blind spot. Macneil complained that most writing about contract, whether by 'legal academics, modern philosophers, or social scientists – especially economists', overlooked 'the real life level of exchange relations', ie their underlying norms and values.)[65]

Macneil's main target was the paradigmatically discrete contract, central to traditional contract *law* (and not-so-traditional Law and Economics). A representative critique:

> Consider such agglomerations of capital and people as corporations, franchises, complex long term supply contracts, families, partnerships, leases, and countless other forms of material relations. In them, reciprocity in the form of exclamation points of 'discrete This for That exchanges', where any exist at all, are merged with more subtle patterns of exchange spread complexly over time …
>
> I turn now to the abstract world of the law …. What a peculiar world is this law of contract! … Upon the sands of this [discrete] abstraction all the other elements of contract law are founded or pretended to be founded. Thus contract law has discarded all the text of human material relations, and retained only the exclamation points! Rarely, if ever, has a major legal conceptualization provided such an incomplete and distorted reflection of the real world to which it relates.
>
> Few today deny the obvious: this abstraction, centred on the exclamation points of discrete exchange, omit vast quantities of the text of the complex material relations in which real people produce, distribute, and use material wealth. And it vastly distorts all the rest.[66]

In the same essay, Macneil pondered why, notwithstanding this 'obvious' truth, barriers to accepting relational contract persisted. Were lawyers brainwashed into accepting the discrete paradigm in their formative education (viz law-school curricula were to blame)? No – the problem was earlier and deeper than that (after all, lawyers constantly discard unrealistic intellectual baggage). Students are acculturated to 'discrete' thinking long before attending law school – by their

[63] Macneil (n 43) 879 (references omitted).
[64] Macneil (1978) (n 20) 898, fn 137 (and repeated in Macneil (1980) (n 46) 70).
[65] Macneil (1983) (n 20) 351.
[66] IR Macneil, 'Barriers to the Idea of Relational Contracts' in Campbell (2001) (n 2) 300–301.

intellectual heritage. The discrete paradigm has dominated western attitudes to contract for centuries. It is consistent with and derived from Hobbes' pessimistic view of human nature in *Leviathan* (1651). Thus, relational theory (ie accurately understanding contract) faces formidable barriers – the need for:

> a fundamental revision for thinking about material relations among people. We must abandon our deepseated conviction that man really is at heart a selfish, nonsocial atom. We must replace it with the conviction that humans are social animals.[67]

Macneil saw his mission as bringing about such a necessary re-education. To emancipate western lawyers and social scientists from their instinctive adherence to the asocial Hobbesian model. In short to 'overcome the impact hundreds of years of history have had on our minds'.[68]

VI. DIFFICULTIES IN APPLYING MACNEIL'S 'ESSENTIAL CONTRACT THEORY'

Relational contract, and Ian Macneil's transformative writing about it, have been much discussed. Noteworthy among numerous contributions are the symposium following Macneil's retirement in 2000,[69] and the 2013 collection of essays in his honour.[70] Stewart Macaulay declares: 'people should not attempt to write about contracts until they have studied Macneil'.[71]

Yet, Macneil's approach and style seem alien to many lawyers. Nor did Macneil precisely specify what the lessons of his Essential Theory were for the law of contract. These difficulties are inherent in the nature of Macneil's project. He obviously did *not* consider himself a 'black-letter lawyer' – departing from the dominant approach to contract law scholarship (in England at least). Considered from the prevailing doctrinal perspective (which was not Macneil's), his scholarship has evident shortcomings. Of course that does not mean Macneil failed in what he set out to achieve. But contract lawyers have struggled to show how contract doctrine should be understood and reformed in the light of Macneil's theory. Such doctrinal scholarship will be considered in the next section. Here we consider reasons for the uncertain reception of Macneil's work. We note stylistic barriers, in addition to Macneil's conscious neglect of contract law doctrine.

First, style. It is telling that even authors who advocate the relational approach (such as Campbell, Feinman and Mitchell) have reservations about how Macneil expressed his ground-breaking ideas. Campbell remarks that

[67] *ibid* 307.
[68] Macneil (1985) (n 23) 485.
[69] (2000) 94 *Northwestern University Law Review* 735–936.
[70] Campbell et al (2013) (n 2).
[71] Macaulay (n 28) 776.

'[Macneil's] imagination is very fecund indeed when it comes to inventing schemes of classification and terms to fill them out' (a specific example being the ten common contract norms, quoted above, which Campbell thinks 'rather elaborate and expressed in terms to which Macneil typically gives rather unconventional meanings').[72] Feinman reports Macneil's limited impact on contract law and scholarship in the US, explicable partly by the unfamiliar vocabulary, style of presentation and complexity of his writing (proceeding from 'highly abstract observations about society and exchange relations within it'), which make it 'difficult to read'.[73]

Catherine Mitchell, another champion of relational contract, also offers equivocal praise. In her monograph, Mitchell concentrates upon Macneil's as 'the most influential, the most original and also the most fully worked-out of all relational theories of contract'.[74] Yet Mitchell accepts that the 'price of [Macneil's] broad engagement with a range of social and contextual factors is indeterminacy and a certain degree of normative emptiness'.[75] We are scarcely reassured to read that 'Macneil was not completely silent on [the] issue of legal reasoning, although his comments are not always helpful or easy to understand'.[76] Not surprisingly, the legal implications of Macneil's theory are 'difficult to tease out'.[77] Mitchell would reform contract law to accommodate relational theory. But she properly concedes that it appears 'radically indeterminate' and 'too amorphous a theory to offer much reliable guidance to a [commercial] judge'.[78]

Nor are objections merely stylistic or terminological. As noted already, doctrinal scholarship was a low priority for Macneil in his mature work (or no priority at all). He focused on providing an accurate account of exchange relations by considering all the human dimensions of real-life contracting behaviour. It seems more a project of sociological description than black-letter analysis. His concern was the practice of contracting rather than contract law itself. And in so far as Macneil built an alternative theory on the rich accounts of contracting behaviour and practice, the impetus was to *uproot and displace* contract law's longstanding 'discrete' paradigm.

The results do not straightforwardly translate into contract doctrine. Macaulay, the friendliest critic imaginable, comments that although 'Macneil's approach has the virtue of avoiding fictions and reflecting actual situations' it

[72] D Campbell, 'Ian Macneil and the Relational Theory of Contract' in Campbell (2001) (n 2) 46–47. *cf* a slimmed-down, non-repetitious account: R Austen-Baker, 'Comprehensive Contract Theory: A Four-Norm Model of Contractual Relations' (2009) 25 *Journal of Contract Law* 216.

[73] JM Feinman, 'The Reception of Ian Macneil's Work on Contract in the USA' in Campbell (2001) (n 2) 63.

[74] C Mitchell, *Contract Law and Contract Practice: Bridging the Gap between Legal Reasoning and Commercial Expectations* (Oxford, Hart Publishing, 2013) 171.

[75] *ibid* 181.

[76] *ibid* 182.

[77] *ibid* 183.

[78] *ibid* 196–97.

'[does] not offer elegant models of contracting behavior. You get a story and multiple factors to consider, but not a simple formula that produces results'.[79]

Macaulay quotes Unger's observation that theorists must choose how much complex descriptive fidelity to sacrifice to simplicity of explanation, according to the theorist's aims.[80] For Macneil it seems that faithful description was paramount, however unwieldy the results. For those with other priorities, Macneil's choice will appear unhelpful. One trying to formulate rules of contract law will reasonably complain that 'amorphous social inquiry' 'does not yield determinate legal principles' and Macneil's 'particulistic' approach would exceed the capacity of courts to apply.[81] Campbell defends Macneil: the strength of traditional 'formally abstract' legal accounts is their resulting clarity of explanation – but at what cost if those abstractions 'fasten on very little that exists in the real world of contract'?[82]

Macneil consistently prioritised that 'real world' over legal abstractions. In his first casebook (1968), Macneil announced his concern with contracts and not (as in standard texts) 'the law as defined by the outcome of contract litigation', warning that 'Contracts and contract litigation are not the same thing'.[83] Thus, Macneil rejected the common lawyer's basic assumption. Nor was the disjunction between formal law and actual practice his only objection to traditional accounts. Macneil also rejected the assumption that 'the law of contract litigation is a relatively neat and logical structure of rules'.[84] The determinacy of the traditional 'discrete' law of contract was overstated. Campbell notes the expanding complexity of post-war contract law, arguing that it has resulted from 'desperate' attempts to accommodate the issues posed by relational contracts – at best a very awkward fit. Campbell suggests that Macneil's reason for 'not [paying] particular attention to these doctrinal shifts' is that he thought them 'superficial responses to the failures of the classical law'[85] – there was little value in considering doctrinal elaboration of contract law's 'present unrealistic framework'.[86] Hence Macneil's concern with contract law's underlying theoretical basis rather than its doctrinal superstructure.

[79] Macaulay (n 28) 775, 779, 782.

[80] RM Unger, *Law in Modern Society: Toward a Criticism of Social Theory* (New York, Free Press, 1976) 11–12.

[81] MJ Trebilcock, *The Limits of Freedom of Contract* (Cambridge MA, Harvard University Press, 1993) 141.

[82] Campbell (n 72) 33.

[83] IR Macneil, 'Contracts Instruments for Social Cooperation in East Africa' in Campbell (2001) (n 2) 352.

[84] *ibid.*

[85] *cf* Macneil's dismissal of supposed innovators ('Fuller, Llewellyn, the [Uniform Commercial Code], Justice Traynor, *Restatement (Second)*, promissory estoppel, Lord Denning and heaven knows who and what else') when compared with static contract textbooks / curricula (Macneil (n 49) 805, fn 320).

[86] Campbell (n 72) 26–27.

Macneil's uninterest in legal doctrine cannot be denied. It is manifest throughout his work on relational contract. Notably, Macneil felt obliged to add a 'postscript' to his seminal article 'The Many Futures of Contracts', already over 100 pages long, to address draft-readers' 'expressed discontent with the absence of some normative or other connection of the [article's] conceptualizations with the real world'.[87] Macneil found it problematic to draw normative implications from an essay whose main goal was 'to free contract from the myth of pure transactionism which so dominates many current concepts'. He offered a 'skeletal' analysis of just two indicative examples. Twenty five years later, in a reflective contribution published at the end of his career, Macneil was no more confident about concrete recommendations for contract doctrine. He noted only the Essential Theory's:

> somewhat general assumption that typically the law will more or less track the common contract behavior and norms. This should not, however, be overread. There may often be good reasons why the law should not track the common contract behavior and norms.[88]

Macneil accepted that a transaction might properly be analysed *as if it were* discrete. 'However important openness to change is in economic relations, there will nevertheless always be a great need for fixed and reliable planning.'[89] To ram home the point that his reluctance was deliberate and not some careless oversight, Macneil added this remarkable statement:

> I challenge to a duel anyone who ... persists in converting my descriptions of relational contract law into prescriptions of what the law should be, particularly prescriptions of some universal application of relational contract law.[90]

VII. ATTEMPTS TO APPLY MACNEIL'S THEORY TO THE LAW OF CONTRACT

Notwithstanding the warning just quoted, many writers have attempted to draw the contours of a relational contract law. The broad outline might appear obvious. But any 'universal' or undifferentiated application of relational doctrine would go further than Macneil himself advocated. In truth there is no absolute binary choice between 'relational' and 'discrete'. Macneil did employ the terms as a contrasting pair. But they were labels for opposite points of a spectrum. The 'sliding scale' must be appreciated. We then see that the question for contract law is not, after all, 'relational or not?' The correct questions are – *how* relational? For *which* contracts? And *who decides*?

[87] Macneil (n 49) 806, see 'Postscript' 805–16.

[88] Macneil (n 43) 893, see further 900: 'I have long recognized limitations on this idea. Nonetheless, it seemed to me a generally sound notion'.

[89] *ibid* 895, fn 69. See, eg, Macneil (1980) (n 46) 63; Macneil (1978) (n 20) 893–94 (considering when 'classical notions [of contract law] may very properly be applied').

[90] Macneil (n 43) 899.

This set of questions does not yield a single clear-cut answer, valid across the board. That is another reason why Macneil's theory does not translate straightforwardly into legal doctrine. Before exploring these nuances and complications, we outline the powerful critique of 'discrete' contract law that Macneil's Essential Theory is taken to provide.

Relational theory contrasts sharply with the classical law (and its underlying assumptions). First, over the insistence that no contract can be properly understood except within the social context of the parties' ongoing relationship. Second, in the centrality of 'solidarity' (or co-operation or trust). The divergence from classical contract law could not be greater. Traditional doctrine emphasises the primacy of the document or text in determining – indeed exhausting – the meaning and content of the parties' agreement; and within the outer limits of force and fraud does not attempt to regulate opportunism ('The question is not what a man of scrupulous morality or nice honour would do …'). There is certainly no attempt to enforce trust or co-operation as a matter of course – no general doctrine of good faith (which would be 'repugnant to the inherently adversarial position of negotiating parties'). In English law at least, such a sketch is by no means caricature. (The dicta parenthetically quoted are of course from leading English cases.)[91]

It is often thought that these 'classical' notions must be discarded, given the relational theory. Feinman accepts the difficulty of translating relational theory into contract doctrine. The practical application of Macneil's abstract scholarship 'is not immediately obvious … and Macneil himself has not devoted much effort to that side of the project, considering how the work might be applied to doctrinal problems'.[92] Furthermore, Macneil's method of analysing relations within the abstract structure of the contract norms 'leads substantially, if not totally, to a rejection of doctrinal method as it is ordinarily practiced, in favor of a method that looks much more like policy analysis'.[93] Still, Feinman suggests, if relational theory is conceived more loosely as an alternative *structure of argument* rather than a rival set of precise rules, it offers a 'competing general account […] of the sources and nature of obligation in contract law'. It emphasises 'the necessity and desirability of trust, mutual responsibility, and connection. Not all of these bonds should be legally enforceable, but beginning analysis by recognizing them is likely to produce a broader set of obligations'.[94]

Others derive more concrete prescriptions from both the main relational norms (context; solidarity). For example, Campbell has long argued that contract law must recognise and enforce the mutual trust and cooperation

[91] Respectively *Smith v Hughes* (1871) LR 6 QB 597, 603 (Cockburn CJ) and *Walford v Miles* [1992] 2 AC 128 (HL) 138 (Lord Ackner).

[92] Feinman (n 73) 63.

[93] JM Feinman, 'Relational Contract Theory in Context' (2000) 94 *Northwestern University Law Review* 737, 743.

[94] *ibid* 748.

that is essential to all contracts (Macneil's 'solidarity').[95] This received important English recognition in the *Yam Seng* case. Leggatt J reasoned that many contracts involving more than a simple exchange (ie in the judge's words 'relational contracts')

> may require a high degree of communication, co-operation and predictable performance based on mutual trust and confidence and involve expectations of loyalty which are not legislated for in the express terms of the contract but are implicit in the parties' understanding and necessary to give business efficacy to the arrangements.[96]

From this premise the Court derived (and enforced) an implied obligation of good faith performance of a distributorship contract. Campbell naturally welcomes judicial acceptance of the 'ubiquity' of good faith. He comments that Leggatt J's reasoning:

> captured what Macneil fundamentally wanted to argue in the relational theory of contract: all contracts are relational in the sense that no contract is the product only of the agreement of the parties but rather is a fundamentally co-operative exchange relationship ... Contracting can take place only within a framework of implicit duties of respect for each party's autonomy which institutionalises that co-operation.[97]

Campbell argues that even cases emblematic of English law's 'individualistic' tradition should properly be understood as relational contracts.[98]

Richard Speidel, another longstanding enthusiast,[99] also argues that contract law should be transformed by Macneil's insights. (Despite conceding that notwithstanding the 'vast and varied literature ... there is still disagreement among the theorists about ... what modern contract law can or should do to respond to it [the relational theory]'.)[100] Speidel's thesis indicates how far a relational duty of good faith might need to go. In his view, what contract law 'can and should do' is to preserve the commercial relationships on which all contracts rest.[101] Speidel first advises how those drafting long-term contracts can 'facilitate governance of the exchange relationship'. But whether the drafters have done this or not, courts hearing disputes about relational contracts should intervene to deter opportunism. Self-interested behaviour threatens the

[95] eg, D Campbell and D Harris, 'Flexibility in Long-term Contractual Relationships: The Role of Co-operation' (1993) 20 *Journal of Law & Society* 166; D Campbell, 'The Relational Constitution of the Discrete Contract' in D Campbell and P Vincent-Jones (eds), *Contract and Economic Organisation* (Aldershot, Dartmouth, 1996).

[96] *Yam Seng Pte Ltd v International Trade Corporation Ltd* [2013] EWHC 111 (QB), [2013] 1 Lloyd's Rep 526 [142].

[97] D Campbell, 'Good Faith and the Ubiquity of the Relational Contract' (2014) 77 *MLR* 475, 482.

[98] D Campbell, '*Arcos v Ronaasen* as a Relational Contract' in Campbell et al (2013) (n 2); D Campbell, 'Adam Smith and the Social Foundation of Agreement: *Walford v Miles* as a Relational Contract' (2017) 21 *Edinburgh Law Review* 376.

[99] See, eg, RE Speidel, 'Court-Imposed Price Adjustments under Long-Term Supply Contracts' (1981) 76 *Northwestern University Law Review* 369.

[100] Speidel (n 40) 824.

[101] *ibid* (passim).

relationship because it violates the 'primary norms of reciprocity and solidarity or the supplementary norms of cooperation or risk sharing'. Indeed, courts should uphold contracts wherever possible. Speidel commends one US court's solution to a dispute about pricing within a long-term contract for carriage: the Court determined a reasonable price for the disputed shipment and ordered the parties to undertake mediation to agree on future prices.[102] For Speidel, '[a] better example of a relational default rule cannot be imagined' than the unprecedented order to mediate.[103] Speidel's general conclusion is that good faith duties (already well-established in US law) should be expanded with the goal of 'facilitating continuing negotiation and agreed adjustment under a contract that is preserved for that purpose'. Such preservation 'protects the transaction-specific investments, preserves expectations, and avoids disrupting relationships that have developed between the parties to the long-term contract'.[104]

Macneil would apparently go even further.[105] Macneil considered how courts should resolve disputes about long-term contracts. He envisaged not just different substantive rules but novel procedures and a radically different judicial role. By contrast with the traditional significance given to the parties' initial agreement:

> In a truly relational approach the reference point is the entire relation as it had developed to the time of the change ... This may or may not include an 'original agreement'; and if it does, may or may not result in great deference being given it.

The parties' formal contract could, perhaps, be seen as the 'constitution' for the commercial relationship – but Macneil was cautious about this. It would be 'relationally dysfunctional' to use that concept 'to resurrect "constitutions" long decayed and made obsolete by less formally established patterns of communications and behaviour'. (If valid, note that the 'constitution' idea imports a distinctive interpretive approach, consistent with Marshall CJ's famous admonition: 'we must never forget that it is a *constitution* we are expounding'.[106])

Macneil's view of procedure also suggests a 'public law' reorientation. He argued that classic adversarial litigation was unsuitable for relational adjustment. Its aim is to *end* the parties' relationship. A relational court should instead follow Chayes' celebrated model of 'public law litigation'.[107] Rather than issuing traditional one-off awards compensating past wrongs (ie breach of contract), the relational court would undertake 'continuing administration' of the commercial relationship. Its decisions would be 'in great (or even entire)

[102] *Ogelbay Norton Co v Armco Inc* 556 NE 2d 515 (Ohio 1990).
[103] Speidel (n 40) 837.
[104] *ibid* 839.
[105] For the points in the next two paragraphs, see Macneil (1978) (n 20) 854.
[106] *McCulloch v Maryland* 17 US (4 Wheat) 316 (1819) (emphasis in original).
[107] A Chayes, 'The Role of the Judge in Public Law Litigation' (1976) 89 *Harvard Law Review* 1281.

measure forwardlooking, fashioned ad hoc on flexible and broadly remedial lines … not imposed but negotiated and mediated'.[108]

Courts would not merely adjudicate about historical breaches. Their role instead becomes a 'legislative' one (for the parties). Procedures would no longer be 'rigidly bilateral', but 'sprawling and amorphous'. Such an expanded function for the court was necessary because:

> 'As contractual relations expand, those relations take on more and more the characteristics of minisocieties and ministates … [with] such broad norms as distributive justice, liberty, human dignity, social equality and inequality, and procedural justice'.[109]

A novel approach (of the 'ongoing-administrative kind') was needed to enforce this 'vast array of norms'.

Thus, Macneil's emphasis on solidarity and trust in ongoing relations could justify far-reaching legal intervention. This could range from the relatively modest *Yam Seng* doctrine (conceptualised in classical fashion as a term implied by the parties' intentions),[110] right up to Speidel's and Macneil's more extravagant recommendations. Macneil especially envisaged a transformation not only in the law of contract, but the very nature of the judicial role. It may not be unfair to identify a characteristic combination of the radical and the vague. As Whitford commented:

> Macneil himself rarely states his specific views about the desirable content of positive law. Certainly Macneil believes the legal system needs to take radically different approaches … [He] counsels greater reliance on proactive administrative agencies that can take account of the many third-party interests at stake and less reliance on courts able to apply regulatory rules only when a disadvantaged party initiates a court procedure. Absent such big changes, however, Macneil rarely indicates how courts should decide cases …[111]

Relational theory's other major tenet holds that relational norms are *every* contract's context. No contract can properly be understood as 'discrete', ie acontextually, aside from the relationship in which it is embedded. The relational theory is 'contextual with a vengeance'.[112] The lesson for contract law again seems clear, and transformative. The text of a formal written contract should no longer be the exclusive nor even the major source of the parties' agreement. The relational context should, wherever necessary, supplement or even override what the formal text says.[113] This would entail major reforms to English law, where

[108] Macneil (1978) (n 20) 892.
[109] *ibid* 898.
[110] For criticism see H Collins, 'Implied Terms: The Foundation in Good Faith and Fair Dealing' (2014) 67 *Current Legal Problems* 297.
[111] Whitford (n 36) 551–52.
[112] Feinman (n 93) 742.
[113] H Collins, *Regulating Contracts* (Oxford, Oxford University Press, 1999) ch 7.

the signature rule and (to some degree) presumption of written exclusivity still prevail.[114] Yet English law seeks to uphold contracting parties' reasonable expectations – it is a matter of pride for the courts to keep contract law consistent with commercial practice and commercial needs.[115] Moreover, on the central question of how written contracts are interpreted and understood, English courts now place greater emphasis on the agreement's context. While the nature, extent and even the basic desirability of the change in interpretive practice has produced heated judicial (and extrajudicial) controversy,[116] the direction of travel has tended towards 'committed contextualism'.[117] This too would appear consistent with the relational theory. As Stewart Macaulay argues, relational contract prioritises agreements' 'implicit dimensions' over formal documents ('the real deal' not the 'paper deal').[118]

Again however, the implications of Macneil's work are not as clear-cut as it might seem. For Macneil accepted that sometimes contracts should legitimately be analysed as if they were 'discrete'. There are situations in which the contractors properly wish to prioritise the norms of planning ('presentiation') – precisely to give the formal contract dispositive status over any disputes. Macneil's concession still differs from classical contract law which assumed (incorrectly) that in *every* case 'discrete' norms predominate. Macneil argued that a prior question must be posed (and answered only by examining the whole course of a given contractual relationship) – viz 'do the formal [contractual] communications indeed reflect the sharp past focus and strong intentions necessary to put these communications high in the priorities of values created by the contractual relation?'[119]

Macaulay acknowledges the resulting problem:

> Macneil has pointed out that there are situations where it is in the interest of the parties, and even perhaps of the economy as a whole, where the law should treat parties as if their relationship was discrete and entirely contained within the borders of a written document. The task is to identify such situations.[120]

[114] For criticism, see, eg, G McMeel, 'Documentary Fundamentalism in the Senior Courts: The Myth of Contractual Estoppel' [2011] *Lloyd's Maritime and Commercial Law Quarterly* 185.

[115] Lord Steyn, 'Contract Law: Fulfiling the Reasonable Expectations of Honest Men' (1997) 113 *LQR* 433.

[116] See, eg, J Sumption, 'A Question of Taste: The Supreme Court and the Interpretation of Contracts' (2017) 17 *Oxford University Commonwealth Law Journal* 301; L Hoffmann, 'Language and Lawyers' (2018) 134 *LQR* 553.

[117] H Collins, 'Objectivity and Committed Contextualism in Interpretation' in S Worthington (ed), *Commercial Law and Commercial Practice* (Oxford, Hart Publishing, 2003). See further, eg, J Wightman, 'Contract in a Pre-Realist World: Prof Macaulay, Lord Hoffmann and the Rise of Context in the English Law of Contract' in J Braucher et al (eds), *Revisiting the Contracts Scholarship of Stewart Macaulay* (Oxford, Hart Publishing, 2013).

[118] S Macaulay, 'The Real and the Paper Deal: Empirical Pictures of Relationships, Complexity and the Urge for Transparent Simple Rules' (2003) 66 *MLR* 44.

[119] Macneil (1978) (n 20) 894.

[120] Macaulay (n 118) 70.

And the task is not easy. Macaulay notes that any categorical distinction between (say) consumer and commercial contracts would be too crude; it is hard to imagine that no commercial contacts are ever understood relationally. Macaulay frames the question in somewhat tendentious terms, 'The hard part … is deciding when courts should honor the work of a corporate lawyer which she has labeled "contract" when there is only second class consent, if that'.[121] Not surprisingly, Macaulay leans towards a contextual solution. Any 'formalist' adherence to the 'paper deal', he warns, runs 'the real risk of defeating actual reasonable expectations of bargainers'. Quite apart from thwarting their expectations, the law's very legitimacy is endangered if it 'comes to symbolise that contract rests on manipulations of forms and courts reject the substance of the real deal'.[122] However, Macaulay's criticism fails to bite where party expectations actually are 'formalist' or 'documentary'. As Macneil and Macaulay both accept, formalism is the proper context for analysing *some* contracts.

Identifying those situations may be still harder than Macaulay allows. Mitchell criticises Macaulay's either/ or choice between 'real and paper deals'.[123] In many situations, parties simultaneously use *both* frames to understand their agreement. Mitchell identifies various functions performed by contractual documents in commercial practice. Given these functions, to enforce the documentary contract cannot simply be dismissed as 'stiff and superstitious formalism' (as a committed contextualist might say).[124]

An interim conclusion: there are many obstacles to a 'relational law of contract'. These go beyond Macneil's studied obscurity on the details of legal doctrine. There are limits in the very nature of legal process (adversarial litigation) that obstruct its usefulness in supporting trust and co-operation. The context of an agreement is important – a point now universally acknowledged. But that cannot justify ignoring formal written contracts entirely. As Macneil accepted, sometimes a relationship is best understood through the planned formal transaction – viz by enforcing the contract documents. Not surprisingly, Macneil tartly rejected suggestions that he had recommended the '*universal* application of relational contract law'.

VIII. THE DOMAIN OF RELATIONAL THEORY: CONTRACTS COMMERCIAL AND PERSONAL

A further controversy concerns the relational theory's legal reach. Macneil's writing considered a wide range of human activity. His theory ranges far beyond

[121] *ibid* 66.
[122] *ibid* 79.
[123] C Mitchell, 'Contracts and Contract Law: Challenging the Distinction between the "Real" and "Paper" Deal' (2009) 29 *OJLS* 675.
[124] D Nicholls, 'My Kingdom for a Horse' (2005) 121 *LQR* 577 (quoting *Wigmore on Evidence*).

the *commercial* transactions at contract law's core. Should the law expand its definition of 'contract' to include non-commercial forms of exchange? Macneil was (again) not explicit on this point. Yet there are important arguments against expanding contract law's jurisdiction. It could be downright harmful (not to say difficult) to 'judicialise' certain relational norms. Can important human institutions like reciprocal gift-giving, or trust and co-operation, function properly when enforced by coercive legal sanctions (rather than social bonds)? There may be good reason for the boundaries of contract *law* to be more tightly drawn than the social category of 'exchange'. Legal enforcement could disrupt and undermine the relevant social norms. At least it cannot be assumed that every social norm requires, or would benefit from, translation into a legal obligation.

Macneil's ambition was identified by Feinman:

> [Macneil] brings within the scope of contract relations those activities that have economic aspects but that are not primarily economic, such as family relations. Relational contract, therefore, is willing to treat an astonishingly wide range of transactions as subject to the same body of theory.[125]

Macneil's reflections on the family and early human societies were significant for his development of the foundational contract norms. Macneil maintained that the values governing contractual relations cannot be reduced solely to monetary value (the profit motive) – not even for contracts in a modern economy. Does this wide theory translate into a broader scope for contract law? Some commentators indicate that it might. Whitford argues that economic factors are only a partial explanation for Macneil's 'recurrent assertion that parties to relational contracts desire to preserve their relationship'.[126] Certain economic incentives do point towards relationship-preservation: the expense of switching suppliers (etc) when understandings have developed with existing commercial partners, and other relationship-specific ('idiosyncratic') investments. Yet this is not the whole story. There is a human dimension too. Someone operating a business franchise sees it as their life's work and part of their identity – the termination of the franchise would therefore involve 'emotional costs well beyond the wealth costs of establishing a new career'. (A point widely accepted regarding dismissal from employment.) Whitford argues that a contractual relationship's values 'beyond wealth' should be considered in disputes about termination, despite this complicating the legal analysis.

Macneil certainly stressed that relational contract values go beyond the narrowly financial. But he angrily denied Teubner's charge that the Essential Theory was 'romantic yearning for a mediaeval unity of the *buon governo*', the unrealistic advocacy of 'the warm, human, co-operative interpersonal relation that overcomes … cold economic instrumentalism with a communitarian

[125] Feinman (n 93) 741.
[126] Whitford (n 36) 550.

orientation'.[127] Macneil rejected this 'distortion'. The Essential Theory attempted only to describe contractual relations accurately, 'as socially neutral as is humanly possible'.[128] If his work had been perceived as *other* than neutral, this demonstrated, rather, the incompleteness of conventional 'discrete' accounts of contract. Received thinking grossly distorted the nature of contracting by 'the exclusion of highly relevant humanitarian factors'. Macneil's concern was simply to 'render humanitarian factors existing in a contractual relation visible to the eye ... rendering visible what is largely invisible in discretist models'.[129] Macneil added (characteristically) that the Essential Theory 'compels no particular conclusions about how to deal with what is revealed'.

Macneil's emphasis on the non-economic values of exchange coheres with his critique of Law and Economics. In contrast with his uninterest in contract doctrine, Macneil devoted considerable energy to attacking 'neoclassical' Law and Economics (perhaps perceiving it as a more important intellectual foundation of the 'discrete' attitude to contract).[130] It can scarcely be denied that the abstract models of such economic analysis leave out much, ie that which cannot be monetised and quantified. Nor was Macneil impressed by economists' attempts to incorporate the realities of contracting behaviour into their models as 'transaction costs'. This was selectively rather than consistently done (and without any empirical basis). Macneil used such criticisms to devastating effect in 'Efficient Breach of Contract: Circles in the Sky'.[131] Macneil there argued persuasively that the most famous of all economic analysis of contract law was a giant exercise in begging the question. Breach of contract was asserted to be 'efficient' purely because breach was *assumed* to be a less costly means for transferring performance, compared to negotiating an agreed release with the original promisee. Well, is that not precisely the comparison that needs to be undertaken (and empirically, rather than deductively)?[132]

The wider debate about the merits of Law and Economics lies outside the scope of this chapter. Macneil's preoccupation with it seems surprising to lawyers in England, where economic analysis has had so little traction that English theorists scarcely bother to oppose it. Of course US legal academia is quite different. It should be noted that one important strand of economics has sought to grapple with Macneil's sort of question: why and when do actors choose to structure their enterprises using depersonalised markets ('discrete' contracts in Macneil's terminology), or long-term contractual arrangements ('relational' contracts), or

[127] G Teubner, 'Contracting Worlds: The Many Autonomies of Private Law' (2000) 9 *Social & Legal Studies* 399, 405.

[128] Macneil (2003) (n 15) 213.

[129] *ibid* 215.

[130] D Campbell, 'Ian Macneil and the Relational Theory of Contract' in Campbell (2001) (n 2) 29.

[131] Macneil (n 22).

[132] *cf* W Farnsworth, 'Do Parties to Nuisance Cases Bargain after Judgment – A Glimpse Inside the Cathedral' (1999) 66 *University of Chicago Law Review* 373.

full integration inside one business ('bureaucracy'). This is uncatchily known as the 'New Institutional Economics'. One leading work's title shows the debt to Macneil's ideas: Oliver Williamson's *The Economic Institutions of Capitalism: Firms, Markets, Relational Contracting*.[133]

Nevertheless, the common law of contract's commercial orientation has deep historical roots[134] – it is not some recent invention of Posnerian Law and Economics (Macneil's primary target). In so far as the emergent sixteenth-century action for assumpsit had any general theory of contractual obligation, it was the doctrine of consideration. This required exchange in a narrowly economic sense. Promises made through gratitude, family ties, moral obligation were deliberately ruled out as 'lacking consideration'. The later doctrine of 'intention to create legal relations' was invented in the early twentieth century to perform much the same function – to keep family agreements (even when cast in financially-reciprocal form) outside the law's jurisdiction.[135] While some 'deletions' of heavily relational areas from the general law of contract (eg insurance or employment law) are recent and statutory, the common law's decidedly *commercial* core is longstanding.

Macneil's definition of 'relational contract' clearly contains much that is not currently contract law's concern (consider Feinman's summary above). Should the law expand to enforce the whole sweep of 'relational contracting'? Yet again, the answer is far from clear. Randy Barnett complains:

> Macneil has adamantly refused to offer his own principled, or at least discernable, distinction between those Macneilian contractual exchanges that merit legal protection and those that do not. This is, however, one of the singular problems that contract theory, as opposed to a more general social theory of exchange, attempts to address.[136]

Macneil's 'overencompassing conception of contract' results from an 'antipathy for providing guidance as to when legal enforcement will result from exchange activity'. Such lack of guidance is problematic. As Barnett says, those engaged in exchange activity should be able to discover whether it generates *legal* obligations – risking 'the weight of legal coercion'. Barnett does not define the limits of contract law himself. (It is a familiar feature of 'Macneil studies' that commentators lament Macneil's incomplete analysis, but do not supply the omission.) Barnett comments merely that 'freedom *from* contract' is an important liberal principle and Macneil overlooks 'the danger of contractual overenforcement – that is, the [legal] enforcement of commitments that ought not be enforced'.[137]

[133] O Williamson, *The Economic Institutions of Capitalism: Firms, Markets, Relational Contracting* (New York, Free Press, 1985).
[134] See J Morgan, 'Bargain' in W Swain and D Campbell (eds), *Reconsidering Contract Law Pedagogy* (Abingdon, Routledge, 2019).
[135] *Balfour v Balfour* [1919] 2 KB 571 (CA).
[136] Barnett (n 55) 1190.
[137] *ibid* 1197.

The common law's commitment to a narrow economic definition of 'contract' has a long pedigree. But that is not a decisive answer to Macneil's challenge. Errors can persist for years or even centuries – and of course Macneil identified society's longstanding assumptions about 'discrete' exchange as a central problem. But the outer limits of the law of contract have received stout defence. The law's commercial focus is not a historical anomaly. Nathan Oman advances a case for the civilising virtues of markets and commercial law (which takes seriously, as Macneil did, the non-financial interests in contractual relations).[138] Melvin Eisenberg, moreover, argues that gift promises are correctly excluded from contract law's scope.[139] Eisenberg contends that it would 'impoverish' gift-giving to make such promises legally enforceable when 'much of the world of gift is driven by affective considerations like love, affection, friendship, gratitude, and comradeship' – and not the desire for profitable trading. Eisenberg is therefore critical of the over-generality of Macneil's theory:

> [Macneil's] massive contractualization of human relationships undesirably obscures critical differences between economic and affective relationships, between explicit and tacit reciprocity, between relationships that should be enforceable by both law and social norms and relationships that should be enforceable only by social norms, and between relationships that are triggered by promise and relationships that are not.[140]

A well-known encapsulation of relational contract states that 'parties treat their contracts more like marriages than like one-night stands'.[141] In each, commitments evolve over time:

> are not frozen at the initial moment of [contracting], but change as circumstances change; the object of contracting is not primarily to allocate risks, but to signify a commitment to cooperate. In bad times parties are expected to lend one another mutual support.[142]

All this is true of contractual relations, and now widely accepted. Yet the marital metaphor again suggests caution about the role of contract *law*.

In actual marriages, the law does not attempt positively to enforce the spirit of harmony, love and compromise that undoubtedly underlies every successful marital partnership.[143] How could this be done? Would compromise imposed on pain of legal sanction anyway be the same thing as voluntary compromises

[138] NB Oman, *The Dignity of Commerce: Markets and the Moral Foundations of Contract Law* (Chicago, University of Chicago Press, 2016).
[139] MA Eisenberg, 'The World of Contract and the World of Gift' (1997) 85 *California Law Review* 821.
[140] MA Eisenberg, 'Why There is No Law of Relational Contracts' (2000) 94 *Northwestern University Law Review* 805, 820.
[141] RW Gordon, 'Macaulay, Macneil, and the Discovery of Solidarity and Power in Contract Law' (1985) *Wisconsin Law Review* 565, 569.
[142] *ibid*.
[143] ES Scott and RE Scott, 'Marriage as Relational Contract' (1998) 84 *Virginia Law Review* 1225.

between spouses? The melancholy fact is that we do not have a law of *marriage* in the relevant sense – only a law of divorce. And while some aspects of divorce law might be designed to encourage reconciliation (or at least to discourage over-hasty dissolution), its primary purpose is to disentangle the partners' intertwined financial and parental rights and responsibilities – to wind up the marriage as a going concern. Although all contracts are relational, and in this resemble marriages, the law of contract deals with breach – divorce – rather than mutual support and co-operation when times are good.

The scope of the law of contract has not expanded to encompass the whole sweep of 'relational contracting'. There seems little appetite for an enlarged jurisdiction. The challenge posed by Macneil's theory is to explain why not. Quite apart from the deep historical roots of contract law's commercial focus, contemporary scholarship has questioned the feasibility and the wisdom of legal enforcement of the relational contract norms. Discussion of the marriage 'contract' makes the point most clearly. It is a paradigm 'relational contract'. But the law has not attempted positively to enforce the norms of solidarity, flexibility, sharing, etc that (without question) govern flourishing spousal partnerships. First it is practically impossible to prove ('verify') to an outsider, like the court, what precise norms have developed within a particular marriage, and who bears primary responsibility for their breach. Second, it is hard to see that the court could by coercive orders restore the solidarity lost in broken marriages. One cannot just order people to trust each other. And that seems as true for commercial partners as for life-partners.

IX. EMPIRICAL EVIDENCE FOR RELATIONAL CONTRACTING

As this chapter suggests, describing relational contract theory is more like traversing the labyrinth of Knossos than strolling down the High at Oxford. Amid the many controversies, most would agree that alongside Macneil's contribution relational theory's second major thread is empirical research into contracting practice, pioneered by Stewart Macaulay.[144] While a detailed account of Macaulay's contribution would be out of place here, we focus on its interaction with (and contrasts with) Macneil's work. The appraisals by Robert Scott and David Campbell are noteworthy.[145] From different starting points these commentators argue that the upshot of Macneil's and Macaulay's ideas is not the irrelevance of the law of contract, but the need for a different, more differentiated contract law. In short, one comprising both 'discrete' and 'relational' rules.

[144] See D Campbell (ed), *Stewart Macaulay: Selected Works* (Cham, Springer, 2020).

[145] RE Scott, 'The Promise and Peril of Relational Contract Theory' and D Campbell, 'What Do We Mean by the Non-Use of Contract?' in J Braucher et al (eds), *Revisiting the Contracts Scholarship of Stewart Macaulay* (Oxford, Hart Publishing, 2013).

Macneil confessed that his relational theory lacked direct empirical support. Despite its genesis in reflection about the social practice of exchange relationships, he had not directly tested its precepts empirically. However, he defended the importance of 'casually empirical' human knowledge.[146] Whitford notes that it would be impossible to test empirically such a wide-ranging account of human behaviour as Macneil's theory.[147] Nonetheless, Macneil's approach receives important if indirect support from studies of contracting practice – the empirical complement to Macneil's abstract theory.[148] Macneil and Macaulay are often hailed together as relational contract theory's co-founders.[149]

Stewart Macaulay's 'Non-contractual relations in business: A preliminary study' is among the most famous contract articles.[150] It is the 'foundation of what is now known as relational contract theory'.[151] Other empirical studies have followed. Space (and our focus on Macneil) rules out a detailed account.[152] Broadly speaking, the empirical research shows that contract *law* plays a far less significant role in business deals than one would expect (if one were a traditional scholar of contract law). Extra-legal norms by comparison prove more significant than lawyers might have expected. Does this confirm 'the Death of Contract'? Grant Gilmore attempted to invest Macaulay as the 'Lord High Executioner' of that movement[153] – but Macaulay declined to accept, arguing that contracting was alive and well in the real world: only *academic* contract was dying.[154]

The empirical picture supports Macneil's theory of relational contract – and Macneil's disparagement of classical contract law. Studies have found innumerable contracts, embedded in commercial relationships and governed by social norms, where the law of contract is more or less irrelevant to them, even alien. But we should hesitate before concluding that the 'non-use' of contract law is a *problem* to be addressed by making the law 'relational'. The research does not find that contract law is never used at all. As Macaulay suggested in his great paper of 1963, we must also ask when and why contractors still use the law.

[146] Macneil (1985) (n 23) 510, fn 115.
[147] Whitford (n 36) 559
[148] Campbell (n 144) 172.
[149] See, eg, Gordon (n 141).
[150] S Macaulay, 'Non-Contractual Relations in Business: A Preliminary Study' (1963) 28 *American Sociological Review* 55.
[151] Scott (n 145) 105.
[152] See, eg, H Beale and T Dugdale, 'Contracts Between Businessmen: Planning and the Use of Contractual Remedies' (1975) 2 *British Journal of Law & Society* 45; J Armour and S Deakin, 'Norms in Private Insolvency: The "London Approach" to the Resolution of Financial Distress' (2001) 1 *Journal of Corporate Legal Studies* 21.
[153] G Gilmore, *The Death of Contract* (Columbus, Ohio University Press, 1974) 113.
[154] 'Steward Macaulay', University of Wisconsin-Madison Law School: https://secure.law.wisc.edu/profiles/smacaula@wisc.edu. See further EL Rubin, 'The Nonjudicial Life of Contract: Beyond the Shadow of the Law' (1995) 90 *Northwestern University Law Review* 107, 131 ('There is a vast world of commercial relations … waiting outside the judiciary's narrow chambers … [and] we must venture forth into that world if we want to avoid the charnel house of intellectual irrelevance').

The studies suggest a perhaps surprising degree of non-use of contract law. But not total desuetude. And other empirical studies show that formal, legally-enforceable contracts fulfil various important functions. For example, Daintith's study of long-term iron-ore supply contracts suggested the following reasons for entering a formal contract: reassuring important third parties (eg lenders, government agencies); providing 'fixed points of reference' for the relationship, if only parameters for its later adaptation; and an unambiguous statement of the parties' mutual commitment to their business relations (which 'gives better, but not absolute, security').[155] Macaulay cites Daintith's study, commenting that it is the *symbol* of commitment that matters rather than legal enforcement.[156] Yet does the symbolism not presuppose and derive from the formal contract's ultimate enforceability (however unlikely in practice)? As seen Mitchell, having discussed a number of further empirical studies showing the business use of formal contracts, argues that the 'paper deal' cannot be dismissed as easily as Macaulay suggests.[157]

Scott argues that Macaulay's 'The Real and the Paper Deal' (2003) is 'equally remarkable' as his famous 'Non-Contractual Relations in Business' (1963). The 2003 article advances towards a solution of the central puzzle. Macaulay accepts that some contracts really are better analysed as 'discrete' or formal contracts, as under classical contract law. Macaulay implicitly rejects the assumption that there is a single set of rules that governs all kinds of contracts. Scott agrees: 'a unitary contract law appropriate to all these environments is a hopeless fiction'.[158] Scott's neo-formalist approach holds that in certain sorts of contractual relations, parties rationally prefer formal (viz 'discrete') legal resolution of their disputes. Scott traces the intellectual basis back to Macaulay's 1963 paper – which invited the question of when parties will rely on social norms and when on law. (By contrast, Scott suggests *Macneil*'s uninterest in law made him less influential: '[Macneil's] views on the role of common law courts in creating a "relational contract law" were tentative at best and, at worst, opaque'.[159] In Scott's view that opaqueness lured incautious scholars to fill the vacuum with oversimplified extrapolations from Macneil's theory, ie assuming that *all* contract law must be relational.)[160]

Campbell suggests that Macaulay's answer to the question 'why do parties ever resort to contract law?' should incorporate another strand of Macneil's

[155] T Daintith, 'The Design and the Performance of Long-Term Contracts' in T Daintith and G Teubner (eds), *Contract and Organisation: Legal Analysis in the Light of Economic and Social Theory* (Berlin, Walter de Gruyter, 1986) 187–88.

[156] Macaulay (n 118) 61.

[157] *cf* text to n 123.

[158] Scott (n 145) 108.

[159] *ibid* 115.

[160] Citing Speidel (n 99); RA Hillman, 'Court Adjustment of Long-Term Contracts' (1987) *Duke Law Journal* 1; L Trakman, 'Winner Take Some: Loss Sharing and Commercial Impracticability' (1985) 69 *Minnesota Law Review* 471.

scholarship. Macneil (in his 'best paper') discussed extensively the contract-drafter's role in planning for the relationship and potential disputes.[161] True enough. But didn't Macneil repeatedly stress the impossibility of planning in relational contracts? Isn't this impossibility an obvious reason for the non-use of formal contracts in business relations? Campbell thinks these points overplayed. First there are many important types of contract which can be planned and governed by 'discrete' rules. Second, even heavily relational contracts *can* be planned – albeit their planning requires conscious departure from the law's usual default approach. In practice, this is very common.

Campbell accepts that classical contract law is well suited to discrete contracts such as commodities sales (which are, *pace* Macaulay, the paradigm contract, not some special example).[162] However, the traditional law remains a poor basis for relational contracts. Remedies that work so smoothly in a commercial sale (damages awarding the difference between the contract and market prices) are horribly complex when applied to breach of relational contracts. In those situations, market substitutes ('cover') are unlikely to be readily available, and relationship breakdowns inevitably result in disputable consequential loss. Moreover, Campbell argues, contract law's basic purpose (enforcing what is agreed at the outset) is inimical to an evolving, co-operative commercial relationship. Is this not again Macneil's point that 'presentiation' is impossible? Yet Campbell argues that *relational planning* is perfectly feasible. He instances the elaborate contractual structures used in large-scale construction projects. These building contracts' primary goal is managing change and variation as the project proceeds, ie not focusing on enforcement. Campbell suggests that much of advanced commercial law is of this nature. Accepting Macneil's point that 'no contract can ever be fully planned',[163] Campbell states that nonetheless 'properly devised contracts could, and to various extents do, provide for necessary co-operation by ousting the classical provisions that militate against [it]'.[164]

Some conclusions on the Macaulay school. First, relational norms are indeed vital in business. Second (therefore) the antagonistic process of contract litigation is seen as an absolute last resort. However, third, that does not mean there is no role for contract planning – a formal contract may play a variety of functions. Fourth, the classical law of contract *sometimes* functions well – see Beale and Dugdale's finding that in business practice as much as in contract law, sellers are expected to pay 'market price' compensation if they fail to deliver goods, and routinely do so.[165] Fifth, although there are still many situations in which the classical law fails to serve the parties' goals, they can anticipate this in their

[161] Campbell (n 144) 173; IR Macneil, 'A Primer of Contract Planning' (1975) 48 *Southern California Law Review* 627.
[162] Campbell (n 144) 178.
[163] Macneil (n 161) 668.
[164] Campbell (n 144) 173. See also 182.
[165] Beale and Dugdale (n 152).

contracts by ousting the law's default approach in favour of more appropriate relational governance. On this view, while the law certainly should not thwart such 'opting out',[166] it does not necessarily follow that it should become relational by default across the board. As Macaulay's 2003 paper accepts, drawing on concessions made by Macneil, *some* contracts should be treated by law as if they were discrete, giving priority to notions of risk-allocation, planning and formality. Again the questions remain – which? And who decides?

X. RESISTANCE TO RELATIONAL CONTRACT

So far this chapter has taken a bracing swim in contract theory, largely American. It is likely that for most practising lawyers in England, including perhaps academic contract lawyers, the characteristic reaction to relational contract theory is to ignore it completely. But even black-letter lawyers have taken notice of 'relational contract' since it was discussed by Lord Leggatt in *Yam Seng*. Whether or not relational values become mainstream in English contract law,[167] the theory can no longer be *ignored*. Yet a theory contrary to English contract law's basic premises will face resistance. As noted, Macneil was disappointed by the reception of relational theory in US contract law. In this section, we dismiss two weak reasons for resistance to relational contract, before considering more persuasive counter-arguments. Consensus may yet emerge over a variegated law of contract, tailored to the needs of particular contractors (whether relational or discrete – or on the spectrum in between).

Hostility to relational contract could perhaps be seen as ideological (one recalls Atiyah's complaint that Freedom of Contract had not Fallen despite his opus of 1979 – blaming its renaissance on 1980s Thatcherism).[168] It is easy enough to suggest political influences on private law, but much harder to prove. The main actors (judges, textbook-writers) would deny *political* inspiration behind the contract doctrines that they elaborate. The average Law Lord seems an unlikely candidate for false consciousness. Still there is always Keynes's claim about the inescapable theory behind every apparently atheoretical approach.[169]

[166] Campbell (n 144) 172 identifies this as a problem in the current law.

[167] See, eg, H Beale, 'Relational Values in English Contract Law' in Campbell et al (n 2) (dubious).

[168] PS Atiyah, 'Freedom of Contract and the New Right' in *Essays on Contract* (Oxford, Oxford University Press, 1988); *cf* PS Atiyah, *The Rise and Fall of Freedom of Contract* (Oxford, Oxford University Press, 1979).

[169] Perhaps too well known to include, but too good to omit:

> The ideas of economists and political philosophers … are more powerful than is commonly understood. Indeed the world is ruled by little else. Practical men, who believe themselves to be quite exempt from any intellectual influence, are usually the slaves of some defunct economist. Madmen in authority, who hear voices in the air, are distilling their frenzy from some academic scribbler of a few years back.

(JM Keynes, *The General Theory of Employment, Interest and Money* (Cambridge, Palgrave Macmillan, 1936) 383).

In the present context Keynes's (somewhat self-serving) argument has particular resonance. Macneil described the deep-seated attachment to 'discrete' contract in western cultural, economic and political thought. It is so pervasive that it is scarcely noticed, and deviations from it (like Macneil's theory) face instinctive rejection.

Or does resistance to relational contract lie closer to (small-c) conservatism – a facet of path dependence?[170] This does play a significant part in legal development. Lawyers have an engrained tendency to defend inherited rules and doctrinal structures, side-lining deviations (like *Yam Seng*?) as anomalies. And there is good sense in this attitude. An uncodified common-law system could not last long without powerful centipedal forces operating to hold it together. All this said, English contract lawyers would be puzzled by the suggestion that they are doctrinaire guardians of immutable rules. As noted above, commercial judges have from at least Lord Mansfield's time prided themselves on harmonising the law with commercial needs. Perhaps their pride is unwarranted; perhaps English contract law sounds less harmonious to the commercial ear than to its judicial composers. Still, given the pragmatic and facilitative imperatives of commercial law it seems unlikely that calls for 'relational' reforms to contract law would be dismissed for novelty alone.

Although we have discounted two dubious reasons for unthinking resistance to relational contract law, others cannot be so lightly dismissed. Interrelated arguments follow from reflection on the role and limits of contract law. Given that litigation exists to *resolve disputes* (rather than to administer ongoing contractual relations), might a 'discrete' framework better describe what the law is designed to do – and what litigants expect it to do? When even heavily relational contracts end, a sharp-edged 'divorce' law might serve better than attempts to enforce the implicit norms that previously governed the relationship. As seen, 'neo-formalists' argue that because of the limits of adjudication, courts are incompetent to enforce relational norms. While *contracts* are 'relational', contract *law* is inherently 'formal'. Courts are ill-suited to discovering the norms of particular relationships, and legal enforcement may even be counterproductive, crowding out trust.

There is empirical evidence that some sophisticated commercial parties do prefer 'formalist' approaches. Direct evidence comes from Lisa Bernstein's studies of certain trade associations' standard forms and dispute-resolution.[171] Quantitative (but indirect) evidence comes from US commercial parties' choice of law clauses' marked preference for New York (the hypothesis being that

[170] Mitchell (n 74).

[171] L Bernstein, 'Merchant Law in a Merchant Court: Rethinking the Code's Search for Immanent Business Norms' (1996) 144 *University of Pennsylvania Law Review* 1765; L Bernstein, 'Private Commercial Law in the Cotton Industry: Creating Cooperation Through Rules, Norms, and Institutions' (2001) 99 *Michigan Law Review* 1724.

whereas New York and (say) California are of comparable economic importance, New York's contract law is formal/discrete, where California's is contextual/relational).[172]

The qualification is important: neo-formalists limit their claims to 'sophisticated commercial parties'.[173] But these should not be thought a monolithic category with homogenous preferences. All complex, long-term contracts involve ongoing co-operation, flexibility and adaptation for the reasons Macneil stressed in his relational theory, ie even between large commercial entities. At the very least, contract law must respect the choice of contractors who expressly draft relational contract terms. (In English law, a *cause celebre* is the enforceability of express duties to negotiate in good faith.)[174] Well-advised contractors can realistically be expected to signal when they want courts to approach disputes 'relationally', by drafting appropriate contract terms. But how many contracts are drafted, bespoke, by and for such parties? Many more are informal, or imposed upon less powerful parties as a non-negotiable form. In such situations the court must decide where on the relational-discrete spectrum to place the contract. It cannot always be left to the parties to choose the correct legal regime.

Traditional 'discrete' contract law remains the appropriate register for understanding *some* contracts. Even Macneil allowed a place for it. But the law should no longer be unthinkingly discrete. Macneil shows that the traditional uniform rules, in traditionally discrete form, are unsuitable in many situations – perhaps even most. At a minimum, contract law must become nuanced and multi-layered, applying relational rules where appropriate to a particular contractual relationship (such as duties to co-operate, negotiate, adapt contracts and even share losses). The law may even become relational by default, albeit permitting parties that prefer a discrete approach to contract back into that regime. The default relational approach would accord with Macneil's insistence that all contracts are relational (even though some are appropriately treated as if they were discrete).

XI. CONCLUSION

How do we assess a scholar's significance? Must we demonstrate 'impact' on the substantive law of contract (in the bureaucratic language of the Research Excellence Framework)? Even by this demanding metric, Macneil proves significant. He might not have written a great treatise still regularly cited a century after its appearance (like Williston) or written the *Restatement (First) of the*

[172] See, eg, GP Miller, 'Bargains Bicoastal: New Light on Contract Theory' (2010) 31 *Cardozo Law Review* 1475.

[173] See, eg, A Schwartz and RE Scott, 'Contract Theory and the Limits of Contract Law' (2003) 113 *Yale Law Journal* 541.

[174] See, eg, G Leggatt, 'Negotiation in Good Faith' [2019] *Journal of Business Law* 104.

Law of Contracts (Williston again),[175] or produced a treatise which dominated the *Restatement (Second) of the Law of Contracts* (Corbin). No doubt these were the direct paths to lasting influence. Perhaps they still are. But Macneil's *indirect* influence has nevertheless been substantial. Even in traditional, pragmatic England, so aloof from *theories* of all kinds (relational or economic or otherwise), the most important doctrinal debates today clearly flow from the challenge of Macneil's relational theory. Controversies about contract interpretation, and duties of good faith, are merely the most prominent.[176]

Perhaps the English suspicion of good faith and commitment to textual construction will re-assert themselves. There are good reasons to retain a 'discrete' approach for certain kinds of contracts and parties – the very disputes that are the English commercial courts' standard diet.[177] This does not diminish the importance of Macneil's theory. That the debate is being had at all – that English courts now explicitly discuss relational contract – is further evidence of the relational theory's influence. Even if it is not accepted with the degree of universality that Macneil (at least sometimes) envisaged, the relational theory of contract has had a permanent impact on the way that commercial contract law is understood. Traditional discrete contract law today needs to be *justified*. Its scope requires careful consideration, not unthinking general application. If influence is measured by a scholar's effect on the intellectual parameters within which the law is debated and understood, Ian Macneil remains one of the most important scholars of contract law today.

[175] For Williston, see Rakoff, chapter seven of this volume.

[176] See Wightman (n 117).

[177] Such parties may deliberately choose *English* law to govern their disputes, precisely because it satisfies their 'discrete' expectations.

13

Professor Brian Coote (1929–2019)

STEPHEN WADDAMS*

I. INTRODUCTION

BRIAN COOTE WAS born in 1929 in the New Zealand town of Cambridge (population about 2,000).[1] After leaving his secondary school he attended what was then known as Auckland University College, New Zealand University, where he graduated with the degrees of LLB in 1953, and LLM in 1954. He was awarded a New Zealand travelling scholarship and went to Cambridge University as a research student, graduating with the degree of PhD in 1959. His thesis, on the topic of exception clauses in contracts, was awarded the Yorke prize, and was subsequently published by Sweet & Maxwell in 1964. He returned to New Zealand to join the Law Faculty of the University of Auckland, where he spent his whole teaching career, serving as dean from 1984–1987.

In the course of his career, he published over 140 articles and notes, mainly on aspects of contract law. His book and his articles were cited in the House of Lords, in the Privy Council, in cases in Canada, Hong Kong and Singapore, and in dozens of cases in New Zealand and Australia. He was, for 20 years, a member of the New Zealand Contracts and Commercial Law Reform Committee, and was principally responsible for reports that led to the enactment of several important statutes reforming contract law. He was appointed a CBE in 1995, made a Fellow of the Academy of the Humanities in 2007, and of the Royal Society of New Zealand in 2009. In 2017 he was awarded the degree of LLD by the University of Auckland – a degree earned on the basis of published work. Twenty two of his articles on various aspects of contract law were collected and republished in two books in 2010 and 2016, and, in the following year, 16 articles on the New Zealand contract statutes were collected and republished.

* I am grateful to Peter Watts, Warren Swain and Alex Pel for their help. Opinions and errors of fact are mine.

[1] New Zealand Government, 'The New Zealand Official Year-Book, 1930', available at www3.stats.govt.nz/New_Zealand_Official_Yearbooks/1930/NZOYB_1930.html.

He died in 2019 in his ninetieth year. The funeral was held at All Saints Church, Ponsonby, Auckland, and obituaries were published in New Zealand,[2] Australia[3] and England.[4] By lifetime gifts, and by his will, he left about NZ$7 million to the law school, which will be used to endow a fund in his name.

In 1995 a special issue of the *Journal of Contract Law* was published to mark Coote's retirement from the University of Auckland. The issue was jointly edited by Professors John Carter and Francis Reynolds, and included an introductory essay by Sir Robin Cooke, the President of the New Zealand Court of Appeal, together with essays on a variety of contractual topics by seven contributors. One of these was the present writer, who received a very gracious letter of thanks from Coote, handwritten by fountain pen, in the best and most courteous academic style. Probably he wrote similar letters to the other contributors. The letter goes far beyond a formal acknowledgment, carefully selecting aspects of the article for praise, despite the fact that Coote would certainly have disagreed with some of it. The letter is not, therefore, necessarily a reliable indicator of Coote's own views, but one passage that may cast light on his view of legal concepts in general is a reference to

> how difficult it is to believe that there can be a unified concept [of good faith]. It's another example of Holmes' dictum that one does not get a new and single principle by simply giving a single name to all the cases to be accounted for.[5]

II. EXCEPTION CLAUSES AND FUNDAMENTAL BREACH

Coote wrote his Cambridge PhD thesis on the topic of what were then usually called exemption clauses (also sometimes called exempting clauses, exclusion clauses, disclaimer clauses or limitation of liability clauses). The thesis was awarded the Yorke prize, and subsequently published under the title *Exception Clauses: Some Aspects of the Law Relating to Exception Clauses for the Carriage, Bailment and Sale of Goods*.[6] The main theme of the book was that many clauses limiting the liability of a promisor could and should be understood as simply ways of describing, or defining, the extent of the promise, and that there was nothing inherently objectionable in defining a promise by the use

[2] P Watts, 'A Legacy in Law' [2019] *Auckland University Law Review* 76; C Howie, 'Obituary' *New Zealand Weekend Herald* (30 May 2020).

[3] P Watts, 'Emeritus Professor Brian Coote, CBE, FRSNZ' (2019) 36 *Journal of Contract Law* 1.

[4] Queens' College Record (Cambridge, 2018–2019) 108.

[5] Letter from Brian Coote to author (1 September 1995) (in author's possession). The reference is probably to OW Holmes Jr, *The Common Law* (Boston, Little, Brown & Co, 1881) 204, quoted by Coote in his valedictory lecture in 1994 and reprinted in B Coote, 'Contract: An Underview' in JW Carter (ed), *Contract as Assumption II* (Oxford, Hart Publishing, 2016).

[6] B Coote, *Exception Clauses: Some Aspects of the Law Relating to Exception Clauses for the Carriage, Bailment and Sale of Goods* (London, Sweet & Maxwell, 1964).

of exceptions. Coote gave the example of the sale of a horse warranted sound except for hunting. Such an exception was, he said, just a convenient way of describing the sale of a 'non-hunting' horse. This approach explains the choice of the phrase 'exception clause', implying not an *exemption* from some independently existing obligation, but a way of defining the primary obligation itself. Coote wrote: 'Thus, where a horse is sold warranted sound "except for hunting" the purchaser will have no primary right to call for a horse sound for hunting'.[7] And, in a later summary: 'So, if I sell a horse warranted sound except for hunting, I accept no primary obligation as to its soundness for hunting'.[8]

These arguments were not made in a vacuum. In 1956, at about the time that Coote started to read for his degree at Cambridge, there had been a notorious and much-discussed decision of the English Court of Appeal, where the seller of a defective used car sought to rely on a clause excluding liability. Denning LJ said in that case that

> the law about exempting clauses has been much developed in recent years, at any rate about printed exempting clauses, which so often pass unread. Notwithstanding earlier cases which might suggest the contrary, it is now settled that exempting clauses of this kind, no matter how widely they are expressed, only avail the party when he is carrying out his contract in its essential respects. He is not allowed to use them as a cover for misconduct or indifference or to enable him to turn a blind eye to his obligations. They do not avail him when he is guilty of a breach which goes to the root of the contract. The thing to do is to look at the contract apart from the exempting clauses and see what are the terms, express or implied, which impose an obligation on the party. If he has been guilty of a breach of those obligations in a respect which goes to the very root of the contract, he cannot rely on the exempting clauses ….The principle is sometimes said to be that the party cannot rely on an exempting clause when he delivers something 'different in kind' from that contracted for, or has broken a 'fundamental term' or a 'fundamental contractual obligation,' but these are, I think, all comprehended by the general principle that a breach which goes to the root of the contract disentitles the party from relying on the exempting clause.[9]

Denning LJ's underlying purpose was to find a way of granting relief to a consumer buyer who had (apparently) entered into a very disadvantageous contract. Coote did not deny that there might be a social problem in some such cases, but he thought that the concept of fundamental breach was not a permissible or defensible way of achieving that result. He thought also, as was the prevailing opinion in England at the time, that it was beyond the proper power of the courts to attempt to solve such a problem, and that any solution should be left to Parliament.

[7] *ibid* ch 1.

[8] B Coote, 'The Second Rise and Fall of Fundamental Breach' (1981) 55 *Australian Law Journal* 788.

[9] *Karsales (Harrow) Ltd v Wallis* [1956] 1 WLR 936 (CA) 940.

In an unpublished paper in 1967 he wrote:

> The point to be stressed here is that there is nothing *intrinsically* unfair or reprehensible about the exception clause as such. It can of course be abused. Claims in large print followed by exceptions in print so small as to be unreadable would be an example. But as a form, it is no more than one mode of expressing the obligations of the parties.[10]

Coote's analogy of the hypothetical case of the horse not warranted for hunting, though logical, was not very promising for the prospects of the buyer of the defective car (in effect, 'not warranted for use as a car'): the implication is that, if the buyer has agreed to pay a large sum of money for a heap of scrap metal, that is no proper concern of the courts. Coote went on to quote Lord Reid in *Suisse Atlantique* on the proper limits of judicial action in a passage itself strongly reflecting Coote's influence:

> Exemption Clauses differ greatly in many respects. Probably the most objectionable are found in the complex standard conditions which are now so common.
>
> In the ordinary way the customer has no time to read them, and if he did read them he would probably not understand them. And if he did understand and object
>
> to any of them, he would generally be told he could take it or leave it. And if he then went to another supplier the result would be the same. Freedom to contract must surely imply some choice or room for bargaining. At the other extreme is the case where parties are bargaining on terms of equality and a stringent exemption clause is accepted for a quid pro quo or other good reason. But this rule appears to treat all cases alike. There is no indication in the recent cases that the courts are to consider whether the exemption is fair in all the circumstances or is harsh and unconscionable or whether it was freely agreed by the customer. And it does not seem to me to be satisfactory that the decision must always go one way if, e.g., defects in a car or other goods are just sufficient to make the breach of contract a fundamental breach, but must always go the other way if the defects fall just short of that. This is a complex problem which intimately affects millions of people and it appears to me that its solution should be left to Parliament.[11]

Exception Clauses received a glowing review in the *Cambridge Law Journal* from Tony Weir (a stern critic[12]), who described the book as 'excellent and of constant interest'. Weir said that 'the inferences from [Coote's] hypothesis are developed with such lucidity that the whole argument is irresistible, once the hypothesis is accepted'. He called the book 'an exemplary monograph, a

[10] B Coote, 'Exception Clauses in Consumer Sales' [1967] *New Zealand Legal Research Foundation Seminar Papers* 4, *Second Business Law Symposium Paper No 3* 27, 30 (emphasis in original).

[11] *ibid* 32, quoting Lord Reid in *Suisse Atlantique Societe d'Armement Maritime SA v Rotterdamsche Kolen Centrale* [1967] 1 AC 361 (HL) 406.

[12] See Collins, chapter ten of this volume, p 274, fn 80.

mini-masterpiece', adding that 'it has an almost Gallic elegance, the result of an enviable style, with just the right degree of aeration, being brought to bear, with a rare singleness of purpose, on a problem neatly defined and authorities thoroughly mastered'.[13]

Following the *Suisse Atlantique* case, Lord Denning attempted to revive the doctrine of fundamental breach, which was then decisively and finally rejected by the House of Lords in 1980. Lord Wilberforce said, however, that the doctrine had served a useful purpose:

> The doctrine of 'fundamental breach' in spite of its imperfections and doubtful parentage has served a useful purpose. There was a large number of problems, productive of injustice, in which it was worse than unsatisfactory to leave exception clauses to operate.[14]

The use of the term 'exception' clauses in this passage (rather than one of the more usual words) clearly indicates Coote's influence. One of his articles was cited in argument.[15]

It is significant that one of the principal reasons that Lord Wilberforce gave for overruling the doctrine was that Parliament had by that time enacted a statute, the Unfair Contract Terms Act 1977, that expressly gave the court power to invalidate unreasonable terms in consumer standard form contracts. It might be said, therefore that, although Lord Denning's method of resolving the problem of unfair use of exemption clauses was disapproved, his ultimate object was approved, and, indeed, reinforced by the legislature.

Lord Denning, had he been called upon to mount a defence of his conduct, would probably have said that, in the legal intellectual climate prevailing in 1956 it was simply not possible to persuade English judges to adopt directly a power to control unfair contracts, and that the concept of fundamental breach was the only tool available that had a prospect of success. In fact, Lord Denning did say almost exactly that in his very last case, issued on the day that his retirement took effect:

> None of you nowadays will remember the trouble we had – when I was called to the Bar – with exemption clauses. They were printed in small print on the back of tickets and order forms and invoices. They were contained in catalogues or timetables. They were held to be binding on any person who took them without objection. No one ever did object. He never read them or knew what was in them. No matter how unreasonable they were, he was bound. All this was done in the name of 'freedom of contract.' But the freedom was all on the side of the big concern which had the use of the printing press. No freedom for the little man who took the ticket or order form or invoice.

[13] JA Weir, 'Book Review' (1965) 23 *CLJ* 301, 302–303.
[14] *Photo Production Ltd v Securicor Transport Ltd* [1980] AC 827 (HL) 843.
[15] B Coote, 'Exception Causes as Dependent Promises' (1977) 40 *MLR* 41; cited by counsel for the appellant in *Photo Production Ltd v Securicor Transport Ltd* (n 14) 839.

The big concern said, 'Take it or leave it.' The little man had no option but to take it. The big concern could and did exempt itself from liability in its own interest without regard to the little man. It got away with it time after time. When the courts said to the big concern, 'You must put it in clear words,' the big concern had no hesitation in doing so. It knew well that the little man would never read the exemption clauses or understand them. It was a bleak winter for our law of contract ….

The secret weapon

Faced with this abuse of power – by the strong against the weak – by the use of the small print of the conditions – the judges did what they could to put a curb upon it. They still had before them the idol, 'freedom of contract.' They still knelt down and worshipped it, but they concealed under their cloaks a secret weapon. They used it to stab the idol in the back. This weapon was called 'the true construction of the contract.' They used it with great skill and ingenuity. They used it so as to depart from the natural meaning of the words of the exemption clause and to put upon them a strained and unnatural construction. In case after case, they said that the words were not strong enough to give the big concern exemption from liability; or that in the circumstances the big concern was not entitled to rely on the exemption clause. … In short, whenever the wide words – in their natural meaning – would give rise to an unreasonable result, the judges either rejected them as repugnant to the main purpose of the contract, or else cut them down to size in order to produce a reasonable result. … But when the clause was itself reasonable and gave rise to a reasonable result, the judges upheld it ….

Fundamental breach

No doubt has ever been cast thus far by anyone. But doubts arose when in this court – in *Karsales (Harrow) Ltd. v. Wallis* … – we ventured to suggest that if the big concern was guilty of a breach which went to the 'very root' of the contract – sometimes called a 'fundamental breach' – or at other times a 'total failure' of its obligations – then it could not rely on the printed clause to exempt itself from liability. … But we did make a mistake – in the eyes of some – in elevating it – by inference – into a 'rule of law.' That was too rude an interference with the idol of 'freedom of contract.' We ought to have used the secret weapon. We ought to have said that in each case, on the 'true construction of the contract' in that case, the exemption clause did not avail the party where he was guilty of a fundamental breach or a breach going to the root. …

The change in climate

In 1969 there was a change in climate. Out of winter into spring. It came with the … Supply of Goods (Implied Terms) Act 1973. In 1975 there was a further change. Out of spring into summer. It came with the … Unfair Contract Terms Act 1977. No longer was the big concern able to impose whatever terms and conditions it liked in a printed form – no matter how unreasonable they might be. These reports showed most convincingly that the courts could and should only enforce them if they were fair and reasonable in themselves and it was fair and reasonable to allow the big concern to rely on them. So the idol of 'freedom of contract' was shattered. In cases of personal injury or death, it was not permissible to exclude or restrict liability at all. In consumer contracts any exemption clause was subject to the test of reasonableness … What is the result of all this? To my mind it heralds a revolution in our approach

> to exemption clauses ....We should set about meeting a new challenge. It is presented by the test of reasonableness.[16]

In summary, there can be no doubt that Coote achieved an outstanding success in bringing about the demise of the doctrine of fundamental breach. His view, reflecting the prevailing English attitude at the time, was that reform of the law was a matter for Parliament, and in England Parliamentary reform had in fact come about, shortly before the final judicial rejection of the doctrine of fundamental breach, in the form of the Unfair Contract Terms Act 1977, which, as we have seen, played an important part in persuading the House of Lords that the doctrine of fundamental breach was no longer needed. But, even assuming that this was a wholly satisfactory development in English law, it should be noted that the abolition of the doctrine of fundamental breach ran the risk of leaving a gap in other jurisdictions that had not adopted legislation comparable to the Unfair Contract Terms Act 1979. In 1981 Coote noted the necessary connexion between the doctrine of fundamental breach and the general question of control of unfair contracts:

> By reaffirming Suisse Atlantique and overruling Harbutt's Plasticene [a case in which Lord Denning had attempted to revive the doctrine], the House of Lords has done what it can to remove two obvious distortions from the law, but neither action, by itself, can solve the continuing problem of unacceptable contractual terms generally. Neither 'construction' nor a third revival of fundamental breach can provide a fully satisfactory answer. The better approach, it is submitted, would be the development of an overall control based on some such test as reasonableness or, much more narrowly, unconscionability. Nor, in logic, should such a control be restricted to only one form of contract term.[17]

This is a significant statement, not typical of a formalist, recognising an underlying purpose of the doctrine of fundamental breach extrinsic to the law itself, namely, to 'solve the continuing problem of unacceptable contractual terms generally' and that a general test was needed of reasonableness, or unconscionability, that would apply not only to exception (or exemption) clauses, but to all potentially unfair contractual terms. The assertion that there was a 'continuing' problem of 'unacceptable' contractual terms that required to be 'solve[d]' indicates a purposive approach to legal decision-making and to legal change, with considerable relaxation of the hostility to adoption of wide judicial powers and to judicial development of the law that had prevailed in English legal thinking, as in Coote's own thinking, in the mid-twentieth century. This question will be discussed further below in the context of Coote's 'formalism'.

[16] *George Mitchell (Chesterhall) Ltd v Finney Lock Seeds Ltd* [1983] QB 284 (CA) 296–99, affd [1983] 2 AC 803 (HL).

[17] Coote (n 8) 803.

III. THE NEW ZEALAND CONTRACT LAW REFORM STATUTES

As mentioned earlier, Coote played an important part in bringing about legislation in New Zealand affecting contractual remedies, mistake, privity and illegality.[18] Unsurprisingly, the statutes gave rise to a number of uncertainties and difficulties of interpretation, and, in 2001, Coote published an article critical, in some respects, of the judicial interpretation of the statutes.

When 'The Security of Contract and the New Zealand Contract Statutes' was reprinted in 2017 in *Coote on the New Zealand Contract Statutes*,[19] the article appeared as Chapter 16, in part VI, which itself had a new title, 'Apologia'. Since part VI contained only one chapter (Chapter 16) the new title attached to the part amounted to an addition to the title of the article itself. The word 'apologia' means defence, as in Cardinal Newman's *Apologia pro Vita Sua*, and need not imply regret, as the word 'apology' usually does in modern English usage. Nevertheless, the use of the word is significant. It indicates, at the very least, that Coote felt called upon in 2017 to offer a defence of his contribution to the New Zealand reform statutes. Further, as we shall see, the article does show marks of regret in several respects.

In the preliminaries to *Coote on the New Zealand Contract Statutes*, there appears a two-page 'Word from the Author,' which includes the following comments:

> All I wish to do, here, is to add some comment to the piece which is reproduced in Chapter 7 ['Chinese Whispers and the Contractual Remedies Act 1979']. Many readers must wonder why a committee of experienced practitioners, Government lawyers, and academics, were apparently so unprepared for what the courts were going to do with the contract statutes. Although many were couched in fairly general terms, I very naively expected that their interpretation would have had regard, for example, to the historic canons of construction. And in response to an attempt on my part, at one point, to urge that a draft be more specific, the comment was made that we could not legislate on the basis that the judges were stupid.
>
> It is interesting that in an article entitled 'Codification, Law Reform and Judicial Development' (1996) 9 JCL 192, Professor S. Waddams addressed the same sorts of issue. He described what has happened in Canada in applying the Canadian Charter of Rights and Freedoms. Our own New Zealand Bill of Rights Act 1990 had not been passed when the Contract Statutes first came before the courts. But the analogy is appropriate nonetheless. The Contract Statutes tended to be more general than the New Zealand courts and practitioners were used to, most previous legislation

[18] Now consolidated in the Contract and Commercial Law Act 2017 (NZ). See W Swain, 'A Reputation for Boldness: Statutory Reform of Contract Law in New Zealand' in TT Arvind and J Steele (eds), *Contract Law and the Legislature: Autonomy, Expectations, and the Making of Legal Doctrine* (Oxford, Hart Publishing, 2020) 107.

[19] JW Carter and J Ren (eds), *Coote on the New Zealand Contract Statutes* (Wellington, Thomson Reuters, 2017).

> tending to be very specific. These issues are dealt with more fully in Chapter 16 and it is for that reason that a conference paper originally headed as 'Security of Contract and the New Zealand Contract Statutes' now appears in the Table of Contents under the part heading *Apologia*.

This passage is worth examining in the present context for the evidence that it may supply of Coote's changing attitudes. On re-reading the 1996 article of mine to which Coote referred, I find that I made only a passing reference to the Canadian Charter of Rights, advancing the (not very original or startling) suggestion that general considerations of justice and policy developed in Charter cases may have affected the court's attitude to questions of private law.[20] The only significance of this reference in the present context is what it may reveal of Coote's changing attitudes. The sentence '*these issues* are dealt with more fully in Chapter 16 *and it is for that reason* that [the article on 'Security of Contract'] now appears … under the part heading *Apologia*' is not entirely easy to follow, and shows some ambivalence on the question of judicial powers and their relation to legislation. The train of thought in the whole passage seems to be that the judges erred in their treatment of the statutes; that the error arose because of the generality of the statutes and the judges' unfamiliarity with the exercise of general statutory powers; that Canadian experience showed that judges accustomed to exercising general powers in one context might transfer their attitudes to other contexts, and that, in the light of these considerations, a defence of the approach taken in the New Zealand statutes was called for. But it is not quite clear whether the implicit conclusion is that, had the future been foreseen, the statutes would have been more specific (restraining wide judicial powers), or, that had the future been foreseen, the statutes would have been unnecessary (accepting wide judicial powers).

A perennial question is when the courts should use their power to modify and develop the law, and when reform should be left to the legislature. It has often been convenient for courts to decline an invitation to modify or develop a legal rule by saying that reform must be for the legislature. This response has the effect of apparently removing from the courts responsibility for unjust and anomalous legal consequences.

There are many possible objections to this line of thinking: it neglects the powers of the court derived from equity, and it neglects the inherent powers of a court of justice; it is often an excuse for inaction, or for avoiding difficult problems; the contemplated legislation may never occur, or it may be long delayed, especially in jurisdictions where the legislature is dominated by business interests; where legislation does occur, it is often limited to particular circumstances,

[20] 'Canadian courts, partly because of their experience with the Charter of Rights and Freedoms, are increasingly showing themselves ready to decide contract cases on broad considerations of justice and policy': SM Waddams, 'Codification, Law Reform and Judicial Development' (1996) 9 *Journal of Contract Law* 192, 199.

leaving large gaps and creating new anomalies, or hedged with complex reservations and exceptions; there is a danger that legislation dealing with particular circumstances may actually reinforce an unjust legal rule in areas falling just outside the scope of the legislation; legislation tends to crystallise concepts that might have been more satisfactorily modified or transcended by judicial development; in federal jurisdictions it is very unlikely that any reforming legislation would be uniform.

There is a further reason: legislation, however general in nature, rarely leaves the court with the flexibility that accompanies judicial change. Principles developed judicially can be reformulated so as to accommodate unforeseen circumstances, but statutory provisions are difficult to amend. As Coote says,[21] in relation to the Illegal Contracts Act, 'the conditions which prompted a reform, and to which they were directed, can be forgotten and an Act [can quickly] take on a life of its own', adding[22] that 'implied constraints which would once have appeared obvious can as quickly be ignored or forgotten'. He says that the results 'have in practice turned out to be significantly different from what the reformers appear to have expected or intended'.[23] The reform, drafting and enactment process of legislation presents many opportunities for unintended consequences. In respect of a section of the Contractual Remedies Act, Professor Coote says that 'the wording of the section appears to contradict what was almost certainly the intention of Parliament in framing it'.[24] He points out that the statutes were drafted against a background understanding of the corpus of the pre-existing law, adding that 'I for one failed to appreciate how quickly familiarity with this background would be lost to the profession'.[25] Since Professor Coote was one of the principal architects of the reforms, his comments carry very great weight. He concludes that the earlier critics of the legislative reforms 'have proved to be much more prescient than I was'.[26]

Sir Terence Arnold, then Solicitor-General and later a judge of the New Zealand Supreme Court, commented, in relation to Coote's 2000 article,[27]

> I return to Professor Coote's observation concerning the contract statutes to the effect that he was surprised at how quickly the 'old' learning disappeared. But surely he should not have been surprised. For new generations of lawyers, the focus is on the contract statutes as interpreted and applied and not upon the common law which preceded them.[28]

[21] Carter and Ren (n 19) 30.

[22] *ibid* 50.

[23] *ibid*.

[24] *ibid* 81. See also the critical comments in F Dawson and DW McLauchlan, *The Contractual Remedies Act 1979* (Auckland, Sweet & Maxwell, 1981) 7–9.

[25] Carter and Ren (n 19) 177.

[26] *ibid* 182.

[27] B Coote, 'Security of Contract and the New Zealand Contract Statutes' (2000) 16 *Journal of Contract Law* 37.

[28] T Arnold, 'Parliament and the Courts: Arm Wrestle or Handshake?' (2005) 3 *New Zealand Journal of Public and International Law* 45, 61.

It must be conceded that there is some force in this comment, particularly in relation to one considering himself to be a formalist. The casting of a legal rule into statutory form affects its substance. A judicially declared rule may be, and often has been, modified by a subsequent court in light of the context of the earlier case, and the principle or principles supposed to underlie the rule, but in the case of a statutory rule the precise words are paramount, unalterable (though subject to interpretation) by the court, and the source of their authority is ordinarily unimpeachable: the reasons that may be supposed to have motivated the legislation are normally irrelevant except in case of ambiguity. An important point, related but distinct, is that judicially declared rules can be modified by equity, as they have been for hundreds of years, and, in case of conflict in the modern court equity prevails,[29] whereas there is no equitable power to modify statutes.

The result of these considerations is to suggest that in an uncodified system there are substantial advantages to judicial development of the general principles of law, particularly in jurisdictions where the legislature is unlikely to act promptly to implement subsequent reforms and where the initial legislation has (as often occurs) produced unexpected, anomalous and unjust consequences. If it is accepted that a general residual power is necessary to modify highly unreasonable contracts, to grant relief for fundamental mistake, to reach a fair result in cases of illegality, to adjust remedies so as to do justice between the parties, or, in exceptional circumstances, difficult to define precisely, where justice requires it, to enforce contracts in favour of non-parties, it is scarcely coherent for the court to plead meekly for legislation that, if and when enacted, could, at best, do no more than to restore powers that the court itself had allowed to fall into disuse, and, at worst, is likely to cause new complexities, anomalies and injustices. Professor Coote's observations may be read as an apt and timely warning to those who recommend waiting for legislation to resolve such problems: they should be very careful what they wish for.[30]

IV. CONTRACT AS ASSUMPTION

Coote, after discussing and rejecting various approaches to contract law (will, bargain, promise, reasonable expectations, reliance and others) proposed that 'in essence a contract is a promise or undertaking in respect of which legal contractual obligation has been assumed by means which the law recognises as effective for that purpose'.[31]

[29] Judicature Act 1873 (UK), s 25(11) and modern equivalents.

[30] Parts of the preceding paragraphs were published in SM Waddams, 'Book Review' (2018) 35 *Journal of Contract Law* 185. Warren Swain, in reference to the Contractual Mistakes Act 1977 (NZ), has spoken of 'the perils of codification': Swain (n 18) 113.

[31] B Coote, 'The Essence of Contract' (1988) 1 *Journal of Contract Law* 91, 183.

This may be welcomed as a valuable perspective, recalling the origins of the modern English law in 'assumpsit', and emphasising the practical value, to individuals and to society at large, of recognition of an effective means of enabling the pledging of credit. It is not to detract from this favourable assessment to add that it seems unlikely that the concept of assumption will displace every other perspective on contract law, or that it will supply a single simple means of understanding the past or of predicting the future: the reference to 'means by which the law recognises as effective' must open the door to other perspectives (including, will, bargain, promise, expectation and reliance) for the law often reaches its conclusions for multiple reasons; the objective principle of contract formation will mean that contractual obligation is sometimes imposed without the conscious or willing assumption of obligation, in the ordinary sense of these words; and retention of the doctrine of consideration means that conscious assumption of obligation will not always be sufficient. Martin Hogg, writing from a Scottish civil law perspective, in fact criticised Coote's proposal on this point on the ground that if assumption of obligation were the relevant test, the doctrine of consideration would (and, in Hogg's view should) be unnecessary.[32]

How much did Coote himself claim for the assumption concept? In his valedictory lecture he said

> All these theories [i.e., other theories of contract law] still have their adherents. All are flawed because each seizes on a feature of some contracts and makes that feature the basis of what purports to be a comprehensive theory. But all is not lost. There is a theory of contract which I like to think is general enough to cover all contracts of every kind, in every legal system, and in every age.[33]

This statement, contained in a lecture to which Coote gave an ironic title ('Contract: An Underview') may perhaps itself be suspected of containing an element of self-deprecating irony. It is unlikely that he thought that he has solved for ever, for all time, and for everywhere all problems of contract law. But, on the other hand, there is no doubt that Coote thought that the concept of assumption offered a useful insight, as he chose as titles for his two books of collected articles, *Contract as Assumption* and *Contract as Assumption II*.

In relation to the decision of the English Court of Appeal in *Williams v Roffey Bros & Nicholls (Contractors) Ltd*,[34] on the problem of one-sided contractual variations (in that case a promise to pay more for performance already due under an earlier contract), he rejected the reasoning of the Court on the basis that it misapplied the doctrine of consideration, saying that 'if that decision is ever affirmed by the House of Lords, the case for any brand of formalism will have been pretty well fatally compromised'.[35] But, surprisingly for one claiming to be

[32] M Hogg, 'Book Review' (2011) 15 *Edinburgh Law Review* 315, 317–18.
[33] Coote (n 5) 214.
[34] *Williams v Roffey Bros & Nicholls (Contractors) Ltd* [1991] 1 QB 1 (CA).
[35] Coote (n 5) 225–26.

a formalist, he approved the result, suggesting that consideration should not be required for variations of contracts.[36] The concept of 'assumption' is evidently capable of performing many tasks and of producing novel and surprising results. Referring to a New Zealand case that had suggested that consideration might not be needed for variations,[37] Coote wrote that 'the concept thus stated will no doubt be further developed by the New Zealand courts'. He added:

> As was recognised in *Roffey Bros*, some other method would be needed by which to limit or control the circumstances in which a variation would still be binding. It would defeat a principal object of the law of contract if a party, having secured a contract (quite possibly in competition with others) and having embarked upon performance, were free to refuse and demand extra payment *merely* on the ground that he had under-quoted for the job or that it had proved to be more difficult than he had expected, let alone just because he wished to extract a larger profit. Fraud and duress are obvious possible controls but the New Zealand court has gone further and referred more generally to 'policy reasons' why the parties should not be bound by the variation … Applied flexibly, that formula could be used to discourage behaviour by contractors which, although short of fraud or duress, took unfair advantage of the other party and so was contrary to good faith, or which otherwise was an abuse of a dominant bargaining position. The security of the original contract would thus receive greater protection, albeit at some cost to certainty.[38]

There is much to be said in favour of a general and flexible judicial power to prevent unfair advantage and abuse of a dominant bargaining position, but these are not concepts usually associated with a formalistic approach, or with Coote's earlier views on judicial development of the law or of judicial discretion. A consequence of such a power would be that often one-sided variations would *not* be enforced, because, in the commercial context, parties rarely promise to relinquish contractual rights if they receive nothing in exchange, unless they are under some sort of economic or other pressure, so the crucial question will almost always depend on the residual power of the court, which may take away with one hand what was apparently given by the other. Such a power could not rationally be confined to one-sided contractual variations: if the party relinquishing valuable rights received a trivial advantage in exchange, there would be consideration, but the variation might still be objectionable as unfair.

Coote's suggestion that variations of contracts should not require consideration was discussed recently at considerable length by the Singapore Court of Appeal, and rejected.[39] The case involved a loan where the money had been

[36] B Coote, 'Consideration and Variations: A Different Solution' (2004) 120 *LQR* 19. See also B Coote, 'Variations Sans Consideration' (2011) 27 *Journal of Contract Law* 185.

[37] *Antons Trawling Co Ltd v Smith* [2002] NZCA 331, [2003] 2 NZLR 23.

[38] Coote (n 36) 63–64 (emphasis in original).

[39] *Ma Hongjin v SCP Holdings Pte Ltd* [2020] SGCA 106 [68]–[73] (unanimous judgment of a panel of five delivered by Andrew Phang Boon Leong JA).

fully advanced, followed by a supplemental agreement under which additional burdens were assumed by the borrower, no additional obligations being assumed by the lender, and no obligations by the lender remaining unperformed. This was not, therefore, a case of performance, or of a promise to perform, a pre-existing duty. The Court unanimously held that the fact that a transaction takes the form of a variation of a prior transaction is insufficient reason, in itself, for departing from the general requirement of consideration. It should be conceded by those who have supported the abolition of the requirement of consideration for variation of prior contracts, that this is a very strong argument: unless the doctrine of consideration is to be abolished altogether, there is no persuasive reason to enforce a one-sided promise merely because it takes the form of a variation. It is, perhaps, somewhat ironic that Coote, known for most of his career as very conservative in his approach to judicial law reform, should now have his views rejected as too radical.

Coote did not retreat from his suggestions on this point. In one of his last published writings, he returned to the question of one-sided contractual variations, and went so far as to suggest that the doctrine of consideration might itself be wholly dispensed with. As indicated in the last paragraph, this might be the logical consequence of abolishing the doctrine in the context of variations. Coote wrote that

> [t]here is nothing in the concept of a contract, as such, which requires consideration as an essential element. The law might well grant recognition to alternative indications of contractual intention as being sufficient to serve the same purpose.[40]

On the need for control in the contest of variations, he added,

> [o]f course ... some alternative form of control is necessary if exploitation is to be prevented. The solution advanced by two [of the cases under discussion] was the possibility of recourse to fraud and duress ... On the other hand, if that approach were considered to be too narrow and restrictive, there is always the rather wider alternative suggestion by the New Zealand Court of Appeal that the promisor should be bound 'in the absence of policy reasons to the contrary'.[41]

As suggested above, these are not the words of a formalist. As Coote also recognised, the concept of assumption of obligation cannot, in itself, resolve the problem of one-sided variations because the assumption of obligation by the party agreeing to the variation is not the only assumption in issue: the assumption of obligation by the opposite party in the original contract also has to be taken into account. But it would scarcely be a credible criticism of the concept of assumption that it fails to resolve all the problems of contract law, since no other concept or proposal has succeeded, or is likely to succeed, in doing so.

[40] Coote (2011) (n 36) 197.
[41] *ibid.*

V. FORMALISM

In his valedictory lecture in 1994, Coote described himself as a 'formalist', using rather striking language:

> But why, you may ask, an 'underview' of contract? The answer is that I belong to a declining academic underclass, what you might call an endangered species. Both in New Zealand and overseas, I'm classified as a 'formalist.' In fact, according to a book published in England in 1987, I'm a quintessential formalist, in the same category, it seems, as Lord Diplock. Well, in the words of Lord Justice Asquith, that is a consequence I must face with such fortitude as I can command.
>
> The word 'formalist,' you'll appreciate, is an academic swear word, a currently fashionable put down. As I apply it to myself, it comprehends those who believe that the answers to most legal questions can be found within the law; that the common law is a more or less coherent body of rules, doctrines, principles and concepts which for that reason, and because of the doctrine of precedent, is reasonably predictable; that ideally, at least, it endeavours to treat like cases alike; and that it ought to develop incrementally rather than by arbitrary fiat or from merely personal predilections of the judiciary.[42]

He went on to say that 'formalists like me have become the Fred Flintstones of the academic world both here and overseas'.[43]

It is not easy to give a precise meaning to the word 'formalist'. The meaning varies according to what is contrasted with it, and according to whether the word is used by writers or speakers of themselves, or of others. It would not, therefore, seem likely to be productive to discuss at very great length the question of whether or not Coote was 'truly' a formalist. The view of the law that he described in the passage just quoted might be held by many who would not describe themselves as formalists, and far less tenable views might be attributed to those who are described (by others) as formalists. But what is significant, I would suggest, is the defiant tone of the comments, showing that Coote felt himself to be embattled. There are certain instances where the tone of a comment may tend to contradict its substance. If, for example, someone self-described as a strict grammarian were to object to a modern linguistic usage (split infinitives, for instance), and were defiantly to insist that proper usage remained unchanged, a commentator might justly say that the defiant tone itself was evidence that usage had indeed changed, and that the grammarian knew it, for otherwise the defiant tone would be unnecessary, and even unthinkable. It is possible that Coote was speaking (in whole or in part) ironically, or, in his valedictory address, playing up to what may have been a somewhat staid and formal image projected (or perceived) at the Auckland law school.[44] Justice Andrew

[42] Coote (n 5) 207.

[43] *ibid* 208.

[44] Jokes circulated imagining Coote as a professional wrestler with the motto 'no consideration given or taken': Watts (n 2) 77.

Phang has suggested that Coote's characterisation of himself as a positivist 'is probably somewhat tongue in cheek'.[45] On the other hand, Coote's very moderate, nuanced and heavily qualified statement of the formalist position, quoted above,[46] reads like a serious attempt to summarise his own actual views: answers to most legal questions found within the law, common law more or less coherent and reasonably predictable, ideally endeavouring to treat like cases alike, and developing incrementally free from arbitrary fiat or from merely personal predilections of the judiciary. Many could subscribe to these propositions without attaching the label of formalism.

As we have seen, Coote's attitudes to statutory law reform changed during his lifetime. So also did the law itself, and the legal intellectual climate, in England and elsewhere. When Coote started to read for his doctoral degree at Cambridge in 1956, he shared the then prevailing English view that stability, predictability and certainty were paramount and highly desirable characteristics of the law, that wide judicial powers were undesirable and that the law could not, and should not be amended except by Parliament. This was a time when the House of Lords still maintained the view that even the House itself (sitting judicially as the Appellate Committee – the final court of appeal) could not overrule its own decisions.[47] But this view was about to change, and two years after the publication of *Exception Clauses* the House of Lords, in a Practice Statement, altered its rule on this point, and announced that, in future, it would entertain the possibility of overruling its own decisions.[48] The far-reaching effect of this change was not immediately apparent. In his inaugural lecture in Auckland in 1967 Coote mentioned the change of practice, without showing great enthusiasm for it, but suggesting that its effect would be slight:

> Lawyers present will know that the House of Lords, which is the highest court of appeal in England, recently issued a note that in future it would not be absolutely bound by its own decisions and this could be the start of a swing toward the American pattern. I know that many of us doubt whether the announcement is going to mean very much.[49]

This prediction turned out to be wrong. Louis Blom-Cooper, reviewing the matter 43 years later, wrote that '[t]he Practice Statement … dropped a pebble into the judicial pool that produced not merely a few ripples but also a seismic wave in English judicial thinking'.[50] The possibility of judicial change was

[45] A Phang, 'Contract as Assumption – The Scholarship and Influence of Professor Brian Coote' (2011) 27 *Journal of Contract Law* 247, 261.

[46] Coote (n 5). See text to n 42.

[47] *London Tramways Co Ltd v London County Council* [1898] AC 375 (HL).

[48] *Practice Statement (Judicial Precedent)* [1966] 1 WLR 1234 (HL).

[49] B Coote, 'A Law Teacher Looks at His Trade' (1968) 6 *Alberta Law Review* 270, 276. The date of the lecture was 19 September 1967.

[50] L Blom-Cooper, '1966 and All That: The Story of the Practice Statement' in L Blom-Cooper, B Dickson and G Drewry (eds), *The Judicial House of Lords: 1876–2009* (Oxford, Oxford University Press, 2009).

introduced into the potential agenda of discussion of every question relating to judicially developed legal rules: even when a judge or commentator advocated statutory change, the possibility of judicial change (if statutory change were not forthcoming) lurked in the background.

As we have seen, *Exception Clauses* was highly influential in persuading the House of Lords to abolish the doctrine of fundamental breach. In reviewing these events in 1981, Coote wrote, as mentioned above, that

> [b]y reaffirming *Suisse Atlantique* and overruling *Harbutt's Plasticene*, the House of Lords has done what it can to remove two obvious distortions from the law, but neither action, by itself, can solve the continuing problem of unacceptable contractual terms generally. Neither 'construction' nor a third revival of fundamental breach can provide a fully satisfactory answer. The better approach, it is submitted, would be the development of an overall control based on some such test as reasonableness or, much more narrowly, unconscionability. Nor, in logic, should such a control be restricted to only one form of contract term.[51]

These are not the words of a formalist. Coote looks to the ulterior purpose that had underlain the doctrine of fundamental breach and points out that the abolition of the doctrine leaves the underlying problem in need of a solution, inviting his readers to agree, on the basis of an argument resting on experience, judgment and persuasion, that there was a serious problem (identified from outside the internal discourse of the law) in need of a solution ('the *continuing* problem of *unacceptable* contractual terms *generally*'). He then points out that techniques of interpretation (construction) cannot supply a satisfactory basis for modifying contracts, and that there is no good reason to limit control to any particular type of contract term. The conclusion is that there should be a general power (presumably to be exercised by judicial or quasi-judicial officers) to control highly unreasonable contractual terms. Then, as though conscious of departing from his earlier views, he added:

> It may be that in a country like Canada, where the approach to law appears to be rather more functional than it is in, say, England, Australia or New Zealand, such a control could be evolved by the courts themselves. But in countries where the approach is more determinist, it would seem far too late, now, to expect any such development to be possible. For such countries, the need is surely for statutory intervention, as Lord Reid indicated in *Suisse Atlantique*.[52]

This qualification does not (it is suggested) entirely restore a perspective that would ordinarily be called formalist. The starting point remains the argument in the preceding paragraph that a general power of control is desirable, and the best means of achieving this objective becomes a secondary consideration that may

[51] Coote (n 8) 803.
[52] Coote, *Contract as Assumption* (n 7) 125.

take into account the legal intellectual climate in different jurisdictions. Coote is ready to accept that in Canada, where he says that the approach to law is 'functional', judicial development might well be the better route. His suggestion that statutory reform would be necessary in England, Australia and New Zealand is based not on the inherent necessity or superiority of statutory reform but on his assessment of the intellectual climate then prevailing in those jurisdictions, which he describes as 'determinist' and of which he says that 'it would seem far too late, *now*, to expect any such development to be possible'. These words do not preclude the view that judicial development, even in the three jurisdictions named, would be desirable if statutory reform were shown to be impossible or impracticable, nor do they preclude the possibility of a change in intellectual climate. Indeed, the use of the word 'now' implies that the intellectual climate may have been different in the past, and may be different in the future.

These comments must be read in the light of Coote's later views of the New Zealand reform statutes, discussed above. He indicated in his article published in 2000[53] considerable reservations about the effect of the reform statutes, and his addition to the title of that article, when it was reprinted in 2016,[54] of the word 'Apologia' shows (whether or not the word 'apologia' is taken to imply regret) that he felt called upon to discuss the merits of statutory, as opposed to judicial, reform, of the law. The implicit framework of the discussion is that the end to be achieved by the proposed reform is the primary objective, and that it then becomes a matter for debate whether judicial or statutory reform is the more desirable and effective method of attaining the objective. This is not what is normally regarded as a formalist approach.

VI. CONCLUSION

It is no reproach to legal scholars to suggest that their opinions have changed over time. On the contrary, there is sometimes reason to view with suspicion opinions held unchanged for 50 years. Changes in facts justify changes in opinions. It is suggested that Coote's views evolved over time, even though he did not always fully acknowledge this himself. The law changed during his lifetime, as did the legal intellectual climate surrounding him, and it is entirely unsurprising, and, indeed, creditable, that his own views also evolved.

Brian Coote could certainly have written an excellent treatise on contract law. But it is not entirely a matter of regret that he did not do so, because, freed from the treatise-writer's attempt (never completely successful) to be comprehensive, he was able, instead, to write more deeply and more cogently on particular

[53] Coote (n 27).

[54] Carter and Ren (n 19) vii, xiv. The word 'apologia' was added as a title to part VI of the book. Part VI contains only one chapter, Coote (n 27).

issues that commanded his, and hence his readers', interest. His article on the performance interest in contract damages, for example, was extensively cited by the House of Lords in a case addressing the rather specialised, and decidedly knotty, problem of damages for defective performance causing loss to a person not a party to the contract.[55] Tony Weir, in his review of *Exception Clauses*, underlined the virtues of particularised legal research:

> It [the book] is, in fact, like the best French books on isolated legal topics, and that already makes it very much better than most legal writing in English .... It is recommended without reservation to all who like reading intelligent and well-written books on important and rather neglected topics.[56]

It is likely that Coote's articles and notes on particular contract topics will be valued and cited long after many of the treatises written during his lifetime have been forgotten, and buried in the remote storage depositories of university libraries. From a broader historical perspective Coote's writings simultaneously reflect, illustrate and illuminate the profound changes in English legal thinking that occurred during the second half of the twentieth century, not least the recognition that one of the characteristics of judicial decision-making is continual change.

[55] *Alfred McAlpine Construction Ltd v Panatown Ltd* [2001] AC 518 (HL), referring to B Coote, 'Contract Damages, *Ruxley*, and the Performance Interest' (1997) 56 *CLJ* 537. Coote was cited by Lord Clyde (534), Lord Goff (548, 551, 556) and by Lord Millett (587); Lords Goff and Millett were dissenting, but their difference from the majority turned on the particular facts of the case. The article was recently cited (though Coote's specific proposals were not adopted) in L Ho and RC Nolan, 'The Performance Interest in the Law of Trusts' (2020) 136 *LQR* 402, 421.

[56] Weir (n 13) 304–305.

14

Professor Patrick Atiyah (1931–2018)

JAMES GOUDKAMP*

I. INTRODUCTION

PATRICK ATIYAH WAS one of the great legal scholars of the twentieth century and a key figure in what is widely regarded as a golden age for law at the University of Oxford. Research active for most of the second half of the century, he produced numerous works of great originality and lasting significance.[1] In contrast with most of the scholars who are addressed in this volume, Atiyah was not concerned exclusively with contract law. He was equally if not better known for his work in connection with the law of torts.[2] However, his contributions to the law of contract were by any measure immense. Foremost among these was his *The Rise and Fall of Freedom of Contract*,[3] which Atiyah regarded as being his 'magnum opus'.[4] Running to almost 800 pages, it chronicles the ebb and flow of the concept of freedom of contract. Its focus was not, for the most part, on doctrinal developments but on the evolution of the economic, intellectual, political and social environment in which contract law operated. Freedom of contract was perceived as a mere experiment that was carried out in the nineteenth century rather than a phenomenon of enduring significance.

* Particular thanks are due to William Twining. With the consent of Atiyah's family, he not only secured my having access to a substantial autobiography that Atiyah wrote but he additionally made available to me a trove of Atiyah's personal correspondence. Most significantly of all, however, William has been a generous critic and sounding board. This chapter also benefitted considerably from often extensive exchanges with Peter Cane, Jonathan Morgan, Edwin Peel, Francis Reynolds and Jane Stapleton. Finally, I am indebted to Peter and Jane, who Atiyah appointed as his 'literary executors', for providing me with voluminous personal documents that belonged to Atiyah.

[1] Atiyah's publications are listed in P Cane and J Stapleton (eds), *Essays for Patrick Atiyah* (Oxford, Clarendon Press, 1991) 375–81.

[2] Regarding Atiyah's tort law scholarship, see J Goudkamp, 'Professor Patrick Atiyah (1931–2018)' in J Goudkamp and D Nolan (eds), *Scholars of Tort Law* (Oxford, Oxford University Press, 2019).

[3] PS Atiyah, *The Rise and Fall of Freedom of Contract* (Oxford, Oxford University Press, 1979).

[4] PS Atiyah, *An Academic Autobiography* (unpublished) 92.

Although Atiyah wrote a good number of formidable doctrinal works and was to a considerable degree a case-orientated lawyer, the fine details of the law were not his central concern. Ultimately, he was interested to understand how the rules that constitute the law of contract came to be and the story that lay behind them. He also had strongly held views regarding the role of legal scholars. In particular, Atiyah considered that academics discharged a vital but woefully under-appreciated (and under-remunerated) function in holding the judiciary to account and in exposing matters to which judges were either oblivious or unwilling to reveal. He also thought that scholars owed an obligation to facilitate public understanding of the law, which he regretted was 'in England regarded as an arcane subject, a husk of technicalities of no real interest or concern to the public'.[5] Consistent with this belief, many of Atiyah's writings, both inside and outside the law of contract, were animated by a concern to improve the law's accessibility. He wrote several works aimed principally at the layperson although not specifically in relation to the law of contract.

II. BIOGRAPHY

Atiyah's life is outlined in a memoir that I wrote regarding him[6] as well as, in far more detail, a substantial and largely unpublished autobiography that he wrote.[7] The latter makes for gripping reading and offers considerable insight regarding Atiyah. It also contains fascinating details concerning the Oxford Law Faculty during the years when Atiyah was an active member of it and, indeed, the state of the legal academy in England, the United States and elsewhere more generally. For present purposes, it must suffice to provide a thumbnail sketch of Atiyah's life. Given the subject of the book of which this chapter forms a part, and in order to minimise travelling over the same terrain again, aspects of Atiyah's professional work that particularly concern his contract law scholarship are emphasised. However, it is necessary to touch periodically on his writings in other fields as Atiyah's scholarship as regards the law of contract cannot properly be understood if it is examined in isolation. That is partly because, as we will see, Atiyah did not perceive the category of contract law to be coherent and considered its separation from, in particular, the law of torts to be symptomatic of outmoded thinking. For him, the law of obligations needed to be radically

[5] *ibid*.

[6] J Goudkamp, 'Patrick Atiyah' (2020) 19 *Biographical Memoirs of Fellows of the British Academy* 149.

[7] Atiyah (n 4). It is difficult to pinpoint precisely when the autobiography was written but all indications point to its having been produced in the early to mid-1990s. Consistent with this is the fact that a small portion of it was published in 1995: PS Atiyah, 'An Autobiographical Fragment' in GP Wilson (ed), *Frontiers of Legal Scholarship* (New York, John Wiley & Sons, 1995).

re-organised, although he never took it upon himself to demonstrate precisely how it should be re-imagined.[8]

A. Early Life

Atiyah was born in England in 1931 but raised in Africa. He attended the Clergy House School in Khartoum and then Victoria College in Alexandria and subsequently in Cairo. His daily companion for much of his childhood was his older brother, Michael, who was two years his senior. From an early age and, indeed, throughout his life, Atiyah regarded himself as living in Michael's shadow, a perception that was reinforced upon Michael's becoming one of the world's most distinguished mathematicians.[9] In 1945, Atiyah returned to England and completed his schooling at Woking County Grammar School for Boys. In 1949, he was awarded an Entrance Exhibition (a type of scholarship) to study Modern History at Magdalen College. In the event, he switched to Jurisprudence shortly before he was due to go up to Oxford.

This change was inspired on account of Atiyah's having had a brush with the law.[10] He had been involved in a minor motor vehicle accident which led to his being charged for driving without due care and attention. Atiyah defended himself in court, which included his cross-examining witnesses. The magistrate convicted him and imposed a nominal sentence of £1. However, the way in which Atiyah had conducted his defence prompted the magistrate to enquire of him whether he was a law student. This caused Atiyah to rethink his plans regarding his studies and, during the train trip home, he resolved to read law. It is a decision that he 'never regretted'.[11] One wonders whether this chance collision inspired not only Atiyah's decision to read Jurisprudence but also whether it had a bearing on his interest in the law of torts and liability for accidents more particularly.

At Magdalen, Atiyah was taught principally by Rupert Cross and John Morris, who are widely regarded as having been one of the most successful law tutor duos in Oxford's history. Atiyah relished his tutorials with Cross. Conversely, he found being taught by Morris, who he described as being 'pompous, severe, and cantankerous',[12] less enjoyable. The antipathy appears to have been mutual with Morris considering Atiyah to be 'brash and bumptious'.[13]

[8] Although see the unpublished paper that is referred to in n 181.

[9] See N Hitchin, 'Sir Michael Atiyah OM' (2020) 69 *Biographical Memoirs of Fellows of the Royal Society* 9.

[10] Atiyah (n 4) 84.

[11] *ibid*.

[12] *ibid* 87.

[13] *ibid* 88. See also *ibid* 98 ('Morris regarded me as conceited if not arrogant') and 125 ('bumptious and arrogant').

Atiyah did little else during his undergraduate years other than study although, 'being an ardent and idealist socialist in those days',[14] he was involved in the activities of Oxford's Labour Club. A sense of the centrality of his studies to his life can be gleaned from the fact that Atiyah regarded participating in the annual dinner moot before Lord Denning as one of the most 'exciting occasions'[15] that he experienced at Magdalen. In 1953, Atiyah completed his undergraduate degree with first class honours. He then studied for the Bachelor of Civil Law, which he was also awarded with first class honours.

B. First Academic Posts

In October 1954, Atiyah started work as an assistant lecturer at the London School of Economics where he delivered tutorials in the law of trusts and the law of contract.[16] Atiyah preferred teaching the latter as he found the former to be 'in many ways exceeding technical, and lacking the excitement of a social dimension'.[17] He remained in this post for only one year during which time he published his first article, which concerned the law of conversion and the defence of *jus tertii*.[18] Thereafter, he held successive appointments as a lecturer and senior lecturer at the University of Khartoum, where he ran the Commercial Law Department. William Twining was one of his colleagues (and neighbours).[19] Twining would, as things turned out, exert a significant influence on the direction of Atiyah's research (Atiyah had a similar impact on Twining's work).

While at Khartoum, Atiyah wrote numerous casenotes for the *Sudan Law Journal*. Most of these were concerned with the law of contract and were predominantly black-letter in nature. They covered topics such as privity,[20] the penalty doctrine[21] and exemption clauses.[22] Atiyah also published a draft Sale of Goods Bill[23] that was loosely based on the Sale of Goods Act 1893 (UK). This last-mentioned project reveals a striking concern with reforming the law that would endure throughout his career.[24] Atiyah also wrote several substantial

[14] *ibid* 89.
[15] *ibid* 92.
[16] *ibid* 100.
[17] *ibid*.
[18] PS Atiyah, 'A Re-examination of the *Jus Tertii* in Conversion' (1955) 18 *MLR* 97.
[19] See the discussion in W Twining, *Jurist in Context: A Memoir* (Cambridge, Cambridge University Press, 2019) 41–42.
[20] PS Atiyah, 'Sid Ahmed Mohamed v. Sudan Mercantile Co' [1956] *Sudan Law Journal and Reports* 55.
[21] PS Atiyah, 'Roughdi Boutros v. Christos Simos' [1956] *Sudan Law Journal and Reports* 93.
[22] PS Atiyah, '*Hassan Khalil Suleiman v. El A'Gig Ali and Christos Simos v. Mohd. Ali Ahmed*' [1956] *Sudan Law Journal and Reports* 94.
[23] PS Atiyah, 'A New Sale of Goods Bill' [1957] *Sudan Law Journal and Reports* 107.
[24] This theme is explored further below: see text to nn 198–205.

articles on topics that similarly fell broadly within contract law.[25] In addition to these periodical publications, he published *The Sale of Goods*.[26] This work was aimed mainly at students and written because Atiyah considered 'that there seemed to be no adequate book on the subject'.[27] The text ended up being 'the most successful and consistent seller'[28] of all of the books that he would go on to write.[29]

In 1958, Atiyah received an invitation to write a book on contract law for the Clarendon Law series. The invitation came from HLA Hart, who was the series' general editor. It appears that Hart approached Atiyah on the recommendation of Rupert Cross.[30] Atiyah immediately accepted the offer and wrote the book – *An Introduction to the Law of Contract* – 'in a little over a year'. In 1959, he travelled to England where he 'went over [the manuscript] carefully' with Hart.[31] 'Scarcely a page of the original draft emerged unscathed from his vigilant scrutiny'.[32] The book was published in 1961. It was aimed at 'law students beginning a course on Contract, and non-lawyers who would like to have some idea of what the law of contract is about'.[33] However, as Neil Andrews observed in a review of a later edition,[34] it did not, despite its title, really provide a mere introduction to the subject. Rather, it was a work in which Atiyah singled out for analysis particular doctrines that he thought were revealing regarding the subject's nature and explored broad trends in and influences upon it. Atiyah would go on to write a total of five editions of the book.[35] Although the work evolved significantly over time as one would expect, it retained its central character. Consistent with this, a reviewer of the fifth edition wrote that

> [t]his is not a work that sets out the law with the authority of Chitty or with the objectivity of Treitel [but is intended] to disabuse the reader of the idea that contract law is simply a matter of applying established legal principles to a given situation.[36]

[25] See, eg, PS Atiyah, 'Couturier v Hastie and the Sale of Non-Existent Goods' (1957) 73 *LQR* 340; PS Atiyah, 'Injustices and Anomalies in the Law of Hire Purchase' (1958) 5 *Business Law Review* 24; PS Atiyah, 'The Liability of Infants in Fraud and Restitution' (1959) 22 *MLR* 273.

[26] PS Atiyah, *The Sale of Goods* (London, Pitman, 1957).

[27] Atiyah (n 4) 119.

[28] *ibid.*

[29] Consistent with this, it is one of his longest surviving books, and numerous editions of it have been produced by other authors. The latest is C Twigg-Flesner and R Canavan, *Atiyah and Adams' Sale of Goods*, 14th edn (Harlow, Pearson, 2021).

[30] Atiyah (n 4) 123.

[31] *ibid.*

[32] PS Atiyah, *An Introduction to the Law of Contract* (Oxford, Clarendon Press, 1961) vii.

[33] *ibid* vi.

[34] N Andrews, 'Book Review' (2006) 65 *CLJ* 727, 727. Consider also A Phang, 'Theory as Practice and Practice as Theory – The Integrated and Integral Contract Scholarship of Professor Michael Furmston' (2014) 31 *Journal of Contract Law* 12, 14.

[35] Atiyah (n 32); PS Atiyah, *An Introduction to the Law of Contract*, 2nd edn (Oxford, Clarendon Press, 1971); PS Atiyah, *An Introduction to the Law of Contract*, 3rd edn (Oxford, Clarendon Press, 1981); PS Atiyah, *An Introduction to the Law of Contract*, 4th edn (Oxford, Clarendon Press, 1989); PS Atiyah, *An Introduction to the Law of Contract*, 5th edn (Oxford, Clarendon Press, 1995).

[36] M Riley, 'Book Review' (1996) 7 *International Company and Commercial Law Review* 116, 116.

C. Civil Service

Although he had developed an enviable publication record while in Khartoum, Atiyah considered that his career would be unlikely to prosper unless he moved on. He regarded himself as toiling in isolation in the Sudan.[37] This led to his applying for two Oxford fellowships and an assistant lecturership at Cambridge. As a result of what must rank as some of the worst decisions ever made by Oxbridge appointment panels, these applications were unsuccessful. It appears that one of the Oxford applications was scuppered by a negative reference written by John Morris[38] who, as discussed above, held some animosity towards Atiyah.[39] No new academic role being offered to him, in 1959 Atiyah moved to Ghana in order to accept a position in the Attorney-General's Department. In that capacity, he carried out a range of legal work for the Government. Among other things, Atiyah found himself 'doing a lot of commercial work, drafting contracts and advising government departments'.[40] Although he initially enjoyed life in Ghana, he became disillusioned with it by what he described as 'the general smell of corruption which hovered over government activities'[41] as well as because of 'the increasing totalitarianism'.[42]

In 1961, Atiyah returned to England in order to take up a position as a legal assistant at the Board of Trade. In this role, Atiyah learned 'a lot about care and accuracy in legal research', which was something that he considered 'the ordinary academic is (perhaps surprisingly) not always very good at'.[43] He was also involved in drafting government bills and, in 1964, transferred to the Parliamentary Counsel's Office. In the event, however, Atiyah did not remain in that post for long. He evidently found it rather dull and regarded himself and the civil service generally as being seriously underworked. Shortly after he had started at the Parliamentary Counsel's Office he received a letter from the Warden of New College, Oxford, effectively offering him a law fellowship, which he accepted (which was apparently the way in which things worked at the time). In 1964, Atiyah thus returned to Oxford.

It is not entirely impossible that Michael Atiyah played some role in New College's reaching out to his brother in circumstances where Michael had been

[37] See W Twining, 'Reflections on Law in Context' in Cane and Stapleton (n 1) 1.
[38] Atiyah (n 4) 125.
[39] See text to nn 12–13.
[40] Atiyah (n 4) 134.
[41] *ibid* 136.
[42] *ibid* 138.
[43] *ibid* 143.

elected to a Professorial Fellowship at the College in 1963. Conversely, Patrick himself seems to have regarded his appointment as being linked in some way with that of Tony Honoré, who accepted a post as a reader at New College in the same year. In somewhat cryptic remarks in a chapter for a *festschrift* for Honoré, he wrote that he 'assumed' that his election 'had something to do with the simultaneous migration of Tony Honoré from Queen's to New College'.[44] Whatever the position, the appointments were an extraordinary triumph for New College. Few if any other Oxbridge Colleges could claim to have pulled off such a hiring coup in a single year.

D. New College

While at New College, Atiyah pivoted, to a degree, from contract law (with which he had been primarily concerned while at the University of Khartoum)[45] to the law of torts. He wrote his first book on the subject, *Vicarious Liability in the Law of Torts*,[46] which was published in 1967. It earned rave reviews[47] and was and still is regularly cited by the courts,[48] which is remarkable given how much that field has developed in the intervening half-century since it was published.[49] Although Atiyah was increasingly concerned with the law of torts during this period of his career, he continued working on the law of contract. Thus, he joined the editorial team of *Chitty on Contracts* and ultimately took part in three editions of that work.[50] Further, while at New College Atiyah became more and more interested in philosophy. He had many discussions with the College's philosophy fellows and 'discovered how fascinated philosophers had been down the ages about the nature of promissory obligations'.[51]

[44] PS Atiyah, 'Form and Substance in Legal Reasoning: the Case of Contract' in N MacCormick and P Birks (eds), *The Legal Mind: Essays for Tony Honoré* (Oxford, Clarendon Press, 1986) 19.

[45] See nn 20–33.

[46] PS Atiyah, *Vicarious Liability in the Law of Torts* (London, Butterworths, 1967).

[47] See, eg, JA Jolowicz, 'Book Review: Vicarious Liability in the Law of Torts' (1986) 26 *CLJ* 150.

[48] See, eg, *Majrowski v Guy's and St Thomas's NHS Trust* [2006] UKHL 34, [2007] 1 AC 224 [11] ('well-known book'); *Biffa Waste Services Ltd v Maschinenfabrik Ernst Hese GmbH* [2008] EWCA Civ 1257, [2009] QB 725 [75] ('seminal work').

[49] In *Various Claimants v Catholic Child Welfare Society* [2012] UKSC 56, [2013] 2 AC 1 [19], Lord Phillips observed that '[t]he law of vicarious liability is on the move'. In *Cox v Ministry of Justice* [2016] UKSC 10, [2016] AC 660 [1], Lord Reed added that '[i]t has not yet come to a stop'.

[50] *Chitty on Contracts*, 23rd edn (London, Sweet & Maxwell, 1968); *Chitty on Contracts*, 24th edn (London, Sweet & Maxwell, 1977); *Chitty on Contracts*, 25th edn (London, Sweet & Maxwell, 1983).

[51] Atiyah (n 4) 182.

In terms of teaching, in addition to providing tutorials for New College, Atiyah delivered a course of lectures on contract. Complete sets of notes for several of these survive to the present day. They are nothing short of meticulous and extraordinarily comprehensive. For example, Atiyah prepared 120 pages of immaculate typed notes for a set of lectures on 'Mistake' and 127 pages of typed text for lectures on 'Misrepresentation'. These notes reveal not only an exceptionally diligent educator but also suggest that Atiyah did not like to go off-piste in his lectures and stuck fairly strictly to a carefully prepared script. Overall, the content was pitched at a high level of sophistication and probably rather far beyond the grasp of the average undergraduate student. Predictably, the lecture notes were not simply descriptive of the law. Atiyah often criticised the law and identified areas where he considered that the courts had gone seriously wrong. He did not spare academics from his attacks, and frequently castigated the authors of leading textbooks for spouting what he regarded as gibberish. His favourite targets were Treitel's *The Law of Contract* and Cheshire and Fifoot's *The Law of Contract*. For instance, he said of the former:

> [I]n *Treitel* I find the proposition that mistake as to the person and mistake as to the subject matter make a contract void if the mistake is fundamental whereas a mistake as to terms makes a contract void even if the mistake is not fundamental. I am bound to say that I think this is nonsense.[52]

To give another example, he said that Cheshire and Fifoot's account of *Couturier v Hastie*[53] was 'not only wrong, but positively mischievous' and ultimately nothing more than 'rubbish'.[54]

E. Canberra

As the 1960s drew to an end, Atiyah grew increasingly dissatisfied with his position at Oxford. He knew that opportunities for promotion were few and far between and the 'unbearable grind'[55] of Oxford's tutorial system was taking a heavy toll on him. He searched out other opportunities and, in the event, accepted the offer of a chair at the Australia National University. He took up that position in 1969.[56] According to *The Canberra Times*, Atiyah was responsible

[52] PS Atiyah, Lectures on Mistake, 51.

[53] *Couturier v Hastie* (1856) 5 HLC 673 (HL). See PS Atiyah, '*Couturier v. Hastie* and the Sale of Non-Existent Goods' (1957) 73 *LQR* 340.

[54] Atiyah (n 52) 98.

[55] Atiyah (n 4) 215.

[56] Upon arriving at the Australian National University, Atiyah wrote a short unpublished paper entitled 'A Few Thoughts on Legal Education at Oxford' in which he wrote that he was 'depressed by the prospects for undergraduate legal education at Oxford' and opined that 'the quality of legal education at Oxford is lower than it should be; it is lower than that at many other English and Commonwealth Universities, including (I think), the A.N.U.' (at 2).

for introducing 'specialised courses in business and commercial law'.[57] His inaugural lecture was entitled 'Consideration in Contracts: A Fundamental Restatement'.[58] It criticised the doctrine of consideration as having become unduly formalistic and divorced from the justice of enforcing promises.

In 1970, Atiyah published *Accidents, Compensation and the Law*.[59] This book was the first in the Law and Context series.[60] In it, Atiyah examined tort law alongside various other mechanisms for providing compensation for accidentally caused personal injury and death. His concern was not with the fine details of torts cases but to understand matters such as the number of accidents and claims, the frictional costs involved in administering the various systems for providing redress for personal injury and death, the significance of settlements, the roles played by insurers and lawyers in the process, the effects of awarding compensation on the behaviour of both injurers and the injured and so on. Nicola Lacey summed up the book well when she said that it 'epitomised [the] intellectual ambition [of the Law and Context series] and commitment to examining legal doctrines and arrangements in the round, in terms of not only their normative details, but also their social roles and meanings'.[61]

An 'instant classic' that 'guaranteed Atiyah's place in the pantheon of the great scholars of Tort law',[62] *Accidents, Compensation and the Law* represented an inflection point in the nature of legal scholarship in the Commonwealth. By eschewing concern with the minutiae of the case law and instead focusing on the social *milieu* of which the law was a part, it departed radically from traditional forms of legal research. As Twining observes, the book 'won almost instant recognition as a brilliantly designed and executed departure from tradition'.[63] The significance of these remarks regarding *Accidents, Compensation and the Law* for present purposes lies mainly in the fact that, and as will be explored in further detail below,[64] Atiyah's expertise regarding tort law significantly influenced his thinking regarding contract law. The contextual methodology also carried over to a degree.[65]

[57] 'ANU Chair for Oxford Fellow' *The Canberra Times* (1 October 1969) 8.

[58] PS Atiyah, *Consideration in Contracts: A Fundamental Restatement* (Canberra, Australian National University Press, 1971).

[59] PS Atiyah, *Accidents, Compensation and the Law* (London, Weidenfeld and Nicolson, 1970).

[60] Twining, one of the series editors, had initially invited Atiyah to write a book for the series on Commercial Law. Atiyah reportedly responded that he was bored with contract and that he wanted to do a number on torts.

[61] N Lacey, 'William Twining and the Law in Context series: A Personal Reflection' (2020) 16 *International Journal of Law in Context* 464, 465.

[62] PRB Fortes, 'An Exploring of Legal Borderlands: A Review of William Twining's Jurist in Context, A Memoir' (2019) 5 *Journal of Institutional Studies* 777, 786.

[63] Twining (n 37) 26. See also the discussion in Twining (n 19) 154–55. See also T Weir, 'Book Review' (1992) 51 *CLJ* 375, 376 ('pathbreaking').

[64] See text to nn 185–86.

[65] See text to nn 163–67.

In July 1973, Atiyah abruptly left Australia.[66] The catalyst for his sudden departure were legal problems that had ensnared his eldest son, Julian. Criminal proceedings had been brought against him and Atiyah had formed the view that the police officers involved were corrupt and the judge who tried the proceedings openly biased and incompetent.[67] While an appeal was pending, Julian was arrested again and Atiyah thought that 'it was not safe for him to remain in Australia, because there was a grave risk of his ending up in jail on some trumped up charge'.[68] Atiyah and his family thus returned to England where he had accepted a chair at the University of Warwick, to which he was attracted because its Law Department 'was pioneering a law degree of a much more overtly social character'.[69] He had been recruited by Twining, who had himself moved to Warwick shortly beforehand.[70] It appears that Atiyah's chair was created because the Law Department wanted to develop greater expertise in socio-legal studies.[71]

F. Warwick

At Warwick, Twining encouraged Atiyah to write a book on contract for, presumably, the Law in Context series.[72] However, for reasons that are unclear Atiyah 'simply did not see how this could be done'[73] and he embarked instead on a different project which would yield his *The Rise and Fall of Freedom of Contract*. As its title makes clear, the book is about the intellectual movement from, as Atiyah saw it, *laissez-faire* philosophy to one in which the role of the free market appeared to be over. Grant Gilmore's *The Death of Contract*,[74] which Atiyah regarded as 'a splendid little book',[75] was the catalyst for the work.[76] Atiyah sent Gilmore tranches of draft text for his comment. Gilmore responded that the book would 'become one of the chief monuments of English jurisprudence in our century'.[77] The project was all-consuming and, 'for a year or two', Atiyah 'neglected [his] family and virtually all other interests'.[78] He spent long

[66] Letter from PS Atiyah to the Register of the Australian National University (2 July 1973).
[67] Atiyah (n 4) 234–41.
[68] *ibid* 246–47.
[69] *ibid* 249.
[70] *ibid* 243.
[71] Atiyah was described in the Warwick law programme as Professor of Socio-Legal Studies, although his chair carried no such title (unpublished paper written by PS Atiyah entitled 'Socio-Legal Studies in the Law School', 1).
[72] Atiyah (n 4) 262–63.
[73] *ibid* 263.
[74] G Gilmore, *The Death of Contract* (Columbus, Ohio State University Press, 1974).
[75] PS Atiyah, 'Book Review' (1977) 71 *American Political Science Review* 636, 636.
[76] Atiyah (n 4) 263.
[77] Letter from G Gilmore to PS Atiyah (29 July 1977).
[78] Atiyah (n 4) 267.

hours in Warwick's library browsing material throughout the social sciences.[79] By 1977,[80] the bulk of the book had been written although it was not published until 1979. Atiyah had originally intended to produce a two-part work.[81] He envisaged that the first would be historical and the latter contemporary and, more specifically, a search for a new theory of contractual liability given the demise of the classical model. *The Rise and Fall of Freedom of Contract* constituted the first instalment. Although Atiyah took extensive notes with a view to writing the second, he never produced it and, sadly, he appears not to have preserved his preliminary work.

While Atiyah was engaged in writing *The Rise and Fall of Freedom of Contract*, Guenter Treitel published[82] a reply, which was regarded as hard-hitting at the time, to the lecture that Atiyah had delivered in 1971 at the Australian National University.[83] It is impractical to explore within the confines of this chapter the details of Treitel's objections. In broad terms, however, Treitel regarded Atiyah as having overlooked key features of the doctrinal landscape. His overall conclusion was that 'Professor Atiyah's suggested Restatement will not lead to any significant improvements in the current position'.[84] The fact that Treitel published this response to Atiyah's lecture so long after the latter had been delivered is probably explained, as Francis Reynolds suggests, by the fact that Treitel held a visiting position at the University of Western Australia at the time.[85]

G. Election to a Chair at Oxford

In 1977, Atiyah was elected Professor of English Law at Oxford and to a professorial fellowship at St John's College, with which College that chair is associated. He regarded this as one of his greatest achievements.[86] Treitel, who had been in the running for the position, was 'severe[ly] disappointed'[87] that the appointment panel had selected Atiyah instead of him.[88] He complained bitterly

[79] *ibid* 265.

[80] *ibid* 275.

[81] Atiyah (n 3) vi.

[82] GH Treitel, 'Consideration: A Critical Analysis of Professor Atiyah's Fundamental Restatement' (1976) 50 *Australian Law Journal* 439. For discussion, see Burrows, chapter 11 of this volume, pp 280–81.

[83] See text to n 58.

[84] Treitel (n 82) 449.

[85] F Reynolds, 'Guenter Treitel' (2020) 19 *Biographical Memoirs of Fellows of the British Academy* 129, 141.

[86] '[R]eading the letter of appointment from the University Registrar was one of the greatest moments of my life': Atiyah (n 4) 271.

[87] G Treitel, 'Vicissitudes of an Academic Lawyer' [2018] *Zeitschrift für Europäisches Privatrecht* 130, 162.

[88] See further Reynolds (n 85) 140.

to colleagues about the decision. The disappointment must have been heightened in circumstances where Treitel was Atiyah's senior. As Atiyah observed, 'Treitel had ... been an Oxford fellow for over 20 years, and indeed had been promoted to Reader the year I had arrived as a mere fellow at New College'.[89] In the event, Treitel's disappointment was assuaged upon his being elected in 1978 to the Vinerian chair.[90]

Although Atiyah's elevation to a statutory chair substantially relieved him of teaching commitments,[91] he assumed a variety of onerous obligations, including serving for six years as the inaugural general editor of the *Oxford Journal of Legal Studies*.[92] He also continued to write furiously and produced a substantial number of formidable pieces of scholarship. These included *Promises, Morals, and Law*,[93] which was concerned with the nature of promissory obligations, and *Form and Substance in Anglo-American Law: A Comparative Study of Legal Reasoning, Legal Theory, and Legal Institutions*,[94] which promoted the thesis that English law was more formal than that in the United States.

It was during this phase of his career that Atiyah rose to international prominence. Invitations to give named lectures across the world, but particularly in the United States, came at breakneck pace. By far the most prestigious of these – and in Atiyah's words 'one of the greatest honours which can be bestowed on a legal scholar in the common law world'[95] – was that to deliver one of the three Holmes Lectures at Harvard Law School in 1981.[96] Charles Fried lobbied Harvard 'with great enthusiasm' for the invitation to be issued,[97] and the letter of invitation makes it clear Atiyah had earned a significant reputation in the United States legal academy on account of *The Rise and Fall of Freedom of Contract*.[98] Atiyah's Holmes Lecture ended up addressing Holmes's contribution to the law of contract, crime and tort from a British perspective.

[89] Atiyah (n 4) 270.

[90] For details, see Treitel (n 87) 163; Reynolds (n 85) 141.

[91] It has been difficult to identify the subjects that Atiyah taught upon his return to Oxford. However, personal papers that have been made available to me make it clear that in 1984 he taught a course entitled 'Remedies in Contract and Tort' and in 1986 he delivered a course of lectures entitled 'The Foundations of Contractual Liability'. Nor, with the exception of Jane Stapleton who read for a doctorate under Atiyah entitled 'Compensation for Disease', has it proved possible to identify who were his research students.

[92] Atiyah (n 4) 286–87.

[93] PS Atiyah, *Promises, Morals, and Law* (Oxford, Oxford University Press, 1983).

[94] PS Atiyah and RS Summers, *Form and Substance in Anglo-American Law: A Comparative Study of Legal Reasoning, Legal Theory, and Legal Institutions* (Oxford, Clarendon Press, 1987).

[95] Atiyah (n 4) 298.

[96] An expanded version of the lecture was published as PS Atiyah, 'The Legacy of Holmes through English Eyes' (1983) 63 *Boston University Law Review* 341.

[97] Letter from C Fried to PS Atiyah (15 August 1980).

[98] Letter from AM Sacks to PS Atiyah (26 June 1980).

H. Retirement

In 1988, Atiyah retired prematurely because of long-standing difficulties with his heart.[99] He moved to Hayling Island where he lived in a relatively modest detached house. It is clear from correspondence that is now available that he did not, however, become completely disconnected from the law. Atiyah continued to read significant judgments. He exchanged letters with several Law Lords regarding cases that they decided. For example, in 2000, Atiyah wrote to one Law Lord regarding the House of Lords' decision in *MacFarlane v Tayside Health Board*,[100] of which he apparently approved. He also continued to publish albeit at a much-reduced rate. In particular, Atiyah wrote *The Damages Lottery*,[101] which was a short book aimed at the layperson in which he severely criticised the tort system and argued for its abolition and replacement with a market solution to the problem of accidentally caused personal injury and deaths. He evidently hoped that the volume would spark some reforms. He even sent, perhaps rather optimistically, a copy of it to Lord Irvine, who was then the Lord Chancellor.[102] Atiyah also continued to give some public lectures. For instance, in 1999 he delivered an unpublished lecture entitled 'Social Change and the Law – the Last Fifty Years' at Christ's College, Cambridge. The focus of this lecture was the vast increase in choice available to consumers over the last half-century and the impact of that increase on the law. Strikingly, he made searing criticisms of the Law Commission on the basis that it focused on abstract principles while ignoring momentous social developments. He queried whether one Law Commissioner 'live[d] in the same world' as him.[103] In 2018, Atiyah died following a cruel battle with dementia.

III. PRINCIPAL WORKS

This section dwells (albeit inevitably briefly given the space available) on Atiyah's principal writings regarding contract law. These are *The Rise and Fall of Freedom of Contract* and *Promises, Morals, and Law*.[104] Paradoxically, neither of these works is centrally concerned with the *law* of contract.

[99] Atiyah (n 4) 328–29.

[100] *MacFarlane v Tayside Health Board* [2000] 2 AC 59 (HL).

[101] PS Atiyah, *The Damages Lottery* (Oxford, Hart Publishing, 1997).

[102] Letter from PS Atiyah to A Irvine (15 November 1997).

[103] PS Atiyah, 'Social Change and the Law – the Last Fifty Years' (unpublished lecture, Christ's College, Cambridge, 1999) 18.

[104] PS Atiyah, *Essays on Contract* (Oxford, Clarendon Press, 1986) is a substantial and important work but, since it is a compilation of various of Atiyah's essays regarding the law of contract written over the course of his career, does not deliver a sustained message in the same way that his monographs do.

A. *The Rise and Fall of Freedom of Contract*

Atiyah's fame as a scholar of contract law rests in significant part on his *The Rise and Fall of Freedom of Contract*. This vast book is, ultimately, a sprawling excursus regarding the concept of freedom of contract in view of the environment in which, according to Atiyah, it flourished and then wilted.[105] The book is divided into three temporal periods. The first is concerned with matters prior to 1770, which Atiyah regarded as the formative period for the idea of freedom of contract. During this stage, there was, Atiyah concluded, no general theory of contractual liability and promises played a merely subordinate role in the creation of obligations. The second spanned the period from 1770 to 1870, which Atiyah called the age of freedom of contract. It was characterised by the flourishing of general principles of contract law that were intimately linked with the development of the free market. The third concerned the next century from 1870 to 1970. This period involved the decline and fall of freedom of contract. A recurring theme was that both '[t]he notion that benefits should be fairly recompensed' and 'the notion that reasonable reliance should be protected' grew in prominence.[106] This trend was matched by a decline of promise-based liability. Indeed, Atiyah suggested that promise-based liability may be nothing more than 'a projection of liabilities normally based on benefit or reliance'.[107] Scholars of contract law were chided for glorifying classical theory despite the world having long since moved on in a way that was incompatible with it. Each of the three parts of the book includes chapters on the social conditions in England and the intellectual background before turning to consider the law.

The Rise and Fall of Freedom of Contract basked in the warmth of numerous glowing reviews and, perhaps surprisingly given that it did not engage extensively with American sources, attracted great interest on that side of the Atlantic. Charles Gray considered that it was 'outstanding both as a synthesis of specialized work by historians and as a commentary on English institutional history and its intellectual counterpoint from the eighteenth century to the present'.[108] Barbara Black wrote that '[t]his volume will superbly serve the reader for whom it is an introduction to the subject; the specialist in the field will find in it an abundance of novel insight and provocative ideas. We have here a major scholarly contribution …'.[109] Keith Uff said that 'it is hardly an

[105] *The Rise and Fall of Freedom of Contract* was preceded by an important article published shortly before the book appeared in print: PS Atiyah, 'Contracts, Promises and the Law of Obligations' (1978) 94 *LQR* 193.

[106] Atiyah (n 3) 714.

[107] *ibid* 4.

[108] CM Gray, 'The Ages of Classical Contract Law' (1980) 90 *Yale Law Journal* 216, 216.

[109] B Black, 'A Tale of Two Laws' (1981) 79 *Michigan Law Review* 929, 946.

exaggeration to say that every page contains some important new and perceptive insight'.[110]

However, the reception was far from unwaveringly positive. John Baker characterised the book 'as a monument of intellectual history' rather than 'an essay in strict legal history'.[111] He considered that the least convincing part of the book was, ironically, its analysis of the law. Atiyah was accused of having committed serious errors in his interpretation of the relevant materials, and resorting to bare assertions about 'what the law must have been' as opposed to basing his analysis on contemporary records.[112] Thus, Baker writes that various features of the law that Atiyah traced to the period from 1770, such as attention being focused on promises as opposed to the claimant's reliance or the defendant's receipt of a benefit, were in fact present in the law well beforehand.[113] Colin Turpin expressed broadly similar sentiments. He wrote that 'Atiyah has written a history of thought, ideas and attitudes, necessarily at a level of generality, and he ventures upon speculations which a close study of records and cases may demonstrate to need correction or qualification'.[114] Charles Fried, although he greatly admired the work,[115] similarly objected to various of Atiyah's characterisations of the law and argued, for example, that Atiyah's account of the doctrine of consideration was 'seriously distorted'.[116] Other reviewers took issue not with Atiyah's handling of the law but perceived shortcomings in the coverage of the intellectual and political background.[117]

In the final chapter of the book Atiyah claimed that freedom of contract in England had 'ceased to be a living issue'.[118] He asserted that it was 'no longer the individual but the Government which largely allocates resources in the British economy',[119] that there had 'been a continuous weakening of belief in the values involved in individual freedom of choice'[120] and that there had been 'a significant move to increase liabilities based on unbargained-for reliance'.[121] Ironically, these claims, which lay at the heart of his enterprise, were largely contradicted by developments that occurred at almost precisely the time that

[110] K Uff, 'Book Review' (1980) 5 *Holdsworth Law Review* 101, 101.
[111] JH Baker, 'Book Review' (1980) 43 *MLR* 467, 469.
[112] *ibid* 467.
[113] *ibid* 467–68.
[114] C Turpin, 'Book Review' (1980) 39 *CLJ* 396, 397.
[115] See text accompanying n 97 above.
[116] C Fried, 'Book Review' (1980) 93 *Harvard Law Review* 1858, 1865.
[117] See, eg, I Duncanson, 'Book Review' (1983) 1 *Law in Context: A Socio-Legal Journal* 126, 129–30 (contending that insufficient attention had been paid to Marxist ideas).
[118] Atiyah (n 3) 716.
[119] *ibid* 717.
[120] *ibid* 726.
[121] *ibid* 771.

the book went to press. In the same year that *The Rise and Fall of Freedom of Contract* appeared in print, Margaret Thatcher became Prime Minister and a fundamental change in the political *zeitgeist* followed. Deregulation and privatisation of industries was emphasised and there was a decline in the significance of unions. The pendulum had swung firmly back in favour of freedom of contract.[122] Atiyah was compelled to acknowledge as much in the fifth edition of his *Introduction to the Law of Contract*,[123] although he queried the extent to which the shift into reverse gear affected the common law[124] and maintained the claims that the law of contract had surrendered territory to tort law and the law of unjust enrichment.[125]

B. *Promises, Morals, and Law*

Promises, Morals, and Law, which runs to a little over 200 pages, is addressed to philosophers interested in the topic of promising and to theoretically inclined lawyers.[126] The book[127] has various related goals. One is to probe the reasons why promises are thought to be morally binding. Atiyah considered the lack of learning on this subject among lawyers was a rather astonishing gap in understanding regarding contract law. Legal scholars had largely taken it for granted, he wrote, that promises were morally binding and that this was at least part of the reason why the law enforced them. Another of the book's functions is to bridge a gap between philosophy and law. Although philosophers had long been absorbed by the concept of promises, much of the relevant scholarship had simply not, Atiyah said, filtered through to lawyers. Condensing matters significantly, Atiyah made two central claims in the book. The first, and the subject of chapters two to four, was that the available explanations for the moral obligation to perform promises were defective. The second, advanced in chapters five to seven, was that, in truth, promises themselves were not morally binding at all. Promises are simply things that appear to generate obligations and that, when

[122] The revival of the idea of freedom of contract is explored in FH Buckley (ed), *The Fall and Rise of Freedom of Contract* (Durham NC, Duke University Press, 1999).

[123] Atiyah (1995) (n 35) 27–34.

[124] *ibid* 27.

[125] *ibid* 33.

[126] Atiyah (n 93) v.

[127] The book was preceded by a lengthy unpublished paper entitled 'The Practice of Promising' that Atiyah wrote while at the University of Warwick. Atiyah scribbled in manuscript on that paper that he 'had drawn on it for' *Promises, Morals, and Law*. It is unclear why Atiyah did not publish it. It may be that he was preoccupied with completing work on *The Rise and Fall of Freedom of Contract*. Another explanation is that he simply continued to ruminate on the analysis and ultimately considered that it required book-length treatment in *Promises, Morals, and Law*.

the situation is properly understood, it emerges that the obligation in issue has an independent source.[128]

On the whole, reviewers, while they readily acknowledged the importance of the book and the novelty of the analysis offered in it, were unconvinced. AWB Simpson, while he considered the book to be a 'very original critical work', concluded that 'Atiyah, having developed the important thesis that moral reasons can be stronger or weaker, carries this too far in claiming that promises as such can never count as moral reasons'.[129] Hugh Collins expressed similar views. He wrote that:

> Atiyah's thesis is based upon some dubious generalisations about the direction in which legal doctrine is flowing, and upon some unconvincing and often unarticulated reasons for accepting a new analysis of the moral rule relating to promises which debases the promise to an evidentiary function.[130]

Joseph Raz considered that Atiyah had been 'led … to an untenable view of promises and to a distorted doctrine of their relation to the law'.[131] In Raz's view, promises are not simply admissions of other obligations but sources of obligation in their own right that the law enforces to protect the valuable social practice of promising.[132] Another reviewer concluded that Atiyah's 'ultimate thesis, that the binding force of promises depends on independent norms, rests on an unpersuasive attack on prior doctrine and an unwarranted faith in the morality of social practices and rules'.[133] In 1984, a joint committee of the Royal Society of Arts and Royal College of Physicians awarded Atiyah the Swiney Prize for the book.[134] It consisted in a silver cup and the sum of £100.

IV. THEMES

This section ruminates on twelve (often interconnected) features of Atiyah's contract law scholarship. To a degree, the discussion is equally applicable to his writings in other areas of the law. That said, there are important and striking differences in the methodology that Atiyah employed in his work as regards contract law and his research in connection with the law of torts. In relation to the former, Atiyah was deeply interested in history and theory (as exemplified by

[128] This theme was present although less forcefully expressed in the unpublished paper referred to in the previous footnote. In that paper, Atiyah argued that one of the principal functions of promises was to 'clarify rather than create obligations' (at 56).

[129] AWB Simpson, 'Book Review' (1982) 7 *American Bar Foundation Research Journal* 537, 541.

[130] H Collins, 'Counsel to Philosophers' (1982) 45 *MLR* 225, 229–30.

[131] J Raz, 'Promises in Law and Morality' (1982) 16 *Harvard Law Review* 916, 938.

[132] *ibid* 927–38.

[133] 'Book Review' (1983) 81 *Michigan Law Review* 899, 903.

[134] Letter from JS Skidmore to PS Atiyah (5 January 1984).

his *The Rise and Fall of Freedom of Contract* and *Promises, Morals, and Law* respectively). Conversely, he was almost completely unconcerned with these aspects of tort law. He said almost nothing about either of them in his published works on tort despite the vast scale of those writings. The reason for this major difference in his approach to the two fields is unclear.

A. Perspective

To a considerable extent, Atiyah was not ultimately concerned with the precise details of contract law and, consistent with this, his works were generally lightly referenced.[135] One senses that the microscopic features of the authorities and statutes did not really hold his attention and that he was far more interested with identifying major arcs in the law. *The Rise and Fall of Freedom of Contract* is emblematic of this approach. This work was fundamentally concerned with shifts in the social context relevant to the idea of freedom of contract rather than with the specifics of individual cases and statutes. Another illustration is Atiyah's *From Principles to Pragmatism*,[136] which was his inaugural lecture at Oxford. The overarching thesis of this work, which was largely developed with reference to illustrations taken from the law of contract, is that the law had gradually become much less concerned with principle and that it had instead increasingly emphasised individualised justice. None of the foregoing is meant to suggest that Atiyah was caviller as regards the minutiae of the law when it mattered. He was clearly comfortable with traditional doctrinal scholarship, as epitomised by his contributing to several editions of *Chitty on Contracts*.[137] The point is that orthodox analysis and comprehensive coverage of the cases was not his central concern.[138]

B. Critical

Atiyah regarded the law, including contract law, not as an inevitability but a decidedly human and hence deficient construct that often cried out for radical reform. Thus, he did not shrink from criticising the law and received wisdom regarding it and from doing so in strident terms. Illustrations abound. For example, Atiyah contended that the traditional view that estoppel cannot give rise to a cause of action was premised on arguments that were 'transparently

[135] A striking example is Atiyah (n 105).

[136] PS Atiyah, *From Principles to Pragmatism* (Oxford, Clarendon Press, 1978).

[137] See text to n 50.

[138] Atiyah expressly stated as much in the preface to the fifth edition of his *An Introduction to the Law of Contract*: Atiyah (1995) (n 35) v.

fallacious'[139] and that '[t]he belief that estoppel is not a cause of action in itself is a myth'.[140]

Another good example is supplied by a well-known and rather incautiously worded casenote that he wrote regarding the decision of the Court of Appeal in *Crabb v Arun District Council*.[141] Atiyah castigated the decision as indicative of 'the extraordinary conceptual morass into which English contract law is falling, largely because of outmoded ideas about the purpose and nature of the doctrine of consideration'.[142] His basic point was that it was extraordinary that the Court of Appeal had considered that the appeal turned on whether there was an agreement yet then proceeded to uphold the claim on equitable rather than contractual principles. The note is notorious partly on account of its having provoked Peter Millett QC (later Lord Millett), who had appeared as counsel in the case, to write a rebuttal of Atiyah's analysis.[143] Because of, among other things, the intensely critical nature of many of Atiyah's writings, they were never dreary. He often challenged dogma and was rarely concerned merely to describe the law. Indeed, simply distilling principles from judgments would, for Atiyah, have yielded a seriously incomplete account of the law since there was often a wide gulf between what judges 'do as compared with what they are saying'.[144]

At times, Atiyah may have assumed the mantle of an advocate a little bit too readily. He was sometimes rather dismissive of, or ridiculed, arguments against his preferred position. Joseph Raz observed that in concluding in his *Promises, Morals, and Law* that there was no good reason for considering that promises themselves generated obligations, Atiyah had addressed only a very limited range of accounts.[145] Raz also considered that Atiyah was overly concerned to demolish rival arguments and that he did not always strive to see the best in them before rejecting them. He wrote of Atiyah:

> He cannot help feeling that natural law and intuitionistic theories are old-fashioned and obscurantist myth spinnings. He tries to deal them quick, fatal blows. But trying to do too much in a space encourages a particular brand of self-defeating overkill. One is tempted to concentrate on the most glaring and oft-recognised shortcomings of familiar theories. At the same time, one is liable to overlook those same theories' hidden strengths … I cannot be the only reader who finds that the view he favours is not discussed at all, while its long defunct relative is yet again exposed to public ridicule by Atiyah's rhetorical questions.[146]

[139] PS Atiyah, 'Misrepresentation, Warranty and Estoppel' (1971) 9 *Alberta Law Review* 347, 370.
[140] *ibid* 371.
[141] *Crabb v Arun District Council* [1976] Ch 179 (CA).
[142] PS Atiyah, 'When is an Enforceable Agreement not a Contract? Answer: When it is an Equity' (1976) 92 *LQR* 174, 174.
[143] PJ Millett, '*Crabb v Arun District Council*—A Riposte' (1976) 92 *LQR* 342.
[144] Atiyah (n 142) 174.
[145] Raz (n 131) 917.
[146] *ibid* 917–18.

C. Radical

Much of Atiyah's work is iconoclastic in nature both inside and outside the law of contract[147] and he sometimes made rather extravagant claims that attracted few or no adherents. A striking illustration is his argument in *Promises, Morals, and Law* that promises often merely evidenced an already extant duty.[148] Promises were, he contended, frequently nothing more than admissions that some pre-existing duty was owed and were not themselves an independent source of obligation. Atiyah illustrated what he had in mind by referring to, among other things, a situation in which a motorist agrees to settle a claim for compensation that an injured road user had made against them. He wrote that 'it seems clear that once the promise of payment is made by the defendant, the promise coincides with, or overlaps with the prior duty to make compensation which is anyhow imposed by law'.[149] The argument is highly original but it is also rather farfetched and seems to have persuaded no one.[150] Limiting our attention to the very example that Atiyah offered in support of his account, it is noteworthy that he fails to mention the fact that when disputes are compromised, the agreement is almost invariably made on the express basis that liability is *not* admitted.

Numerous other of Atiyah's works demonstrate his willingness to challenge orthodoxy. To give just one further example of a direct attack on a basic tenet, consider chapter four of his *An Introduction to the Law of Contract*.[151] It is entitled 'Contracts Made by the Courts'. The title, as Atiyah observed was, 'according to traditional contract theory, a solecism'.[152] It was and remains dogma[153] that the courts do not make contracts for the parties but merely give effect to their agreement. Atiyah argued, however, that this received wisdom was 'misleading'.[154] To his mind, '[a] great many … contracts … are imposed on the parties who are or have been negotiating with each other … but do not arise out of any actual agreement or contract the parties may have made'.[155] He added that '[j]udges have rarely hesitated to use whatever instruments they can lay hands on in order to achieve a just result in a particular case; and the law of contract is one of those instruments'.[156]

[147] See, further, J Goudkamp and D Nolan, 'Pioneers, Consolidators and Iconoclasts: The Story of Tort Scholarship' in J Goudkamp and D Nolan (eds), *Scholars of Tort Law* (Oxford, Hart Publishing, 2019) 27–28.

[148] Atiyah (n 93) 184–202.

[149] *ibid* 185.

[150] For a prominent critique, see Raz (n 131) 921–27.

[151] Atiyah (1995) (n 35).

[152] *ibid* 89.

[153] 'We do not make contracts; we enforce them when they are proved': *Wild v Woolwich Borough Council* [1910] 1 Ch 35 (CA) 42 (Farwell J).

[154] Atiyah (1995) (n 35) 89.

[155] *ibid*.

[156] *ibid* 90.

D. Originality

Atiyah is widely regarded as having advanced novel ideas both as regards the law of contract and other legal fields. As a reviewer of one of his books observed, 'striking originality … marks much of [his] work'.[157] Even when relying heavily on the analysis of others, he was often able to shine a new light on things or, as another reviewer aptly put it, 'to demonstrate the remarkable potential of the familiar'.[158] One example of this, which Tony Weir singled out as Atiyah's 'most famous contribution … to contemporary discussions of the law of obligations',[159] is the claim, the fullest statement of which is found in *The Rise and Fall of Freedom of Contract*, that reliance-detriment and benefit-received were stronger bases for imposing liability than a failure to honour a promise. Atiyah was drawing here on the writings of a range of other scholars,[160] but he painstakingly constructed from a great mass of materials a remarkably full case in support of his thesis in a way that others had not been able to achieve. Fried vividly referred to the 'power and sweep of [Atiyah's] synthesis'.[161]

E. Context

Early in his career Atiyah was perceived by some as a black-letter lawyer.[162] However, he quickly shook off that image and exhibited a fundamental concern with context and many of his writings are a powerful antidote to purely inward-looking accounts of contract law. To give just one example, the opening chapter of the first edition of Atiyah's *An Introduction to the Law of Contract*[163] is not addressed to rules such as those governing offer and acceptance but is entitled 'The Development of the Modern Law of Contract'. It examined the functions that the law of contract discharged in modern societies, the enduring influence of ideas inherited from the nineteenth century cases, the relevance of changing social and economic conditions, the retreat of the *laissez-faire* philosophy and the rise of and problems created by standard-form contracts. In the preface to the fifth edition of the same work, Atiyah wrote that the book 'tries to supply a basic introduction not merely to the law of contract but also to theories and

[157] S Lee, 'Book Review' (1987) 103 *LQR* 484, 484. See also Collins (n 130) 226 ('highly innovative').

[158] Black (n 109) 930. See also Turpin (n 114) 397 ('even when, as quite often, [Atiyah] traverses well-known ground … he does so freshly and from his own angle of vision').

[159] Weir (n 63) 376.

[160] In particular, Atiyah drew here on LL Fuller and WR Perdue, 'The Reliance Interest in Contract Damages: I' (1936) 46 *Yale Law Journal* 52 and LL Fuller and WR Perdue, 'The Reliance Interest in Contract Damages: II' (1937) 46 *Yale Law Journal* 373.

[161] Fried (n 116) 1860.

[162] See the discussion in Twining (n 37) 2–3.

[163] Atiyah (n 32) ch 1.

policies and ideas underlying the subject'.[164] Despite his interest in the environment in which contract law was situated, he never took context quite as seriously as he could have done. Twining uses a contrast to illuminate the point. He observes that whereas in *Accidents, Compensation and the Law* Atiyah broke away from torts as a category and instead used 'accidents' as his organising device,[165] he 'stayed with Contract as a way of designating a field'.[166]

F. Policy

Atiyah considered that whereas lawyers in the United States tended to deploy policy considerations openly, English lawyers often concealed recourse to policy behind the law's concepts or simply ignored them. This was not always the case. Prior to the 1850s, English lawyers, Atiyah thought, were far more receptive to influences that were external to the law. However, from around the middle of the nineteenth century they generally eschewed recourse to policy factors. Law and policy, he wrote,

> became totally divorced, at least in conscious formulations of legal argument and legal justification. Even in cases [decided in the inter-war period] involving the most important economic issues ..., a series of decisions were made ... in which all the arguments floundered in a conceptual morass.[167]

In the context of the law of contract, he argued that law and policy became separate domains 'partly because lawyers could no longer find their answers in broad theories about society, or political economy, or moral principles' with the result that 'they increasingly turned inwards to the law itself'.[168] Atiyah considered this to be a retrograde development. A persistent theme in his writings, as regards contract law, tort law and the substantial body of work that he produced concerning the role of judges more generally, was that policy factors should be brought into the open. Doing so would ensure that convincing policy factors were not overlooked and appropriately weighed, and it would permit unconvincing factors to be exposed as such.[169] He had no time for the notion that

[164] Atiyah (1995) (n 35) v.
[165] See text to nn 59–65.
[166] Twining (n 37) 24.
[167] Atiyah (n 3) 662–62.
[168] *ibid* 660.
[169] See, eg, *ibid* 665; PS Atiyah, 'Judicial Techniques and the English Law of Contract' (1968) 2 *Ottawa Law Review* 337, 359–62; PS Atiyah, 'Judges and Policy' (1980) 15 *Israel Law Review* 346. Another particularly striking illustration is a lengthy unpublished paper that Atiyah wrote regarding the decision of the Court of Appeal in *Dorset Yacht Co Ltd v Home Office* [1969] 2 QB 412 (CA). He argued that the courts should disclaim any power to change the law if they were unwilling 'to discuss issues of policy in a rational and sophisticated manner ...'. It appears that he withdrew the paper from the *Cambridge Law Journal* when it turned out that the *Journal* could not move swiftly enough to publish it prior to the hearing of the Home Office's appeal to the House of Lords.

policy was the exclusive province of the legislature rather than the judiciary. One suspects that it would have regarded as contrived and unreal the arguments that corrective justice and other rights theorists promoted from the late twentieth century to the effect that policy was incompatible with the structure of private law[170] and the nature of the judicial role.[171]

G. Comparative

A recurring feature of Atiyah's writings is the concern with the law in other jurisdictions. Atiyah was particularly interested in the law in the United States,[172] with which he was perhaps especially familiar on account of the many working visits that he made to that country.[173] In his autobiography he wrote that '[a] serious specialist must these days … be prepared to keep up with developments in other countries. Nobody in modern times can be a serious academic lawyer in England without some attempt to master American legal writing'.[174] Unusually for a British legal scholar, Atiyah wrote numerous articles for American law journals.[175] Also atypically for an English academic (both in his day and now), Atiyah had a formidable reputation in the United States. His work was very regularly referenced in the American periodical literature[176] and textbooks, and Atiyah maintained a steady stream of correspondence with United States academics and judges. Overall, he greatly admired the law and legal tradition in

[170] See, in particular, EJ Weinrib, *The Idea of Private Law* (Cambridge MA, Harvard University Press, 1995).

[171] See, eg, R Stevens, *Torts and Rights* (Oxford, Oxford University Press, 2007) ch 14.

[172] This culminated in Atiyah and Summers (n 94), in which Atiyah and his co-author compared and contrasted legal reasoning in Britain and the United States.

[173] American universities at which Atiyah spent semesters include Yale Law School (1968), the University of Texas at Austin (1969 and 1979), Harvard Law School (1982–1983) and Duke University (1985). While at Harvard, he delivered a course entitled 'Comparative No-Fault Compensation'. Atiyah also delivered lectures at other United States universities. For example, he presented a fully-formed paper entitled 'Liberalism and the Social Framework — The English Experience, 1776–1914' at Princeton. Regrettably, it was never published.

[174] Atiyah (n 4) 215.

[175] See, eg, PS Atiyah, 'Book Review' (1976) 45 *Cincinnati Law Review* 340; PS Atiyah, 'Liability for Railway Nuisance in the English Common Law' (1980) 23 *Journal of Law & Economics* 191; PS Atiyah, 'No-Fault Compensation: A Question that Will not Go Away' (1980) 54 *Tulane Law Review* 274; PS Atiyah, 'Book Review' (1981) 95 *Harvard Law Review* 509; PS Atiyah, 'The Theoretical Basis of Contract Law: An English Perspective' (1981) 1 *International Review of Law and Economics* 183; PS Atiyah, 'Book Review: The Principles of Social Order' [1983] *Duke Law Journal* 669; PS Atiyah, 'Lawyers and Rules: Some Anglo-American Comparisons (1983) 37 *Southwestern Law Journal* 545; PS Atiyah, 'Book Review' (1983) 132 *University of Pennsylvania Law Review* 187; Atiyah (n 96); PS Atiyah, 'Book Review' (1985) 33 *American Journal of Comparative Law* 342; PS Atiyah, 'Medical Malpractice and the Contract/Tort Boundary' (1986) 49 *Law & Contemporary Problems* 287.

[176] As of 22 January 2022, Atiyah was cited in 742 discrete articles available on the US-centric database HeinOnline.

the United States. He was particularly enamoured with its systems of teaching and research,[177] and regarded Harvard 'as perhaps the greatest law school in the world'.[178]

H. Cross-Fertilisation

Atiyah's research interests were unusually broad and extended far beyond the law of contract. In particular, they encompassed the law of torts, in which his expertise rivalled or even exceeded that which he had in relation to the law of contract. He was also deeply concerned with matters such as the relationship between the common law and legislation[179] and the processes by which law is made and developed and the respective roles played by the various institutions involved.[180] Atiyah had a significant interest in legal education.[181] In these circumstances, it is unsurprising that his writings often traversed traditional legal categories. A good example is his Holmes Lecture, which covered criminal law, tort law and contract law in equal measure.[182]

Focusing specifically on his contract law scholarship, a noteworthy feature of it is that it is regularly punctuated with reference to other fields and especially the law of torts. Unsurprisingly, Atiyah, heavily influenced by Gilmore,[183] regarded the relationship between contract law and tort law as being highly porous. For example, in his essay 'The Modern Role of Contract' he argued 'that contract law as a whole … is increasingly merging with tort law into a general law of obligations'.[184] His article 'Misrepresentation Warranty and Estoppel' was largely devoted to considering whether liability for misrepresentation was truly contractual or belonged instead to the domain of tort law.[185] Atiyah's view of the nature of promises that he promoted in *Promises, Morals, and Law* is consistent with his belief that the divide between contract and tort was significantly overstated and that the law of obligations needed to be restructured along different lines. If promises are not an independent source of obligation but simply evidence of pre-existing obligations as Atiyah

[177] For discussion, see Atiyah (1995) (n 7) 39–40.

[178] Atiyah (n 4) 97.

[179] PS Atiyah, 'Common Law and Statute Law' (1985) 48 *MLR* 1.

[180] See, eg, PS Atiyah, *Pragmatism and Theory in English Law* (London, Stevens & Sons, 1987).

[181] See, eg, PS Atiyah, 'Legal Education in the Sudan' (1958) 4 *Journal of the Society of Public Teachers of Law* 137. Among other works, he also wrote (seemingly in the early 1970s while he was at the Australian National University) a substantial and apparently unpublished paper entitled 'The Teaching of Tort Law' in which he advocated for redrawing the boundaries of courses on Tort and Contract and argued for subjects on Accident Law to be introduced.

[182] Atiyah (n 96).

[183] Gilmore (n 74) 92–96.

[184] Atiyah (n 104) 8.

[185] Atiyah (n 139) 349–68.

contended,[186] they can hardly mark out the law of contract as distinct from tort law and other fields.[187]

Atiyah's interests were unusually broad not only in the sense that he was concerned with more than one field of law but also in the sense that although his focus was usually on the law, he regularly relied upon sources outside the law. This is exemplified by his *The Rise and Fall of Freedom of Contract*. In one sense, the book entails a search for relationships between phenomena in several different disciplines: economics, history, law, philosophy, politics and sociology. One reviewer observed that it displayed 'extraordinary mastery of literature from many fields'.[188] Atiyah's *Promises, Morals, and Law* supplies another illustration in that it draws heavily on philosophy. Thus, in a review article, Raz observed that:

> the book fulfills its promise in being a genuinely interdisciplinary study. Atiyah is not a philosopher using a few legal cases as illustration, nor is he a lawyer who uses the occasional philosophical argument. He is a great legal scholar who has studied the philosophical issues in detail and who speaks with confidence in both fields.[189]

I. Style

Atiyah took particular care to ensure that his scholarship was accessible. A good illustration of this emerges from the following passage in the preface to the third edition of his *An Introduction to the Law of Contract*:

> The ideas may seem advanced, but that is no reason why they should be made difficult to understand, or written about in a complicated fashion. I have therefore … tried to write of these matters in as simple and intelligible a way as possible.[190]

Thus, sentences that run to more than four or five lines of text are hard to find in his work and, despite his prodigious output, most of his publications were relatively compact. He eschewed complicated prose and obscure terminology. Illustrations that he selected in support of his analysis were generally easy to understand.[191] The result was that his readers were rarely if ever required to re-read the text in order to understand the point that he was making. Impressively, Atiyah ensured that his work was eminently readable without rendering the analysis superficial or simplistic. These qualities shone through even in his

[186] See text to nn 126–28.
[187] See the valuable discussion on this point in Collins (n 130) 225, 228.
[188] Gray (n 108) 231.
[189] Raz (n 131) 917.
[190] PS Atiyah, *An Introduction to the Law of Contract*, 3rd edn (Oxford, Oxford University Press, 1981) v.
[191] Raz (n 131) 916 (referring to Atiyah's use of examples in *Promises, Morals, and Law* as being 'non-technical and judicious, and present[ing] no difficulty for a nonlawyer').

most substantial works. Thus, Fried wrote of *The Rise and Fall of Freedom of Contract* that '[e]very argument is clear, and illustrated with examples and quotations so aptly chosen that one admires not only the compendiousness of the author's learning, but his wit and imagination as well'.[192]

Relatedly, Atiyah was particularly concerned to promote public understanding of legal issues. Thus, he wrote a short book aimed at helping the layperson grasp fundamental features of the law and the legal system.[193] Atiyah also participated in the production of television programmes about the law although it appears that these never aired.[194] He was an avid contributor to *The Times*, especially later in his career. In one of his longer letters to the editor he stressed, in the context of litigation concerning steel strikes,[195] that judges do not simply discover and apply existing law when deciding cases but need to choose between competing views by reference to 'policies' and 'value judgments'. He added that:

> One does not know, in many cases, what policies influence judges, for they usually do not wish to tell us. Apparently Lord Scarman thinks that it would lower the public's respect for the law if they knew. Perhaps it would; but that too is a policy argument, and a highly debatable one.[196]

J. Reformist

Atiyah was deeply concerned not only with improving the law's accessibility[197] but also the rules that constitute it. Thus, he provided extensive comments to the Law Commission on certain of its projects[198] and many of his published writings contained suggestions for reform, especially in so far as the law of torts was concerned.[199] In the preface to the first edition of *The Sale of Goods* he

[192] Fried (n 116) 1860.

[193] PS Atiyah, *Law and Modern Society* (Oxford, Oxford University Press, 1983).

[194] Atiyah (n 4) 290–94.

[195] See *Express Newspapers v McShane* [1980] AC 672 (HL).

[196] Letter to the Editor, *The Times* (12 February 1980).

[197] See text to nn 194–97.

[198] For example, he provided 15 pages of comments to the Law Commission on its Working Paper 61 (Law Commission, *Penalty Clauses and Forfeiture of Money Paid* (1975)) and Working Paper 65 (Law Commission, *Law of Contract: Pecuniary Restitution on Breach of Contract* (1975)), 19 pages of comments on Working Paper 73 (Law Commission, *Non-Disclosure and Breach of Warranty in Insurance Law* (1978)) and 11 pages of comments on a draft that became Working Paper 81 (Law Commission, *Minors' Contracts* (1982)).

[199] By far the best illustration of this is found in Atiyah's work regarding tort law and accident compensation. He lobbied extensively for what is now generally known as the Pearson Commission to be established: see *Report of the Royal Commission on Civil Liability and Personal Injury*, Cmnd 7054 (London, HMSO, 1978). Atiyah's work in this regard culminated in the publication of *The Damages Lottery* (n 102), in which he argued for the abolition of the tort system in so far as it concerned negligently caused personal injury and death. He considered that this would allow a market-based mechanism for ensuring compensation for accidents to flourish in its place. For discussion, see Goudkamp (n 2) 319–30.

wrote that he had 'not been slow to criticise the existing law where it appeared to me to be unsatisfactory, and to suggest possible reforms'.[200] Atiyah appears, however, to have had little or no impact in this regard. There do not appear to be any instances where his proposals were implemented or even given serious consideration by the legislature or courts as potential models for reform. This is perhaps unsurprising given the often radical nature of his work and substantial indifference of the courts to academic scholarship during the period of time when Atiyah was research active.

In order properly to understand Atiyah's mindset in offering suggestions for change, it is important to appreciate the role that he regarded legal academics as discharging. He considered that scholars had played a vastly more significant role in the development of the law than is generally acknowledged. Thus, Atiyah wrote that 'modern contract law was very largely *created* by the academic writers of the late nineteenth century, especially Sir William Anson and Sir Frederick Pollock'.[201] He also argued that academics played a formal role in the legal system. Far from their remit being simply to teach,[202] he regarded modern-day academics as being the ultimate check on the power wielded by the judiciary.[203] He also envisaged judges and academics substantially to share the obligation to keep the law in shape, with the former being charged with 'the often very pragmatic business of deciding cases' and the latter having 'primar[y] responsib[ility] for the part played by reason and theory in the law'.[204]

K. Individualistic

Almost all of Atiyah's writing, both inside and outside the law of contract, was done as a sole author. There were only a handful of exceptions.[205] Perhaps the most noteworthy is an article that Atiyah wrote with Treitel on the Misrepresentation Act 1967 (UK),[206] which was a singularly odd collaboration given their radically different styles. It reflects a good deal of compromise. The sometimes intemperate language in it is more in line with Atiyah but the attention to detail is consistent with Treitel's style. That Atiyah joined forces with other writers only sparingly is readily explicable. His ideas were often sufficiently radical that many other scholars would have been reluctant to commit to his claims. Perhaps more significantly, co-authored work inevitably requires

[200] Atiyah (n 26) viii.
[201] Atiyah (n 136) 170 (emphasis in original).
[202] *ibid* 165–84.
[203] *ibid* 183.
[204] *ibid* 184.
[205] They are PS Atiyah and FAR Bennion, 'Mistake in the Construction of Contracts' (1961) 24 *MLR* 421; PS Atiyah and GH Treitel, 'Misrepresentation Act 1967' (1967) 30 *MLR* 369; and Atiyah and Summers (n 94).
[206] Atiyah and Treitel (n 205).

that concessions be made and Atiyah was sufficiently dogmatic that one senses that he would not have wanted to varnish his writing. Another potential factor is that jointly authored work was simply much less common in Atiyah's time than it is today.

L. Realist

Much of Atiyah's writing exhibits pronounced realist tendencies. Indeed, he self-identified as a realist. Thus, Atiyah wrote that he was

> as willing as any realist to discount much of what is said in legal opinions on the ground that judges often intuitively feel their way to a conclusion, but are unable or unwilling to articulate very convincingly why they have reached a result.[207]

He regarded the law's labels and concepts as well as the reasoning in judgments as being frequently obfuscatory. To give just one example drawn from his contract law scholarship, he argued that:

> One need only think of the ordinary supermarket cash purchase to appreciate how brainwashed we have become with regard to defining contracts in terms of agreements or promises. The man in the street would assume that when he buys something for cash in a supermarket, he is exchanging his money for the goods. Only the lawyer insists that this transaction is an exchange of promises, surely a grotesque example of the way in which we reinterpret facts to fit our concepts.[208]

V. CONCLUSION

Atiyah was one of the finest legal scholars of his or any other generation. His contributions to the law of contract (as well as to several other branches of the law) were on a staggering scale. He was a 'giant'[209] of the field who produced 'masterly'[210] works regarding it. His particular strengths included synthesising vast masses of material from both inside and outside the law and in identifying order and connections within it where others saw none. Although sometimes Atiyah went too far in his claims and was perhaps too quick to dismiss rival contentions, his work was unfailingly interesting and compelled serious reflection upon what the law of contract was all about.

[207] Atiyah (n 96) 368.
[208] *ibid* 371.
[209] Andrews (n 34) 727.
[210] Raz (n 131) 917.

15

Afterword: Understanding Contracts – A Realist Perspective

WILLIAM TWINING[1]

'See it fresh, see it whole, see it as it works' (Karl Llewellyn)

I. INTRODUCTION

IN AN EMPIRICAL study of the ideas and practices of Canadian Contract(s) teachers[2] David Sandomierski paints a picture of a deeply conflicted group who believe one thing about their subject but teach quite another.[3]

[1] Most of the ideas presented here have been explored at greater length in earlier works, especially W Twining, *Jurist in Context: A Memoir* (Cambridge, Cambridge University Press, 2019); W Twining, *Karl Llewellyn and the Realist Movement* (London, Weidenfeld & Nicolson, 1973); 2nd edn (Cambridge, Cambridge University Press, 2012); W Twining, *General Jurisprudence* (Cambridge, Cambridge University Press, 2009); W Twining and D Miers, *How To Do Things With Rules*, 5th edn (Cambridge, Cambridge University Press, 2010). This chapter focuses on Contracts scholarship on domestic/municipal state law in conventional markets and excludes from consideration regional, transnational and global law, non-state law, informal or underground markets and other topics that are relevant to broader approaches to what is involved in understanding law within our discipline and beyond.

[2] In neither J Goudkamp and D Nolan (eds), *Scholars of Tort Law* (Oxford, Hart Publishing, 2019) nor the present volume is much significance attached to whether the labels Tort(s) or Contract(s) are designated in the singular or plural. Given that Leake, Langdell, and Macneil used Contracts, but Williston, Treitel and others used Contract and some used both, I shall not dwell here on such nuances, although I personally favour Torts and Contract(s). I shall use Contracts here as the name of a field of law, whether its scope is interpreted narrowly or broadly. Sometimes the difference is significant. For example, Grant Gilmore was not talking about the death of contracts and contracting, but about the impossibility in his view of claiming any coherence for the Law of Contract (doctrine) as a single field (see n 13).

[3] D Sandomierski, *Aspiration and Reality in Legal Education* (Toronto, University of Toronto Press, 2020). This book is concerned with teaching, whereas the present volume, including this chapter, is mainly concerned with scholarship. The two are historically closely intertwined: see E Mertz, *The Language of Law School: Learning to 'Think Like a Lawyer'* (Oxford, Oxford University Press, 2007).

To simplify, they are anti-formalists in their ideas but formalistic in their teaching.[4] As Canadian legal cultures in such matters can be located with Australia approximately in the mid-Atlantic, his study throws light on the differences between American and English Contract(s) scholarship and teaching that are brought out in the preceding chapters. Similar ambivalences are exhibited on both sides of the Atlantic, but the story that has been told in the present volume suggests that some kinds of formalism are still dominant in England and Wales and in different ways in Continental Europe, with Scotland representing a halfway house. The American story is significantly different. In this chapter I shall argue that formalism/anti-formalism is a false dichotomy for present purposes and that there is a middle ground that can open the way to a quite nuanced rapprochement between seemingly conflicting conceptions of and approaches to Contract(s) as a field.

Scholars of Contract Law ('*SCL*') joins *Scholars of Tort Law* ('*STL*') as very welcome additions to the literature about legal scholarship in general and private law in particular. They add significant biographical and contextual detail to the study of private law and the histories of (largely) Anglo-American legal scholarship and give a plausible account of variations in the self-perceptions and genre and style of literature by Contracts scholars, their rather narrow audiences and patterns of deep and superficial differences and disagreements. They are also revealing about the similarities, differences and reactions to each other of modern English and American Contracts scholars, but no individual fits neatly into Sandomierski's account of conflicted Canadian Contracts teachers.

I was privileged to attend nearly all of the discussions on both volumes, not because of my expertise, but because of my age. I was first invited because I was a lifelong colleague and friend of Patrick Atiyah and I helped with the chapter on him in the Tort volume. I continued to be involved because as a student or colleague I had encountered several of the individuals discussed in the current volume and as a jurist interested in American Legal Realism, I had interviewed some and had got to know others, mainly in connection with my work on Karl Llewellyn. For this reason the editors have encouraged me to

[4] Sandomierski presents his analysis in terms of the idea of the 'Revolt Against Formalism' in the United States in the early twentieth century. This idea was popularised by Morton White in his classic book of that name (M White, *Social Thought in America: The Revolt against Formalism*, 2nd edn (Boston, Beacon Press, 1957)). There the term referred to a very broad trend in American intellectual life reacting against excessive 'scientism' and 'eager to come to grips with life, experience, process, growth, context, function'. It transcended several disciplines. This may be adequate for Sandomierski's purposes. However, 'formalism' in legal discourse has generally been more narrowly conceived especially in respect of judicial reasoning about questions of law (see Rakoff, chapter seven of this volume). There is an extensive and convoluted theoretical literature on formalism in law, including PS Atiyah and RS Summers, *Form and Substance in Anglo-American Law* (Oxford, Clarendon Press, 1987) and Brian Tamanaha's controversial B Tamanaha, *Beyond the Formalist/Realist Divide* (Princeton, Princeton University Press, 2009). A Robertson and J Goudkamp (eds), *Form and Substance in the Law of Obligations* (Oxford, Hart Publishing, 2019) illustrates the complexities.

combine the anecdotal with the analytical. However, I am not a private lawyer. I retired from teaching Torts in East Africa in 1965 and I have never taught the Law of Contract. Nevertheless, like nearly all members of society I have extensive practical experience of contracts and contracting. Here I am more like an ethnographer observing a vaguely familiar group or caste (Contract(s) scholars) with a view to studying them more systematically. My observations, impressions and even critical comments are more like hypotheses than evidence-based findings, focusing on the field as a whole rather than details.

II. A REALIST PERSPECTIVE

My standpoint here is generally that of an outsider to Contract(s) scholarship, a theorist who is interested in bridging the seeming divides between different species of 'formalist' and 'realist' perspectives. I claim to be a 'legal realist' in a quite specific sense. My starting-premise is that the mission of Law as a discipline, as of other scholarly disciplines, is the advancement and dissemination of both knowledge and understanding of the subject-matters of the discipline. These subject-matters are vast, varied and constantly changing. Understanding Contract(s) as an academic field involves conceptual, normative, doctrinal and empirical elements each of which is necessary but not sufficient for advancing knowledge and understanding of the field as a whole.[5] As interpreted here, the main message of 'realism' is to right an imbalance in the heritage of Western traditions of academic law by insisting that the empirical dimensions of understanding contractual relations have been relatively neglected, but that they are also a necessary, but not a sufficient, condition of advancing knowledge and understanding of the field. Conceptual, normative and doctrinal aspects are also each necessary, but not sufficient, conditions of understanding contracts within the discipline of Law. Nearly all enquiries involve combinations of these four aspects or strands in many ways.

For present purposes the following formulation of the concept of 'legal realism' can serve as a starting-point: 'That knowledge and understanding of empirical dimensions of law and justice are relevant to (weak), an integral part of (moderate), necessary/essential to (strong) understanding law and legal phenomena'.[6]

[5] Twining (2019) (n 1) ch 13.

[6] *ibid* 166. Here my conception of a 'realist' perspective is clearly distinguished from ideas that are commonly (mis)attributed to 'the' American Legal Realists between the two World Wars. On the bad history and poor analysis of the American Legal Realists and about 'realism' as a concept, see *ibid* ch 13, and W Twining, 'Legal R/realism and Jurisprudence: Ten Theses' in E Mertz et al (eds), *The New Legal Realism: Translating Law-and-Society for Today's Legal Practice: Volume I* (Cambridge, Cambridge University Press, 2016) 121–46. Suffice to say here that concern about the relationship between theory and practice and being 'realistic' about law have never been an American exclusive, that the American Realist Movement of the 1920s to 1940s is best treated as an historical phenomenon and that we need to take 'realism' as an analytical concept seriously, freed from the confusing associations of that complex episode.

This conception of realism distances itself from American Legal Realism which is best treated as an historical phenomenon. This version does not involve commitment to (i) strong versions of rule scepticism or normative indeterminacy; (ii) a view that doctrine is unimportant; (iii) a view that the doctrinal tradition needs to be caricatured in terms of 'black-letter law' or 'school rules' views of law or crude interpretations of formalism. It does, however, mean that it involves criticising the *dominance* of the doctrinal traditions in Western academic law and ideas of *self-sufficiency* or *exclusiveness* of legal dogmatics (strong versions of doctrinal legal science).[7]

In this interpretation 'legal realism' is a matter of *focus*; it begs most epistemological questions about 'reality'. It says no more than that for purposes of understanding it is often (weak)/usually (moderate)/always (strong) necessary to be in touch with empirical dimensions of law and justice and legal phenomena. Like jesting Pilate it may ask 'What is reality?', but it does not stay for an answer. Put simply, understanding law involves concepts, values, facts and doctrine: each is necessary but not sufficient for understanding legal phenomena and ideas. In most legal discourse two or more of these are intertwined and difficult to separate. The central concern of the modern realist should be to strengthen the empirical dimensions of law and justice and better integrate them into mainstream legal studies.[8] This is exactly what the New Legal Realism is trying to do and it applies significantly to modern Contracts scholarship.[9]

III. ENCOUNTERS WITH THE TRIBE

A theme running through both *SCL* and *STL* is the contrast between committed doctrinal scholars and others who in different ways were interpreted as being

[7] Twining (2019) (n 1) 24, ch 13.

[8] See *ibid* ch 13. The term 'law in context' is an aspect of legal realism. It has been variously interpreted. Here three views are especially relevant: some interpret the term to mean 'doctrine in context'; often that implies that one must know the doctrine before it can be set in context. An alternative view is that rules and doctrine can be viewed as responses to 'mischiefs', that is as attempted responses to perceived problems and that it is more illuminating to consider context first (Twining and Miers (2010) (n 1) 74–76). If a broader view of 'law' is assumed, for instance to include institutions, processes, personnel and technology as well as doctrine, this leads to a third interpretation of 'law in context', which I personally prefer. All three interpretations are quite common and need to be distinguished.

The idea for the label of the 'Law in Context' series of books was borrowed from A Mueller, *Contract in Context* (Brooklyn, Foundation Press, 1951), a student book which was organised around the *transactions and problems* encountered in *Mr Blandings Builds His Dream House*, a popular novel by Eric Hodgins (1946) and film (1948) starring Myrna Loy, Cary Grant and Melvyn Douglas. Mueller's book did not sell well (Twining (2019) (n 1) 91–92).

[9] On the New Legal Realism, see E Mertz et al (eds), *The New Legal Realism: Translating Law-and-Society for Today's Legal Practice: Volumes I & II* (Cambridge, Cambridge University Press, 2016); D Campbell (ed), *Stewart Macaulay: Selected Works* (Cham, Springer, 2020) 495–551 and the *Journal of Empirical Legal Studies*. For a selective list of empirical works on contracts associated with the New Legal Realism, see n 94.

part of a general 'revolt against formalism'. As is clear from this book, there was great variety within each category and some have tried to reconcile the two. I have experienced several varieties of both kinds at first hand in different relationships, as mentors and gurus, as authors, teachers, interviewees, biographical subjects, colleagues and some as personal friends.

In Oxford my main textbooks were *Anson* and *Cheshire and Fifoot*; along with Treitel and Atiyah, who were contemporaries, these were almost my only encounters with English subjects of this volume.[10] My American experience was quite different: in Chicago I was taught by Llewellyn, Mentschikoff, Steffen and Sharp; my research on Llewellyn involved close encounters with Kessler, Corbin, Gilmore and Duncan Kennedy among others; and as a visitor to several American Law Schools I came to know Speidel, Macaulay and Summers as friends and allies, as was Ian Macneil whom I met in East Africa in the mid-1960s.[11] Contracts, especially business contracts, were a key focus of American Legal Realism and Duncan Kennedy encouraged his fellow 'crits' to capture first year Contracts courses 'in the belly of the whale' to get at the soul of the common law. None of this makes me an expert on Contract doctrine but gives me a sense of the culture of English and American Contracts scholars as a tribe or caste.

After my book on Llewellyn was published, in the late 1970s I gave two light-hearted lectures called 'Some Contracts Teachers are People' at Northwestern Law School.[12] These were stimulated by Grant Gilmore's *The Death of Contract* (1974)[13] and the popularity among law students of the film

[10] However, I coincided with Treitel in Chicago in 1963–64 and kept in touch with him thereafter. Francis Reynolds and I were also together in Chicago in 1957–58. I have no memory of Pollock being mentioned in respect of Contract during my time as an undergraduate. Some have suggested that Pollock can be credited with the dominant theory of the Law of Contract in England. He was probably most influential through his commentary with Mulla on the Indian Contract Act 1872, which diffused through most British dependencies during the Victorian age and was the only successful attempt to codify the English Law of Contract. It still survives with little modification in a number of jurisdictions. F Pollock and DF Mulla, *Commentary on the Indian Contract and Specific Relief Acts* (London, Sweet & Maxwell, 1905) went rapidly through five editions until 1925 and was treated widely as a work of authority in East Africa in the 1960s.

[11] On Ian Macneil and East Africa, see pp 398–400.

[12] These lectures were never intended for publication. A handout and some rough notes survive. The tone is indicated by the fact that I very probably recounted how Robert Heuston, with whom I had corresponded in his role as editor of *Salmond on Torts*, told me that he was so irritated by KN Llewellyn, *The Common Law Tradition* (Boston, Little, Brown and Co, 1962) that after a few pages he threw his almost pristine copy over an Irish hedge. Having struggled for some months to make some sense of that book, I sympathised.

[13] In the early 1970s Grant Gilmore proclaimed the death of Contract in the United States. What died? Actual contracts and contracting were as alive as ever, the Uniform Commercial Code was settling down, commercial arbitration was expanding, 'Law and Economics' were trying to colonise Contract doctrine, and critical legal studies, led by Duncan Kennedy, was also focusing on Contract doctrine, not to announce its death but rather to show up its ideological underpinnings and internal contradictions. Gilmore's thesis was that the courts had for centuries developed specialised laws of Contracts, such as Sales and Negotiable instruments, and it was Langdell who had 'inadvertently' created an artificial theory of Contract Law without doing any theorising (by claiming that Contract

The Paperchase (1973) which, as one reviewer put it, was *Love Story* without memorable music or Ali McGraw and with a Contracts teacher instead of leukaemia as the villain.[14] My cast was Langdell, Holmes, Williston, Corbin, Llewellyn and Gilmore. The central theme was that in spite of rejecting Langdell's conception of the Law of Contracts, the leaders of 'The Revolt against Formalism' prolonged the life of the Langdellian case method, including the idea that almost all the material was available in printed books, viz the law reports.[15] Many contract(s) teachers claimed to be teaching every student 'to think like a lawyer' but continued to assume that all lawyers think in the same way about the same things, ie questions of law.[16] Some still make that unrealistic claim. It is clear that in teaching, Corbin, Llewellyn, Gilmore and even Macneil treated the law reports as their main source and helped to perpetuate the fiction of a national American Private Law based on cases, with a few intrusions by state legislatures.

As is clear from the preceding chapters, many common law Contract(s) scholars have been obsessed with the law reports. Langdell,[17] Corbin,[18] Treitel[19] and some others confined their attention almost entirely to reported cases, supplemented (or distorted) by fragmented legislation. My image of this kind of Contracts scholar was based on Corbin, whom I was privileged to interview twice in 1965 shortly before his death:

> By then Corbin was in his 80s, his hearing was impaired and he could only read with considerable effort. He had just completed work on a supplement to his monumental treatise on contracts. Beside his chair was a box of manila cards on which each new

doctrine could be reduced in a scientific way to a few underlying principles). This theory was developed by Holmes and Williston but demolished by Corbin whose treatise was 'the greatest law book ever written'. Some of the historical details of Gilmore's thesis have been contested and Contract(s) remains almost unchallenged today as an organising concept (see pp 400–402). Gilmore influenced Atiyah's historical work, but the latter became quite critical. However, Gilmore was surely right in maintaining that a uniform law of Contract in the United States was an artificial construct underpinned by the growth of national law schools and the felt need for a unified 'American Law'. My thesis was similar to Gilmore's, but I considered aspects of his argument to be overstated and my perspective was more ethnographic.

[14] BF Brody, 'A Movie Review' (1974) 26 *Journal of Legal Education* 605. It was rumoured that the domineering Professor Kingsfield was modelled in part on Lon Fuller. As earlier chapters make clear, Fuller was influential on several of the subjects of this volume. Llewellyn and Fuller had a combative, but friendly, correspondence until they both got telephones in their offices.

[15] Ian Macneil made a similar point, but I was unaware of it at the time.

[16] Twining (2019) (n 1) 126–34.

[17] The successors of Langdell, such as Joseph Henry Beale, insisted that all of the main courses should be taught in this way. Beale almost declined the Deanship of the University of Chicago Law School because Ernst Freund, who had tenure, already had established courses on Legislation and Administrative Law, which would dilute the pure stream of Langdellism; see further Twining (2012) (n 1) 445, fn 8. Administrators gave strong support to this approach as they realised that the Kingsfield model was helping to subsidise the university by providing a very cheap way of keeping very large classes cowed by a reign of terror that was respectable.

[18] See Klass, chapter eight of this volume.

[19] See Burrows, chapter 11 of this volume.

> decision affecting contracts was noted with care in longhand as the advance sheets came in. In the previous six months, Corbin said, he had noted approximately two thousand cases in this fashion. Long after most scholars would have handed over such 'mechanical' work (Corbin would have rejected this description of it) to younger men, he had ploughed on relentlessly and had only stopped when it became a physical impossibility to continue.[20]

As with many others before me, he became one of my heroes despite his idiosyncratic jurisprudence.

IV. FORMALISM AND REALISM – AVOIDING CARICATURES

Throughout this book a broad distinction has been made between realists and those who in different ways are broadly associated with 'formalism' in American legal thought. 'Formalism' in relation to social thought covered a very wide spectrum of views across several disciplines. In Law it has had a less abstract and more agonised history.[21] I suggest that in respect of Contracts Scholarship formalism/realism is a false dichotomy because several leading 'American Legal Realists' (including Kessler, Gilmore and Llewellyn) were clearly doctrinal scholars, that is to say that doctrine was at the centre of their interest in Contract(s).[22]

Doctrine in this context needs to be distinguished from crude versions of 'black-letter law' or extreme 'formalism'. All of the individuals considered here would have rejected crude versions of the idea that law consists solely of legal rules that could be stated in propositional form.[23] Andrew Halpin suggests a 'richer notion' of doctrine that includes not only rule-formulations, but also

[20] This passage was written almost contemporaneously and published in Twining (2012) (n 1) in 1973 (see now 2nd edn, 451, fn 12). Corbin not only allowed me to record the interview, but also sent me two substantial handwritten documents: (i) some answers to questions I had sent him in advance (12 pages, Letter from A Corbin to author (October 1965)) and (ii) 'An account by AL Corbin of association with KN Llewellyn' (16 pages, Letter from A Corbin to author (26 September 1965)). These proved invaluable for my research as well as being an example of Corbin's encouragement of the young.

[21] See Todd Rakoff's excellent discussion of the ambiguities of 'formalism' (Rakoff, chapter seven of this volume); see also Twining (2019) (n 1) ch 13; Tamanaha (n 4); and Robertson and Goudkamp (n 4).

[22] I pass over here the relationship between modern doctrinal scholars and analytical legal theorists who conceptualise 'law' in terms of commands, rules, norms, normative principles or other prescriptions that can be expressed in propositional form. Most of our canonical jurists in the analytical tradition, including Bentham, Austin, Kelsen, Hart, Finnis, Raz and Dworkin can be categorised as 'doctrinal jurists' in that they tended to equate 'law' with propositions of law. I also leave open the question whether this is a convenient symbiosis or something more complex: see Twining (2019) (n 1) 169–74.

[23] 'Black-letter' is used here to refer to legal publications in which principles or rules of law in propositional form are printed in bold face. The term is sometimes used in the United States to refer to clearly established principles or rules, but it is also sometimes used in a derogatory sense to suggest that such accounts are dogmatic or simplistic. The point here is to emphasise that by no means all 'doctrinalists' are culpable in such ways.

'principles, differentiated conceptions of interpretive roles and informed conceptions of the nature of legal materials that are normally "beneath the surface"'.[24] This can help us to avoid crude caricatures of leading expositors, who are best exemplified by the great pioneering American and Scottish treatise writers and include many mainstream Contracts scholars. Anyone who claims to be a doctrinal scholar, especially those with some practical experience, can be expected to have sophisticated, usually tacit, knowledge of Halpin's constituents of doctrine as part of their working assumptions.[25]

American Legal 'Realism' has been subjected to as much caricature as 'formalism'. The most common faults are attributing shared ideas to unnamed 'Realists' and conflating historical accounts of 'the Realists' (often over unspecified periods of time) with analysis of 'realism' as an analytical concept rather than as a very crude label.[26] The most harmful caricature was the famous claim that Realists believed that 'talk of rules is a myth'.[27] This was expressed rather loosely by Herbert Hart and followed by an extraordinary number of British commentators. The precise meaning of this phrase is unclear. If it suggests that (some) Realists believed that all rules are non-existent or radically indeterminate or obfuscations or unclear, then none of the subjects of earlier chapters in this book count as 'Realists'. Similarly, if 'realists' and 'doctrinal scholars' are mutually exclusive categories, where does that leave 'R/realism'?

If most 'Realist' scholars interested in Contract(s) were also doctrinal scholars and most doctrinal Contracts scholars[28] accepted some approximation to Halpin's conception of 'doctrine', both categories belong to the moderate ends of formalism and anti-formalism. This does not mean that there were no

[24] A Halpin, *Definition in Criminal Law* (Oxford, Hart Publishing, 2004) ch 1, discussed in Twining (2019) (n 1) 171.

[25] Much of such tacit knowledge tends to be quite local (for example, 'know your court' as a first principle of advocacy) and so the idea of a unified American law had to shed some of these elements. On tacit knowledge: see Twining (2019) (n 1) index.

[26] *ibid* ch 13 provides an analysis and overview of the similarities and differences between the American Realist Movement (ALR) and 'Law in Context' in the UK as historical phenomena. For a critique of common errors in interpreting ALR ideas: see W Twining, 'Talk about Realism' (1985) 60 *New York University Law Review* 329. Today I would place more emphasis on the point that most discussions of ALR use or modify Llewellyn's list of 1931 thereby omitting scholars who came to prominence after that date, such as Willard Hurst, Grant Gilmore, Malcolm Sharp and the young Myres MacDougal, who further complicate 'the ALR story'.

[27] HLA Hart, *The Concept of Law* (Oxford, Clarendon Press, 1961) 133 quietly retracted in several places, eg, HLA Hart, *Essays in Jurisprudence and Philosophy* (Oxford, Clarendon Press, 1983) 128.

[28] If a doctrinal scholar is defined as someone for whom doctrine is important and a central, but not necessarily an exclusive, focus of attention, then nearly all of the English individuals featuring in this book can be so characterised. Of the Americans, Williston, Corbin and Kessler clearly belong in this category and I would add Langdell, Llewellyn, Gilmore and Summers to this list. I discuss Atiyah, Macneil and Macaulay in more detail below.

differences and disagreements. Clearly there were. What they were differing or disagreeing about is not always clear.[29]

In relation to Contract(s) there are two additional concerns that are particularly important. First, the idea that the Realists believed that talk of rules is a myth or that (some) Legal Realists believed that all or most rules are radically indeterminate. Second, that 'realism' involves a denial that legal doctrine is an important part of the subject-matter of understanding Contracts. I know of no evidence to suggest that any of the Contracts scholars studied in this book subscribed to either of these views. Indeed, all of them with the possible exception of Macneil can be classified as doctrinal scholars in that Contracts doctrine was the main or at least a very important focus of their attention.[30] The only one who got near to this position explicitly was Corbin when he said: 'Pared-down principles there must of course be – "the law"; but it seldom struck me that the ones I saw in print were *the* ones.'[31] Corbin's main concern was an accurate exposition of 'tentative working rules'. This was not scepticism about the existence or determinacy of rules in general, but rather about their over-abstract and over-confident formulation in expository works.

V. FIRST IMPRESSIONS: ARE MOST ANGLO-AMERICAN PRIVATE LAWYERS CASE-MAD?[32]

In his lectures that became *The Bramble Bush* (1930), the young Karl Llewellyn openly acknowledged that he had been seduced by the 'threat of the available'.[33] By this he meant that his main justification for focusing on appellate cases was that the law reports are accessible, wonderful anthologies of real life human stories, intellectual puzzles and skilful arguments – authentic, detailed, interrelated, well-organised and continually renewing themselves and as such wonderful materials of law study.[34] Thirty years later, in his last major work, *The Common Law Tradition: Deciding Appeals* (1962), he acknowledged that he was focusing narrowly on what was only one part of a much bigger

[29] On different underlying conceptions of law: see n 22.

[30] On Macneil, see pp 398–400.

[31] Letter from A Corbin to KN Llewellyn (1 December 1960)(emphasis in original).

[32] On Colebrooke as an extraordinary exception, see McCunn, chapter two of this volume.

[33] KN Llewellyn, *The Bramble Bush* (New York, Oceana, 1931) ch 5. The longest discussion is in 'Legal Tradition and Social Science Method – A Realist's Critique' (1931) reprinted in KN Llewellyn, *Jurisprudence: Realism in Theory and Practice* (Chicago, University of Chicago Press, 1962) ch 3.

[34] The reasons for 'appellate court-itis' have been in some ways different in England, where their value as authority is stronger, and in the United States because of the Constitutional arrangements, the efficiency of the system of advance sheets and other factors.

picture.[35] Again he felt that this focus needed justification, this time on the grounds that the law reports have great advantages just because of their accessibility and because they had unexploited potential for a variety of purposes: lawyers generally regarded them as 'repositories of doctrine'; jurists and social scientists had been blind to them 'as a curiously valuable, accessible and time-cheap fountain of instruction about life'.[36] Thus through most of his career Llewellyn focused on reported cases, mainly in appellate courts and he in effect admitted that he had succumbed to 'appellate court-itis'.[37] In his law jobs theory Llewellyn treated disputes as important phenomena in themselves.[38]

I also believe that the law reports are a wonderful resource and a very useful pedagogical tool which is underused as well as overused.[39] But it is widely acknowledged that on their own they serve as a distorting lens not only on law in society but on law itself. A classic statement is by Otto Kahn-Freund:

> Is it not in the nature of the lawyers' work that his mind concentrates on phenomena which are socially marginal? Legal thinking must, I think, be constituted that way – this is perhaps the principal difference between law as an academic discipline and other social sciences which are concerned with typical and not with marginal situations. Above all: litigation is a pathological phenomenon in the body politic. The reported cases are the cases of the most serious diseases, and the leading cases are often the worst, and least typical of all … Is legal education based on case law not like a medical education which would plunge the student into morbid anatomy and pathology without first having taught him the anatomy and physiology of a healthy body? More than that, is the concentration on decided, and especially on reported cases not like a clinical education that would enable the doctor to diagnose

[35] KN Llewellyn, *The Common Law Tradition: Deciding Appeals* (Boston, Little, Brown & Co, 1960) 355. Llewellyn was very clear that his detailed research for this book was focused, unusually, on state appellate courts, and he also emphasised the special value of the law reports as a source not only for lawyers: *ibid* 355–62 and Appendix B.

[36] Twining (2012) (n 1) 246.

[37] Jerome Frank's term. Frank, who emphasised the importance and uncertainty of adjudicative fact-finding at first instance, focused on contested, mainly jury, trials, and could be similarly accused of 'court-itis'; as could Oliver Wendell Holmes, whose Bad Man was concerned to predict what *the courts* of Massachusetts would do, without taking into consideration all the intermediate decisions and events which might keep him from ever finding himself before a court or even arrested (W Twining, *The Great Juristic Bazaar: Jurists' Texts and Lawyers' Stories* (Routledge, Abingdon, 2017) ch 3). There are many denials that 'realism' is only of significance in relation to appellate adjudication, adjudication or even litigation: see Twining (2012) (n 1) passim. However, Frank is rightly acknowledged as one of the main progenitors of 'The New Evidence Scholarship' (Twining (2019) (n 1) ch 14).

[38] See, eg, this much-cited passage: 'The case of trouble, again, is the case of doubt, or is that in which discipline has failed, or is that in which an unruly personality is breaking through into new paths of action or leadership, or is that in which an ancient institution is being tried against emergent forces. It is the case of trouble which makes, breaks twists or flatly establishes a rule, an institution, an authority … not only the making of new law and the effect of old, but the hold and thrust of all other vital aspects of the culture, shine clear in the crucible of conflict' (KN Llewellyn and EA Hoebel, *The Cheyenne Way* (Norman, Oklahoma University Press, 1941) 29).

[39] See W Twining, *Blackstone's Tower* (London, Sweet & Maxwell, 1994) ch 5, esp 98–105.

> and treat some complicated brain tumour without ever telling him how to help a patient suffering from a simple stomach upset?[40]

This eloquent passage is much cited. I agree with the general thrust but would gloss it in three ways: 'the lawyer' in the first line is barrister-oriented; 'legal thinking' is equated with thinking about disputed questions of law; and no mention is made of criticisms that are made of medical science and practice in so far as they emphasise diagnosis and treatment of diseases rather than their prevention – a science of medicines rather than of health. These points fortify the argument that contracts are primarily instruments of dispute prevention and that those concerned with contracts in action are more like solicitors than barristers, not only in the work they do but also in their numbers.

Even for the strictest doctrinalist in the UK, legislation is much more important than case law in political, social and legal life and most legislation, whether primary or subordinate, never gets near the courts. However, interpreting and applying legislation (broadly conceived) probably forms at least 50 per cent of modern reported cases.[41]

In formal legal education, for teachers and students alike law reports are much more alluring than the statute book or other sources, such as actual contracts or whole statutes. However, this seductiveness alone cannot explain why almost all of the literature on 'legal reasoning' is exclusively confined to reasoning about questions of law.[42]

VI. *SCHOLARS OF CONTRACT LAW*: WHAT DID I LEARN?

Before studying the text in detail my first move was to follow the advice of Karl Llewellyn and take a fresh look at Contracts as a field from my own prior knowledge. On the basis of my initial education, researches on Llewellyn and American Legal Realism, my M Jourdain-like practical experiences as a member of society, and personal encounters with leading Anglo-American Contracts scholars, four points immediately stood out.

First, Contracts is a huge field that penetrates almost all corners of social life and relations. Contracts and contracting in a broad sense as an aspect of social co-operation fit comfortably in most ways of classifying them, for example, business, consumer, employment, housing, family, community and transnational relations and relationships. Standard taxonomies of fields or branches of Contracts echo all these categories quite closely.

[40] O Kahn-Freund, 'Reflections on Legal Education' (1966) 29 *MLR* 121, 127.

[41] This has long been recognised. See, eg, G Calabresi, *A Common Law for the Age of Statutes* (Cambridge MA, Harvard University Press, 1985). In a survey by David Miers of cases reported in the *All England Law Reports* for 1998 and 2008, 306 out of 498 cases involved interpretation of legislation (Twining and Miers (2010) (n 1) 272); see also *ibid* 196–98.

[42] See Twining (2019) (n 1) 263–65; *cf* Mertz (n 3).

Second, as mentioned above, because of this nearly all members of society have a vast amount of direct, varied, practical and observational experience of contracts and contracting through six of the seven ages of man.[43] Contractual behaviour and much of its discourse, basic ideas and vocabulary are part of 'general experience' as well as general knowledge.[44] For this reason many of the basic concepts of contract doctrine reflect familiar normative and social categories: for example, 'Contracts' as a field can be subsumed under social co-operation or dispute prevention and processing;[45] important normative categories such as promise, reliance, agreement, fraud, mistake, fairness are part of ordinary discourse;[46] probably many doctrinal categories such as offer, deal, misrepresentation, breach, damages are also broadly understood. A few, such as transaction costs, free trade and regulation, may require some elementary social science literacy, but on the whole they do not set up great barriers to understanding.

Third, as a social institution only a very small proportion of actual contracts are ever disputed to the stage that other actors are publicly involved. Of disputed contracts only a tiny number reach the point of formal litigation; of these only a small proportion reach adjudication on questions of fact, let alone of law; only a few of the latter reach the law reports and by no means all of these can

[43] As an infant, muling and puking, I bartered, promised, blackmailed, and experienced what it was to be the weaker party; by the age of four I understood the differences between promise, agreement, reliance, unfairness and disappointed expectations, and though I did not have a word for it, unconscionability. Thereafter I followed an ordinary bourgeois academic career. My readers can fill in the next stages of such a life from their own experience. Now in the seventh age of life I am learning about another range of pre-death and post-mortem transactions. Of course, many adult citizens with extensive practical experience of contracts may not be articulate about this experience or precise in their use of basic concepts.

[44] The field of Evidence in legal contexts has an illuminating literature on 'common sense' and social 'stocks of knowledge/beliefs', and extensive analysis of concepts such as general experience, cognitive competence, cognitive consensus and judicial notice: see T Anderson et al, *Analysis of Evidence*, 2nd edn (Cambridge, Cambridge University Press, 2005) ch 10. The title of Wigmore's extraordinary book which contained his theory of Evidence was JH Wigmore, *The Principles of Judicial Proof as found in Logic, Psychology and General Experience* (Boston, Little, Brown & Co, 1913); JH Wigmore, *The Science of Judicial Proof as found in Logic, Psychology and General Experience*, 2nd edn (Boston, Little, Brown & Co, 1937). In this context the concept of 'general experience' ranged from well-settled, evidence-backed scientific generalisations or generally accepted facts to legends, myths and popular fallacies. Today it would include 'fake news' if it is widely believed.

[45] M Palmer and S Roberts, *Dispute Processes*, 3rd edn (Cambridge, Cambridge University Press, 2020) makes clear the minor role that litigation generally plays in dispute prevention and settlement and illustrates how other factors in addition to law play important roles in dispute prevention and social co-operation.

[46] In so far as there is widespread agreement that the normative bases for contractual obligation are pluralist and cannot be reduced to a single reductionist moral 'foundation' these terms represent the main candidates for inclusion: see G Klass et al (eds), *Philosophical Foundations of Contract Law* (Oxford, Oxford University Press, 2014) and J Morgan, *Great Debates in Contract Law*, 3rd edn (Oxford, Hart Publishing, 2020).

reasonably count as appellate cases worth appealing.[47] Of those reported not all get treated as precedents. In so far as the main function of contracts and contracting is to further social co-operation as a social institution, it appears to be extraordinarily successful. However, it has a 'dark side' in that many contracts are instruments of oppression, coercion or exploitation. Nearly all Contracts scholars have been concerned to a greater or lesser extent to right unfair imbalances of power to protect the weaker party. However, questions do arise whether classical doctrinal scholarship has tended to play down or obscure the extent and significance of the 'darker side'.[48]

Fourth, one lesson that I learned as a student, which was repeatedly reinforced in later encounters, was that comparisons about English and American 'common law' can serve to gloss over very significant socio-economic, cultural and institutional differences by emphasising a partly shared early history and linguistic and conceptual heritage. Atiyah and Summers in *Form and Substance in Anglo-American Law* (1987) brought out some of these very clearly, but I have long felt that they did not go far enough. To give one example: the idea of a unified 'American common law'. In the American federal system private law is mainly a matter for individual states, but the great bulk of American contract scholarship is focused on a fictitious body of doctrine, the American Common Law of Contract.[49] The urge to maintain the unity of the common law in a multiplicity of jurisdictions was institutionalised in the law schools (which nearly all still teach the American Law of Contract) and in the American Law Institute's *Restatements* and model statutes and the work of the National Conference of Commissioners on Uniform State Laws and like bodies. The *Restatements* were an ingenious device of 'private legislation' designed to bypass

[47] Appellate cases not worth appealing are according to Llewellyn, following Cardozo, those that are 'foredoomed' and often constitute a high proportion of appeals in the United States (Llewellyn (n 12) 189–90, discussed in Twining (2012) (n 1) 48–50). This is related to, but different from, the notion of 'easy' (as opposed to hard) cases in that it is from the standpoint of the judges involved in the relevant cases.

[48] I am grateful to David Sugarman for providing this footnote. There is an extensive but fragmented literature on contract's other (darker) roles and effects, such as coercion, domination, exploitation, taking advantage of an imbalance of power and wealth. See, eg, the historical and empirical literature on employment contracts such as P Craven and D Hay, 'Master and Servant in England and Empire: A Comparative Study' (1993) 31 *Labour/Le Travail* 175–84; P Craven and D Hay, 'The Criminalization of "Free" Labour: Master and Servant in Comparative Perspective' (1994) 15 *Slavery & Abolition* 71; K Foster, 'From Status to Contract: Legal Form and Work Relations 1750–1850' (1979) 3 *Warwick Law Working Papers* 44; D Hay, 'The State and the Market in 1800: Lord Kenyon and Mr Waddington' (1999) 162 *Past & Present* 101; K Orren, *Belated Feudalism: Labor, the Law and Liberal Development in the United States* (Cambridge, Cambridge University Press, 1991); R Steinfield, *Coercion, Contract, and Free Labor in the Nineteenth Century* (New York, Cambridge University Press, 2001); W Steinmetz (ed), *Private Law and Social Inequality in the Industrial Age: Comparing Legal Cultures in Britain, France, Germany, and the United States* (Oxford, Oxford University Press, 2000); C Tomlins, *Freedom Bound: Law, Labor, and Civic Identity in Colonizing English America* (New York, Cambridge University Press, 2010).

[49] Twining (2012) (n 1) 272–74.

the state legislatures,[50] but most of the Uniform Acts had to be passed by each state legislature, as is illustrated by the convoluted history of the enactment and attempts at revision of the Uniform Commercial Code. In respect of Contract doctrine this has led to local regulatory interventions often being downplayed as minor incursions into the great stream of the common law – thereby elevating case law and major treatises over legislation as sources of law. Moreover, in so far as much 'context' is local, a fictitious homogeneity is imposed. There is a problem, it is well-understood by lawyers, but the solution is messy and persistently controversial.[51]

A careful reading of these chapters has been a rewarding experience. They are a significant contribution to legal history, filling gaps in our knowledge and casting new light on some familiar figures. They are especially revealing about the fluidity and complexity of seemingly fixed genres and authors' shifting perceptions of their roles as scholars. In the sister volume, the editors divided Tort scholars into *pioneers*, *consolidators* and *iconoclasts*. The present volume illustrates in fascinating detail the problems of identifying their conceptions of their role, their perceived and actual audiences, and the genres of their main works. All these vary and shift and are more or less nuanced in complex ways.[52] Doctrinal Contract(s) scholars appear to have had more varied roles in respect of their stated aspirations and scholarly practices. This book adds especially to the already quite sophisticated secondary literature about legal textbooks, treatises and institutional works.[53] None of this small band of individual scholars conformed very closely to a simple set of ideal types of genres of such works: some books grew fatter, a very few became thinner; some evolved from elementary introductions for beginning law students or reference works for 'practitioners' into something quite different: for example, Treitel's *The Law of Contract* started as a basic textbook in 1962, segued into an 'advanced' text, and then to an example of 'practical doctrinal scholarship' addressed primarily to appellate judges and their satellites[54] – a prestigious,

[50] At the first meeting of the American Law Institute ('ALI'), John W Davis stated: 'None of us here, I fancy, certainly none of those familiar with Congress or the forty-eight legislatures of our states, anticipate that this labor should be committed to their charge' (ALI, *Proceedings: Volume II* (Philadelphia, American Law Institute, 1923) 112). On 'surface law' and the *Restatements*: see Twining (2009) (n 1) ch 10.

[51] P Winship, 'Unification of Law in the United States: An Updated Sketch' (1996) 1 *Unification Law Review* 633.

[52] Goudkamp and Nolan (n 2) ch 1.

[53] See, eg, AWB Simpson, 'The Rise and Fall of the Legal Treatise: Legal Principles and the Forms of Legal Literature' (1981) 48 *University of Chicago Law Review* 632; D Sugarman, 'Legal Theory, the Common Law Mind and the Making of the Textbook Tradition' in W Twining (ed), *Legal Theory and Common Law* (Oxford, Basil Blackwell, 1986); and M Lobban, *A History of the Philosophy of Law in The Common Law World, 1600–1900* (Dordrecht, Springer, 2016).

[54] Burrows, chapter 11 of this volume, builds on the extensive debate on 'practical doctrinal scholarship' stimulated by HT Edwards, 'The Growing Disjunction Between Legal Education and the Legal Profession' (1992) 91 *Michigan Law Review* 34, 42–43 (deploring the decline of the genre); see also R Posner, 'The Triumphs and Travails of Legal Scholarship' in R Posner, *Overcoming Law* (Cambridge MA, Harvard University Press, 1995) 86. Note that all

but very narrow, audience. Others starting as compendia of cases became academicised over time with legal practitioners broadly conceived as the main market.[55] Some now labelled as monographs were mainly addressed to other Contracts scholars.[56] It is dangerous to generalise in this complex area, but it seems broadly true that the primary audiences of scholarly works on the Law of Contract (doctrine) did not include non-lawyers, a topic to which I shall return.

I was not familiar with the work of Colebrooke or Leake or Coote. Although I knew about Chief Baron Gilbert as the main target of Bentham's attack on all rules of Evidence, Michael Lobban's masterly account of his work on Contracts, only recently published, was a revelation.[57]

My impressions of those individuals whom I had encountered as a student, researcher or colleague were very largely confirmed and enlarged, with a few minor exceptions. The most significant gloss is that I felt that more emphasis could be placed on the differences between Williston and Corbin. As the two relevant chapters highlight, both were highly respected scholars, their major treatises were very different in conception and style and method and it is surprising that they collaborated amicably on the *Restatement (Second) of the Law of Contracts*.[58]

three of these authors have been senior judges. The complex topic of the notional centrality of adjudication in common law culture is explored in a forthcoming paper on 'Reasoning in Legal Contexts'. Interestingly, Jane Stapleton has advocated in her Clarendon lectures (J Stapleton, *Three Essays on Torts* (Oxford, Oxford University Press, 2021)) that young scholars of Torts should adopt an approach similar to 'practical doctrinal scholarship', treating senior judges as their main audience. This echoes a similar departure by Patrick Atiyah towards the end of his life (see Goudkamp, chapter 14 of this volume). This reached me too late for comment, except to say that we differ about this as advice to young scholars.

[55] If a biography of a work rather than of its original author(s) were allowed, I would have chosen *Chitty on Contracts* (1824 to the present, the latest edition being the 34th) now edited by a team led by Professor Hugh Beale. Significantly, the publisher's claim that it is the 'most trustworthy reference for *drafting, negotiating & disputing* contracts' (emphasis added): www.sweetandmaxwell.co.uk/chitty/key_reasons.html. A course for intellectual property practitioners (Intellectual Property Agreements: Law and Practice) makes similar claims: ucl.ac.uk/short-courses/search-courses/intellectual-property-ip-transactions-law-and-practice.

[56] Compare Stuart Macaulay's uncharacteristically sharp comment: 'Perhaps classic contracts scholarship can safely ignore the way the contract system works. This scholarship may be irrelevant to most of practice, and so it does not matter how articles are written. However, this scholarship has influence in some instances, and this leaves us with a puzzle. In the face of many scholars challenging its descriptive accuracy, many scholars and theorists continue to paint a simple instrumental picture. … Descriptive accuracy requires us to confront the dark side of the society and its legal system' (Campbell (n 9) 412); see *ibid* 441–42 where he suggests that 'we will do better if we attempt to fashion doctrines more or less suited to specific types of contracts rather than trying to fabricate one grand contract law'.

[57] See Lobban, chapter two of this volume.

[58] Williston was persuaded by Corbin to accept Hohfeld's conceptual scheme as a useful analytical tool but refused to adopt his terminology. Similarly, he opposed the enactment of the Revised Sales Act because it involved 'restating the law even where no substantial change is desired' (letter from S Williston to KN Llewellyn (19 May 1949)). He continued: 'You will pardon an old hunker like me citing as authority Lord Thurlow's reply to a band of dissenters who sought amelioration of their political disabilities: "I am against you by God, sir, I'm in favor of the established church; and if you get your damned religion established I'll be in favor of that too"'. (Discussed in Twining (2012) (n 1) 289–90.)

I think that they were also very different in respect of their intellectual backgrounds and their approaches to reported cases: while Williston was clearly a product of the Harvard tradition, Corbin claimed that he knew nothing of Langdell. His intellectual heroes were not jurists, but rather Charles Darwin, John Stuart Mill and William Graham Sumner out of whose ideas he fashioned his idiosyncratic evolutionary and inductivist approach to doctrine. Corbin read and used reported cases as fragments of evidence of the state of the piecemeal bit-by-bit evolution of doctrine. He noted each case as if he were constructing a headnote, emphasising the facts and the outcomes and treating the reasoning as secondary. Williston, on the other hand, was selective in his treatment of cases, treating them loosely as authoritative, paying attention to the reasoning as much as the outcomes and, it is rumoured, when updating encouraged his assistants to find cases which quoted his treatise to supplant earlier precedents. Moreover, Corbin is a key part of the American Realist story, strongly influencing Llewellyn, Kessler and Gilmore among others and providing at Yale the start of an alternative to the Harvard interpretation of Langdellism.[59]

It is correct to say that Corbin denied being a 'Realist',[60] but that was in order to distance himself from some younger colleagues at Yale in the late 1920s and early 1930s who were seemingly playing the role of rule-sceptics in neighbouring streams of the first year course on Contracts.[61] Corbin was Llewellyn's chief mentor who supported him and claimed basically to agree with him throughout his career. He was a profound admirer of his student, who is generally regarded as the most important Realist scholar and perhaps the only recognised legal theorist among them.[62] Corbin clearly influenced the formulation of Llewellyn's 'starting-points of Realism' in 1931, especially in relation to the idea of 'narrower categories'.[63] Llewellyn and his wife Soia Mentschikoff both called

[59] Twining (2012) (n 1) ch 2.

[60] See Klass, chapter eight of this volume, p 202.

[61] Corbin's targets were Lee Tulin, Robert Maynard Hutchins and Leon Green as the very young colleagues who shocked him when they were teaching Contracts at Yale. The first two hardly feature as central 'Realists' in most myths about American Legal Realism. Could it be that they were mainly hiding the ball, as Nicholas de Belleville Katzenbach (later as Federal Solicitor-General and Attorney-General, a great upholder of the Rule of Law) did to us in Chicago in 1957–58? ('There are no rules of Conflicts of Laws'). Leon Green was perhaps the nearest of those discussed here to being a 'rule sceptic', especially in his attacks on the *Restatement* project, which he dismissed as 'blackletter law'. However, his main focus was on doctrine, he used law reports as his main source and he produced a number of casebooks. For a good account see J Steele, 'Professor Leon Green (1888–1979): Word Magic and the Regenerative Power of Law' in Goudkamp and Nolan (n 2).

[62] See, eg, W Twining, '"Looking Back, Looking Forward": A Letter from Arthur Corbin to Soia Mentschikoff upon the Death of Karl Llewellyn' (2015) 47 *Yale Journal of Law and Humanities* 101.

[63] Corbin's main complaint against the mainstream Contracts literature was that it relied too much on abstract categories. This was probably a main influence on the seventh in Llewellyn and Frank's nine starting-points of Realism in 1931: 'The belief in the worthwhileness of grouping cases together into narrower categories than has been the practice in the past'. This was a major theme in Llewellyn's work on Sales. For example, his pioneering casebook included an index where cases are classified by commodities, bananas, oranges and coal rather than 'goods' or even fruit (Twining (2012) (n 1) ch 7), which he used especially in his famous analysis of risk and title.

him 'Dad' (father-in-the-law, not father-in-law).[64] Remove Corbin and Llewellyn from one's account of American Legal Realism from the late 1920s to the 1940s and what is left?[65]

Before reading this book, I had tended to assume that Contracts and Torts were both closely related and very similar as important fields of law. And that is broadly how they are treated by the contributors. They are often paired together in legal education, in theoretical discussions of the foundations of liability and responsibility, and as leading fields in Private Law and the Law of Obligations. There are clear historical reasons for this. However, this pairing obscures important differences between these two areas of scholarship as phenomena: actual contract(s) are economically, socially and statistically much more important than torts and torticles; 'Torts' is a very fragile organising concept,[66] whereas Contract(s) is stable and robust; the main function of contract is dispute prevention; the Law of Torts has some deterrence and preventative functions, but its main function is compensation; perhaps most significant is that contracts are much more firmly part of the general experience of ordinary members of society than are torts. Gilmore's idea of 'the death of Contract' hardly refers to the practices of contractual behaviour;[67] whereas in several common law jurisdictions the Law of Torts has been largely superceded or even abolished.[68] There are both similarities and differences between Contracts and Torts as fields of law, but from a realist point of view the differences between their subject-matters (actual contracts and torts) and their scholarship as phenomena are greater. They are not twins or even siblings, but more like second cousins sharing a common ancestor. There has been a tendency among Contracts scholars to emphasise the similarities and play down the differences.

The editors of this volume had a difficult problem of selection. To some extent they allowed authors to choose their subjects. There is a good spread across time; although the focus is on English and American scholars, the chapters on Colebrooke and Coote provide a reminder that the English Law of Contract has had a distinctive life or lives in the days of Empire and the Commonwealth; preference has generally been given to candidates who have not been the subject of significant studies elsewhere (for instance, studies of Pothier, Mansfield, Pollock,

[64] Twining (2012) (n 1) 95.

[65] On post-1931 Realists see n 26.

[66] Twining (2019) (n 1) 153–55.

[67] On Gilmore, see n 13.

[68] Goudkamp and Nolan (n 2) 33–35, 186. I do not pursue here the theme that in attempts to provide a moral basis for responsibility for liability in Tort, the main focus is also on personal injuries with most of the previously included torts and torticles filtered out or, as in the case of defamation, treated as a distinct field. I am more concerned here with claims that Contract Law is a semi-autonomous field that excludes the study of actual contracts or the processes of negotiating, constructing, adjusting and drafting actual contracts – the kinds of activity that are central to the work of many office lawyers, business persons and, others. This brings us back to the question: what is involved in understanding Contract doctrine? See further the works on Contract and Tort in the Philosophical Foundations series, both of which focus almost entirely on doctrine.

Langdell, Holmes, Llewellyn and Macaulay are readily available); American deviants from the classical mainstream are represented and there is a reasonable spread. I might have chosen Chalmers, Macaulay, one or two feminists and, of course, Llewellyn,[69] but that is a matter of judgement.[70]

It is hardly surprising that this selection of individuals is remarkably homogeneous in respect of gender, race, intellectual abilities, class (one Scottish laird as an exception) and conformity to their own legal cultures; the modern ones divide fairly clearly into those who were dedicated specialists (Corbin, Williston, Macneil, Kessler, Treitel) and those for whom writing a Contracts textbook was a side-line from activities for which they were better known (Anson, Cheshire, Fifoot); Atiyah is perhaps an exception to the last point: although very much a common lawyer he ranged quite widely across legal theory and history; the striking differences between his works on Torts and Contracts being at least in part explicable as having two different target audiences, law reformers for the former and senior judges for the latter.[71] Atiyah was also keen to change legal education and advance public understanding of the law.

So far as one can tell the academics had their students' needs and concerns at heart and several were popular or even revered as teachers. Less obvious, perhaps, is that the economic base of their scholarly activities was teaching and this has sustained a continuous and intimate relationship between teaching and scholarship, illustrated by the point that a very high proportion of the leading works discussed here envisaged first year law students as their primary audience. Demand for teaching restrains the focus of scholarship.

As already noted, it is striking that nearly all the authors were litigation-oriented, the English ones all being barristers in a broad sense. They mostly treated their students as if they were potential litigators (moots rather than exercises in drafting, or negotiating or adjusting contracts) and have showed little interest in the information needs and problems of the vast majority of lawyers and others for whom formation, negotiation, drafting, management and dispute avoidance are their main concerns.[72]

The core of this book lies in the detailed treatment of each individual. Kessler, Macneil and Atiyah represent the main deviants from the classical doctrinal tradition. Of these I was closest to Patrick Atiyah as we were career-long friends

[69] Alan Schwartz rightly criticises me for failing to do justice to Llewellyn's articles on Contracts, especially the brilliant series published in 1937–39. In 1973, I pleaded lack of expertise. Schwartz has admirably filled the gap in a paper which can be read as a supplement to this book (AR Schwartz, 'Karl Llewellyn and the Origins of Contract Theory' in JS Kraus and SD Walt (eds), *Jurisprudential Foundations of Corporate and Commercial Law* (Cambridge, Cambridge University Press, 2000)). I did, however, give a detailed account of Llewellyn's coursebook KN Llewellyn, *Cases and Materials on the Law of Sales* (Chicago, Callaghan & Co, 1930) (famous inter alia for its index of commodities) which, like so many such works, marked an important point in his intellectual development.

[70] See n 88.

[71] Among his papers, Atiyah preserved a selection of correspondence with senior judges and hardly any other professional letters. See Goudkamp, chapter 14 of this volume.

[72] See n 68.

from 1958 until his death in 2018, including being colleagues in Khartoum and Warwick, neighbours in Khartoum, Leamington Spa and Iffley village at different periods and in a significant editor-author relationship. James Goudkamp has done extensive careful research on Patrick Atiyah and I have assisted in some of the writings about him. Here we can take Goudkamp's informative chapter (chapter 14) as my starting-point. I agree that Atiyah is difficult to categorise and in respect of his political beliefs either ambivalent or changeable or inclined pragmatically to adjust to the *zeitgeist* of the time.

Atiyah was clearly a doctrinal scholar, addicted to the law reports, but concerned to be realistic about the law in action. In Khartoum in the late 1950s he regularly complained about being cut off from finding out what English businessmen (sic) thought about Contract doctrine ('do they really take consideration seriously?'). As far as I know he never undertook systematic empirical research, but he made use of it skilfully from sources in several disciplines and his experience as a civil servant in Accra and London in several capacities gave him a good sense of how governments work.

Atiyah's most notable books belong to different genres and address different primary audiences. An *Introduction to the Law of Contract* is not a textbook, but a general introduction to Contracts specifically addressed to beginning law students and the general reader, a contribution to public understanding of English law.[73] *Accidents, Compensation and the Law*[74] was an academic reconceptualisation and disruption of a central part of a major field; It was mainly focused on English law, but its general aspects were relevant to common law countries generally.[75] *The Rise and Fall of Freedom of Contract*[76] is essentially an academic monograph.[77] Most of Atiyah's other books fall into one of these three categories. All were recognised as involving a distinctive voice and original ideas, but it is difficult to extract from them a clear overall vision of the field of Contracts within the discipline of Law. *Rise and Fall* purported to be a prolegomenon to a major doctrinal volume. I long suspected that, like Thayer's influential *Preliminary Treatise on the Law of Evidence* among others, the promised second volume would never be written but the preliminary one would be influential. My prediction was correct, but Goudkamp reports that Atiyah

[73] Like Macneil's and a very few others this work starts with a brief survey of the social functions of contracts rather than with basic concepts or norms of Contract Law. On public understanding see Twining (2019) (n 1) 269–73.

[74] PS Atiyah, *Accidents, Compensation and the Law*, (Cambridge, Cambridge University Press, 1970).

[75] For further discussion, see Twining (2019) (n 1) 154–55.

[76] PS Atiyah, *The Rise and Fall of Freedom of Contract* (Oxford, Oxford University Press, 1979).

[77] Atiyah was disappointed that the publication of *Rise and Fall* coincided with the rise of Thatcherism (see Goudkamp, chapter 14 of this volume, p 366). This did not invalidate his historical argument except perhaps in so far as he seemed to suggest that the fall of freedom of contract was permanent.

did in fact make extensive preparatory notes for this,[78] which it may be possible to interpret what he had in mind – a general theoretical overview of the Law of Contract or, more likely, a comprehensive doctrinal treatise as a rival to Treitel's *magnum opus* or something else? There are suggestions that it might have been intended as a work of 'practical doctrinal scholarship' with the higher judiciary in England as the main intended audience.[79]

Despite writing mainly about English Law, Atiyah greatly admired aspects of the American legal tradition, especially its greater openness about policy and substantive reasons and the leading American law schools. In turn he was greatly admired by leading American scholars, including some who strongly disagreed with him. He considered the invitation to give one of the Holmes Lectures at Harvard as 'one of the greatest honours which can be bestowed on a legal scholar in the common law world'.[80] However, he did not fit any recognisable model of American or English legal scholarship. As his friend, I found him restless, volatile and reactive rather than someone whose thinking stemmed from a single central vision.

I remember Fritz Kessler as a very friendly host at Yale in 1963–64 rather than as a Contracts scholar. He was a disciple and friend of Arthur Corbin and a regular visitor to his home in later years. It was he who arranged for me to have access to Corbin when he was very frail and these were among my most productive interviews in my Llewellyn research. I discussed Llewellyn, American Realism and the *Restatements* with Fritz, but at the time did not realise that he was responsible for the nearest publication to a Realist coursebook on Contracts, co-edited with Malcolm Sharp who had taught me at Chicago and whom I much admired.[81] If I learned anything about Kessler's ideas on Contracts from our relationship it was probably by osmosis. However, as we shall see, there are important links with Ian Macneil, Malcolm Sharp and Stewart Macaulay.

My relationship with Ian Macneil was rather unusual. He arrived in Dar-es-Salaam in 1965, just after I had left. We got to know each other when I visited. We got on well and kept in touch for many years, with only occasional meetings. I do not recall discussing his relational theory with him, but we did discuss Karl Llewellyn, American Legal Realism, the Uniform Commercial Code, the American *Restatements*, and what kind of legal education was

[78] See Goudkamp, chapter 14 of this volume, p 361.

[79] It is striking that senior British judges were the main recipients of much of his professional correspondence in his later years.

[80] See Goudkamp, chapter 14 of this volume, p 362.

[81] F Kessler and M Sharp, *Contracts: Cases and Materials* (New York, Prentice Hall, 1953). Later editions were published in 1970 and 1986. *cf* Llewellyn's *Cases and Materials on the Law of Sales* (n 68). I took a seminar with Malcolm Sharp in 1957–58 but it was on Jurisprudence, not Contracts. At the time I had no idea that Sharp was associated with American Legal Realism. On Sharp and Macaulay, see p 401.

needed in newly independent countries in Africa. More significantly, I became familiar with his book *Contracts: Instruments for Social Co-operation – East Africa*[82] which was printed in Dar-es-Salaam, but published by Fred B Rothman in the US. This is a remarkable phenomenon in several ways. It involved an extraordinary amount of research into local materials, mainly reported cases nearly all from East Africa; the Indian Contract Act 1872 and a few Indian precedents; and some materials from newspapers, government reports and the like. It was soon recognised as the most substantial work of scholarship produced in the early years of the Dar-es-Salaam Law Faculty.[83] It worked well with his own students, who contributed to its development, but proved to be too novel for his successors in teaching Contracts in East Africa and was hardly used after he left. The book, perhaps understandably, focused on the state law of the main East African jurisdictions; this was mainly 'city law' or 'expatriate law', because the vast majority of actual contractual relations and agreements by the local population in a predominantly agricultural country operated under customary law or no law at all. Clearly Macneil did not have time to do field work on customary law, but I was disappointed that he included less than three pages on the topic and barely mentioned the already quite developed literature on 'African Law' and legal anthropology and the interesting debates about the codification and 'restatement' of customary law in the region.[84] The significance of this is that, although Macneil did provide some general social context, the structure of the book is rather like an American casebook and consists almost entirely of reported cases and his approach was not very different from that of other American law teachers who spent a short period teaching in Africa, except that he was more assiduous than most in collecting local materials.

Even more surprising is that, so far as I can tell, after his return to the United States Macneil made almost no reference to his East African book nor the significance of his East African experience in his intellectual development, whereas most people who taught law in the region in the heady days of Independence found it a transformative experience. The East African book is a

[82] IR Macneil, *Contracts: Instruments for Social Co-operation – East Africa* (South Hackensack, Fred B Rothman, 1968).

[83] The other work of substance emanating from Dar-es-Salaam in the early years of the Law Faculty was Y Ghai and JPWB MacAuslan, *Public Law and Political Change in Kenya* (Nairobi, Oxford University Press, 1970) which is still a leading monograph in Kenya after 50 years.

[84] There were lively debates in the 1960s about the nature of 'customary law' and attempts to codify, unify or restate it. The literature of 'African Law' and legal anthropology were already quite well-developed in the region. Relevant works included TO Elias, *The Nature of African Customary Law* (Manchester, Manchester University Press, 1957); AN Allott, *Essays in African Law* (London, Butterworths, 1960); School of Oriental and African Studies, *Journal of African Law* (1957–2016); L Mair, *Primitive Government* (Baltimore, Penguin Books, 1962); and M Gluckman, *Judicial Process among Barotse* (Glencoe, The Free Press, 1955) and other works, including his famous debate with Paul Bohannan about the translatability of African and English legal concepts: see P Bohannan, *Justice and Judgment among the Tiv* (Oxford, Oxford University Press, 1957).

clear precursor of the first edition of Macneil's American casebook[85] which was published in 1971 three years later. My suggestion is that Macneil might have been stimulated in Dar to include ideas about informal economies and customs and other norms. Thus if he had paid more attention to the social context of contract in East Africa, the already established literature on African Law and legal anthropology in the region and the lively local debates about 'restatement' and codification of customary law,[86] he might have been bolder in his approach to contracts in the US rather than focusing on one major theme about relational contracting and one central idea of exchange. His distinction between relational and 'discrete' contracts has very important implications for Contracts as a field, but is not sufficient on its own to ground an alternative to the classical tradition. My admittedly speculative conclusion is that far from being too radical, Macneil was not radical enough in that he drew back from advancing a genuinely coherent alternative to the classical view of contracts and contracting in America based on the idea of social co-operation. Thus I agree with David Campbell that Macneil did not follow through on his basic insight and that he would have done better to root his vision in a broad, perhaps Weberian, theory of social co-operation rather than a more restricted one of exchange.[87]

It might be objected that this suggestion would turn Macneil's vision into a sociological theory rather than a legal one. Apart from relying on a dubious distinction this misses the point. For my suggestion is that Macneil could have developed a coherent theory of contracts and contracting *as part of the discipline of Law*. Macneil was a lawyer, both practising and academic, throughout his career; the main audiences of his writings were legal and he was reacting against the dominant doctrinal tradition of Contracts scholarship, his main bases were mainstream American law schools and in teaching first year Contracts he was under strong pressures to conform. In his teaching and in his work in arbitration he was not practising Sociology. Such an objection would be based on the false assumption that concern with understanding actual contracts and contracting behaviour falls outside the discipline of Law.

I cannot do justice here to Stewart Macaulay. I would have selected him for this book instead of Macneil as he is an important leader of the New Legal Realism and its most influential Contracts scholar.[88] He preceded me at Chicago

[85] IR Macneil, *Cases and Materials on Contracts: Exchange Transactions and Relationships* (Mineola, Foundation Press, 1971). There is an extensive literature on relational theory. In addition to Jonathan Morgan's excellent chapter 12 of this volume, see D Campbell, L Mulcahy and S Wheeler (eds), *Changing Concepts of Contract: Essays in Honour of Ian Macneil* (Basingstoke, Palgrave MacMillan, 2015). For a useful recent analysis of three strands in relational contract theory and its implications for courts, see Z Xing, 'Disrupting Doctrine? Revisiting the Doctrinal Impact of Relational Contract Theory' (2019) 39 *Legal Studies* 98.

[86] See n 84.

[87] D Campbell, 'The Social Theory of Relational Contract: Macneil as the Modern Proudhon' (1990) 18 *International Journal of Sociology of Law* 75.

[88] Macaulay's essay (S Macaulay, 'Non-Contractual Relations in Business: A Preliminary Study' (1963) 28 *American Sociological Review* 55) is generally treated as the start of studies of the gap

by a year in 1956–57 where he was strongly influenced by Malcolm Sharp.[89] He conducted two major empirical projects on contracts, one of which resulted in his classic essay 'Non-Contractual Relations in Business',[90] which is treated by many as the starting-point of empirical studies of Contracts. He has continued as the leading theorist of empirical approaches to contracts and contracting, has been a major figure at the University of Wisconsin Law School and the mentor of many important socio-legal scholars.[91] We have been friends and allies mainly by correspondence for over 60 years. I will confine myself here to two points.

First, Macaulay is sometimes treated as a sociologist rather than a lawyer, perhaps because he has emphasised the very limited role that Contract Law (doctrine) has played in contracts practice. However, like Macneil, Macaulay has been an academic lawyer for the whole of his career: he studied law at Stanford and Chicago, his main base has been at the University of Wisconsin Law School, his main audiences have been legal and socio-legal, many of his articles were published in law journals and, like Macneil, he taught first year Contracts to law students and, even at Wisconsin, he had to conform and teach doctrine mainly through reported cases.[92] Brian Bix sums up his contribution as follows: '[he] taught contracts scholars to focus on practice not theory, on relationships not models, and on the power and politics behind everything'.[93]

Second, Macaulay has focused mainly on systematic empirical research rather than on the broader idea of empirical understandings of all kinds. He has usefully distinguished between several distinct streams and traditions within this broad area.[94] Movements such as Law and Society, Socio-legal Studies, and the New Legal Realism have emphasised disciplined empirical *research* which

between Contracts doctrine and contracts and contracting behaviour in the US. It is a classic study of the gap between doctrinal scholarship and the law in action. About 20 years later Macaulay revisited and updated this essay and provided a succinct overview of what he thought constituted the gap (S Macaulay, 'An Empirical View of Contract' [1985] *Wisconsin Law Review* 465). He has continued to publish essays around this theme and has been a leading figure in the New Legal Realism: Campbell (n 9) collects together most of his relevant essays. See further n 94.

[89] He even arranged for the title of his post at Wisconsin to be renamed the Malcolm P Sharp Chair, even though Sharp had only spent a year at Wisconsin.

[90] Macaulay (1963) (n 88).

[91] There are excellent appraisals of his work in Campbell (n 9).

[92] For example, when I wrote asking him about the history of a space called 'Reality checkpoint' in the University of Wisconsin Law Library, he not only provided a detailed answer but commented: 'What a wonderful way to avoid work this is! I am supposed to be grading 30 Contracts 2 exam answers dealing with what may be a breach of an installment contract if the late performance is not excused by a force majeure clause that might have been part of the final contract under Karl Llewellyn's wonderful/terrible § 2–207 of the UCC dealing with the battle of the forms. This was much more fun.' (Letter from Stewart Macaulay to author (14 May 2013).)

[93] B Bix, 'Stewart Macaulay and the Law of Contract' in Campbell (n 9).

[94] In a very useful paper Juliet Kostritsky summarises Macaulay's contribution and surveys writings of an impressive range of scholars who have been influenced by or responded to that contribution, including Robert Gordon, Brian Bix, Robert Scott, Mitu Gulati, Lisa Bernstein, David Campbell, Matthew Jennejohn, Barak Richman, Edward Rubin, Robert C Ellickson, Gillian Hadfield and Iva Bozovic, and Thomas Palay (J Kostritsky, 'A Paradigm Shift in Comparative Institutional

in my view, though desirable, cannot hope ever to cover more than one part of what is needed. As Karl Llewellyn said repeatedly, 'knowledge does not have to be "scientific" to be useful and important'.[95] For many purposes we often have to be satisfied with extrapolations from other disciplines, the lessons of practical experience and even impressions of participants or casual observers. The 'evidence-based' movement has given a boost to this kind of perspective, especially since it has broadened out from medicine and other STEM sciences to include enquiries that involve normative as well as empirical elements, such as policy-making and nursing practice.[96] The basic precept is 'use the best information that is available'. This is a difference of emphasis rather than disagreement, but it is an important one in the context of this chapter. Macaulay and I are close allies, but have different ideas about what a coherent view of Contracts as a major field within the discipline of Law would encompass.[97]

Do these impressions suggest any generalisations about Anglo-American Contracts scholars as a caste or class? Let me try some tentative suggestions.

We have already seen that many common law scholars tend to be obsessed with the law reports (Colebrooke being a notable exception); that contract scholars are not and cannot be empirical virgins about contracts and contracting, though some did not allow much empirical knowledge to intrude explicitly; and that genres of expository works are rather more fluid and complex than is suggested by standard categorisations of student works, treatises and monographs.

The individuals selected broadly confirm my original impressions of Contracts as a field of law: that they tended to have quite narrow conceptions of their audiences; that all of them assumed that doctrine was a necessary element of understanding contracts; that nearly all leading contracts scholars were centrists in respect of alleged divides between formalism and anti-formalism, individualism and communitarianism, freedom of contract and state regulation, although they differed among themselves about the hows and whys of limiting imbalances of power and ensuring a modicum of fairness. The main explanation for this has been that social co-operation is recognised as a necessity

Governance: The Role of Contract in Business Relationships and Cost/Benefit Analysis' [2021] *Wisconsin Law Review* 385). Other significant works include J Kostritsky, 'Why Choose LTAs [Long Term Agreements]? An Empirical Study of Ohio Manufactures' Contractual Choices Through a Bargaining Lens' (2020) 9 *American University Business Law Review* 337; CA Hill, 'Why Contracts are Written in "Legalese"' (2001) 77 *Chicago-Kent Law Review* 59; M Gulati and R Scott, *The Three and a Half Minute Transaction: Boilerplate and the Limits of Contract Design* (Chicago, University of Chicago Press, 2012); J Whitford, *The New Old Economy: Networks, Institutions, and the Organizational Transformation of American Manufacturing* (Oxford, Oxford University Press, 2005); and J Morgan, *Contract Law Minimalism* (Cambridge, Cambridge University Press, 2013). A good starting-point is Mertz (n 3). See also Campbell (n 9).

[95] See, eg, Llewellyn (1962) (n 33) ch 3; Twining (2012) (n 1) ch 3; Twining (2009) (n 1) ch 8.

[96] For a useful discussion of the issues, see P Cairney and K Oliver, 'Evidence-Based Policymaking is Not Like Evidence-Based Medicine, So How Far Should You Go to Bridge the Divide between Evidence and Policy?' (2017) 15 *Health Research Policy and Systems* 35.

[97] Macaulay doubts that Contracts can usefully be conceived as a single field (see n 56). If James Gordley's historical thesis is correct, I disagree.

as well as a good by nearly all actors and scholars; that all treated 'contract' as a stable and workable organising concept, although some wanted to patrol the boundaries (eg in respect of quasi-contract/restitution); that most of the doctrinal concepts treated as basic have been seen as serviceable as tools of contracts discourse, and that only a few (such as consideration) differ sharply from ordinary English usage. From a realist perspective I would suggest that none of these predecessors offers a satisfactory template for twenty-first century Contracts scholars looking for a role model, especially early career academic lawyers who wish to try to bridge the divide between narrower and broader approaches.[98]

What is needed to achieve this? Here I can only outline some tentative suggestions: broaden the vision of Contracts as an academic field to include contract formation and contractual behaviour; broaden the audiences of Contracts scholarship to include all human beings, especially those who in their work are concerned with creating and preserving social co-operation rather than focusing on clearing up messes; extend the use of sources for understanding contracts and contracting to actual contracts, standard forms, relevant findings and insights of socio-legal scholarship and accessible data about different contexts of social relations; do not assume that data is mainly relevant for the light it throws on doctrine; acknowledge the dark side of contracts and the existence of alternative markets; better integrate Contracts and Commercial Law and test all generalised statements about doctrine against different contexts and different kinds of contractual relations; emphasise the differences as well as the affinities between Contracts and Torts as fields of law; recognise that Contracts is a very large, varied and important field and deserves more space in the legal imagination.[99]

Most Contracts scholars are specialists and rightly so. They should in the ordinary course of things assimilate legal, conceptual and other materials

[98] There are two main reasons for suggesting that none of the subjects of this book is now a suitable role model for an early career Contracts scholar in England or the US in 2022. The first is that none of the subjects of this book offered a coherent alternative vision to the dominant, but ill-conceived, classical tradition of the importance and the potential of Contracts scholarship to understanding law. The second reason, and probably the more important, is that the context of legal scholarship, including Contracts, has changed and is changing radically in England and the US. Some of the factors are summed up in Richard Susskind's futurology: 'Tomorrow's world, as predicted and described here, bears little resemblance to that of the past. Legal institutions and lawyers are at a crossroads, I claim, and are poised to change more radically in less than two decades than they have over the last two centuries. If you are a young lawyer, this revolution will happen on your watch' (R Susskind, *Tomorrow's Lawyers*, 2nd edn (Oxford, Oxford University Press, 2017) xvii).

[99] Pressure of space precludes detailed treatment of these ideas. I hope in a longer version of this chapter to deal in more detail with specific topics relating to some themes, including audiences (eg, those involved in negotiating, constructing and managing contracts: is canned doctrine all that they need?); sources (eg, actual contracts, contextual case studies (Simpson et al); existing and potential data banks and services); non-doctrinal concepts (eg, basic economic and social science concepts, relational/discrete contracts, non-contractual relations, etc); ideological differences (eg, individualism, communitarianism, socialism); philosophical concerns (eg, moral monism and pluralism); workable taxonomies; and wider perspectives (eg, transnational relations, non-state law, underground and shadow economies, etc).

relevant to their specialism. But it is also useful to set these in the context of broader views of the landscape and histories of contracts and contracting and what is involved in understanding contracts in respect of concepts, values, empirical information and doctrine.

VII. ANTICIPATING SOME OBJECTIONS

To the objection that we want to preserve the integrity of doctrinal scholarship, the realist reply is that doctrine is central to understanding contracts, but that the role of scholars is to advance understanding as well as knowledge and doctrine cannot be understood without reference to context.

To the objection that my observations about the worlds of contracts and contracting are obvious and familiar to every Contracts scholar. Of course, they are; but that they are part of 'the forgotten obvious' is illustrated by the tendency to gloss over differences between Contracts and Torts as fields of law, or silences about the limitations of law reports or lack of emphasis on the familiarity of contracts to ordinary members of society.

To the objection that such broadening of focus will involve mastering a new language, the reply is that this argument is easily overstated. Doctrinal scholarship has a rich and stable heritage of concepts, but it needs a few additions and distinctions.[100] Many of these are part of the ordinary vocabulary of a citizen who is competent to vote, act as a juror, magistrate or witness or negotiate and enter into contracts without expert help.

To the objection that it is not the role of Contracts scholars to serve non-legal audiences, who are catered for by other providers of information, one may answer that this is only true if such works are not misleading or perpetuate fallacies, such as that 'discrete' contracts can be treated as the paradigm case of all contracts or that reported cases on disputed Contracts are representative of the world of contracts and contracting or that the Law of Contracts is a Law of disputed contracts or that understanding contracting behaviour is not part of the field of Contracts within the discipline of law.

To the objection that introductory books on Contracts traditionally served as basic building blocks for more specialised studies of particular spheres or kinds of contracts, one may answer that this is partly true but assumes that doctrine on its own is the *best starting-point* for law students or other beginners to understand the subject.

To the objection 'we are lawyers, not sociologists' the answer is that as legal scholars you are not necessarily expected to undertake empirical research but

[100] For example, relational/discrete contracts, real deal/paper deal; regulatory state/limited state, private government, informal economy; collective bargaining; bureaucracy; discrete contracts; course of dealing, usage of the trade, even unconscionability.

you should know how to find and to use relevant data and other information and observe the mantra of evidence-based policy to use the best available information even if it is not 'scientific'.

To the objection that this approach is unmanageable, the answer is that it is true that Contracts is a huge field and most Contracts scholars are specialists, but they need to be able to relate their own work to the field as a whole and to adjacent aspects of it, in order to make comparisons, generalisations and informed judgements about apt levels of generality. Such context-setting can often be quite broad brush and approximate, more like medium term climate maps than ephemeral weather ones. Often such maps will exist already and be accessible.

VIII. CONCLUSION

My main conclusion is that Anglo-American Contracts scholarship has a rich heritage in respect of concepts, ideological debates and doctrinal analysis but it has not done so well on the empirical side. What is needed is a steady breath of realism, as interpreted here, not a revolution. In short social co-operation and dispute prevention rather than dispute settlement are at the core of understanding what contracts are all about. That is an important part of the mission of the discipline of Law.

Index